Information Processing Systems
for Management

**The Irwin Series in
Information and Decision Sciences**

Consulting Editors

Robert B. Fetter
Yale University

Claude McMillan
University of Colorado

Information Processing Systems for Management

Donna Hussain
K. M. Hussain
New Mexico State University

Second Edition

1985

RICHARD D. IRWIN, INC.
Homewood, Illinois 60430

628339

ISBN 0-256-03209-2

Library of Congress Catalog Card No. 84–81734

Printed in the United States of America

1 2 3 4 5 6 7 8 9 0 MP 2 1 0 9 8 7 6 5

Preface

Few businesses have been left untouched by the computer revolution. The computer is being increasingly used for operations, control, and planning as well as to improve office efficiency. Managers today need to know how computers work and how they can be applied to a firm's operations.

The purpose of this book is to provide managers and students of management with a basic understanding of computer processing systems. Use of this textbook does not require a course prerequisite. The book is a stand-alone text, written for the upper division undergraduate or the master's student. Though the text includes a brief overview of hardware, software, peripherals, and communications, the primary focus is on the development and administration of information systems and how managers can use computers on the job. Omitted is an explanation of the internal workings of a computer, flowcharting, how to program, and the history of computers; topics commonly presented in introductory computer science texts.

Three new chapters have been written for this Second Edition: Microcomputers: Home and Business Use; The Impact of Computers on Management; and Computers in Our Future. In addition, all of the chapters have been revised and updated. Subjects added include: spreadsheets, windows, privacy concerns, local area networks, videotex, 4GLs, expert systems, public online data bases, automated integrated factories, information specialists, fifth generation computers, intelligent management information systems, and future trends in computing. Colored photographs now supplement the text and the annotated bibliographies that follow each chapter have been revised to include publications from the 1980s.

An instructor's manual has been prepared to accompany the text. The manual has been expanded for this Second Edition as well. It now includes sample student answers to the discussion questions that follow each chapter. In addition, more than 1,000 multiple-choice questions for reviews or exams are provided.

Like the text, this data base has been updated and rewritten. Supplementary diagrams and summary lists in the form of transparency masters for use in the classroom are also part of the instructor's package.

The authors wish to thank colleagues and reviewers who read the manuscript and provided helpful comments and corrections. We are particularly indebted to Marvin Rothstein, Leslie Spencer, Deane Carter, Steve Hallam, Mark St. Paul, Don Cartlidge, and David Carlson for their constructive criticisms. A special word of gratitude must also be given to our secretaries Stella Rodriquez and Karen Cavert.

Donna Hussain
K. M. Hussain

Contents

Information Processing Systems
for Management

COMPUTER HARDWARE AND SOFTWARE

PART

1

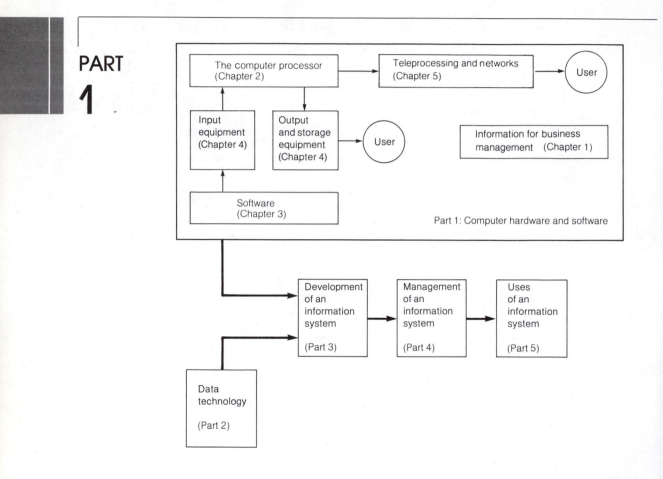

The computer processor (Chapter 2)

Teleprocessing and networks (Chapter 5)

User

Input equipment (Chapter 4)

Output and storage equipment (Chapter 4)

User

Information for business management (Chapter 1)

Software (Chapter 3)

Part 1: Computer hardware and software

Development of an information system (Part 3)

Management of an information system (Part 4)

Uses of an information system (Part 5)

Data technology (Part 2)

Computer technology required for a computerized information system is the subject of Part 1. The relationship of the chapters of this part is shown in the diagram.

Central to all computer technology is the computer itself. Students of management for whom this text is written need general knowledge about computers, not technical details of how computers are constructed and operate. They are like car owners who can be good drivers without understanding the design and mechanics of internal combustion engines. Chapter 1 discusses the impact of information technology on business. In Chapter 2, the main components of a computer and component capabilities in general terms are described. The chapter also tells what computer equipment can and cannot do.

Given input, computer programs are needed to instruct the computer in processing so that desired results are achieved. These programs, called software, are the subject of Chapter 3. Again, technical details are omitted. Instead, the chapter presents an overview of types of programs used in processing. Also given is an introductory classification of languages that are used to write programs. Languages used most frequently in business processing are identified, and their capabilities and limitations briefly discussed.

Chapter 4 discusses input and output equipment and how output is stored for later use. Once programs process data, the output generated must be transmitted to a manager or user. The destination for the output is sometimes remote from the place of processing. Equipment and a set of procedures for efficient, effective, and secure transmission of output are required. Chapter 5, on teleprocessing, deals with this subject.

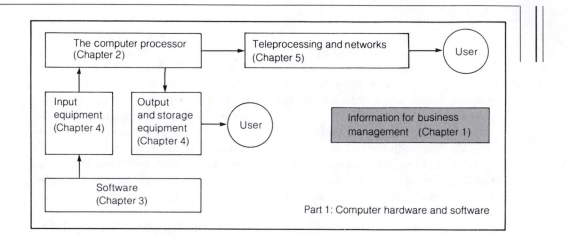

Part 1: Computer hardware and software

Information for business management

1

To live effectively is to live with
adequate information.

Norbert Weiner

Ages, such as the stone, bronze, medieval, and industrial ages, have been used to describe the passage of human history. The dramatic development of computers in recent years has led to the birth of a new age, the age of information. In this chapter, the technology of information as it relates to business management is examined.

Growth of information technology

Businesspeople first felt the impetus of the age of information in the 1950s, when electronic computers reached the market. The first computer, the ENIAC, made calculations in milliseconds, matching in one day 300 days of manual computation. Today, computers execute instructions in nanoseconds (billionths of a second). Business applications such as those listed in Figure 1.1 are now solved in only a fraction of a second. No longer must businesses be run by hunch and intuition. Information on which to base decisions can now be processed by computer at incredible speeds.

Everyone recognizes that technological advances in transportation in the last century have reshaped the American lifestyle. We are no longer limited to walking, but travel by jet, an increase in speed by a factor of 100, from 4 mph to roughly 400 mph. The speed of processing information by computer, however, has increased by a factor of one million. Accessibility of information will ultimately transform society as profoundly as did the invention of the jet or the internal combustion engine.

Speed is not the only aspect of computer development to make prodigious improvement in recent years. Computers are getting smaller. Even purse and pocket models can now be purchased. Other characteristics such as system reliability and cost-performance ratios have also improved greatly as shown in Ta-

5

Figure 1.1
The computer performs its functions at incredible speeds

Courtesy International Business Machines Corporation

ble 1.1 In spite of inflation, the purchase price of computer equipment has dropped as well. In 1950, the first computer cost $5 million. Today many models cost less than $100.

Although information can be processed at reduced cost, total expenditures for data processing are on the rise as a result of increased demand for information, rising salaries of computer personnel, and the expense of sophisticated software. This is a good indication of how the business community values information as a

Table 1.1
Relative changes in hardware characteristics

	1950s	1960s	1970s	1980s	1990s*
Size (number of circuits per cubic foot)	1,000	100,000	10 million	1 billion	Many billions
Speed (time to execute an instruction in CPU)	300 ms	5 ms	80 ns	25 ns	5 ns
Reliability (mean average in between failures in CPU)	Hours	Tens of hours	Hundreds of hours	Thousands of hours	Tens of thousands of hours
Relative cost (for 1 million basic instructions)	28	1	0.02	0.001	Less than 0.001
Relative cost (of storage)	2.61	0.85	0.05	0.001	Less than 0.001

ms = Microsecond (millionth of a second).
ns = Nanosecond (billionth of a second).
*Estimated.

resource. Experts predict that by the late 1980s, some 8 million computers will be installed in the United States. That is 7 times the number in use when the decade began (See Figure 1.2)

Many improvements in computers can be traced to the development of integrated circuitry and the use of small chips made of silicon, an element second to oxygen in abundance, on which circuitry is crammed. Modern technology also enables us to send data by satellite at 1,200 million bits per second compared with an average of 1 to 1 million bits per second on a telephone line. Data storage devices are needed when transmitting such large amounts of data, but again, costs are dropping per unit stored and the devices themselves are becoming smaller and more compact. Figure 1.3 illustrates how space requirements for one million characters in storage have been reduced in time. Improved storage tech-

Figure 1.2
Growth in computer numbers

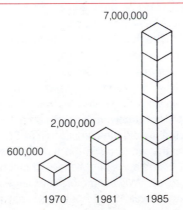

7,000,000

2,000,000

600,000

1970   1981   1985

Figure 1.3
Space for one million characters of storage over time

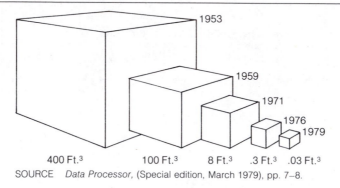

SOURCE   *Data Processor,* (Special edition, March 1979), pp. 7–8.

nology has enabled data bases to grow in size. Today, data bases of over a trillion bits of stored data (one million million bits) are not uncommon.

Of course, computers have limitations. They lack human skills such as intuitive reasoning, associative recall, creativity, recognition of all patterns in written and spoken words, hearing, smelling, feeling, and tasting. Also, computers require human intervention. Without direction they cannot operate. Through research, however, some of these limitations may be eliminated in the near future. For example, prototype models are being developed to follow voiced instructions and have some "intelligent" capabilities.

Predictions for the future

The potential of computers is vast. Future computers may think and teach themselves to do new tasks, like HAL, a computer in the film, *2001: A Space Odyssey.* Factories may be automated to operate on the basis of programmed decisions produced in automated offices, as predicted by the Nobel prizewinner Herbert Simon. Shopping may be done on home screens instead of at shopping centers. Advertising and news may be produced on computer terminals rather than on the printed page. Society may become cashless and checkless, with funds transferred electronically. The convergence of the computing and telecommunications industries may result in computers being as common and necessary for businesses as telephones are today. Constraints on these developments are more organizational, political, and regulatory than technological or economic, making it difficult to forecast when such projections will become commonplace.

It is harder to predict future misuse of computer technology. Will computers attempt to take control as did the computer in *2001,* or team up with foreign computers to take over the world as in the film *Colossus, the Forbin Project*? Will computers become monsters as in Michael Crichton's *The Terminal Man* and Ira Lewis' *This Perfect Day*? Will computers and large data banks monitor people's lives as perceived by Orwell in *1984* or direct a spy network as in Len Deighton's *Billion-Dollar Brain*? Will the ultimate robot prove ultimately uncontrollable as in

John Barth's *Giles, Goat Boy*? Or become a lover as in Karl Bruchner's *The Hour of the Robots*? Will Karl Capek's play, *R.U.R.,* which depicts a dehumanized computerized version of man as a technological slave become reality? Will man no longer be dominant in society but become a markedly inferior species as in Olaf Johannesson's *Tales of the Big Computer*? Is it possible that fiction will become fact? No one can answer these questions with certainty, but knowledge of computer technology and information systems should help readers evaluate the likelihood of such imaginary scenarios becoming reality.

Since it generally takes a 5– to 20–year gestation period from invention to commercial application of new computer technology, professionals studying past trends and current research and development can make generalizations about the performance of computer systems to be marketed in this century with some measure of certainty. It is predicted that:

1. Computers will be more convenient for access, more compact, and more compatible with computer-related equipment manufactured by a wide range of vendors.
2. Computers will be simpler to use. For example, they will be conversational in mode, carrying on dialogues with users to help determine their needs, making it easy for nontechnical personnel to communicate with the computer system. Voice recognition equipment, optical character recognition equipment, and the development of computer microfilm technology will help make the computers faster and cheaper as well.
3. Languages and the control of data bases will evolve, helping human-machine interface.
4. Copiers will have their own memory and intelligence, and will be integrated into computer systems for both on-site and remote-site processing.
5. Computer processing and copier technology will converge with teleprocessing to make instant correspondence and transfer of information between offices economically possible even when long distances separate them.
6. Interorganizational communications will be electronic, bypassing the post office in many cases.
7. Teleconferences will be held by management at all levels, decreasing the time and cost of business traveling.
8. Transmission of data will be done by satellites. For on-land transmission, glass optic fibers will be used that are 1/200th inch in diameter, having a capacity a billion times that of scarce copper wire used commonly in telephone cable.
9. Robots will increasingly displace manufacturing personnel, and computers will be used in the areas of numerical control, process control, and computer-aided design, thereby increasing both efficiency and productivity.
10. Computers designed for special purposes will be compact, reliable, and cheap enough to be part of many household and industrial products.

To take full advantage of these trends, knowledge of computer technology and computerized information systems is essential for managers of the future. Providing this background is the purpose of this text.

Impact of information technology on business

Formerly the two principal economic resources of business were capital and labor. A third primary resource has now been added: information. Access to information enables management to answer questions and solve problems and, in so doing, achieve corporate goals. Without information, decisions are intuitive and expedient, but not necessarily economically rational. The information provided by computer systems not only makes decision making more effective than in the past, but enables businesses to realize objectives never before possible. For example, a mail order company with the objective of good customer relations was never able to satisfy this aim when using manual inventory control, for customers were frequently inconvenienced by out-of-stock notices. When a computer system was installed to monitor warehouse contents and reorder items when a predetermined stock level was reached, the new system resulted in prompt fulfillment of orders and satisfied customers.

But information system technology places a burden on managers. They must understand what information systems can do, and actively participate in the development of systems for their own special needs. This requires the ability to define problems, objectives, and constraints, specifically, in operational terms. Without this ability, managers will be unable to take full advantage of computer technology.

Though managers may not suffer as did the father in W. W. Jacob's story, "The Monkey's Paw," there is a lesson to be learned from this story. The plot concerns a man awarded three wishes as owner of a magical monkey's paw. The man's first wish was for $200 as recompense for the life of a son mangled while operating a machine. The second wish, for the son's return, was granted in the form of a mutilated ghost knocking at the door. The man's third wish, for the disappearance of this ghost, left him as bereaved as at the beginning. The father really wanted the return of his son as he was before the accident, but he had failed to express that wish precisely.

Managers, like the owner of the monkey's paw, must learn how to express their wishes. An information system produces only what is asked, but this may not be what the manager really wants. In order to exploit information technology, knowledge about computers and their capabilities is required. New skills and new patterns of decision making must be learned. A different cadre of business managers from managers in the past is in demand.

Role of management in developing information systems

What information is needed, why, for whom, and when are specifications on which the design of an information system is based. Determining such specifications is the responsibility of management, though analysts and consultants may assist in this determination. Implementation of the system is more technical, a responsibility of computer personnel, though liaison with management is necessary when making organizational changes required for the new system. Implementation transforms design specifications into the desired finished product: the new information system.

A distinction between user (management) and developer (systems analyst) is often made when discussing the development of information systems, but it is the authors' position that both groups are developers. They must cooperate, understand each other's capabilities and limitations, and support one another throughout the development process. Development is a highly interactive process. But too often in the past top management had relinquished its responsibility by allowing computer personnel to determine their own objectives, set up their own standards, and measure their own performance. This is management by default.

A lack of interest on the part of management can lead to serious undesirable consequences. According to one commentator, managers who are not willing to invest some of their time in the development process are not likely to use a management control system well, and their system, in turn, is likely to abuse them.

To effectively discharge their role in the development of information systems, managers should understand basic analytic tools. They should have fundamental knowledge of information systems and data organization, and should comprehend the process of developing an information system. This book discusses all of these topics.

Outline of book

The text is divided into five parts. Part 1 presents computer technology needed for a computerized information system. The discussion of the basic components of computers and computer-related equipment does not require any previous computing background or experience to be understood. The section on computer hardware in this part includes a look at input, output, and storage equipment, and the use of telecommunications for transferring data and information. Computer software (programs to instruct the computer on the processing of data) is also introduced.

Though much of the information in Chapters 1–5 can be found in introductory textbooks, the emphasis in this book is on recent developments. For example, Chapter 2 includes a discussion on microelectronics; Chapter 3, dialogue and interactive languages; and Chapter 4, scanners, COM (computer output on microfilm), voice recognition, and terminals with intelligent, graphic, and interactive capabilities. Chapter 5 is on the subject of telecommunications and networks. Many computerized business applications depend on this technology.

Data, another component of an information system, are defined and the related technology discussed in Part 2. Since the cost per bit of random access storage of data has dropped steadily since 1970 with every indication that this trend will continue, businesses today are collecting increasingly large amounts of data. To use data effectively requires a basic knowledge of data organization, storage, and retrieval techniques, all described in this part of the text.

The development of an information system is the subject of Part 3. No two information systems are alike because every organization has unique output needs, but common to all systems are procedures for determining the needs of the information system and specific steps for designing and implementing the system, testing it, and converting the old to the new. The activities in each of these stages are presented.

The management of an information system is also important if the system is to be effective and economically efficient. Part 4 discusses how to operate, maintain, evaluate, control, and organize an information system.

Information systems in businesses have many applications. These are discussed in Part 5. Sample functional applications are presented, integrating the principles and concepts described in the first four parts of this text. Also introduced are the use of computers for planning and control by top and middle management, numerical control, robots, process control, computer-aided design, electronic fund transfer, electronic mail, teleconferencing, and word processing. One chapter includes a discussion of the electronic office and the use of microcomputers for business as well. Home applications of microcomputers are also examined.

The book closes with chapters describing the impact of computers on society, and a look at information systems of the future. Though predictions about technology often prove near-sighted, particularly in a fast-paced field such as computer science, the authors do attempt to alert readers about some of the social and economic implications of tomorrow's computerized society.

A more detailed outline of the contents of this book can be obtained by reading in a series the part introductions which describe chapter contents within each part, or reading the summaries that appear at the end of each chapter.

A list of key terms and concepts introduced in the text and a set of discussion questions are at the end of each chapter, followed by a selected annotated bibliography for further study. Some chapters have a set of exercises as well. A contextual definition of terms and concepts presented in the book is found in the Appendix, "Glossary in Prose."

Discussion questions

1. Why should business students study computer processing and computerized information systems?

2. Need a businessperson know about a computer? What understanding of a computer and a computer system is necessary? Why?

3. Is the need for information systems for business increasing or decreasing? What is the future trend? How does it depend on the nature, size, and complexity of the business?

4. What is the difference between mechanization, automation, and computerization?

5. Give examples of users of computerized information in business and industry.

6. Why might a business without a computer fail?

7. What are the major trends in computers and computing in terms of speed, reliability, cost-effectiveness, and size? Are these trends expected to continue? If so, for how long and to what extent?

8. Distinguish between user and developer.

9. State briefly your view of the limitations of computers and your agreement or disagreement with the many fictional views described in this chapter.

10. Would you agree that persons who like computers tend to be technologists, scientists, and mathematicians, and those who dislike computers, humanists?

11. Our current dependence on computers is dangerous. Do you agree with this statement? Why?

12. Give examples of misuse of information technology.

13. What is the role of a manager in the development and maintenance of an information system?

14. What abilities must a manager have in order to effectively participate in the development of an information system?

15. What are some of the potential capabilities of information technology?

Exercise

1. Read the article by Harold J. Leavitt and Thomas L. Whistler, "Management in the 1980s," *Harvard Business Review* no. 6 (November–December 1958), and a follow-up by J. G. Hunt and P. F. Newell, "Management in the 1980s Revisited," *Personnel Journal* 16, no. 1 (January 1971). Both these articles are printed in Gordon B. Davis and Gordon C. Everest, *Readings in Management Information Systems* (New York: McGraw-Hill, 1976) pp. 266–84.

   Identify the predictions made regarding information technology and the effect advances in technology will have on management, business organization structure, and management information systems. Have predictions mentioned in these articles already become a reality? Are the authors' assumptions wrong? Do you anticipate that the predictions will become true in the 1980s? Why is it difficult and dangerous to predict advances in computer technology and the implications of such advances?

Selected annotated bibliography

Baer, Robert M. *The Digital Villain.* Reading, Mass.: Addison-Wesley Publishing, 1972.

The subtitle of this book is: *Notes on the Numerology, Parapsychology, and Metaphysics of the Computer.* Despite the forbidding subtitle, this is a delightful book on computers in fiction. It cites extensively from many books, films, and plays where a computer is usually the villain. It also discusses the social implications in the event that fiction becomes reality.

Bryce, Tim. "Information Systems—A Field in Transition." *Journal of Systems Management* 34, no. 8 (August 1983), pp. 6–13.

An overview of the challenges to be faced by management when applying information technology. The challenges identified are retraining at all levels, active user participation, and executive management commitment when developing information systems and establishing information policies and controls.

Cushing, David. "Computer Literacy for Managers." *Training/HRD* 20, no. 2 (February 1983), pp. 22–25.

The author discusses how managers can achieve computer literacy.

Dolotta, T. A., et al. *Data Processing in 1980–1985: A Study of Potential Limitations to Progress.* New York: John Wiley & Sons, 1976. 191 pp.

There are seven authors of this book, all from industry, including representatives of the computer industry. They focus on the mainstream of large, general-purpose, business-oriented data processing systems and predict changing demands on both the data processing industry and on management. The appendix has a set of tables that includes predictions on expenditures and personnel required for 1980–1985.

Goleman, Daniel. "The Electronic Rorschach." *Psychology Today* 17, no. 2 (February 1983), pp. 36–43.

A delightful and refreshing view of the uneasy relationship between humans and machines. The title refers to the author's thesis that people project their faith or distrust of older technologies onto newer ones. Goleman also addresses the computer literacy issue and concludes that such literacy is becoming as essential as reading, writing, and arithmetic.

Laughery, Kenneth R., ed. *Information Technology and Psychology.* New York: Praeger Publishers, 1982, 260 pp.

This book is a collection of 12 articles that emerged from a symposium. The articles discuss the implementation of computer technology in the future. Training and human factor studies are also considered.

Martin, James. *Telematic Society: A Challenge for Tomorrow.* Englewood Cliffs, N.J.: Prentice-Hall, 1981, 244 pp.

This book discusses the implications of computer technology in our society and in the world.

Simon, H.A. "What Computers Mean for Man and Society." *Science* 195, no. 4283 (March 18, 1977), pp. 1186–91.

The author looks into the present and the future of computers and their impact on society, especially in relation to control and privacy, the nature of work, and shifts in the structure of business employment. The author, a Nobel prizewinner in economics, has been a keen commentator on decision making and artificial intelligence, and the relationship between the two.

Turkle, Sherry. "Computer as Rorschach." *Transactions in Social Sciences and Modern Society* 17, no. 2 (January–February 1980), pp. 15–24.

This article is well written and provocative. Turkle looks at the computer as a metaphor and suggests that the subjective side of the computer presence is highly relevant to understanding issues concerning computation and public life. People have stronger feelings about computers than they realize and find the impersonality of computers threatening, according to Turkle. Any discussion on computers raises "tense questions on what is man and what is machine."

Turn, Rein. *Computers in the 1980s.* New York: Columbia University Press, 1977. 257 pp.

This book is a set of predictions by a senior analyst at RAND corporation. The author looks at developments in CPU hardware, peripherals, communication systems, and computer systems until 1990 and tells the reader how to revise these predictions as certain developments occur. The forecast assumes no supertechnological breakthrough.

In Part Four of the book the author discusses specific innovations which include modularity of systems and networks, software transferability, greater failure-tolerant systems, and increased viability of human-machine interface.

Weil, Ulric. *Information Systems in the 80s.* Englewood Cliffs, N.J.: Prentice-Hall, 1982, 383 pp.

This book discusses products, markets and vendors. The effect of Japanese competition on public policy in relation to the computer industry is also examined.

Yarrish, Edward B. "Computer Literacy: A New Requirement for Managers?" *ABA Banking Journal* 74, no. 3 (April 1982), pp. 52–56.

Yarrish makes a convincing argument for the need for computer literacy and discusses a five-point strategy to achieve it.

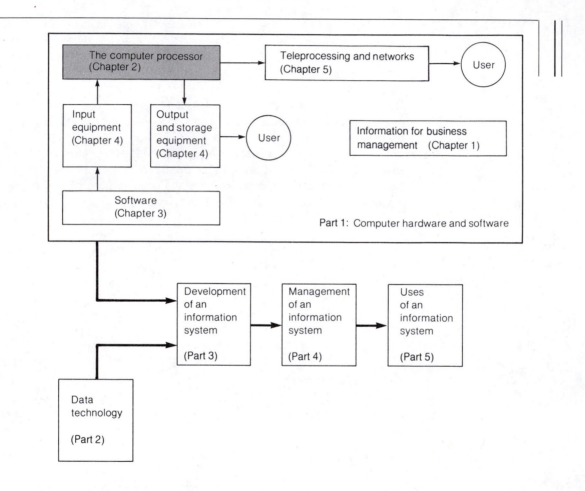

The computer processor (Chapter 2)

Teleprocessing and networks (Chapter 5)

User

Input equipment (Chapter 4)

Output and storage equipment (Chapter 4)

User

Information for business management   (Chapter 1)

Software (Chapter 3)

Part 1: Computer hardware and software

Development of an information system (Part 3)

Management of an information system (Part 4)

Uses of an information system (Part 5)

Data technology (Part 2)

The computer processor

2

An information system is an organized set of components designed to produce intelligence required for decision making. In a business context, the information is for management. The system itself has four main components: input, output, computer programs, and the processor. The relationship between these parts is shown in Figure 2.1. The subject of this chapter is the processor. The other components and the design of the system will be discussed in chapters that follow.

Justification for computer processors

Following a transaction, data on the event must be handled according to predetermined procedures and decision rules to generate desired information. This can be done by hand, called **manual processing,** but when computations are complex and large in volume, such processing can be slow, monotonous, inaccurate, and costly. Machine processing is then recommended, often called simply **data processing.**

Data processing was first used by Herman Hollerith to speed up processing of 1890 census data. The machine processing was done with greater accuracy and in one third the time that manual processing had required.

Hollerith developed a card on which data could be represented by holes, a card known as the **Hollerith card,** which has since been produced in such massive quantities by IBM that it is more commonly called the **IBM card.** When data processing was in its infancy, these cards often contained data for one record, such as all sales data for one transaction, so that processing cards became known as **unit record processing.** The machines used were electrical and performed primarily accounting operations, which explains why they were called **electrical accounting machines** or **EAM** equipment. As the amount of data to be processed increased, this equipment proved slow and expensive to use. It was re-

Figure 2.1
Main components of an information system

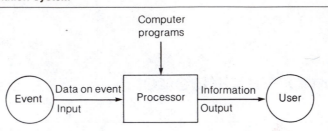

placed by the electronic computer for **electronic data processing,** known as **EDP.**

Although both EAM and EDP require the initial investment of costly equipment, large-volume data processing reaches a **break-even point** where use of the equipment is economically justified. Savings in processing occur for added volume beyond this point. Figure 2.2 illustrates this concept. In this figure, variable costs are shown by the slope of the total cost lines. It will be noted that the slope of *AB* for manual processing is steeper than *CD,* the slope of machine processing. (*CD* includes EAM and other office machines such as bookkeeping equipment.) That means that the variable cost per unit processed is higher in manual processing, though the fixed cost *OA* (desk, pencil, paper) is lower. The break-even point, *P,* representing volume processing, *OE,* is the point beyond which machine processing is warranted. For lower volume, manual processing remains

Figure 2.2
Break-even points for machine and computer processing

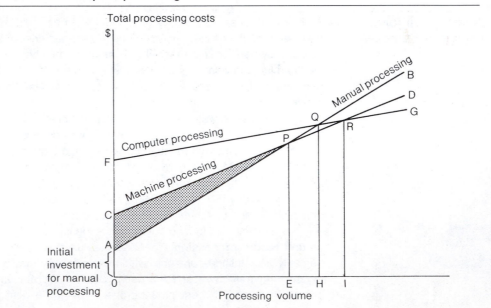

COMPUTER HARDWARE

This microcomputer consists of a CRT screen, a single disk drive for a floppy disk, a keyboard, and a phone for the transmission of data or voice to another terminal, computer, or other data processing device. *Courtesy of Mitel.*

Mainframe computers, like this one, range in cost from a few hundred thousand dollars to several million. Generally mainframes are general-purpose computers capable of performing most of the information processing needs of the organizations they serve. *Courtesy of Electronic Data Systems Corporation.*

Some personal computers enable a user to delete a line, edit a sentence, change a worksheet, or initiate commands by simply touching the screen. *Courtesy of Carroll Touch Technology.*

COMPUTER HARDWARE

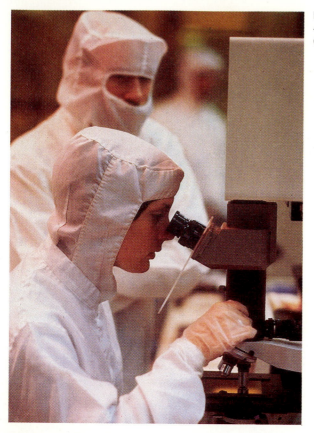

Microelectronic circuits are inspected under 400X microscopes in the clean room facility at GE. *Courtesy of General Electric.*

A digitizer, a hand-operated device, is moved over a picture. Coordinates are keyed by the user. This information is stored. When later processed, a computer can re-create the picture or manipulate the data concerning the digitized picture. *Courtesy of Sanders Associates, Inc.*

Data network management is provided by this turnkey communications system. It provides managers with the capability to control, monitor, and restore even the largest networks from a central site. *Courtesy of Racal-Milgo.*

This light-weight portable microcomputer, designed for businesspersons, fits into an attaché case. *Courtesy of GRiD SystemsCorporation.*

Bar codes are frequently used in making high-security, machine-readable identity cards. *Courtesy of Ericsson.*

A wand is used to enter data into a library computer. It reads book identification codes when charging and discharging books. *Courtesy of IBM.*

COMPUTER HARDWARE

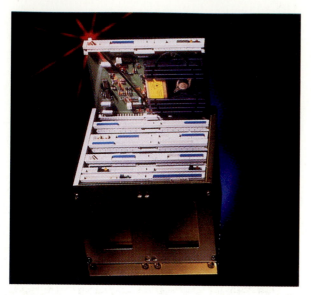

Highly sophisticated optical fiber systems are used in urban network linking. *Courtesy of Ericsson.*

These photographs show future executive workstations. A single workstation may be combined with other similar workstations, creating a conference room or a teleconferencing area to be used by more than one person. In both cases note the absence of stacks of paper. This is a paperless environment.

more economical, the shaded area showing the savings that would accrue if manual instead of machine processing were used.

The slope of computer processing is even flatter, though initial costs are higher. The break-even point compared to manual processing (*AB*) is *Q,* for volume *OH.* A much higher volume of data processing (*OI*) is needed when compared to machine processing (*CD*) before EDP becomes economically justified.

This figure is merely a model. In an actual case, the starting point on the *X* axis would depend on the equipment used, and the slope of manual processing would depend on the wage scale. But the general concept that this figure illustrates would still apply. As the volume of data processing increases, the switchover from manual to machine to computer processing becomes economically justified. For large volume processing, beyond *OI* in Figure 2.2, computer processing is the cheapest way to generate information.

The digital computer

Computers may be classified in terms of the type of data processed. When data is discrete (separate, made up of distinct parts: e.g., counting units coming off an assembly line), a **digital computer** is used.[1] When data is processed continuously (e.g., monitoring temperature, pressure, and flow of liquids in manufacturing), an **analog computer** is used. A **hybrid computer** handles both discrete and continuous data. Since businesses usually deal with discrete digital data, digital computers are most commonly used for management decision making.

The main components of a digital computer system are shown in Figure 2.3. The **central processor (CPU)** in this system has three parts: the **arithmetic and logic unit,** the **memory and storage unit,** and the **control unit.**

Input data is stored in the memory until it is ready to be processed. Also stored are instructions concerning computations to be performed—calculations such as addition and multiplication which are carried out by the arithmetic unit, which also does logical operations, for example, comparisons. The control unit coordinates the sequence of instructions and flow of data between units.

Intermediate calculations and other information related to the transformation of input are also stored. If the volume of data to be stored is too large for the **internal memory** or **main memory,** it can be stored in **external memory** or **secondary storage** on such devices as magnetic tapes or disks. Some manufacturers have developed **virtual memory,** which enables secondary storage to be treated as an extension of the internal memory, thereby effectively expanding internal storage capacity.

Digital computers have changed greatly since the UNIVAC computer became commercially available in 1951. The changes came in large jumps of performance, referred to as **generations** of computers, instead of slowly and gradually

---

[1] According to Webster's dictionary, this sentence should be written, "When data are discrete. . . ." However, in computer terminology, data is usually considered a singular, collective noun.

Figure 2.3
The organization of a digital computer system

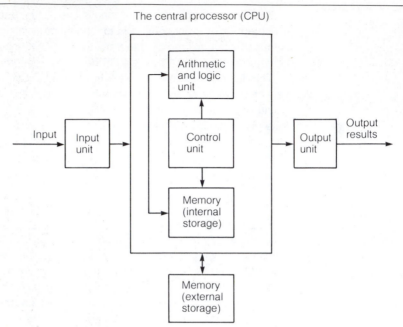

as might be expected. In the first generation, **vacuum tubes** were used; in the second, **transistors;** in the third, **integrated circuits;** and in the fourth, **large-scale integration (LSI)** of circuits. We expect fifth generation computers in the near future. These computers will be characterized by very very large-scale integration, will operate at speeds measured in trillionths of a second, and have "intelligent" processors (processors that can make inferences). A time line of computer generations appears in Figure 2.4. A comparison of generation characteristics is found in Table 2.1.

| CPU advances | All digital data can be represented by unique arrangements of the digits 0 and 1. These **binary digits,** called **bits,** can be represented by two states (on and off in a switch, different states of electrons in a vacuum tube, or by high and low voltage in a transistor). The answers to true-false statements, for example, can be coded in binary digits; that is, off = false, on = true. The British mathematician Boole designed algebra (Boolean algebra) using the true-false concept for a logical analysis that is electronically represented in gates. A **gate** controls the flow of information by providing an output signal only when the input signals are in prescribed states. Combinations of gates enable such computations as addition, subtraction, multiplication, division, and comparisons. It is the production method of these gates that changed with the generations of digital computers. The first vacuum tube gates proved unreliable. These gates were replaced by the transis- |

tor which proved 1,000 times more reliable. Transistors were in time replaced by integrated circuits that proved 100 times more reliable still. Thus, the progression to integrated circuits from the vacuum tube represented an improvement of reliability by a factor of 100,000.

While reliability was advancing, costs were decreasing. The vacuum tube gate

Figure 2.4
The relationship of component development and computer generations in time

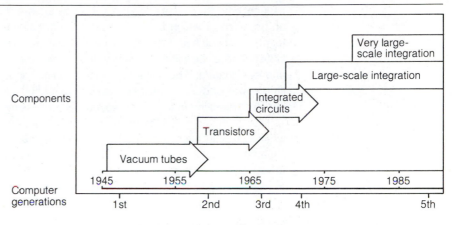

Table 2.1
Comparison of computer generations

Major characteristics	First generation	Second generation	Third and fourth generation	Fifth generation
Introduced	1950s	1960s	1907s–80s	1990s
Electronic circuitry	Vacuum tubes	Transistors	Integrated circuits (IC, LSI, VLSI)	Very, very large scale integration (VVLSI)
Size	Room size	Closet size	Desktop to chip	Not known
Speed	Millisecond	Microsecond	Nanosecond	Picosecond
Most common languages used	Symbolic or machine language	High level, e.g., FORTRAN, COBOL	High and higher level, e.g., query languages	Artificial intelligence-oriented language
Main memory	Magnetic	Magnetic	Solid state	Solid state
Reliability Relative	1	1,000	100,000	Infinity
Failure	1 every few hours	1 every 100–1,000 hours	1 every million hours	Approaching 0
Applications	Scientific and engineering	Business	Integrated	Artificial-intelligence-oriented
Early examples	ENIAC IBM 650	IBM 1401 Honeywell 200	IBM 360 IBM 370 NCR 395 Minis Micros	Super super-computer

cost about $10. Only one cent was required for an integrated circuit gate in the late 1970s.

Other characteristics of digital computers have been affected by technological developments as well. The early vacuum tubes were large, consumed much electrical power, and generated considerable heat. Air conditioning and frequent maintenance were required. Transistors are smaller, cheaper, generate less heat, and consume less power. Integrated circuits made quantum jumps in all these areas, but especially in size. The technology that made this possible was **microelectronics,** a photolithography process for fabricating millions of elements of circuitry onto thin wafers of silicon. The wafers are divided into individual **dice** or **chips,** each of which forms at least one complete electronic circuit that is photographically etched. Integrated circuitry contains many interconnections that previously had to be joined manually; thus there is a saving in labor and materials and less chance of human error causing malfunction. Integrated circuits consume little power and their small size means that short distances of circuitry must be traveled, resulting in increased speeds of processing.

Chip technology is also used in memory units. A three-quarter-inch diameter wafer can hold over 100 square silicon chips, each able to store 64,000 bits of information. 256 K RAM chips are beginning to be commercially available. By 1987 annual sales for these chips will be an estimated $3.5 billion.

Modes of processing

Batch processing

In the first generation of digital computers, **batch processing** was used. This technique is still employed though faster processing methods have been developed. Many persons use batch processing when paying bills. They do not write checks immediately upon receipt of bills, but collect them waiting until the monthly paycheck arrives at which time all bills are paid at once. Writing checks in a batch saves time since checkbook, pen, stamps, and envelopes must be located and put back only once a month instead of numerous times. In computer batch processing, either the computer operator or the system itself collects jobs in batches, resulting in a significant reduction in overhead costs since repetitive handling of each job is eliminated. Batch processing of data reduces processing costs, though a processing delay of hours or days may result.

Delay in batch processing is compounded when the source of data is remote from the computer. The use of **telecommunications lines** (the telephone, for example) to transfer data to the CPU reduces this delay. Special control programs for receiving, checking, scheduling, and observing priorities for data processing services are added to the system when **remote processing** is employed. Businesses that have multiple sources of data generation use remote processing for input **(remote job entry).**

Equipment not directly connected to a computer is called **offline. Online** means users have direct access to the computer system for both input and output. That is, user terminals are either plugged into the CPU or connected by a telecommunication line, such as telephone or satellite.

Time sharing

The slow speed of telecommunications equipment for input and output relative to computer processing speeds has led to the development of a processing system called **time sharing.** With time sharing, several users share a block of computer time. The computer actually processes each user's data in sequence, but the response time of the computer is so fast that it seems as if all processing is being handled simultaneously.

Time sharing usually requires fair-use rules, rules to establish processing priorities. These rules are used in scheduling when many users want service or when a single user has a complex problem to solve that requires a great deal of processing time. Some time-sharing systems operate on a first-come, first-served basis. The disadvantage is that users with small jobs have to wait until users with long jobs are serviced. Sometimes priority depends on the status of the user or the urgency of the job. **Round-robin service** gives all users a small slice of computing time in turn. Second generation computers, which first used round-robin service, had such fast processing speeds that most users were under the illusion that the computer was dedicated to their sole use.

Time sharing has proved particularly valuable to small businesses unable to afford computers and software equipment of their own. Another group of users is found among firms that have switched from batch processing to time sharing, attracted by the convenience and speed of time sharing, even though the cost of information processed by this mode is higher. Time sharing is widely used, although problems with data security and priority processing can arise. A summary of the advantages and disadvantages of time sharing appears in Table 2.2.

**Table 2.2
Time sharing**

Characteristics
   Central computer accessible to multiple users for input and output.
   Telephonic connections between computer and user at remote sites.

Advantages
   Enables small user to have access to a large computer system, sharing overhead costs
      with other users.
   Reduces overhead cost even for large user.
   Provides access to data bases and generalized applications programs.
   Faster response than batch.
   Enables interactive and conversational use of computer.
   No geographic restriction except for cost of transmission.
   Convenience of use.

Disadvantages
   When system is down, all users sharing the system are affected.
   Higher cost than batch processing.
   Loss of security. Data is subject to violation either due to accident or design.
   Response time can drop with increase in number of users, especially those with large
      scientific problems to process.
   Possible loss of priority when large competitive demands are placed on system.

Time sharing does not always provide immediate access to computing power that some businesses require. For example, banks may want quick access at all times to the status of a customer's current balance. For instantaneous processing and continuous updating of the data base, **real-time systems** were developed in the second generation of computers.

Real time

Real-time systems process input and deliver output continuously and simultaneously. They are used to monitor data and to detect undesirable deviations from predetermined standards and then provide feedback information for control. For example, the computer may process continuous data on an industrial process and issue instructions for controlling that process, such as monitoring pressure and shutting off valves when pressure gets too high. Though real-time processing is instantaneous, the speed of output will depend on need, taking only a fraction of a second in some cases or minutes in others, depending on the time required to make the necessary correction or the urgency of information processed. Such a system must be online; hence it is called an **online real-time** system or **OLRT.**

Distributed processing

Distributed data processing, the relocation and distribution of computing capability from a central location to remote sites (such as branch offices, warehouses, and plants), is one of the results of the development of third generation computers. Giving local levels more autonomy through distributed processing results in decentralization, changing the organizational structure of firms and their patterns of decision making. The impact of such processing on management will be discussed in Part 4 at length.

Two technological developments have made distributed data processing feasible: teleprocessing (see Chapter 5) and microelectronics including microprocessors, microcomputers, and minicomputers. Microelectronics, in drastically reducing computing cost, have made one-site data processing practical. The nature and implications of microelectronics are the subject of the remaining parts of this chapter.

Microelectronics

Microelectronics became possible as a result of advances made in solid-state physics and integrated circuitry. In the early stages of microelectronics, the concentration of circuit components that were integrated was small, called **small-scale integration (SSI).** Conventional transistor circuitry as found in radios was used. This circuitry consumed much electric current and developed heat which limited the number of transistors that could be put on one chip. These problems were overcome by **metal oxide semiconductor (MOS) technology** which enabled greater concentration of circuitry per chip, or large-scale integration (LSI). A comparison of LSI and SSI appears in Table 2.3.

In 1964, Gordon E. Moore, then working for Fairchild, noted that the number

Table 2.3
Summary of SSI and LSI

Characteristic	Small-scale integrated circuits	Large-scale integrated circuits
Components per circuit	1–32	1,000–262,000
Size of computer	Desk or desk-top size	Typewriter size to chip size
Speed of computer	100 nanoseconds	5 nanoseconds
Main memory	Magnetic core	LSI circuits
Mode of processing	Time sharing Online real time	Distributed processing Microprocessors Microcomputers Minicomputers

of components per circuit had a linear relationship over time. He correctly predicted that circuit complexity would double each year. Technology still hasn't reached the limits imposed by the laws of physics. Further miniaturization is still possible.

Microprocessors

LSI technology means that an entire CPU can now be placed on a single chip. **Microprocessors,** designed to perform specific functions in products and to make needed adjustments necessary for changed conditions, utilize this miniaturization. Through **sensors,** a microprocessor can collect input on performance, evaluate it against preset standards, and through an actuator, make control adjustments. For example, in cars, a microprocessor can optimize consumption of fuel by sensing the air environment (temperature, velocity, density) and adjusting the mixture of air and fuel accordingly. A user may also change the microprocessor's **microcode** (program) from one control application to another.

Table 2.4 is a list of products where microprocessors are commonly used. Many of these need more than one micro. Uses of microprocessors in an airplane are shown in Figure 2.5. Table 2.5 summarizes current and potential use of microprocessors in automobiles. A study by Arthur D. Little predicts that by 1987 the microprocessor industry will have 400 million chip-based consumers.[2]

Microcomputers

When microprocessors are given additional memory and input/output capabilities they are called **microcomputers** (often called a **micro,** although the term **micro** can also refer to a microprocessor). Unlike a microprocessor designed for a spe-

[2] A single copy of the results of this $2-million study cost costs $35,000. A report of this study appears in the *Economist* 270, no. 7073 (March 24–30, 1979), p. 49.

Table 2.4
Uses of microprocessors

Industrial products	Consumer products
Aircraft subsystems	Automobile subsystems
Blood analyzers	Blenders
Cash registers	Burglar alarms
Communication devices	Calculators
Copying machines	Cameras
Dictating machines	Clocks
Gasoline pumps	Clothes dryers
Lab equipment control	Dishwashers
Machine control	Electric slicing knives
Measuring instruments	Fire alarms
Medical diagnostics	Food blenders
Pacemakers	Hair dryers
Robots	Heating systems
Scales	Microwave ovens
Scanners	Monitoring of home utilities:
Taxi meters	fuel/heat/water/light
Telephone switching	Ovens
Testing instruments	Pinball machines
Traffic lights	Radios
TV cameras	Refrigerators
Vending machines	Slow cookers
and so forth	Stereo systems
	Telephones
	Television sets
	Washing machines
	Watches
	and so forth

cific application, a microcomputer is a general-purpose computer. A microcomputer can be constructed on a chip or chips and may be much smaller than a fingertip, as illustrated in Figure 2.6. One of these chips can be a microprocessor, an enlarged photograph of which appears in Figure 2.7 with its main functional components identified. A functional representation of this microprocessor within a microcomputer, shown in Figure 2.8, corresponds with the basic components of a computer illustrated in Figure 2.3. The term **bus** in these figures refers to circuits used for transmitting data or power. A **register** is a temporary storage device.

The sale of desk-top microcomputers to businesspersons and homeowners as **personal computers** is a potentially explosive market. Software is being developed for entertainment (games) and computing applications such as checkbook balancing, keeping a calendar of events, calculating income taxes, monitoring investments, updating address lists, and typing letters. A California Supreme Court justice has even used a personal computer to index data from a trial. Neither cost nor hardware technology limits the widespread use of microcomputers at present. It is, rather, a reluctance to learn how to use computers and a lack of appropriate software that is slowing sales. When these problems are overcome, there will be a revolution in the way we live, work, and do business.

Figure 2.5
Use of microprocessors and microcomputers in aircraft

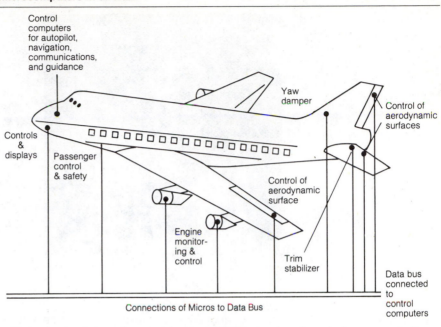

Control computers for autopilot, navigation, communications, and guidance

Yaw damper

Control of aerodynamic surfaces

Controls & displays

Passenger control & safety

Control of aerodynamic surface

Engine monitoring & control

Trim stabilizer

Data bus connected to control computers

Connections of Micros to Data Bus

Modern jet aircraft depend on a variety of sophisticated subsystems for navigation, communication, music, passenger comfort and safety, engine control, and the control of aerodynamic surfaces. At present, the sensors that monitor these various systems transmit their data to related central computers. The cable lengths required for such centralized systems have become a significant portion of the total cost of modern aircraft avionics. Various aircraft subsystems can be controlled locally by microprocessors using data bus or multiplexing techniques. A savings in cable costs, increased reliability, increased computing power, and lower life-cycle maintenance can result. Such distributed computing networks are under active examination for a wide variety of similar applications.

Table 2.5
Uses of microprocessors in an automobile

Accessory control	Exhaust gas control
Air conditioning control	Locking doors
Belt buckling control	Maintenance analysis
Braking control	Skid control
Collision avoidance system	Speed control
Comfort control	Steering control
Control of subsystems such as level of fuel,	Theft deterrent control
driver's seat, and mirror adjustments	Trip information (distance to
Emission control	destination, driving range,
Engine control	and so forth)
Air-fuel mixture	Vehicle diagnosis
Ignition timing	Vehicle performance analysis

Figure 2.6
A microcomputer on a chip placed against a fingertip

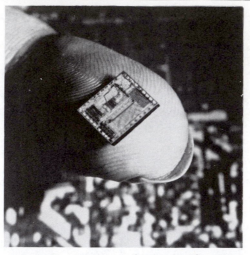

Courtesy Intel Corporation

Minicomputers (mini)

The term **mini** originally meant smaller in memory capacity; lower in cost; slower in speed; and smaller in size than other computers on the market. However, when microcomputers were developed, they were much smaller than minis. Nevertheless, the term *mini,* continued to be used. Minicomputer describes general-purpose computers smaller than mainframes, but with more computing power than most microcomputers.

Today minicomputers are not small as the name implies. The PDP-11 is six feet high and occupies 14 by 18 inches of floor space. This does not include a printer but does include storage devices like the **magnetic cassette** and the **floppy disk.** (The nonrigid floppy is preferable to former disks which required large disk drive units and had to be extremely level for operation.)

Minis have added to their computing capability in recent years, incorporating technological advances of the last decade. In fact, modern minis are more powerful than the large computers manufactured 10 years ago so that the term *mini* is indeed a misnomer. Though the line of division between minis and larger models is less clear-cut than formerly, minis still have lower processing speeds, a relatively small memory, fewer peripheral units for input-output (I/O), and less software support than medium or large-scale computers. The low speed is the result of an architectural characteristic: small **word** size where a word is a unit of storage. This small width of word reduces the number of instructions that can be fetched from memory at one time. The word size varies between 8 and 18 bits. If a mini has 16 bits per word, and floating point calculations (with decimal numbers) are being computed, this requires 64 bits; that is, four fetches from memory, instead of one fetch with a 64-bit machine, resulting in low speed of processing.

Figure 2.7
Components of the Intel 8086 microprocessor

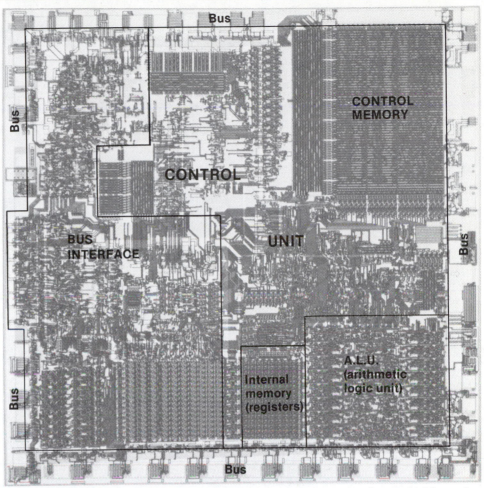

Bus

Bus

CONTROL
MEMORY

CONTROL

Bus

BUS
INTERFACE

UNIT

A.L.U.
(arithmetic
logic unit)

Internal
memory
(registers)

Bus

Bus

Courtesy Intel Corporation

The CPU and memory of minicomputers can be built from microprocessors and chips. Different **configurations** can be constructed for varying applications as shown in Figure 2.9. As prices for microprocessors drop, it may become possible to have hundreds or even thousands of processors working in parallel on a common problem. This would increase the processing capability of machines and hence be a contribution to machine intelligence (artificial intelligence).

Because of the adaptability and flexibility of minicomputer configurations, over a third of the production is bought by companies called **original equipment manufacturers (OEMs)** who resell the minis with their own software as a **package** with applications in accounting, sales, control of manufacture, and other specialized business functions. Such packages enable small businesses with low budgets and nontechnical personnel to purchase and use a computer.

The characteristics, advantages, and limitations of minicomputers are summarized in Table 2.6. Both minis and micros are least effective when applications are complex. For simple problems, the price performance ratio of a microproces-

Figure 2.8
Basic components of a microcomputer

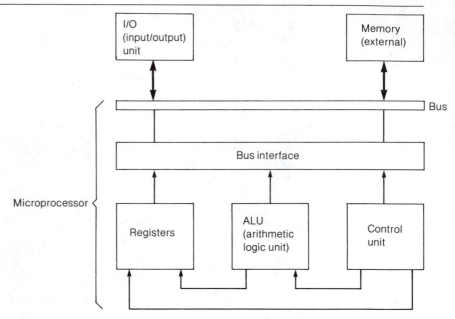

Table 2.6
Common characteristics, advantages, and limitations of a minicomputer

Characteristics
  16-bit word
  4–28000 word storage
  Low cost ($10–25,000)
  Integrated circuit technology used for both CPU and memory

Advantages
  Ease of use
  Low cost (compared to mainframe)
  Flexibility through external programs
  Adaptability to different configurations

*Limitations**
  Cannot perform complex programs
  Slow speeds of computing due to small word size and limited software support
  Many manufacturers are new to the field
  Has limited peripherals

Many of these limitations are being overcome in newer models.

Figure 2.9
Configurations of micro and mini hardware

Micro hardware hierarchy		Capabilities	Typical uses and users
Level	Representation		
Chips	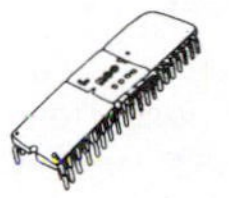	Custom design of a hardware system for particular need	Hardware designers
Modules	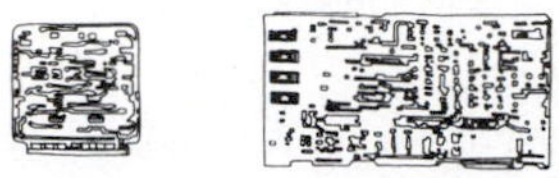	Small development system for learning microprocessor characteristics Small-user programs (under 1 K)	Beginning users of microprocessors Elementary prototyping User evaluation of microprocessor
Small computer system (SCS)	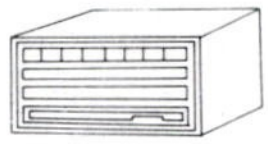	Intermediate-complexity applications programs (1-10 K) Some higher-level language capability (e.g. BASIC)	Personal computer Hobbyist
Full development system (FDS)	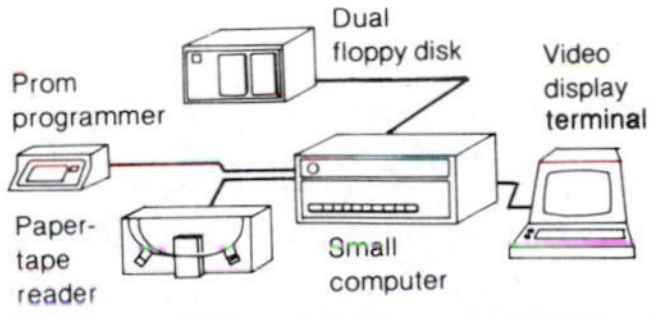	Full software development Hardware debugging Higher-level language programming	Software-applications programming Debugging of hardware target system
Multiprocessor system	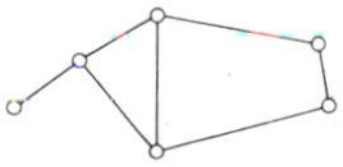	Distributed computing Tightly coupled parallel processing	Process automation Coordination and control on a distributed and local basis

Microprocessor systems can be arranged in an ascending hierarchy of hardware and software in which smaller components are assembled into successively larger systems with more powerful capabilities. The building blocks are the families of chips designed for various functions. To solve an application problem, for example, the control system of an airplane, designers usually assemble modules or small computer systems and provide them with a suitable program for the task. Chips and modules have become so cheap (less than $30 for a microprocessor and less than $300 for a single-board module) that a major cost in engineering an application is the cost of developing the software to create the final program for the "target" system. Improvements in semiconductor technology are steadily making it possible for systems at each level to include more of capabilities once assigned to level above.

SOURCE   Adapted from Hoo-Min D. Toong, "Microprocessors," *Scientific American* 237, no. 3 (September 1977), pp. 154–55.

Table 2.7
Uses of microcomputers and minis

Badge and credit-card checking	Passenger movement control
Bank terminals	Personal computer
Bartenders	Physician control of
Blood analyzer	information on patients
CAI (computer-assisted instruction)	Plant schedule control
Cash register	Printing
Communication	Editing
Storing and forwarding messages	Typesetting
Monitoring telephone lines	Page layout
Education	Process control
Elevator control	Security and access control
Gas pump control	Shopping scales
Input validation on terminals	Simulation
Instrumentation	Stock and commodity applications
Medical diagnosis	Stand-alone computer for small
Mixers (e.g., paint and other substances)	businesses
Numerical control	Text editing
Online calculations in hotel	Typewriters
Bill	Vending machines
Restaurant	
Tip	

sor is least (best). As complexity increases, micros and minicomputers become cost effective until a point is reached where only large-scale computers are economically justified.

Uses of microcomputers and minis are listed in Table 2.7. It is predicted that by 1990, the price of many micros will drop to less than $100. This will be primarily due to better exploitation and integration of LSI, greater demand for distributive processing, and pressure on manufacturers and software houses for better price performance ratios.

Research directions

In the 1970s, microtechnology was largely responsible for advances in computer performance. First, there was a 4-bit machine. This was followed by an 8-bit, then a 16-bit, and then a 32-bit machine. The latter has over 450,000 transistors on a single chip.

Improvements have also been made to silicon chips.[3] We now have **wafers** 3 to 4 inches in diameter made of 100 silicon chips linked together by what is called **wafer-scale technology.** Chips often contain over 100,000 transistors and other electronic elements, compared to a few thousand in earlier chips. The close proximity of the chips means communication between them is fast and efficient. Fewer circuit connections exist as well. As a result, there has been increase in computer

[3] The area south of San Francisco where many electronic and computer firms are located is commonly called Silicon Valley. This name reflects the importance of silicon chips to the local economy.

reliability (faulty connections are often the cause of malfunction). An additional advantage of wafers is that space is available for circuits that can be used to diagnose and correct problems. We now have computers with self-repairing capabilities.

In the future, silicon chips may be commonly replaced by chips made of **gallium arsenide,** a material that allows electrons to move five times faster than silicon. A computer with such chips will, therefore, require less power. The disadvantage of gallium arsenide is that it is difficult to handle—it tends to vaporize at temperatures tolerated by silicon. Another factor that may slow the switch to the new chips is the expense of retooling equipment to produce gallium arsenide chips.

A **distributed array processor,** using thousands of microprocessors in parallel, is another computer innovation under development. This processor, however, has limited speed, for it depends on conventional integrated circuits. Another major problem is that it requires considerable power. A 250 mips computer with conventional architecture would consume around 20,000 watts and would melt as soon as it was turned on. Circuitry problems may be resolved by VLSI (very large-scale integration) and VHSIC (very high-speed integrated circuits). Chips are projected that are one hundredth the width of human hair, containing lines half a micron in size. A single chip could contain entire systems for a radar network, a library, or factory. We may someday have an information-system-on-a-chip, or an office-on-a-chip.

Research isn't limited to arrays of microprocessors. Pipelines or multiprocessors are also being studied. In addition, the Japanese government and its computer industry have announced that they are joining forces to produce a fifth-generation computer by the 1990s, a supercomputer with 10 times the speed of fourth-generation computers.

This news has alarmed the U.S. computer industry. Fearful that Americans may lose dominance in computing to the Japanese, a research corporation, **Microelectronics and Computer Technology Corporation,** jointly funded by 10 top U.S. computer companies, has been formed. This corporation will concentrate on four research areas: (1) integrated-circuit packaging; (2) computer architecture; (3) software technology; and, (4) computer-aided design and manufacturing systems. The corporation is for research only—development of products will be left to individual member companies.

Benefits from such research will not reach the marketplace immediately. It takes time to develop products with computing advances, time to develop secondary technologies needed for such products, and time to gain the confidence of consumers. Furthermore, technical feasibility does not necessarily mean a product will be manufactured. Economic factors often determine what products reach the market.

In addition, exploding demand for chips has meant that chips have been in short supply. This has slowed the introduction of new products using microtechnology. Many firms that manufactured chips in-house in the past now buy chips on the open market because of production problems at their own facilities, adding to demand.

One reason why companies manufacturing chips have not kept prace with demand is that the semiconductor industry has not earned enough profits to finance its own phenomenal growth. Investment costs for chipmaking equipment are staggering. A basic facility for the manufacture of chips could be built for $2 million in the 1960s. In 1980, the same facility cost at least $50 million. Intel, a leader in semiconductors, spent $275 million from 1981 through 1983 on chipmaking equipment.

Certainly the next decade will see an increase in the use of microchips. However, the increase may not constitute a microelectronic revolution as was once predicted.

Summary and conclusions

This chapter has discussed the evolution of computers. Minicomputers have more computing capacity than the first electronic computer, ENIAC. They are 20 times faster, have a larger memory, are thousands of times more reliable; consume the power of a light bulb rather than that of a locomotive, and occupy 1/30,000 the volume. They also cost less than 1/10,000 as much. (See Figure 2.10 for a comparison of components per chip and cost per component.) Minicomputers can be purchased by mail order or at local hobby stores. The trend is continuing toward further miniaturization, faster speeds, greater reliability, and lower costs. Past improvements were due to technological changes in the basic components of the

Figure 2.10
Trends in microelectronics

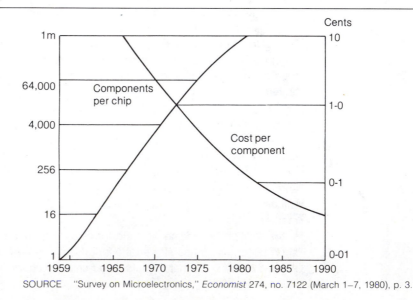

SOURCE "Survey on Microelectronics," *Economist* 274, no. 7122 (March 1–7, 1980), p. 3.

CPU, which evolved from the vacuum tube to transistors, and from SSI to LSI and chip technology. Technological advances have resulted in increased concentration of circuitry (gate density) by a factor of 100, or two magnitudes (10^2). Another two orders of magnitude are predicted for the 1980s. Yet another order of magnitude is necessary to approach the gate density of the human brain.

Micros are being incorporated in home products making them "smart." That is, they are able to evaluate the environment and the desires of the user and activate correcting adjustments where necessary. In the future, they will commonly appear in clocks, thermostats, light switches, radios, toasters, vacuum cleaners, and so forth. Micros and minis will also appear in industrial products, in the factory, and in communications. These applications will be discussed at greater length in Part 5.

Micros, minis, and **maxis** (large) computers can only do what they are programmed to do. Their intelligence is based on the instructions that tell the CPU how to process data. This subject, programming, is examined in Chapter 3.

Key words

Analog computer	Integrated circuits
Arithmetic and logic unit	Internal memory
Batch processing	Large-scale integration (LSI)
Binary digits	Magnetic cassette
Bits	Main memory
Break-even point	Manual processing
Bus	Maxi
Central processor (CPU)	Memory and storage unit
Chips	Metal oxide semiconductor
Configuration	technology (MOS)
Control unit	Micro
Data processing	Microcode
Dice	Microcomputer
Digital computer	Microelectronics
Distributed array processor	Microelectronics and Computer
Distributed data processing	Technology Corporation
Electrical accounting machines	Microprocessor
(EAM)	Mini
Electronic data processing (EDP)	Minicomputer
External memory	Offline
Floppy disk	Online
Gallium arsenide	Online real-time (OLRT)
Gate	Original equipment manufacturer
Generations	(OEM)
Hollerith card	Package
Hybrid computer	Personal computer
IBM card	Real-time systems

Register
Remote job entry
Remote processing
Round-robin service
Secondary storage
Sensor
Small-scale integration (SSI)
Telecommunication lines

Time sharing
Transistors
Unit record processing
Vacuum tubes
Virtual memory
Wafers
Wafer-scale technology
Word

Discussion questions

1. What are the economic considerations and conditions that can justify the use of computers?

2. Distinguish between manual, machine, and computer processing in terms of:
   a. Equipment used.
   b. Economic justification.

3. Distinguish between batch, time-sharing, online, and online real-time processing. Give an example of each mode of processing in business.

4. List the main advantages of computer processing over:
   a. Manual processing.
   b. Machine processing.

5. Are computers capable of making logical choices? Explain.

6. What is the effect of an increase in:
   a. Volume of processing.
   b. Fixed cost.
   c. Variable cost.

   on the break-even point between computer processing and other means of processing?

7. Give three examples from business and industry for each of the following modes of processing:
   a. Batch.
   b. Online.
   c. Online real time.
   d. Time sharing.
   e. Offline.

8. Distinguish between:
   a. Business and scientific computer.
   b. Analog and digital computer.
   c. Discrete and continuous computations.
   d. General-purpose and special-purpose computer.
   e. Small and large computer.
   f. Microcomputer and microprocessor.
   g. Microcomputer and minicomputer.

9. What is meant by the microelectronic revolution? Has this revolution affected you? How? Will it affect businesses? How?

10. What unique hardware features are required for a system operating in an OLRT environment rather than a batch environment?

11. What is meant by computer generations? How have computer generations affected the user in business?

12. What affect will the following have on managerial decision making:
    a. Gallium arsenide chips?
    b. Wafer technology?

13. What will be the impact of fifth-generation computers on:
    a. Foreign trade?
    b. World leadership in computers?
    c. Productivity?
    d. Employment?

14. Advances in microtechnology are occurring faster than we can absorb the new technology. Comment.

Exercise

1. In the table below, check the appropriate column for the best mode of processing for each application listed.

		Mode of processing		
Application	Batch	Time sharing	Online	OLRT
Airline reservations				
Hotel nationwide reservations				
An auto dealer				
Accounting				
Contract calculations				
with buyer				
Instructor keeping grades				
University keeping grades				
University admissions				
University registration				
University computing for class				
University alumni records				
Retailer point-of-sales				
credit checking				
Bank account status				
monthly ledger				
Wholesale inventory				
For perishables				
For nonperishables				
and stable demand				
Large data base computing				
and computing for sale				

Selected annotated bibliography

Boraiko, Allen A. "The Chip." *National Geographic* 162, no. 4 (October 1982), pp. 421–76.

A superb article on computers and how they work with many colorful and well-explained photographs on the production of computers.

Forester, Tom. *The Microelectronics Revolution.* Cambridge, Mass.: MIT Press, 1980, 581 pp.

This is an excellent selection of some 40 articles organized into eight chapters, each chapter ending with a guide to further reading. The selections are well balanced between such optimists as Herbert Simon, and critics like Joe Weizenbaum. Microelectronics is such a fast-moving field that anything written soon becomes obsolete. This book, however, is valuable as a reference.

Healey, Martin. "Junking the Mainframe." *Datamation®* 29, no. 3 (August 1983), pp. 120–32.

The author argues that the mainframe will not die but fade away in the next 10 years as the micro takes over. Teleprocessing networks, specifically LAN (local area networks), will be largely responsible.

Immel, A. Richard. "Small Business Computing: The Micro-Mainframe War," *Popular Computing* 2, no. 8 (June 1983), pp. 46–60.

The author describes the encroachment of micros on mainframe turf in corporate America. The conversion from mainframes to micros is also discussed.

Kibbin, Wendy Lea. "Awaiting the Intelligent Computer." *Infosystems* 30, no. 8 (August 1983), pp. 96–99.

Expert systems, automatic programming, and natural language applications are discussed. The author concludes: "Theoretically, there is no task to which an expert computer could not be assigned."

Levine, Ronald D. "Supercomputers." *Scientific American* 246, no. 1 (January 1982) pp. 118–35.

Many illustrations in this article help explain the working of supercomputers.

Pournelle, Jerry. "The Next Five Years in Microcomputers." *Byte* 8, no. 9 (September 1983), pp. 233–44.

You may not agree with Pournelle's predictions but you must admire him for daring to predict the future in such a volatile and dynamic field.

Roland, John. "The Microelectronic Revolution." *The Futurist* 13, no. 2 (April 1979), pp. 81–90.

A futurist view and an optimistic one. Roland discusses the applications of microcomputers in business and everyday life, applications in which the security and privacy of information are protected. A provocative look at micros and their effect on society.

"Thanks for the Memories." *Datamation* 28, no. 10 (September 1982), pp. 27–52.

This article appears in a special issue of *Datamation* celebrating the magazine's 25th anniversary. The contributions of Amdahl, Backus, Cray, Davis, Eckert, Mauchly, Forrester, Hewlett, Packard, Hopper, Lautenberg, Palevsky, Shockley and others are discussed.

An article by Michael Cashman, "Products of Their Times," pp. 127–34, providing an interesting walk through the history of computer products, also appears in this issue.

"The Battle of the Supercomputers: Japan All-out Challenge to the U.S." *Business Week,* no. 2812 (October 17, 1983), pp. 156–166.

A good discussion of supercomputer number crunchers under development in both the United States and Japan.

Utal, Bro. "The Coming Glut of Semiconductors." *Fortune* 109 no. 6 (March 19, 1984), pp. 125–133.

The author discusses the current soaring demand of chips and warns against an inevitable shakeout in 1986. Though chipmakers are learning from a similar boom-bust cycle in the near past, there will be overproduction followed by price slashing. The article provides a good discussion of current microtechnology trends, both production and use.

Verity, John W. "Alas, Poor Mini." *Datamation* 28, no. 10 (September 1982), pp. 223–28.

The author asks the question: "Is the mini doomed to extinction?" He concludes that the mini may live on in spirit, having helped create a marketplace for small processors.

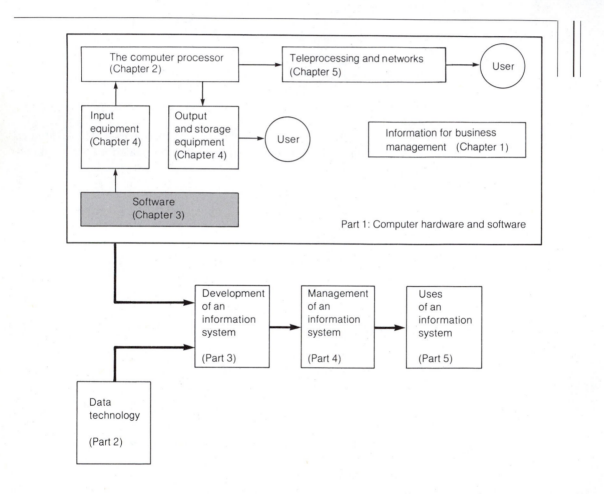

The computer processor (Chapter 2)

Teleprocessing and networks (Chapter 5)

User

Input equipment (Chapter 4)

Output and storage equipment (Chapter 4)

User

Information for business management   (Chapter 1)

Software (Chapter 3)

Part 1: Computer hardware and software

Development of an information system (Part 3)

Management of an information system (Part 4)

Uses of an information system (Part 5)

Data technology (Part 2)

Software

Computer programming as a practical human activity is some 25 years old, a short time for intellectual development. Yet computer programming has already posed the greatest intellectual challenge that mankind has faced in pure logic and complexity.

Harlan D. Mills

3

Computer hardware is circuitry and metal. What gives life to a computer, the ability to perform calculations and process information, are **programs.** Programs are sets of instructions and decision rules for processing. Unlike **hardware** that is physical, hard, and something that can be touched, programs represent decision logic, the intellectual process for solving problems. Being the antithesis of hardware, programs are called **software.**

In this chapter, two principal categories of software will be discussed: **operating systems** and **application programs.** Some authors list a third classification, **data base management systems (DBMS),** since these programs are needed to administer large data bases. Because of the importance of DBMS to business, an entire chapter, Chapter 9, is devoted to this subject.

Every computer has an operating system unique to that model that is often provided by the manufacturer. Programs for operation usually concern only data processing personnel, not users. However, since their functions should be understood by managers, an overview of operating systems is included in this chapter. Application programs consist of detailed instructions for processing and generating information, serving as the interface between user and hardware. All programs are written in **programming languages,** many of which are technical. Though the actual instructions are written either by EDP personnel, analysts, or programmers working for the users, the objective of each program and the logic used are decisions that should be made by management. Only by understanding the capabilities of different programming languages and their comparative advantages can managers participate wisely in program preparation. A section in this chapter compares and evaluates the main languages for business processing to give future business managers this needed background.

As the price of computer terminals continues to drop, a new class of software is emerging which enables users to directly converse and interact with computers, using English-like languages. Because of the ease in using these new languages, they offer great promise. This chapter concludes with sections on **terminal interactive languages** and natural language research.

Data processing

A computer does computations by using arithmetic **operators** (add, subtract, multiply, and so forth). But what operators to be used, what data must be processed, and the sequence of operations to be performed must all be specified by programs. The composition of data and how it is processed are factors that determine how programs will be written and what programming languages are most appropriate. But in order to explain this further, the structure of data first needs to be discussed.

Structure of data

The most elemental data used by management is numeric (0–9), alphabetic (A–Z), or special symbols (i.e., /, $, %, and including the operators $+$, $-$, $\div$, $\times$). Variables that users need to record, such as name, date, price, and so forth are called **data elements,** the values of which are expressed by a combination of **characters.** For example, alphabetic characters are used to represent the data element *name,* and a combination of numeric characters and alpha characters would represent the data element *invoice number* (e.g., AC325).

Related data elements constitute a **record.** An accounts payable record might consist of a vendor's name, identification number, and amount of sale. All accounts payable records for all vendors would constitute a **file,** an accounts payable file. Businesses generally have many functional files, including a payroll file, a production file, an asset file, and so forth.

A function that includes transactions, events like goods delivered or received, or accounts paid or received, has a **transaction file** in which transactional data of a temporary nature is recorded. Permanent data on the function is kept on a **master file,** which is periodically updated from the transaction file, the latter being destroyed or kept as backup once updating takes place. The updated master is used in processing.

Updating requires processing of two files, transferring relevant information from the transaction file to the master. If data on both files were at random, merging the two would be a complex task. As an analogy, imagine placing one thousand letters, each addressed to a specific customer, in preaddressed envelopes which are in no special order. The task would be simplified by **sorting** and stacking both letters and envelopes in alphabetical order by last name of customer, then matching and merging the two piles while stuffing the envelopes. In batch processing, records on both the transaction and master file must be sorted before data on the two files can be merged. In real-time processing, where transactions are entered at random (as they occur) on the transaction file, only the master

Table 3.1
Updating a master file

Unsorted records on master file
3000510	Hall, A. E.	$120.00
3285000	Adams, J. M.	210.00
2003250	Jackson, K. M.	150.00

(Each record has ID number of vendor, name of vendor, and amount payable, in that order.)

Master file
(Sorted by vendor number in ascending sequence)
2003250	Jackson, K. M.	$150.00
3000510	Hall, A. E.	120.00
3285000	Adams, J. M.	210.00

Transactional file
(Sorted by vendor number listing amounts paid)
2003250	$100.00
3285000	110.00

Master file after updating
2003250	Jackson, K. M.	$ 50.00
3000510	Hall, A. E.	120.00
3285000	Adams, J. M.	100.00

Updated master file resorted into alphabetic sequence (output)
Adams, J. M.	3285000	$100.00
Hall, A. E.	3000510	120.00
Jackson, K. M.	2003250	50.00

must be sorted. Sorting of computer data is seldom done by name because names are long and not unique (two Robert Joneses may exist). Instead, an assigned vendor number or other unique identification will be used.

Table 3.1 shows data in a master file before and after sorting by identification number. This sorting is not done manually but by computer program. Data on the transaction file is also sorted by vendor number. The application program then instructs the computer to deduct the amounts paid listed on the transaction file from the corresponding record of amount due on the master file. In order for this updating to take place, a data element common to both files, called a **key data element,** must exist. The computer can then match and merge the files and perform prescribed computations on data in the two files.

The master file, when updated, is then ready for additional processing. In Table 3.1, processing concluded with a printout made of the updated master resorted alphabetically. Other processing might be performing computations with master file figures such as calculating totals, balances, or averages. The results might then be **classified** into categories, **summarized** and **reported** for use by different levels of management. All of these operations, summarized in Figure 3.1, are common business applications done by computer according to programmed instructions. These instructions are written in a form a computer can understand, called a **programming language.** How these languages work will now be explained.

Figure 3.1
Basic business operations by the CPU

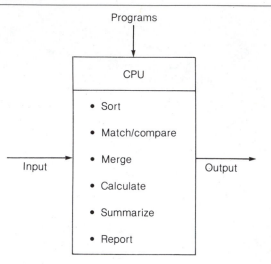

Programs

CPU

- Sort
- Match/compare
- Merge
- Calculate
- Summarize
- Report

Input

Output

Programming

Signals (*off* and *on* of electric current, or two levels of voltage in a transistor) are used in computers to represent the **binary digits** 0 and 1. These digits are the only digits used in the binary number base; therefore all numbers commonly used in the base 10 number system rewritten in binary configurations will be recognized by the computer's circuits in the CPU (for example, $1001 = 9$, $10011001 = 153$).

Machine language was the first programming language developed. Instructions in machine language are a series of base 10 numbers that are converted internally by the computer into binary digits recognized by the CPU. Figure 3.2 shows a machine language instruction for an early computer, the IBM 1620. The instruction has three parts. The first two digits represent the operation code (add, subtract, move data, and so forth). In this example, code 21 represents *add.* The data will, therefore, be channeled through circuitry that will perform addition (other circuitry exists for other arithmetic operations). The second and third parts are **operands,** where data is stored, called a **storage location** or **address.** In this case, the data in storage location 14000 is 120; the data in storage location 12002 is 30. The machine instruction 211400012002 means: find data stored in operand 1, add it to data stored in operand 2, and then store the result in operand 1. That is, take the data 120 (which in this case is regular weekly pay in dollars), add it to data 30 (overtime pay), and store the result 150 in location 14000.

Writing programs in **machine language** has many drawbacks.

1. It is necessary to keep track of storage locations and their contents, for contents keep changing, as in the example above. Location 14000 switched from regular daily pay to total weekly pay.
2. It is necessary to remember operation codes.

Figure 3.2
An example of machine language instruction

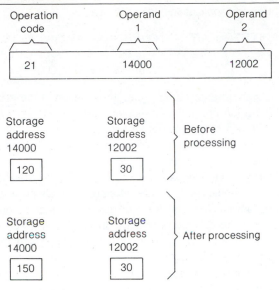

3. There are many instructions to write, one for each machine command.
4. The language is **machine dependent.** Each CPU has a unique circuitry design so that the form and structure of instructions used may vary from one manufacturer to another, and possibly from one model to another as well. A machine language program is written for a specific computer, sometimes even for a specific model. It is usually not **portable** from one computer to another.

To overcome some of these problems the first **assembly language** was developed in the 1950s. An instruction in this language, also for the IBM 1620, with the same meaning as the previous example, 211400012002, is: A RGP OTP. Here the numeric operation code 21 is replaced by the alphabetic code A, and the addresses have been replaced by variable names RGP (regular pay) and OTP (overtime pay). The computer has an internal program, called an **assembler,** to convert alphabetic letters (and symbols) into binary digits. The assembler also converts storage location names when new variables are stored there: RGP becoming TP (total pay). In other words, the assembler converts the assembly language program, the **source program,** into its machine language equivalent, the **object program.** This process is shown in Figure 3.3

Assembly programs are less difficult to write than programs in machine language, for the need to remember storage locations and contents is eliminated. Also, alphabetic operation codes are easier to remember than numeric codes, especially when the abbreviations are meaningful. But criticisms 3. and 4. remain: a large number of instructions still must be written and the language is nonportable.

As a result, **high level programming languages** have been developed, languages closer to English. Instructions in COBOL, a language commonly used for business applications, look like this:

ADD REGULAR-PAY, OVERTIME-PAY GIVING TOTAL-PAY
or PAY = REGPAY + OVTPAY
or PAY = RGP + OTP

As with assembly languages, a translation of these instructions is done internally before the program is executed. But for high level languages, the translation is done by a **compiler,** not an assembler. This translation process is shown in Figure 3.4. Table 3.2 lists common high level languages and compares their features.

High level languages overcome all of the drawbacks of machine languages. The computer keeps track of storage locations and contents. Operation codes are familiar symbols. A major gain over machine or assembly languages is that few instructions are necessary. In 1957, when FORTRAN was developed, a set of 47 FORTRAN instructions equaled approximately 1,000 machine language commands. Furthermore, high level languages are portable, provided the other computer has an appropriate compiler. In addition, because instructions resemble English, high level languages are easier to learn, quicker and less tedious to write and modify, and easier to check for errors. In addition, many such languages are self-documenting.

The number of high-level languages available is steadily increasing. A classification of high-level languages and a discussion of a selected few commonly used

Figure 3.3
Assembler language translation process

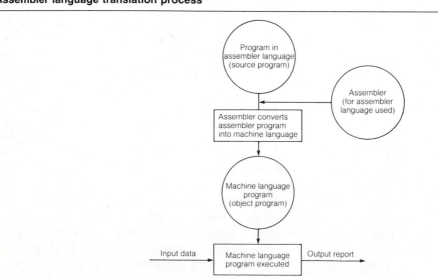

Table 3.2
Common high level programming languages

Ada: Originally developed by the Department of Defense for use in embedded system applications in the military services. Used today for many other applications as well (e.g., payroll). Named after Ada Augusta, the Countess of Lovelace, considered by many to be the first programmer.

ALGOL (**ALGO**rithmic **L**anguage):   Designed by an international group of mathematicians, intended for use of those involved in scientific and mathematical projects. Modular structured language. Used extensively in Europe.

APL (**A** **P**rogramming **L**anguage):   Conceived by Kenneth Iverson who worked at IBM to develop it. An interactive, powerful language for scientific and mathematical computations. Can perform complex operations with a minimum of coding. Requires a large memory and a special keyboard. Available only on large- or medium-sized machines.

BASIC (**B**eginners' **A**ll-purpose **S**ymbolic **I**nstruction **C**ode: Developed at Dartmouth College for use with time-sharing systems. Easy to learn. Originally intended to be used by universities for instructional purposes, but has been adopted by many firms for their data-processing needs. Requires small internal memory and is, hence, available on most microcomputers.

C Language: C language first appeared in 1983 and is often referred to as a portable assembly language. It is used both by manufacturers and software developers for writing operating systems, utilities, and applications including the animation of the film, *Return of the Jedi*. It has been used on small microcomputers as well as supercomputers like CRAY-1. It has many of the advanced, structured programming features found in Pascal.

COBOL (**CO**mmon **B**usiness **O**riented **L**anguage):   Designed for business applications with a large amount of input/output but few complex calculations. Machine independent. English-like. Strong file-handling capabilities. Required on all Department of Defense computers. This makes COBOL the most commonly available language on mainframes.

FORTRAN (**FOR**mula **TRAN**slation):   First commercial high level language. Introduced by IBM in 1954, designed primarily for scientific and engineering applications. Algebra-like, highly structured format. Not a good business language since it has limited ability to process alphabetic data and files.

GPSS (**G**eneral **P**urpose **S**ystem **S**imulation):   Designed by IBM. Graphic-oriented. Used for business simulation problems.

Pascal: Named after Blaise Pascal, French mathematician of the 17th century. Powerful, easy to learn language first developed to teach programming concepts but rapidly extended to business and scientific applications. Uses structured IF-THEN-ELSE, WHILE-DO, and REPEAT-UNTIL. Available on microcomputers.

PL/1 (**P**rogramming **L**anguage—version **1**):   High level language developed by IBM. Designed to be the *lingua franca* of programming but not used widely. An all-purpose, procedure-oriented language for both scientific and business applications. Has powerful features that make it good for systems programming. Facilities allow use of structured programming techniques. Large amount of storage required for compiler prohibits use on small computers.

PROLOG (**PRO**gramming in **LOG**ic):   Lends itself to inference-making. Used extensively in artificial intelligence. Gained in popularity after the Japanese announced it as the language for their fifth generation computers.

RPG (**R**eport **P**rogram **G**enerator):   Problem-oriented language originally designed to facilitate the output of business reports. Easy to learn and use. Commonly used to rearrange and format reports and process files for accounts receivable, general ledgers, and inventory.

in business processing will appear later in this chapter. But first, other types of software needed to run a computer and an information system will be discussed.

Classification of software

There are two main types of software: **operating system software** and **application software.** The latter generally is custom-made for a particular problem or environment, whereas the former is concerned with the operation of the CPU and its peripheral equipment. The classification of all software is shown in Figure 3.5. These subdivisions are discussed next.

Operating system software

The operating system for a small computer may consist of only a few control and processing programs. For large computer systems, however, a complex set of programs is required to coordinate, control, and allocate the systems resources. These programs are provided by the vendor of the CPU and are especially necessary for systems that handle large volumes of interrelated data and for systems using communications networks, real time, time sharing, or distributed processing. The objectives of operating software are to maximize efficiency of operations, minimize human intervention, and facilitate the task of the programmer in accessing data and/or peripheral equipment. To achieve these objectives, two main sets of programs exist: **control programs** and **processing programs.**

Control programs
The **supervisor,** also called the **executive, monitor,** or **controller,** is the most important control program of a computer system. It coordinates all the hardware of the computer system and handles job scheduling, queuing, and storage allo-

Figure 3.4
Language translation by compiler

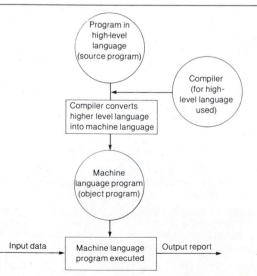

**Figure 3.5
Types of software**

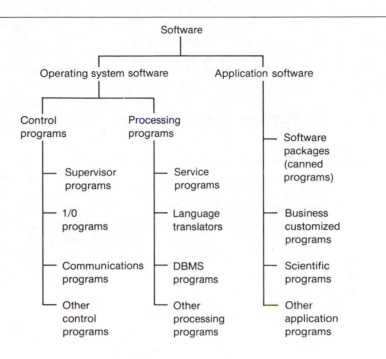

cation. It also keeps logs and does job accounting for each job processed. Finally, the supervisor communicates with the human operator through the console regarding the status of computer system operations.

I/O control programs are a collection of subroutines for the input of data and output of information dealing with the actual physical location and format of data and its logical organization into data elements, records, and files. These programs handle input/output scheduling, error corrections, and various functions necessary to create and maintain files. For business applications, I/O control programs may constitute between 30–45 percent of all programmed instructions.

Communications programs perform message switching and remote inquiry. Other control subroutines exist for specialized functions. But, in essence, control programs manage data (input, output, storage, and retrieval), execute processing programs, and govern job preparation and scheduling.

Some manufacturers offer control program facilities. For example, IBM's Systems Management Facilities (SMF) provides the base for user written control programs for monitoring jobs and utilization of equipment. SMF also collects the necessary data for user specified analytical reports for accounting and costing purposes.

Processing programs

Service programs are a subclassification of processing software, performing calculations and other repetitive routines such as sorting and merging needed so frequently in business applications. **Housekeeping** and **utility programs** fall into this category. These consist of programs needed for standard and frequent operations such as listing data in storage, called **dumping,** or converting data from one storage medium to another. Other service programs include automatic program testing and debugging software. Many service programs are unique to a machine, manufacturer, or environment so they will not be specifically mentioned due to the lack of generality in their use.

Another set of processing programs, a **data base management system (DBMS),** is used to administer large data bases.

Application software

Software packages

Many firms have similar information requirements. Programs using common decision rules to perform statistical computations, sorting, merging, and standard applications (such as payroll and inventory control) can serve many organizations. Businesses needing such programs can save development costs and time by purchasing predeveloped **software packages** with self-supporting documentation for their needs. These programs may require modification, but generally they are ready for immediate use, a convenience that parallels that of canned food. Hence the term **canned programs** is used. The advantages and limitations of canned programs as well as criteria for their evaluation are shown in Table 3.3.

Software packages are available for **scientific** and **business programs,** and also for DBMS. Many computer vendors provide such packages free as a service to their customers. Other packages can be leased or purchased from **software houses,** companies that develop software.

**Table 3.3
Software packages**

Advantages
   Time is saved by the organization (compared to tailor-made system).
   Time and worry over debugging reduced.
   Cheaper because the development cost is distributed over many users.
   System analysts, a scarce resource, are freed for other tasks.
   Necessary modification requires less commitment of resources than initial development.

Disadvantages or limitations
   Programs for complex applications are often too generalized to be useful. When specific, they may need extensive modification to fit local needs.
   Programs may require unavailable hardware.
   Resistance to canned programs is common. Users prefer programs developed for their own special needs.
   Purchase hampers the development of in-house program design and implementation capability.

Criteria for evaluating package
   Quality and completeness of documentation.
   Ease of installation.
   Ease of use.
   Vendor technical support.
   Throughput.
   Efficiency.
   Amount of training required.

An example of packaged software widely used in business is a **spreadsheet** program. Users specify the values of parameters (the *Y* axis), the values to be computed (the *X* axis), and the relationship between the *X* and *Y* axes. The program then calculates all of the values for the cells of the matrix. A sample application for a spreadsheet would be budget forecasting for different time periods based on parameters that affect the forecast, for example, inflation and/or prices.

The placement of expenses by line item in one column and then use of a spreadsheet program to calculate other columns by geographic area or administrative unit is another spreadsheet application.

Spreadsheet packages vary from vendor to vendor. Not all have identical features. Some are stand-alone spreadsheets while others integrate the spreadsheet with word processing so that the output is presented in text. Many packages have graphic capabilities. Still others feature windows. A **window** means that the user's screen will display data sets or output from two or more programs simultaneously (the screen is subdivided into small display areas for each data set output). The user is able to switch back and forth between windows without disturbing the data in the windows or operation of the programs themselves. Windows of information on the screen can be moved about much like papers can be shuffled at a desk. That explains why the windowing capability is often called an *electronic desktop.*

Selection of a software package from a particular vendor will depend on a user's need, features offered, price, documentation, compatibility with user hardware, and the degree of modification needed to fit the particular user's environment.

Business programs

Although software packages exist for many general applications, programs must be customized for specialized or unusual applications. Businesses may have unique requirements for even common programs such as sales reporting or payroll, in which case, in-house programs must be written.

A large number of languages exist for business applications. In 1969, Jean Sammet characterized the overabundance of such languages as Tower of Babel (see Figure 3.6). But her implicit warning has been ignored. In recent years, languages have proliferated, adding to the confusion of users and dividing the ranks of professionals. Even languages for special applications such as artificial intelligence, query, and text processing have multiplied. Among the leading languages for business problems are APL, BASIC, COBOL, FORTRAN, PL/1, and RPG. For a comparison of these and other common languages, see Table 3.4.

Scientific programs

In the past, a clear distinction existed between application software for scientific problems and for business problems. In the natural sciences, complex formulas involving numerous computations were common, but input and output were relatively small. In contrast, business applications in the past generally required the handling of large volumes of input and output but the actual computations were

Figure 3.6
The tower of Babel of programming languages

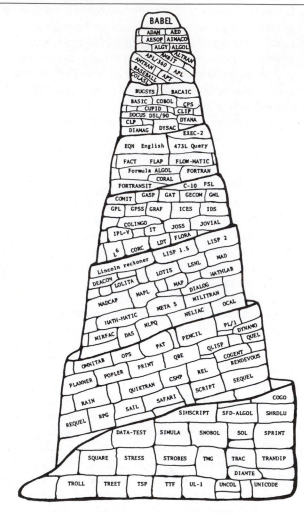

And the Lord said, . . . let us go down, and there confound
their language, that they may not understand
one another's speech (Genesis, 11: 6-7)

SOURCE   Adapted from Jean E. Sammet, *Programming Languages: History and Fundamentals* (Englewood Cliffs, N.J.: Prentice-Hall, © 1969), front cover. Reprinted by permission.

Table 3.4
Comparison of common programming languages

	Ada	ALGOL	APL	Assembler language	BASIC	COBOL	FORTRAN	Pascal	PL/1	PROLOG	RPG	Dialog/query
Machine dependent				X								
Procedure oriented	X	X			X	X	X	X	X			
Problem oriented										X	X	X
English-like						X			X			X
"Structured"	X	X						X	X			
Mathematic/ scientific orientation		X	X				X					
Business oriented						X					X	X
Multipurpose	X	X		X	X			X	X			
Good character manipulation	X		X	X	X	X		X	X			X
Interactive capability			X		X			X		X		X
Requires main-frame	X	X	X			X			X	X		
Standardized	X				X	X	X	X	X			

relatively simple and repetitive. As a result, computer hardware and software were designed for either scientific or business applications.

This distinction is fading. Computers are now designed to meet both scientific and business needs and programming languages available today claim capability over the entire range of problems.[1] Furthermore, many business applications in the area of planning and control have scientific characteristics. For example, planning is often computation-intensive, involving statistics and regressive equations found in scientific programming, though a large volume of input and output

---

[1] Traditionally, degrees 25 percent of applications (or 90 degrees of a pie) were scientific applications and 75 percent (270 degrees) were business oriented. When IBM manufactured a computer that served 100 percent of users' needs (or 360 degrees of the pie), the computer was called the IBM 360.

must still be processed as in other business applications. Calculating the optimal mix of production levels (linear programming) is another business problem involving complicated scientific formulas. Equations like the following must be solved:

$$a_{i1}x_1 + \cdots + a_{ij}x_j + \cdots + a_{in}x_n \leq b_i$$

where:

a_{ij} = amount of resource i (first subscript)
required to produce one unit of product j
(second subscript)
x_j = *level of product j*
b_i = available resource i
n = total number of products

Languages used in business

Today, many business problems involve hundreds of equations for tens of products resulting in complex matrix calculations. These applications use a scientific-type language such as FORTRAN. APT and ADAPT are other languages used for business applications with a scientific orientation such as numerical control (automated production).

Business problems that involve probabilities (such as the probability of customer arrival and of customer sale) that cannot be solved by models like linear programming or regression equations must be **simulated.** That is, the problems must be repeatedly solved for different values of variables to answer the question, "What if this variable changes x percent?" Though **simulation programs** can be written in FORTRAN, specialized programming languages have been developed that facilitate repeated calculations for "What if?" type questions. The most common of such simulation languages in the United States are GPSS and SIMSCRIPT.

The features of FORTRAN IV, GPSS, and SIMSCRIPT are listed in Table 3.5 and the performance of each when used to solve a queuing and an inventory problem are compared. SIMULA, a mathematically powerful simulation language with similar capabilities, does not appear in the table though this language is used extensively in Europe. The SIMULA compiler is not readily available in the United States.

RPG (Report **P**rogram **G**enerator) is a language designed to extract data from a file or a data base and format it into a desired report. This language is used extensively in business. Some RPGs are independent of data base or query facilities, while others are an extension of data-base query languages.

Report generators may have arithmetic and logic capabilities, but instructions have to be written for implementing these capabilities. This is avoided in **applications generators,** which call modules to perform the functions of an application. The input specifics which arithmetic and logical operations are to be performed, what data to use, and the output to be generated. This greatly speeds up application development. When an application requires operations which the

Table 3.5
Comparison of simulation languages used for business

General characteristics	FORTRAN IV	GPSS	SIMSCRIPT 2.5
Availability	Available on almost all computers	On IBM equipment only (provided by vendor)	Available from CAI (a software company)
Compiler internal storage requirement	Relatively small	Medium	Relatively large
Easy to learn	Very easy	Easy	Difficult
Readability of program	Medium	Easy	Medium
Self-documenting	No	No	A little
Run time characteristics	*FORTRAN IV*	*GPSS*	*SIMSCRIPT 2.5*
Queuing problem			
Time to learn (hours)	10	6	15
Time to write (hours)	8	4	12
Time to validate (hours)	8	12	15
Execution time (seconds)	1.64	1.53	2.21
Number of instructions	148	22	85
Max core used (kilobyte)	128	128	288
Large capacity storage (kilobyte per hour)	0.05	0.34	0.92
Inventory problem			
Time to learn (hours)	12	8	17
Time to write (hours)	10	5	15
Time to validate (hours)	8	10	12
Execution time (seconds)	3.92	2.44	3.19
Number of instructions	167	15	142
Max core used (kilobyte)	128	128	288
Large capacity storage (kilobyte per hours)	0.12	0.51	0.97

SOURCE   Y. S. Fang, "Comparison of Simulation Languages" (1979), unpublished paper.

**Table 3.6
Language comparison**

Characteristics	APL	BASIC	COBOL 1974	FORTRAN IV	PL/1	RPG II
Number of instructions	6	10	62	12	21	27
Number of characters	150	250	1,550	300	525	675
Entry time	1.2	2	12.4	2.4	4.2	4.6
Compile time (minutes)	0.066	0.024	0.03	0.012	0.033	1.5
Time to validate (seconds)	0.024	0.0144	0.123	0.0144	0.124	1.5
Time to write (days)	0.5	0.9	5.6	1.1	1.9	2.4
Self-documentation	No	No	Yes	No	Yes	No
Easy language rule	Moderate	Difficult	Easy	Moderate	Easy	Easy
Easily readable	No	Moderate	Yes	Moderate	Moderate	No
Widely available	Moderate	Moderate	Yes	Yes	Moderate	Moderate
Machine independent	Moderate	Moderate	Yes	Yes	Moderate	Yes

SOURCE   Adapted from Perry Edwards and Bruce Broadwell, *Data Processing: Computers in Action* (Belmont, Calif.: Wadsworth Publishing, 1979), pp. 284–85, © 1979 by Wadsworth, Inc. Used by permission of the publisher.

application generator cannot create, the generator is still useful because it allows the inclusion of routines written in a program language.

Special languages are also being developed to facilitate the display and manipulation of data on graphic terminals. Some **graphic languages** enable users to ask for data and specify how they want it displayed. Like report generators, some graphic packages have arithmetic and logic capabilities.

Some languages have modified versions. FORTRAN IV and COBOL '74 are examples. The chart in Table 3.6 is an evaluation by Edwards and Broadwell of the six languages most commonly used in business. Comparative programming costs are shown in Figure 3.7. Note that the initial fixed cost for program development is low for APL, BASIC, and FORTRAN, and high for PL/1, RPG, and COBOL. For a small number of runs (up to point *A*), APL is cheapest, BASIC is most economical from point *A* to *B,* and thereafter COBOL is least costly in spite of its high development cost.

Both APL and BASIC have an advantage not listed in Table 3.6 or shown in Figure 3.7. They are **interactive languages.** The problem is stated, a specific key on the terminal is pressed, and the answer is computed. There is no need to specify the format of input or output as required when using the other four languages. APL is also powerful mathematically. For example, one command will produce a set of random numbers or compute statistics. But additional mathematical characters have been added to the language to generate this computing power, the use of which often makes business programmers uneasy. Many prefer BASIC, a simpler language to learn, available on many minis, but understandably less powerful.

Though FORTRAN does not solve many business problems efficiently and is too mathematical for many business programmers, it is still commonly used for both operations and planning in business. One reason is that the language is taught at most universities, providing a large cadre of FORTRAN programmers. Also, the FORTRAN compiler is widely available.

Figure 3.7
Cost of programming selected languages

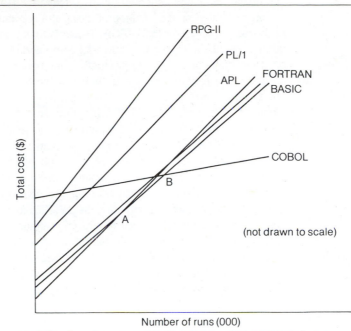

SOURCE   Perry Edwards and Bruce Broadwell, *Data Processing* (Belmont, Calif.: Wadsworth Publishing, 1979), p. 287, © 1979 by Wadsworth, Inc. Reprinted by permission of the publisher.

Both COBOL and RPG are more business-oriented than FORTRAN. Of the two, COBOL has better computational capability. It also includes special features like the SORT verb (which enables sorting of data), and its design permits it to handle and manipulate large input and output files. When the Department of Defense required COBOL for all its computers, computer manufacturers started supplying COBOL compilers. By the 1970s, COBOL had become the most widely used business language.

IBM attempted to develop a programming *lingua franca* with PL/1. This language has business as well as scientific capabilities and is also a very high level language. Among the special features included is text processing. PL/1 has not become a universal language as was once predicted, however, in part because its features have made it so complex. Meanwhile, as hardware has evolved and the costs of terminals have dropped, interactive languages have gained in appeal. Also the emergence of DBMS has made it possible to access large data bases with much of the data manipulation and processing handled by the system. Language needs have consequently changed. Many businesses need terminal interactive languages that permit nontechnical personnel to query the system from a terminal for information needed in decision making.

At the present time, much language research is being conducted to make languages easier to write. Already **fourth generation languages (4GLs)** are being introduced, languages such as FOCUS, NOMAD, RAMIS, and MANTIS that are nonprocedural in nature. Instead of giving the computer commands that tell how to process information (as in FORTRAN, COBOL, and ALGOL), these new languages employ a small set of powerful commands that tell the computer what to do. Not only is programming productivity increased, but end users with no prior programming experience can do their own programming, enter their own data, and run their own reports without relying on data processing personnel. (It is estimated that 75 percent of all 4GL programming can be done by users with only two days of training.) Special programmers, however, are still needed to handle complex applications and to fine tune the main nonprocedural code.

In spite of the advantages of 4GLs, a negative reaction to these languages is exhibited by many computer processing departments. This is due, in part, to fear of the unknown and to resistance to change. Managers of computing who have gained their seniority by the old methods don't like to see their power bases eroded, their budgets reduced, or their control over standards diminished—all of which occurs when programming is transferred to end users. It is the enthusiasm of users that is promoting 4GLs, and the fact that 4GLs are helping to wipe out application backlogs. With further language research, we may even reach a point in time when programming becomes automated, eliminating programmers and programming languages entirely.

Terminal interactive languages

A separate section is being devoted to terminal interactive languages since these languages are relatively new and gaining in popularity in the business sector. These languages have a special capability: computer-directed or computer-promoted queries assist clerks in data entry. They also assist managers in information retrieval and decision making. The questioning that appears on the terminal may be menu selection, fill in the blanks, or parametric requests.

Question and answer techniques

Menu selection
In **menu selection,** the user is offered a list of choices. For example, three reports, each numbered, will be briefly described. The user merely types 2 if the second report is the one desired. The advantage of this method of retrieval is that no knowledge of the system or data base is required. The disadvantage is slowness, for all of the choices must be explained.

Fill in the blanks
A checklist of questions with blanks to be completed prods the user into supplying all of the necessary input in this method of data collection. Intelligent terminals or real-time terminals may have the added capability of validating the data as soon as it enters the system. For example, the system may be programmed to provide the exact format of input to reduce possible errors. A nine-digit number

required as input might be requested by a set of nine boxes, making any omission obvious.

This technique requires some training or knowledge to operate the system (e.g., ten digits might be required for a social security number, the last being a check digit). Careful programming, however, can train the user online by providing explanations or rephrasing questions when users make entry errors or need assistance.

Parametric requests

This technique is a form of dialogue between user and machine. The values of specific parameters are entered, the computer responds, new parameters are added, another response given, and so forth, until the transaction is completed.

Query languages

The questioning in the abovementioned techniques must be in an English-like language in order for persons with little programming knowledge to enter and retrieve data. Examples of **query languages** that have been developed include ADAM (A Data Management System), MODEL 24, and SYSTEM 2000, all of which feature quick retrieval; COLINGO (Compile On Line and Go), which can be easily programmed online; FLORAL and QUERY BY EXAMPLE, two calculus-based languages; CUPID, FLORAL LP and SQUARE which use two-dimensional notation; DSL/ALPHA which enables operations to be expressed in a relational data base; IQF (Interactive Query Facility language); and QUEL and SEQUEL II, which are key-word-based languages. Table 3.7 demonstrates how a statement in English is translated into a sample few of these languages.

Table 3.7
Examples of query languages

a. English:
Find employees working for Smith who make under $20,000.

b. SEQUEL: SELECT NAME
FROM PERSONNEL
WHERE MANAGER='SMITH'
AND SALARY <20000

c. SQUARE: EMP   ('SMITH',<'20000')
           NAME   MANAGER,SALARY

d. QUERY BY EXAMPLE:

PERSONNEL	NAME	MANAGER	SALARY
	P*	Smith	<20000

e. IQF: (1) FROM PERSONNEL FILE
      (2) FOR SMITH MANAGER
      (3) AND FOR SALARY <20000
      (4) LIST NAME

*P stands for print, identifying desired output.

A study comparing the effectiveness of SEQUEL and SQUARE, two IBM languages listed in the table, found that the error rate for nonprogrammers using SEQUEL, a key-word language, as 51 percent whereas the rate for SQUARE, which features an explicit composition operator, was only 34 percent. Programmers got about two thirds of their queries correct in either language. With both user groups, 50 percent of the errors were judged clerical rather than conceptual. Each language required 10 hours to learn.[2]

QUERY BY EXAMPLE, evaluated by Thomas and Gould, showed a query accuracy rate of 67 percent.[3] Less than two hours were required to learn this language. The effectiveness of IQF, studied by Gould and Ascher, showed an overall accuracy by nonprogrammers of 34 percent and an error rate of 28 percent.[4]

It is often assumed that, ideally, computers should be programmed in natural languages. This is possible at the present time, though processing is costly and computer time is inefficiently used. This postulate has been refuted by Small and Weldon who studied English versus SEQUEL, concluding:

> The common assumption that ordinary, everyday English is the ideal way to communicate with computers is not supported by the present results. Subjects were not realiably more accurate using English than using SEQUEL. They were reliably faster using SEQUEL, suggesting that the structured language is easier to use.[5]

Schneidermann, not satisfied with Small and Weldon's experimental design, questioned this finding.[6] He objected to the fact that subjects were required to use tables, feeling this constrained them in formulating questions to resolve problems. Scheidermann experimented on his own, asking subjects to choose a department where they would like to be transferred, based on departmental information acquired by query from a data base, such as employees' names, salaries, managers, job descriptions, age of personnel, and years of employment. Fourteen percent of the queries were invalid using SEQUEL, 55 percent invalid using English. Imaginative questions, ones that had no answers in the data base, were asked in English, such as, "How often are raises awarded?" "What is the personality of managers?"

The above studies indicate that a formal query language helps structure user requests. English may be too flexible, inappropriate for queries. Or perhaps a natural language is not a natural query language. Certainly factors such as the

---

[2]P. Reisner, R. Royce, and D. Chamberlin, "Human Factors Evaluation of Two Data Base Query Languages: SQUARE and SEQUEL," *IBM Technical Report* (RJ 1478, 1974).

[3]J. Thomas and J Gould, "A Psychological Study of Query-by-Example," *AFIPS Natiopnal Computer Conference Proceedings* (Montvale, N.J.: AFIPS Press, 1975), pp. 439–45.

[4]Gould and R. Ascher, "Use of an IQF-like Query Language by Non-Programmers," *IBM Research Report* (RC 5279, 1975).

[5]D. W. Small and L. J. Weldon, "The Efficiency of Retrieving Information from Computers Using Natural and Structured Query Languages," Rep. SAI-78-655-WA. (Arlington, Va.: Science Applications, 1977).

[6]Ben Schneidermann, "Improving the Human Factors Aspect of Database Interactions," *ACM Transactions on Database Systems* 3, no. 4 (December 1978), pp. 433–37.

quantitiative background of users and their abilities (right-brain visual intuitive thinking versus left-brain verbal deductive thinking) affect individual success with formal query languages. The function for which the language is used (for example, production and inventory control) also plays a role. The ideal may prove to be formal languages as an alternative to, not as a substitute for, natural language programming.

Natural language research

At the present time, much language research is being conducted. Natural languages have an obvious advantage: no training in programming language structure is required, though users must still understand the function of a computer and be able to formulate, organize, and analyze problems. Research is also being conducted in this area. It is hoped techniques will be developed to help users identify needs and formulate problems so that computers can be of assistance.

For example, there are several prototype languages under development that engage the user in a dialogue, trying to determine what information is needed through questions and answers. The assumption here is that the user either doesn't know or can't express needs in terms the computer understands. A sample output of one such language, RENDEZVOUS, appears in Table 3.8. Note that the menu technique is used in this example. The computer's method of restating and clarifying the user's request is called a **clarification response.** The program also utilizes a **stroking dialogue,** congratulating or sympathizing with the user (in this sample, "Good!"), a technique found in diagnostic and psychiatric discourse.[7]

Another dialogue technique, not inluded in Table 3.8, is the **contributive response,** where entirely new information is introduced by the computer such as, "These parts are also supplied by the foreign firm ABC."

Using a mix of the above techniques, the user is guided in framing a request for information while being reminded of the range of options available. In the case of RENDEZVOUS, the main objective of the program is to understand the user's requirements and to match this need for information with what the system and its data base can provide.

IBM, the developer of RENDEZVOUS, also uses dialogue in a system to customize applications for accounting. An example of such a dialogue is shown in Table 3.9. Yet another example is NPGS work done at Yale University, a sample output of which appears in Table 3.10. Here a problem on queuing is expressed in English and the equivalent simulation language in GPSS is automatically generated. This shows how powerful specialized languages like GPSS in simulation can be used by a manager without programming knowledge of that language, though in this case, some understanding of queuing was obviously required.

The results of the above research projects, and of other similar projects, such

---

[7] For an early classical example, see the work by Joe Weizenbaum and his ELIZA program, J. Weizenbaum, "ELIZA—A Computer Program for the Study of Natural Language Communication between Man and Machine," *Communications of the ACM* 9, no. 1 (January 1966), pp. 36–45.

Table 3.8
Sample query dialogue with RENDEZVOUS

SYSTEM: Please proceed.

USER: Give me a list of the part numbers, quantities, and suppliers of Houston parts.

SYSTEM: You are requesting (among other things) a listing of quantities of parts. Do you want:
1. Quantities on hand
2. Quantities on order
3. Quantities shipped?

USER: I want quantities on order.

SYSTEM: Fine! Now, with regard to "Houston parts," do you mean:
1. Parts supplied by Houston suppliers
2. Parts supplied to Houston projects
3. Parts associated with Houston in some other way?

USER: I mean Item 2.

(NOTE: Nothing prevents the user from responding in a manner which is incomprehensible to the system—for example, *"le deuxième"*—but if he does, the system tightens up the dialogue by: "Please reply by means of one of the numerals 1 or 2 or 3." How response 3 would be treated is discussed later.)

SYSTEM: Good! I need one more piece of information. In the listing of part numbers, quantity on order, and suppliers, how do you want suppliers to be identified:
1. By number
2. By name
3. Some other way?

USER: By name and by city.

SYSTEM: O.K. This is what I understand your query to be: "Find all combinations of part number, quantity on order, supplier name, and supplier city such that the supplier supplied the part to a project located in Houston." Is this what you intended?

(We now follow two possibilities. Case 1: the user is satisfied.)

USER: Yes.

SYSTEM: Do you want the listing to be ordered in any special way?

USER: Yes, by part number and then by supplier number.

This ends the dialogue in Case 1. The system now proceeds to interpret the relational calculus formula for the user's query—a formula that it has been synthesizing in its store, partly from the original statement by the user, and partly from the succeeding dialogue. (Case 2: the user is not satisfied.)

USER: I have changed my mind.

(NOTE: The system does not understand this idiom, but is fully aware of its inability to understand, so it tightens up the dialogue as follows.)

SYSTEM: Please select item 1 or 2 below:
1. The restatement is satisfactory.
2. The restatement is *not* satisfactory.

USER: 2.

SYSTEM: If your intent can be expressed by making minor changes in my restatement, please type it in with your changes incorporated. If your change is major, you may re-state your query in your own terms.

This is where we leave the dialogue in Case 2.

SOURCE E. F. Codd, "Seven Steps to RENDEZVOUS with the Casual User," in *Data Base Management*, J. W. Klimbe and K. L. Koffeman, eds. (Amsterdam: North-Holland Publishing, 1974), pp. 181–82.

Table 3.9
Hypothetical customizing dialogue (IBM)

IN ORDER FOR ME TO CREATE A BILLING PROGRAM FOR YOU I WILL NEED TO GET CERTAIN INFORMATION FROM YOU ABOUT WHAT YOU WANT. FEEL FREE TO ASK QUESTIONS AS WE GO ALONG.

WOULD YOU LIKE YOUR SYSTEM TO BE TRANSACTION ORIENTED OR BATCH ORIENTED?

what is a transaction oriented system?

IN A TRANSACTION ORIENTED SYSTEM AN INVOICE IS PRODUCED IMMEDIATELY WHEN AN ORDER ARRIVES.

i want invoices to be produced just once a day at 5 p.m.

DO YOU WANT A SEPARATE INVOICE FOR EACH ORDER OR DO YOU WANT THE ORDERS GROUPED BY CUSTOMER?

separate invoices.

ARE THE CUSTOMERS' NAME AND ADDRESS FURNISHED ON EACH ORDER OR MUST THEY BE LOOKED UP IN THE CUSTOMER MASTER FILE?

looked up; is it possible to specify a different address on an order?

NO, NOT IF THEY ARE TO BE LOOKED UP IN THE CUSTOMER MASTER FILE.

how would i handle an order from a new customer?

BY "NEW CUSTOMER" DO YOU MEAN ONE WHO IS NOT IN THE MASTER FILE?

yes.

YOU WOULD HAVE TO MAKE AN ENTRY FOR HIM IN THE CUSTOMER MASTER FILE BEFORE THE ORDER IS PROCESSED.

okay.

DOES THE SAME TAX RATE APPLY TO ALL CUSTOMERS?

yes, 5%.

TO SUMMARIZE YOUR REQUIREMENTS:
    INVOICES ARE TO BE PRODUCED IN A BATCH AT 5 PM EACH DAY.
    A SEPARATE INVOICE WILL BE PRODUCED FOR EACH ORDER.
    THE CUSTOMER'S NAME AND ADDRESS WILL BE LOOKED UP IN THE CUSTOMER
      MASTER FILE.
    A TAX RATE OF 5% APPLIES TO ALL CUSTOMERS.

DO YOU HAVE ANY FURTHER QUESTIONS?

what does an invoice look like?

(SYSTEM PRINTS A SAMPLE INVOICE)

how is extended price calculated?

THE EXTENDED PRICE FOR AN ITEM IS CALCULATED BY MULTIPLYING THE UNIT PRICE BY THE QUANTITY.

that's all.

SOURCE   G. E. Heidorn "Automatic Programming through Natural Language Dialogue: A Survey," *IBM Journal of Research and Development* 20, no. 4 (July 1976), p. 309, © 1976 by International Business Machines Corporation. Reprinted with permission.

Table 3.10
Problem statement in NPGS

1. when a vehicle arrives at a station, it leaves there immediately if the length of the line at a pump in the station is not less than 2.
2. 75 percent of the vehicles are cars and a fourth are trucks.
3. there is just 1 pump.
4. a simulation run time of 8 hours is desired.
5. ask questions for further info.
6. HOW OFTEN DO THE VEHICLES ARRIVE AT THE STATION?
7. the arrivals of vehicles are normally distributed with a mean of 8 minutes.
8. WHAT IS THE STANDARD DEVIATION OF THE NORMAL DISTRIBUTION?
9. 1 minute.
10. OTHERWISE, WHAT DO THE VEHICLES DO?
11. what?
12. AFTER ARRIVING AT THE STATION, IF THE LENGTH OF THE LINE AT THE PUMP IN THE STATION IS NOT LESS THAN 2, THE VEHICLE WILL LEAVE THE STATION. OTHERWISE, WHAT DO THE VEHICLES DO?
13. they are serviced.
14. WHERE ARE THE VEHICLES SERVICED?
15. at the pump.
16. HOW LONG ARE THE VEHICLES SERVICED AT THE PUMP IN THE STATION?
17. vehicle service times are exponential.
18. THE TIME FOR THE VEHICLES TO BE SERVICED AT THE PUMP IN THE STATION IS EXPONENTIALLY DISTRIBUTED. WHAT IS THE MEAN OF THE EXPONENTIAL DISTRIBUTION?
19. 5 minutes for cars and 9 minutes for trucks.
20. AFTER BEING SERVICED AT THE PUMP IN THE STATION, WHAT DO THE VEHICLES DO?
21. leave the station.
22. WHAT IS THE BASIC TIME UNIT TO BE USED IN THE MODEL?
23. 30 seconds.
24. THE PROBLEM STATEMENT IS COMPLETE.
25. how often does a vehicle arrive at the station?
26. THE TIME BETWEEN ARRIVALS OF THE VEHICLES AT THE STATION IS NORMALLY DISTRIBUTED, WITH A MEAN OF 8 MINUTES AND A STANDARD DEVIATION OF 1 MINUTE.
27. the standard deviation of the time between arrivals should be 2 minutes.
28. are vehicles serviced at the pump?
29. YES, THE VEHICLES ARE SERVICED AT THE PUMP IN THE STATION.
30. state the complete problem in english.
31. THE VEHICLES ARRIVE AT THE STATION. THE TIME BETWEEN ARRIVALS OF THE VEHICLES AT THE STATION IS NORMALLY DISTRIBUTED, WITH A MEAN OF 8 MINUTES AND A STANDARD DEVIATION OF 2 MINUTES. 75 PERCENT OF THE VEHICLES ARE CARS, AND THE REST ARE TRUCKS. AFTER ARRIVING AT THE STATION, IF THE LENGTH OF THE LINE AT THE PUMP IN THE STATION IS LESS THAN 2, THE VEHICLE WILL BE SERVICED AT THE PUMP IN THE STATION. OTHERWISE, THE VEHICLE WILL LEAVE THE STATION. THE TIME FOR THE VEHICLES TO BE SERVICED AT THE PUMP IN THE STATION IS EXPONENTIALLY DISTRIBUTED, WITH A MEAN OF 5 MINUTES FOR THE CARS, AND 9 MINUTES FOR THE TRUCKS. AFTER BEING SERVICED AT THE PUMP IN THE STATION, THE VEHICLES LEAVE THE STATION.

   THE SIMULATION IS TO BE RUN FOR 8 HOURS, USING A BASIC TIME UNIT OF 30 SECONDS.

SOURCE   G. E. Heidorn, "Automatic Programming through Natural Language Dialogue: A Survey," *IBM Journal of Research and Development* 20, no. 4 (July 1976), p. 303, © 1976 by International Business Machines Corporation. Reprinted with permission.

as LSNLIS, NPL, RAIN, REL, REQUEST, as well as SHRDL, are impressive and promising. However, it must be recognized that these programs apply only to a limited set of problems. The language used is a restricted subset of English with a narrow vocabulary and conceptual range. Natural language dialogue with computer recognition of the full range of grammatical subtleties and syntactic diversities of English is still under research. What is needed is a computer that can converse with a user on any subject, interpret requests for information meaningfully, and one that can learn from the dialogue how the user makes decisions (frame of reference, style of management, even idiosyncracies) so that the data supplied is appropriate.

There is a danger, however, that natural language communication wil give users the illusion that the computer fully understands their problems, and that solutions proposed are indisputably correct. Further research is necessary not only in language development, but in techniques for evaluating computer solutions and testing for correctness.

Future of software

In 1970, in an out-of-court settlement, IBM agreed to price and sell hardware and software separately. This decision enabled small innovative software houses to enter into competition with computer giants and, as a result, a large number of application programs with a variety of capabilities and options appeared on the market. In the future application software will become even more "friendly," that is, designed for users with little knowledge of computer systems; the former cryptic terminal responses replaced by conversational exchanges; and the coding and command structure simplified. A greater use of parameters will let users state a need with the computer itself translating this need into computer language and guiding the user toward a programmed solution.

As software becomes increasingly sophisticated, a larger percentage of the total system cost will be software costs, up from 10 percent to 40–50 percent for minis, approaching 90 percent (up from 50 percent) for larger systems. More special-purpose packages and small systems with improved reliability will appear, many packages being sold off-the-shelf. The user will also benefit from greater discipline in design and improved techniques in programming, for example, structured programming.

In addition, there may be a noticeable shift in the comparative popularity of programming languages. Pascal, competing with BASIC for minis, is gaining converts for all types and sizes of computers. This language, named after a French mathematician, was first developed by Niklaus Wirth in the 1960s. It retains the block structure of ALGOL but gave up ALGOL's cumbersome grammar and syntax for free-form coding, elegance, and simplicity. It is a powerful and easy language to use, falling somewhere between FORTRAN and COBOL.

Another reason for Pascal's importance is that it serves as a base for other languages. One example is Ada, a language named after Ada Augusta, the

Countess of Lovelace, the world's first programmer. Ada, developed and implemented by the U.S. Department of Defense, is designed for numerical applications, systems programming, embedded programs, and real-time applications. Many forecast Ada to be the language of the future. This is largely due to the fact that the Department of Defense is a major user of computers. In the 1970s, over $3 billion a year was spent by Defense on software, and every indicator points to greater allocations in the future. Ada, however, is not as appropriate as COBOL for business processing and lacks COBOL's elegant data structures. COBOL has survived competition in the past, and may well remain the favorite language of the business community in the future. As expressed by one business programmer:

BASIC is easy,
PL/1 is powerful,
FORTRAN is fast,
but COBOL's the one.

Summary

Business data processing includes sorting, merging, calculating, summarizing, and reporting. To perform such processing, software is needed: application software which specifies decision rules and sequencing necessary for processing; operating software necessary for translating application programs into machine language; and software for operating computer hardware. Figure 3.8 shows the hierarchy of communications with computers from the movement of electrons to query languages.

Figure 3.8
Hierarchy of communication with computers

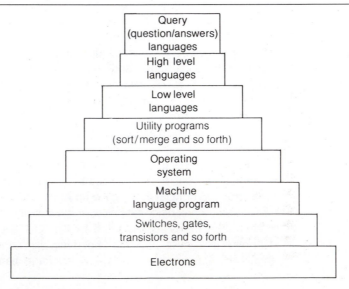

Figure 3.9
High and low level language spectrum

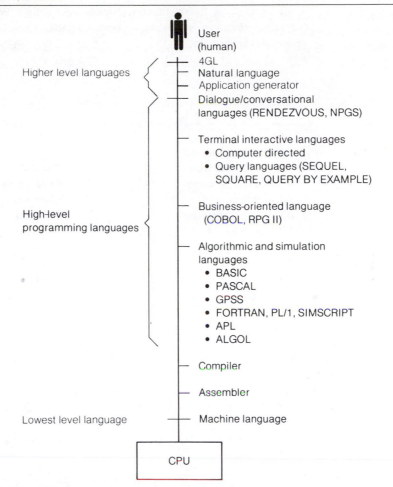

Implementing programs requires programming languages. The most efficient to run in terms of computer time is machine language, but this language is complex and difficult to learn. Languages closer to natural languages take more computer running time, but are easier to learn and faster to write. Because skilled programmers are an expensive, scarce resource while computer time is becoming cheaper, a distinct shift is being made from machine efficiency, favoring inefficient but high-level languages. Even operating systems are no longer written in machine language. Users have always preferred high-level languages for business application programs, the higher the better, though language ranking within the high level category is subjective, depending on one's need and background. The languages discussed in this chapter are arranged according to the authors' view of their levels in Figure 3.9.

Software that will enable a manager to enter data (input) and generate output from a terminal in a conversational mode and in a language close to English is the trend of the future. Businesspeople want simple, versatile programs that are reliable, readable, verifiable, and maintainable. Research in this direction is active and promising.

Key words

Address
Application generators
Application programs
Application software
Assembler
Assembler language
Binary digits
Business programs
Canned programs
Characters
Clarification response
Classify
Communications programs
Compiler
Contributive response
Controller
Control programs
Data base management systems (DBMS)
Data elements
Dumping
Executive
File
4th generation languages (4GL)
Graphic language
High level programming languages
Housekeeping programs
Interactive languages
I/O control programs
Key data element
Machine dependent
Machine language
Master file
Menu selection

Monitor
Object program
Operand
Operating systems software
Operating systems
Operators
Portable
Processing programs
Programming languages
Programs
Query languages
Record
Report
Report Program Generator (RPG)
Scientific programs
Service programs
Simulated
Simulation program
Software
Software houses
Software packages
Sorting
Source program
Spreadsheet
Storage location
Stroking dialogue
Summarize
Supervisor
Terminal interactive languages
Transaction file
Updating
Utility programs
Window

Discussion questions

1. Describe (*a*) in narrative and (*b*) by flowchart, the basic steps in the logic for processing data for a particular application such as payroll or accounts receivable.

2. What is an operating system? Why is it sometimes called the "underwear" system to the hardware and software system?

3. What is the difference between a natural language, such as English, and a formal programming language? Under what circumstances would it be desirable for programming languages to approach natural languages?

4. Name two compiler-based languages used in business. How are they different? When would each be used?

5. Which programming languages are most suitable for business applications? Give examples.

6. What factors must be considered when selecting a programming language for a given specific business problem?

7. Which programming language would you recommend for an application that is primarily:
   a. Computational (using a mathematical model).
   b. A problem in simulation.
   c. A problem in retrieval.
   d. Rearranging data.
   e. Generation of a report.
   f. A combination of (*d*) and (*e*) with some computations?

8. What is a utility program? Are such programs useful in business processing? Give three examples. Where would you obtain a utility program?

9. What is a software package? Give three examples. How are packages used and where can one obtain them?

10. Would software packages be more appropriate for small rather than large businesses? Why? What are the limitations of such software packages? What are some advantages?

11. Why is COBOL a common programming language used in business? Will it be superseded by Ada?

12. Can a computer language resemble natural language? Should it?

13. What are the limitations of translator- or compiler-based languages?

14. What are the advantages and disadvantages of a machine language? When are machine languages used for business applications?

15. What knowledge of programming is essential for a middle or top business manager? If a language must be learned, what language would you recommend for each level of management?

16. What is an interactive programming language and interactive processing? How is interactive processing different from batch processing?

17. Distinguish between:

a. Source and object program.
b. Low- and high-level languages.
c. Application and system programs.
d. System and utility programs.
e. Interactive and intelligent terminals.

18. What are the major categories of software?

19. Does every computer application require a computer program? Explain.

20. What are interactive and conversational computing? Are online, real time, and/or time sharing necessary for interactive or conversational computing?

21. Distinguish between a transaction and master file. Give examples from files for a marketing department, accounting office, and university.

22. Comment on this statement. Computers are neutral and unbiased. They only do what they are instructed to do. Who then is responsible for a computer error?

23. Comment on this statement: Computers and information are amoral.

24. How does sorting, merging, and updating vary in complexity between batch and online real-time systems? What additional resources are required for the additional complexity?

25. In what business environment would the following languages be appropriate?
a. Ada.
b. FORTRAN.
c. COBOL.
d. RPG.
e. SQL.

26. When would it be appropriate for a businessperson to use:
a. Spreadsheet?
b. SQL?
c. High level language?
d. Low level language?
e. Windows?

Exercise

1. An interactive system involves a set of activities that must be performed in a specific sequence. Rearrange the steps below to meet the sequence requirements:

a. User types in a reply (to the question).
b. User thinks about the questions for a while.
c. Computer asks a question.
d. Computer asks another question.
e. The above steps are repeated.
f. Computer does some processing.

Selected annotated bibliography

Arblaster, Andrew. "Human Factors in the Design and Use of Computing Languages." *International Journal of Man/Machine Studies* 17, no. 2, August 1982, pp. 211–24.

A broad review of computing linguistics. The author believes that high-level programming languages make it easier for people to read and understand programs. Perceptual, lexical, syntactic, semantic, and pragmatic levels of languages are explored. An extensive bibliography is included.

Berard, Edward V. "Ada Steps Out." *Datamation* 29, no. 9, (September 1983), pp. 114–28.

The author states that the characteristics that make Ada cost effective for military systems also make it attractive to the commercial software developer. What is lacking at present is the availability of validated, production-quality Ada compilers. This problem will be solved in time. Ada will affect more software professionals in the 1980s than COBOL did in the 1960s and 1970s.

Canning, Richard G., ed. "Query Systems for End Users." *EDP Analyzer* 20. no. 9. (September 1982), pp. 1–14.

This article concentrates on software for human-machine interface. Menus, forms, command languages, free-form natural language systems, and multi-query systems are discussed. Criteria for evaluating end-user interface include comfort, helpfulness, efficiency, forgiveness, and ease in remembering procedures and codes.

Chapanis, A. "Computers and the Common Man." In *Information Technology and Psychology: Prospects for the Future*. eds. R. A. Kasschan et al. New York: Praeger Publishers, 1982, pp. 106–32.

This article focuses on user-software problems associated with computers. The author believes that sensitivity to the needs of users and a willingness to develop computer software to meet those needs (not additional psychological research) will make computers a useful tool for everyone.

Edwards, Perry, and Broadwell, Bruce. *Data Processing*. Belmont, Calif.: Wadsworth, 1979, pp. 173–292.

This is a module on programming languages including a sample business-type problem solved in BASIC, FORTRAN IV, COBOL 1974, RPG II, PL/1, and APL and an evaluation of these languages. Well written with enough detail to appreciate the special characteristics of each language.

Ehrenreich, S. C. "Query Lnaguages: Design Recommendations Derived from Human Factors Literature." *Human Factors* 23, no. 6, (December 1981), pp. 709–25.

A well-written summary of research on query languages. Includes recommended readings on background material.

Martin, James. *Application Development Without Programmers*. Englewood Cliffs, N.J.: Prentice-Hall, 1982, 250 pp.

The author does not predict or propose the elimination of programmers as the title suggests. Instead, he proposes approaches and tools to complement current application development methods. These include methods to help users develop their own applications, the purchase of preprogrammed software packages, consulting support for users, the development of fourth-level languages, systems prototyping, and the establishment of information centers. The author also discusses APL, NOMAD, MAPPER, DMS, and ADF.

McClennan, Stephen T. "The End of the Hardware Era." *Datamation* 30, no. 6, (May 1, 1984), pp. 122–34.

McClennan is a professional journalist and Wall Street analyst. He argues that the future in computing lies in software—the era of hardware is past.

McMullen, Barbara E. and John F. "The Super Spreadsheets: How Do They Compare?" *Personal Computing* 2, no. 8, (June 1983), pp. 112–20.

This article evaluates, feature-by-feature, Visicalc Advanced Version, Multi-plan, and Supercalc.

Sammet, Jean E. "An Overview of High-level Languages." In *Advances in Computers*. ed. Marshall C. Yovits. New York: Academic Press, 1981, pp. 200–60.

Jean Sammet also wrote a highly respected text in 1969: *Programming Languages: History and Fundamentals*. This article discusses the relationship of languages to software technology and identifies programming trends.

Schneidermann, B. "Improving the Human Factors Aspect of Database Interactions." *ACM Transactions on Database Systems* 3, no. 4, (December 1978), pp. 417–39.

This is a survey of query languages. It classifies interaction modes, types of users, query features, and methods of retrieval. Field studies in evaluating the effectiveness of the natural and query languages are discussed. Also a good list of 52 references is included.

Sheil, B. A. "The Psychological Study of Programming." *ACM Computing Surveys* 13, no. 1, March 1981, pp. 101–20.

An in-depth review of psychological studies of programming, assessment of findings, and lessons for the future.

Thiel, Carol T. "New Packages Spark Change." *Infosystems* 30, no. 3, (July 1983), pp. 44–46.

This article is one of *Infosystems'* semiannual reviews of 35 categories of software packages. DBMS, MRP, teleprocessing, project management, DSS, spreadsheets, and functional applications, such as architecture, are among the topics discussed.

Wegner, Peter. "Programming Languages—the First 25 Years." *IEEE Transactions on Computers C–25,* no. 12, (December 1976), pp. 1207–25.

The author discusses 30 milestone in the history of programming. Thirteen milestones concern development. Evaluated are assemblers, FORTRAN, ALGOL 60, COBOL 61, ALGOL 68, SIMULA 67, and LISP. Ten milestones are programming concepts and theories, and the remaining seven concern software engineering technology. The article is descriptive with the technical portion separated so that it can be easily skipped. The author captures the sense of excitement and the enormous variety of activity that was characteristic of the first 25 years of programming.

Welty, Charles, and David D. Stample. "Human Factors Comparison of a Procedural and a Nonprocedural Query Language." *ACM Transactions on Database Systems* 6, no. 4, (December 1981), pp. 626–49.

This article discusses two experiments testing the ability of subjects to write queries in two different query languages: SQL and TABLET. The experiment showed that subjects wrote difficult queries better using the more procedural language (SQL). A good bibliography of 43 references is included.

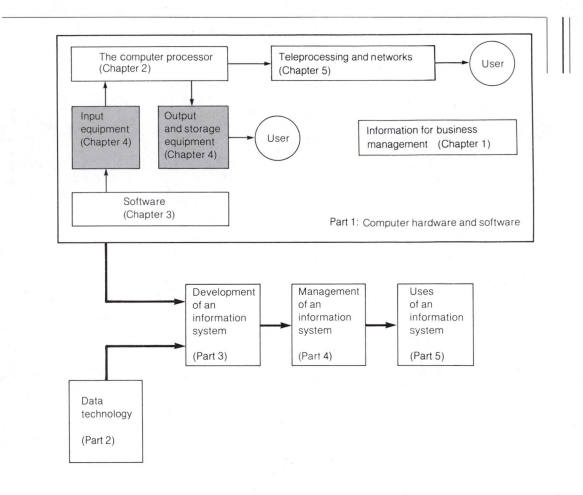

Input, output, and storage equipment

If computers are so fast, why do we spend so much time waiting around the computer center?

Computer Graffiti

All computers need **peripheral devices** to support the CPU. These include equipment for input, output, and storage (the topic of this chapter) and communication equipment (the subject of Chapter 5). It is important that students of business understand the capabilities and limitations of peripherals since they constitute the major share of hardware costs, sometimes as much as 90 percent. Formerly these devices were technical, the jurisdiction of data processing personnel. But the trend is toward less expensive, easier to operate machines. Managers today help select peripherals and supervise their use. Of these peripherals, input equipment is the most troublesome from management's point of view since input is human-intensive, prone to error. Users, not skilled EDP operators, prepare input and operate input equipment, often at remote sites where technical assistance is unavailable. Minimizing errors and seeing that the equipment is used efficiently is management's responsibility. The effectiveness of storage devices also depends on input equipment, for most output placed in storage becomes input at a later point in time. Furthermore, input equipment is the greatest bottleneck in computing operations. CPU speed is measured in nanoseconds, input speed in seconds. **Input bound** systems result when data waiting to be processed by high speed computers becomes backlogged due to the slowness of input equipment. Correcting this situation through purchase of new devices or revised approaches to input preparation is also a problem for management.

Before examining input, output, and storage devices in detail, the relationship between these peripherals, as depicted in Figure 4.1, should be explained. An example may prove helpful. A transaction file **(cards, tape,** or **disk)** is input; an updated master (also cards, tape, or disk) is output. This master will be stored until it serves as input for subsequent updating and processing. For example, the updated master of the day's transactions would serve as input for the next day's processing. Thus, the master has two states: **intermediate output** and input.

Figure 4.1
Input, output, and storage

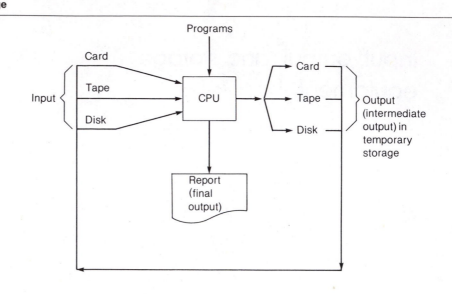

Figure 4.2
Input conversion to machine-readable form

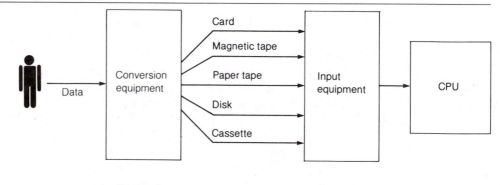

• Keypunch

• Magnetic tape converter
  (key to magnetic tape)

• Paper tape converter
  (key to paper tape)

• Disk converter
  (key to disk)

• Cassette converter
  (Key to cassette)

• Card reader

• Magnetic tape reader

• Paper tape reader

• Disk drive or floppy disk drive

• Cassette reader

Output, such as a journal listing, might also be in a **terminal** (final) state, a finished product that would not be stored.

This chapter examines the characteristics and uses of input, output, and storage devices, including specialized and advanced equipment since such machines will reduce, possibly eliminate, the problem of I/O bound systems in the future.

Input conversion

Input is generated by humans who collect data to be processed by the computer. Coding this data onto a machine-readable medium such as cards, disk, or tape is done by **conversion equipment.** Then the data is read by input equipment before being processed by the CPU. Figure 4.2 shows this process. Input devices may be **offline,** not directly connected to the computer, or **online,** in which case the devices are plugged into the computer or connected by a communication line, such as telephone or satellite.

Input devices

Cards are still used for input in some organizations. Figure 4.3 shows some of the conversion equipment needed before cards can be machine-read. Note that

Figure 4.3
Equipment to convert data to cards as machine-readable input

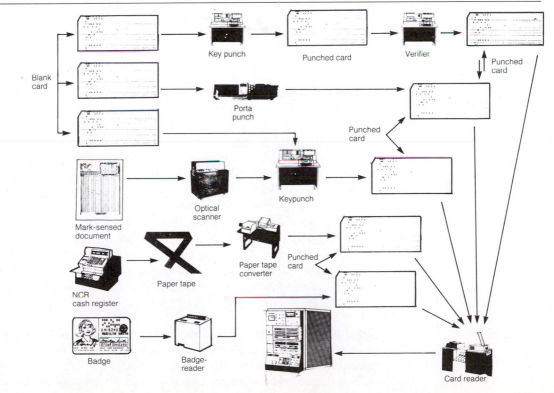

Figure 4.4
Examples of input devices

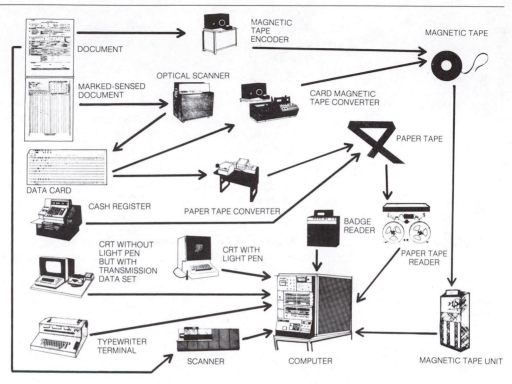

sometimes two machines are required. For example, an **optical scanner** and a **keypunch** are needed when cards are produced from a mark-sensed document.

Other examples of input to a computerized system are illustrated in Figure 4.4. The top path, in which a document is encoded on **magnetic tape,** is an example of offline input. The same document can be converted and input online (bottom path) by a scanner since the scanner transmits directly to the CPU. **Badge readers** used in production plants and terminals such as a **CRT (cathode ray tube terminal)** are other online input devices.

The characteristics of sample input devices are summarized in Table 4.1. Online input is reducing in price, becoming increasingly competitive with labor-intensive offline equipment. Another advantage of online input is that the opportunity for human error is reduced since the input is handled less by clerks and operators. A discussion follows of different types of online terminals.

Terminals

Terminals connected to the computer CPU can be used exclusively for input or for both input and output. Figure 4.5 shows the variety of terminals available. An **intelligent terminal** is one that is programmable. It might incorporate a microcomputer capable of performing computing tasks independent of the central CPU,

Table 4.1
Characteristics of sample input devices

Equipment	Media	Primary functions	Typical storage capacity	Major advantages and/or disadvantages
Card reader/punch	Punched card	Input/output	80 or 96 characters per card	Low cost, but slow-speed and bulky media
Paper tape reader/punch	Paper tape	Input/output	10 characters per inch	Simple and inexpensive, but fragile and bulky
Magnetic ink character recognition reader (MICR)	MICR paper documents	Reads input of MICR documents	—	Fast, high reliability reading, but documents must be preprinted, and the character set is not alphabetic
Optical character recognition reader (OCR)	Paper documents	Reads input from OCR typed documents	—	Direct input from paper documents, but limitations on input format
Mark-sense scanner	Mark-sense documents	Prepares input	One mark-sense sheet	Faster and more reliable than cards, but more expensive and limited to reading "marks"

Figure 4.5
Classification of terminals

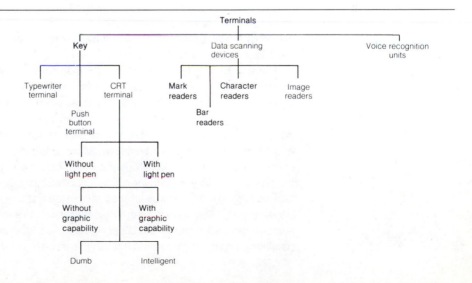

such as editing and validating data at the point of entry, a feature that helps reduce operator errors. Such intelligent terminals are useful in banking, reservations at hotels, car rentals, insurance, and accounting applications where data entry volume is large. A **dumb terminal** lacks such computing capabilities but can still be used to enter data and programs for processing by the central computer.

Teletype terminals (a typewriter terminal) can have both input and output capabilities. They may be used for entering data by keying the input or using push buttons for calling upon programs from the central computer facility to solve problems, and even for typing new programs into the system. Slowness is the major problem with this device. Input is limited by the operator's typing ability, and output by teletype speed.

A **cathode ray tube (CRT)** displays input or output on a screen resembling that of a television set. Information may appear character by character, or page by page. In either case, each character can be **addressed** (accessed) for making changes. The screen is a grid with characters at intersections of two coordinates. An operator can move a **cursor,** a symbol such as a dash, to locations on this grid by pressing a specific key. Wherever the cursor is stationed, a character may be entered, filling the space or replacing an existing character. In some systems, the pointer used to identify positions on the screen is controlled by a lever called a **joystick** or a device called a **mouse** which is a box that can be rolled on a flat tabletop.

The page image will fade unless it is **refreshed** (continually redisplayed), a process that requires extra hardware capability, increasing the price of the CRT unit. There is the additional cost of an add-on printer if a hardcopy is desired. All the applications of a typewriter terminal can be done on a CRT, but the latter is faster and quieter, and eliminates reams of paper. Ordering merchandise, recording inventory states, and accounting are examples of business applications for which the CRT is particularly well suited.

Some CRTs also have **graphic capabilities.** Lines and curves can be drawn on the tube so that vectors rather than characters are displayed. These are generated by a computer program which locates points on the screen matrix and joins them in the desired pattern.

There are many types of graphic CRT devices. They differ in cost and sophistication, some having more control over image manipulation than others. Users can also select from a potpourri of special features including: a **data tablet** that digitizes the coordinates of points of a hand-drawn sketch; **blinking characters** (for emphasis), brightness, and color choice; **zooming** and **scaling** (enlargement and reduction); **character reversal** (black character on white background becoming white on black); **scroll display** (the lines move upward, disappearing from the top of the screen with new lines continuously added to the bottom); **protected formats** (prevention of inadvertent alteration or erasure); partial screen transmission; control over image placement on screen; and the ability to underline or overstrike a character. Other features available include communication capabilities; access to programming languages and editing; choice of storage devices; printing facilities; and automatic answering where residing programs enable responses to messages without human intervention.

The use of graphic CRTs for production design is an application that has been used extensively in the automotive and electronics industries. Visual display is also appropriate for computer-assisted instruction, drafting and mapping, chart preparation (for example, flowcharts, organization charts, or planning and scheduling charts such as Gantt, PERT, or CPM), blueprints, and layouts.

The cursor can be replaced by a **light pen** which resembles a pencil attached by cable to the CRT. The light pen, hand-held for operation, has a photosensitive element hardly larger than a pinhead at one end which creates electric impulses that are recognized by the CRT when the screen is touched. The CRT can be programmed so that this tool can draw on the screen or indicate a choice from a menu presented on the screen. For example, in a query dialogue, the question,

How do you want suppliers identified?
1. By number.
2. By name.
3. Some other way.

might be answered by touching the light pen on 2 if name identification is desired. In other systems, the cursor might have to be brought into position for keying 2.

The light pen is deceptive in cost. The pen itself is not expensive, but the software that must accompany it is.

Data scanning terminals

Some terminals scan such documents as inventory tags, plastic credit cards, or badges, converting the data on these into machine-readable form and storing the information for later processing. The data—unique marks or special **fonts**—needs to be preprinted on the object to be scanned. Such online input terminals eliminate the labor and error of operator data conversion, and reduce the time required for data entry. However, documents in poor condition (smudges, creases, tears, or dirt) can be misread.

Scanning terminals read three classifications of data: **marks, bars,** and **characters.** The advantages and disadvantages of equipment to scan these media are summarized in Table 4.2.

One scanning device is a portable **wand,** resembling a plastic pistol connected by cable to the data collection terminal. The wand captures data through a sensor at its tip when waved past a bar tag or other encoded data (the Universal Product Code, for example). In one NCR model an audible beep registers that the data has been read. In one Singer machine a key lights up. Such systems are used extensively in retail stores. In the early 1980s, Montgomery Ward had approximately 16,000 wands in use in over 500 stores.

Voice recognition

Another pattern recognition terminal used for input is **voice recognition equipment.** These terminals are conceptually similar to optical scanners in that pat-

Table 4.2
Comparison of scanning terminals

	Mark-sense reader	*Bar code reader*	*Character reader*
Media	Marks on cards or documents	Bars on document or product	Characters on document
Speed	Fast	Application of UPC reader limited by clerk speed	Fast
Readable by human	Yes	Not easily	Yes
Accuracy	Depends on care in marking	Very high	High
Information density	Low (binary)	Medium (digital)	High (character)
Complexity of equipment	Simple	Simple	Complex, specialized
Cost	Low	Low	High
Problems	Marks are specialized	Bars must be preprinted	Format size is restricted
Advantages	Less danger of being misread Easy to complete Straightforward Errors known can be corrected easily	Easily and quickly read	Direct way to process printed documents like insurance premiums and turn-around documents Reduces stacks of paper
Disadvantages	Special documents required Sometimes requires special markers/pencils Unsuitable for extensive alphabetic data Assumption of careful entering not valid Inappropriate for volatile data	Bars must be preprinted Requires standardization in production of bar-coded products	Special input preparation equipment required Handprinting not foolproof to read Problems of standardization
Applications	Market research Testing (multiple-choice exam grading) Inventory Meter reading for billing and accounting Time sheets Order forms	Supermarket checkout (UPC) Credit card checking Badge reading for factory floor or library use Tag reading for point-of-sale use in retail stores	Office work Turn-around documents Stock/shares Payroll data Mail sorting

terns are traced and represented by a set of numbers (0 and 1 bits). However, converting speech, an airborne signal, into digital data is a far more complex process than reading marks or bars, since voice patterns include variables in sound, pitch, tone, and loudness. Voice data, once digitized, is then compared to a voice profile stored in the memory of the computer.

A major problem in voice recognition is that pronunciation varies from individual to individual, and a person's mood, circumstance, or health can also affect speech characteristics. Furthermore, telephone lines distort voice signals, as do factors such as humidity. An exact match of voice patterns is, therefore, almost an impossibility.

One method of overcoming some of the above problems is to store **voice profiles** of individual users. In a get-acquainted session the computer flashes on a screen vocabulary words which the user repeatedly vocalizes. The voice profile stored in the computer is, therefore, the user's own. Another approach is to store a set of standard voices for a limited vocabulary, a vocabulary chosen according to clients' use of voice recognition equipment.

At present, voice recognition is effective only for limited applications. Each word pronounced by a client must be surrounded by an overlay of silence extending $\frac{1}{10}$ to $\frac{1}{4}$ second. A string of words in a sentence or words spoken quickly require a storage capacity and processing time far too expensive for practical use. In the future, however, advances in technology of voice reproduction and reduction in memory costs will undoubtedly make voice recognition units even for large vocabularies cost-effective.

Voice recognition devices are currently in use in factories where the hands of an employee are busy so that data entry by typewriter or optical scanner would break hand motion, reducing throughput. The worker voices input through a headset, continuing prescribed hand tasks. Mail sorting in post offices and in large firms (such as Monsanto, a major chemical company, which processes 25,000 pieces of mail per day) is another practical application.

Voice recognition can also be used for identification purposes in restricted areas of factories, or as security in banking or cash dispensing. These examples, however, are better served by pattern recognition of signatures, fingerprints, and hand forms. These, surprisingly, are more unique than voice patterns, and vary less over time. The steady drop in the price of minicomputers required for processing pattern recognition will ensure the manufacture and use of such devices in the future.

Storage devices

Characteristics of the main storage devices on the market today are summarized in Table 4.3. The **cassette** and **floppy disk** are products of recent technology. Both are compact, cheap, and very simple to operate, though of the two, the floppy disk (or **diskette**) is more useful because it allows random access. The floppy comes in different sizes (5 to 8 inches in diameter) with single or double side, and has a capacity of up to 5 million bytes. This capacity can be increased by

Table 4.3
Characteristics of external storage equipment

Equipment	Media	Primary functions	Major advantages and/or disadvantages
Magnetic tape drive	Magnetic tape	Secondary storage (sequential access) and input/output	Inexpensive with a fast transfer rate, but only sequential access
Magnetic tape cassette	Magnetic tape cassette	Secondary storage and input/output	Small, inexpensive, and convenient, but only sequential access
Magnetic strip storage unit	Magnetic strip cartridge	Mass secondary storage	Relatively inexpensive, large capacity, but slow access time
Magnetic disk drive	Magnetic disk	Secondary storage (direct access) and input/output	Large capacity, fast direct access storage device (DASD), but expensive
Floppy disk drive	Magnetic diskette	Input/output and secondary storage	Small, inexpensive, and convenient, but slower and smaller capacity than other DASDs
Magnetic drum unit	Magnetic drum	Secondary storage and input/output	Fast access time and large capacity, but expensive

adding more floppy disk drives. The floppy represents a definite advance over storage devices of the 1960s which were bulky, had limited capacity, and required extremely level disk drives during processing. Today's floppy rotates freely within its jacket and can be handled, even transported in a notebook or attaché case without being damaged. It is readily replacing cards, cartridges, and even cassettes for cheap medium-size storage, complementing new storage technology of bubble memory, charged coupled devices (CCD), and random access memory (RAM) using metal-oxide-semiconductor technology (MOS) which provides fast access to large memories. A detailed discussion of the technology of such large memories is beyond the scope of this book. But a brief look at bubble memory will give the reader some insight into recent developments in this area.

Bubble memories store information on a thin film of garnet in areas where the magnetic polarity can be reversed, a reversal that represents the binary states 0 and 1. These areas, when seen under a microscope, appear as bubbles, for which the memory is named. The great advantage of this device is that stored data is unaffected by a power failure. At present, bubble memory costs less than CCDs and RAMs with MOS technology, and the fact that its price is expected to tumble greatly in the next few years means that bubble devices will commonly be used for large memories in the late 1980s. Technological advances are harder to predict for CCDs and RAMs. At present, the former is 100 times faster than bubble memory; RAMs with MOS technology are 10,000 faster. But cost is a factor limiting their use.

Output peripherals

Figure 4.6 illustrates common **output devices** and media. The characteristics of major output equipment are summarized in Table 4.4

Note that terminals and CRTs discussed earlier in this chapter as input de-

Figure 4.6
Output devices and media

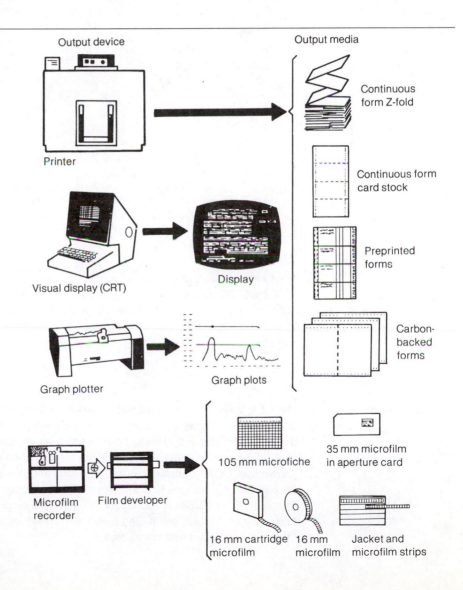

Output device

Output media

Printer

Continuous form Z-fold

Continuous form card stock

Visual display (CRT)

Display

Preprinted forms

Carbon-backed forms

Graph plotter

Graph plots

Microfilm recorder

Film developer

105 mm microfiche

35 mm microfilm in aperture card

16 mm cartridge microfilm

16 mm microfilm

Jacket and microfilm strips

Table 4.4
Characteristics of major output equipment

Equipment	Media	Primary functions	Major advantages and/or disadvantages
Line printer	Paper (hard copy)	Printed output of paper reports and documents	Fast and low-cost hard copy, but inconvenient and bulky
CRT terminal	"Soft" display	Keyboard input and output	Convenient and inexpensive, but limited display capacity and no hard copy
Plotter	Paper	Output	Important when graphic output is needed; expensive, especially the table model that can plot back and forth
Computer output, on microfilm, (COM)	Microfilm spool/ strips/cartridge Microfiche Aperture card	Output that has archival significance	See Table 4.5

vices serve for output as well. A **printer** is an example of equipment used solely for output. The disadvantage of computer printouts is that they can be so voluminous that information which a manager needs is not always readily accessible. To overcome this problem, a terminal to **page** or **scroll** the output on a CRT screen can be used.

Computer output on microfilm

Output representing historical data needed for infrequent processing (for example, violation records of a police department, invoice files, student records at a university) or output that must be preserved as stipulated by law (for example, utility company records) can be produced on **microfilm** or **microfiche.** Figure 4.7 shows how **COM (computer output on microfilm)** is prepared, stored, and retrieved. The advantages and limitations of COM are summarized in Table 4.5. At the present time, COM is cost-effective only when output volume is large and the frequency of retrieval small. The computerized retrieval and display of microfilm information is called **micrographics.**

Figure 4.7
COM—computer output on microfilm

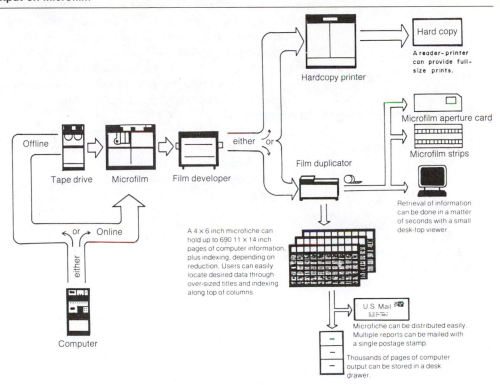

Hardcopy printer

Hard copy

A reader-printer can provide full-size prints.

Offline

Tape drive   Microfilm   Film developer   either or

Microfilm aperture card

Microfilm strips

Film duplicator

Retrieval of information can be done in a matter of seconds with a small desk-top viewer.

either   or   Online

A 4 × 6 inch microfiche can hold up to 690 11 × 14 inch pages of computer information, plus indexing, depending on reduction. Users can easily locate desired data through over-sized titles and indexing along top of columns.

either

Computer

U.S. Mail

Microfiche can be distributed easily. Multiple reports can be mailed with a single postage stamp.

Thousands of pages of computer output can be stored in a desk drawer.

Voice output

An output device that will become more common in the 1980s is **voice output.** This equipment reverses the process of voice recognition discussed earlier. Digitized data of the human voice for a given vocabulary is stored in the computer memory. To verbalize a message, a microprocessor selects the desired words, strings them together, draws the digitized data for these words from the memory, and converts the data to an analog signal through filters and amplifiers. The advent of microprocessors and reduced costs for large memory capacity have resulted in recent improvement in speech synthesis. No longer is the output monotone as depicted in many movies. Computers can speak with variable pitch and loudness. They can phrase sentences with appropriate pauses and even reproduce regional and local accents.

One can expect voice output to increasingly replace dials and display boards in factories, airplanes, and even in the family car as the cost of this equipment drops in response to technological advances. ("Fasten your seat belt, please," instead of that annoying buzz.)

Voice output has numerous educational applications as well. It can supplement visual display in **computer-assisted instruction,** or aid in teaching and translating foreign languages. In data processing, validation of input by audio feedback improves efficiency. Errors often pass undetected when operators check input documents against input entry on a CRT screen with eyes shifting from document to screen. Errors are caught more easily during audio validation when the eyes of the operator focus solely on the input document. However, voice output raises noise levels, a good example of how the solution to one problem creates another.

Eventually speech synthesis and voice recognition devices will be integrated in one piece of equipment, permitting verbal computer responses to voiced inquiries. One major benefit will be extended service to clients outside 8–5 working hours, for automated responses to phoned questions at any hour of day or night will be possible.

Peripherals of the future

The development of faster and less labor-intensive peripherals is essential. Otherwise bottlenecks in creation of data, storage, and output production will restrict the performance of the powerful CPUs. To speed input, data will be increasingly collected by scanners and optical readers, eliminating the current step of keying data which is not only time-consuming but subject to human error. Present identification systems are also inadequate for transactions like fund transfers. Recognition of fingerprints, hand forms, signatures, and voice prints will replace the plastic identification card used today. Though such devices are technologically feasible at the present time, their cost is too high for common business use. For example, in 1980, signature analysis equipment was approximately $1,000; biometrics (analyzing the shape of the hand) $3,000; voice analysis $5,000; and fingerprint analysis $9,000. Based strictly on cost, signature analysis seems most promising, but voice recognition equipment has other business applications as

Table 4.5
Advantages and limitations of COM

Advantages:
> Reduces printed paper volume dramatically (space occupied by film cassette or microfiche is 1 percent and 0.05 percent, respectively, of the paper equivalent) and hence is cheaper to store (cost of facility, insurance, security, and so forth) and mail.
> Fast in preparation—over 1 million frames per month in one shift.
> Faster (and much cheaper to retrieve than a paper document (⅑ the time).
> More reliable; less down time than printer.

Disadvantages:
> Requires special equipment to read and to print hard copy. Media, uncomfortable, causing eyestrain for some readers.
> Updating is expensive and time-consuming. Not appropriate for operational data.
> User cannot mark pages or make notes on microfilm or microfiche.
> Poor file integrity (continuity) with microfiche. If one COM is removed and misplaced, its loss is difficult to detect. (Not so with microfilm.)
> Large capital investment needed.
> Can raise organizational questions. In which department will the COM be located?

well. Data entry is one example. As a result, voice recognition equipment will be increasingly common in the 1980s.

The technology of sensors for input has not kept pace with CPU technology, in part because the market of suppliers is fragmented, but also because of the difficulty of finding venture capital for manufacturing such equipment. Besides, once data is recognized by sensors, there still remains the problem of interpreting and using this information.

CRTs, the mainstay of the terminal market in the 1970s for both input and output, may well be displaced in the future because of user dissatisfaction with their flicker which causes eyestrain after one or two hours of work. The electronic beam scanning across the screen fades and needs to be refreshed: hence, the flicker. The CRT has also been opposed by unions for alleged dangerous X-ray emissions. The **plasma display** may be the CRT replacement. This device is essentially a grid of conductors between glass plates surrounded by neon gas. When a point on the screen is part of a desired image, the conductors intersecting at that point are energized making the gas there glow brightly and steadily. At present, plasma displays are more expensive than their CRT counterpart, but as demand increases in the 1980s, the price should drop. A major disadvantage of plasma displays is that they lack the color and graphic capabilities of the CRT. Color graphics, especially interactive color graphics, have many applications for management at the control and planning level, providing information in a manner that is easily absorbed and understood especially when the terminal has adaptive keys for routines (of computations and figures), and a variety of character sets (special symbols, foreign alphabets, and so forth).

In the next decade, reduced costs for greater storage capacity can be expected, including archival mass storage systems that can store up to 470 billion characters (equivalent to 27 million pages of a typical newspaper). Lasers may also be used to record information for storage. However, the lasers burn the medium, which cannot then be reused, a major disadvantage.

Optical memories are also under development. One such device selling for $100,000 in the mid–1980s had a capacity of 4 gigabytes (4 billion characters); another costing $100 stored 1 gigabyte. The melting of tiny pools of metal on the surface of a recording medium, changing the metal pools from a crystalline to noncrystalline state (or vice versa) is one approach to erasable optical memories. A laser detects the difference between the surface reflectivity of the two metal states and thereby recognizes and reads the digital codes recorded.

Magnetic storage devices are still faster than optical memory devices (a million bytes can be stored in a third of a second). However, optical memory cuts storage costs by a third (from 15 cents per million bytes to 5 cents). One can expect great cost reductions and faster speeds for optical memory in the future.

Stored data has little value unless it can be efficiently retrieved. This requires an effective word-matching algorithm and software to implement the algorithm. A records manager is being developed that matches key words in a query (concerning a letter or a memo) with words in the files and allows not only for a change in order of words but also for misspelling. The records manager computer has its

Figure 4.8
Summary of input, output, and storage media and peripherals

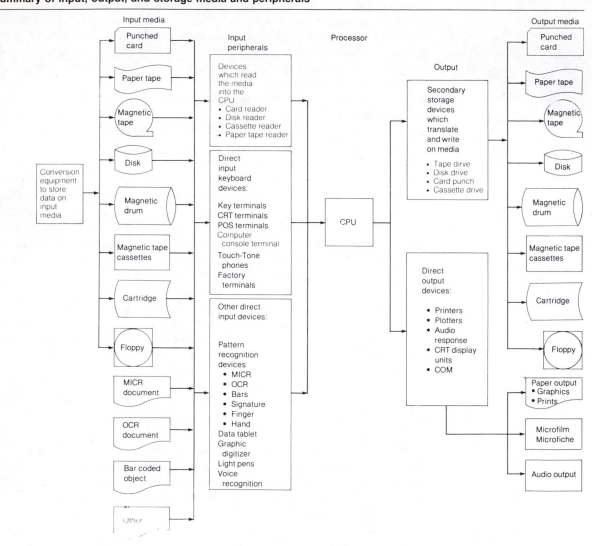

own display and printer and has a storage capacity of 75,000 full pages, holding information equivalent to information stored in 60 file cabinets, yet is smaller in size than a single-tier filing cabinet. When debugged and commercially available at cost-effective prices, it will have a great impact on the office of the future.

Another important change in peripherals of the future will be in the terminal market. The dollar value of terminals will increase an estimated 50 percent in the decade ending in 1988, while the expected number of terminals will double due to falling terminal prices. Furthermore, the mix of terminals will change. Dumb terminals and **point-of-sale(POS) terminals** have peaked in their demand and will be replaced by intelligent and specialty terminals, custom-built for applications such as brokerage terminals, industrial badge readers, hand-held portable terminals, and voice units, albeit those with limited functional vocabulary.

Summary

All computers require equipment for input and output. In cases where processing is spread over time, information needs to be stored. Equipment for input, output, and storage varies in structure and performance depending on the media of data handled. Figure 4.8 summarizes both available media and peripherals.

Some peripherals are both expensive and technical, acquired and maintained by EDP personnel though shared by all users in an organization. These include printers, plotters, large storage devices, and input conversion equipment. Other equipment, such as optical character readers and COM devices, though technical, may be under the user's jurisdiction. User responsibility is generally for media and equipment that is compact, easy to operate, and inexpensive—equipment that can be employed in conjunction with minis and micros in a distributive processing environment such as point-of-sale terminals (POS), data entry terminals, floppy diskettes and diskette drives, and scanners.

In discussing peripherals, no attempt has been made to identify actual equipment models, manufacturers, or prices because the industry is extremely volatile, with new competitors and equipment continually entering the market. Technological advances mean that performance is improving while prices are dropping, even with current inflation. When peripherals are needed, a cost-benefit study should be made of available equipment to determine which models are cost-effective in view of an individual firm's requirements.

Key words

Address	Disk
Badge reader	Diskette
Bars	Dumb terminal
Blinking characters	Floppy disk
Bubble memory	Font
Cards	Graphic capability
Cassette	Input bound
Cathode ray tube terminal (CRT)	Intelligent terminal
Character reversal	Intermediate output
Characters	Joystick
COM (computer output on microfilm)	Keypunch
Computer-assisted instruction	Light pen
Conversion equipment	Magnetic tape
Cursor	Marks
Data tablet	Microfiche

Microfilm

Micrographics

Mouse

Offline

Online

Optical memory

Optical scanner

Output devices

Page

Peripheral devices

Plasma display

Point-of-sale terminal (POS)

Printer

Protected formats

Refresh

Scaling

Scroll display

Tape

Teletype terminal

Terminal

Voice output

Voice profile

Voice recognition equipment

Wand

Discussion questions

1. What is the difference between online and offline devices? Give three examples of each. What circumstances favor each?

2. What peripherals have you personally used? Was your use multipurpose or for input, storage, or output?

3. Compare OCR with MICR. Cite examples in business where each has a comparative advantage.

4. Compare printers, CRTs, and COMs as computer output devices. Cite business examples where each has the comparative advantage. Explain.

5. Compare typewriter terminals and CRTs as I/O devices. Under what conditions would one be more desirable than the other?

6. When would voice input and voice output be appropriate? Why is voice recognition equipment limited in use at the present time?

7. How are checks processed in a modern bank using computers? What special equipment and input characteristics are required?

8. What is a light pen? Why is it not universally used?

9. Distinguish between:
   a. Remote and console terminals.
   b. Inquiry and response terminals.
   c. Badge and audio terminals.
   d. Visual and voice terminals.
   e. Tape and disk storage.

10. What peripherals would you use for an OLRT system in a large firm with a diversified set of sources for raw materials, many products, and a variety of production processes?

11. Are peripherals essential to the operation of a computer? Do they cotribute to the performance of a computer? What is the proportion of peripheral cost to the total cost of hardware?

12. What is currently the main constraint to computer performance, CPU, or peripherals? Cite examples.

13. What developments in the peripheral industry are expected in the next few years? What is the main obstacle to peripheral technological advance?

14. What are the factors that influence the selection of peripheral equipment?

15. How would selection of peripherals differ for OL and OLRT systems?

16. What are the advantages and disadvantages of using a:
    - a. Mouse?
    - b. Cursor?
    - c. Joystick?

17. What is the significance to a person in business of advances in:
    - a. Optical memories?
    - b. Bubble memories?
    - c. Micrographics?
    - d. COM?

18. How can a manager benefit from the following features?
    - a. Paging.
    - b. Zooming.
    - c. Refreshing.
    - d. Scaling.

Exercise

1. Visit a computer room. Draw a block diagram of the hardware located in the computer room. Identify and label each hardware in terms of devices for input, output, storage, processing, or multipurpose use.

Selected annotated bibliography

References evaluating specific computer equipment soon become outdated. Readers are advised to read such periodicals as *Datamation, Mini-Micro Systems,* and *Infosystems* for surveys and articles about peripherals on the market.

Cakir, A.; D. J. Hard; and T. Stewart. *Visual Display Terminals*. New York: John Wiley and Sons, 1980, 257 pp.

This is a manual covering the following aspects of visual display terminals: ergonomics, workplace, design, health and safety features, and task organization.

Computer Technology Review.

An excellent journal on peripheral equipment. Articles are not limited to hardware, but discuss software implementation and the integration of peripherals in a computer system as well.

Datapro Research Corporation. *Datapro*.

This is a looseleaf reference service on computer equipment, software, media, and supplies. New products are described and evaluated. A special volume is devoted to peripherals. In addition to product briefs, there is a periodic update section called "All about—." Some of the topics, covered are display terminals, printers, disk drives, disk packs, data entry devices, key entry, and data collection equipment, COM, optical readers, and plotters. In each case, the state of the art is reviewed, the advantages and limitations discussed, vendors' names and addresses listed, and most important of all, models on the market are evaluated in detail.

Datapro is a consumer's guide written in nontechnical language. In a competitive and innovative industry, this is a valuable reference for anyone planning to acquire computer equipment. *Data World* is a similar reference service.

Dean, M. "How a Computer Should Talk to People." *IBM Systems Journal* 12, no. 4 (1982), pp. 424–53.

This is an easy-to-read article on human-computer interaction. It discusses messages generated by programs for users and paths for successful interface.

Edmonds, Ernest. "The Man-Computer Interface: A Note on Concepts and Design." *International Journal of Man-Machine Studies* 16, no. 3 (April 1982), pp. 231–236.

A British view, but still valid for the American scene. This article is addressed to the designer of interactive systems and stresses the central role of human-computer interface in such systems. Types of processors and the components of interface are identified. Directions for future research are also suggested.

Friend, David. "Graphics for Managers: The Distributed Approach." *Datamation* 28, no. 7 (July 1982), pp. 76–96.

This article is more on graphics than DDP. It discusses the characteristics of transaction and decision input data and how they can be expressed in graphics. It also examines CPU and storage hardware needed for graphic representation and cost tradeoffs of equipment.

Information Management 17, no. 4 (April 1983), pp. 18–38.

This issue has a special section on microfilm, electronic filing, COM, and OCR. The discussion is both descriptive and prescriptive for the 1980s.

Mehlmann, Marilyn. *When People Use Computers: An Approach to Developing an Interface*. Englewood Cliffs, N.J.: Prentice-Hall 1981. 142 pp.

This book is pleasing to the eye and challenging to the mind. There are good sections on the design and implementation of the screen image (screen layout with examples of frame templates) and dialogues.

Webster, Edward. "Figuring the Economics of the New Page Printers." *Datamation* 24, no. 5 (May 1978), pp. 171–77.

A look at the benefits and cost of any peripheral is important. One does not have to be an economist to follow the analysis of this article. The evaluation procedure for printers used by Webster could be adapted to all equipment acquisition.

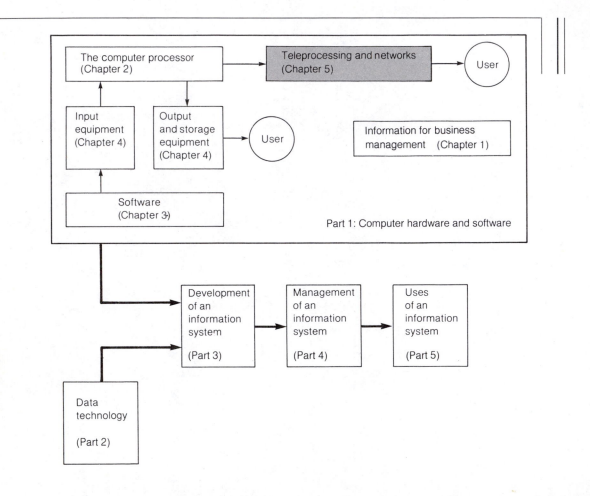

The computer processor
(Chapter 2)

Teleprocessing and networks
(Chapter 5)

User

Input
equipment
(Chapter 4)

Output
and storage
equipment
(Chapter 4)

User

Information for business
management   (Chapter 1)

Software
(Chapter 3)

Part 1: Computer hardware and software

Development
of an
information
system

(Part 3)

Management
of an
information
system

(Part 4)

Uses
of an
information
system

(Part 5)

Data
technology

(Part 2)

Teleprocessing and networks

5

In 1899, the director of the U.S Patent Office urged President William McKinley to abolish his department. According to the director, everything that could be invented had been invented.

Although processing by computers is measured in nanoseconds, the user may not get the full benefit of this speed because of the time lapse in moving input data to the computer and output to the user. Cards and paper printouts create delays due simply to their bulk. Even if this problem is overcome by the use of more compact tape, disk, and cassette, the transfer of information is still time-consuming when dispersed locations such as sales offices, branch offices, warehouses, and plants of a business all use a centralized computer.

Teleprocessing to instantly record input and output is one method of speeding up operations. This involves the transfer of data and information between computers and remote points by telephone, satellite, or other communication channels. The term *teleprocessing,* first used by IBM, is often used as a synonym for telecommunications, data communication, or information communication. The term is also used to include communication of data and its related processing. Businesses that want instant information on inventory levels, production status, or bank balances find teleprocessing invaluable. So do airlines, hotels, and car rental agencies that require immediate reservation confirmations.

This chapter will consider data transmission channels, computer equipment configurations, functions of teleprocessing systems, and communication networks.

Data transmission

Data transmission is the transfer of data to and from the computer through telecommunication channels. The movement may be a few feet within a single office building or over thousands of miles. Transmission methods can be characterized by three main variables: **types of channels, speed of transmission,** and **mode of transmission.**

Figure 5.1
Types of channels in telecommunications

Type	Transmission direction	Graphic representation	Example
Simplex	One direction only	 A ⟶ B	• Radio • Television
Half-duplex	One direction only at any one time. Can be in both directions in sequence	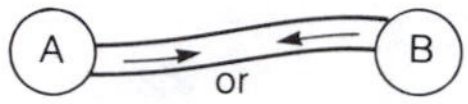 A ⟶ or ⟵ B	• Walkie-talkie • Intercom
Duplex or Full duplex	In both directions simultaneously	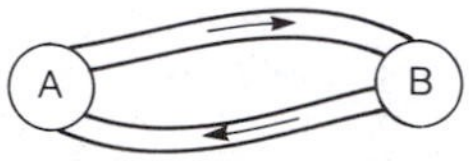 A ⟶ ⟵ B	• Picture-telephone • Dedicated separate transmission lines (such as a presidential "hot-line")

Types of channels

A communication line or **channel** can be simplex, half duplex, or full duplex. These channels are compared in Figure 5.1. The **simplex** enables communication of information in only one direction, from source to computer or from computer to user. No interchange is possible. There is neither indication of readiness to accept transmission nor any acknowledgment of transmission received. A **half-duplex** system allows sequential transmission of data in both directions but this involves a delay when the direction is reversed. The ability to transmit simultaneously in both directions requires a **duplex** or **full duplex** system. Though more costly, this system decreases processing time because it enables output to be displayed on a terminal while input is still being sent.

Speed of transmission

Transmission of data is measured in **baud.** (Baud is both a singular and plural word, named after the inventor.) In most communication lines, a baud is one bit per second. The capacity of the channel is a data rate called **bandwidths** or **bands.** This gives a measure of the amount of data that can be transmitted in a unit of time. Table 5.1 compares different bands of transmission with their respective speeds and uses. Combining speeds, bandwidths, and types of channels, one has a spectrum of capabilities, the cheapest and most limited being a simplex telegraphic grade channel, the most versatile and expensive being a full duplex broadband system.

Modes of communication services

Different modes of communication services are summarized in Table 5.2. Carriers in the United States are licensed by the Federal Communications Commis-

Table 5.1
Types of transmission of data

Channel bandwidth	Speed	Use
Telegraph grade	75 b/s (bits per second)	Printer and keyboard devices
Subvoice grade	45–180 b/s	Teleprinter, also used for telephone
Voice grade	600–9,600 b/s	Communication (telephone)
Broadband	Usually 4,800–9,600 b/s, may go as high as 500,000 b/s	Computer-computer communications

sion (FCC), which regulates transmission by wire, radio, satellite, telephone, television, telegraph, facsimile (documents), and telephoto.[1] There are over 2,000 telecommunication carriers in the United States, the largest being AT&T for telephone, and Western Union for wire and microwave radio communications. In addition, there are specialized **common carriers,** such as MCI and Datron, that provide point-to-point or switched services in heavy traffic areas. These services send data over public lines passing through exchanges and switching facilities, so the term **switched line** is used. In contrast, there are private or **leased lines** which have full access to the line. Some companies with private lines connecting branches and plants refer to these lines as **tie lines.**

Some telecommunication services split data into **batches** or **packets,** transmitting over routes that are less busy during slack periods, and using routes that take advantage of the difference in time between the East and West Coast. The data is then reassembled at the receiving end. This concept is illustrated in Figure 5.2. Here, a company wishes to transmit data between points 1 and 2. Instead of having its own communications system, the company pays for the services of a carrier that has the packet switching capability added to its transmission line. A carrier of this type is called a **value-added carrier.** The carrier can select one of many routes on its packet-switched network, such as ABE, ACE, or ADE. The packets transmitted could all follow the same route but alternate with other customer packets in transmission, or the packets could follow different routes according to line availability. The combination of routing and interspersing of packets is **transparent** to the user since the user does not necessarily know how it is done. This routing and sequencing of packets add security because it is difficult to intercept an entire **message** since it is split into parts.

The FCC, concerned with competitiveness in telecommunications, regulates the carriers and services offered. One of its far-reaching decisions was to allow

---

[1] For an excellent discussion of public carriers both in the United States and abroad, see R. J. Halsey et al., "Public Networks: Their Evolution, Interfaces and Status," *IBM Systems Journal* 18, no. 2 (1979), pp. 223–43.

Table 5.2
The services offered by principal carriers in
telecommunications

Name of service	Characteristics of service	Carrier
DATAPHONE	Uses telephone lines.	Bell System
WATS (Wide-Area Telephone Service)	Uses telephone lines but restricted to geographic area. Has fixed charges. Can be used with DATAPHONE.	Bell System
TWX (Teletypewriter Exchange Service)	Each subscriber has individual line with TWX number. Charges are based on length of call, time used, and established minimums. Used for low-speed business machines.	Bell System and other telephone companies
TELEX	Similar to TWX except for limit on digits (7) that can be dialed. Has no minimum charge.	Western Union
ACS (Advanced Communication System)	Able to switch computer data between terminals at different speeds and formats.	AT&T (parent company of Bell)
SBS (Satellite Business System)	Intra-company communication for large businesses via satellite.	IBM, Aetna Life, and Communications Satellite Corp.
VIEWDATA	Offers information services through the television.	Agency of British Government

a consortium, including IBM, to initiate a system for transmission of data between large organizations via satellite, a system in competition with AT&T. Competition between AT&T, IBM, and Xerox will benefit the consumer by providing a greater variety of services at competitive prices. This will lead to the widespread use of the electronic office, the merging of office equipment technology and computers with data communications. Adequate technology and corporate resources are available. Progress in this direction will in part depend on the consistency and liberalness of FCC policy.

Figure 5.2
Packet switching

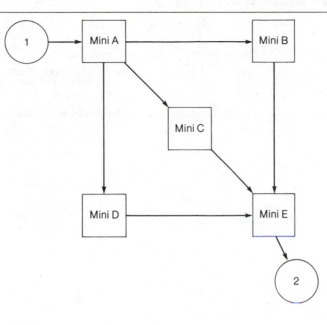

Equipment at the user's end

A user needs a **terminal,** a **multiplexer** or **concentrator,** and a **modem** when transmitting and receiving data to and from a computer over a communication line.

Terminals

The types of terminal equipment used for sending and receiving data are summarized in Table 5.3. Some of these are only input equipment (Touch-Tone, voice, and badge reader), some are only output equipment (printer, COM, and audio response), while others have both input and output capabilities (keyboard and CRT terminals).

Special software is often needed for adding processing capabilities to the terminal and for polling the terminals. **Polling** is a set of rules by which each terminal is queried to determine whether or not it is ready for use.

Multiplexers

One problem with terminals is that their maximum speed of transmission is much less than that of a telecommunication line. To improve efficiency, a multiplexer is used to combine multiple lines from terminals of slow transmission speeds with one fast broadbeam transmission line. The multiplexer functions at the terminal end in both receiving and transmitting data. This is illustrated in Figure 5.3 A multiplexer also performs intelligent functions, such as routing messages and checking for errors.

Table 5.3
Terminals and other devices used for sending and receiving data

Device	Feature and capability of device
Terminal keyboard	Typewriter terminal.
Intelligent	Verifies data and enables correction prior to transmission. Could be a minicomputer with peripheral devices such as tape or disk.
Nonintelligent	Simple input and output device.
Video display unit	Has a video tube like a TV. Can have alphanumeric or graphic capability. Can also have a hard copy unit for printing.
Touch-Tone phone	Used for numeric data transmission by persons such as sales representatives.
Voice input	Acoustic features of person speaking can be checked for bona fide user. Expensive and relatively modern. Useful where identification of input source is essential.
Input reader	Card or tape readers.
Badge reader	Reads specially coded badges, such as identification cards carried by factory and other workers.
Printer	Only for output.
COM	Computer output on microfiche or microfilm.
Audio response	Audio output only.

Figure 5.3
Multiplexer

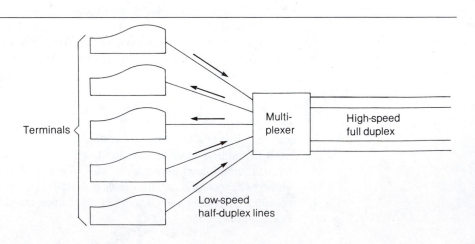

Figure 5.4
Digital and analog signals

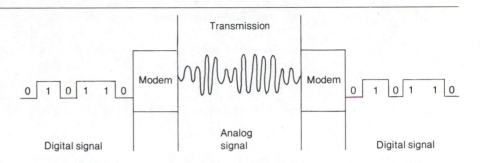

Concentrator

A multiplexer assumes that all terminals need equal priority of access and have equal density of use. When some terminals operate less frequently than others, resulting in under-utilization of transmission lines, slow terminal lines are concentrated into a few faster channels for transmission. This is done by a device called a **concentrator.**

A concentrator serving many terminals will poll each terminal. If one is ready to transmit or needs to receive data, it is then engaged. A user may also initiate a request for service. If all channels are engaged, the user will get a busy signal and must wait in turn. Terminals share a channel, unlike multiplexing where each terminal has its own channel.

The number of channels and terminals per concentrator depends on the frequency of terminal use, the average time spent per usage, the cost of equipment, and cost of waiting by a user. A manager can specify limits to waiting time and maximum queue length and then use a queuing model to determine the optimal number of channels and terminals.

Modem

Data from a terminal or a computer is in **digital signals,** while the transmission is often in **analog signals** (recent transmission modes, such as satellites, excepted). A digital-analog converter, called a **modulator,** is used for sending data and an analog-digital converter, called a **demodulator,** is used for receipt of data. The modulator/demodulator is a **modem,** also commonly known as a **data set.** An illustration of the digital and analog signals and the conversions by a modem is shown in Figure 5.4.

Equipment at computer end

Though a modem is not used in satellite telecommunication, systems need **interface equipment** between data transmission and the CPU to perform the following functions:

1. To compensate for the relatively slow speed of transmission compared to the speed of the computer.

2. To check security authorization.
3. To translate transmission codes.
4. To exchange recognition signals with the terminal, referred to as **handshaking.**
5. To detect errors and take corrective action where necessary.
6. To edit and preprocess data.
7. To route messages according to priority of messages.
8. To buffer and store information before routing, if necessary.
9. To keep communication and teleprocessing statistics.

Front-end processor

The interface can be performed by most general-purpose computers equipped for remote communications. But as the number of terminals serviced and the volume of data processed increase, the channels become clogged, and the **buffer** (a storage device) becomes swamped with messages for the CPU. Consequently, the efficiency and effectiveness of the computing system drop below acceptable levels. To alleviate the problem, teleprocessing functions are transferred from the CPU to special processing equipment called a **front-end processor** which can be programmed to relieve the CPU or host computer of teleprocessing responsibilities. The front-end programmable processor is cheaper and more easily maintained, programmed, and modified than the host computer because of its more limited and specialized functions and because of its detachment from the CPU.

Figure 5.5 shows a front-end processor having many ports or connection points

**Figure 5.5
One configuration of a front-end processor**

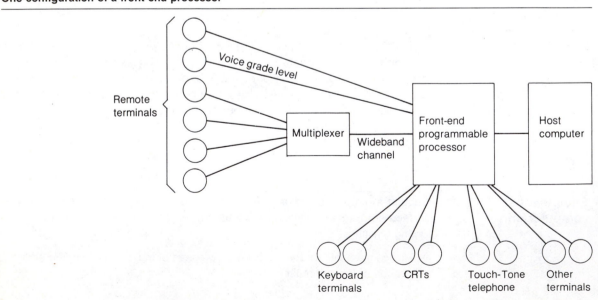

for transmission lines and showing many terminal devices. But this is only one configuration. Many designs, with varying capabilities, are possible. Some of these capabilities are:

1. Message switching between terminals.
2. Performance of stand-alone data processing when the teleprocessing load is low or absent.
3. Acceptance of messages from local lines and mixed communication modes of transmission.
4. Performing the function of multiplexers and concentrators.
5. Providing access to external storage and other peripherals.
6. Facilitating time sharing.
7. Supporting network processing.

Figure 5.6 illustrates the equipment needed by users and a computer center in a telecommunication system.

Network processing

Computers can stand alone—but with increasing demands, and demands from physically dispersed locations—computers belonging to the same organization often need to share and exchange information. This requires that the computers be interconnected. Examples of possible configurations are shown in Figure 5.7. One is the **star network** which enables centralized control and sharing of resources. A disadvantage of this configuration is that breakdown of the central computer will affect the entire system. To provide backup, a network may include more than one computer connected in a **ring.** If a computer breaks down, it can then be supported by a connected computer. But if the computers on both sides and/or

Figure 5.6
Equipment needed in teleprocessing

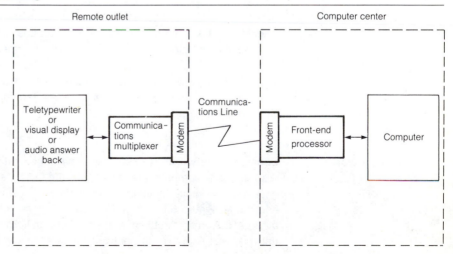

Figure 5.7
Computer network configuration

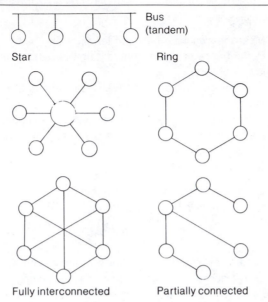

the transmission lines fail, the network will no longer be effective. To reduce the effect of breakdown an **interconnected system** is needed. Added interconnections increase the cost of equipment and transmission lines, but backup is provided. As minicomputers become cheaper and more powerful, they will be used increasingly as interconnected computers in the network and as front-end processors.

The actual network configuration selected by management will depend on the reliability and promptness of responses required from the system. For example, a reservation system will have a greater need for fast response time than will a warehouse of durable goods. The cost of a network (including the possibility of a standby additional system) must be weighed against the benefits. In one sense, the selection is determined by the function performed by the teleprocessing system.

Telecommunications can link computing facilities over short distances (called local area networks), or can link processors, terminals, and other peripheral devices that are far apart.

Local area networks

Local area networks (LANs) may serve organizations within a community that wish to share computing resources, or they can be established by a single organization wanting to connect workstations in various locations with remote equipment. Figure 5.8 shows the types of services that could be interconnected by a LAN. A major problem is ensuring compatibility of equipment served by the network. For example, the network must allow for code conversion and speed

Figure 5.8
Computing resources that can be integrated by a communications network

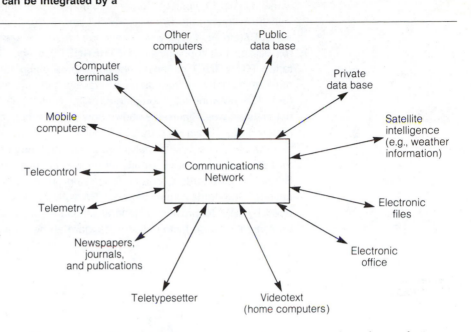

differences among linked devices manufactured by a number of manufacturers. It must also accommodate different user requirements for security and backup.

Coaxial cable (twisted pair of wires) may be used to connect processing centers in a LAN. However, such cable has a limited capacity. It cannot handle high-speed transmission and is inappropriate for video, audio, and fascimile processing. Only 8- and 16-bit computers can be linked by coaxial cable and then only for intermittent service. Furthermore, coaxial cable is ineffective over distances greater than 2,000 feet.

Another LAN alternative is a **baseband** transmission system. Baseband networks transmit digital data, but only one device can transmit at a time. It allows packet switching and utilizes a bus or ring network.

Broadband systems assign messages to particular bandwidths and channels, allowing multitransmission of messages. Because of higher throughput than baseband systems, broadband is more efficient in handling voice, data, or video transmissions. Another advantage is that broadband can transmit both analog and digital signals simultaneously.

(PBX) (Private Automatic Branch Exchange) is still another LAN approach. This system utilizes a central controller and is the basis of most in-house telephone-switching systems. It is particularly appropriate for voice transmission. Disadvantages include high initial cost, limited transmission speeds, and the use of a star network that is vulnerable when failure occurs at the center.

Many companies have developed networking systems for the market. These systems vary in their hardware, software, procedures, and protocols. Wang-Net, developed by Wang Labs, utilizes the huge bandwidth of cable television networks. Digital Equipment Corporation markets Decnet, which links its equipment with IBM equipment. Both Honeywell and Burroughs have other network versions. Britain's University of Cambridge has developed the Cambridge Ring. Xerox utilizes bus topology in its **ETHERNET,** perhaps the most popular network today. ETHERNET connects not only Xerox equipment, but equipment of most other manufacturers through an interface costing approximately $500 (1984 $ figure). The network links computers, peripherals of all types, and clusters of peripherals as well. Figure 5.9 shows how workstations, processors, and output peripherals can be serviced by ETHERNET.

Few standards exist for network architecture though such standards are needed for the establishment of a national (or international) network infrastructure. The Bureau of Standards is one body working on the problem; so is the ISO (International Standards Organization). SNA (Standard Network Architecture), developed by IBM to provide a general structure for varying configurations of IBM equipment, is a de facto industry standard at the present time.

Figure 5.9
ETHERNET

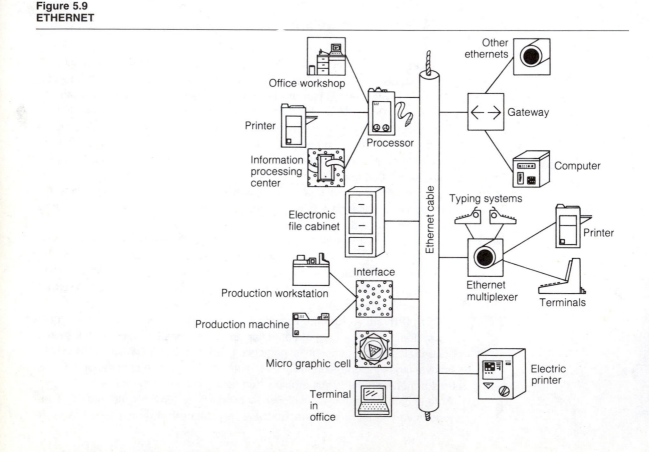

Figure 5.10
Linked LANs

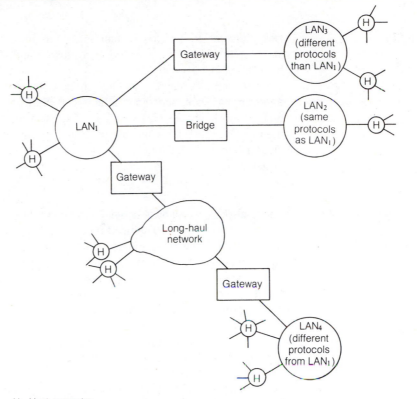

H = Host computer

Linked LANs

By linking local networks through satellite or other transmission modes, an integrated information system can be obtained. The links are termed either bridges or gateways.

A **bridge** is a simple connection between LANs that shares the same protocols. (**Protocols** are codes, conventions, and procedures.)[2] No modification of the content or format of the message packet is made, and no identification or control data is added.

When heterogeneous equipment and protocols are involved or message modification takes place, a **gateway** is required. Gateways can connect LANs that are close to one another or separated by long distances. Address schemes, routing rules, error recovery procedures, packet constraints, and interface requirements are provided by gateways.

Figure 5.10 illustrates the role of bridges and gateways in connecting LANs.

---

[2] For more details on the subject of protocols, see P. E. Green, "An Introduction to Network Architectures and Protocols," *IBM Systems Journal* 18, no. 2 (1979), pp. 202–22.

Functions performed by a teleprocessing system

There are two main functions performed by a teleprocessing system: **data entry** and **inquiry and transaction processing**

Data entry

Using telecommunications to enter data on a remote terminal avoids transporting input to the site of the computer. It saves time and also reduces errors since the handling of input is minimized.

Examples of terminals used for remote data entry would be badge readers in an assembly plant, sensors in a factory to measure variables that must be controlled, and keyboard or Touch-Tone terminals for recording sales in a department store. These terminals are used as input devices to collect data for immediate use in an OLRT (online real-time) system or for later processing by a batch system.

Inquiry and transaction processing

Terminals connected by telecommunications to a computer can be used to make a query such as: Are 10 items of product X in the warehouse? If not, how many are available? When can the complete order be filled? Can two reservations be confirmed on Flight TWA 311 on January 6? What is the bank balance of account 7614? When a decision is made based on the computer response, the transaction is processed using the data base and a set of programs, and the dialogue ends. Then the initiator of the inquiry is informed that the transaction has been completed.

In this application, the terminal is used as an input-output device. Typewriter terminals are sufficient for short cryptic or coded messages. A CRT terminal is appropriate for longer output.

Remote job entry, (RJE) is another type of query processing. In RJE, a user enters data on a terminal and expects a solution from the computer. The program is sometimes provided on the terminal or called from external memory, but no updating of a data base is necessary as with a warehouse or reservation application. RJE might be used by an engineer solving a problem on a terminal in an office, for example, when the computer itself is located elsewhere. The terminal could be keyboard, CRT, or a graphics terminal.

Other functions

The above modes of teleprocessing are not mutually exclusive. Many businesses, especially those with dispersed plants, warehouses, and sales offices, use all three.

The actual functions performed and the equipment used will vary between industries and even within an industry, and will depend not only on size and complexity of the business but on management and its use of equipment. For example, within a plant, there might be use of a computer as a calculator for RJE, but the terminals could be keyboard terminals or CRTs with "bells and whistles," such as light pens, attached printer, COM devices, or even color graphics. In some cases, these terminals might be replaced by minicomputers.

Once the devices have been selected, there are still many choices to be made. Should a half-duplex line with a public carrier or a full-duplex leased private line be used? Would the ACS system by AT&T serve, or would the satellite transmission by IBM's SBS be preferable? Are individual terminal channels with a multiplexer needed, or should channels be shared? These choices must be made uniquely for each business, depending on the frequency and density of transmission, the need for security, and access to a private line, and finally, the offerings of services and cost by the different public carriers.

Security

Security is providing controlled access in order to maintain the confidentiality of data. One must guard against intrusion at the terminal when transmission is initiated or during transmission.

One method to ensure security at the terminal end is the use of a predetermined signal of recognition called a **handshake.** The computer must recognize the signal before transmission of data can take place. Protocols for user identification and dialogue termination are also used. These are often specified by manufacturers of equipment, particularly producers of multiplexers and concentrators.

The violation of security during transmission occurs when a line is intercepted and eavesdropping takes place. To prevent interception, the message is sent in predetermined code. **Encoding** or **encrypting** (a word from the Greek root *crypt:* to hide) can be done in one of two ways: **transposition** or **substitution.** In transposition, characters are exchanged by a set of rules. For example, the third and fourth characters might be switched so that 5289 becomes 5298. In substitution, characters are replaced. The number 1 may become a 3, so that 514 reads 534. Or the substitution may be more complex. A specified number might be added to a digit, for example, a 2 added to the third digit, making 514 read 516. Decrypting restores the data to its original value. This process is illustrated in Figure 5.11.

The key used in Figure 5.11 for coding the message is derived from a **key base** (base of data). It could be a random number key, or a key based on a formula or algorithm. The key base and the algorithm must be kept a secret, accessible only to bona fide users. As in all codes, the key must be difficult to break. Frequent changing of the key adds to the security of data.

The U.S. government is as concerned as business regarding security of telecommunications. The 1974 Privacy Act entrusted the National Bureau of Standards with the security of federal data. The Bureau has produced a **data encryption standard (DES)** which has been accepted by most manufacturers of teleprocessing equipment. DES incorporates transposition and substitution repeatedly in each encryption.

In addition to DES, some computer manufacturers have developed their own encryption products

. . . IBM encryption products feed back part of the immediately proceeding, already transformed message and combine it with the plain text about to enter, and their sum is enciphered under control of the key. . . . Such is the security offered by that arrangement that its project work factor is considerable: the time needed to decipher the message encrypted by it would engage the most powerful of all present computers for many years, in which time the value of the information would have long faded and the key many times changed.[3]

This quote is based on the capabilities of computers in the 1970s. In coming years decrypting may be faster, taking only weeks, possibly merely days, hours or even minutes. When billions of dollars are at stake, as in the electronic transfer of funds, the ingenuity of intruders and the resources allocated to theft will increase.

In 1978, telecommunications security was broken by a computer consultant to a bank, enabling him to transfer the bank's money to a Swiss account for the purchase of Russian diamonds. The FBI, which broke the case, will not state whether the bank was using DES or encrypting equipment. But certainly there is evidence that present-day security is not foolproof in spite of our knowledge of protocol, DES, and encrypting devices. This case was unusual in that it had a happy ending, at least for the bank. When the diamonds were resold, the bank's profit was more than the potential rate of return had the funds been legally invested in a savings account.

Figure 5.11
Encrypting and decrypting of data in teleprocessing

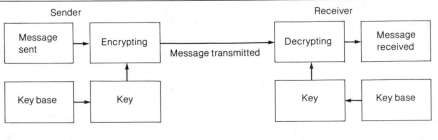

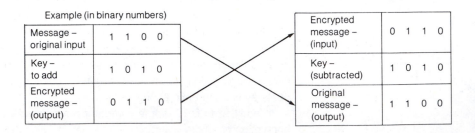

---

[3]L. Sandek, "Privacy, Security and Ciphers," *Data Processor,* 21, no. 1 (January 1978), p. 5.

Errors

In teleprocessing, errors may be the result of **noise,** the addition of unintended signals caused by switching equipment of the transmission carrier, or noise caused by natural events such as a surge impulse due to lightning. **Fading,** the reduction of signals due to weak transmission, may also cause mistakes. Both noise and fading occur frequently on public telephone and telegraph lines. **Leased dedicated lines** are less prone to noise and fading, but the cost of transmission on these lines is greater. In deciding which lines to use, management must compare this additional cost to the cost of losses in transmission.

One method of facilitating error detection is the odd (or even) **parity check.** A bit of data is added to each set of bits representing a character so that the total number of 1 bits is odd (or even). Upon receipt of the transmission, the bits are added and compared to the parity rule. When an error is detected, a signal is sent for retransmission of the data.

Checking for the use of a prescribed pattern of ones and zeros to represent characters is another method of tracing errors. Automatic checking of prescribed patterns of bits in a code makes this a self-checking code. This raises costs, however, since additional check bits must be transmitted and processed.

Fortunately, improved technology such as large- and small-scale integrated circuitry (LSI and SSI) is reducing the error rate in communications lines and improving reliability.

Future of telecommunications

The 1980s will be a period of great activity in satellite telecommunications, a period both of challenges to the FCC and of court battles regarding integration of computers with satellites. Once regulations are clarified, competition between corporate giants (IBM, Xerox, AT&T), and other firms (for example, General Telephone and Electronic Corporation, and Continental Telephone Corporation) should spur the development of numerous equipment configurations for satellite teleprocessing. One such configuration, shown in Figure 5.12 has two earth stations both at the sending and receiving end. Whatever the configuration, satellites will transmit data, voice, video, and facsimile at a rate of 60–1200 million bits/second. The constraint in speed is the earth relay from satellite station to user. Telephones, for example, can only transmit 1 to 1 million bits/sec. Here, the high technology of optical fibers, replacing conventional copper wire, is very promising. Optical fiber can transmit pulses of information in the form of laser-emitted light waves. The light waves are detected and decoded at the receiver end by photo diodes, technology produced by the semiconductor industry. The transmitting medium in between is glass fiber that is thinner than human hair, stronger than steel, and 80 times lighter than an equivalent copper conductor. Its capacity is one billion times the capacity of copper telephone wire in bits/second. The fibers have proven immune to electrical disturbances such as storms and disturbances from surrounding communication links. They are amenable to transmission of digital computer data and require fewer repeater stations than copper cables. The security

Figure 5.12
One configuration of a satellite communication

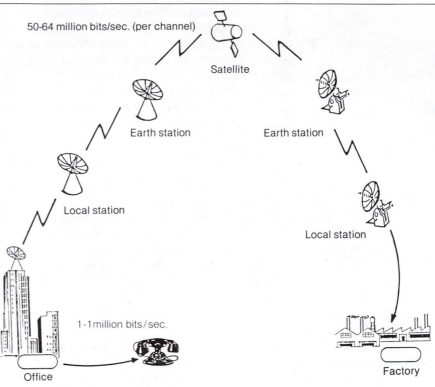

50-64 million bits/sec. (per channel)

Satellite

Earth station

Earth station

Local station

Local station

1-1million bits/sec.

Office

Factory

is also tighter (light waves are hard to decode and light wave interception equipment does not yet exist). But replacing existing telephone lines with glass fibers will be expensive. It is estimated that the cost will be equivalent to the entire U.S. space program (allowing for inflation). And, of course, firms with vested interests in existing equipment will resist changes in equipment standards. The fibers are being used in wired cities, such as Hi-Ovis in Japan. Over 50 million meters have already been installed in the United States.

Once the costs of glass fibers drop and line losses are reduced, it is conceivable that fiber optic cables may even prove more economical than satellite communications over high-density routes. Satellites, however, will retain a comparative economic advantage over long distances and rough terrain.

Summary and Conclusions

Teleprocessing is the use of telecommunications lines for transferring computer data between remote points. It is used for data entry as well as inquiry and transaction processing. It is also essential for remote batch processing, time sharing, and distributed data processing. The channels used may be simplex (one direction only), half-duplex (both directions sequentially), or full duplex (both directions simultaneously). The speed of transmission, measured in baud (bits/second), determines use. Data may be sent by public, leased, or private lines. Value-added carriers have packet switching capabilities that permit batches of data to be transmitted over a choice of routes for reassembly at the receiving end.

Transmission can be by telephone lines, sea cables, radio, or satellite. These are shown in Figure 5.13, along with different input-output equipment options available. Devices and procedures required specifically for telecommunications are summarized in Table 5.4.

A major cost of teleprocessing is the equipment needed by user and computer

Figure 5.13
Examples of transmission modes and input output devices

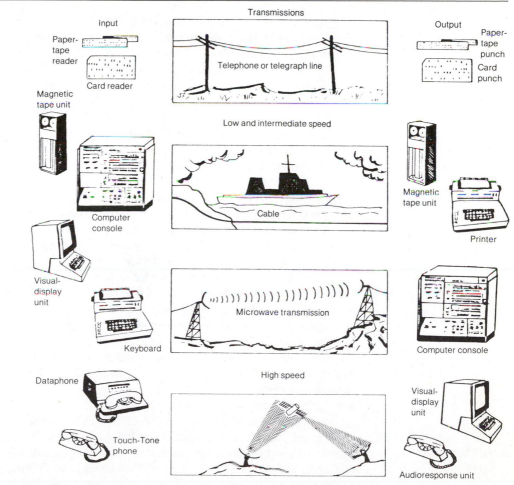

SOURCE   Adapted from Andrew Vazsonyi, *Introduction to Data Processing*, 3d ed. (Homewood, Ill.: Richard D. Irwin, 1980), p. 223, © 1980 by Richard D. Irwin, Inc.

Table 5.4
Devices and procedures needed for telecommunications

Interfacing
  Modems
  Terminal interfaces
  Equipment interfaces

Bandwidth sharing
  Concentrators
  Multiplexers
  Software multiplexing—polling

Switching
  Store-and-forward switches
    Message
    Packet
  Circuit or line switches

Distribution of information
  Front-end processors
  Concentrators
  Line Controllers
  Protocols

Network control
  Testing
  Diagnostics
  Error detection

which must be added to the communication channel. A variety of terminals for transmitting data is available. Some are input equipment only (card and tape readers, badge readers, Touch-Tone telephones); some are exclusively for output (printers, card punch, COM, audio response units); and some (kayboard terminals and CRTs) are used as both input and output devices. A multiplexer or concentrator is required so that a fast wideband channel may be used, and a modem is needed to convert signals (digital-analog-digital). A front-end processor that can be programmed (possibly a minicomputer) is also used to interface the transmission signal with the computer. The relationship of this equipment is illustrated in Figure 5.14.

Teleprocessing costs include costs of transmission, security measures, protocols, error detection, special software, job control procedures, and backup. These expenses must be weighed against savings made by the elimination of the physical movement of data and savings as a result of sharing processing facilities, computer programs, and data bases. In deciding whether or not to invest in teleprocessing, a business must consider the volume, density, direction, and distribution of its messages. It must also analyze the urgency of transmission and receipt of data. Available equipment must be examined, and choices made regarding the degree of security needed and acceptable error rates.

In the future, telemail, teleconferences, telediagnostics, invisible money, teleshopping, telenews, and telelectures served by satellite transmission and telepocket radios are possible applications. Since telecommunications channels are regulated by the FCC, the direction and development of teleprocessing in business will be largely shaped by this agency.

The effect of teleprocessing on organizations will be considered in Part 4, with present and future business applications examined in Part 5. But, before investigating the use of information, this text will explain what data is, how it is identified, collected, validated, organized, and managed (Part 2); and how data information systems are developed and operated (Parts 3 and 4).

Figure 5.14
A teleprocessing system

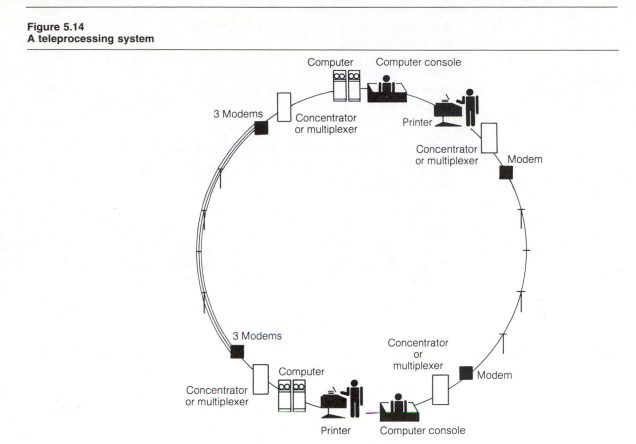

Key words

Analog signal	Data set
Band	Data transmission
Bandwidth	Demodulator
Basebound	Digital signal
Batch	Duplex
Baud	Encoding
Bridge	Encrypting
Broadband	Ethernet
Buffer	Fading
Channel	Front-end processor
Coaxial cable	Full duplex
Common carrier	Gateway
Concentrator	Half-duplex
Data encryption standard (DES)	Handshake
Data entry	Inquiry and transaction processing

Interconnected system

Interface equipment

Key base

Leased dedicated line

Local area network (LAN)

Message

Modem

Mode of transmission

Modulator

Multiplexer

Network processing

Noise

Packets

Parity check

Polling

Private Automatic Branch Exchange (PBX)

Protocol

Remote job entry (RJE)

Ring network

Security

Simplex

Speed of transmission

Star network

Substitution

Switched line

Teleprocessing

Terminal

Tie line

Transparent

Transposition

Types of channels

Value-added carrier

Discussion questions

1. What is the difference between telecommunications, teleprocessing, and teletransmission?

2. Why are telecommunications important to computer processing?

3. What functions do the following perform: modem, multiplexer, concentrator, front-end processor?

4. Contrast:
   a. Half-duplex and full duplex.
   b. Modulation and demodulation.
   c. Multiplexer and concentrator.
   d. Transmission and communications.
   e. Analog and digital signals.
   f. Encryption and decryption.

5. What are the advantages and disadvantages of a satellite system? Can the disadvantages be overcome with time and technological advances?

6. Discuss the factors which a firm must consider in choosing the type of telecommunication system to use.

7. What are the main componnts of a telecommunications system? Draw a diagram showing these components and their interrelationships.

8. What are the functions performed by a front-end processor? Under what circumstances is a front-end processor necessary or desirable? Give examples.

9. What are the different types of terminals used in teleprocessing? Why would

you recommend each type? What other equipment could be used instead of a terminal?

10. Discuss a teleprocessing network. What functions does it perform? How is it controlled? What happens if there is a breakdown in one of the paths?

11. What is an intelligent terminal? Why and when would it be used?

12. Identify and compare at least three network designs in terms of cost, reliability, ease of implementation, and special equipment required. Give business or industrial examples were each type of network might be used.

13. What are the organizational and managerial considerations of a telecommunications network?

14. What types of networks are most common in business? Give examples of their use.

15. What network would you recommend for each of the following applications. (The number of computers in each network is in parenthesis.)
    a. Hotel reservation network (4).
    b. Airline reservation network (24).
    c. Warehouse network (3).
    d. Production plants (5).
    e. Insurance company (3).
    f. University (10).

16. What are current trends in telecommunications?

17. What are the obstacles in exploiting existing telecommunications technology? Why the delay?

18. Teleprocessing is one of the most important growth sectors of the computer industry. Do you agree or disagree with this statement? Explain.

19. Why are there more legal and regulatory problems with telecommunications systems than with on-site processing? What are the problems?

20. What elements in a telecommunications system are not found in a batch system?

21. What is the significance of a LAN to a business user of computers when the business is:
    A. Small?
    b. Medium-sized?
    c. Large?
    d. Multinational?
    e. Large, with regional subdivisions within the United States?

22. Why is ETHERNET so popular?

23. Successful implementation of LANs requires the development of standards. Comment.

24. Why haven't LANs been widely adopted in the United States?

Selected annotated bibliography

Canning, Richard R. "A New Approach for Local Area Networks." *EDP Analyzer* 19, no. 1 (November 1981), p. 14.

A good survey of LAN with helpful classifications, descriptions, and comparisons of modes of communication.

FitzGerald, Jerry, and Tom S. Eason. *Fundamentals of Data Communications*. New York: John Wiley & Sons, 1978.

An excellent text, covering communication concepts, hardware, software, and errors, as well as networks and common carriers.

Franta, W. R., and Imich Chamtac. *Local Networks*. Lexington, Mass.: Lexington Books, 1981. 481 pp.

A good text on organizational structure, operating systems, modeling measurement, and interconnections of local area networks.

IBM Systems Journal 18, no. 2 (1979), pp. 186–350.

This is a special issue on telecommunications, including IBM's own use of telecommunications, one of the most advanced telecommunications systems in existence, with 8,200 devices, applications, and its communication architecture, the SNA. Also discussed are emerging international telecommunications standards and three excellent nontechnical articles by Halsey et al. on public networks, their evolution, interfaces, and status; an article by Frazer on the future of telecommunications; and a tutorial on network architecture and protocols by Greer.

IBM Systems Journal 22, no. 4 (1983).

This issue is devoted to design considerations and implementation features of Systems Network Architecture (SNA). Included are articles on SNA distribution services, interconnecting SNA networks, logical problems determination for SNA networks, performance and ability measurement, SNA routing, and flow control in SNA networks with satellite links.

Martin, James. *Telecommunications and the Computer*. 2d ed. Engelwood Cliffs, N.J.: Prentice-Hall, 1976.

This book has detailed sections on transmission, switching, and imperfections. The latter includes noise and distortion, line failures, delays, and data errors. The book is readable, well organized, and generously illustrated with photos and colored diagrams.

———. *Future Developments in Telecommunications,* 2d ed. Englewood Cliffs, N.J.: Prentice-Hall, 1977.

This is the fourth book written by the author on teleprocessing. It discusses the use of teleprocessing, its synthesis and technology. Like other Martin books, this one is well-organized and illustrated.

———. *Telematic Society: A Challenge for Tomorrow*. Englewood Cliffs, N.J.: Prentice-Hall, 1981, 244 pp.

An excellent discussion of telecommunications technology, including the social implications of teleprocessing in medicine, news, and shopping.

Mayo, John S. "The Role of Microelectronics in Communication." *Scientific American* 237, no. 3 (September 1977), pp. 192–208.

A well-illustrated, nontechnical discussion of a technical subject. This issue is a special one on microelectronics as it relates to computing. It is also available in a separately bound volume as a *Scientific American* Book. Highly recommended as a tutorial on microelectronics, microprocessors, and microcomputers.

Scherr, A. L. "A Perspective on Communications and Computing." *IBM Systems Journal* 22, no. 1&2 (1983), pp. 5–10.

The dynamics of the relationship between computing and communications technologies are discussed. Communications protocols, network management, data base design, and the transformation of batch to online processing are also discussed.

This issue of *IBM Systems Journal* is devoted to the subject of telecommunications. Other articles are on the following topics: X-25, Teletex, token-ring networks, satellite communications controller, SNA networks, videoconferencing, and network management of a large computing service. An annotated bibliography of rare sources is also given.

Wicklein, John. *Electronic Nightmare: The New Communications and Freedom.* New York: Viking Press, 1981, 282 pp.

The author discusses the danger that social relationships will be adversely affected by telecommunications technology. For example, individual privacy may be threatened and the poorer nations may find themselves at the mercy of multinational corporations as a result of superior technology.

White, Wade, and Morris Holmes. "The Future of Commercial Satellite Telecommunication." *Datamation* 24, no. 7 (July 1978), pp. 94–102.

An excellent, well-illustrated article on a little-documented subject. Has details on one system: TDMA (Time-Division Multiple Access).

DATA TECHNOLOGY

PART 2

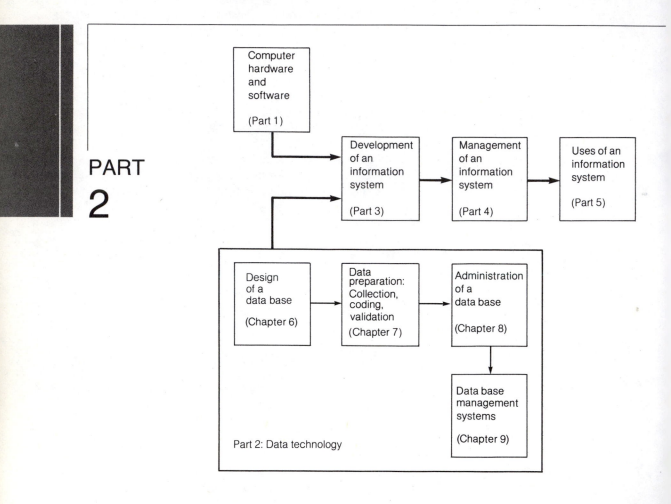

Technology relating to data, how data is created, organized, prepared, stored, accessed, maintained, and controlled is the subject of Part 2. Such technology is becoming increasingly important to business, for the reduced cost of hardware for data storage means that firms can afford large data bases comprising billions of characters of data. These data bases are the foundation on which management information systems are built. Though many of the activities related to data bases are technical and the responsibility of EDP personnel, managers must be involved in these activities to ensure that data needed for decision making is included in the base. and to ensure quality, security, and easy retrieval of needed data. The background knowledge provided in the chapters in Part 2 is a prerequisite to understanding how management information systems are developed and maintained, the subjects of Parts 3 and 4.

The chapter layout for Part 2 is shown in diagram form. The design and content of data bases are the subject of Chapter 6. Chapter 7 examines three aspects of data preparation: data collection, coding, and validation. Data directories and the organization of a DED/DD system for implementing the data base are discussed in Chapter 8. The role of a data base administrator and the resources needed for data management are also reviewed. Program sets for automating many of the responsibilities of data base administration are called data base management systems (DBMS). Chapter 9 introduces DBMS to the reader.

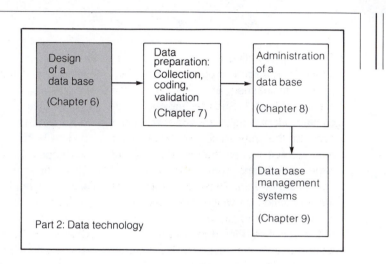

Design of a data base

6

Knowledge is of two kinds: we know a subject ourselves or we know where to find information upon it.

Samuel Johnson

The data for a computerized information system must be in a machine-readable form and according to prescribed conventions. Such data is called a **data base.** A **common data base** consists of data shared by organizational units within a business, a sharing that is of great value when different units need to correlate data for effective decision making.

Managers should be involved in both creation and maintenance of a data base since the information obtained from the base is for their use. Furthermore, the quality of information derived is directly related to the quality of the data base itself. There is a cliché in data processing, GIGO: garbage in, garbage out. The design of the base for a management information system should not be left to computer technicians either by delegation or default since technicians lack the expertise, judgment, viewpoint, and motivation of managers, the ultimate users of the system. Managers themselves should be active in the design. But this requires that the manager understand how data bases work. Providing such an understanding is the objective of this chapter.

This chapter opens with a definition of data and then outlines the types of data elements commonly collected by business and industry. How to determine the exact data elements an information system requires is then explained. To avoid misinterpretation of data elements, data element dictionaries must be prepared. The design and content of such dictionaries are, therefore, described. Finally, the difference between logical and physical organization of data within a data base is clarified, and the comparative advantages of cards, tape, and disks for input are reviewed.

Data and data elements

Data is a fact or an observation. The data 3528 is abstract, meaningless unless it can be related or associated with a specific entity. This might be an invoice

Table 6.1
Classification of data elements

Data elements by function	Person with prime responsibility
Transaction Reference	} Manager
Planning Linking Control Security	} Manager and analyst
Identification Checking Other data elements	} Analyst

Data element by source
Raw data
   Observation
   Fact
   Assignment
Derived
Estimated
   Hunch
   Guesswork
   Statistical techniques
	} Manager

number, an account number, a machine part number, or the number might represent an employee, Mr. Jones. Data on other attributes about Mr. Jones might also be gathered, such as age, marital status, or address. An attribute for which data is collected is called a **data element.** Thus, the sex of employee Jones is a data element, the value of that data element being MALE, or the data element is a code representation meaning male—such as 2. Name of the employee is also a data element. In this case, the value is JONES. If an employee works seven hours, 7 is the value of the data element "hours worked." If the seven hours of work and the male employee Jones are related, they would form a logical grouping of data elements yielding the information: Jones is a male employee who has worked seven hours. If these data elements were associated with other data elements, such as academic record and date appointed, more information could be produced, creating a **logical record** of employee Jones.

There are many kinds of data elements. A summary list appears in Table 6.1. The list identifies data elements by function and source, and shows the person primarily responsible for their determination. Each data element in this table is explained below.

Data elements by function

Transactional data elements

Most data elements in a common data base are created by transaction. For example, hiring an employee is a transaction that generates a whole series of values for data elements such as name, address, sex, and previous employment. When work hours are recorded or salary checks issued, additional **transactional**

data is created. Purchase of raw materials or the sale of a product would create values for still other transactional data elements.

Reference data elements

Sometimes data elements are needed for purposes of reference. Consider a transaction regarding the purchase of supplies. When the supplies are received, the vendor is paid an agreed amount and the transaction is recorded in the financial file. But occasionally the transaction must be traced and the invoice checked. To do this, the data system must include some means of reference to the invoice, such as the invoice number. This means of reference is a data element.

Other examples of **reference data elements** include purchase order numbers, personnel employment form sequential numbers, and transaction numbers.

Data elements for planning

If variable and fixed cost coefficients are used to predict costs in the planning process, these are **planning data elements.** Other examples of planning data elements are future production coefficients or projected estimates of variables such as future sales. These data elements can be derived from historical data, may be based on the planner's value judgment, or may be normative and reflect what is wanted or hoped.

Linking data elements

Linking data elements are unique identifiers to permit integration of files. For example, a payment recorded in a receipts file can be deducted by computer from the balance owed by that same customer in the accounts receivable file when a link, such as the customer's account number, is used in both files. Linking data elements will be discussed in greater detail later in this chapter.

Control-related data elements

Some variables in production are regulated by upper and lower control limits, predetermined maximum and minimum allowable values. When a variable exceeds or even approaches these limits, management is informed. These limits constitute values for **control-related data elements.** Other control limits or values are set in budgeting, advertising, sales, and quotas. Violation of these limits is defined as an exception, and an **exception report** is generated. The exception is then traced and resolved.

Security-related data elelents

To prevent unauthorized access to data, users often need to be assigned codes. One code may be used to identify a user's access to a certain file and another may specify what the user can do with the file (read, modify, delete, and so forth). These codes are values of special data elements related to the security of the system.

Identification data elements

Transactional data needs to be **identified** as to where and when the transaction occurred and where the data is stored. For example, payroll needs to be identified by week, month, or year; sales by month or even day. Another type of identification could be that of data from different divisions, or even committees, of an organization.

Checking data elements

Many transactions need to be checked for completeness and accuracy. This is sometimes done by matching a total that is provided as data with a total generated by the computer for the same set (or batch) of transactions. For example, a cashier may make transactions on a cash register and send these to be processed by computer along with a total generated by the cash register. The computer adds each transaction in the set and compares the total with that of the cash register. If it is the same, further processing takes place. If not, the inconsistency is identified, to be later traced and resolved. In this case, the total is the value of a **checking data element.** A checking data element does not appear in the output for the user but is nonetheless necessary.

Sometimes entries of numbers which are long or crucial for other computations need to be checked. The accuracy of social security numbers or employee numbers is a good example of such a problem. These numbers, used when making salary payments to employees, must be recorded accurately as input. To prevent input errors, a specific additional character or **check digit** is calculated by a special formula and is attached to each employee number. This check digit is recalculated by the computer each time the number is encountered in processing and compared with the original check digit added to the identification number. Any discrepancy is noted as an error in the input and processing is terminated until the error is corrected. In order for the check digit to be used by more than one user, the formula for generation needs to be defined and accepted by all users.

Other data elements

There are other specialized data elements related to processing which are primarily of interest to EDP personnel. These will be mentioned briefly in a section on descriptors which follows later in the chapter.

Data elements by source

Raw data

Earlier, data was defined as an observation or a fact. The value JONES was given as an example of a value for the data element "name of employee." Sometimes coded values are assigned to data, such as codes to denote the professional classification of an employee or the department where the employee works. Both facts and **assigned data** are **primitive data,** data not derived from other data elements nor the result of processing. Primitive data is also called **raw data.**

Derived data elements

Derived data is determined by manipulating or processing data elements. For example, the data element "average number of hours worked per week per employee" is calculated by dividing the data element "total number of hours worked" by the data element "number of employees."

Another example would be values for the data element "age of employee." The value of this data could be derived from the employee's date of birth and the current date.

Though the actual computation is done by computer program, management is responsible for specifying derivation rules. In the above examples, the rules are obvious, but in many instances alternative ways of deriving data exist. For example, firms differ in procedures for calculating markups and discounts. When derived data is included in the data base, the formula or algorithm used must be defined and documented.

Estimated data element

Estimated data elements are neither primitive nor derived. The future cost of production, for example, cannot be observed, nor is it a fact. This data element must be calculated by a formula such as:

$$Y = bX$$

where Y = future cost of production
   X = units of production
   b = future cost coefficient (variable cost per unit produced).

The coefficient b is the relationship between Y and $X (Y/X)$ and will be estimated by statistical techniques based on historical data of Y and X, by hunch, or by the manager's perception of the relationship of Y and X. This data element b is an estimated data element. When multiplied by X, the answer is the estimated data element "future cost of production."

In this discussion of data elements, the original definition of data has been extended. Data can now be defined as raw data (an observation, fact, or assignment), derived data, or estimated data.

Selecting data elements for collection

The identification of specific data elements needed in an information system is deduced by studying the informational needs of management and output. For example, if a personnel report is expected to list the number of female professional employees with masters degrees as output, the input for such a report must include data on the academic qualifications and sex of each employee. Similarly, if a report on accounts receivable is to show the distribution of aging of accounts (that is, the distribution of the time the accounts are outstanding), the input for the report must include the invoice dates so that aging can be calculated. If a report were to compare dollar value of sales for each sales representative with quotas, then both sales and quotas would have to be entered as input.

In a data base, data elements will often be used for generating more than one report. (A single report may be generated from one file. More often a report is generated from more than one file and a file contains data elements for many different reports.) Data elements needed for new reports may already exist in the common data base. To identify these existing data elements, an **input/output table (I/O table)** can be used, a technique developed by the economist W. Leontief.

An example of an I/O table is shown in Table 6.2. The table has a horizontal axis listing output reports and files. The vertical axis lists data elements necessary for these reports. When new reports are added to the system, new columns are added to the table. Data elements already existing in the system required for these reports are checked off. These can be shared, resulting in economies in storage and processing. If the new report requires data never before collected, a new row to the I/O table may be necessary. Sometimes, however, needed data can be derived from existing data in the system. For example, if the company represented in Table 6.2 were to require the age of each employee for a new report, this information could be calculated from the date of birth already in the data base. However, if this new report were to be generated by a new file, File 3, this file would have to be linked to File 1 in order to derive age. That is, a common data element would have to appear in both files so that the computer could access information in the two files when processing. Derived data elements are not listed in an I/O table since they do not require the collection of additional data.

Other data elements excluded from an I/O table include the report heading names or column headings that appear on output. Also excluded are data elements written into the application programs such as norms for checking value weights and control-related data. Page numbers and subtotals of totals (derived data) would also be created by programs. In addition, the computer generates

Table 6.2
Partial I/O table

Data elements	File 1		File 2
Files	*Report 1*	*Report 2*	*Report 3*
1. Employee ID (identification no.)	x	x	x
2. Name	x	x	
3. Address	x	x	
4. Date of birth	x	x	
5. Sex		x	
6. Academic qualifications			x
7. Field of specialization			x
8. Years of experience			x
9. Year of first employment		x	

Figure 6.1
Analysis of information needs

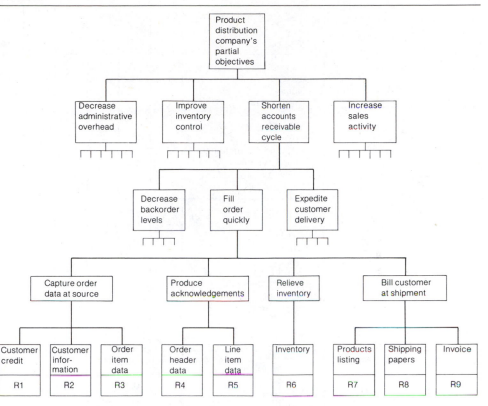

data such as time and date which appear on printouts at the time of processing. None of these data elements is included in an I/O table. Though the I/O table does not name all the data elements in the system, every data element that is listed in the table must exist in the data base.

To identify elements needed in a company's data base, corporate goals and the informational needs of management at all levels will have to be studied to arrive at the reports a computerized information system should produce. Thereafter an I/O table can be used to identify which data elements must be added to the data base.

An illustration of this process is shown in Figure 6.1. Here the information needs of a product distribution company are analyzed.[1] A chart has been prepared listing company goals; decreased administrative overhead, improved inventory control, shortened accounts receivable cycle, and increased sales activity. For simplicity's sake only one of the goals is subdivided in Figure 6.1, that of shortening

---

[1] For details, see Thomas R. Finneran and J. Shirley Henry, "Structured Analysis for Data Base Design," *Datamation* 23, no. 11 (November 1977), pp. 99–113.

Table 6.3
I/O table for a distribution company

Data elements	R1	R2	R3	R4	R5	R6	R7	R8	R9
Each customer record									
ID	x	x	x	x				x	x
Name	x			x				x	x
Credit rating	x								
Credit unit	x								
Sold-to address		x		x				x	x
Ship-to address		x		x				x	x
Shipping instructions		x		x				x	x
Product number		x		x				x	x
Sales tax rate		x		x					x
Territory code		x							
Each item record									
ID			x		x	x	x	x	x
Description			x		x	x	x	x	x
Order quantity			x		x	x	x	x	x
Price/unit			x		x				x
Ship from warehouse			x						
Warehouse location						x	x		
Discount					x				
Each shipment record									
ID							x	x	x
Ship date							x		
Bill location							x		
Ship warehouse location							x		
Ship quantity								x	x
Weight								x	
Freight class								x	
Net amount									x
Sales tax									x

the cycle of accounts receivable, and only one of these subgoals, filling orders quickly, is further traced to the report level. From the reports identified in the chart, an I/O table, Table 6.3, has been prepared. This I/O table would be merged to an I/O table previously compiled for data elements in the firm's data base (if one exits). By studying the table, analysts can learn which data elements need collection for the new reports and which already exist in the data base.

Data elements for future requirements should also be included in a data base. Adding data elements after a common data base has been organized can be a costly and disruptive process, analogous to adding plumbing and electrical connections to a house after the walls have been painted. So data elements for future use should be incorporated in the base when the system is designed. However, predicting such elements is a far more difficult task than studying an I/O chart and deducing what data elements need collection for current reports. It is management's responsibility to make such predictions, to chart the company's future. Data element needs must be anticipated for the estimated life of the information system.

Managers and analysts designing the data base must be cognizant that future changes in management may occur or that shifts in the style of current decision makers may take place. The data base must be flexible in content and format to allow for such changes. For example, today's manager may want an analysis of sales in dollars per sales representative. In the future, the same manager or a later replacement may demand dollar sales per product. Such shifts in need for information must be possible within the framework of the data base.

Data element dictionary

Data for operations, control, and planning may be shared by several levels of management (Figure 6.2), or sharing may occur along organizational lines (Figure 6.3). In both cases the use of the data varies from level to level.

For example, the value of the data element "dollar sales" by sales representative Smith is used at the control level to evaluate the performance of Smith, and over a period of time this data may determine whether a bonus is given or Smith is released. Smith's data reclassified in terms of products sold, combined with sales data from the other sales representatives, is used at the planning level for future sales projections. The data could also be used to generate derived data, such as average sales by sales representatives per month per product—data used in control and planning. This sales data may also be used at the regional, national, or international headquarters of the company. Thus, the value of Smith's dollars sales is data that is used at all levels of decision making. However, this shared use of data is possible only if all users interpret the data elements in the same manner, agreeing on data element definitions.

Figure 6.2
Flow of data between levels of management

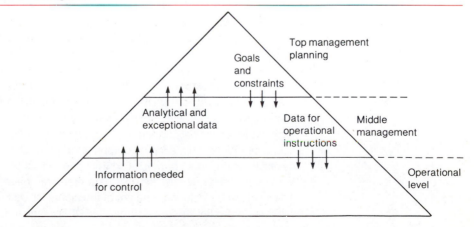

Figure 6.3
Flow of data along organizational lines

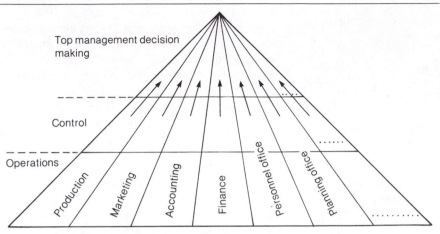

The need for common definitions arises whenever people wish to communicate with each other and have a large or complex vocabulary. Dictionaries are a reference for word definitions in natural languages, such as English and French. Data elements are also defined in dictionaries so that all data users know their exact meaning. A **data element dictionary (DED)** has to be designed for every information system using data elements.

Most spoken languages have words with more than one meaning and words that are synonyms. In designing a DED, one must try to avoid such linguistic ambiguities. But since users generally prefer to retain their natural language words as names of data elements, and agreement on the meaning of technical terms is lacking in the field of data processing, data elements must be defined with enough detail in the DED so that no misinterpretation is possible. For example, a data element cannot be called *"date,"* for there are many types of dates used to generate reports: date of birth, date of sale, date of employment, and so forth.

Sometimes a single data element may have several commonly used names. For example, the purchasing department may use the term *"item"* for what the inventory department calls a *"part."* In such cases, the dictionary must provide cross-references, referring users to the exact name of the data element used by the information system.

A sample page from a DED is shown in Figure 6.4 A DED is simply a collection of pages of data element definitions. But unlike single-volume French or English dictionaries, data element dictionaries are often in many volumes corresponding to functions, such as personnel or production. In addition, each level of decision making in an organization will have a dictonary set that differs in content from sets at other levels, for only data elements needed for decision making at that level will be included. The set of functional DEDs needed at the division level will therefore differ in content from the DEDs required by the corporation head-

Figure 6.4
Sample page of a DED

ABC COMPANY
DATA ELEMENT DICTIONARY

Name of Data Element	Marital status
Variable Name	MARISTATUS
Definition	Indicates whether or not a person is legally and currently married
Classification & Coding	1. Unmarried 2. Married 3. Other
Uses	For calculation of tax, deductions, and personnel profile
Derivation Rules (if any)	Source is Personnel Form 201A to be completed by person concerned.
Units (if any)	None
Format	Numeric

Format		Justification	N.A.
Width of Field	One digit		

Validity Rules	Required [X] Definite Error	Range 1-3	Content	Other
	Optional [ ] Possible Error			

PERSON PROCESSING FORM	Diana Sandalian
Date Issued	02/10/81
Status	Already implemented
Comments	The "other" category is expected to be less than 5%. If more, or another category is needed such as divorced, further coding subclassification is advisable.

quarters, though there will be many data elements common to both sets. Definitions, however, must be consistent at all levels in all the functional DEDs. This consistency gives data **upward compatibility** and lets data collected at the operational level of the organization be uniformly interpreted when used at higher levels of the organization.

Small systems may use preprinted DED pages, filling in the blanks by typing in information on each data element. In larger systems, the DED will be in machine-readable form, stored in the computer, and accessed by programs for screen display, or printout pages (corresponding to the sample). Computer programs can also use the information in the DED to generate reports and tables for analysis when the DED is in machine-readable form.

Descriptors of a DED

Data elements are described in a DED by characteristics and attributes called **descriptors.** Not all DEDs use the same descriptors and the order and design of a DED page may vary. Every information system has unique requirements and limitations. The DEDs are prepared with these specialized needs in mind. Constraints of space, the relative importance of descriptors, and logical groupings of descriptors (that is, technical descriptors) will also influence DED design.

The main descriptors of interest to managers are: name, definition, derivation algorithm, units, format, width of field, validity rules, version of issuance, identification, and status. These are discussed below.

Name

The **name** of a data element must be unique, unambiguous, and easy to use and remember. Names must also be logical and meaningful terms.

Long names chosen to eliminate ambiguities may prove too cumbersome for convenience and efficiency in processing. As the name length increases, more storage and processing time is required. Therefore, long data element names are often abbreviated. An abbreviation will also fit easily on a printed computer report when space is limited. If abbreviations are used, they must be defined in the DED.[2]

Definition

The **definition** explains the meaning of the data element. Examples of a practical application of the element may be included in the definition for added clarity. Other data elements with similar or contrary meanings may be mentioned and the root of the term explained.

The origin of the data element should also be included in the definition. If a data element is raw data, the division originating the raw data should be mentioned. This will help users assess possible bias. If the data element is estimated, the manner of estimation is relevant.

The data element should be defined at the lowest level of aggregation in case this detail is needed at some future date. For example, sales information collected at the county level can be aggregated for state, regional, or national sales statistics. But if sales data is initially collected only at the state level, the data cannot provide management with information on county sales. When deciding what level of aggregation should be collected, one must weigh possible benefits from

---

[2]For standard abbreviations of states and names of countries, see ANSI (American National Standards Institute) publications. ANSI is the source of most computer-related standards in the United States, including standards on codes, magnetic disks, magnetic tapes, data communication, and computer programming. For details, write: ANSI Inc., 1430 Broadway, New York, N.Y. 10018.

lower levels of aggregation against the cost of including possible nonessential data elements in the DED and the added cost of processing these data elements.

Derivation rule

If data is derived, the **derivation rule** must be specified. In calculating ratios and coefficients, for example, the numerators and denominators in equations must be defined in unambiguous terms. This not only eliminates confusion and misunderstandings, but is essential for the programmer who will have to write the program instructions to derive the data.

In deriving data values, it is also necessary to specify the level of accuracy required. For example, should a percentage value be calculated at one, two, or three decimal places? How should values be rounded to the first significant digit? Rounding is especially important when calculating financial values, for the rounding rule can make a significant dollar difference when values are repeatedly used in other calculations.

Problems of derivation also occur with alphabetic data. For example, in using the data element "name of employee," many computer programs limit the surname to 10 characters even though many names are longer. How should a business abbreviate an 11-character name like Thorneberry? Let the employee choose an abbreviation or develop guidelines applicable to all names? What abbreviation guidelines should be selected? Initials? Truncations? The abbreviations rules used for data element values must be explicitly defined.

Units

The **units** of measure for the data element must be specified. For example, the data element "weight" with a value of 10 needs a unit descriptor. Is it 10 pounds or grams? The data element "length" must have a descriptor specifying FPS or metric units. Sometimes the units are included in the name of the data element, such as "dollars sales." If not, a separate unit descriptor is needed.

Format

The **format** of how the data elements are stated is also a descriptor to be included in the DED. This need arises in group data elements. A **group data element** is a composite data element of several individual data elements. For example, the data element "date of birth" (120565) is a composite of the data elements month, day, and year. The usual format is:

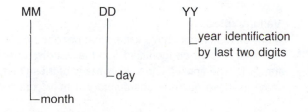

If this format, MMDDYY, is the desired format, it should be so stated. Otherwise a possible misunderstanding might arise. DDMMYY is the format used in England; other European countries use YYMMDD.

The format of a name is also important. A DED that defines an employee's name as a combination of surname, first name, and middle initial does not have an adequate definition since the format must convey the order of the name components as well as the separators between the component parts. Blanks used as separators can be confusing because they sometimes occur within a surname, as in Mac Donald or Van der Kamp. The format for additions to the surname such as Jr. or Sr. must also be expressed. Should shortened names (Liz for Elizabeth) or nicknames be allowed? This is not hairsplitting. A detailed specification is necessary. Names will not match in computer processing if the same format is not used consistently; that is, the same order of components, the same separators, and the exact same spelling.

Another formatting problem that must be clarified in the DED is the placement of data in a field wider than the data itself. Should the data start from the left or the right of the field? In the case of alphabetic data, it is customary to start from the left, called **left justified.** This facilitates reading a list of alphabetic data and is needed when sorting alphabetic data by computer. In contrast, numeric data starts from the right, called **right justified,** so as to avoid interpreting blank spaces in the field as zeros. For example, 345 appearing in a five-character field that is left justified could be read by the computer as 34500. Left or right justification of the values of each data element must be stated.

Width of field

The DED definition should also specify the **width of field** for each data element (The term *field* refers to the space allocated data on a storage medium, such as cards, tape, or disk.) Most width determinations are technical, made by analysts. Adding a check digit to a social security number is the type of technical decision an analyst would make. But many widths must be determined by management. Determining potential maximum values for the data elements, for example. How many characters should be allowed for the data element "dollar value of sales per customer?" An amount of $2,000 would require a four-character field width. If the amount increased to $10,000 or more, the allowed field would be inadequate. On some computer printouts, the value of $12,003 would appear as 2003 if the field specification were four characters, ignoring the most significant digit. It is the manager's responsibility to predict maximum values so an adequate width of field will be allowed.

Validity rules

Many data elements have values that need to be checked for validity. These data elements should be identified and the **validity check rules** should be stated in the DED. The analyst can specify many of these rules. For example, a name field may not have numeric characters but may contain symbols such as hyphens, whereas the data element "weight" must have a numeric value. Some check rules, however, should be determined by managers instead of analysts. These include checks as to probable ranges of data element values. For example, a firm's check rule for age of employee could identify values under 15 and over 75 as definite errors and ages between 15–18 and 70–75 as possible errors. A manager can best state such ranges and can best identify which data elements need to be checked for allowable ranges. Managers also know what data is essential and cannot be missing from the input data.

Indentification

Each data element is assigned a coded label to enable a unique and fast **identification.** A blocked decimal code structure has been successfully used for this purpose. An example of such a label is:

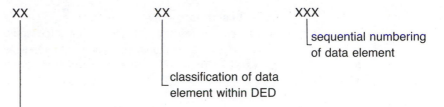

The first character or two characters identifies in which dictionary, within the set of DEDs, the data element appears. The next subfield identifies how the data element is classified within the DED. For example, one subclassification in the payroll file might be the rate: rate of pay, the tax deducation rate, the medical service deduction rate, and so forth. The third subfield can be a sequential identification of the data element itself. An example of this coding structure is shown in Table 6.4. In this chart the data element "health deduction rate" (02) is classified under payroll rates (06) located in the staff DED (03). Its code identification number is 03.06.02.

The main purpose of subfields is to facilitate reference, processing, and analysis. For example, in searching for payroll rates in the staff file, one need only search the codes 03.06 without being concerned with the remaining subfield codes.

In order to find a specific data element definition in a DED without knowing its identification code, an alphabetical index by data element name can be used. This index is generated by computer program once the DED sets are completed.

Status

The **status** of data elements must also appear in the DED. A data element may be operational or under consideration for adoption. If the latter, it should be stated whether the data element has been approved but not yet implemented, or merely proposed. Some data elements have the status "superseded" but are still recorded for reference purposes.

Table 6.4
Example of coding for data element identification

DED identification	Classification of data elements	Sequencing of data elements
03 Staff	01 Name • • • 06 Payroll Rates	01 Surname 02 First name 03 Middle name 04 Jr. and Sr. identification 01 Rate of pay 02 Health deduction rate 03 Tax deduction rate

Other descriptors

The descriptors mentioned above are basic descriptors. But the list is by no means complete. Some additional descriptors of interest to the analyst and programmer are listed in Table. 6.5. A manager may not use these technical descriptors but they appear in the DED since the dictionary is designed for all users of the information system.

Organization of data

Once data *is* identified and defined in DEDs, it must be organized so that later processing and retrieval will be fast and efficient. There are two types of organization: logical and physical.

Logical organization is the grouping of data elements according to the user's view of data interrelationships for purposes of input and output. For example, the grouping of all data elements relating to payroll. Logical organization is a major concern of management, determining the facility with which data elements serve the informational needs of the user.

Table 6.5
Selected list of descriptors of interest to analysts and programmers

User relationship
Creation/specification responsibility
Transaction relationship
Program names
Synonym
Codes
Mode
Security code
Billing code
Access limitation
Logical/physical relationship
Medium of storage

Physical organization, on the other hand, concerns technical personnel: programmers and data specialists. It is the physical storage on the data base's storage media of data elements in the data base. For example, when a logical set of data is stored on tape, the tape is the physical representation of data. How the data is stored on tape (e.g., order) concerns the physical organization of data. Since technicians, not management, are responsible for planning the storage location of every bit of data and for providing access to that data for retrieval and processing, only a brief discussion of the physical organization of data on data storage devices will be included in this chapter.

Logical organization

There are many steps to the logical organization of data. First, data elements required to produce a specified output must be determined. Then a **record** is formed by joining the related data elements with one another. An employee record would consist of related data elements, such as name of employee, address, date of birth, department, and salary code. An invoice record might include customer identification, customer address, item(s) bought, purchase date(s), and price(s). All related records are then grouped into a **file.** An employee personnel file, for example, would be a collection of all employee records. A business may have an advertising file, a payroll file, a marketing file, a production file, and so forth. The data files, when integrated or linked to share data, form a **common data base.**

A graphic representation of data organization from data element to the data base is shown in Figure 6.5. Thoeretically, there is no limit to the number of data elements in a record, the number of records in a file, or files in a data base. In practice, however, the values of *k, m,* and *n* in Figure 6.5 are constrained by factors such as storage space on a tape or disk. Efficiency poses additional restraints. A file used primarily for accounts payable is more efficient when limited to data elements relevant to that application. Interdepartmental rivalry in many

Figure 6.5
Data organization from data element to data base

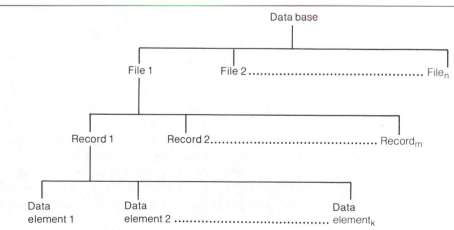

Table 6.6
Data elements in each record in each file

Customer file Data elements for each customer **ID (customer)** Name Address Credit rating Credit limit Territory code Sales tax code	*Invoice header file* Data elements for each invoice **ID (customer)** **Invoice no.** Ship-to address Shipping instructions Purchase order number **Warehouse code**
Order line item file Data elements for each item **Invoice no.** **Item number** Order quantity	*Inventory file* Data elements for each item **Warehouse code** **Item number** Item description Item price Discount rate

businesses also tends to limit file size. A unit which has created a file for a specific purpose may resist the enlargement of that file by other departments, fearing that the expansion will result in loss of control over that file.

A common data base consists of **linked files.** Table 6.6 helps illustrate the concept of linkage. Key data elements in each file are in bold print, since these data elements appear in two or more files. They enable the computer to integrate information in disparate files. For example, the data element "item number" appears in the inventory and order files. Given an item number, a computer program can locate the invoice number and order the quantity from the Order Line Item File and can also list the item description, as well as price and discount rate, information stored in the Inventory File. The use of a common data element in two or more files is, therefore, the link that permits file integration.

Figure 6.6 is another schema showing linkage. It also identifies the key data elements which integrate the files in Table 6.6. Note that there is no direct link between the Inventory and Customer Files, whereas the Order Line Item File is directly linked with two other files.

Data elements organized into records, files, and data base constitute levels of data, part of the **hierarchy of data.** The hierarchy of data can be further disaggregated into a set of characters. The characters may be alphabetic (a–z), numeric (0–9), a combination of letters and numbers as commonly seen on license plates, called alphanumeric or alphameric, or special character symbols (such as / * − , ' % #). Since a computer cannot store characters per se, a still lower level of data organization is required. A character is represented by a set of **bytes,** each byte consisting of **bits,** (binary digits) generally eight bits to a byte. In most machines, bytes are aggregated further into **words** for efficient access on storage devices. The hierarchy of data is shown in Figure 6.7.

Only binary digits can be recognized by the computer. The conversion of a character to a bit is done by input equipment so a manager is seldom concerned with data organization below the character level. The input which is collected and arranged in logical order by the manager, and the output which crosses the manager's desk, will be in characters, not bits or bytes.

**Figure 6.6
Linking of files**

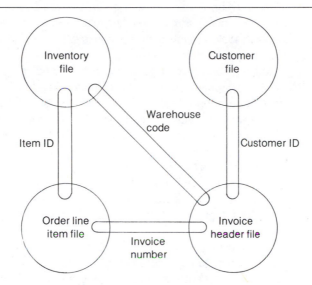

**Figure 6.7
Hierarchy of data for logical records and physical records on storage files**

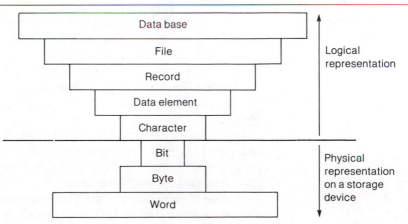

Physical organization of data

Some logical records are long, requiring many physical units of data, units such as cards, tapes, or disks. These units are called **physical records.** Physical records are grouped into **physical files** just as logical records are grouped into logical files.

To clarify the relationship between logical and physical files, imagine that a student taking Mktg. 310, Acctg. 329, and CS 330 keeps notes for these classes in separate notebooks. Mktg. 310 in one notebook would constitute one logical file in one physical file (one-to-one relationship). If the student kept notes for all three courses in a single notebook, the person would have three logical files in one physical file, a many-to-one relationship. If a second notebook were purchased when the first filled, the student would have three logical records in two physical records, a many-to-many relationship. In the latter case, the student would have to look through both notebooks when reviewing for an exam in marketing to find course material. The search would take less time if the notebook pages had been numbered and a list kept of page numbers containing marketing notes.

For computerized data, the computer needs a similar aid to locate data belonging to a logical file in one or more physical files. Data is located by an **address** which "points" to the data's location on the physical file, thereby maintaining the continuity of the logical file just as the student notation of page numbers would indicate directions to all marketing notes in different notebooks.

The space allocated a data element on a physical record is called a **field.** The group data element "date of birth" with the value 010375 has a field of six digits consisting of three **subfields** (day, month, and year); each subfield composed of two digits. Figure 6.8 illustrates the relationship between a data element field and subfields.

In data processing, physical records are sometimes **cards** and the physical space is measured in **columns** per card. In planning, the physical number of columns, called **width of field,** and the allocation (spacing or relationship) of the assigned columns are specified on a **data layout sheet.** Field width must be planned with care. An unnecessarily wide field will result in a waste of computer storage space and processing time. An insufficient width of field will necessitate restructuring the data base before data can be processed. For example, if only four columns are allocated to number of employees and the firm subsequently grows over 10,000, data on the cards will have to be shifted to allow an additional column for the information. Then all the computer programs which use the data elements involved will have to be modified, for processing cannot take place unless the application programs know the correct location of data on each physical record.

The card layout form in Figure 6.9 shows how the personnel file of John Doe, a logical record, is assigned space on a physical record. Each row represents a computer card. In this case, Doe's personnel file requires two cards, that is, two physical records for one logical record.

The use of cards becomes cumbersome when a logical record requires many physical records (10 cards per record are not uncommon); when a large number of logical records need processing (payroll for a firm of 120,000 employees, for

Figure 6.8
Field and subfields for data element *"date of birth"*

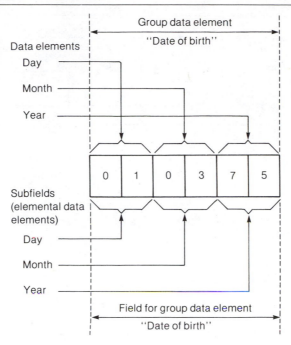

Figure 6.9
Card form layout

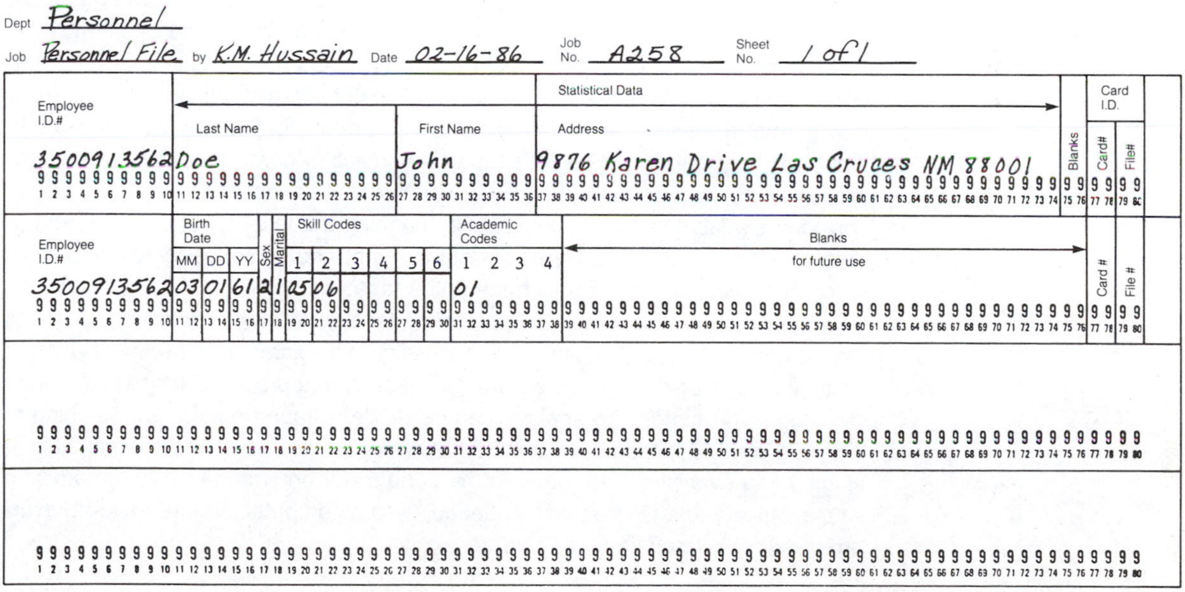

Figure 6.10
Transformation of two physical cards for one employee
record into one logical tape record

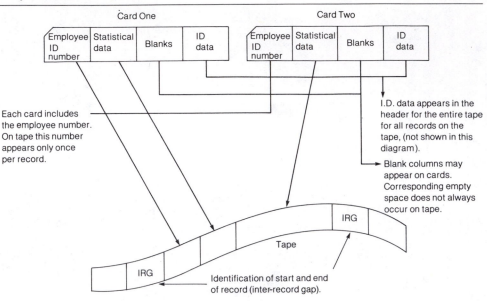

example); and when processing is frequent (once a week or even once a month). In such cases, logical records on **tape** are preferable.

Figure 6.10 shows the transference to tape of a logical record stored on cards. Note that the employee number appears only once on tapes, whereas it must be restated on each card of the logical record. The data ID, identifying sequencing of cards, is also eliminated because its purpose is to identify related cards of each logical record. Instead a **header label** is used at the beginning of each tape to identify the logical records on the tape. The logical records themselves are separated by an **inter-record gap (IRG)** which identifies the end of one logical record and signals the start of another. In planning the location of data on tape, a data layout is used to identify each data element and its sequencing. Data is located in processing by searching the entire tape.

The use of magnetic tape is appropriate for **sequential processing** when all logical records in a logical file need processing; for example, the reconciliation of bank accounts or payroll processing. But tape is inappropriate for handling individual logical records. An analogy can be made to taped music. For listening to a series of songs, tapes are excellent. But tapes do not let the listener hear a single song over and over, nor can the song order be changed. When data of a single logical record is frequently needed, then a computer **disk** (a **random storage device**) is used instead of tape.

Figure 6.11
Storage of a logical record on a disk (physical record)

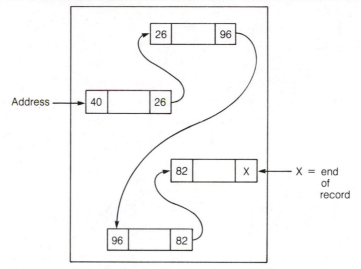

A logical record need not be stored contiguously on a disk. The record can be stored in parts wherever there is space. The problem is one of connecting the disjointed parts. This is done by *pointers*. A pointer is a code located at the end of each stored segment which indicates the address of the record's continuation. In the above diagram, arrows are used to depict this chaining.

A representation of a logical record on magnetic disk is shown in Figure 6.11. The data is stored on tracks on the disk wherever there is space, so the logical record may appear in several discontinuous parts. The order for storing the logical record is not prescribed. Space availability and the time of data collection will determine the location of the data on the disk. However, the entire logical record can be retrieved since each segment ends with a pointer indicating the address where the data is continued on the disk.

Random processing (also called **direct access**) is essential when data must be retrieved quickly. However, this shortened response time costs more. Sequential processing is the most time-consuming but costs least. In between are other forms of data processing which vary in response time and cost performance.

Figure 6.12 shows the relationship of time and cost for three types of processing. Sequential processing with magnetic tape can be used economically when response time is not critical. As response time is reduced and random processing is used, the cost increases rapidly. Eventually, processing with an indexed sequential file (where data is stored sequentially on a disk, but indexed with the indexes being accessed randomly) becomes less expensive since it allows skipping over inactive portions of the file and thus reduces input/output time.

Figure 6.12
Cost as a function of response time and mode of processing

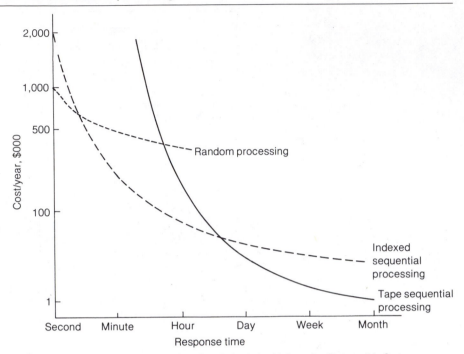

SOURCE   Adapted from J. Emery, "Cost/Benefit Analysis of Information Systems," in *Systems Analysis Techniques,* eds. J. Daniel Couger and Robert W. Knapp, (New York: John Wiley & Sons, 1974), p. 415.

Common data base

Stored data when integrated makes up a **data base.** A **common data base** is merely a data base that has pooled data integrated for common use as a shared resource. A business may have one or more common data bases but need not place all its data in a common pool. Excluded may be specialized data, data used by only one group or department.

Determining what data to include in a common data base is often an arduous process. Users do not always agree on what is and what should be common data. They fear that security and privacy of data is endangered in a common pool. Managers who have built up an empire of data resist losing control over that data. They may not want others to know such data exists or share in its use. There may be genuine problems in reaching agreement on data element definitions and difficulties in coordinating the timing of data creation. Standardization means each may have to change practices in collecting and handling data.

In deciding what constitutes a common data base, all potential users of that base should participate. When consensus is not possible, conflicts must be resolved or arbitrated by management at a higher level. Unfortunately, interorganizational politics too often determine what data is placed in the common data base when, instead, the decisions should be based on technological and economic factors.

Though user resistance may slow the formation of a common data base, its evolution should be systematic and progressive, for the advantages of a common pool of data are many. Data required by many users needs to be collected only once. A single operation will update data for all users. Standardized procedures are established for gathering and recording data for a common pool, making the data itself more reliable. And finally, communication improves because a common terminology defined in the DED is used by both analysts and managers.

Summary

Data may be used for transactions, reference, planning, linking, control, security, identification, and checking. All of these functions have business applications. One method of determining which data elements are required for each application is to trace the input needed for every data element in the output. To see if the data base contains the needed data, an input/output table is used where each output is represented by a column and every data element by a row. If the data elements identified do not already exist in the I/O table and in the base, they must be added to the data base for the new application. Other data elements needed for processing, such as those required for linking, identification of data, security, and control, are determined by analysts.

Data elements must be defined in a DED, a data element dictionary. The descriptors for each data element will vary, but typically they include: label of identification, name of data element as it appears to the user and as it appears in the computer program, description, derivation rule, units of measure, format, width of field, and rules for validation.

Once the data elements for an application are identified, they must be conceptually organized into a logical entity. Related data elements constitute a record, related records constitute a file, and related files are a data base. The data is then collected. If the data is collected on cards, each card is a physical representation of one or more parts of the logical record. A set of cards can represent a set of records in a file. In cases of large amounts of data, the file can be on tape, which is appropriate for sequential processing, or on a disk, which is best for random processing. Whatever the form of storage, files must be linked by a common data element if they are to be related and the data shared. This common sharing of data reduces redundancy, storage space, processing time, data preparation, time and effort, and improves security and standardization. This sharing of a common data base also enables the data of different divisions to be correlated for preparation of computerized reports. But it does cause organization problems because users do not always want to pool data and are often unwilling to submit to the standardization and discipline required for such sharing.

Key words

Address	Identification
Assigned data	Input/output table (I/O table)
Bit	Inter-record gap (IRG)
Byte	Left (right) justification
Cards	Linked files
Characters	Linking data elements
Check digit	Logical organization
Checking data element	Logical record
Columns	Name
Common data base	Physical file
Control-related data elements	Physical organization
Data	Physical record
Data base	Planning data elements
Data element	Primitive data
Data element dictionary (DED)	Random processing
Data layout sheet	Random storage device
Definition	Raw data
Derivation rule	Record
Derived data	Reference data elements
Descriptor	Sequential processing
Direct access	Status
Disk	Subfield
Estimated data elements	Tape
Exception report	Transactional data
Field	Unit
File	Upward compatibility
Format	Validity check rules
Group data element	Width of field
Header label	Word
Hierarchy of data	

Discussion questions

1. Distinguish between data and information.
2. Classify types of data and give two examples of each.
3. Describe the hierarchy of a data base.
4. What is the difference between a data base and a common data base?
5. Conflicts arise when establishing common data bases. What are they? How can they be reduced or eliminated?
6. What are the benefits of a common data base?
7. What is the difference between the physical and logical structure of data?

8. What is meant by the phrase "bit and byte level" of a computer? What is a manager's relationship to this level?

9. Why is numeric data preferable to alphabetic? Why are numeric identifications preferable to names of individuals?

10. Why is a social security number a useful identification in computerized processing? What are the limitations of social security numbers?

11. The social security number is used as a personal identifier mainly for economic reasons. Do you agree with this statement?

12. The social security number has been printed on T-shirts to suggest depersonalization of the human being. Is that a justifiable image? Who is to blame for such an image? How can it be corrected?

13. Distinguish between:
    a. Alphabetic and alphameric field.
    b. Fixed and variable length of data field.
    c. Physical and logical files.
    d. Raw and derived data.
    e. Size and format of data.
    f. Identification and reference data elements.
    g. Direct and random access.
    h. Bit and byte.
    i. Header and IRG.
    j. Data element and data field.
    k. Left and right justification.

14. Compare planning data with data for control and operations in terms of:
    a. Reliability.
    b. Source.
    c. Contribution to decision making.

15. Is data privacy a right? How can privacy be protected? How can this protection be enforced?

16. Compare random processing with sequential processing. Give examples from business for each approach.

17. What is a subfield? Give an example other than dates where subfields occur? Why are subfields needed?

18. What are the special factors to be considered in designing a common data base (features not needed in a local data base)?

19. What are fixed and variable costs in designing a file? Why should the cost of maintaining the file be evaluated carefully? How do maintenance costs depend on the content of file? Give examples. How can maintenance costs be reduced?

20. How are decision rules used for determining which data elements to include and which to exclude in a data file?

Exercises

1. Design a personnel file for the following data elements:
    Name
    Home address
    Date of birth (correct to the day)
    Sex
    Marital status
    University major
    Fixed monthly salary
    Commission rate

2. What type of processing would you recommend for the above file? Random, sequential or index sequential? Why? Explain.

3. If the personnel file above were used by managers to print lists of sales by each salesperson (with additional sales information provided), would you use random or sequential processing? Explain. What additional data is needed?

4. Trace one character used in a personnel data base (specify one if you do not have access to a personnel data base) through all the levels of hierarchy. Draw a diagram showing your hierarchy of data.

5. Check the most appropriate storage device and processing mode for the applications listed below.

	Storage media		Mode of processing	
Application	*Tape*	*Disk*	*Random*	*Sequential*
Airline reservations				
Hotel nationwide reservations				
An auto dealer Accounting				
Contract calculations with buyer				
Instructor keeping grades				
University keeping grades				
University admissions				
University registration				
University computing for class				
University alumni				
Retailer point of sales credit checking				
Bank account status monthly ledger				
Wholesaler inventory Perishables				
Nonperishables and staple demand				
Large data base and computing for sale				

6. In the table below, check the data elements that should be included in a bank deposit file, production inventory file, and accounts payable file.

Data element	Bank deposit file	Production inventory file	Accounts payable file
Name of part			
Name of depositor			
Account number			
Address of vendor			
Address of deposit			
Part description			
Name of vendor			
Discount code			
Unit price			
Amount deposited			
Vendor account number			
Quantity ordered			
Quantity of goods			
Amount withdrawn ($)			
Safety check			
Price			
Invoice number			
Current stock on hand			
Balance ($)			
Invoice date			
Quantity sold			

Selected annotated bibliography

Chorafas, Dimitris N. *Databses for Networks and Minicomputers*. New York: Petrocelli, 1982. 281 pp.

This book focuses on organizational steps necessary to prepare text and data assets of a firm for online distributed processing. Topics covered include planning a data base, architecture, design prioritieis, protocols, data dictionaries, and data base integration.

Curtice, Robert M, and Paul E. Jones, Jr. *Logical Data Base Design*. New York: Van Nostrand Reinhold, 1982, 272 pp.

Practical guidelines for data base design. The author developed these guidelines while consulting for Arthur D. Little over a period of 14 years.

House, William C., ed. *Interactive Decision-Oriented Data Base Systems*. New York: Mason/Charter, 1977, 470 pp.

This book has many contributions on the general subject of data bases, including concepts and design.

Kroenke, David M. *Database Processing: Fundamentals, Design, Implementation*. 2nd ed. Chicago: Science Research Associates, 1983. 607 pp.

Chapter 6, pages 205–41, on logical data base is recommended. The chapter discusses logical design structures, the essential features of the semantic data model, and illustrates SDM concepts by describing the logical schema design for Sally Enterprises.

Szewczak, E. J. "Two Approaches to Strategic Database Design." *Data Base* 14, no. 2 (Winter 1983), pp. 19–23.

Both descriptive and prescriptive approaches to data base design are described. The underlying assumptions and tradeoffs for each approach are discussed.

Walsh, Myles E. "Update on Data Dictionaries." *Journal of Systems Development* 29, no. 8 (August 1978), pp. 28–39.
The author discusses recent dictionaries on the market as to their facilities and capabilities, including those relating to security of data.

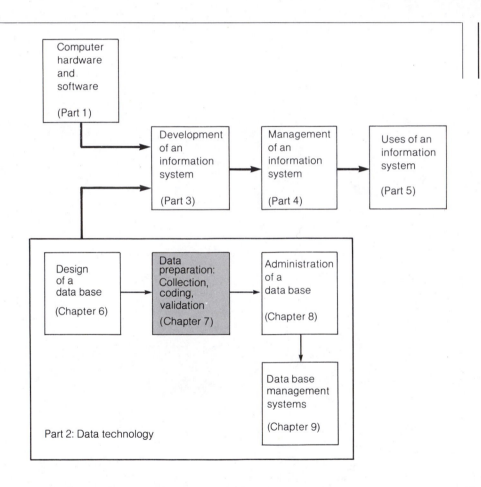

Computer
hardware
and
software

(Part 1)

Development
of an
information
system

(Part 3)

Management
of an
information
system

(Part 4)

Uses of an
information
system

(Part 5)

Design
of a
data base

(Chapter 6)

Data
preparation:
Collection,
coding,
validation

(Chapter 7)

Administration
of a
data base

(Chapter 8)

Data base
management
systems

(Chapter 9)

Part 2: Data technology

Data preparation: Collection, coding, and validation

7

One of the major drawbacks of the collection of information is the human temptation to use it, and in some instances to misuse it.

Unknown

Once the data base is designed, the data itself must be collected, coded, converted into machine-readable form, and validated before it can be used. These procedures, shown diagrammatically in Figure 7.1, are called **data preparation.** Quality output of a management information system depends on quality input. It is up to management to provide guidelines for data preparation to ensure that data is complete and coded for maximum processing efficiency and validity. Managers who participate in the development of information systems and utilize the reports generated need knowledge of this aspect of data technology. Aspects of data preparation described in this chapter are data collection, coding, and data validation.

Data collection

There are many methods of collecting data for a data base. Forms are commonly used. For example, data on a prospective employee, such as name, address, phone number, and so forth, can be collected by a job application form. Logs are also a source of data. An employee on an assembly line may log each completed task, time of completion, and equipment used. Data in the log may subsequently serve as data input.

In addition, peripherals may be used in **data collection.** Such peripherals can be classified into two general categories, **online** and **offline collection** devices, as shown in Figure 7.2. The characteristics and major advantages and disadvantages of these input devices were described in Chapter 4. Identification of the person entering input data is particularly important for online systems when banking or POS terminal fund transfers are involved. Card identification is not foolproof because stolen cards can be used to breach the system's security. More unique identification, such as pattern recognition equipment, is required, but such devices are expensive and not totally reliable at the present time.

Surprisingly, most data collected for a data base is still derived from documents. This data must be converted into machine-readable form, such as cards, disks, or tape, before being entered into the data base. The equipment required for this conversion was discussed in Chapter 4.

All input data, whether collected on forms or directly by equipment, must have a prescribed format. Procedures and rules governing input are documented in an **input manual.** This manual is prepared after the output of an information system is decided and after the system's specifications have been determined. The process of deciding what data to collect for input is described in Chapter 12.

Codes

Codes are used for many purposes. During the Revolutionary War, two lanterns were hung in North Church in Boston to warn that British troops were arriving by sea. A more elaborate set of symbols is the Morse Code used for transmitting messages over wire or by flashing lights at sea. A kick under a bridge table can

Figure 7.1
Overview of data preparation

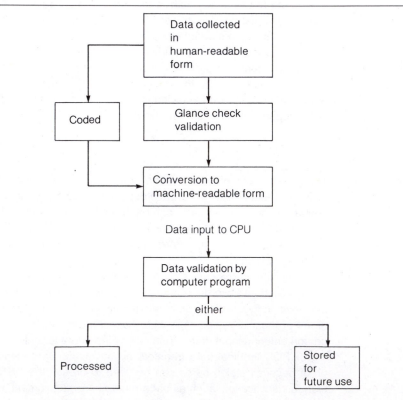

**Figure 7.2
Data collection**

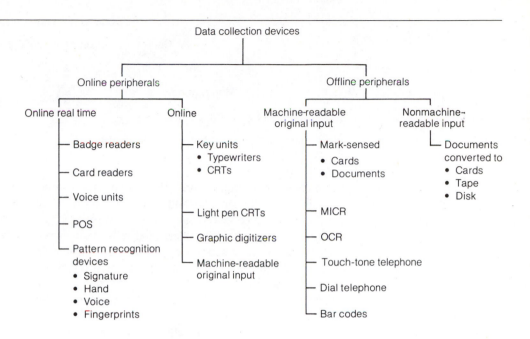

be a coded signal. A more subtle player was once expelled from a tournament for using finger signals, conveying high points by the way the cards were held.

Codes are also used in information systems. In this context, a code is a system of symbols for identifying attributes of data elements, simplifying natural language identification.[1] That is, a character or set of characters replace the natural language value of the data element. A firm might number its divisions, for example, and then substitute the number code for the division name in personnel records.

Codes can also abbreviate natural language messages. The information, "Elida Glass, a female employee, born in December 1947, is working in the Welding Department of the Production Division," can be shortened by coding. Miss Glass can be identified by her social security number (585281928), her sex coded as 2, her birth month identified by number (12 for December), the year of birth coded by the last two digits (47), the Division of Production coded as 14, and the Department of Welding as 09. The coded record would be as follows:

---

[1] According to G. W. Patterson, "The most fundamental idea concerning a code is that of the existence of two languages, the source language (historically a natural language such as English) and the code language (usually made up of special signals created for the purpose at hand). . . . The code, properly speaking, is the system of rules that enables messages in the source language to be encoded into the code language." G. W. Patterson, "What Is a Code?" *Communications of the ACM,* 3, no. 5 (May 1960), p. 315.

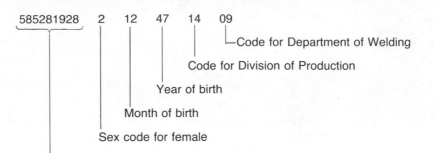

This coded form requires only 18 data characters (the input omits spacing) instead of the 118 characters and spaces of the English statement.

The use of a code also saves time when recording the data in machine-readable form, such as keypunching, and when transmission of data is necessary. But the main use of codes is to facilitate classification of data and to speed processing. If codes are used to categorize data regarding product composition, for example, information on all wood products can be quickly retrieved by use of the wood code. Search and computing time for noncoded data is substantially more time-consuming. Though the time saved must be weighed against the time spent preparing codes and using them, the net savings in processing alone is often sufficient to economically justify coding.

Another advantage of a code is that it provides unique or near-unique identification. Much noncoded information is subject to semantic vagueness. It is possible for two employees to have the same name, and even the same middle initial. When duplication must be eliminated, a code, such as an employee number or social security number, would make each employee's record distinct. (Uniqueness of identification is not necessarily provided by a social security number, however, for some individuals have been issued two social security numbers by the government.)

Coding sometimes appears as output. This occurs when large amounts of data must be compressed onto one page. Generally, however, coded data is decoded by computer program for output reports. The computer simply scans a table to determine the meaning of each code in the output and prints the decoded information, a procedure called **table lookup.** The program will also determine format of the decoded information, providing spacing and the addition of symbols, such as dollar signs, to make the output readable.

It should be mentioned that the terms *code* and *coder* have more than one meaning in the computing field. In this chapter, the conversion of data from natural languages to code characters according to a set of rules is called **coding** or **encoding.** The person performing this operation is a **coder.** The special form used for this purpose is called a **coding sheet.**

In programming, another set of definitions is used. An abbreviated programming instruction is also called a code, and a programmer writing such an instruction will use coding sheets and be called a coder. Programmers, however, have a wider responsibility than coders as defined in the first definition. They design programs and specify program logic by preparing flowcharts in addition to coding instructions.

Types of codes

Alphabetic and numeric codes

The binary system used by computers to represent numerical concepts is one type of code. The number 9 coded as 1001 in binary appears a longer representation than the noncoded 9, but in fact speeds processing since the computer will process binary digits but not decimal numbers.

A **mnemonic symbol** is a code chosen to aid memory. M for male is an example of an alphabetic mnemonic symbol; 1 for single and 2 for married are numeric mnemonic codes. **Alphabetic codes** are often preferred by coders because their meaning seems so obvious, but in fact they are often misinterpreted when they appear as output. An M might mean married or manager to a user. Even MA, a two-letter code, would be ambiguous in this case.

Arbitrary **numeric codes** might instead be assigned. The disadvantage is that such codes are hard to remember. A common coding technique combines the advantage of mnemonic clues with numeric uniqueness, giving data elements **alphameric** (or **alphanumeric)** coded values. The product code CRB162 for a crib and a customized license plate, such as HAL62, are examples. Some commercial banks identify customer accounts by the first five characters of the surname followed by first and middle initials`and a two-digit number. Using this scheme, the account of Arthur James Carswell could be coded as CARSWAJ63.

Yet even alphanumeric codes can be misinterpreted unless designed with care. A firm which coded the Henry Building as H, and the O'Hare Building as OH printed the following room assignment for an important conference: 23OH. Some participants went to 23 O'Hare, the rest to 230 Henry. Caution must also prevail when using alphabetic characters so that undesirable permutations are not formed. Inept coding of the Sam Oliver Building (by using its first letters as a code) could cause a flood of complaints.

Sequential codes

Numbering accounts **sequentially** is a conceptually simple **code.** A unique identification is provided and the number shows the relative age of accounts, but that is all. No classification information is provided. Another weakness of numbering is apparent when employee numbers are assigned sequentially from an alphabetic personnel list. The names of new employees cannot be added to the alphabetic list without renumbering unless, when the sequential code was designed, numbers were skipped to allow for later insertions.

Block codes

The use of **block codes** is a more effective technique, permitting subclassification of data elements. The mail zip code is a good example. The first number identifies geographic area, the next two permit sorting within that area, and the final two digits identify the local post office from which a letter is to be delivered.

Blocks with assigned subfields for each subclassification of a data element are called **group classification codes.** Each subfield is coded independently. Numbers can, therefore, be repeated in one or more subclassifications, their position in the block determining code meaning. By adding subfields, more and more information can be conveyed. The number 93015181 might represent a straight-back wooden chair with side arms and green leather upholstery if the code were a composite of the following code groups:

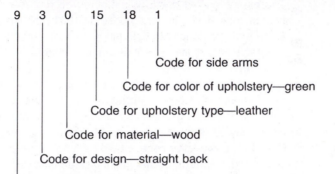

9   3   0   15   18   1

Code for side arms

Code for color of upholstery—green

Code for upholstery type—leather

Code for material—wood

Code for design—straight back

Code for type of furniture—chair

The size for each subclassification should be designed to allow for the addition of other codes at a later date. For example, if the furniture manufacturer expanded operations, producing 14 types of furniture, a block size with only one digit for type of furniture would not be wide enough.

Subclassifications facilitate processing for purposes of statistical analysis and other computations, but a blocked code often results in a long code. When the range of choices to be coded is small, a serial set of codes may expedite processing.

Another problem with group classification is that each subfield has to be wide enough to accommodate the maximum code value. If that maximum seldom occurs, the space is underutilized, making both storage and processing of the data element more expensive than necessary. To overcome this problem, some subclassifications are designed to have variable width, while keeping within the total width constraint of the code. For example, publishers use ISBN (International Standard Book Number) throughout the world. A sample book in this code is 0-256-01834-0.

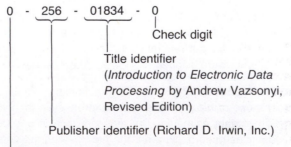

0 - 256 - 01834 - 0

Check digit

Title identifier
(*Introduction to Electronic Data Processing* by Andrew Vazsonyi, Revised Edition)

Publisher identifier (Richard D. Irwin, Inc.)

National and geographic identifier (U.S.A.)

Only a few countries have a single digit for national identifier. Those chosen for the single digit are countries with many publishers and hundreds of titles printed per year, such as the United States and Britain. Countries with a smaller publishing industry are given wider identification blocks (Spain, 84; Indonesia, 929) and narrower publisher and title subfields. Certain numbers in the first block are codes which identify field widths. But in all cases, the total width of the code remains the same. The code ensures that book orders will be filled with the titles, authors, and editions requested.

Within the United States, the first code is deleted. American wholesalers and retailers use the truncated code, calling it SBN (Standard Book Number) when ordering from U.S. publishers.

Decimal codes
Decimal codes are also used for subclassifications. One example of this coding structure is the Dewey Decimal System used by libraries. According to this system, a textbook on EDP would be numbered 651.84.

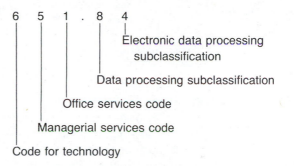

The primary advantage of decimal codes is their expandability.

Magnetic ink character code
A major application for magnetic ink character codes is in banking. Codes written in **magnetic ink characters** are preprinted at the bottom of checks. In processing, the dollar amount of the written check is keyed manually on an **encoder** (similar to keypunch) which converts this figure into magnetic ink characters which are placed in the lower right-hand corner of the check, as in Figure 7.3. The check then passes through a **magnetic ink character recognition (MICR) reader** which validates the characters for completeness and readability. Invalid checks such as those that are torn or smudged are sorted into a pocket for later manual processing. The rest are sorted by the MICR equipment according to block codes in the preprinted characters for routing, bank identification, account number, and process control, with the characters sending sorting signals to the MICR equipment as they pass the read-head. The data is then transferred to a storage device, such as a disk, which is later used for processing the bank's daily transactions.

Figure 7.3
Sample of MIC (magnetic ink character code)

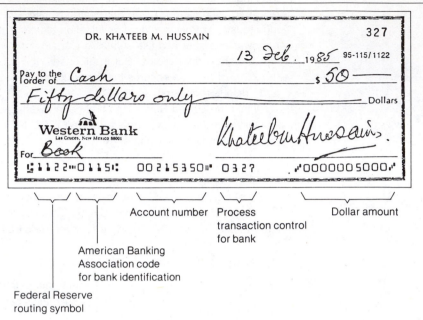

Bar codes

Bar codes have a variety of applications. The **Universal Product Code,** developed for retailing, is an example. This code, read by a scanner, is most commonly found on products in grocery stores. The manufacturers ID and the product or part ID, both numeric codes, are represented in each UPC symbol by a combination of black and white bars (the white bars being spacing). The correspondence between each of the 10 numeric digits and their bar codes is shown in Figure 7.4.

Once the scanner reads the code, identifying manufacturer and product, the computer searches a price list stored in its memory to determine price of the item. The directness of this operation reduces the speed of checkout by an estimated 30 percent.[2] The U.S. Postal Service is considering the use of bar codes for the machine processing of mail. It is estimated that this will reduce the error rate of misdirected mail from 2.2 percent to less than 1 percent and will speed processing at reduced cost.[3]

Another application is for library cards, as shown in Figure 7.5. Still other applications are listed in Table 7.1. Since computer printers are now capable of

[2] *Computer World,* 9, no. 8 (February 19, 1975), p. 1.
[3] James Rawlings Sydnor, "Bar Coded Unique ZIP Codes Solve Postal Problems," *Journal of Systems Management* 29, no. 7 (July 1978), p. 18.

Figure 7.4
Universal product code

A UPC contains a number system character, 10-data characters, and a check character. In addition, guard bars appear on each side and separate the two halves of the code.

Table 7.1
Sample applications of bar codes

Accounts payable
Accounts receivable
Order processing
Production control
Scheduling
Inventory control
Mail
Retail stores
Sorting and routing
Vehicle identification

Figure 7.5
Library use of bar code

727-3150-6
UNIVERSITY PUBLIC LIBRARY

03 01 031456 2 5

Name: FRANK D. WILLIAMS
Street: 7145 WATERMAN
City: U. CITY, MO. 63130
Phone: 726-5171   Expires: SEPT. 1988

is responsible for all use made of this card

printing bar codes on labels, and laser scanners to read the codes can do so accurately from as far as six feet away, even when the object with the code is moving as on a production assembly line, we can expect the use of bar codes for many new applications in the future. As the number of applications expands, special equipment will be designed to produce and read the codes at low cost— low cost because of economies of scale.

Miscellaneous codes

The coding systems described above can be combined into a variety of permutations. The code CARSWAJ63 mentioned earlier is a combination of name and sequential codes. Sequence codes can also be added to block and decimal codes.

Sometimes codes have embedded information. The personal ID code in Sweden includes year of birth. Some product codes include prices. The first four digits in product 35402620 might be the suggested sales price ($35.40), the last four the wholesale price ($26.20). This innocent-looking code can be used to calculate markup.

Color codes are also common. One prestigious university is now sending letters of acceptance on paper with a pink border and rejection letters bordered in black after a computer center mixup of address tapes which caused accepted students to receive rejection letters and vice versa. The color codes now alert computer operators, mail personnel, and the control clerk as to the nature of the letter so that extra care in computer processing will take place.

Selection of coding structure

The coding structure used for a data element must be chosen with great care. It affects error rates in coding, readability, and processing, as well as the morale of coders. The hardware and software components of an information system may also have to be modified. Van Court Hare states:

> The selection of a particular code that will be used, even though unique, offers a classic example of economic trade-offs. On the one hand, some capacity or investment in facilities is required to transmit, process, and manipulate codes. On the other hand the capacity required in each of these phases of processing is affected by the choice of code format. In general, the shorter the code, the smaller the cost of transmission storage, data entry, sorting and human handling. The longer code, however, requires less translation and "lookup" capacity and processing and often provides greater versatility in data extraction, statistical analysis, and category combination.[4]

Decisions on coding structures and data element subclassifications should not be delegated to analysts. Management should participate in the design of coding schemes and in code implementation.

---

[4]Van Court Hare, Jr., *Systems Analysis :A Diagnostic Approach* (New York: Harcourt Brace Jovanovich, 1967), pp. 494–95.

Principles of code design

Once a code structure has been selected, codes must be assigned within the structure. The following are principles of code design.

1. Codes should be logical and meaningful whenever possible. Arbitrary alphabetic codes that have no relation to names, such as rug coded CN, can be confusing to coders and result in inaccuracies. Numerical codes should also make sense. 1 for married and 2 for single should be reversed, for example.

2. Codes should be neutral, evoking no emotional response on the part of coders or users. Women's groups have objected to the use of 1 for male and 2 for female in sex coding. Many coders dismiss the number 13 as a coding option.

3. Codes should identify the lowest level of measurement or aggregation that will be needed during the lifetime of the coding structure.

4. Long codes should include a self-checking feature to ensure that codes are correctly transcribed and converted into machine-readable form. (An explanation of check digits appears later in this chapter.)

5. The code design should allow for expansion of data attributes. Lack of planning for such needs may require reprogramming and restructuring of data files to incorporate changes at a later date. The U.S. Postal Service plans to add four digits to the zip code to help identify postal routes and set of postal boxes. A small Connecticut business has calculated that it would need to change 85 computer programs, expand 40 disk files, reprint 6 input documents, and recompile 81 control procedures for a 9-digit zip code. The nationwide cost of this code expansion will be high, not to mention the confusion and disruption that such a change will entail.

6. Codes should incorporate supplemental information embedded in the code wherever possible. For example, a personnel number that includes year of employment in two digits added to sequential numbering is a code that identifies employee records uniquely while providing useful information for statistical reports.

7. An "other" category that can be subclassified at a future date should be provided, since it is not always possible to anticipate all attributes of a data element that need coding.

8. Hyphens, decimals, or spaces should be added to long codes to help users remember them. The grouping of digits in social security numbers assists memorization, for example.

9. A standard coding system should be adopted and codes defined in the DED for each data element that is coded. This will ensure that data elements within a firm's data base are uniformly coded. Imagine the confusion that would arise if a warehouse assigned color codes to products that differed from the color codes used by salespersons.

Problems

A major disadvantage of coding is that errors are frequently made converting data to code, errors that are not always easily detected. Computer programs can be written to check data entry against a list of accepted codes so that nonexistent characters will be spotted, but a legitimate code used incorrectly will pass undetected.

The credibility of data is often directly related to the origin of coding. Coding at the data source may lead to inadvertent errors due to a misunderstanding of the coding structure or carelessness in applying valid and relevant codes. Trained coders, selected and supervised with care and motivated as to the importance of their job, make fewer errors. Their work can be checked by sending a copy of the coded record to the division that collected the data, but this approach depends on the cooperation of individuals at the data source. What if the data were unfavorable to that division? Would motivation to make corrections exist? A statistical sample of a coder's work should be regularly checked. If the coder's error rate exceeds previously set standards, that person should be fired or relocated. An information system with incorrect data as a result of incorrect coding has little value.

Validation

Data (either coded or uncoded) ready for input should first be **glance-checked.** Once converted into machine language, content and meaning can be further validated by computer program. In computer science literature, validation is often called editing, but these two terms should not be interchanged. **Editing,** strictly defined, is correcting syntax by adding hyphens, dollar signs, or commas to make output readable, or eliminating zeros, as in the number 0032—changes that can be made by programs during processing. **Validation,** however, concerns checking compliance of data with preset standards and verification of data correctness.

This validation may be of input, checking data on forms or CRT screens at the time of data collection. For example, an incorrect entry on an employment application might be caught by a clerk, and called to the applicant's attention for revision. Data converted into machine language can further be validated by computer program. If errors are detected, data must recycle back to the error source, as shown in Figure 7.6.

Invalid data may be the result of:

1. Incorrect or outdated source documentation (form or manual).
2. Entry error by data collector.
3. Misinterpretation of documentation during input preparation.
4. Coding errors.
5. Operator errors in data conversion (the largest single cause of input error).
6. Errors in data transmission and data handling (for example, lost data or incorrect sequencing).

Validity checks

Data should be checked for completeness, format, range, reasonableness, consistency, sequence, and transaction count. The self-checking code should also be validated. It should be emphasized that decision rules for all validity tests need

**Figure 7.6
Data validation**

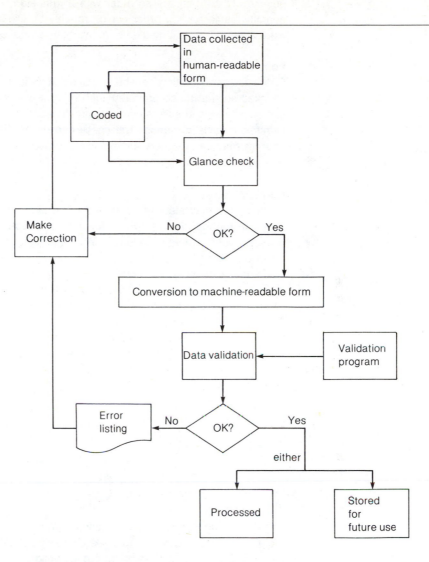

to be stated with care. Errors in data should not pass undetected nor should correct data be identified as invalid. The perspective of managers is needed in deciding which data elements require validation, and what validation rules should be applied.

Completeness

Data should be **complete.** When data has a prescribed length, such as nine digits for a social security number, all characters should be expressed. Completeness checks are necessary only when missing data will affect results. The computer could not process an order with a truncated product number or one with quantity blank, but the order could probably be filled if the client's middle initial were absent or a digit omitted from the client's phone number.

Format

Character configuration can be specified in validation programs, and the data checked against these predetermined rules. For example, a validation program can be written to identify as an error an alphabetic character in a dollar data field, or numeric data in names. The check can divide the **format** into subfields. An address may be assigned numeric fields for house number and zip code, but alphabetic blocks for street and city.

Range

A check rule may state that data entry is limited to predetermined values, or a **range of values.** If M and F are used as sex codes, only these two characters would be vaid in the sex code field. Any other letter or number would be listed as an error. Similarly, a range of values could be specified. If a firm's minimum wage/hour rate were $4 and the maximum $9, the computer could be programmed to identify as invalid data with values under or over these amounts, errors called **definite** or **fatal errors.** The computer might also be programmed to identify **possible** or **suspected errors,** data near the limits of acceptable values. For example, if few employees earned over $8, a listing of employees in the $8–9 range could be provided for recheck. The validation rule would be as follows:

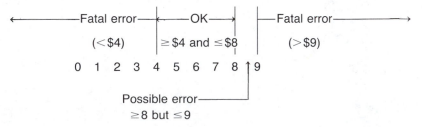

Fatal errors identified by the validation program would have to be traced and corrected. The data would then be reprocessed. An overriding code would permit processing of suspected data that proved valid.

Reasonableness

In any given situation a number of checks for **reasonableness** could be postulated. Date of employment cannot predate a worker's birth, the total of accounts receivable cannot be negative, a probationary student cannot graduate with honors, and so forth. The cost of processing such checks must be weighed against losses (monetary and credibility), should errors pass undetected. Such judgments require management's expertise.

Table 7.2
Transaction data

	Invoice number	Quantity (units)	Price $	Value $	Batch total	Hash total
	320	16	3.20	53.20		392.40
Batch 1	321	8	4.10	32.80		365.90
	323	21	1.90	39.90	125.90	511.70
	324	25	4.00	100.00		363.00
Batch 2	325	31	4.20	130.20		490.40
	326	9	5.80	52.20		393.00
	327	5	6.10	30.50	312.90	681.60
				438.80	438.80	

Consistency

Data values can be checked by verifying them from more than one source. This may mean collecting the same raw data from two or more principals, or generating the values of a data element from input to be matched with the keyed value for that same data element. The latter method is used to check totals, for example. If the information on Table 7.2 were keypunched, a computer validity program could add $53.20, $32.80, and $39.90 in Batch I and match the total with the batch total $125.90 entered as input. Or each invoice total could be calculated by computer (price times quantity) and the product compared to the figure listed in the value column. Any discrepancy would be identified on an error listing. Most frequently, invalid data is a mistake in keying the input.

A **hash total** entered as input is also a useful check for **consistency.** All the data in one transaction is totaled even though the units are not the same. The computer then totals the "hash" independently, $(320 + 16 + 3.20 + 53.20$ in the first transaction in Table 7.2) and compares the total with the keyed hash total of $392.40. Since many transactions involve 80 to 100 characters, the hash total is an important validity check.

Duplicate processing is another method of checking for consistency. A firm which needed to determine a coefficient to two decimal places from complex calculations for the allocation of over $4 million used both COBOL and FORTRAN to make the calculations. Because of the large amount of money involved, it was helpful to compare calculations made by the two compilers which differed in rounding and truncation rules.

Sequence

In Table 7.2 invoice 322 is missing. A validity test for **sequencing** would identify this situation. The document may have been mislaid or lost, in which case corrective action, such as recollection of the data, would take place. But often an explanation, such as a cancelled order, will be traced. In processing payrolls, logs are kept of checks damaged, destroyed by the printer, or checks left blank—a record that is searched when a sequence validity test flags an error.

Transaction count

When a given number of transactions are to be processed, this total is entered as input. The transactions are again counted during processing. An invalid state will be identified if the totals do not match. This will alert operators to a lost document, or records stuck to one another, or possibly even multiple processing of the same transaction.

Check-digit validation

A code is sometimes used to check for transposition of data or data entry errors, situations that often occur in data elements consisting of a long string of digits. This code, called a **check digit,** is calculated by a prescribed set of rules based on the value of the digits in the number and their locational relationships. The code is then added to the data element number and recalculated every time that data element is processed. If the recalculated value does not coincide with the original check digit, an error is identified.

Modulus 10 is one technique for calculating a check digit. In this technique, the position of digits in a number is significant. Digits in odd positions (such as first, third, fifth, and so forth) are added for a subtotal. Digits in even positions are multiplied by 2 and the digits in the products added together for a second subtotal. The subtotals are then added and divided by ten. The number that must be added to the remainder to make it divisible by 10 is the check digit.

For the number 142796539, the check digit, according to these rules, is 2. To demonstrate the derivation of the check digit, the number will be aligned in two rows, digits in odd positions separated from digits in even positions. The calculations are then performed as follows:

	Multiplied by 2	Subtotal of digits in row
1 2 9 5 9	No	$1+2+9+5+9 = 26$
4 7 6 3	Yes	$8+(1+4)+(1+2)+6 = 22$
		Total $= 48$

$$\text{Remainder when total is divided by } 10 = 8$$
$$\text{Number to be added to remainder to equal } 10 = 2$$
$$\text{New check digit} = 2$$

$$\text{New number} = 1427965392$$

To test the working of the check digit, study the following example in which the value of one digit is changed.

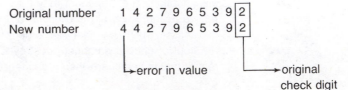

Original number   1 4 2 7 9 6 5 3 9 |2|
New number   4 4 2 7 9 6 5 3 9 |2|

→ error in value   → original check digit

	Multiplied by 2	Subtotal of digits in row
4 2 9 5 9	No	$4+2+9+5+9 \quad = 29$
4 7 6 3	Yes	$8+(1+4)+(1+2)+6 = 22$
		Total $\quad = 51$

Remainder after dividing total by $10 = 1$

Number to be added to remainder to equal $10 = 9$

New check digit $= 9$

Original check digit $= 2$

New check digit does not equal original check digit.
Therefore, an error exists.

In the following example, two adjacent digits are transposed.

Original number   1 4 2 7 9 6 5 3 9 2
New number   4 1 2 7 9 6 5 3 9 2 ← check digit

└→ error from single transportation

	Multiplied by 2	Subtotal of digits in row
4 2 9 5 9	No	$4+2+9+5+9 \quad = 29$
1 7 6 3	Yes	$2+(1+4)+(1+2)+6 = 16$
		Total $\quad 45$

Remainder after dividing total by $10 = 5$

Number to be added to remainder to equal $10 = 5$

New check digit $= 5$

Original check digit $= 2$

The new check digit does not equal the original digit.
Therefore, an error exists.

    The problem with **Modulus 10** is that double transposition can take place without affecting the check digit (that is, 5431 transposed as 3154). **Modulus 11,** another method of calculating a check digit, overcomes this problem. In Modulus 11, digits in the value of the data element are assigned weights such as numbers in an ascending or descending scale. Each digit is then multiplied by its corresponding weighted value, and the products are totaled. The number that must be added to this total to make it divisible by 11 is the check digit. All types of transposition (double, triple, and so forth) and data entry errors are caught by this technique.

    An application of Modulus 11 is in ISBN numbers (International Standard Book Numbers). Use of the check digit guards against more than 99 percent of ordering errors caused by transposing or miscopying book numbers.

    An example of how the ISBN check digit is calculated for Hussain and Hussain, *Information Processing Systems for Management,* 1981 edition, appears below.

ISBN number	0	2	5	6	0	2	4	8	2
ISBN weights	10	9	8	7	6	5	4	3	2

Weighted
values   0 18 40 42 0 10 16 24 4
(ISBN number multiplied by ISBN weight)

Weighted total: $0 + 18 + 40 + 42 + 0 + 10 + 16 + 24 + 4 = 154$

Number to be added to total to make it divisible by $11 = $ 0

Check digit $= $ 0

ISBN number $= 0{-}256{-}02482{-}0$

If the check digit had been calculated as 10, an X would have been used instead of the number since only one character is assigned to the check digit. ISBN 0-256-02121-X, for James A. O'Brien's text, *Computers in Business Management: An Introduction,* 1979, fits this pattern.

The use of a check digit has disadvantages. It adds to the length of numbers and increases data preparation effort, the time required for processing, and storage space requirements. The longer number is also harder to remember. But when reliability is important and the number is repeatedly used in processing, detection of errors may be worth the inconvenience and cost. Self-checking codes are commonly the last digit in identification numbers for employees, vendors, customers, accounts, and parts. Their use will identify posting of transactions to wrong accounts.

Summary

Three aspects of data preparation have been discussed in this chapter: data collection, coding, and validation.

Forms, logs and equipment, such as badge readers or point of sale terminals, can be used to collect data for system input.

Coding is a brief unique representation of data used to facilitate classification, speed processing, and reduce costs in data preparation and storage. Each application requires codes tailored to the environment. That is why management should participate in code design. Technicians may have coding skill but lack perspective regarding the goals and operational limitations of the firm, factors that should be considered when designing coding for input and retrieval.

Computer validation of data takes place after it is coded in machine language. The rules of validation should be specified with care by management. Underspecification may lead to undetected errors, causing the system to produce unreliable information. Overspecification adds unnecessarily to processing costs. Validation tests include checks for completeness, format, range, reasonableness, consistency, sequence and transaction count, and recalculation of check digits.

Some errors will still escape detection—such as mistakes of data entry that fall within allowable ranges. But validation tests will improve the quality of information by reducing, even eliminating, obvious errors in input and output.

Key words

Alphabetic codes	Group classification code
Alphameric (alphanumeric) code	Hash total
Block code	Input manual
Check digit	Magnetic ink character code
Coder	Magnetic ink character
Coding	recognition (MICR) reader
Coding sheet	Mnemonic symbol
Complete	Modulus 10
Consistency	Modulus 11
Data collection	Numeric codes
Data preparation	Offline collection
Decimal code	Online collection
Definite error	Possible error
Duplicate processing	Range of values
Editing	Reasonableness
Encoder	Sequencing
Encoding	Suspected error
Fatal error	Table lookup
Format	Universal Product Code (UPC)
Glance check	Validation

Discussion questions

1. What are the principles of code design?

2. What are the disadvantages of using codes?

3. What approach to data collection would you advise for each of the following situations? Identify both input media and input equipment.
   a. Bank.
   b. Warehouse.
   c. Production plant.
   d. Sales office.
   e. Accounts payable.

4. What is the UPC? What are its advantages and disadvantages? Why is it not used universally in retail stores?

5. What are some of the applications of a bar code in industries other than the retail industry?

6. Identify situations in business and industry where optical scanning can be used effectively.

7. What is the need and significance of editing or validation? At what point in processing must they be performed? What additional resources are necessary?

8. Can the following errors be caught by validation? In each case state the validation rule.
   a. $93A2.4.
   b. DR. HUSS3IN.
   c. $3 2.64.
   d. WAGE $1686 per hour.
   e. Account number incorrect.
   f. Age incorrect by one year.
   g. Age incorrect by 100 years.

9. Within a firm, coding methods should be standardized or else there will be confusion and inefficiency. Comment. How can coding methods be standardized?

10. Describe how data is converted into machine-readable form. Why is this conversion important? How can data from a meter be converted into machine-readable form?

11. What are the rationale for coding data? What costs are involved?

12. What national attempt has been made at standardized codes? Why? What are the main obstacles to standardization?

13. Distinguish between:
    a. Data code and program code.
    b. Block code and group code.
    c. Code and coder.
    d. Decimal code and classification code.
    e. Alphabetic and numeric code.
    f. Alphameric and alphanumeric code.

14. When should a file be verified? Must all the contents be verified in each verification run?

15. What is the difference between verification of new data for content errors and editing for format errors? How is each done? Must each be done?

16. When is a check digit useful? Why? Give examples.

17. Why are codes used in information systems?

18. Explain six validation rules for data.

19. What are common causes for invalid data?

20. Given that validation is important to data manipulations, describe some potential problems involved in validation.

Exercises

1. Design codes for the data elements in Exercise 1, Chapter 6. Use alpha characters only for the month subfield code, use a block code to identify uni-

versity, college (e.g., Business Ad), department (e.g., Economics), and major (e.g., Micro Economics).

2. Find the ISBN number for this text. Decode it. The identifier for the country of publication is the first digit, the publisher identifier the next three digits. All Irwin books should have these same digits. The title identifier is the next five digits. Compare this ISBN number with other business books published by Irwin. What digits are the same?

3. The last digit of the ISBN is a check digit. Figure out the algorithm used for this book. Try the algorithm on another Irwin book. Does it work?

4. Calculate the check digit for the number 362815 using Modulus 11 with 1, 2, 3, 4, 5, and 6 as weights. What is the new number with the check digit?

5. Compare the UPC code on a can of Campbell's Cream of Chicken Soup with the code from some other product by Campbell. What parts of the codes are identical? Why? Which parts differ? Why?

Selected annotated bibliography

Anderson, Lauek, et al. "Self-Checking Digit Concepts." *Journal of Systems Development* 25, no. 9 (September 1974), pp. 36–42.

A detailed description and comparison of seven check digit formulas, including Mod 11.

Clifton, H. D. *Business Data Systems*. Engelwood Cliffs, N.J.: Prentice-Hall, 1978, pp. 229–35.

A good systematic discussion of coding classification and design.

Daniels, Alan, and Donald Yeates. *Systems Analysis*. Palo Alto, Calif.: Science Research Associates, 1971, pp. 62–71.

An excellent discussion on functions of codes and design considerations. Sequence codes, group classification codes, block codes, significant digit codes, the Dewey Decimal Code, and nine types of check digit codes are reviewed.

Kohn, B. *Secret Codes and Ciphers*. Engelwood Cliffs, N.J.: Prentice-Hall, 1968, 63 pp.

This is a small book with a large print, many diagrams, and amusing illustrations—a delight.

Lasden, Martin. "Update on Data Entry." *Computer Decisions* 13, no. 4 (April 1981), pp. 74–96.

Lasden argues that the new technologies present the manager with both opportunities and responsibilities for data entry.

Savir, D., and G. L. Laurer. "The Characteristics and Decodability of the Universal Product Code." *IBM System Journal* 14, no. 1 (1975), pp. 16–34.

An excellent discussion on the development of the UPC, including characteristics, errors, and decoding. The decoding presentation is mathematical, but that part can be skipped and still much gained by the general reader.

Schultz, Gaymond. "An Intelligent-Workstation Approach to Office Automation." *Mini-Micro Systems* 16, no. 6 (May 1983), pp. 193–204.

A technical discussion of one workstation with voice capability used for data preparation. Necessary software is described.

Way, Peter. *Codes and Ciphers*. London: Aldus Books Ltd., 1977, 144 pp.

A nontechnical book with many illustrations with an interesting description of how codes have been used (successfully and unsuccessfully) during wars and in espionage.

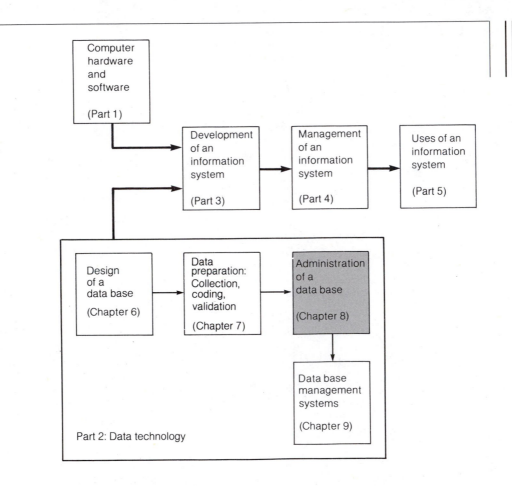

Administration of a data base

8

The extension of man's intellect by machine, and the partnership
of man and machine in handling information may well be the technological advance dominating this century.

Simon Ramo

As data grows in volume within a business, a system is required to keep track of
and manage all the elements in the common data base. The data base itself can
be utilized efficiently and effectively only when procedures for its control and use
are well designed.

Knowledge of this aspect of data technology is needed when developing and
implementing information systems. For example, a manager may wish to know
which reports would be affected if values for a specific data element were no longer
collected. A listing of who accesses data, and why, might prove useful. The ability
to identify units creating data, or programs and files using particular data elements, might also be required. This information can be generated by a set of programs that draws on all knowledge about the elements stored in the data element
dictionaries of the firm and available in the data base. The tables or lists generated make up a **directory.**

Because of the close relationship between dictionaries and data directories,
the two are often developed together, forming a **data element dictionary/data
directory system (DED/DD system).** (The acronym is sometimes shortened to
DD/D for **data dictionary/directory.**) But the dictionary could be produced first
and a directory added at a later date. Some software firms and computer manufacturers put together DED/DD systems which they provide to customers. Many
businesses, however, develop unique DED/DD systems for their own use.

Technicians are responsible for most of the activities in creating and maintaining a common data base, including generation of directories, although a manager, pesonally, or through a committee, oversees these activities. For large and
complex systems, a data base management system and the hiring of a data base
administrator are advisable. This chapter presents a brief nontechnical discussion of how data bases are implemented and administered.

Directories

Directories are lists or tables that facilitate quick reference to pertinent information. Consider a directory we utilize every day—a telephone directory. We refer to it for phone numbers and addresses. The **key word** or **index** in this case is family name. Data systems also have directories. These index data elements and provide such information as where data elements are located in the files, which programs and transactions use the elements, and who uses the information derived from the data elements. In data system directories, the key word indexed is either the data element name or a **label,** the latter being a short, unique, and easy-to-process identifier substituted for the name. For example, F.I.C.A. (for Federal Insurance Contributions Act) is a label commonly used in place of the data element name of *social security tax.* Since some programming languages have restrictions on the choice of label (FORTRAN limits the number of characters per label), it is advisable to keep programming rules in mind when labels are designed.

Because dictionaries and directories both provide organizational information about data elements, the two are closely related. In some cases, directories also define data elements, so they perform the function of dictionaries. The distinction between directories and dictionaries has been further clouded by many data processing practitioners who define **fixed data elements** (such as sex) in dictionaries, and **variable data elements** (such as marital status) in directories. However, not all data elements can be easily categorized in this manner. Some data elements are fixed over a period of time and then change, such as a name that changes upon marriage. Data element definitions may also change when managers change. There simply is no universally accepted distinction between dictionaries and directories in the data processing profession. By referring to dictionaries and directories jointly, as a DED/DD system, the need for making a hard and fast distinction between the two is avoided.

DED/DD systems have two primary functions: they serve as a repository of information for data processing personnel and users, and as an information source for application and system programs. Just how they facilitate and control the use of the data base is described below.

Information repository for users

Indexes

One important function of a DED/DD system is that it documents information related to processing. This documentation also serves as a set of standards governing the creation and use of the data.

Accessing this information may prove laborious in large systems. An **index** can facilitate access, particularly when searching for data elements with compound or long names when one has forgotten the exact title or spelling of the element. In such cases a **KWIC (Key Word in Context)** or **KWOC (Key Word out of Context)** index is helpful. The former is more commonly used because it identifies in alphabetic sequence every data element word without changing the order of words. Table 8.1 shows excerpts from a sample KWIC that would help a user trace the data element "employee job startdate." In the alphabetic se-

Table 8.1
KWIC extracts

	Data element number
EMPLOYEE-HISTORY-DATA	1.1.10
EMPLOYEE-JOB-STARTDATE	1.3.18
EMPLOYEE-JOB-STATUS	1.3.19
EMPLOYEE-JOB-TITLE	1.3.20
EMPLOYEE-NAME	1.2.02
EMPLOYEE-NUMBER	1.2.03
PAST-EMPLOYEE-NUMBER	1.2.13

•
•
•
•
•

INVOICE-CREDIT	3.2.02
INVOICE-DATE	3.2.04
INVOICE-NUMBER	3.2.04
JOB-NUMBER	1.3.02
EMPLOYEE-JOB-STARTDATE	1.3.18
EMPLOYEE-JOB-STATUS	1.3.19
EMPLOYEE-JOB-TITLE	1.3.30
JOB-WAGE-RATE	1.3.24

•

quence, this data element would be listed three times: under E for employee, J for job, and S for startdate. The data element could therefore be traced if only one of the three words in its name were recalled.

This multiple indexing technique has other business applications as well. It may be employed in indexing a user's manual, a procedures manual, or even a chart of accounts.

Since some data element names are ambiguous or have names chosen for convenience rather than relevance, a descriptor called a **designator** is often added to the definition of a data element and is used for indexing that element. This descriptor is a set of **key words** reflecting the content and meaning of the data element. A convention is generally followed for ordering words in the designator name: the most general key word appears first, the most specific last. Thus, if the words "shortened name of employee" were chosen for the designator, the convention would require that this be written as "name employee shortened" since "name" is the most general key word and "shortened" the most specific. "Of" would be eliminated entirely.

Some key words occur frequently. These are designated **classwords** and should be used wherever applicable. This helps reduce synonyms. Examples of classwords are amount, salesperson, and part number.

Using designators and using key words in data element names and designators result in the grouping of similar data elements in indexes. Such groupings greatly facilitate the identification of duplications, synonyms, and inconsistencies in a DED. A manager administering a data base may be alerted to the need for modification or even reconstruction of the firm's DED by analyzing directory indexes.

Table to identify users of data elements

A DED/DD system can generate a directory to represent the relationship of each data element in the data base with users. Data elements form one axis, and user (current or potential) the other. The letter may represent organizational units, reports, models, or individuals. A matrix of this type (see Table 8.2) can help streamline the data base by identifying data elements that should be dropped (data elements collected but not used) and can help assess the relative importance of data elements in the system, an assessment of value to management for control, since heavily used data elements will require more careful monitoring than those used infrequently. For example, since PIN is a data element used by all organizational units in Table 8.2, the need for validation procedures of PIN input might be deduced from this matrix.

Matrix to identify data creators

DED/DD systems may also generate a directory to identify organizational units that create and/or maintain each data element. This matrix tells management which units are responsible for correct, complete collection of data on time. When superimposed on the matrix showing organizational users, managers can identify data elements that are both created and used by a single organizational unit (see Table 8.3). The quality of data in such cases is generally high, for the creator as a later user has a vested interest in accuracy and completeness. Units that serve merely as collectors of data for others are less motivated and may become lax in the quality of data generated. The matrix is therefore a useful tool in data base administration since it helps monitor quality by pointing to potential weaknesses in data collection.

Transaction matrix

It is sometimes desirable to identify the data elements used by each transaction. In the matrix, transactions can be either formal input documents and printed forms, or output forms. This matrix is generated to determine which transactions would

Table 8.2
Matrix to identify users of data elements

Data elements	Users				
	Organizational unit (departments coded)				
	1	2	3	• • •	• • •
PIN of employee (personal ID number)	x	x	x		
Name	x		x		
Address	x		x		
Sex	x		x		
Marital status	x		x		

Table 8.3
Matrix to identify creators and users of data elements

Data elements / Users	Organizational unit (departments coded)				
	1	2	3	• • •	• • •
PIN of employee (personal ID number)	x	x	x		
Name	x		⊗		
Address	x		⊗		
Sex	x		⊗		
Marital status	x		⊗		
Educational highest degree		⊗			
Experience code		⊗			
Years of experience		⊗			
Language code	x				
State of birth	x				
Year of birth	x				
Medical benefit		⊗	⊗		
Deduction codes		⊗	⊗		
Tax code		⊗	⊗		
Wage rate		⊗	⊗		
Key: x = creator ○ = user					

be affected if a data element were redefined or deleted. Such information is useful in form and document control.

Information repository for software

Access directory

In processing, the computer sometimes uses tables generated by the DED/DD system. For example, the computer may check the level of security code needed for access to specific data elements or files before processing a user's job—information that is stored in a directory. In addition, the table referenced might specify the type of access permitted, that is, read or write. In a terminal environment, the data elements accessible by each terminal might also be listed, as well as the time of day when access is permitted. Special user access limitations and user account numbers for purposes of billing might also be drawn from the directory in processing. Computers programmed to refuse access to those not authorized generally log all requests to use the system, a log that will help alert managers to attempted security violations of the system.

Programs may be written for printing directory information stored in computer memory. For example, a manager or auditor may wish a printout of information in the security/access directory used by the computer in processing. The exact format of the printout would depend on the programmed instructions since the information could be printed in a variety of sorting orders. A sample access directory is shown in Table 8.4.

Table 8.4
Access directory

User identification: 076–835–5623 Access limitation: 13 hours (of CPU time for current fiscal year) Account No.: AS5842				
Data elements	*Type of access*	*Security level*	*Terminal number*	*Time lock*
Customer No.	Read	10	04	08.00–17.00
Invoice No.	Read	10	04	08.00–17.00
Cash receipt	Read/Write	12	06	08.00–12.00

Processing information

The form of a data element, such as its mode of data representation, format, and compaction (if it is compacted), is information needed in processing. Though this is usually specified by programs, it may prove more economical to have this information in a directory that is machine-readable. In such cases, every time that data elements in the common data base are used, information necessary for processing is referenced from the DED/DD system.

A somewhat similar situation may arise in validating input data values for data elements entered into the system by several terminals. Instead of independent validity programs testing the input values, the validation rules can be stored in the DED/DD system and referenced by a DED/DD-driven validator. If the data does not pass the validation tests, diagnostics of error are sent to the originator of the data. Valid data is added to the data base and subsequently used in processing applications programs. This process is shown in Figure 8.1.

Locational information

Once data is validated, it is stored on a storage device and the location is recorded. A stored set of data constitutes a **physical record.** When the data is a set of logically related values, it constitutes a **logical record.** Physical records, therefore, become repositories of stored logical records. When access to a logical record is needed, its physical location must be known. This information can be provided by a directory. DED/DD systems with locational information enable programmers to merely name logical records or data elements needed in processing without having to specify location. **Data mapping,** illustrated in Figure 8.2, referenced from a directory is particularly useful in a multistorage device system.

Generation of test data

The rules for data validation discussed earlier include information on character composition and the permissible range of data values. This information, plus information on format available in the data dictionary, enables DED/DD systems to generate sample data needed to test computer programs before live data is collected. Even after live data is available, DED/DD generation of sample data is

Figure 8.1
DED/DD-driven centralized validator for input data to data base

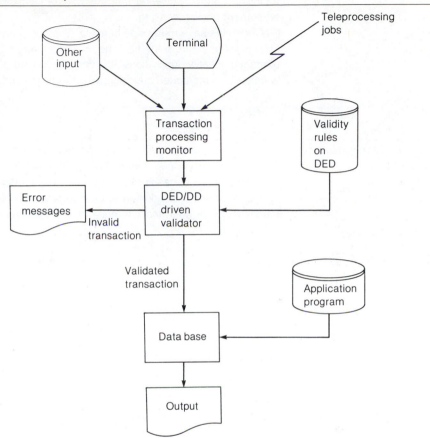

useful for maintenance programs which can then be tested without disturbing the live data stream.

The sample test data should be statistically designed (for example, a stratified random sample). It should include boundary conditions and exceptional values, information which is available in the DED/DD system.

Code file
Definitions of data elements can be extended to include subclassifications. A DED/DD system can then generate a **code file** from these definitions, listing names and codes of all subclassifications, a file to be referenced whenever the data element name or code is unknown.

Some argue that a code file should contain only large sets of frequently used codes, such as a chart of accounts of a diversified firm. Short, frequently used codes, such as a sex code, should be excluded (may be defined externally or in programs used). Others favor inclusion of all codes in a code file to facilitate data definition control, believing that this control justifies the higher cost required for equipment and processing.

Code files have many side benefits. The computer can generate updated code listings for users from the file. The file serves as an authority on codes and helps managers identify duplications of codes which need purging. Users must first check whether existing codes are applicable to their needs before adding new codes to the system.

Adding descriptors to the DED

Only a few of the many directories and indexes that can be produced by a DED/DD system have been mentioned. The information itself is generated by computer programs. In most cases, this requires a trivial effort.[1] But there is an important cost component: the addition of descriptors to the DED to define terms and relationships needed in the reference tables. Examples of such descriptors include

Figure 8.2
Physical and logical mapping of data

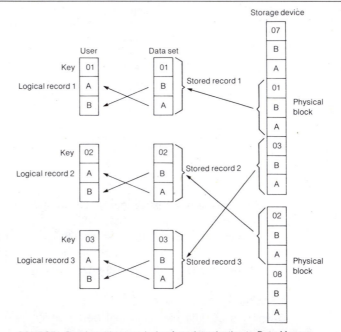

SOURCE   Reprinted by permission from *Introduction to Data Management*. Student Text, No. SC20–8096–0, p. 37, © 1980, International Business Machines Corporation.

---

[1] The effort of writing a program that will generate a directory is not trivial in itself, but such programs can be purchased, or they are provided by vendors of computer equipment. Their use requires a trivial effort.

designator, synonym, user, data creator, codes for subclassification, mode (bit string, character string, packed decimal, and so forth), logical/physical relationship, and medium of storage. One large firm studied listed 250 descriptors required for its use of COBOL, assembler source programs, Job Control Language, and operating system and software packages. This firm, however, is an exceptional case, requiring far more descriptors than usual. Commonly used descriptors for DED/DD systems are listed in Table 8.5.

Organization of a DED/DD system

A DED/DD system requires considerable organization and control. In many firms, a DED/DD committee is responsible for the content of the system and decides what equipment and software are required for developing and maintaining the system, what qualifications are desirable for personnel using equipment and software, and what procedures and mechanisms are needed for control, and so forth.

Control procedures are diagrammed in Figure 8.3. Although the ultimate authority to authorize change to the data base may rest with a DED/DD committee, as shown in this figure, in reality change commonly involves a sequence of approval steps in which users, programmers, analysts, and data processing management play a role. The exact personnel involved will depend on the organization's procedures in the past, the system's complexity, and personalities. For example, when a report is requested by management for which a new program is written, the programmer may find that data elements not in the data base are needed. This may be brought to the attention of a data processing manager who will then request approval of the DED/DD committee for the additions. Some firms may skip this intermediate step, however, authorizing the programmers to approach the committee directly.

Not shown in Figure 8.3 is the duty of the committee to periodically review the existing DED for redundancies and duplications, and the important committee role

Table 8.5
Common descriptors used in DED/DD systems

Names	Last date changed
Definition	Designator
Derivation algorithm (including accuracy level)	Synonym
	User relationship
Units (where relevant, e.g., dollars, meters)	Creation/specification responsibility
Format	Transaction relationship
Justification	Potential use relationship
Width of field	Codes
Validity rules	Mode
Identification	Security code
Version of issuance	Billing code
Date of issuance	Access limitation
Status (effective, proposed or approved)	Logical/physical relationship
	Medium of storage

Figure 8.3
Mechanism for controlling the DED/DD

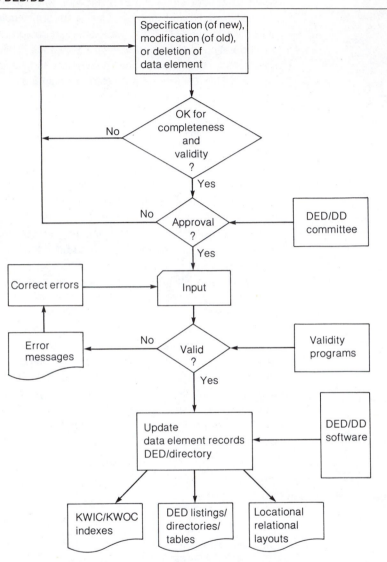

in recognizing the need for revision of the DED due to changes in organizational needs, structure, and personnel.

In controlling the content of the DED/DD system, the committee also has the responsibility of resolving the differences which arise between organizational units. This duty can best be performed when the committee is a consortium of users with high level management positions so that the committee has the operational power and respectability to enforce decisions made—that is, power to overrule unilateral actions by users, to adjudicate conflicts, and to overcome resistance.

The committee must also state policy and provide guidelines for creating, maintaining, and monitoring the DED/DD system. Since implementation is often complex and technical, the committee may delegate this responsibility, retaining merely a supervisory role. The delegated responsibility often goes to a **data base administrator** (sometimes called a **data manager** or **data controller**), a new position in many organizational structures.

The bottom half of Figure 8.3 shows validation programs (discussed in Chapter 7) to control data input, and directories to keep track of data elements in the system.

Data base administrator (DBA)

As mentioned above, a data base administrator is often delegated authority to coordinate, monitor, and control the base and accompanying software, and responsibility for administering the total DED/DD system. Table 8.6 summarizes the data base administrator's duties. Data maintenance, the upkeep of active data, the storage of historical data, and the purging of useless data are primary tasks. Authorized changes to the data base must be made to dictionaries and directories under the data base administrator's supervision. Such changes may require moving data from one storage medium to another, a move that entails careful logging and tagging if data is to be quickly and effectively accessed. Maintenance also includes checking for continuity and completeness of data. Continuity is especially important for planning data with longitudinal integration (integration over time). The modification of historical files is required when definitions of data elements and classifications change. Continuity is threatened by breakdowns in processing, particularly those of online systems where loss of data may result. Procedures for backup, recovery, and restart for all possible types of breakdowns, including natural disasters, must be planned.

A DBA is also responsible for the quality (accurateness and reliability) of the data base. **Logging** and **auditing** procedures should be established, and performance (access, utilization, cost, and response-time performance) monitored. Screening procedures to identify authorized users at minimal cost and inconvenience should be devised to protect the data from misuse. Security of access can be achieved through passwords or passkeys, and directories listing data to be accessed, the time of permissible access, and place.

Both legislative and executive powers are needed by data base administrators. They must not only make rules regarding data base content, access, security, recovery, logging, dumping, and auditing, they must also be able to enforce these rules for all users at all levels of the organizational hierarchy. This authority must extend even over data processing management and vice presidents, for individuals in these positions have been known to break the system for personal financial gain, as shown in Table 8.7. A supervisor or committee should oversee the data administrator, safeguarding against abuse of such authority.

Governing a data base requires many talents. A DBA must be a ". . . technician, politician, [and] consultant . . . who speaks with equal fluency the lan-

Table 8.6
Functions of a data base administrator

Data base design
  Content
    Creation
    Reconciling differences
  Dictionary/Directory
    Create
    Maintain
  Data compression
  Data classification/coding
  Data integrity
    Backup
    Restart/recovery

Data base operation
  DED custodian/authority
    Maintain
    Add
    Purge
  Data base maintenance
    Integrity
      Detect losses
      Repair losses
    Recovery
    Access for testing
    Dumping
  Software for DED/DD
    Utility programs
    Tables/indexes for
      end user
    Storage
    Physical record structure
    Logical-physical mapping
    Physical storage device
      assignments
  Security/access
    Assign passwords
    Assign lock/key
    Modifying passwords/keys
    Logging
    Cryptography
    Modification

Retrieval
  Search strategies
Statistics
  Access
  Frequency of processing
  Space use
  User utilization
  Response time
Design operational
    procedures
  Access to data base
  Access for testing
  Interfaces
  Testing system

Monitoring
  Quality of data
    validity
  Performance
  Efficiency
  Cost
  Use/utilization
  Security/privacy
  Audit
  Compliance
    Standards
    Procedures

Other functions
  Liaison/communications with:
    End users
    Analysts/programmers
  Training on data base
  Consultant on file design
  Design operational
    procedures
    Access to data base
    Access for testing
    Interfaces

guages of both computers and human beings."[2] But since it is difficult to find all of these qualities in one person, data base administrators in large organizations generally select a balanced staff of assistants including data specialists with expertise in public relations and liaison work, and personnel qualified as trainers/educators.

Since data base administrators and staff are usually classified as data processing technical personnel, some organizational theorists recommend that they report to a data processing manager. Others argue that the data base adminis-

---

[2]C. M. Travers, "Data Base Administrator—the Emerging Position," *Proceedings of the College and University Machine Records Conference* (1973), p. 8.

trator should report to a user committee. This gives users the feeling of being "custodians" of the data base.

Resources for data administration

Special equipment (e.g., cryptographic equipment) and special software are used to administer a data base. The terminal in the data base administrator's office may be the only terminal with authority to make changes to the DED/DD system, for example. In security-sensitive systems, the data base administrator's terminal may list all changes to the system that need to be monitored. Some systems will alert the DBA when a user tries many access codes from the same terminal in a short period of time since this may indicate an attempt to break a code. A timely response by the administrator may prevent breach to the system's security.

Software is also needed to generate reports related to use, operation, and monitoring of the data base. A list of reports and programs which support a DED/DD system appears in Table 8.8.

Summary

Data directories are extensions to the DED, providing reference information regarding data relationships of data elements defined in the DED. Data element relationships are of interest and importance in the maintenance of data, in de-

Table 8.7
Distribution of embezzlers by position

Position	Number of embezzlers*
Operations vice-president, manager, clerk	32
Loan officer, manager	29
Teller	22
President	14
Cashier	8
Director, stockholder, officer	5
Vice president, EDP	4
EDP clerk	3
Bookkeeper	3
Trust officer	3
Programmer	3
Computer operator	3
System analyst	2
Chief teller	1
Auditor	1
Vice-president	1
Proof department supervisor	1

*Includes 17 cases of collusion.

SOURCE   Donn B. Parker, *Crime by Computer* (New York: Charles Scribner's Sons, 1976), p. 52. Copyright © 1976 by Donn B. Parker. Reprinted by permission of the publisher.

Table 8.8
Reports and programs to support the DED/DD system

Listings of DED
KWIC/KWOC indexes
Listings of directories
Testing data generator
Data division generator
JCL generator
Implementing hardware and software changes
Data validator
Access controller
Data definition controller
Data structure converter
Data storage assigner
Statistical reports on utilization
Comparison routine
Utility routines
  Logging
  Editing
  Dumping
  Garbage collector

signing data collection, and in reports. Each relationship can be expressed in tabular form like an input/output table, with the data element on the X axis, and the Y axis representing whatever organization, transaction, file, or program needs to be defined in terms of data elements. DED/DD software enables generation of printed lists and tables in response to simple commands.

Most comprehensive DED/DD systems contain information about and maintain relationships between entities in the following categories:

Application programs	Physical data base
Data base schema	Report
Data base subschema	Source document
Data item	Transaction
Data field	User
Data file	

Centralizing all information on data elements in a DED/DD system improves efficiency in monitoring and control of data. All information regarding security and validity of data can be readily accessed, information that is needed by a data base administrator given responsibility for integrity, reliability, and operations of the data base.

DED/DD systems can be used by businesses with data bases at any level of sophistication. The most basic use would be a DED as a repository of definitions of data elements. Directories and DED/DD software could be added for more developed bases. Large and complex data systems require a data base management system, the subject of the next chapter.

Key words

Classword	Data base administrator
Code file	Data controller

Data dictionary/directory (DD/D)

Data element dictionary/data
 directory system (DED/DD)

Data manager

Data mapping

Designator

Directory

Fixed data elements

Index

Key word

Key word in context (KWIC)

Key word out of context (KWOC)

Label

Logging

Logical record

Physical record

Variable data elements

Discussion questions

1. What are problems of security and privacy in a data base system for business firms?

2. What power accrues to the person responsible for the common data base? How can this power be misused? Can misuse be avoided? How?

3. What is the difference between a DED and a DD system?

4. What software is required (if any) to operate the DED, DD, or DED/DD system? Should such software be developed internally in each firm or be purchased from a vendor or software house?

5. List characteristics that are common in software for these systems:
   a. DED.
   b. DD.
   c. DED/DD.
   What factors should be considered in selecting such software?

6. What special resources are required by a data base administrator?

7. List users of a:
   a. DED.
   b. DD.
   c. DED/DD.
   Give examples of use of each of these systems.

8. List tables in a data directory that are useful to:
   a. A user-manager.
   b. A programmer.
   c. Programs.
   d. A DBA.

9. How can access to a common data base be controlled? Discuss problems of access control.

10. To whom should the DBA report? Explain your answer.

11. A DBA needs staff assistance to manage a large and complex common data base. If only three staff members were assigned to a DBA, what assignments would you recommend each be given?

12. What are the problems that are faced in the use of DED and DD systems?

Exercise

1. Prepare a sheet for a DED for the data element "date of birth." Include in your descriptors the validity rules for each of the subfields for the data element "date of birth." If you feel you do not have sufficient information to do this exercise, then make a reasonable assumption, state it, and justify your assumption. How can this information in the DED be used by a data directory?

Selected annotated bibliography

Adam, Robert G. "The Changing Fabric of Data Base Technology," *ICF Software Business Review* 12, no. 2 (February–March 1983), pp. 38–45.

The author suggests that a DBMS affects the design of information systems, the selection of computers, the organization of data structures, the location of data, and the use of automated information. According to the author, data element dictionaries (not the DBMS) provide the glue that holds together the information resources of an organization.

Another article of interest in this magazine describes how to acquire the best DBMS for you (pp. 84–88).

Allen, Frank, W.; Mary E. Loomis; and Michael V. Manning. "The Integrated Dictionary/Directory System." *ACM Computing Surveys* 14, no. 2 (June 1982), pp. 245–86.

A detailed and somewhat technical discussion of the DED/DD system. Has a bibliography of 41 references and a listing of 32 current DED, DD, and DED/DD systems.

Chorafas, Dimitris. *Databases for Networks and Minicomputers*. New York: Petrocelli Books, 1982, 282 pp.

This book has an excellent coverage on the design, integration, and management of data bases. It is not as specialized as the title implies. Most textbooks on data base design include sections on a DBA as this one does. (See pages 161–70 and 175–88.)

Lyon, John K. *The Data Base Administrator*. New York: John Wiley & Sons, 1976, 170 pp.

The author discusses the responsibilities of a data base administrator and tools used on the job. This book is written by a practicing computer scientist at Honeywell who has written extensively on the subject of data bases.

Martin, James. *An End-User's Guide to Data Bases*. Englewood Cliffs, N.J.: Prentice-Hall, 1981, 144 pp.

Any data base installation that does not model its data in a logical form before doing the physical design is throwing money down the drain, according to Martin. Advice on how this modeling should be done is given in this book. Excellent chapters on ownership of data and considerations that affect machine performance are also included.

Uhrowczki, P. P. "Data Dictionary/Directories." *IBM Systems Journal* 12, no. 4 (1973), pp. 332–50.

One of the earliest and still authoritative articles on the subject. It has a good discussion and diagrams on physical organization, logical organization, and reports generated by DED/DD systems. A good appendix on definitions of data base terms is included.

Walsh, Miles E. "Update on Data Dictionaries." *Journal of Systems Management* 20, no. 8 (August 1978), pp. 28–39.

This article discusses the concept, implementation and use of data dictionaries and DED/DD systems. It has many samples of dictionary reports.

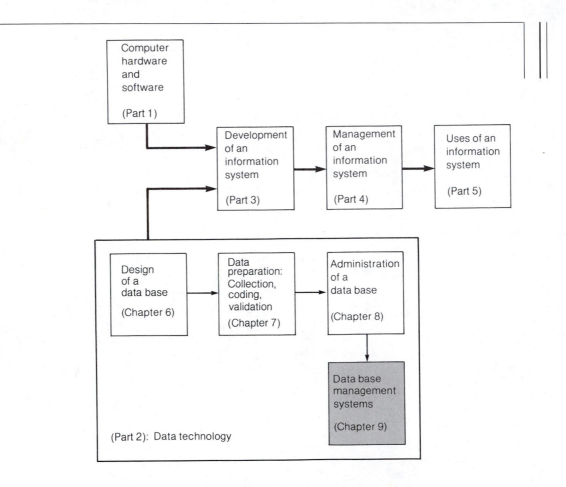

Data base management systems

9

Sooner or later, data base management systems will be on all computers.

Aaron Zornes

Management of large data bases servicing a large number of users is an exceedingly complex task. Fast retrieval by programs using different languages is often needed. Remote access adds to problems of privacy and security of data. Users' programs must be protected should the data base grow and need restructuring. In order to modify a large data base, the logical and physical organization of data must be known. Software to perform these functions is called a **data base management system (DBMS).**

In this chapter, the evolution of DBMS will be traced. The structure, features, and operation of such systems will be discussed, and both resources and problems of implementation will be examined. The chapter is an extension of Chapter 8 since a DBMS is essentially a way of facilitating the control and access of the data base. The subject matter is somewhat technical, but managers should be knowledgeable about this aspect of data technology to participate effectively in both development and implementation of information systems.

Overview of DBMS

The very first computer-based information systems were simple applications using programs with their own sets of data as depicted in Figure 9.1. Though User 1 might have had need of information generated by both application programs A_1 and A_2, the data required by the programs was not integrated. Likewise, application programs A_1 and A_2 both used some common data elements without any integration. Data elements such as *a* and *c* had to be collected, verified, and stored for more than one program, a wasteful duplication of effort.

The inefficiency of independent processing runs was replaced by integrated applications when common data bases were established. This required the corollary development of input/output routines and basic operating systems to manage the data base and to facilitate data access. The schema in Figure 9.2 shows this revised organization. Users no longer had exclusive control of data, but integration meant additional systems using the data were feasible.

With the growth of common data bases and an increase in users, operating systems proved inadequate. Software to provide greater integration of data, com-

Figure 9.1
Early configuration of data by many users

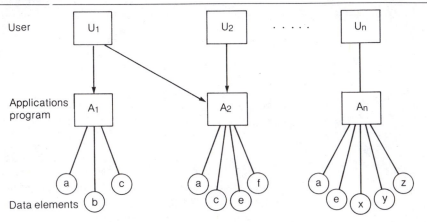

Figure 9.2
Common data base and many users

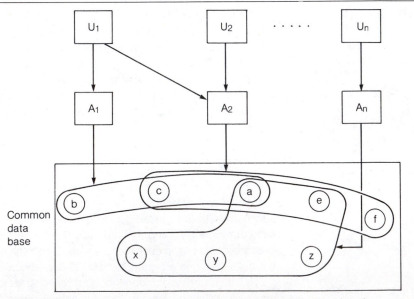

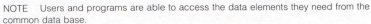
NOTE   Users and programs are able to access the data elements they need from the common data base.

Figure 9.3
DBMS as an interface

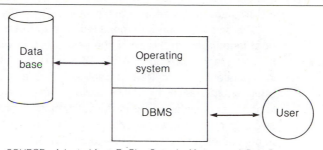

SOURCE   Adapted from R. Clay Sprowls, *Management Data Bases*
(New York: John Wiley & Sons, 1978), pp. 71–72.

plex file structures, and online access was in demand. Additional facilities for data base reorganization, data privacy, breakdown recovery, and independence of applications programs were needed. Supplementary software was developed to fulfill these needs, software called a data base management system (DBMS). The relationship of a DBMS to the data base, operating system, and user is shown in Figure 9.3.

Access to large and complex data bases is facilitated in DBMS by a **data manager.** The manager is not a person as the word suggests, but software which describes the logical and physical organization of the data base and enables manipulation of the base by programmers. This software, an interface between the data base and high level languages (e.g., FORTRAN, COBOL, or PL/1) employed by users, comprises a **data description language (DDL)** and a **data manipulation language (DML).** The word language in DDL and DML is confusing since DDL and DML are interface software, not names of programming languages, such as FORTRAN. The relationship of DDL and DML to the data base and user is shown in Figure 9.4.

What the figure attempts to show diagramatically is that users may write programs in high level languages, DDL and DML convert these instructions into information that the operating system requires, while the data base manager guides

Figure 9.4
The data base manager, DDL, and DML

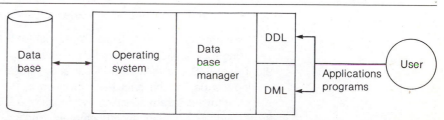

SOURCE   Adapted from R. Clay Sprowls, *Managment Data Bases* (New York: John Wiley & Sons, 1978), pp. 71–72.

the operating system in retrieving the needed data by keeping track of the logical and physical organization of all data in the base. (Other features and functions of a DBMS are described later in this chapter.)

DDL and DML can be embedded as a **guest** in high-level languages, called **host languages.** In this case, the user program would be a mixture of both the host language and statements of DDL and DML. Some independent languages incorporate DDL and DML capabilities. These are called **self-contained languages** (GIS, MARK IV, TDMS, and UL1 are examples). Both host and self-contained languages are used in the batch mode. For terminal use where rapid answers to questions are needed, a query language is used that communicates through a teleprocessing monitor attached to the DBMS.

To date, no standard implementation design for a DBMS has been accepted by original equipment manufacturers (OEMs) or users. Groups which differ in approach have worked on the problem. The **Data Base Task Group (DBTG),** a subcommittee of the Committee on Data Systems Language (CODASYL) composed of volunteer professionals, has concentrated on specifics of design. **GUIDE/SHARE,** a coalition of business and scientific users of IBM equipment, has adopted a more conceptual approach, focusing on determination of requirements based on users' desires. These two groups have both published major sets of reports with proposals for implementation. DDL and DML, described in the preceding section of this text, belong to the data base management system of Data Base Task Group. GUIDE/SHARE proposes DBDL (Data Base Description Language) and DBCL (Data Base Command Language) with equivalent capabilities. The two groups also differ in terminology. Neither has developed a complete and definitive system. For example, Data Base Task Group has identified many areas where software is lacking, such as a device media control language to assist data administrators in assigning storage devices and the need for additional recovery techniques, but has left these areas to the realm of individual implementors.

It will take time for a common stand and a single DBMS implementation design to emerge. Since the work of all parties engaged in DBMS research cannot be covered in a single chapter, the sections that follow concentrate on DBMS design features developed by Data Base Task Group, a group known in the field by its acronym, DBTG.

Operations of a DBMS

The operation of a DBMS is shown in Figure 9.5. Each step is identified by a numbered arrow and takes place in the sequence shown.

1. User program 1 (UP 1) issues a request for the retrieval (or storage) of data using a DML (Data Manipulation Language).
2. The DBMS analyzes the request and extracts structural information regarding the part of the data base involved in the request from a stored **data-structure-diagram** specified by means of a DDL.
3. Based upon request and structure information, the DBMS will call on the operating system to perform one or more read or write operations.

**Figure 9.5
Conceptual DBMS**

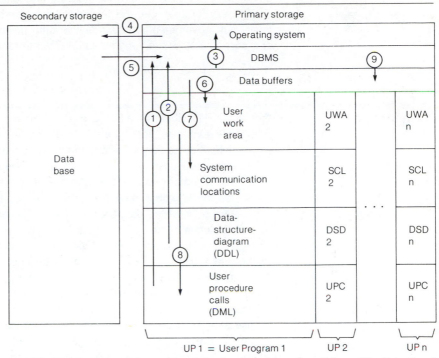

SOURCE This diagram and the text description is adapted from Sven Eriksen, "The Data Base," *Honeywell Computer Journal,* (1971), p. 16; and Harry Katzan, Jr., *Computer Data Management and Data Base Technology* (New York: Van Nostrand Reinhold, 1975), p. 210.

4. The operating system establishes contact with the data base.
5. The operating system may transfer data requested between primary and secondary storage, using one or more data buffers. (A **buffer** is a temporary storage device.)
6. The DBMS will transfer data between data buffers and a particular **user work area** (memory space for user).
7. The DBMS will also transfer various status information on the operation performed. This information is available to the user in some **system communication locations (SCLs)** in the user program.
8. Data will be available for further processing in the user work area.
9. The DBMS will control all data buffers which are common to all programs interrogating the data base. It will also provide the answers and results requested.

In essence, the Data Base Task Group has designed a structure to facilitate the association and retrieval of data. The hierarchy of data has been redefined and new levels added. Many terms, such as *file management* (the mapping of logical files to physical storage space), a capability encompassed in the DBMS, have definitions that are widely accepted by others (see Table 9.1 for sample definitions), but other terms with multiple meanings in the field have specialized definitions. For example, the term *data management* means an administrative position in government, comprehensive data packages to software manufacturers, access methods to vendors, and DBMS to others.

Architecture

One set of definitions in the DBTG report concerns architecture. Applications programmers generally need not view the entire data base, the **schema,** but only a logical subset of the base, a **subschema.** Many applications may invoke the same subschema, subschemas may overlap, or they may even encompass the entire data base. Programmers that deal with a subschema have a **local view** of the data base, not a **global view.** Both local and global views consist of DDL entries that define parts of the data base required. The one-step separation of application from schema allows for logical and physical data independence. That is, changes can be made to the schema of the data base or to the physical structure and representation of the data without affecting applications as a result of the DDL interface. This is of great importance because hardware changes and data modifications occur constantly and they are now insulated from the applications user. Remote terminal users may invoke the global schema or a local subschema by use of a **query language.** Two additional levels of DBMS architecture are defined: the **storage schema** and the **device level.** These latter levels concern the physical representation of data. Figure 9.6 is a graphic representation of the levels of DBMS architecture.

Data relationships are expressed by models in the DBTG's design of a DBMS. To explain model details fully would require a separate textbook on data structures. Briefly, there are three main data models: **hierarchical, relational,** and

Table 9.1
Some definitions from the DBTG (CODASYL)

An Area is a named subdivision of the addressable storage space in the data base and may contain occurrences of records and sets or parts of sets of various types.

A Data-item is the smallest unit of named data. An occurrence of a data-item is a representation of a value.

A Data aggregate is a named collection of data-items within a record.

A Record is a named collection of zero, one, or more data-items or data aggregates.

A Set is a named collection of record types. As such, it establishes the characteristics of an arbitrary number of occurrences of the named set. Each set type specified in the schema must have one record type declared as its OWNER and one or more record types declared as its MEMBER records. Each occurrence of a set must contain an arbitrary number of occurrences of each of its member record types.

SOURCE   "CODASYL Data Description Language," *NBS Handbook* (Washington, D.C.: Government Printing Office, January 1974). This source stresses the evolutionary nature of these specifications.

**Figure 9.6
Levels of DBMS architecture**

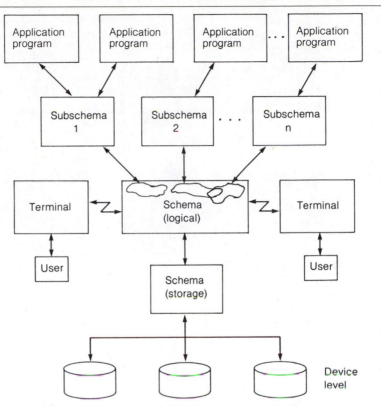

SOURCE   S. M. Dean, *Fundamentals of Data Base Systems* (Rochelle Park, N.J.: Hayden Book Co., 1977), p. 51.

network.[1] Each model is evaluated by the user for its degree of data independence, for the danger of creating anomalies, for performance, and other criteria of relevance to use in determining which model is appropriate for each application.

A data model not only represents the schema but also subschemas. This is shown in Figure 9.7, where three applications (manufacturing, financial, and personnel) illustrate model use. The users and language facilities at each level are also identified.

---

[1] For an early survey and comparison of data models, see *ACM Computing Surveys* 8, no. 1 (March 1976). For more recent discussions, see chapters devoted to data models in the many texts reviewed in the annotated bibliography at the end of this chapter. For a breezy survey of data model selection, see Christopher Coulson, "Putting the Pieces Together— Solving the Puzzle of How to Buy the Best DBMS for You," *ICP Software Business Review* 2, no. 1 (February/March 1983), pp. 84–88.

Figure 9.7
DBMS architecture, showing data models, users, and language facilities

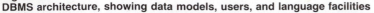
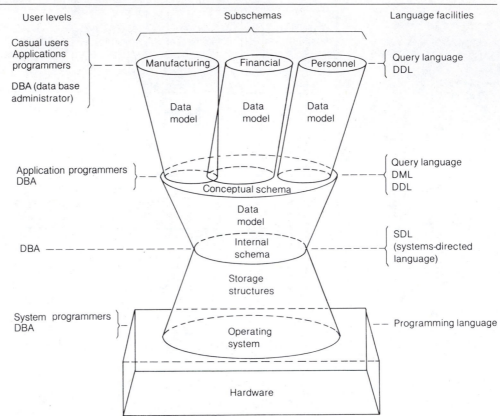

SOURCE   Adapted from D. C. Tsichritzis and I. H. Lechovsky, *Data Base Management System* (New York: Academic Press, 1977), p. 97.

Features and functions of DBMS

Two important features of the DBTG design for a DBMS have already been mentioned in this chapter: data independence and data models. Other features and a list of DBMS functions appear in Table 9.2. The data manager, which performs many of the support functions listed in the table, has been well described by Gordon C. Everest.

The database manager is the single, controlling door through which all access to the database is accomplished. It is the run-time module providing data services for programs while they are in execution; it is the module which responds to all requests to access and manipulate data in the database; it is the security guard which intercepts and checks all such requests for proper authorization as well as syntactic and semantic legality; and it is the auditor who keeps a log of all events and changes affecting the database. Providing a single door for the availability functions is desirable for improved performance, but it is mandatory for integrity control.[2]

Data base administrator

Although a **data base administrator (DBA)** has many duties (see Chapter 8), administering the DBMS is a major responsibility. For a large DBMS, a staff will be required since no one individual can perform all the necessary activities. The duties of a DBA and staff in a DBMS environment are listed in Table 9.3. Most

Table 9.2
Features and functions of DBMS

Data creation and structure
    Data definition, creation, and revision
    Data models
    Data independence

Support
    Access control
    Security
    Auditing
    Integrity control
    Performance monitoring
    Usage monitoring
    Data base administrator

Retrieval
    Interrogation
    User facilities

Table 9.3
Duties of DBA and staff in a DBMS environment

Design and administration
    Define schemas and subschemas
    Select and maintain data model
    Select and maintain DBMS software

Administration
    Liaison with users
    Training and assistance of users

Operation
    Formulate and enforce procedures for security and privacy
    Initiate and enforce procedures for recovery and integrity
    Define, create, update, and retire data

Monitoring
    Measure and monitor performance of DBMS resources
    Log and monitor usage of DBMS resources
    Schedule usage
    Monitor security threats

[2]Gordon C. Everest, "Data Base Systems Tutorial," *Readings in Management Information Systems* (New York: McGraw-Hill, 1976), p. 170. Also, see Jacob Karszel et al., "Integrity Checking in Data Base Systems," *Information Systems* 8, no. 2 (April–June 1983), pp. 125–36 and E. B. Fernandez et al., *Database Security and Integrity,* Reading, Mass.: Addison-Wesley, 1981, 320 pp.

Figure 9.8
Areas of DBA responsibility in a DBMS environment

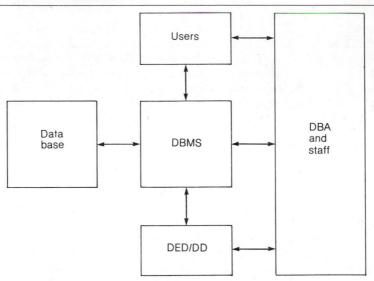

of the activities are self-explanatory but a few comments about integrity and backup will be helpful.

Integrity of data is a broad concept. Data must be accurate, complete, and continuous, which means that it must be protected from failure of the system. This integrity can be achieved by control over validation criteria and parameters, control over updating, and procedures for **backup** and recovery, should data be lost due to midstream termination of transactions. Some systems make periodic backup copies of the data base and restart from the backup point in the event of failure. A DBA must study the vulnerability of the data and make a cost-benefit analysis of possible recovery procedures and then initiate and enforce procedures to protect the data base.

Figure 9.8 is a representation of a DBA's responsibilities in a DBMS environment.

Retrieval

DBMS retrieval may be in the batch mode or online responses to queries. The language in which queries are made will depend on the type of query and the class of user demanding information. The query itself may be one of several types. These are discussed below.

Types of queries

A **projection query** is a request for a whole set of data elements. For example: List the names of all sales representatives. A query might also be for a listing of values for a data element that have one attribute in common. This is called **map-**

ping. An example of this type of query would be: What are the names of all sales representatives in California? Or, what are the names of all sales representatives who sold more than 100 percent of their quotas?

Boolean operators like OR/AND/NOT can be added to the listing request. A **Boolean query** might be: List sales representatives in California who did not sell more than 100 percent of their quotas.

A user may require retrieval of information on a whole set of related data elements. This is called a **selective query.** An example would be: Give the record of sales representative John Dole.

Values of given **functions** can also be queried. For example: Print the sum of sales made. Software for driving frequently used functions (MAXIMUM, MINIMUM, AVERAGE, RANGE, and SUM, for example) are available on call by programs.

Combination queries actually involve two outputs, one being input for the other. For example: Find the sales representatives who sold more than 100 percent of their quotas and print the names of their sales territories.

There are other types of queries that require some mathematical sophistication. For example, an understanding of predicate calculus, and knowledge of programming and the data base. These technical queries are used less frequently by management and so will not be discussed.

Query languages

The characteristics and requirements of languages suitable for queries of a DBMS have been the subject of much research.[3] Managers with programming expertise may use host or self-contained languages for information retrieval but nonprogrammers, dependent on intermediaries to translate their requests into machine language, have urged development of computer-directed languages or natural language software. Research has shown that artificial query languages, such as SEQUEL, may actually be more effective than natural languages for retrieval purposes. For example, Schneidermann, one researcher in the field, has found that artificial languages structure queries so that users are far less likely to pose unanswerable questions than when using natural languages. His conclusions are worth quoting.

> These results should not be interpreted as a condemnation of natural language usage, but as an aid in determining which applications are suitable for natural language front ends and what training users should be given. User knowledge of the applications domain seems to be critical: without this prerequisite, natural language usage would be extremely difficult. Secondly, user

---

[3] See Phyllis Reisner, "Human Factors Studies of Database Query Languages: A Survey and Assessment," *Computing Surveys* 13, no. 1 (March 1981), pp. 13–32, and Charles Welty and David W. Stemple, "Human Factors Comparison of a Procedural and Nonprocedural Query Language," *Transactions on Database Systems* 6 no. 4 (December 1981), pp. 626–49. More references on query languages appear in Chapter 20 when query language use is discussed.

knowledge of the structure of the data in the computer and what each item means appears to be vital. Finally, experience in asking questions against a specific database is probably helpful. Thus the ideal candidate for natural language usage may be the experienced frequent users of a manual information system, but these users are likely to appreciate the simplicity, brevity, and precision of a structured query language. The casual user with little knowledge of the application area, understanding of the data structure, and experience in posing queries may find natural language facilities more confusing. Realistic applications for natural language would be situations where people have familiarity with the application area, data structure, and queries, but are infrequent users. Typical situations that fit this description include library card catalogs, airline schedules, or banking transactions. More research is necessary to support these hypotheses.[4]

In retrieving information, questions must be framed in the same form as data is stored in the data base. This is true regardless of the query language used. For example, the answer to the question, "Who was hired before 1980?" would require that values for the data element "year of hire" be stored in the data base. If the question were rephrased as "Who has served more than 10 years?" the system would be unable to answer. Thus the structure of the data base does affect the validity of queries.

Classes of users

No single query language is appropriate for all users of a large information system since users vary in background, mathematical knowledge, and programming skills. Data processing professionals concerned with efficiency in processing generally employ host or self-contained languages. The type of information requested requires mathematical knowledge and familiarity with the data base. Skilled, frequent users are generally less concerned with machine efficiency than with minimizing time spent programming. These users frame Boolean or combination-type queries using computer-directed languages. Clerks and other users at the operational level with little or no knowledge of programming are dependent on the computer-directed mode for listings, built-in functions, selection, and projection-type queries. Casual users are the most difficult group to please. These users are generally intimidated by computers, preferring that human intermediaries retrieve information on their behalf. If they must query the system directly, they favor natural languages or natural-like languages. This class of user needs help framing requests in terms understood by the system, help that the prompting of the dialogue mode can provide. Of the four groups of users mentioned, this group is potentially the largest.

---

[4] Ben Schneidermann, "Improving the Human Factors Aspect of Database Interactions," *ACM Transactions on Data Base Systems* 3, no. 4 (December 1978), p. 437, © 1978, Association for Computing Machinery, Inc. Reprinted by permission.

Figure 9.9
Costs and stages of EDP evolution

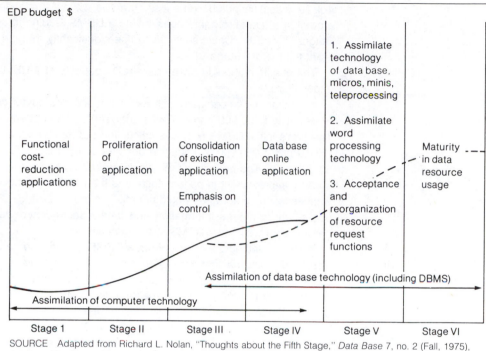

SOURCE Adapted from Richard L. Nolan, "Thoughts about the Fifth Stage," *Data Base* 7, no. 2 (Fall, 1975), pp. 6 and 9.

Costs and benefits of a DBMS

Personnel is one high-cost component in a DBMS. Another is hardware, especially for storage, although the unit cost of storage is dropping significantly. Yet 500,000 characters of main memory for a DBMS are not unusual, and three times more extra disk memory is required for a DBMS than for an information system without a DBMS. Hardware for this much storage represents a considerable investment. And DBMS requires a larger CPU. Another expensive component is DBMS software. In addition, DBMS processing is costly. A study at Ford Motor Co. showed that 70 percent of instructions executed involved DBMS overhead. All of the costs of a DBMS can be reliably measured. It is well established that EDP budgets increase significantly with implementation of data base technology. Figure 9.9 illustrates the upward shift in cost during the stages of EDP evolution. This figure is based on a hypothesis of Nolan regarding growth stages of information systems.[5] Note that EDP expenses rise sharply at the end of Stage II and

---

[5] Richard L. Nolan, "Thoughts about the Fifth Stage," *Data Base* 7, no. 2 (Fall, 1975), pp. 4–10. This subject is discussed again in Chapter 21. For a more recent view by Nolan, see his *Managing the Data Resource Function,* 2d ed. New York: West Publishing, 1982, pp. 8–20.

during part of Stage III. The proliferation of applications at this stage means maintenance becomes cumbersome, and development starts getting out of control. New applications become less attractive without a change in technology. At a point in Stage III, organizations initiate a DBMS, adding to the system through Stages III and IV. Costs continue to rise significantly through Stage V, leveling off at the mature Stage VI.

The question should now be asked: Do benefits of a DBMS warrant such an expenditure?

A representative company with a medium-scale computer and a budget of approximately $750,000 annually was analyzed by McFadden and Suvey in 1978. The firm's initial DBMS cost was calculated at $525,000: the 5-year total cost of DBMS as $1,080,000. Cumulative benefits during this period were estimated at $3,289,250.[6] The benefits were calculated from increased sales, savings in production, improvement in performance, and the reduction of operating costs. A firm with less diverse activities would benefit less from a DBMS. Companies with few users, where shared information and data independence were not major concerns, might well find a DBMS system uneconomical.[7]

However, intangible benefits from a DBMS should also be taken into account. Improved discipline that results from company efforts to organize and support DBMS is hard to measure. Integration of data and online retrieval, two additional benefits of a DBMS, are also hard to quantify. We also lack the tools to give a dollar value to improved availability, accessibility, and timeliness of information.

It has certainly been demonstrated that a DBMS raises EDP to a high level of sophistication, a level that justifies the expense in many business applications. Data base technology may even prove to have far reaching effects on society. James Martin predicts that:

> In centuries hence, historians will look back to the coming of computer data banks and their associated facilities as a step which changed the nature of the evolution of society, perhaps eventually having a greater effect on the human condition than even the invention of the printing press.[8]

Implementation

Management must first define its decision system and information needs in operational terms so that these needs can be adequately addressed by a DBMS. Then installation of the DBMS can take place. Overcoming organizational resistance to the new system and promoting dialogue and cooperation between technicians and users are two areas of implementation that test managerial skill. As E. Sibley, chairman of CODASYL, has stated, "There are hardly any technical problems involved with installing a DBMS, only people problems and managerial

---

[6]Fred R. McFadden and James R. Suvey, "Costs and Benefits of a Database System," *Harvard Business Review* 56, no. 1 (1978), p. 138.
[7]For a good discussion on not using a DBMS, see George Schlussel, "When Not to Use a Data Base," *Datamation,* 21, no. 11 (November 1975), pp. 82, 91, 98.
[8]James Martin, *Computer Data-Base Organization* (Englewood Cliffs, N.J.: Prentice-Hall, 1977), p. 2.

problems."[9] The subject of human resistance to computer technology in general is a subject discussed in detail in Chapter 17.

Finding technical personnel to run the system poses additional difficulties since the supply of experienced data base technicians has not kept pace with the demand. DBAs, analysts, and system programmers are all scarce commodities. Training technicians in-house is both time-consuming and costly. It takes 4–8 months for a programmer to learn to use a DBMS, and 6–9 months to turn an analyst into a DBA.

When to implement

The decision to implement a DBMS should be based on a cost/benefit analysis. The need for a DBMS is generally indicated when a firm needs at least three of the following:

1. An integrated data environment.
2. Rapid retrieval of data from large files.
3. A query/update language for use at terminals.
4. Sophisticated backup and recovery procedures.
5. Elaborate privacy/security protection.
6. Handling of complex data structures.

Preparing for implementation

Once a decision is made to implement a DBMS, management should take steps to ensure success of the new system. These include:

1. Authorizing a central authority with total control over data definitions and all DBMS-related activities.
2. Identifying organizational and transitional problems on which management should focus to minimize company disruption and resistance to the new system.
3. Establishing auditing standards and auditing independence.
4. Instituting DBMS training for users and all levels of management.
5. Anticipating privacy and security issues and establishing policies and procedures for control.

Growth of DBMS

The use of data base management systems is steadily on the rise. The first system was introduced at General Electric in 1961. By 1970, there were 100 users of DBMS; by 1975, 300, or roughly 10 percent of data processing organizations.[10] Some experts have predicted that by the late 1980s, 75 percent of data processing organizations will be DBMS users.

This increase can be explained in part by the decreasing cost of minis and the growing availability of DBMS software for minis.[11] Both factors make a DBMS at-

---

[9] From a paper presented at the 1977 IFIP Congress and quoted in *EDP Analyzer,* 16, no. 5 (May 1978), p. 3.
[10] Schlussel, "When Not to Use a Data Base," p. 83.
[11] Armond Inselberg, "Database Management Systems," *Mini-Micro Systems* 16, no. 14 (December 1983), pp. 193–205.

tractive to small businesses.[12] Not all minis, however, run large data base management systems efficiently because of their small word size and range of instructions. Some of the sophisticated features of data handling must, therefore, be sacrificed. But since small businesses do not always have large data files, the reduced capabilities (for example, restricted query capabilities and less data independence) do not adversely affect operations. Many of the stripped features may not have been applicable to a small business environment in the first place.

The availability of DBMS software for small organizations does not permit firms to skip the agonizing early stages of EDP evolution depicted in **Nolan's growth hypothesis** (Figure 9.9).[13] Experience has shown that firms trying to leapfrog directly into Nolan's third or fourth stage lack the proficiency to implement the requisite technology. The organizational and technical experience of coherent systems planning that is gained in Stages I and II is needed to absorb the "upheaval factor" of a DBMS and to control the new system.

However, advances in data base technology may make leapfrogging a possibility in the future. Computer equipment with operating systems integrated with DBMS are being planned; and special separate CPUs to control access to the data base are envisioned. Such equipment would let firms leap to Stages III or IV without experiencing previous growth phases. Also projected is a computer specially designed for a DBMS, a **data base machine,**[14] that would have optimum performance and data security designed in its architecture.

Distributed data bases and distributed DBMSs will be more common in the future.[15] (These subjects will be discussed in Chapter 18.) Deciding what data to distribute and what data to keep centralized will pose new problems for management as will control of distributed data bases. There is also hope that the near future will see the development of more models, additional generalized languages for DBMS, such as EUFTG (End user facilities) and DBAWG (Management tools for DBA), standards for data technology, and DBMS oriented toward the casual user.

Summary and Conclusions

Interface between a large and complex data base and the user can be provided by a DBMS. This interface necessitates hardware, software, and personnel re-

---

[12] Irene S. Nesbit, "DBMS on Personal Computers—Big Power in a Small Package," *Computer Decisions* 16, no. 5 (April 1984), pp. 178–84.

[13] For a more recent view on the age hypothesis, see R. L. Nolan, "Managing the Crises in Data Processing," *Harvard Business Review,* 57, no. 2 (March–April 1979), pp. 115–126

[14] This subject is discussed in Jan Snyders, "DBMS: The More You Get, The More You Want," *Computer Decisions* 10, no. 2 (February 1984), pp. 124–46 and in Terry Bridges, "Data Base Machine: What and Why," *Data Management* 20, no. 11 (November 1982), pp. 14–16.

[15] For more discussion on this subject, see W. F. Franla et al., "Real-Time Distributed Computer Systems," in Marshall C. Yovick ed., *Advances in Computers,* New York: Academia Press, 1981, pp. 47–48 or Benjamin W. Wah, *Data Management on Distributed Data Bases,* Ann Arbor, Michigan: University Microfilm International, 1981, 291 pp.

sources. Hardware requirements include more storage and processing capability by the CPU and terminals than are needed for non-DBMS information systems. The software consists of a data base manager, an extension of the operating system, and both DDL and DML to provide data independence, user access to the base, and a vehicle for schema and subschema description.

A DBMS is used to request listings or responses to Boolean queries, projection queries, selective queries, built-in functions, or combination queries. Users with programming knowledge may employ high level languages (like COBOL, FORTRAN, or PL/1, which host DDL and DML), or self-contained languages for retrieval. The nonprogrammer can retrieve information through a human intermediary (expensive in pesonnel cost), or may use a natural language (expensive in CPU time and not very effective) or a computer-directed language. Casual users favor natural languages. Clarification dialogues to help frame requests in terms understood by the computer are helpful when casual users query the system.

A data base administrator supervises the hardware, software, and personnel of a DBMS. A staff of assistants may be required if the system is large. The duties of a DBA include control of the DED/DD system and formulating definitions for schemas and subschemas. Monitoring security, privacy, integrity, operations, and user liaison are other areas of DBA responsibility. The job requires authority over all data definitions and all DBMS activities.

The cost of a DBMS includes the acquisition of hardware, specialized software, and technical personnel, the latter often proving the most expensive and scarce resource of all. Some of the benefits of a DBMS are largely intangible: data independence, fast retrieval, and better integration of data. Factors such as the amount of shared data and the diversity of functions are more important than the size of the data base when assessing the need for a DBMS.

The availability of DBMS software for inexpensive minicomputers has recently made DBMS feasible for small businesses. The main constraint is that small businesses often lack the organization and technical expertise with EDP to successfully implement a data base management system.

Though use of DBMS is on the rise, many firms are hesitant to make the large capital and organizational commitment required. They prefer to await the emergence of DBMS standards, the abatement of debate on data models, and the production of data base machines. At the present time, much research is being conducted on DBMS topics, including research on query languages, graphic interfaces, data base definitions, data base restructuring, data and applications migration, and distributed data bases. Results should be forthcoming in the next few years. The 1980–90s will undoubtedly see widespread and profitable use of DBMS in business and industry.

Figure 9.10 is a summary diagram of activities related to the data base, activities discussed in the preceding chapters of Part 2. This diagram shows both the sequence of activities in establishing a common data base and the supplementary software and personnel needed to administer the base. Information systems, the development of which are described in Part 3, are based on data technology.

Figure 9.10
Activitives related to a data base

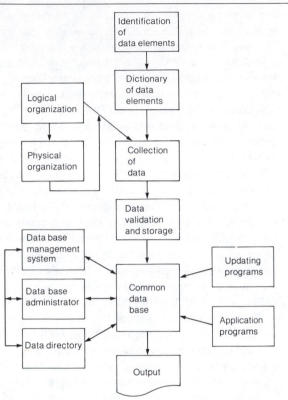

Keywords

Backup	Function
Boolean query	Global view
Buffer	Guest language
Combination query	GUIDE/SHARE
Data base administrator (DBA)	Hierarchical model
Data base machine	Host language
Data base management system (DBMS)	Integrity
	Local view
Data Base Task Group (DBTG)	Mapping
Data description language (DDL)	Network model
Data manager	Nolan's growth curves
Data manipulation language (DML)	Projection query
Data-structure-diagram	Query language
Device level	Relational model

Schema
Selective query
Self-contained language
Storage schema

Subschema
System communication location
  (SCL)
User work area (UWA)

Discussion questions

1. What is the difference between the users' view of the data base and the programmers' view of the data base?

2. What is the difference between a schema and a subschema?

3. What is the difference between the logical schema and the storage schema in a data model? Identify the user and the language facility for each.

4. What is the role of the DBA in relation to a DBMS?

5. What are the main components of a DBMS?

6. Under what conditions in a business is a DBMS justifiable?

7. What are the managerial implications of a DBMS?

8. What is the role of a DBMS in a EDP system?

9. List the advantages and limitations of a DBMS seen from the viewpoint of a:
   a. User of output.
   b. DBA.
   c. Programmer.
   d. Data clerk.

10. What are the role of the DBTG and GUIDE/SHARE in the development and standardization of a DBMS? Have they helped or hindered standardization, or have they just added to the confusion surrounding the DBMS?

11. What is the role of a data model in a DBMS? Why are there so many different models? Does it add to flexibility and choice for the user, or merely add to the uncertainty and confusion surrounding the DBMS?

12. List types of query languages you would use for each of the following situations:
   a. Clerk preparing and retrieving data.
   b. Manager requiring output.
   c. Client retrieving relevant information.
   d. Programmer accessing data base.
   e. Engineer using data base.

13. Is it desirable to have a natural language to access the data base? Why? What are the limitations?

14. How does the role of a DBA differ with and without a DBMS?

15. Explain the three main disadvantages or limitations of a DBMS.

16. What are the social implications of widespread DBMS usage in business?

Exercise

1. Draw a diagram showing the interrelationship of the following:
   a. Data manager.
   b. Data base.
   c. DDL.
   d. User.
   e. Query language.
   f. High level language.

Selected annotated bibliography

ACM Computing Surveys 8, no. 1 (March 1976).

This is a special issue on data base management systems. It has an introductory survey of the evolution of DBMS followed by detailed discussions on three data models: relational, CODASYL, and hierarchical. A final article is a comparison of the relational and CODASYL data models.

The articles are by experts in the field and written for the nontechnical person. Highly recommended reading.

Atre, S. *Data Base: Structured Techniques for Design, Performance, and Management*. New York: John Wiley & Sons, 1980, 442 pp.

Atre discusses the design, implementation, administration, and performance of models. Two good case studies are included: a bank and a university.

Bradley, James. *Introduction to Data Base Management in Business*. New York: Holt, Rinehart and Winston, 1983, 606 pp.

This book discusses the concept and design of data base models. An unusual chapter on data base teleprocessing is also included.

Bridges, Terry. "Database Machines—What and Why." *Data Management* 20, no. 11 (November 1982), pp. 14–16.

Bridges argues that data base machines can relieve systems of using up computing resources to handle a conventional DBMS.

Everest, Gordon C. "Database Management Systems—A Tutorial. In *Readings in Management Information Systems,* edited by G. B. Davis and G. C. Everest. New York: McGraw-Hill, 1976.

An excellent tutorial written by a member of the CODASYL Systems Committee who authored the *Feature Analysis of Generalized Data Base Management Systems*. Discusses the concepts and functions of a DBMS.

Hawryszkiewycz, I. T. *Database Analysis and Design*. Chicago: Science Research Associates, 1984, 578 pp.

An excellent text on models, design, evaluaton, and choosing design methodologies.

Holland, Robert H. "The Executive Guide to Data Base Management Systems." *ICP Software Business Review,* 2, no. 2 (February–March 1983), pp. 46–54.

The author suggests that DBMS technology harnessed and integrated with other electronic technologies will produce 100-fold jumps in productivity in the next decade. A checklist of what to do to achieve such a productivity jump is included.

King, Judy M. *Evaluating Data Base Management Systems*. N.Y.: Van Nostrand Reinhold 1981, 296 pp.

As of 1981, this is the only book describing DBMS from the viewpoint of applications for an organization. The emphasis is on determining when to use a DBMS, how to justify costs, and implementation. The book is valuable, though has a bias toward IBM.

Kroenke, David. *Database Processing*. Chicago: Science Research Associates, 1983, 605 pp.

This book concerns data base fundamentals, their design, and implementation. Relational and CODASYL data models are discussed. A useful description of a DBA is also included (pages 536–54). Appendixes discuss Data Language/I, TOTAL/IMAGE, and MicroRIM.

Martin, James. *Computer Data-Base Organization*. 2d ed. Englewood Cliffs, N.J.: Prentice-Hall, 1977.

A well-organized textbook on both physical and logical data structures and DBMS. The tracing through problems using different colors makes it easy to follow. It places technical material in boxes as supplementary reading without breaking the continuity of the text.

"Planning for DBMS Conversions." *EDP Analyzer* 16, no. 5 (May 1978), pp. 1–13.

Discusses case studies and "war-stories" on DBMS conversions. Outlines steps for implementing a DBMS.

Spiegler, Israel. "MIS and DBMS: Where Does One End and the Other Start?" *Journal of Systems Management* 34, no. 6 (June 1983), pp. 34–42.

The author classifies the purposes of information systems four ways: data bank, prediction, decision making, and decision taking. He then examines how these purposes affect the data base, a DBMS, decision-support systems, and management. Helpful diagrams are included.

DEVELOPMENT OF AN INFORMATION SYSTEM

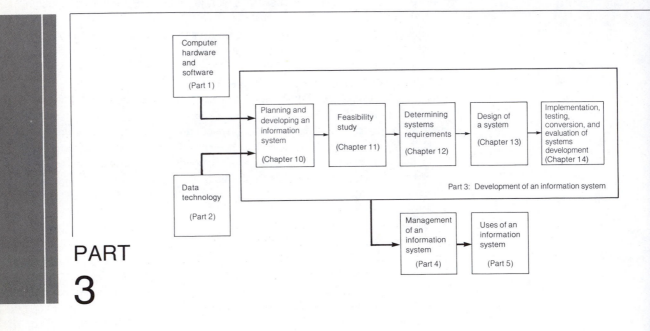

PART

3

Parts 1 and 2 discussed hardware, software, data, and telecommunications. All are components of information systems. This section, Part 3, tells how to mobilize these components to provide the informational needs of a business organization.

System development takes careful planning. First, the output needed for decision making must be ascertained. Then a feasibility study needs to be conducted to determine whether or not a system can be designed to produce the desired output given the firm's objectives and constraints. Systems specifications must next be defined in operational terms. Computer programs need to be written, forms for collecting data designed, and operational procedures established. Once the system is tested and the results are satisfactory, conversion must take place. This entire process is called the development of an information system, the subject of Part 3. A schematic view of the chapters in this section is shown in diagram form.

Chapter 10 introduces the reader to information system development, providing a general overview of planning and developmental activities. Subsequent chapters in Part 3 discuss development in detail. The feasibility study is the subject of Chapter 11, Chapter 12 discusses determination of systems requirements, Chapter 13, design, and the final chapter, Chapter 14, deals with implementation, testing, and conversion.

Planning and developing an information system

10

Here and elsewhere we shall not obtain the best insight into things unless we actually see them growing from the beginning.

Aristotle

A computing time of a few seconds is all that is required for many reports produced by information systems. But to generate these same reports may take months or years of development. This is because the planning, design, and implementation of every computer output requires a set of activities that must be performed in a predetermined sequence.

Planning **information systems (IS)** and the cycle of their development are the subjects of this chapter. Each main development activity will be introduced and those activities for which the manager in a business has prime responsibility will be identified. This chapter presents an overview of developmental activities. Subsequent chapters will discuss the activities in detail.

Systems planning
(Activity 10–20)

Planning is a framework for orderly development of information systems. Generally a planning officer or a special committee is assigned to the task of planning (often called the MIS Committee, Steering Committee, or some similar title). The size of an organization, its experience with EDP, and the complexity of the firm's information systems will determine whether an individual or a committee does the planning. Planning committees are usually composed of functional vice-presidents who will be users, computer center professionals, and representatives from top management.

Inputs that planners must consider are shown in Figure 10.1. User's information needs, both unfulfilled and projected needs, must be studied. The competitive environment should be analyzed. What information and facilities would be competitively advantageous? Technological trends should be evaluated and political realities assessed. Are there legal and regulatory restraints? What will people accept? What is feasible, given the corporate power structure? In addition,

223

**Figure 10.1
Inputs to the planning process**

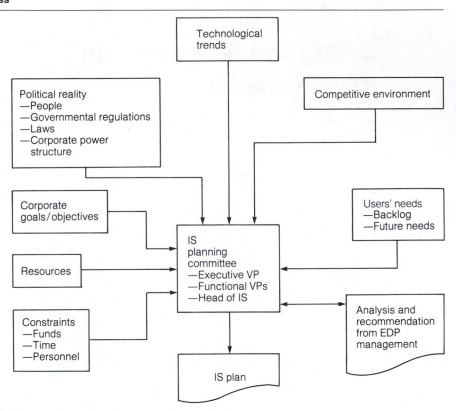

the firm's goals, resources, and constraints should be reviewed. Planners must also consider planning priorities. Given limited resources, what information projects should be implemented first?

Planning will include long-range ideas for system development looking four to five years in the future. (The fast pace of technological advance in the computer field limits the usefulness of planning much farther ahead.) Medium-range plans (two to four years in advance) and short-term plans (to cover a one-year period) will also be formulated.

A planning document is then submitted to corporate management. This document should include a statement of corporate objectives and should outline how information technology can serve these objectives. Projects for information systems development should be described in order of priority. Personnel requirements, equipment, facilities, expenditures, and reorganization to implement proposed projects should be detailed in this document.

Corporate management makes the decision of whether or not to implement proposals of planners. When a given project is given the green light, the development cycle of an information system is initiated. The main activities in this cycle are shown in Figure 10.2. Although the figure does not show recycling (an integral part of development), it is a useful frame of reference in the discussion of development activities that follows.

The development process

Feasibility study (Activity 20–30, Figure 10.2)

Once a decision to add a new system is made, the next stage in a system's development is a **feasibility study.** The study will determine whether the problem can be solved by traditional manual methods or whether a computerized information system is indeed necessary. If the latter, different approaches to a solution are formulated and the organizational environment is checked for constraints. Many alternatives are eliminated at this point as unfeasible. For each approach that is feasible within the given constraints, the costs and benefits are identified and evaluated. Then the best alternative in the judgment of the manager is selected for implementation.

Specifying systems requirements (Activity 30–40)

Following the decision to implement a solution, the problem needs to be defined more precisely than it was in the feasibility study. At this stage the objectives, policies, and constraints of the user must also be stated completely and in operational terms. These statements and the detailed job specification constitute the **systems requirement statement.**

Design (Activity 40–50) and implementation (Activity 50–60)

The systems requirement statement is the basis of a blueprint developed by a system analyst detailing the following: **data base, physical preparation, procedures,** and **program solutions.** The design and subsequent implementation of each of these four areas can sometimes be done in parallel. The complete system is an assembly of all four implemented parts of the blueprint.

Data base

The contents of the data base must be determined after a careful analysis of the output needs and must be responsive to the changing environment and needs of

**Figure 10.2
Development of an information system**

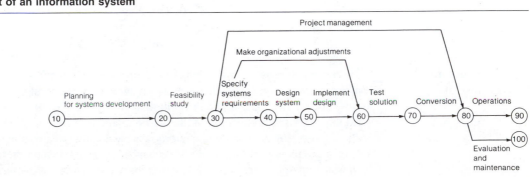

the user. Too much data leads to inefficiency in storage and processing; too little will lead to ineffectiveness because the desired output will not be available. The data must be organized and stored so that it can be readily retrieved and used as a shared resource by many managers. This sharing across division and department lines complicates data base design specifications because not all users will have the same needs for reliability, validity, integrity, and security of data.

Physical preparation

The **physical preparation** for a system is primarily the selection and installation of equipment (that is, computer equipment and peripherals). This usually involves technical choices made by specialists and consultants, but the final decision on equipment procurement must be made by the manager since this requires a large commitment of funds (one-time and recurring costs) and the allocation of space.

Procedures

A **procedure** states how, why, and when a function is to be performed. Procedures for the information system need to be designed, implemented, and tested. The manager who is responsible for procedures when the system is fully operational should participate in this developmental activity.

Programs

Programs are computer instructions prepared by professional programmers. However, managers, with the aid of analysts, must specify what the programs should achieve and must define the decision rules necessary in reaching the solution. This requires some knowledge on the part of management of program capabilities and limitations.

Organizational adjustments (Activity 30–60)

The implementation of an information system requires **organizational adjustments.** These might encompass transferring, adding, retraining, or firing personnel. Such changes may result in a broadened (or narrowed) span of control for managers and alterations in the organization chart of the business. This activity, involving user personnel, need not wait until the technical design and implementation of the system are completed. It can and should be done in parallel with Activities 30–40, 40–50, and 50–60. This helps reduce the overall time needed to prepare the system for testing.

Testing the solution (Activity 60–70)

Once the solution is programmed, procedures prepared, physical preparation completed, and organizational changes implemented, the system is ready for **testing.** There are many approaches to testing. The new system may be tested while the old is still operational, or it may be tested by a pilot system on a small scale. Testing may also be done in progressively comprehensive stages. Another testing approach would be the use of statistical sampling; testing of sample data from which inferences can be made about the whole system. Whichever method is used, the test results are then compared with the specifications stated in the determination of the systems requirement stage. If unsatisfactory, the system is redeveloped. If satisfactory, the system is ready for operation.

Conversion (Activity 70–80)

Conversion is often the most traumatic phase of developing a new system. At this stage, personnel, procedures, manuals, forms, files, and equipment of the old system are changed to meet the requirements of the new system. The dislocations, readjustment, and forging of new relationships make conversion a difficult but crucial activity in the new systems development.

Project management (Activity 30–80)

By the time the conversion of a new system is complete, a large number of activities have been performed. For each main activity shown in Figure 10.1, many subactivities will have taken place. For example, installing new equipment might require a false floor and rewiring of the electrical system. One actual case showed 242 subactivities related to equipment installation alone. Each subactivity needs to be scheduled, allocated resources, and completed within time constraints. The entire set of activities and subactivities from the feasibility study through conversion needs planning and coordination. This is called **project management.** In developing large information systems, project control techniques, such as the Gantt chart, CPM, or PERT, will be required. These techniques utilize computer programs to calculate the **critical path,** or paths of development, that is, the sequence of activities that cannot be delayed without prolonging the entire project.

Operation (Activity 80–90) and evaluation (Activity 80–100)

Once the system is operational, it should be evaluated. If evaluation indicates that the system is unsatisfactory, the system must be **redeveloped.** Once redeveloped, the system is reevaluated. The cycle of evaluation and redevelopment continues until the system is operating efficiently and effectively. Reevaluation also occurs periodically throughout the life of the system as part of regularly scheduled maintenance checks.

Recycling

Evaluation is not the only stage in the development process that may trigger **recycling.** A negative answer to the questions, ''Is the proposed system feasible?'' or ''Are test results satisfactory?'' will also lead to redevelopment of the system. Figure 10.1 does not identify the points where logical decisions leading to recycling are taken because this is a PERT chart and the universally accepted notation of PERT charts does not show recycling although it is implied. Recycling, also referred to as **looping,** can be shown using GERT (Graphic Evaluation Review Technique), but since there are not as many computer programs for implementing a GERT chart as there are for CPM or PERT, GERT is used less frequently. To identify logical decisions leading to recycling in the development process of an information system, see Figure 10.2

Figure 10.3
Flowchart for systems development and redevelopment process

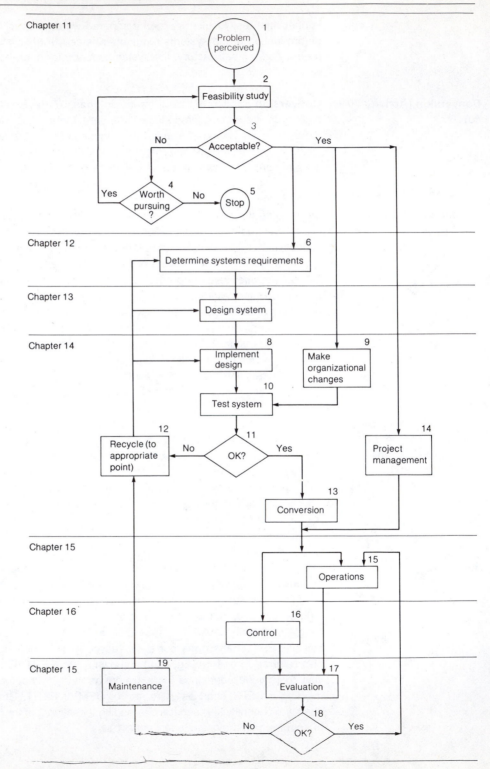

The perception of the need of a new system (Circle 1 in Figure 10.3) may come from the manager or the system analyst. The need initiates a feasibility study (Box 2). The proposed system is then tested for feasibility (Symbol 3). If unsatisfactory (NO exit, Symbol 3), it is examined for potential of further study (Symbol 4). If the proposed system is totally unfeasible, the effort is terminated (Circle 5). For example, if the minimum resources required for a minimum system are more than the resources available, the study is terminated. If, however, another design of the system with revised objectives and constraints is feasible, then a second feasibility study would be conducted (Box 2) and the process would recycle (from Symbol 4, to 2 and 3) until the proposed study is accepted as feasible (YES exit, Symbol 3) or the project is terminated (Circle 5).

If the feasibility study is approved (Exit YES, Symbol 3), then the stages of determining the systems requirements (Box 6) through the testing of the solution (Box 10) are executed along with the parallel set of activities on organization changes (Box 9). These activities correspond to those shown in Figure 10.1 discussed earlier in this chapter. If the test proves unsatisfactory (Exit NO, Symbol 11), then the process will begin to recycle (Box 12). Recycling may start with a minor change in the implementation procedures (Box 8), or change in the design of the system (Box 7), or even a redetermination of the systems requirements (Box 6). The system is then tested (Box 10) and recycled until the test results prove satisfactory (Exit YES, Symbol 11). After conversion (Box 13) the new system is operational (Box 15). A large or complex system will be controlled under project management (Box 14) until the system is operational.

While the system is operational, it is controlled for quality of information (Box 16) and is evaluated (Box 17). If the evaluation is satisfactory (Exit YES, Symbol 18), operations continue. If unsatisfactory (Exit NO, Symbol 18), then maintenance (Box 19) or recycling (Box 12) is initiated. The development recycle may start at any of Boxes 6, 7, or 8, depending on the nature of the problem involved. The recycling may even start with a new feasibility study (Box 2) if the situation has changed radically and another feasibility study is required.

The **cycle of development** shown in the flowchart should be followed for all information systems, large or small, simple or complex. It should be noted, however, that names for the activities in this cycle may vary, and that several activities may be combined. For example, the feasibility study may be called the "study phase" or "preliminary system analysis." Evaluation may be called "post audit" or "control." Other variations are shown in Table 10.1. These are predominantly differences in terminology, not conceptual differences. Sometimes projects require additional development activities because of the specialized nature of the project. For example, when development is subcontracted, an activity called "contract analysis" might be added to the development cycle.

Role of managers

An important resource in the development of an information system is the investment of time and effort by company personnel at all levels. The level of management involved will depend on the type of information system under develop-

Table 10.1
Alternative names* for developing activities

Awad (p. 344)
Feasibility study
Analysis
Design
Testing
Implementation

Burch et al. (p. 19)
Systems analysis
General systems design
Systems evaluation and justification
Detail systems design
Systems implementation

Briggs et al. (pp. 13–19)
Systems planning
   a. Initial investigation
   b. Feasibility study
Systems requirements
   a. Operations and systems analysis
   b. User requirements
   c. Technical support approach
   d. Conceptual design
   e. Alternatives evaluation
Systems development
   a. Systems technical specs
   b. Technical support development
   c. Application specs
   d. Application programming and testing
   e. Users procedures and controls
   f. User training
   g. Implementation planning
   h. Systems conversion
   i. Systems test
Systems implementation
   a. Conversion and phased implementation
   b. Refinement and tuning
   c. Post implementation review

Carter (pp. 105–14)
Feasibility study
Information analysis
System design
Program development
Procedure development
Conversion
Operation and maintenance
Post audit

Gore and Stubbe (p. 16)
Study phase
Design phase
Development phase
Operation phase

Gross and Smith (p. 46)
Preliminary systems analysis
Preliminary systems design
Systems engineering and design engineering
Systems development, testing, and implementation

Haden (p. 123)
Recognition of need
Conception of possible solution
Feasibility evaluation
Systems-analysis
Programming
Control

Senn (p. 359)
Need for information systems change
Feasibility assessment
Requirements analysis
Logical systems design
Physical systems development
Testing
Implementation and evaluation
Maintenance

*SOURCES   Elias M. Awad, *Introduction to Computers in Business* (Englewood Cliffs, N.J.: Prentice-Hall, 1977).

John G. Burch, Jr., Felix R. Strater, and Gary Grudnitski, *Information Systems: Theory and Practice,* 3rd ed. (New York: John Wiley & Sons, 1983), 632 pp.

Charles L. Briggs, Evan G. Birks, and William Atkins, *Managing the Systems Development Process* (Englewood Cliffs, N.J.: Prentice-Hall, 1980), pp. 13–17.

Norman H. Carter, *Introduction to Business Data Processing* (Belmont, Calif.: Dickenson Publishing, 1968).

Marvin Gore and John Stubbe, *Elements of Systems Analysis for Business Data Processing* (Dubuque, Iowa: William C. Brown, 1975).

Paul Gross and Robert D. Smith, *Systems Analysis and Design for Management* (New York: Dun-Donnelley Publishing, 1976).

D. Haden, *Total Business Systems: Computers in Business* (St. Paul, Minn.: West Publishing, 1978).

James A. Senn, *Information Systems in Management,* 2d ed. (Belmont, Calif.: Wadsworth Publishing Company, 1982), p. 359.

Figure 10.4
Management's role in development of an information system

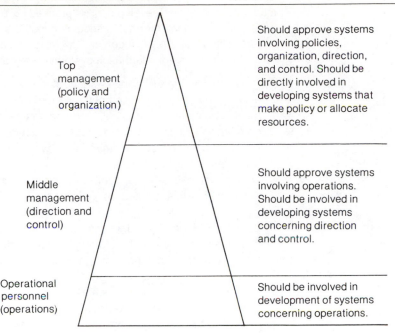

Top management (policy and organization)

Should approve systems involving policies, organization, direction, and control. Should be directly involved in developing systems that make policy or allocate resources.

Middle management (direction and control)

Should approve systems involving operations. Should be involved in developing systems concerning direction and control.

Operational personnel (operations)

Should be involved in development of systems concerning operations.

ment. Generally speaking, managers approve the development of systems one level below them in the organization structure, and participate in developing systems at their own functional level. Operational personnel should assist in the development of operating systems. This set of rules is depicted in Figure 10.4.

According to Figure 10.4, systems which affect only operational matters do not need the approval of top-level managers. For example, a business spending $20,000 per year at the factory for production could automate this function within the $20,000 without involving top management. The approval of a middle-level administrator such as the manager of production would suffice. However, if the system required additional resources—even on a one-shot basis, if the change affected institutional policies in the organization, if it violated institutional constraints, or if it might create interdepartmental rivalries, then approval of top management would be needed.

The value of manager participation in developing information systems has been borne out by empirical evidence. For example, John Garrity studied 27 different companies in 13 different industries using computerized information systems. He divided the companies into two groups: companies that were unmistakably successful in their use of computer systems and those that had had marginal success at best. Garrity found that companies that are successful in their use of computer systems are characterized by managerial review of development plans to ensure that computer effort is focused on high-leverage applications. Time is not spent on technical problems, but on integrating the computer system under development with ongoing activities in the firm. In addition, progress reviews are made to ensure that development is proceeding on schedule. When problems arise, managers look for trouble spots and institute corrective action.

The attitude of top management toward computerized systems also contributes to the success of information systems development. According to Garrity:

> Obviously, the close involvement of operating management is essential if a company is to apply computer systems effectively to inventory management, equipment scheduling, demand forecasting, and the like. The lead companies (successful companies) have achieved it by a combination of factors, including productive missionary work by the technical staff. But top management's attitude seems to be the principal ingredient. Where top management has fostered a tradition of effective line-staff relations, where top management has created an atmosphere favorable to an innovating, inquiring approach, operating executives have been much more willing to participate in the effort. Indeed, in some cases they have been the prime movers.

> But over and above this indirect encouragement, top management in most lead companies has specifically spelled out to operating executives the corporate commitment to the computer effort, its objectives, and operating management's resonsibility for achieving the anticipated return. One operating manager commented: "I did not volunteer to be a guinea pig for the computer. But the message came through loud and clear. I was expected to use the computer and show results.[1]

Table 10.2 shows the activities in the development cycle for which management has prime responsibility. However, managers should also understand and oversee the activities delegated to analysts (also listed in Table 10.2). In fact, a

Table 10.2
Personnel responsible for development activities

Activities of development	Person with prime responsibility
Feasibility study	Manager*
Systems requirements	Manager*
Design system	Analyst
Implement system	Analyst
Test system	Analyst and manager*
Organizational changes	Manager*
Conversion	Analyst
Evaluation	Manager*
Maintenance	Analyst

*Manager of the relevant application area or manager directly involved.

---

[1] Reprinted by permission of the *Harvard Business Review*. Excerpts from "Top Management and Computer Profits" by John J. Garrity (July–August 1963), p. 10. Copyright ©, 1963 by the President and Fellows of Harvard College; all rights reserved.

smooth and successful developmental process depends to a large extent on a close working relationship between management and technical personnel. This is difficult because the two groups have differences in background, training, and perspective. The two often disagree in their perception of what can be done and what should be done. Problems of interpretation and communication arise. The cartoon in Figure 10.5 shows what can happen when objectives are not clearly understood by the technician. A common vocabulary and knowledge about the

Figure 10.5
Lack of communication in project development

As proposed by the marketing department.

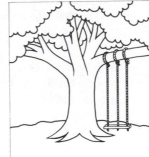
As specified in the product request.

As designed by the senior designer.

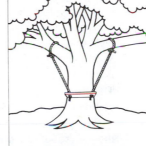
As produced by manufacturing.

As used by the customer.

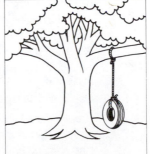
What the customer wanted.

developmental process of information systems will usually minimize such misunderstandings and reduce the noise in communications. One of the purposes of this text is to provide this common foundation.

Many managers in business complain that the promises of an information system are rarely achieved. Two reasons contribute to this credibility gap: system analysts often promise more than they can produce, and managers, in ignorance of information systems, often expect too much. The computer is not a magic machine that will produce instant results. Misconceptions on the part of business managers and the overenthusiasm of system analysts reinforce one another with the result that managers feel let down. This can be avoided to some extent if management understands and participates in all the activities in the development of the information system.

Summary

All information systems must be developed by a prescribed set of activities. These are: perception of need, the feasibility study, specification of the systems requirements, design, implementation, testing, conversion, and operations. Paralleling the activities, from the feasibility study through conversion, are management control and implementation of organizational changes. After conversion and during operations, the system must be controlled for quality of information and evaluated. If the evaluation is found unsatisfactory, the system recycles. This recycling may also begin during the testing activity.

During the development process, the manager must make decisions concerning the systems specifications, implementation, and evaluation. If the manager abdicates this responsibility, these decisions will be made by default by the analyst with the result that the system developed may not meet the manager's needs.

Managers and analysts each have prime responsibility for different activities. But in all phases of development, managers and analysts should work together. This can only be done if they know one another's perspective and understand a common body of knowledge relating to the development of information systems.

The sequence and naming of activities of the development cycle will vary with the nature of the business and the style of managers and analysts. One sequencing expressed in poetry as follows:

(*Canto the first: Proposal*)
"An information system," said the president, J.B.,
"Is what this company sorely needs, or so it seems to me:
An automated, integrated system that embraces
All the proper people, in all the proper places,
So that the proper people, by communications linked,
Can manage by exception, instead of by instinct."

(*Canto the second: Feasibility study*)
They called in the consultants then, to see what they could see,
And to tell them how to optimize their use of EDP.
The consultants studied hard and long (their fee for this was sizable)

And concluded that an information system was quite feasible.
"Such a system," they repeated, "will not only give you speed,
It will give you whole new kinds of information that you need."

(*Canto the third: Installation*)
So an information system was developed and installed
And all the proper people were properly enthralled.
They thought of all the many kinds of facts it could transmit.
And predicted higher profits would indeed result from it;
They agreed the information that it would communicate
Would never be too little, and would never be too late.

(*Canto the last: Output*)
Yet when the system went on line, there was no great hurrah,
For it soon became apparent that it had one fatal flaw:
Though the system functioned perfectly, it couldn't quite atone
For the information it revealed—which was better left unknown.[2]

Key words

Conversion
Critical path
Cycle of development
Data base
Feasibility study
Information systems (IS)
Organizational adjustments
Physical preparation
Planning

Procedure
Programs
Program solutions
Project control techniques
Project management
Recycling
Redevelop
Systems requirement statement
Testing

Discussion questions

1. Do all information systems go through the same stages of development? Why do many stages have multiple names? Is this confusion over names avoidable?

2. Why is the development of an information system a cycle? When (if ever) does the cycle end?

3. What phases of the development process must be recycled? Why does recycling take place?

4. How long does it take to develop an information system? What are the factors that determine the lapse time for development?

5. Does every information system require a development cycle? Explain the conditions under which a development cycle is essential.

---

[2] Marilyn Driscoll, "An Information System," *The Arthur Young Journal,* (Winter 1968), p. 318.

6. What is the role of a manager in the development cycle of an information system? How does it conflict with or supplement (or both) the role of analysts?

7. What background, knowledge, and experience is necessary for a manager to participate effectively in the development of an information system?

8. How do the stages in the development of an information system differ from stages in a redevelopment cycle?

9. List the stages of development of an information system in sequence. Under what circumstances can some of these stages be omitted?

10. Explain factors that lead to the development of an information system. Explain factors leading to redevelopment. Who initiates development and redevelopment? What units are responsible for implementation?

11. What flow of communication is needed between the various levels of management and the analysts for the successful development of an information system?

Exercises*

1. Draw a chart showing activities in the development of an information system for generating a monthly report which identifies sales per salesperson by product and sales area, and for comparing these figures with quotas for each sales representative. Specify any simplifying assumptions of the environment that you make.

2. Assume that the report prepared in the above exercise has been used for three years and needs to be modified in format. Draw a diagram showing the activities needed for such modification.

3. Draw a diagram for the development of an online real-time information system for a large warehouse with five sites annually handling 500 different products worth $5 million.

Selected annotated bibliography

Alvarez, Joan. "A Business Systems Plan." *Journal of Information Management* 4, no. 2 (Winter 1983), pp. 29–38.
  The BSP method, an IBM method, is examined as an approach to evaluating the impact of change in the direction of a business and to ensure that the systems plan is consistent with changes in direction.
Biggs, Charles L; Evan G. Birks; and William Atkins. *Managing the Systems Development Process*. Englewood Cliffs, N.J.: Prentice-Hall, 1980, 408 pp.
  The authors of this book are consultants for Touche Ross and Co., a con-

*Note: Keep your solutions to all the above exercises. Do the same exercises after studying Part 3 and again after Part 4. You will probably find many differences in your answers. Analyze these differences.

sulting firm with much experience developing information systems. The book has an overview chapter on the process of systems development followed by chapters that elaborate on each development phase.

Cleland, David I., and William R. King. *Systems Analysis and Project Management.* New York: McGraw-Hill, 1975, 398 pp.

This book discusses the process and principles of project management.

Davis, Gordon B. *Management Information Systems: Conceptual Foundations, Structure, and Development.* New York: McGraw-Hill, 1974, pp. 413–39.

A tightly written description of the development cycle with a good discussion of the human factors involved in development.

Kanter, J. *Management-Oriented Management Information Systems.* Englewood Cliffs, N.J.: Prentice-Hall, 1977, pp. 92–133.

This chapter discusses three main sets of activities in the development and implementation cycle: analysis, synthesis, and implementation. Detailed activities are also identified. Unfortunately, the pie diagrams used do not emphasize the sequential and cyclic relationship of the activities. There is, however, an excellent discussion of economic analysis as part of the feasibility study.

Lundeberg, Mats. *Information Systems Development—A Systematic Approach.* Englewood Cliffs, N.J.: Prentice-Hall, 1981, 337 pp.

This book offers a nontraditional approach to systems development. The ISAC approach advocated has been developed at the Royal Institute of Technology in Stockholm, Sweden over a 10-year period.

"Prototyping in the System Development Cycle." *System Development* 3, no. 10 (October 1983), pp. 4–5.

The article suggests that one of the advantages of prototyping is that a team spirit is fostered that contributes to successful development.

Ruth, Stephen R. "Getting Too Much System: An Avoidable Tragedy." *Journal of Systems Management* 34, no. 3 (October 1983), pp. 14–17.

According to Ruth, assessing system benefits before acquisition of system resources is very important. Such prior assessment avoids poor design and costly mistakes.

Sanders, Norman. *Manager's Guide to Profitable Computers.* London: AMACOM, 1978, 261 pp.

Development is as good an excuse as any to read this delightful book full of analogies and anecdotes. It totally lacks the formalism of usual texts on this subject, having no footnotes or bibliographies. It is a pleasant, readable book on a difficult, serious subject. The illustrations by Tony Hart add to the humor.

Welke, R. J., and B. R. Kronsyski. "Technology, Methodology and Information Systems: A Tripartite View." *Data Base* 14, no. 1 (Fall 1982), pp. 41–57.

The authors discuss the components of DP systems and user interaction with such systems. The authors conclude that there "are large gaps in our knowledge."

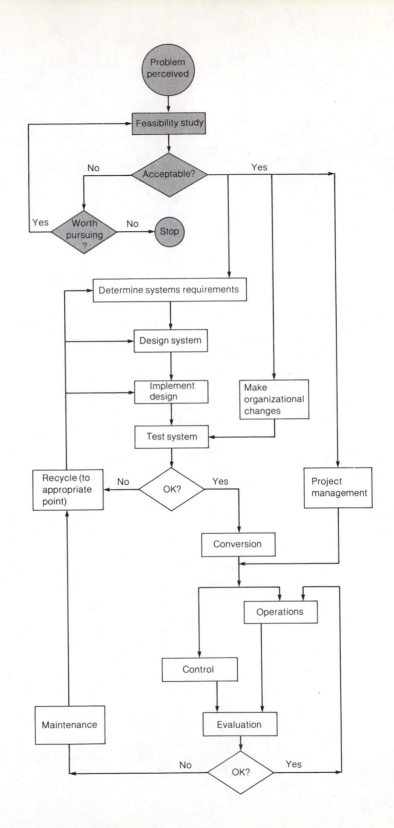

Feasibility study

11

Desultory studies are erased from the mind as easily as pencil marks; classified studies are retained like durable ink.

P. Cooper

Once the need for a new information system is perceived, a **feasibility study** determines whether or not desired objectives of a proposed information system can be achieved within existing constraints. The study identifies the cost of proposed changes (monetary and organizational) and estimates the benefits of the new system. On this information the manager decides whether to implement the new system or discontinue the study.

A feasibility study is usually recommended when a proposed system involves major change, such as the installation of a faster data processing system (with computerized processing). But feasibility studies are themselves costly. Many experts feel that they are a waste of valuable time, talent, and money. They argue that unless a firm is breaking new ground or desires to be on the cutting edge of technology, it is wiser to follow the lead of firms that have already developed systems for achieving the desired objectives. Before a firm commits scarce resources to a feasibility study, it is generally advisable to undertake a preliminary study to decide whether to adopt the solution of another firm or to undertake development of a new system by reviewing objectives, ascertaining company resources and constraints, and surveying existing solutions. A preliminary recommendation to proceed with development of a customized information system would then lead to a detailed feasibility study.

Although a feasibility study postulates a new system, it does not guarantee success. The system may still fail in the testing phase of implementation. This risk, however, is minimized since the study identifies and anticipates problems to be solved.

There are four phases to a feasibility study:

1. Organizing for the feasibility study.
2. Search for a solution.

3. Feasibility analysis.
4. Choice of a solution.

Phase One: Organizing for a feasibility study

The first phase in any feasibility study is preparing for the study itself. A flowchart representation of this organization is shown in Figure 11.1 This phase may be initiated by a manager when the need for a new information system is recognized (Box 2, Figure 11.1). Triggering the redesign may be:

1. Changes in organizational goals, plans, and information requirements.
2. Changes in organizational structure (e.g., appointment of new top management).
3. Changes in the environment (e.g., legislation requiring the company to supply new data to government agencies).
4. Changes in technology that may make new systems feasible.

Figure 11.1
Phase One: Organizing for feasibility study

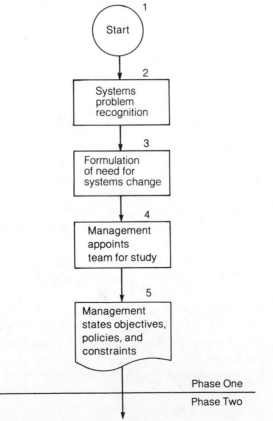

Phase One may also be initiated by systems personnel who may be first to recognize potential benefits to the firm of technological developments in the computer industry. In addition, a firm with an operate-now-integrate-later approach to information systems development may rely on systems personnel to signal the need for expanding subsystems within the overall system.

Once the need for change has been recognized, the problem must be defined and formulated by management (Box 3, Figure 11.1). Then personnel must be appointed to make a feasibility study of problem solutions (Box 4, Figure 11.1). Members of the study team should have the following qualifications:

1. Knowledge of systems techniques. Whether this should be knowledge of operation research, statistics, computer science, information science, business functions (i.e., accounting, marketing, finance, and production) or a combination of these will depend on the nature of the problem. Experience with computer systems (hardware and software) is useful, especially if the systems change involves designing a large or complex information system. A specialist in computer systems is not always essential, though an understanding of the potentials and limitations of computer systems is helpful in making full use of technological developments.
2. The ability to work with people. Projected systems changes disrupt the status quo. People often feel their jobs threatened and manifest this insecurity by lack of cooperation, even open hostility, toward the feasibility study group. Working in this environment requires tact and discretion.
3. An understanding of the organization, its structure, philosophy, objectives, policies, and operations.
4. Skill in perceiving the overall picture combined with a willingness to handle details.
5. A position in management. This provides the status and authority necessary to elicit cooperation when collecting information for the study from all organizational levels.
6. Experience in the type of project under consideration.

The above qualities are seldom found in one individual but all should be represented in the team. Often a firm will not have personnel experienced in the systems change under review. In such cases consultants will have to be hired and added to the team. Their presence has the advantage of bringing an outsider's scrutiny and a certain objectivity to the study.

Team size generally varies from two to eight. There is greater division of labor on large teams and more flexibility in staffing, making it easier to ensure that all the desired qualities are found in the membership. But as size increases, so does the potential for personality conflicts, conflicts that can delay decision making and hinder the team's functioning. The elected committee chairman must be skillful in managing groups, and also be knowledgeable about the firm's goals and policies since the team may need guidance in interpreting the organizational environment. Experience has shown that feasibility studies have more impact when the chairman is drawn from the upper levels of management for large and complex systems.

After the team has been appointed, management must state the objectives of the study and specify related policies and constraints (Box 5, Figure 11.1). This step is delayed until the feasibility study group has been assembled because a team-management dialogue is necessary during this organizational phase. The team's questions about variables and demands for clarification and/or elaboration help management define the study objectives in operational terms. Without this interaction, objectives tend to be stated in ambiguous, generalized terms such as "more accurate information" or "faster reporting." A team will demand specifics. What error rate is permissible? To how many decimal points should results be calculated? Does a response time of two weeks constitute faster reporting time or is one day, or one hour required? Sometimes management is reluctant to state goals, not knowing what can realistically be achieved. But the purpose of the study is to determine feasibility of goals. If the development of technology and the firm's resources make the goals infeasible, management will be so informed and the goals can accordingly be scaled down, or resource constraints relaxed so the objectives can be achieved.

A good example of a seemingly unrealistic goal was stated by American Airlines in 1954. Realizing that the company was losing potential profits because the airline lacked timely information on the availability of seats on their flights, the following objective was formulated: The new system should provide company agents anywhere in the United States with immediate reservation confirmation and accurate information on schedules and seat occupancy. Such fast response time was technologically impossible at the time. Yet this objective was achieved in 1963 by the SABRE System[1] and today computerized reservation systems are taken for granted by the airline industry.

Discussions between team and management during the organizational phases of the feasibility study will also ensure that the resources available for the project and the limits of acceptable organization change are specified. Personnel policies regarding displacement or unemployment resulting from possible acceptance of a new system should also be stated in advance of the study. Without such a policy, valuable employees who feel their jobs threatened may leave the firm. Usually the best workers leave first, even before the new system is installed, thereby adding to the problems of conversion. Policies regarding reclassification of jobs, retraining, and transference of personnel, when stated well in advance of the actual feasibility study, can help alleviate unemployment fears and might contribute to keeping needed workers in the company's employ.

Authorization to cross departmental boundaries for collecting information should be granted the study team during the organizational phase. In cases of complex systems changes, this authority must come from top management.

Phase Two: Search for solutions

A flowchart for the steps in Phase Two is shown in Figure 11.2 The first step in the search for a solution is usually to study the existing system, then to collect

[1]R. W. Parker, "The SABRE System," *Datamation* 11, no. 9 (September 1965), pp. 49–52.

Figure 11.2
Phase Two: Search for solutions

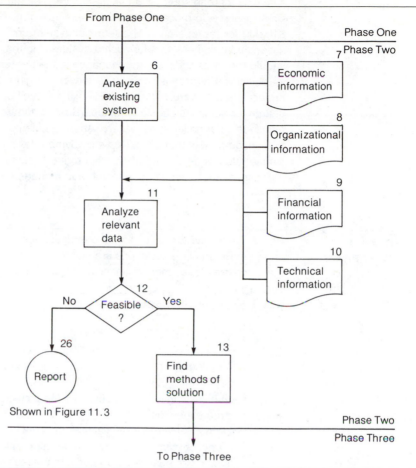

and analyze all relevant information on the environment so that the current performance can be evaluated, and required changes determined (Box 6, Figure 11.2). However, some system analysts feel that teams become biased when such a detailed study is made and argue that a fresh approach, disregarding existing systems, is needed. They suggest that the team skip Box 6, and focus on collected information (Box 7–10) to develop entirely new solutions. A look at the objectives and constraints of management will usually guide the team in how to initiate the study. When subsystems within the basic structure are to be changed, the first approach, a study of the existing system, is generally appropriate. For major overhauls, the fresh approach is usually advisable.

In either case, the team must decide on the detail and depth of its study, and how much information should be collected and analyzed (Boxes 7–11, Figure 11.2). If implementation follows the study, the committee's groundwork will prove useful, but should the study terminate, the time and effort invested are lost. For this reason, only a broad survey-type analysis should be made at this stage to determine whether or not to proceed further. For example, if management has allocated only $10,000 for the operation of a terminal system and the team discovers that the minimum equipment cost for such a system is in the range of $30,000, the team should report its findings, and management either terminate the study or restate its objectives and constraints. If, however, no glaring reasons for declaring the project infeasible are apparent (YES exit for Symbol 12, Figure 11.2), the broad search for solutions should continue, (Box 13, Figure 11.2) with the collection of additional information if necessary. An infeasible project terminates with a report to management to that effect (NO exit, Symbol 12, and Circle 26). In some cases, simple rules of decision making will produce solutions. In other cases, sophisticated models of operations research and management science will be required.

Phase Three: Feasibility analysis

Phase Three, the formal testing of alternative solutions derived in Phase Two, is shown in Figure 11.3. Solutions are tested (Box 14, Figure 11.3) against four primary constraints: economic, financial, organizational, and technical (Box 15–19, Figure 11.3).

Economic feasibility

Theoretically, **economic feasibility** is conceptually simple: a cost-benefit analysis. The expected benefits must equal or exceed the expected costs. However, in designing information systems, the cost half of the equation is rarely computed with accuracy during the feasibility stage. Users' requirements tend to be understated so that costs invariably increase as the project develops, and analysts often underestimate expenses.

Assigning a precise monetary value to the benefit side of the equation is equally difficult in practice since most benefits of information systems cannot be measured in dollars. For example, how can one measure the value of analysis of consumer preferences, or timely information on sales or production? Fortunately, it is not always necessary to measure the **cardinal utility** of benefits. **Ordinal utility** is sufficient: that is, the benefits must be of a higher order than the cost. If an information system is projected to cost $20,000, the manager need only decide whether expected benefits are worth the price, a decision that can be made on an intuitive basis.

Another way to estimate benefits is to ask management how much the company would be willing to pay to an outside firm for the information.

One technique for comparing costs with benefits is to state costs in terms of an **operational variable.** For example, the cost of the information system may be equated with a 0.2 percent increase in inventory turnover, or a 3 percent increase in sales. The value of information derived from the proposed system (management's judgment of intangible benefits plus the tangible benefits) would then be compared to the necessary increase in operations required to offset this calculated cost.

Figure 11.3
Phase Three: Feasibility analysis

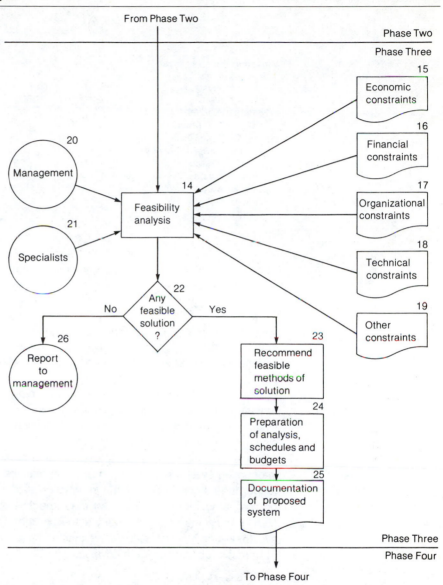

Estimations of costs and benefits are generally **range estimates,** with probability assessments for the values within the range. Managers will choose either pessimistic or optimistic values or an in between value within the range, depending on their aversion to risk. The benefits costs analysis that follows will be based on these expected values.

Where benefits can be quantified, the computed benefits can be placed on a

Table 11.1
Calculations of benefits (in $000)

	Year				
	1	2	3	4	5
Marketing benefits					
Sales forecast					
Present system	20,000	21,000	22,000	23,200	24,300
New system	20,000	21,500	23,700	26,000	28,600
Increase in sales	0	500	1,700	2,800	4,300
Increase in profits	0	50	170	280	430
Production benefits					
Inventory carrying costs					
Finished goods	0	25	25	25	25
In production	0	60	60	60	60
Replenishment avoided	0	125	0	0	0
Factory labor	0	0	20	30	50
Total production benefits	0	210	105	115	135
Other benefits					
From purchasing and other agents	0	60	70	70	70
Total benefits	0	320	345	465	635
Cumulative net benefits	0	320	665	1,130	1,765

table similar to Table 11.1, a hypothetical but fairly realistic case study.[2] The figures derived in the table can then be weighed against costs, as in the **benefits-cost analysis** in Table 11.2. The sample Tables 11.1 and 11.2 show that the project under consideration would be profitable within an approximate pay-back period for four years.

Not all benefits-costs analyses are this simple. Many refinements would be required in a more sophisticated capital budgeting decision. Expertise in business finance and accounting is generally needed when making a benefits-costs analysis for determining economic feasibility.

An additional comment about benefits is in order here. Since the goal of any information system is to reduce a decision maker's uncertainty by predicting the future, the potential value of the information system under development should be compared with a calculation of the **expected value of perfect information (EVPI)** sometime during the early stages of the feasibility study. Of course, no system will be a crystal ball, but if expected benefits prove far from the ideal, the system is probably not worth developing.

Financial feasibility

Often a proposed system with a high benefits-costs ratio is economically feasible, but a lack of money prevents implementation. **Financial feasibility,** checking costs against available funds, is therefore an essential at this stage.

[2]This data and the following section on financial feasibility is adapted from Harold J. McCormack, "Measuring the Benefits of an MIS and a Case" (unpublished), 1979. The basic data came from Fred R. McFadden and James D. Suver, "Costs and Benefits of a Data Base System," *Harvard Business Review* 56, no. 1 (January–February 1978), pp. 131–39.

Table 11.2
Benefits-cost analysis (in $000)

	Year				
	1	2	3	4	5
Costs					
Hardware					
CPU	$150				
Central memory	75				
Data storage	60				
Terminals	15	$15			
Software and conversion					
DBMS	100				
Communications	15				
Training	20	5	$5		
Conversion	25	25	25	$25	
Other (mostly personnel)					
DBA-related	75	90	90	90	$90
Maintenance	20	20	20	20	20
User costs	20	20	20	20	20
Total costs	575	175	160	155	130
Cumulative costs	575	750	910	1,065	1,195
Cumulative benefits (from Table 11.1)	0	320	665	1,130	1,765
Cumulative benefits less costs (net cash flow)	$−575	$−430	$−245	$65	$570

The study team often considers economic and financial constraints jointly, issuing a single decision on economic and financial feasibility. But, conceptually, two feasibility decisions have been made. Though computer analysts assist in determining costs, users determine economic feasibility. Financial feasibility, on the other hand, requires technical advice from people knowledgeable about the availability of capital and methods of financing. Decisions on whether borrowed money would be available for the project, whether internal financing would suffice, or whether a combination of external and internal financing would be advisable are decisions that can only be made by financial experts.

Capital budgeting decisions in large firms generally require complex calculations to determine the relative merit of projects competing for funds. For example, management might have to choose between allocating available resources to R&D, to plant renovation, or to the development of a new information system. In the feasibility study for an information system, the time value of money, the accounting rate of return on investment, the discounted return on investment, and the profitability index might be calculated and be decisive factors in recommending the system's implementation or rejection. These calculations are described briefly below.

Time value of money
The benefits-costs analysis is meaningful only when the estimated benefits are discounted to determine their present value, for the value of money changes over

time due to inflation, changing rates of interest, and so forth. Costs are incurred when a project is initiated. Benefits come later. A comparison of benefits with the **present value (PV) of future amounts** is determined by the following formula:

$$PV = \frac{\text{amount in future}}{(1 + \text{discount rate})^n}$$

where n = number of years from present. For example, $100 two years in the future discounted at 22 percent would be $67.19 ($100 \div (1.0 + .22)^2 = 100 \div 1.4884 = 67.186$). (The 22 percent discount rate in this example is the rate estimated to reflect the changing value of money over a two-year period. This esimate would vary among businesspersons and would change in time as financial conditions and the cost of capital varies.)

Net present value (NPV)
Calculations can be performed to discount the entire cash flow for a project to **net present value (NPV).** The formula for this calculation is:

$$NPV = \sum_{n=1}^{\text{years}} \frac{\pm (\text{cash flow})_n}{(1 + \text{rate})^n}$$

The data in Table 11.2 discounted at 22 percent to determine *NPV* yields a total positive benefit of $67,000 (see Table 11.3). That total benefit figure would then be weighed against benefits that might accrue from other projects that are competing for the limited financial resources of the firm. It would be during the financial feasibility study of a projected information system that this comparison would be made.

Return on investment (ROI)
Return on investment (ROI) is the percentage return for a project based on the PV of benefits. Conceptually, ROI is the interest rate that makes the investment produce the expected returns. Mathematically, ROI is the discount rate which brings the NPV of the project to zero, calculated by iteration for various rates until one is found which satisfies:

$$\sum_{n=1}^{\text{Years}} \frac{\pm (\text{cash flow})_n}{(1 + \text{rate})^n} = 0$$

Table 11.3
Calculation of NPV (in $)

	Year				
	1	*2*	*3*	*4*	*5*
Net cash flow (see Table 11.2)	−575	145	185	310	505
NPV at 22 percent	−575	119	124	171	228

Total positive benefits = 119 + 124 + 171 + 228 − 575 = 67
(i.e., $67,000)

The calculations for the formula on page 248, using the data from Table 11.3, are shown below.

	1	2	3	4	5	NPV
Net cash flow	−575	145	185	310	505	
27 percent PV factors $(1+0.27)^n$	None	1.27	1.6129	2.0484	2.6014	
PV =	−575	114.17	114.70	151.34	194.13	−1≈0

Since *NPV* at 27 percent = 0, therefore the ROI = 27 percent.

The above calculations (which assume that money is due or spent at the beginning of the year) gives *NPV* closest to zero. Other iterative calculations that do not give a zero NPV are:

NPV at 22 percent = + $67,000
NPV at 32 percent = − $58,000
NPV at 26 percent = + $12,000

The ROI for the information system (synonymous with **IRR, internal rate of return**), would be compared with the ROI of other projects under consideration and be a factor in deciding priorities for a firm's financial resources.

Accounting rate of return (ARR)

Accountants use the average net income over the life of a project divided by the value of the investment as a supplement to ROI. Net income is directly affected by accounting conventions, such as depreciations that are excluded from the cash measures. Five years is the life of information systems generally used in the calculation since advances in computer technology make most systems obsolete after that length of time. This rule of thumb is applied to software as well as hardware since systems are generally redeveloped within a five-year time period.

Using the data in Table 11.2, the **accounting rate of return (ARR)** on investment is 40 percent [(145 + 185 + 310 + 505)/5] ÷ 575 = 229/575 = 40 percent.

Profitability index (PI)

Another index used when comparing the relative merits of projects is the **profitability index (PI)** calculated by the formula:

$$PI = \frac{\text{Present value of benefit returns}}{\text{Present value of investment}}$$

For data in Table 11.1 and Table 11.3, the PI = 1.12 (119 + 124 + 171 + 228)/575 = 1.12).

Criteria selection

Whether ROI, PV, and/or other criteria are used in economic and financial feasibility studies depends on the personnel conducting the study. The figures in Table 11.4, based on a study by Petry, show the percentage of surveyed companies using ROI, PV, NPV, and ARR. Most firms used more than one calculation when comparing projects competing for funds. The average number of criteria were 2.24, which explains why the total percentage in Table 11.4 exceeds 100 percent.

Organizational feasibility

Proposed solutions must also be tested against **organizational constraints.** For example, when a new information system requires combining two departments into one, the manager of the absorbed department may strenuously object. If top management agrees that the merger is inadvisable, an organizational constraint exists. Sometimes the person who would be responsible for the new system lacks the qualities necessary to make the change viable. Clerical personnel may be unwilling to prepare data by the new method. A new system is feasible only when personnel with technical and administrative competency are available, and when employees are willing to make changes in procedures, to accept experimentation, to operate in an atmosphere of change, and to accept the risk of making errors, should the system design prove faulty.

Major systems change needs the support of top management. Support at operational and middle management levels is also important. Without such support, it requires courage to implement a new system. The availability of qualified systems personnel is a less decisive factor in deciding whether or not to adopt a new system, since that situation can often be corrected. Consultants can be hired to select, employ, and train needed personnel. It should be recognized, however, that the full support of management is necessary to attract and retain competent personnel. At the present time, the demand for analysts exceeds supply and this shortage is expected to continue in the near future. Instead of fighting nonsystems-oriented management, analysts will choose employment in a supportive working environment, assuming pay incentives are equal.

Sometimes corrective action can be taken to make a proposed system feasible in spite of the opposition of a key manager at the operational or middle management level. Top management might remove the incumbent, either by transfer or dismissal, change the job (e.g., withdraw duties from one position and assign

Table 11.4
Preferences of investment criterion

	Percent
ROI—Return on investment (discounted)	61
PB—Payback period	58
NPV—Net present value (discounted)	33
ARR—Accounting rate of return (undiscounted)	
on initial investment	33
on average investment	27
Other approaches	12

SOURCE   Glenn H. Petry, "Effective Use of Capital Budgeting Tools," *Business Horizons* 19, no. 5 (October 1975), p. 58.

Table 11.5
Decision table for testing organizational feasibility

	Rule 1	Rule 2	Rule 3	Rule 4	Rule 5	Rule 6	Rule 7	Rule 8
Top manager support	N	N	N	N	Y	Y	Y	Y
Operational and middle management support	Y	Y	N	N	Y	Y	N	N
Experienced analysts available	Y	N	Y	N	Y	N	Y	N
Discontinue study		X	X	X				
Hire consultants (assume available)						X		X
Train analysts						X		X
Continue study with caution	X						X	X
Continue with enthusiasm					X			

Key: Y = Yes.
N = No.
X = Action to be taken.

them to others), or, preferably, change the incumbent's views to support of the system through counseling and training. Ways in which management can mobilize employee support are described in Chapter 17. Indeed, the key to success in utilizing computer technology in decision making is often dependent on the ability of management to motivate people involved with the new system rather than on the solution of technical problems regarding machine integration. Because of the importance of human relationships in an information system, an entire chapter (Chapter 17) is devoted to this subject.

Table 11.5 is a decision table used to determine organizational feasibility. The table shows what action to take, given a set of conditions. For example, if the conditions in Rule 1 exist (operational and middle management support and experienced analysts available, but top management support lacking), then continue the study with caution.

Technological feasibility

Sometimes no solution is feasible because of **technological constraints.** Examples include the present lack of mathematical and statistical techniques for determining optimal solutions in some unstructured decision-making situations, and the lack of equipment to perform certain types of operations, such as machine reading of handwriting.

Other feasibility considerations

Additional constraints, both internal and external, may also exist. One example of an **internal constraint** is time. A project may have little or no value unless completed by a given date. Competition or national unions may impose **eternal constraints,** as may federal and state regulatory agencies.

Feasibility decision

Feasibility deliberations in Phase Three are made by the study team, though management and specialists may participate as advisers and counselors (Symbols 14, 20, and 21 in Figure 11.3).

When a number of alternatives are possible, the study team must develop priorities for ranking solutions. For example, in selecting one of many departments to be automated, a unit that is the source of basic data for other departments in the organization might be given preference. Weight might be given to small and isolated departments since automation could provide experience in systems change without adversely affecting the rest of the organization in the event of miscalculation. The team may decide to start with small jobs having a high probability of success, situations where a high volume of repetitious work is done by clerks. Systems designers generally prefer jobs where the assignment is well defined and there is adequate time for planning and implementing the change. They prefer to avoid areas where employees are strongly opposed to change.

Once solutions have been weighted with priority values, the study team will choose and recommend to management the adoption of the highest ranking feasible solution with the best probability of success (Box 23, Figure 11.3). But alternate solutions in order of preference should also be presented with documentation for each possibility included (Boxes 24 and 25, Figure 11.3). The report should list:

1. Dollar resources required
    a. Developmental costs
        Equipment
        Personnel
        Space
        Other
    b. Recurring costs
        Personnel
        Other
2. Anticipated consequences of proposed project
    a. Organizational changes
        Structural
        Personnel
        Procedures
    b. Informational changes
    c. Anticipated problems
3. Limitations of proposed project

4. Benefits of project
   a. Economic
   b. Organizational
   c. Overall systems
   d. Other
5. Time schedule
   a. Time schedule of project
   b. Priority reassignment of other jobs.

The above information should be supported by examples of output and performance figures from other case studies. In addition, a detailed statement of the objectives and the scope of the feasibility study should be prepared for management to accompany the recommendations.

A report to management is also necessary when the study team finds no feasible solution (Circle 26, Figure 11.3).

Phase Four: Choice of a solution

The fourth and last phase of the feasibility study, shown in Figure 11.4, is initiated when the study team presents its findings to management (Box 26, Figure 11.4). Before management adopts the proposed systems change the team's recommendations must be studied with care (Box 27, Figure 11.4). It is management's responsibility to ensure that all relevant variables are specified and that all estimates are checked. Consulting help may prove advisable at this stage. It should be recognized that overruns on expenses and delays in schedules are the norm in the history of information systems, especially in the area of computer installations, so provision for such miscalculations should be made. In their defense, systems personnel claim that they cannot make predictions or estimates with accuracy since their job is developmental, untried, and full of uncertainties. There is some truth to this assertion. But in recent years, the profession has gained experience. Many new techniques and rules for predicting costs have been developed. Some business firms exist solely by preparing and marketing computer systems for determining costs. Feasibility teams should be able to provide management with more reliable time/cost figures than in the past.

Management must also carefully study the feasibility report so that bias or omitted considerations are noted. For example, studies that dismiss organizational impact as unimportant should be viewed with skepticism. Many system changes have organizational implications, especially on future job classifications and employment. These must be anticipated and plans for the future carefully prepared.

Although the feasibility team's recommendations are generally accepted, the final decision on whether or not a new information system should be adopted rests with management. Management should have participated in the team's deliberations when costs and benefits were weighed, when values to intangible vari-

Figure 11.4
Phase Four: Choice of solution

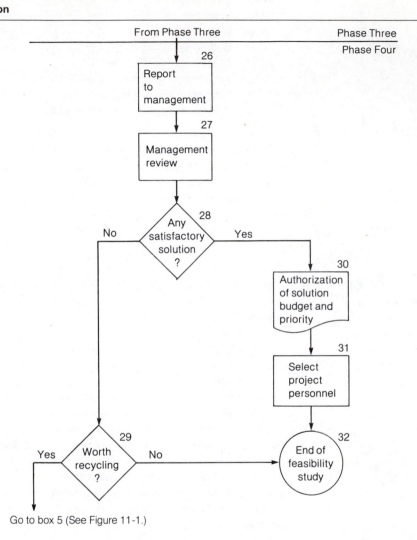

Go to box 5 (See Figure 11-1.)

ables were imputed, when effects of conflicting factors were estimated, and trade-offs evaluated, but a reassessment of these value judgments after the study is complete is advisable. Committing the firm's resources to a new system is, in the final analysis, a policy decision that only management can make. In selecting projects to be implemented, the short- and long-range significance of each project must be considered and a balance between subsystem and total system implementation maintained. Management must guard against the tendency of combatting local brush fires while neglecting overall long-range planning needs. Some firms allocate systems personnel exclusively for long-range systems planning, but this requires top-level commitment of resources and may prove too costly for small organizations.

When management decides that the proposed solutions are unacceptable (Exit NO, Symbol 28; Figure 11.4) recycling may be initiated (Exit YES, Symbol 29 to Box 5, Figure 11.1). Constraints might be relaxed or objectives scaled down in order to find an acceptable feasible solution. A positive acceptance of a solution from the alternatives proposed by the feasibility study team (YES exit, Symbol 28) must be followed by decisions necessary for implementation (output Symbol 30, Figure 11.4) such as authorization of a budget, the establishment of a time schedule, framing necessary policy and procedural changes, and possibly even reassigning existing priorities of systems effort. In some cases, statements concerning organizational policies on personnel are necessary.

In authorizing a new system, management must take actions necessary to ensure that the promised benefits of the system are fully realized. There are many cases on record where a department manager has supported the claim of savings made in the feasibility study, such as the replacement of clerks, but once the system has been implemented, no savings appear. The clerks have merely been assigned unproductive work, what economists call disguised unemployment. This can be prevented if management sets a date when the funds representing the promised savings resulting from the new system will be withdrawn from the department concerned. If this is organizationally feasible, then the action has two important effects. One, it ensures that the savings from the new system are realized and, two, it motivates departments concerned to cooperate with systems personnel so that the proposed project can be completed effectively and on time.

Selecting project personnel

The final step in Phase Four is the appointment of a **project director,** one with knowledge and proven experience in managing systems changes, and assignment of a development team. The team will determine the requirements of the system, analyze and design the new system, and oversee implementation and conversion (Box 31, Figure 11.4). It will be disbanded and given new assignments when the system is turned over to users and operational personnel.

There are several approaches to the organization of this development team. A **functional organization, project organization,** or **matrix organization** are possibilities.

Traditional management philosophy is based on line and staff concepts with a vertical flow of authority and responsibility. The project team might be organized as a functional unit with assigned development responsibilities, keeping traditional line-staff relationships.

However, most information system projects require cooperation and resources from many line units. As M. Stewart states:

> The essence of project management is that it cuts across, and in a sense conflicts with the natural organization structure. . . . Because a project usu-

ally requires decisions and actions from a number of functional areas at once, the main inter-dependencies and the main flow of information in a project are not vertical but lateral. . . . Projects are characterized by exceptionally strong lateral working relationships, requiring closely related activity and decisions by many individuals in different functional departments.[3]

When functional organization is inappropriate, **project organization,** the creation of a separate organizational unit for the sole purpose of completing the project, may work. In this schema, professional, technical, and administrative staff are hired for the duration of the project. But there are serious problems in attracting competent personnel when projects are organized in this manner. Project jobs are temporary, with fluctuating work loads. Professionals are unwilling to join projects that offer no job security.

A **matrix organization** combines functional and project approaches to project management. In a matrix organization, the staff is "borrowed" from functional divisions. In the case of a development team, the team members might be drawn from the accounting division, marketing, operations research, the EDP department, and so forth. Which employees are borrowed is negotiated by the project manager with functional department heads, the choice usually being based on the availability of personnel and the qualifications demanded by the project. Sometimes department heads are reluctant to release competent personnel, but there are advantages to being represented on the development team that most department heads recognize. Certainly the department's interests will be promoted by having a representative on the team.

However, the matrix organization means that project members have two bosses. They are responsible to the project manager for work assignments, yet their permanent supervisors retain jurisdiction over such personnel matters as salary and promotion. The two "bosses" may clash in values and objectives, with the project member caught in between. This potentially explosive situation can be defused if ground rules are negotiated between the project manager and functional heads regarding shared authority and responsibility over project members before the team is constituted.

The advantages of matrix organization may be summarized as follows. Matrix organization:

1. Provides a project manager with authority to cut across vertical organizational divisions.
2. Involves functional departments, and is responsive to their needs, because representatives of most departments will be on the project staff.
3. Has access to the resources in functional departments (on a negotiated basis).
4. Provides a "home" for the project personnel after the completion of the project.

---

[3]M. Stewart, "Making Project Management Work," in *Systems, Organizations, Analysis, Management: A Book of Readings,* D. I. Cleland and W. R. King, eds. (New York: McGraw-Hill, 1969), pp. 295–96.

5. Does not permanently disrupt organizational subgroupings or the continuity of fringe benefits.

When a development team must be chosen for complex projects, a User and Administrative Committee is often formed to aid the project leader in interpreting the firm's policies and in clarifying users' needs. This committee may also monitor the progress of the project at predetermined checkpoints.

Once a systems change is authorized and the project leader and team appointed, with responsibilities clearly defined, the feasibility study is terminated (Circle 32, Figure 11.4).

Duration of a feasibility study

The feasibility study may take a few days if the system change is a simple one, or years if the proposed system change is complex. The duration of the study is also a function of systems personnel and managers, the state of documentation of the existing system, the amount of detailed analysis to be prepared, the number of departments involved in the study, the urgency of the project, and the systems orientation of personnel involved. The study should not be rushed at the expense of quality and thoroughness, for it serves not only as the basis for a decision on implementation, but as the basis for design and evaluation after the feasibility decision is made. Additional time spent on the study may well contribute to the relevancy and effectiveness of the project and furnish materials for starting systems development after approval.

Summary

A feasibility study is primarily a fact-finding effort that provides the information necessary to make the decisions whether or not to implement a new information system. A secondary function is to provide the basic data necessary for the design, evaluation, and scheduling of the system, should it be adopted. Potential benefits and related problems will be identified during the course of the study.

There are four phases to a feasibility study: the organization of the study, a search for solutions, the feasibility analysis, and the decision on implementation. Steps in each of these phases and their interrelationships are shown in Figure 11.5.

Proposed solutions are checked for economic, financial, organizational, and technological feasibility, though not necessary in that order. For example, when new equipment is under consideration, a technological decision must be made before economic and organizational feasibility can be examined. In some cases all feasibility checks are done in parallel.

The lack of necessary funds is the most frequent reason for rejecting a systems change. Economic infeasibility—costs exceeding benefits—comes next. Noneconomic reasons include time constraints, the lack of necessary organizational environment, or the technological inability to achieve objectives.

Two important documents must accompany the decision to implement a new

Figure 11.5
Flowchart for feasibility study

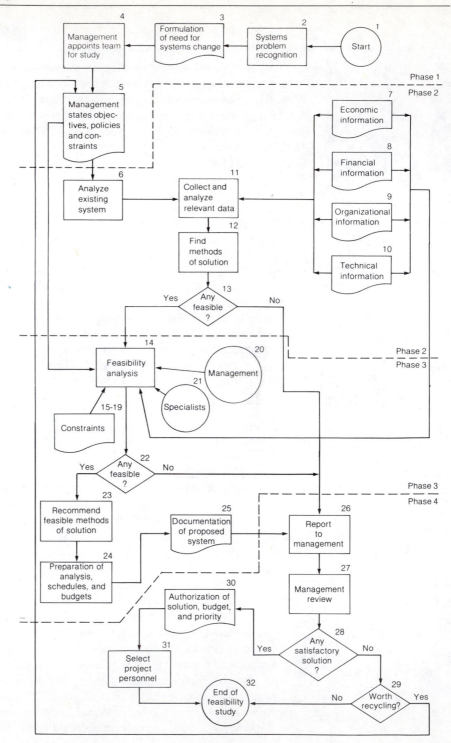

system. One identifies what can be achieved and the resources required, a document prepared by systems personnel. The second is authorization for the project, management's commitment, stating resources available and outlining policies for procedural and organizational changes necessary for implementation.

Figure 11.5 identifies three important decision points. Two are taken by the feasibility team, Symbols 12 and 22, where recommendations to either continue or terminate the feasibility study are made. The third is management's, Symbol 28. This decision is crucial. If management errs and decides to discontinue the study when the project should have been implemented, the firm has lost benefits that could have accrued from a systems change. An implementation when the project should have been discontinued will result in a loss of the firm's resources and unnecessary organizational disruption.

Feasibility studies are costly and time-consuming but they are of value. If properly conducted they reduce the risk of making a wrong decision. When the team fails to anticipate problems or recommends a solution that later proves unfeasible, the cause can usually be attributed to one or more or the following errors:

1. The team used a crash approach which did not provide sufficient time for all the phases of the study.
2. A nonintegrated approach was used, the team failing to consider the role of change in the long-range plans of the firm.
3. Poor leadership and poor staffing of the feasibility team existed.
4. Objectives and constraints were not adequately specified.
5. The feasibility study lacked organizational support.
6. Incorrect estimations were made by the team. These generally include errors in estimating organizational resistance to change, in underestimating the difficulty of the problem to be solved, in incorrectly stating resource requirements, or failure to recognize the organizational impact of the project.
7. User management in the application area did not participate and review objectives of the project.

Key words	
Accounting rate of return (ARR)	Net present value (NPV)
Benefit-cost analysis	Operational variable
Cardinal utility	Ordinal utility
Economic feasibility	Organizational constraints
Expected value of perfect information (EVPI)	Present value of future amounts (PV)
External constraint	Profitability index (PI)
Feasibility study	Project director
Financial feasibility	Project organization
Functional organization	Range estimates
Internal constraint	Return on investment (ROI)
Internal rate of return (IRR)	Technological constraints
Matrix organization	

Discussion questions

1. Distinguish between tangible and intangible benefits. Give examples of each.

2. It is not sufficient to concentrate solely on development costs in a feasibility study. What other considerations should be taken into account?

3. What are the potential costs and benefits of an information system?

4. Describe and compare methods of determining financial feasibility.

5. List examples of intangible costs and intangible benefits. How would you calculate or estimate each?

6. Distinguish between:
   a. Objectives and constraints.
   b. Technical and organizational feasibility.
   c. Economic and financial feasibility.
   d. Economic and financial constraints.
   e. Feasible and optimum solution.

7. Describe how you would organize a development team to design and implement an inventory control system for six warehouses and a $30 million volatile inventory? Would the team composition change if the system were to be OLRT as opposed to a batch system?

8. Is a feasibility study important in the development of an information system? Why? Is it essential for all information systems?

9. What types of feasibility should be examined?

10. Who should initiate a feasibility study? When should the study be initiated?

11. Give two examples each of economic, financial, organizational, and technical constraints.

12. Compare different approaches to capital budgeting for computer resources. Cite one example when each of the approaches might be used. Substantiate your choice.

13. What considerations lead to a GO decision following the feasibility study? Who makes that decision? Which approach is most suited for an EDP environment? Substantiate your position.

14. What project organization would you choose for an inventory project estimated at $800,000 over a span of three years and involving approximately 20 worker years? What types of persons would you want on the project team? Why?

15. What qualifications and qualities would you recommend for the project manager in Question 14.

16. Why are the future returns discounted in the economic criteria used to evaluate investment proposals for an MIS?

17. Explain why more than one financial criteria might be used to evaluate proposals for a MIS?

18. What are the potential financial costs and benefits of an information system?

Exercise

1. Two MIS proposals are competing for a limited capital budget. They have the following net cash flows.

Net cash flows ($000)

	Year					
	1	*2*	*3*	*4*	*5*	*6*
Proposal 1	−440	100	180	180	200	220
Proposal 2	−180	60	80	20	160	200

The company has a target rate of return on investments of 24 percent before considering taxes. Using the financial criteria discussed in this chapter, evaluate these two proposals. Treat all cash flows as occurring at the *end* of each year and discount them at the end of year 1.

Selected annotated bibliography

Couger, J. Daniel; Mel A. Colter; and Robert W. Knapp. *Advanced Systems Development/Feasibility Techniques*. New York: John Wiley & Sons, 1982, 526 pp.

This book is an update of the author's 1974 book *Systems Analysis Techniques*. Five generations of systems development are classified. An excellent reference.

Freilink, A. B., ed. *Economics of Informatics*. New York: North-Holland Publishing, 1975.

This book is on proceedings at an international symposium held in Germany. Especially good are the papers by Dorothy Pope on cost estimation of EDP (pp. 304–13) and by Frank Land on "Criteria for the Evaluation and Design of Effective Systems" (pp. 239–50).

King, John Leslie, and Edward L. Schrems. "Cost-Benefit Analysis in Information Systems Development and Operation." *ACM Computing Surveys* 10, no. 1 (March 1978), pp. 19–34.

A good discussion of the elements in estimating costs and benefits and how to avoid the major problems encountered. The article has a flowchart, a table, and some equations but nothing too technical. A good survey of 27 references.

Klein, Robert T., and Ralph Jamaro. "Cost/Benefit Analysis of MIS." *Journal of Systems Management* 33, no. 9 (September 1982), pp. 20–25.

The authors advocate a phased approach to a cost/benefit analysis. The nature of each phase and management action required in each phase are identified.

Parker, M. M. "Enterprise Information Analysis: Cost-Benefit Analysis and the Data-Managed System." *IBM Systems Journal* 21, no. 1 (1982), pp. 108–23.

The author discusses financial justification for a system based on an assessment of intangible costs and benefits, technological change, risk, and uncertainty.

Phister, Montgomery, Jr. *Data Processing Technology & Economics*. Santa Monica, Calif.: Santa Monica Publishing, 1974, pp. 167–238.

An excellent discussion of cost components: hardware costs, development costs, sales and marketing costs, maintenance costs, and life-cycle costs.

Rosenblatt, Meir J., and James V. Tucker. "Capital Expenditure Decision Making: Some Tools and Trends." *Interfaces* 9, pt. 1, no. 2 (February 1979), pp. 63–69.

A discussion of the use of discounting methods, the determination of discount and cut-off rates, the use of mathematical programming and capital rationing, and approaches to risk and uncertainty. The discussion is based on 15 surveys of the actual use of these approaches in business and industry.

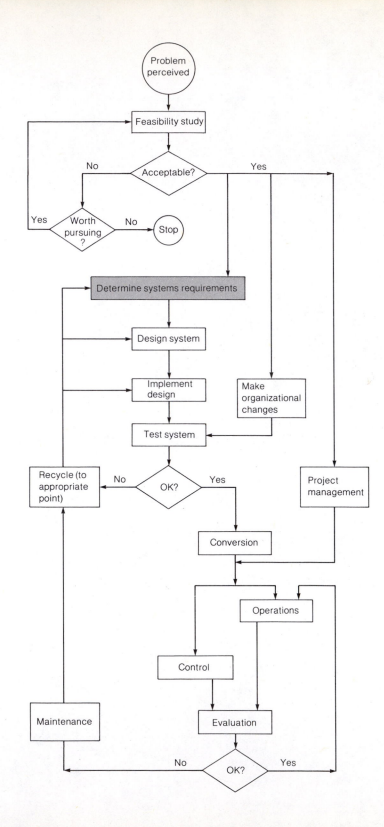

Determining systems requirements

12

Systems analysis is a new wine in an old bottle.

Gerald Weinberg

Determining users' needs and preparing systems specifications follow the feasibility study. At this stage, the objectives stated in general terms in the feasibility study are restated in greater detail to provide the operational framework for the systems design.

According to managers and systems professionals, the identification of information needs of management is the most critical factor associated with successful management information systems. Deficiencies in information systems can be partially avoided by properly defining the required content of the system. The steps in this crucial phase of development are shown in Figure 12.1.

In order to determine systems requirements, a series of design sessions are held so that top and supervisory management, as well as operating personnel, can express their informational needs as users (Boxes 3, 4, 6). System analysts participate in these sessions but primarily as coordinators, catalysts, and documentors. A final design session (Box 7) resolves conflicts between users' groups.

There are two basic strategies that can be used in defining systems design: bottom-up analysis or top-down design. In a **bottom-up approach,**[1] the need for subsystems is identified, and modules are designed and tested as independent units and then integrated into a total system. The approach is evolutionary in nature since operational modules of transaction files can first be designed, with later additions of modules for updating, control, and planning as the need develops.

The **top-down approach,** also called **structured design,**[2] starts by defining

---

[1] For a discussion of this approach, see Sherman Blumenthal, *Management Information Systems* (Englewood Cliffs, N.J.: Prentice-Hall, 1969), pp. 20–24. Blumenthal also discusses the approaches of organization chart, data collection, data bank, integrate later, and integrate now.

[2] For a discussion by one of the earliest and strongest proponents of the structured approach, see Edward Yourdon and Larry L. Constantine, *Structured Design* (Englewood Cliffs,

Figure 12.1
Determining systems specifications

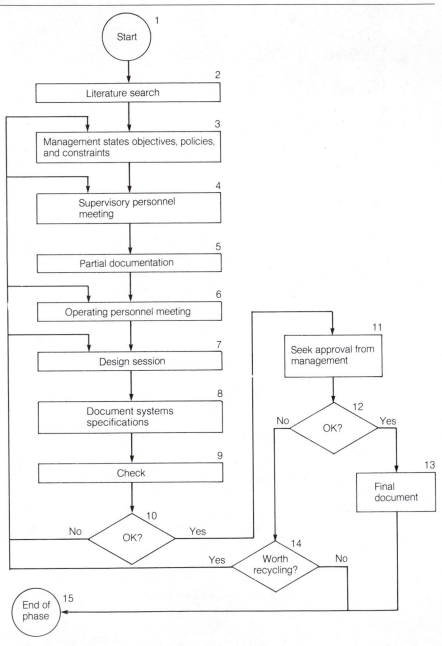

goals of the organization, the means to achieve these goals, the actions necessary to implement the means, and finally, the information needed for these actions. This approach is one of elaboration and clarification. The skeletal version of the new system is first designed before the system is subdivided into manageable components for development.

A distinction should also be made between the **structured methodology** of systems specification and **prototype methodology.** The first approach, also called **structured analysis,** involves specific dos and don'ts and a formal set of procedural steps. It is a rigorous and disciplined approach to systems specification.

Prototype methodology, on the other hand, is informal and experimental.[3] Convergence between need and specification is faster with this methodology. Specifications evolve as users interact with analysts. There is an iterative process of stating need and searching for solutions. A systems model will be proposed and modifications made as needs become clarified. An analogy might be made to using an airplane model in a wind tunnel to experiment with aerodynamic features. However, the prototype methodology for developing information systems is less scientific than structured methodology, and there is a tendency among users not to alter a working status quo even when improvements are advisable. Too often slipshod systems, untested and undocumented, result. The thoroughness of structured methodology minimizes this possibility.

The best method of determining systems specifications would be to utilize both prototype and structured methodology to take advantage of the strengths of both approaches.

At the design sessions, users must decide specifications for the new system, including:

1. Objectives, goals, and criteria of performance.
2. Outputs to be produced.
3. Inputs to be used.
4. Processes to be performed.
5. Resources to be available.
6. Procedures to be followed.
7. Organizational and other constraints to be met.

The key to determining users' requirements is data collection since only by gathering facts and opinions about operating procedures and changes needed can designers draw up a list of such specifications.

N.J.: Prentice-Hall, 1979), 473. See also Tom D. Marco, *Structured Analysis and System Specification* (New York: Yourdon, 1978), 352 p., and Chris Gane and Trish Sarson, *Structured Systems Analysis: Tools and Techniques* (Englewood Cliffs, N.J.: Prentice-Hall, 1979), 231 pp.

For a comparison of the structured approach with other approaches—Jackson Methodology, META Stepwise Refinement (MSR), and Higher Order Software (HOS)—see Lawrence J. Peters and Leonard L. Tipp, "comparing Software Design Methodologies," *Datamation* 23, no. 11 (November 1977), pp. 89–94.

[3] For more on prototyping, see Bernard H. Boar, *Applications Prototyping: A Requirements Definition Strategy for the '80s.* (Somerset, N.J.: John Wiley & Sons, 1984).

This chapter opens with an analysis of three alternative approaches to data collection that can be employed to gather information needed in the design sessions. It is followed by a discussion of the tools and techniques used in each approach. The method of drawing up systems requirements is also explained and approval procedures outlined. Finally, a brief discussion on project management is presented.

Data collection

The traditional approach

The main thesis of the **traditional approach** to data collection in determining users' needs is that no new information system can be designed without first considering the organizational and operational environment to be changed. An analysis of the current system identifies problem areas and areas of potential gain, and provides clues to system solutions. The detailed fact-gathering required aids not only in the analysis but in the subsequent design of the new system.

The list which follows shows the kinds of questions that must be asked when the existing system is studied.[4]

1. Related work
   What related work is being done?
      How is it being done?
2. Preparation and processing
   Who originates source data?
      Who prepares documents?
      How often is processing performed?
      How long does it take?
      Where is the processing performed?
      Who performs it?
      What equipment and supplies are used?
      How many copies are prepared? Who receives them?
      Is there unused processing capacity?
      What is the volume of documents (maximum, minimum, and average?)
      What has been the historical growth rate?
3. Form and timeliness of documents
   Are documents in a useful form?
      What are their limitations?
      Is exception reporting used?
      Can two or more documents be combined?
      Is greater accuracy needed?
      Can lesser accuracy be tolerated?
      Is faster reporting desired? Is it needed?

---

[4] Adapted from G. B. Davis, *Computer Data Processing* (New York: McGraw-Hill, 1974), p. 468.

4. User of documents

Who receives the document?

Does the document initiate decision? What decision? By whom?

Is there a part of the document that is ignored or rarely used?

What additional information is needed?

What processing is performed by the user of the document?

What is the flow of the document?

5. Storage and retrieval

Is the document retained? How? For how long?

What are the procedures for retention and purging?

How often is data purged and updated?

How often is it retrieved?

What are the procedures for retrieval?

How large is file (in number of records and average size per record)?

6. Cost

What is the cost of processing the document?

What is the change in cost resulting from a change in frequency or accuracy of processing?

How much of present cost of processing will be eliminated by computer processing?

What is the cost of storage and retrieval?

The main disadvantage of this list is its length. Gathering information in so much detail is a very time-consuming task, especially for firms that have accumulated many forms and lack updated documentation on procedures. It took 10,000 hours, an equivalent of about five human-years, for a firm of only 300 employees to collect such information when considering a systems change.

One reason the traditional approach is favored is that many users want only to match current performance when a new system is designed, preferring to continue the existing pattern of decision making and processing existing instead of trying something new. They do not even attempt to find optimal solutions nor do they look ahead to predict future information needs.

Because so many users specify that new systems should simply match the old, many firms fail to take advantage of advanced technology. Too many information systems merely duplicate manual, card, and noncomputer data-information systems. The equipment used represents an outdated generation of technology, an inefficient and wasteful use of resources. But a fresh look at systems, discovering a new approach to achieving corporate goals while optimizing performance through the exploitation of technical advances, is difficult when the traditional approach to data collection is used.

The innovative approach   In this approach, systems designers do not examine in-place systems, which may compromise their objectivity and channel their thinking. Instead, the systems favored by other firms with similar operations are studied and the latest computer technology searched. Novel ideas are considered, ideas that might be dismissed as impracticable by those who had first studied existing procedures. Users specify what information is desired even though this might seem idealistic and unobtainable. A drawback to this approach is that resulting systems often require changes in company policies and procedures, and organizational restructuring. The risk and disruption of such major overhaul make firms hesitant to use the **innovative approach** when determining systems requirements.

The hybrid approach

The **hybrid approach** combines the two preceding methods of determining users' needs. First, a totally new system is explored (innovative approach), then the tentative specifications are checked to make sure the new system matches the performance of the old (traditional approach). A variation of the hybrid method is to supplement the traditional approach with recent innovative tools for data collection such as ADS (Accurately Defined System) discussed later in this chapter. The main disadvantage of the hybrid method is that it compounds the weaknesses of the traditional approach: it is both time-consuming and costly.

The choice of method in data collection depends on the nature of the problem, the resources (money and personnel) available, the orientation of management, and the attitudes of systems personnel. The traditional approach is most commonly used. It has, therefore, been chosen as the basis for the flowchart in Figure 12.1.

Tools and techniques of data collection

A literature search, interviews, meetings, the Study Organization Plan, and Accurately Defined System are ways of collecting data to assist users in defining their needs.

Literature search

A **literature search** may be used by management to review and update knowledge of information systems. Systems personnel may study the firm's annual reports, catalogs, and publicity material in order to learn about the organization, its size, operations, products, internal structure, and stated objectives. A search might also be made of monographs, periodicals, professional journals, house organs, and books to learn of systems used in other firms.

An important aspect of the literature search is to help establish a common vocabulary of technical terms for developmental personnel. Lack of agreement on terminology is often a source of confusion, resulting in inaccuracies and wasted effort. The profession is too young and changing too rapidly for a settled body of definitions to exist. Yet development requires common definitions by users and technicians. A literature search should acquaint both groups with terms and be the basis for arriving at definitions early in the project.

Interviews

Interviews are used extensively in the social sciences as a means of collecting data. Structured interviews of users, asking a predetermined set of questions, help ensure that essential data is collected, that nothing important is left out. Unstructured interviews are much more time-consuming, but often their impromptu and spontaneous nature provides insights that result in better systems design.

Meetings

The system design sessions themselves can prove a fruitful technique of data collection. Brainstorming—gathering a group of people with different backgrounds and training for discussions—is a method businesses and industry successfully use in problem solving. When determining users' needs, the meetings would involve managers, systems personnel, and specialists, including consultants when needed. Design sessions also provide an occasion for exchanging reservations, concerns, and objections, and for resolving differences in design philosophies. The strengths of management and systems personnel can be identified and supported, and compensation made for weaknesses. During the course of the discussions, management must ensure that the systems objectives and organizational policies are not compromised unnecessarily and that systems personnel acquire a good conceptual understanding of the problem. An important side effect of such meetings is that all parties usually become interested and involved in the project and gain a better appreciation of interrelationships that affect successful operation of an information system.

Design sessions can be held at many points in the system's development. The flowchart in Figure 12.1 shows only one such meeting (Box 7), but additional sessions could be held following meetings with top management and supervisory personnel.

In all cases, design sessions should be conducted after careful planning and preparation. The participants should be selected with care, the meetings should have a suggestive and provocative agenda, and all relevant documents should be made available, with adequate lead time for study. For complex systems projects, the design sessions may last from two hours to two weeks. Experience has shown that the meetings are more productive when they are held without constant interruptions.

Design sessions on systems changes tend to result in flowcharting and decision tables. A useful technique is to photograph these to provide documentation for the ideas that emerge from the discussions.

Study Organization Plan (SOP)

SOP is a systematic method of collecting information and designing a new system developed by IBM. It was originated for breakthrough types of information systems and has been used with great success. SOP consists of three phases: understanding the present system, determining systems requirements, and designing the new system. Phases 1 and 2 correspond to this chapter, Phase 3, to the next chapter in this book. Phase 1 determines "what is done in the existing system, using what inputs, with what resources, and to achieve what results. Information is collected and organized into a meaningful pattern to permit an accurate understanding of the business as it presently operates and reacts to its environment." Phase 2 "reviews the input of these basic questions about the new system. What must it do? How well must it do it? What resources have management specified be used? To answer these questions and to arrive at a valid set of systems requirements, Phase 2 blends known facts about the present system with projections concerning the future."[5]

The SOP method involves the completion of a number of forms: the Resource Usage Sheet showing the resources (personnel, equipment, and materials) consumed by each organizational unit; the Activity Sheet identifying the inputs, outputs, and file usage of each activity; the Operation Sheet listing the volumes and lapse times of each operation; the File Sheet specifying each file's characteristics; the Message Sheet identifying recorded or unrecorded communications entering or leaving an operation; the Input-Output Sheet showing the input-output specifications; the Required Operation Sheet recording details of operational elements within flowchart diagrams; and Resource Sheets providing quantity and cost data on each resource used.

The SOP method is the traditional approach to data collection. Like other traditional approaches, it is time-consuming and costly, but it is also systematic and thorough. The detailed data collected does help analyze bottleneck areas and identify areas where change can bring added efficiency and effectiveness. It also provides a sound basis for the design activity to follow.

Accurately Defined System (ADS)

The National Cash Register Company has designed **Accurately Defined System (ADS)** for data collection. One version uses five forms for collecting information on outputs, inputs, data files, computations, and systems logic. The forms are designed to make certain there is consistency among data fields; to identify relationships of input, computation, and output; to determine validation rules and ranges of values; and to specify the boundaries of the system.

Other instruments of data collection

Process charts, an additional technique for gathering information, need explanation. The sample process chart in Figure 12.2 is used to analyze an accounts receivable procedure. Each step is traced, the time taken is recorded, and the volume handled noted. An analysis of the chart will quickly identify bottlenecks as well as duplicate and redundant steps, suggesting areas of potential savings in time and effort.

Other instruments of data collection are **flowcharts, data flow diagrams,** and **decision tables,** all of which have been employed in this text and need no further comment. Forms and charts for design can also be purchased from equipment and form vendors.

---

[5] *IBM Study Organization Plan, The Method Phase I,* No. 7–20–8136–0, and *The Method Phase II,* No. F 20–8137–0, pp. 38 and 27, respectively.

Figure 12.2
An example of a process chart

PROCESS CHART WORK SHEET

Please read instructions on other side before completing this form.

Job: Accounts Receivables   Page 1 of 1

Charted by: J. Williams   Date: 02-05-80   Procedure ___ **Method**

Number	Details of Step	Delay	Operation	Transportation	Storage	Check/Control	Time Required	Number	Comment
1	Wait for daily receipts and log them		●	□	△	▽	2-3-4 h		
2	Wait for batch	●	○	□	△	▽	2-3-4 d		
3	Glance verification	○	○	□	△	▼	50-90-120 m		
4	Corrections made	○	●	□	△	▽	2-4-7 h		
5	Sent for keypunching	○	○	■	△	▽	1-2-4 h		
6	Keypunching	○	●	□	△	▽	2-3-4 h		
7	Sent to Computing Center	○	○	■	△	▽	10-20-60 m		Recycled 2
8	Run edit program	○	○	□	△	▼	1-2-8 h		times at an
9	Return diagnostics to A/R	○	○	■	△	▽	1-2-4 h		average
10	Errors await correction	●	○	□	△	▽	1-4-16 h		
11	Correct errors	○	●	□	△	▽	40-60-120 m		
12	When no errors, logged	○	●	□	△	▽	5-10-12 m		
13	Records stored	○	○	□	▲	▽	5-8-10 m		
14	Payment sent to bank	○	●	□	△	▽	4-8-10 m		
15	Enroute to bank	○	○	■	△	▽	4-4-8 hrs		
16		○	○	□	△	▽			
		○	○	□	△	▽			
		○	○	□	△	▽			
		○	○	□	△	▽			

<u>Abbreviations used</u>   d = days   h = hours   m = minutes

Documentation

SOP and ADS are essentially techniques of **documentation,** but other instruments of data collection, especially interviews and design sessions, should also be documented. This must be done soon after the event, while memories are fresh, and should be verified by the individuals involved. Analysts should prepare this documentation periodically as shown in Boxes 5, 8, and 13 of Figure 12.1.

The need for documentation cannot be overemphasized. It should be a complete recording not only of discussions, but of definitions used and assumptions made. This will prevent later misunderstandings.

Identifying users' objectives, policies, and constraints

On the basis of collected data using the approaches and tools discussed in the preceding sections of this chapter, users' requirements must be identified at each organizational level shown in Figure 12.1: top management (Box 3), the supervisory level (Box 4), and the operational level (Box 6). This means defining **objectives** (what the user wishes to accomplish), **policies** (guidelines that determine the course of action for accomplishing the objectives), and **constraints.**

Stating objectives, policies, and constraints

Stating objectives is often difficult but it must be done. Information systems should be uniquely designed for each organization, and this can be accomplished only in context of the specific goals of each firm. The importance of defining objectives on the performance criterion is emphasized by R. N. McKean:

> There is a great danger of forgetting, or at least neglecting, the significance of criteria selection. If extreme care is not exercised in this part of the task, all the researcher's ingenuity and scientific tools may be wasted in deriving right answers to wrong questions—which are sometimes diametrically wrong answers to the real questions.[6]

Theoretically, a study of stated policies should help clarify objectives. In practice, however, policies are often not helpful. Policy manuals either do not exist or they are outdated. The missing information is usually crucial, for that is what caused them to be outdated in the first place. The process of determining short- and long-range objectives means examining how the system project fits into the organizational plan and verbalizing unwritten policies, prefererences, priority rankings, biases, and prejudices. Constraints imposed on the system by either internal or external factors, must also be specified.

Consider, for example, a business with the objective of reducing the length of its check-out lanes to specified limits. This is a classic problem in queuing theory that can be solved, provided the value of several rates and cost coefficients are known. One cost coefficient required is the hourly cost of clerks servicing each station. This is a known value: the wage rate (plus fringe benefits) per clerk. The

[6]R. N. McKean, "Sub-Optimization Criteria and Operations Research," in *Organizational Decision Making* eds. M. Alexis and C. Z. Wilson (Englewood Cliffs, N.J.: Prentice-Hall, 1967), p. 165.

other cost coefficient needed is the value of the customer's time while waiting to be served, a difficult if not impossible value to state. One might use the average hourly wage of the average store client (if that is known), but what about psychic costs, the annoyance, and inconvenience to customers? How can the loss of income be determined, should a customer, irritated by the queue, begin shopping at a competitor's store? How could you assign a value to grumbling that might make the other buyers leave? A crude estimation of the cost of waiting might be derived from the store records and interviews. But this is often not possible. The usual method is for the manager to assign a figure, the amount the business would pay to avoid customer waiting. It is this latter type of value judgment that must be formalized by management when stating objectives. If not, systems personnel will make the judgment by default.

Performance specifications

Objectives, policies, and constraints as they relate to users' requirements must next be specified in operational terms at desired performance levels. The following list shows the detail required.

Output: Content, format, quantity, availability, response time, frequency, distribution list, retention.
Processing: Decision rules, accuracy, ratio or absolute range, significance of results, current and future capacity.
Input: Source, media, procedures, validity checks.
Security: Input, organization, maintenance, decision rules, output, nature of access, list of those allowed access, control of access, identification, hardware, software, audit, general or specific, internal or external.
Backup system: Items needing backup, nature of backup procedures, and maintenance.

The preceding list is a general list of specifications. Each problem will vary in actual specification needs. The following sample, a partial list of systems requirements, shows the detail that was required in defining users' needs when the Universal Product Code (UPC) was developed by the Symbol Standardization Subcommittee of the Uniform Grocery Product Code Council, Inc.[7]

Mode	online real time
Size of code	12 decimal characters
Area of symbol	⊁ (not more than) 1.5 square inch
Speed of scanning	⊁ 100 inch/sec
Scanning reject rate	⊁ 0.01 percent
Undetected error rate	⊁ 0.0001 percent
Normal conditions of abrasion, dirt, and so forth allowed.	

[7] For details, see D. Savir and G. J Laurer, "The Characteristics and Decodability of the Universal Product Code Symbol," *IBM Systems Journal* 14, no. 1 (December 1975), pp. 16–34.

Output, processing, input, and security, the major headings in the performance specification list, have been mentioned earlier in this text and are examined further in Chapters 15 and 16. Users must also consider **backup.** What happens if the new system breaks down, if input data is physically destroyed or lost during computer processing? Can the data be recreated at the source or must the system have the capability of regenerating such losses? Keeping backup data is one solution to this problem but adds to the cost of the system. During this phase, systems personnel can estimate backup costs and users can decide what backup is advisable, but the final decision whether or not backup is worth the cost is the responsibility of management.

Approval procedures

Once users' requirements have been expressed and documented as **systems specifications,** the proposal should be checked for factual and statistical accuracy and the procedures analyzed to make sure they accomplish stated objectives. Then a series of approval decisions must be made on the proposal. The users and systems personnel who participated in the project must first decide whether the systems specifications are adequate (Symbol 10, Figure 12.1). If information is missing, the job recycles to the relevant point in the flowchart (Boxes 3, 4, 6, or 7). Management next evaluates the proposal (Box 11). If dissatisfied, recycling may be initiated (Boxes 3, 4, 6, 7). Management may also decide at this point to terminate the project (Exit NO, Symbol 14). This may be the result of disapproval with the systems specifications or could be due to reevaluation of the project in light of changed environmental conditions, such as the unavailability of expected resources, changes in assumptions made during the feasibility study, changes in priorities, or the appointment of new personnel in management.

Only if management decides to implement the project (Exit YES, Symbol 12) will the document on systems specifications be finalized. This completes the stage of determining systems requirements. The final document, the bill of goods the users want from the new system, outlines the framework for the design of the new system which follows.

Project management

Determining systems requirements is just one of the responsibilities of the development team. **Project management,** initiated after the feasibility study, continues through conversion. (Development of an information system is treated as a project since it begins and ends at target fixed points in time, and because special resources, techniques, and methodology are required.) Successful development is accomplished not through providential guidance nor through any unique expertise, but rather through the application of time-tested methods which are wholly dependent on adequate resources, both personnel and financial, and on a well-developed plan.

Project management is not used exclusively for systems development. Busi-

Figure 12.3
Network diagram of activities related to project management

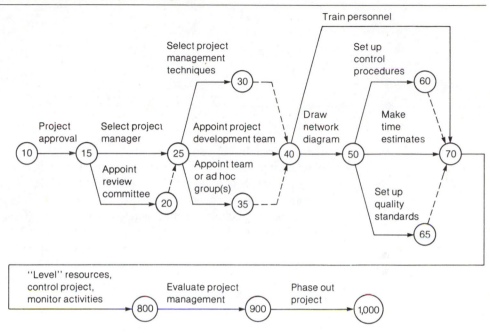

nesses apply project management techniques to complex projects of many types. This discussion in this text, however, is limited to information systems development.

The essence of project management is planning: selecting management techniques, establishing standards and procedures for quality control, and drawing up a schedule with time estimates for each activity of development. The project director oversees the work of the development team, making sure standards and schedules are met. All of the activities of project management are shown in the network diagram, Figure 12.3.

Selection of project management technique

There are many formal techniques of project management. The simplest is the Gantt chart where every activity is represented by a horizontal bar on a time scale. But if one activity is delayed, there is no way of telling which other activity or activities will be affected. A path or network diagram may be used instead. These show interrelationships, clearly establishing which activities must be completed before others can begin. The critical path can also be calculated (that is, the set of activities where delay retards the entire project); this information is needed to determine how long the project will take. If the time for each activity is known with certainty, **CPM (Critical Path Method),** a computerized technique for scheduling, can be used. When times can only be estimated, **PERT (Program Evaluation**

**Figure 12.4
Illustration of GERT**

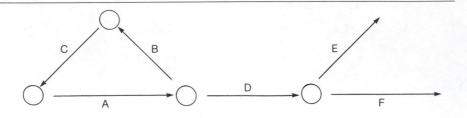

Review Technique) can be applied. This latter technique allows for three types of time estimates: optimistic time, pessimistic time, and most likely time. PERT is more commonly used than CPM in project management for information systems because the time needed for development activities is generally uncertain.

Another computerized scheduling technique, **GERT (Graphic Evaluation Review Technique)**[8] is frequently favored over PERT because it allows **looping.** A loop occurs when three activities (A, B, and C) must be completed before another (D) is initiated, but A must be done before B, B before C, and C before A, as depicted in Figure 12.4. Such loops frequently occur in information systems development. GERT also allows alternative paths (either E or F in Figure 12.4), whereas PERT conventions require that all activities be performed in a set sequence. That is, PERT allows AND relationships, whereas using GERT, one can specify the probability of alternative paths in an OR relationship, such as E or F in Figure 12.4. The time of project completion is then calculated with probability (p) associations. For example, the completion time might be 20 weeks with $p = .6$, and 26 weeks with $p = .8$. This additional information is valuable for scheduling and control in project management.

GERT has disadvantages, however. It requires more data than PERT (data on probabilities that are difficult and expensive to collect), and few computer programs exist for calculating GERT. Computer programs for PERT are readily available[9] and many include refinements such as optimization (of cost and time) as well as management and equipment leveling. PERT is, therefore, more commonly used than GERT for information system development. It is perfectly adequate as long as the user makes allowance for its limitations. For example, when calculating time estimates, the PERT user should include time estimates for possible looping.

[8]For an excellent introductory discussion, see E. R. Clayton and L. J. Moore, "GERT vs. PERT," *Journal of Systems Management* 2, no. 2 (February 1972), pp. 11–19. For a detailed discussion, see the book by L. J. Moore and E. R. Clayton, *GERT Modeling and Simulation* (New York: Petrocelli/Charter, 1976), 227 pp.
[9]For a survey of 43 software packages and a critical discussion of such software, see Perry Peterson, "Project Control Systems" *Datamation* 25, no. 7 (June 1979), pp. 147–148 ff.

Summary

The stage in the development process after the feasibility study is the specification of systems requirements. It is in this stage that users at different levels decide what, why, how, and when information is needed. Figure 12.1 shows the activities in determining systems specifications. Users must identify objectives and constraints during the course of these activities, and specify inputs, outputs, resources, processes, security, and backup to be used. Needed data on which to base specification decisions may be gathered by the traditional, innovative, or hybrid approaches, using literature searches, interviews, meetings, SOP, ADS, and other instruments of data collection.

The goal in this phase of a new system's development is to define users' needs completely and accurately. Since these needs are forever changing and expanding, the process can continue indefinitely at great cost. The other extreme, defining users' needs hastily, is equally unwise for the system developed may prove ineffective. A judicious middle ground should be found.

Once the feasibility study is terminated, development activities must be planned and scheduled. The Gantt chart can be successfully used for small projects. More complex projects with many interrelated activities require a planning technique that shows sequencing and precedence, and calculates the critical path of project completion. PERT and GERT are two techniques commonly used with computer programs for scheduling and control.

Key words

Accurately Defined System (ADS)	Looping
Backup	Objectives
Bottom-up approach	Policies
Constraints	Process chart
Critical Path Method (CPM)	Program Evaluation Review
Data flow diagram	Technique (PERT)
Decision table	Project management
Documentation	Prototype methodology
Flowchart	Structured analysis
Graphic Evaluation Review	Structured design
Technique (GERT)	Structured methodology
Hybrid approach	Study Organization Plan (SOP)
Innovative approach	Systems specifications
Interviews	Top-down approach
Literature search	Traditional approach

Discussion questions

1. What information is relevant when specifying users' needs? How is this information gathered and synthesized?

2. What is systems analysis? What are essential features? Why is systems analysis important when developing a computerized information system?

3. What are some of the tools and techniques of systems analysis to be used for EDP?

4. How are informational requirements influenced by:
   a. Function (that is, planning, control, and so forth)?
   b. Level of management?
   c. Size of organization?
   d. Types of decisions?
   e. Style of management?

5. Why do analysts study existing systems prior to studying alternate solutions? What other approaches can be used?

6. Distinguish between:
   a. Literature search and study of existing system.
   b. Innovative and hybrid approach.
   c. System requirements and users' requirements.
   d. Objectives and requirements of system.
   e. Structured methodology and prototype methodology.

7. Who should state the objectives and constraints of the future system? In what detail should specifications be made?

8. How is the user and system specification at this stage different from specifications drawn up during the feasibility study?

9. Empirical studies have shown that the user specification stage is the most difficult developmental stage. Why?

10. What is the difference between ADS and SOP? Which would you prefer? Would your choice depend on the project? If so, why?

11. Why is a process chart a useful technique for data collection? Cite two examples when the chart could be used.

12. What are differences between Gantt, CPM, PERT, and GERT? Which would one use for an EDP project that is:
    a. Large and complex with most time estimates known with certainty?
    b. Small, simple?
    c. Large and complex with only probability time estimates known?
    d. Complex with much looping and alternative branchings?

13. What other approaches to analysis might be tried?

Exercises

1. Specify in detail a reporting system for Exercise 1, Chapter 10 for use by a manager:
   a. For reference of salesperson's performance.
   b. For posting information on each salesperson by name or number. Assume that there is a unique ID number of 10 digits.
   c. For other purposes, such as ranking salespersons and calculating bonuses.

2. Read Russell L. Ackoff, "Management Misinformation Systems," *Management Science* 14, no. 4 (December 1967), pp. B147–B156, and Alfred Rappaport, "Management Misinformation Systems—Another Perspective," *Management Science* 15, no. 4 (December 1969), pp. B133–B136. (Both articles are available in books of readings, including U. T. Dock et al. *MIS, A Managerial Perspective* (Chicago: Science Research Associates, 1977), pp. 119–30.

   Why does Ackoff argue that managers do not know what they need? What information do managers need, and why? Who understands these needs? Do Ackoff's statements made in 1967 hold true in the 1980s? Does Rappaport effectively answer arguments?

3. State the specifications needed for an office terminal to perform calculations for production and finance. These specs should be detailed enough to be used as a basis for bids.

Selected annotated bibliography

Burch, John G., Jr., et al. *Information Systems: Theory and Practice,* 2d ed. New York: John Wiley & Sons, 1979.

This textbook has an extensive coverage of the development cycle including the phase of specifying users' needs. A case study includes flowcharts, calculation memos, and documentations generated. A good nontheoretical presentation.

Canning, Richard G., ed. "Progress in Project Management." *EDP Analyzer* 15, no. 12 (December 1977), pp. 1–14.

Project management systems packages are discussed. The experiences of the city of Tacoma with SPECTRUM–1 and the Airborne Freight Corporation with SDM/70 are discussed.

———, ed. "The Analysis of User Needs." *EDP Analyzer* 17, no. 1 (January 1979), pp. 1–13.

Two techniques are discussed: IA (Information Analysis) used extensively in Europe and SA (portion of Structured Analysis and Design Techniques). These techniques are not yet automated but may soon be.

Cleland, David I., and William R. King. *Systems Analysis and Project Management,* 2d ed. New York: McGraw-Hill, 1975.

This book is not specifically on information system project management but is nonetheless relevant to such projects. The first edition of the book got the McKinsey Foundation Award. The second edition is updated and has excellent coverage on the project environment and how to plan and organize for it.

Couger, J. Daniel; Mel A. Colter; and Robert W. Knapp. *Advanced Systems Development/Feasibility Techniques.* New York: John Wiley and Sons, 1982, 526 pp.

This book is an update of the authors' 1974 book, *Systems Analysis Techniques.* The new title is somewhat misleading since the book is essentially about techniques of analysis and design. The authors classify systems development and cost effectiveness analysis techniques in five generations. The coverage is comprehensive, though all readers may not agree with the authors' classification of generations. An excellent reference.

Davis, G. B. "Strategies for Information Requirements Determination." *IBM Systems Journal* 21, no. 1 (1982), pp. 4–30.

Various strategies of obtaining information on systems requirements are surveyed. The constraints on humans as specifiers of information requirements are explored. The contingency approach is also discussed.

DeMarco, Tom. *Structured Analysis and System Specification.* Englewood Cliffs, N.J.: Prentice-Hall, 1979, 93 pp.

The author discusses structured English, decision tables, pseudo code, decision trees, the DED, Data Flow Diagram, and his own approach to structured analysis. A well-written and readable book.

Gane, Chris, and Trish Sarson. *Structured Systems Analysis: Tools and Techniques*. New York: Improved Systems Technologies, 1977, 373 pp.

An excellent discussion of the subject. Decision tables, decision trees, structured English, pseudo code and tight English are examined. A good discussion of problems of expressing logic is also included.

Munro, Malcom C., and Gordon B. Davis. "Determining Management Information Needs: A Comparison of Methods." *Management Information System Quarterly* 1, no. 2 (June 1977), p. 43–54.

This is a comparison of the effectiveness of decision analysis (top-down) and data analysis (bottom-up). The results of information obtained by these methods, evaluated by college executives for values and other attributes, are discussed.

Taggart, W. M., and M. Tharp. "A Survey of Information Analysis Techniques." *ACM Computing Surveys* 9, no. 4 (1977), pp. 273–90.

This article surveys 29 references on the subject and includes an annotated bibliography of an additional 40 references. It also suggests directions for profitable research in the future.

Weinberg, Victor. *Structured Analysis*. New York: Yourdon, 1980, 328 pp.

This book is limited to the structured approach, but is a good coverage of structured methodology, analysis, and design.

Yandav, Surya B. "Determining an Organization's Information Requirements: A State of the Art Survey." *Data Base* 14, no. 3 (Spring 1983), pp. 3–20.

A superb survey of a very important, but nebulous, phase of development. Sixty-four references are cited. The author concludes that more research in determining systems requirements is needed. ". . . the literature provides insights but they cannot be considered as systematic aids for determining information requirements of an organization. . . . Very little work has been done on the process of deriving information requirements."

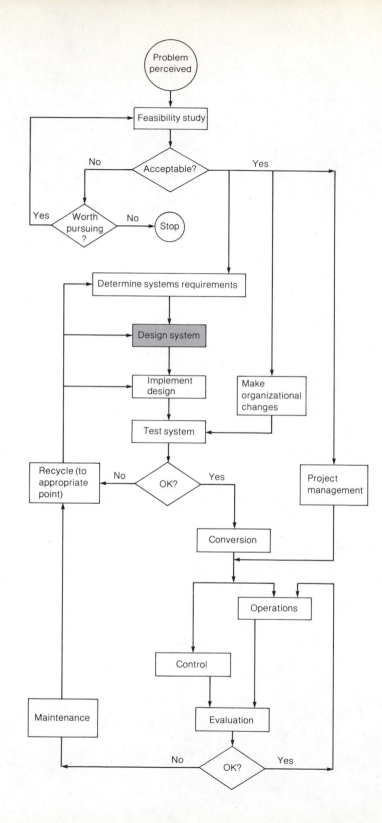

Design of a system

13

Surely we can spend a few minutes before rushing off to spend our money or write programs. Isn't that extra hesitation the essence of design?

Gerald Weinberg

The design phase of a new system's development is the detailed specification of the systems requirements. This phase is analogous to preparing blueprints for the construction of a new house. Once users' needs have been determined (general house layout, square footage, style), particulars must be decided (roof slant, room dimensions, location of electrical outlets). When designing a new system, a development team draws up users' requirements in specific operational terms, designating input, output, the flow of information, standards for personnel, forms to be used, and equipment performance required. Computer programming specifications and system test specifications must also be determined and the role of the new system defined in the overall system plan for the organization.

Figure 13.1 is a network diagram showing the activities in this phase of development. Since the activities are performed in parallel from 300 to 390, dummy activities (requiring no resources or time) are inserted in some paths so a numbering system that uniquely identifies each activity is possible.

Users should participate in the development team in this phase to ensure that the final version of the system's design reflects users' needs. Since implementation of the completed design is the responsibility of the technicians, the activities described in this chapter end active user involvement until testing and conversion.

Design management (300–390) Figure 13.1

As standards and specifications are detailed during the design phase they must be checked to see that they comply with overall system objectives Also, projects need to be kept on schedule. It is the responsibility of the project director to oversee and coordinate the many activities that take place during this stage of development.

Figure 13.1
Network diagram for design stage in system development process

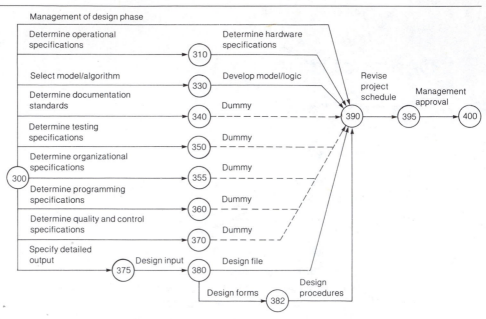

Operational and hardware specifications (300–310–390)

In the design phase, technical decisions regarding standards and hardware characteristics are made. In many instances, the firm will already have adequate computer facilities so no new computer hardware is needed. But specifications on input and output equipment will still have to be made. For example, if scanning equipment for reading input data has been recommended, operational specifications prepared in the design phase might be:

> Speed > (more than) 1600 documents/hour
> Error rate = 1/10,000 markings
> Maintenance ≯ (no more than) 24 hours at any one time

Hardware specifications might include:

> Cost ≯ (no more than) $4,000/year
> Capability = Read markings on document, up to 400 markings per document.
> Document size up to 8½″ × 11″.
> Medium darkness of markings should suffice.

The development team generates a document with such detailed specifications for the use of technicians responsible for physical preparation, programming, and testing of the new system.

Model selection and development (300–330–390)

The **model** necessary for computation must be selected (300–330) and developed (330–390). It defines mathematically the manipulation of variables leading to a solution. In simple applications—such as payroll, accounts payable, or generating reports—flowcharts and decision tables can be used as long as relationships are stated in detail and all decision rules necessary for computation appear. For planning purposes, complex linear programming models may be required. Computer applications needed for management control, such as inventory control, queuing, and scheduling, use complex models. The use of models will be discussed in Chapter 20.

Documentation standards (300–340)

In developing a new information system, standards for documentation should be established in the design phase.

Documentation in this context is a written description of choices and decisions during the development process. There is both **developmental** and **project control documentation.** The former is a description of the system itself (objectives, characteristics, decision rules); the latter concerns project development organization (personnel, time, materials, money). Developmental documentation is needed for operation and use of the new system. Control documentation is for auditing and evaluating the project.

If properly prepared, the documentation package has many advantages.

1. It is a record and evidence of all the commitments and expectations.
2. It helps initiate and train newcomers to the system.
3. It provides information needed to change the system should the environment or management's needs alter.
4. It prevents dislocation and cost which occurs when knowledge of the system is centered in a few individuals who subsequently resign, relocate, or are assigned to other duties.
5. It facilitates routine evaluation, auditing, and control.

Programmers and system analysts have a reputation for disliking documentation and for procrastinating over its completion. They find it tedious and time-consuming work. They often argue that they are too busy, or that documentation should wait until the system stabilizes. Since systems are constantly redesigned, stabilization occurs over a long period of time and documentation tends to be indefinitely postponed. Some companies will contract a system job for a 20-percent reduction in cost if no documentation is required. This is a penny-wise pound-foolish proposition. Documentation is too important to be compromised.

The fact that documentation is not a popular activity means that the development team must carefully spell out documentation standards and insist upon compliance. When standards for preiously developed systems exist, they should be checked by the team to make sure they are applicable to the system under development. It may be necessary to supplement these standards to meet the unique needs of the new system.

Documentation should be divided into four manuals: a **Systems Manual**—general information on the system and its objectives; a **Programmer's Manual**—description of programs; an **Operator's Manual**—directions for running programs; and a **User's Manual**—procedures for use of the system, including data flow diagrams, decision tables, and program descriptions written in terms that users will understand. This division allows simultaneous access to documentation information by groups with differing needs. No single user can withdraw all documentation from circulation. The development team must prescribe what material is to be contained in each manual and establish the format for recording information. Abstract, detailed, and summary documentation should appear in each manual. The team should also specify the timing for completion of the documentation since it loses its value if not available when needed. The dates of documentation completion should be included in project planning charts.

Testing standards for the documentation should also be outlined by the development team. Persons who prepare documentation are often so immersed in the system that assumptions are taken for granted. It is helpful to have people unfamiliar with the system try to operate it on a test basis by following documentation guidelines. Incompleteness, inadequacies, and ambiguities will soon be revealed.

Finally, the team should establish control standards for the documentation. Personnel (librarians) responsible for the manuals should be assigned and given authority to control access, and a physical location for the manuals must be chosen. Persons authorized to use and/or modify the documentation must be identified, and procedures for documentation revision and validity testing should be set.

Documentation standards should be sent to all personnel involved in the development of the new system. This will include personnel in project management, programming, operations, testing, physical preparation, and also personnel responsible for organizational changes.

Testing specifications (300–350)

As part of the design of an information system, testing standards and requirements must be determined. This includes the choice of an approach to testing. One approach is a **pilot study.** The new system is designed and tested on a small scale and only after it is found to be successful does full-scale system implementation take place. This reduces and localizes the losses and disruption that may result from design errors.

When a pilot study is not feasible, testing may be a **parallel** or **dry run.** This involves testing the new system while the old is still in operation. This approach lets management observe the new system and check performance standards before discontinuing the old. Management may insist on this approach if skeptical about the new system, or if the consequences of system failure are so great that a trial run is essential. There is, however, a price that must be paid for test assurance. Two systems running simultaneously often cause confusion. Time and personnel costs are involved. Both pilot studies and dry runs produce considerable organizational strain.

Sometimes management chooses no testing after weighing testing costs against consequences should the system fail to perform. In automated information systems, however, this course is not recommended because one unidentified variable, one unstated decision rule, one transcription error, or one incorrectly stated programming instruction can cause the entire system to malfunction.

One design policy that makes a system suitable for testing and conversion is modularity. This subject will be further discussed in Chapter 14.

New systems need a **factor of safety,** a factor determined by the development team and used in testing. For example, if an information system were designed for 10,000 employees, a safety factor of 2 would require that the system be tested for 20,000. Designing a system to function under unexpected conditions assures management that it can operate when conditions are normal. The magnitude of the safety factor should be decided by the team after weighing incremental costs against benefits.

In this design phase, what to test and how to test are determined. For example, for an online terminal system, the stated requirements for a particular output might be a response time of no more than five seconds. When the new system is implemented, performance will be checked against this specification or, using a factor of safety of 2, a response time of no more than 2½ seconds. Establishing such testing rules and standards is the responsibility of management working in conjunction with the development team.

Test design would also include the assignment of personnel to perform the tests, identification of control points and controls to be used in testing, the establishment of procedures for recording results, and finally, the setting up of a liaison between user and systems personnel for the purpose of evaluating test results.

Organizational specifications (300–355)

New systems require changes in a firm's organizational structure. Some jobs will be eliminated. Others will be created. Existing personnel may have to be retrained and/or new employees hired. Not all staff needs will be known at this stage in the development process. For example, the number and skills of operational personnel required for the new system will depend on the equipment selected. But as soon as these requirements are known, the persons responsible for personnel planning should be informed.

Since a general knowledge of the information system is needed if it is to be operated effectively and efficiently, the development team should specify what types of educational programs are necessary and who should participate. Employees requiring intensified retraining should be identified. In some cases, specifications for staffing may call for a retrenchment of personnel. Since a long gestation period is usually needed when making organizational changes, the development team should document personnel requirements as early as possible to ensure that employees are trained and available when it is time for conversion to the new system.

Programming specifications (300–360)

Programming specifications should include information on the capability and features of the programs to be written. The programming language(s) to be used should also be stated. Sometimes language choice is constrained by limitations of equipment. Too often, programmers simply use the language they know best, a language which may not be the most efficient or effective for the demands of the new system. This happens because programmers, under pressure of production work, have little time to keep abreast of their fast-moving field. Time should be spent in language evaluation before the team makes the final language selection. For example, many languages, especially machine languages, are machine-dependent though these languages have certain advantages, such as fast processing time. Machine-independent languages provide flexibility, facilitating future changes in computer systems. Programmers for such languages are also easier to find. The development team must evaluate such trade-offs in their choice.

Establishing programming standards, such as structured programming, is another responsibility of the development team. Uniform standards have been widely adopted and undoubtedly the firm has incorporated them for other systems in use. Or they can be found in textbooks or manuals. Standards should facilitate interchangeability between programmers.

Quality and control specifications (300–370)

Quality and control are related because the function of control is to ensure specific levels of quality. This is achieved by setting up quality standards and making sure that they are met.

Control is exercised with each systems component, such as input, output, and processing. Control is discussed in different sections of this chapter when design of components is considered There is, however, one important aspect of control that affects all components of the system, the **audit trail.**

An audit trail is the path of data flow in a transaction. In manual processing, points are established along this trail for recording information about the transaction, permitting, for example, a given monetary transaction to be traced from original entry to its termination in the general ledger. The records are then later examined by auditors. In a manual accounting system, arithmetical accuracy and correct posting of figures from one set of documents to another would also be checked as part of quality control.

Audit trails also exist in computerized systems, but control is different since the computer has eliminated the detailed recording that is done in manual processing. Auditors concentrate on verifying input documents and seeing that subsequent procedures are carried out as planned. They are more concerned with checking the system than in checking the indidual items being processed by the system. When designing a new information system, costs versus benefits of audit trails must be evaluated and the degree of trailing must be decided. Management may have little choice, however, for government and regulatory agencies specify auditing requirements for many applications.[1]

---

[1] The subject of auditing is discussed later in Chapter 16.

Control and quality specifications generate a document that is sent to testing personnel who make sure that the quality standards set are met by the new system. The document is also sent to the programming group so that these capabilities can be programmed.

Input and output specifications (300–375–380–382–390)

In a functional sense, input comes before output. But from a design viewpoint the order is reversed. It is necessary to know output requirements first because these determine the input that is required. File design (needed in processing) generally comes last since input determines the records which constitute the file, though in some cases, a preliminary file will be designed before input.

Output (300–375)

In specifying detailed output, users on the development team should be sure that the new system provides all the information that is needed for both current and future use. The incremental cost of producing added information is relatively small at the design stage compared to the cost of redesigning the system at a later date. An analogy would be including a public address system in the blueprints for a building under construction as opposed to the high renovation cost of adding such a system to an existing structure.

But care must be taken not to overspecify output needs. Users should not demand output that is simply nice to have. Unnecessary information can be a burden and have a negative benefit. It can crowd out needed information, making essential information difficult to find and use. There is also a cost involved in producing useless information. The development team must weigh the benefits of output against costs before determining exactly what output the new system should produce.

The details of content of the output may have already been determined as part of the users' requirements. If not, then details must be specified now. For example, parameters and input variables for each computation required for the output should be stated along with their spatial relationships, if these are desired. Such requirements as totals, subtotals, and figures in absolute values or percentages must also be specified.

One characteristic of good ouput is that it can be understood and accurately interpreted by any user, even one who has not participated in the development of the system and is ignorant of the environment. The output can be checked by asking: Is the output readable? Does it have an adequate, unique, and meaningful title? Are the different types of reports easily accessible? Are pages numbered? Are all abbreviations and codes adequately identified? Are assumptions clear? Is the period for which the data is relevant apparent? Is the output dated? Is the run number given when more than one run is made per day? Is the output complete? Is it accurate? Is it easy to store and retrieve?

These questions may seem trivial but attention paid to seemingly small and inconsequential matters often determines the effectiveness of an information system. For example, a university using an information system to produce a class schedule discovered that many students were attending class at the wrong time or going to the wrong room at the start of the semester. The format of the schedule made it hard to read. The eye had to move across ten columns of course information (course number, section number, credit hours, instructor, and so forth) before reaching the columns for time and location. The close spacing of horizontal lines caused the students' eyes to wander to the line above or below before reading the final columns. In this case, faulty output design meant ineffective use of the information produced by the system. The problem was corrected by reformatting the output, keeping relevant information, such as room number and class times in the left-hand columns and lengthy and less consequential information, such as course title, in the right-hand columns. A further solution was to leave spacing at the end of each department's course information, and to use output paper with colored horizontal stripes.

The design of output will vary with the user's style of management. The mode of processing (real time versus batch) and the nature of output (printed versus terminal, or print versus graphic) will also influence design. Nevertheless, there are some basic design principles that apply to all output. They are as follows:

1. Legends, headings, and output formats should be standardized whenever possible.
2. Acronyms, abbreviations, and terms used in the output should be defined. Examples and explanations may serve this purpose. Or a glossary can be appended.
3. Algorithms and assumptions on which calculations are based should be available to users of the output. This assures correct interpretation of output.
4. Output should be hierarchical in presentation so that the user can access data easily at each level required without having to search through all the data.
5. The amount of data, its accuracy, and precision should be governed by how the output is to be used. For example, too much output can overload the user and prove as ineffective as too little.
6. Exceptional data should be displayed in a manner that facilitates comparison of actual values with expected values, the comparison being in meaningful units. For example, percentage increase or decrease in dollar sales might be more useful than absolute dollar values.
7. The contents of the output should be listed in a menu, especially when output appears on a terminal.
8. Users have psychological and intellectual constraints in the amount of data that can be absorbed at any one time.[2] These constraints should be rec-

---

[2] See George A. Miller, "The Magical Number Seven, Plus or Minus Two: Some Limits on Our Capacity for Processing Information," *The Psychological Review* 63, no. 2 (March 1956), pp. 81–97.

ognized and taken into consideration when designing the quantity and format of output data displayed per frame.[3]

9. Users needs should govern the level of aggregation of output.
10. The age of data affects the usefulness of output. Outdated information, data no longer needed for decision making, should be excluded.

Output specifications, once determined, are sent to personnel involved in programming, physical preparation, and testing. The specifications are also prerequisites for the next set of activities to be performed, the design of input.

Input (375–380)

As with output, there is input data that is not essential but nice to have. It is tempting to collect such data because the incremental cost of added input is often very small. However, useless input has the same negative benefit as useless output. Data for future use should be collected but users must be able to show benefits for such input.

Care must be taken to collect data at the lowest level of aggregation needed for present and future use. For example, data on total sales per month per sales representative could not be used to generate a report on company sales for each state unless the input also included information on the location of each sale. What if management five years hence requires historical information on sales per product? The system will be unable to produce such a report unless the input of sales data includes information on products sold.

Files (380–390)

The development team must determine the nature of **files** required for the new information system, the content of each file (what data elements are to be used) and the storage media for each file.

The concept of files was discussed in Chapter 6. Every application will use at least one file. When multiple applications and files exist, they need to be integrated with other files in the data base. For **horizontal integration,** that is, integration between files, one or more linking data elements are needed. For **vertical integration,** integration between the different levels of management, a common set of data elements is required. For **longitudinal integration,** data compatibility over the years is needed. These integrations must be approved and coordinated by the data base administrator. The topic of integration will be discussed in greater detail in Chapter 21.

Within one functional file or subsystem (that is, sales, manufacturing, advertising, or personnel), there may be many related or derived files, as shown in Figure

---

[3]For designs of display output, see James Martin, *Design of Man-Computer Dialogues* (Englewood Cliffs, N.J.: Prentice-Hall, 1973). For a discussion of human factors in output design, see Lance A. Miller and John C. Thomas, Jr., "Behavioral Issues in the Use of Interactive Systems," *International Journal of Man-Machine Studies* 9, no. 5 (September 1977), pp. 509–36.

13.2. The **master file** is designed to contain all basic operational information and should also contain current information on transactions by being regularly updated from the **transaction file.** Updating adds to the master file. It would soon become bulky and inefficient unless stripped of data no longer needed for processing. Stripped historical data, including that used in occasional operational processing and data kept merely for the record, should be stored in an **archive file.** In government-regulated industries, such as utilities, length of time records must be stored is specified by law.

A master file containing data for the current year may still prove cumbersome. Files of 10,000 to 50,000 records, each containing up to 500 characters, are not uncommon for employee, vendor, or customer files. Since only part of these records affect transactions, a **summary master file** can be extracted for regular updating and frequent use, while the complete master is updated less often and processed only when required.

Backup is needed for the master file when the loss of data on that file would disrupt or interfere with operations. If the master file is processed daily, retention of the superseded file would constitute one level of backup (first generation). Yesterday's file would be a second backup (second generation), and the file from the day before yesterday would serve as the third generation of backup. These respective files are commonly called **son, father,** and **grandfather files.** They should be stored in secure and disperse locations. If the location of the master makes it vulnerable, the amount of backup and the degree of security required are factors to be decided by management and the development team. Allowance should be made for accidental master file loss due to operational errors, loss due to natural disasters (such as fire or flood), and possible sabotage or theft. But

**Figure 13.2
Types of files**

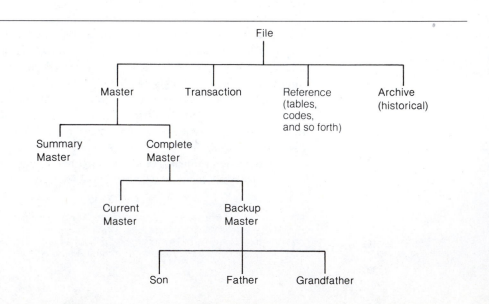

creation of backup will be tempered by processing costs necessary to create backup and the cost of storage.

Figure 13.2 also shows a **reference file.** Generally tables and codes are kept in a reference file because they are commonly shared by several programs, or because they are too lengthy to be incorporated into a program. The tables and codes to be included in the reference file are also design specifications.

Forms (380–382)

Output and input often require preprinted forms. There are principles of design that apply to all forms. They must be unambiguously titled and worded; the color of the forms should be chosen for emphasis and ease of reading (light brown and light green print have been found empirically to be easy on the eye); the forms should be shaded for horizontal reading of lines of data without the drifting of sight; the print must be spaced to facilitate reading; related data should be grouped together; the form size should fit into standard binders and file cabinets; no information should be lost when the form is punched or bound; and finally, the paper used should satisfy requirements at minimum cost.

Other **form design** principles that apply specifically to output were covered in the discussion on output in this chapter. In checking design of input forms, the following questions should be asked.

1. Are the instructions for completing the form adequate and easily understood?
2. Are input codes (if used) unique and unambiguous?
3. Is there sufficient space for completing information without crowding?
4. Are the questions worded unambiguously?
5. Are the questions in proper sequence to avoid confusion?
6. Are lines to be filled in by typewriter spaced to conform to typewriter spacing?
7. Is the vertical alignment on forms to be typewritten such that clerks can use the typewriter tabular-stop device?
8. Does the form provide larger spaces for handwritten data than for typewritten data?
9. If the form is to take information from, or pass information to, another form, do the items appear in the same order on both forms?
10. Does the form have all recurring items printed so that only variable values need to be filled in?
11. Is all known and fixed information preprinted?
12. Have all relevant facts been collected?
13. Is the form designed so that no information is lost when the form is filed or bound?
14. Is the form printed on the size and weight of paper that meets the requirements of the form without being more expensive than necessary?
15. Can the form be easily referenced by document number, date of origin, or some other identification?

The importance of careful form design cannot be overemphasized. A firm with an application asking for name, address, birthdate, father's name, and date of high school graduation found that many persons entered their father's date of graduation whereas the information desired was the applicant's own high school graduation date. In this case, poor sequencing of questions or poor clarification of the question resulted in misinformation. Such problems should be anticipated. Careful design should minimize such misunderstandings. Pretesting a form by sample users is one method of detecting such errors.

The entry of numbers on forms is a frequent source of errors. For example, handwritten *ones* and *sevens* often look alike. The use of boxes on forms for numerical data seems to encourage the average user to write numbers legibly. Data processing personnel commonly use the European convention of placing a dash on the stem of a seven (7̶) to distinguish it from a one. They also place a dash on the Z (Z̶) so it won't be mistaken for a 2, and a slash through the zero (Ø) to distinguish it from the letter O. (Unfortunately, this latter convention is the opposite of the practice in the military).

Date entries such as 3/1/82 can also cause problems of interpretation since the American convention of month/day/year is reversed for Europeans. Here again the use of boxes is advisable. By using the box form design the danger of re-

versing the date order is eliminated, though there still remains the possibility that *Mo,* meaning Monday, may be filled in as day of birth. But well-written instructions for filling out the form, coupled with sample correct and incorrect responses, should eliminate such errors.

The box technique has other advantages. It can keep units separate, such as cents from dollars, and can also ensure that all digits of a number are entered, such as the nine digits of a social security number. An empty box assigned to a social security number can be detected more easily by a glance than a missing number in a string of nine numbers written on a line.

Boxes are also used for coding. Some forms have a space reserved on the right-hand column with boxes used by a coder to code information written on the left-hand side of the form. The form is then used as a document for direct input entry.

Another variation is a series of boxes which users check to indicate a condition. One such example is:

MARITAL
STATUS ☐ 1 ☐ 2 ☐ 3 ☐ 4
SINGLE MARRIED DIVORCED OTHER, SPECIFY_____

Input boxes are also used on machine-readable forms, though these boxes must be marked by a special pencil. This technique, called **mark-sensing,** reduces processing time and inaccuracies in processing since data need not be manually converted into machine language.

Forms are costly. They must be designed, printed, processed, stored, and controlled. Yet forms have a tendency to proliferate. In designing a new system, the development team should carefully scrutinize not only the design of forms but their need, guarding against the collection of unnecessary information or duplication of information previously gathered.

Procedures (382–390)

In using an information system, especially when using equipment preparing input or disseminating output, a specific set of steps and instructions called **procedures,** must be followed. These procedures are:

> . . . a predetermined sequence of actions which should be taken to carry out some task or job, specifying what shall be done, how it shall be done, who shall do it and when. . . . System procedures provide a link among the men, machine, and computer programs within the system, a link which can be used to orient and educate the users before the system is installed and operated, and which will guide them when it is put into use.[4]

The above definition emphasizes the descriptive and prescriptive nature of procedures. But procedures also have a heuristic character, since they are exploratory methods for solving a problem and are improved by evaluation and experience.

The importance of procedures can perhaps best be illustrated by a case study. Figure 13.3 shows the procedures used by a large firm for handling accounts receivable. Careful analysis by the reader should reveal a major procedural weakness costing the firm loss of interest income. According to the flowchart, no check is sent to the bank until all check data is validated (Box 9). In this firm, only 6 percent of the entries needed recycling, yet they held up the deposit of all accounts receivable an average of four days. By changing the decision rule in Symbol 6 to OK? Instead of ALL OK?, valid checks could be sent to the bank immediately to earn interest and only bad entries recycled. This change gave three days of previously lost interest on the valid checks to the firm, and increased cash flow.

Batch collection (Box 2) may also result in a loss of interest income if processing is delayed until a large number of checks are received. If batch size is small, response time will improve but the overhead cost of processing may be more than the interest accrued by faster processing. The procedures should therefore specify optimal batch size. This can be calculated, given the cost of processing, the average rate of arrivals, and the average amount per check. In

---

[4]L. A. Friedman, "Design and Production of Systems Procedures," in *Developing a Computer-Based Information System,* ed. P. E. Rosove (New York: John Wiley & Sons, 1967), pp. 201, 203.

Figure 13.3
Procedure for processing accounts receivable

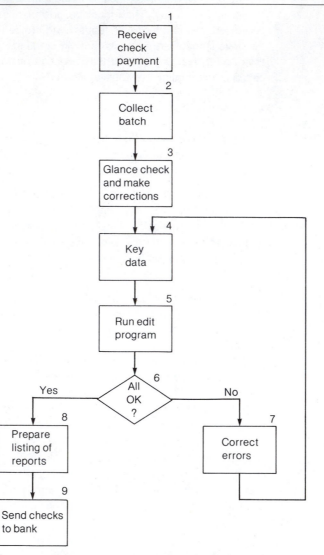

some cases, the batch size will be one, in which case an online real-time system is needed, as found in many warehouses and large urban banks.

As shown by the above example, procedures affect cost and response time. They also affect accuracy and the effectiveness of the system so they must be designed with care. Since many procedures are custom-designed, the participation of management is needed on the development team to interpret the organizational environment and to decide which procedures best serve the interests of the firm.

Some principles of procedure design are:

1. Human considerations should not be overlooked when designing procedures. Tasks should not be monotonous and the opportunity for job enlargement should exist.
2. Skills required for each procedure should be indicated. If special authorization is required, such as security clearance, this should also be stated.
3. The boundaries and domain of each employee's job and responsibility should be well defined. Rules must be established yet rules should allow for flexibility of action. Priorities should be stated. The degree of specificity of procedures will vary with the nature of the environment and projected external disturbances, such as illness, strikes, or natural disaster.
4. Procedures should be standardized whenever possible.
5. Similar procedures, having only slight modifications to fit particular circumstances, should be performed by different individuals. For example, when data for a system being tested must be coded simultaneously with coding for the existing system, yet each system uses different codes, two individuals—a coder for each system—should be assigned. If only one employee is available, processing of the similar procedures should be staggered in time. Switching back and forth between procedures that are alike causes confusion resulting in inaccuracies.
6. Procedures should allow for feedback and evaluation. Statistics should be maintained on the frequency of errors by type of error so that information is available for procedure evaluation. For example, statistics on high error rates in coding might later be used to trace a coder who is poorly trained or incapable of meeting operational standards.

A member of the development team, an analyst or a technical writer assigned the task, should document all procedures in a clear, complete, and unambiguous manner in a **Procedures Manual.** This manual should be tested before being used and periodically evaluated to ensure continued validity.

Formal design techniques

Some techniques of systems design are integrated with computer program development. That is, a computer will generate the necessary sets of programs for the implementation of an information system, given the system's specifications as input. PSA (Program Statement Analyzer) and HOSKYNS (named after the designer) are examples of such an automated design technique. So is a decision table processor that produces COBOL code from a decision table specification. PSA does not go as far as to produce program code but does produce program specifications.

Other techniques such as HIPO (Hierarchy Plus Input Process-Output) integrate design with stages of system analysis and system specification. Still other design techniques include programs for optimizing design. SODA (System Optimization and Design Algorithm) claims to generate an optimal design and hardware specifications from a statement of processing requirements. ISDOS (Information System Design and Optimization System) automates systems development, operations, and maintenance.

Although all these design techniques are technical, generally implemented by system analysts, management should be aware of their capabilities and limitations in order to ensure that the design technique adopted will produce desired results.

Revise project schedule (390–395)

An additional activity in the design phase is revising the project schedule. Once detailed design specifications have been determined, more accurate time estimates for completing activities can be made. Also, some activities may have been added which were not anticipated when the schedule was first drafted.

Management approval (395–400)

The revised schedule, the system definition and the specification documents, are presented to management for approval at the conclusion of the design phase. Although management may have been represented on the design team, a review of the total design package by user management is needed at this stage, and a formal decision on implementation must be made. Lack of approval of the system definition means either termination of the project or recycling of those activities designated unsatisfactory by management. Approval is followed by implementation, the subject of the next chapter of this text.

Figure 13.4
Internal and external environment affecting systems specifications

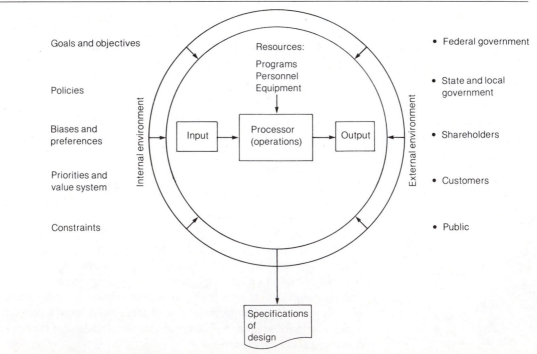

Summary

This chapter is conceptually a continuation of the previous chapter. Both chapters concern systems specifications. There are, however, two main differences: detail and responsibility. In Chapter 12, overall specifications, determined primarily by users on the development team, were examined. In this chapter, detailed specifications, made primarily by system analysts on the team, are described. But in both these phases of development of the new system, analysts and management should work closely together to ensure that the real objectives of the system change are fully achieved. Both are needed to interpret the internal and external environment in which the new system will operate. Factors in these environments influencing systems design are summarized in Figure 13.4.

The discussion of design activities in this chapter has followed the generic network diagram in Figure 13.1 In actual practice, system design may deviate somewhat from this schedule of activities. For example, programming and testing design specifications may be combined for small systems, and no need may exist for making organizational changes or for determining hardware specifications.

The product at the end of the design phase is the set of specification documents listed in Table 13.1. These are sent to various groups, also identified in the table, where they serve as the basis for implementation.

Table 13.1
Users of documents generated in the design phase

Documents	Programming group	Physical preparation group	Testing group	Organizational change group	Other development personnel	Data base administrator
Overall systems plan	*	*	*	*	*	*
Systems specifications	*	*	*	*	*	*
Operational specifications	*	*	*			*
Hardware specifications	*	*	*			*
Documentation specifications	*	*	*	*	*	*
Testing specifications	*	*	*	*	*	*
Organization specifications				*		
Programming specifications	*		*			*
Quality and control specifications	*	*	*			*
Model definition	*		*		*	
Output specifications	*	*	*			
Input and file specifications	*	*	*			*
Forms and procedures specifications	*	*	*			*
Revised schedule	*	*	*	*	*	*

Key words

Archive file
Audit trail
Backup
Developmental documentation
Dry run
Factor of safety
Files
Form design
Horizontal integration
Longitudinal integration
Master file
Model
Operator's Manual
Parallel run

Pilot study
Procedures
Procedures Manual
Programmer's Manual
Programming specifications
Project control documentation
Reference file
Son, father, and grandfather files
Summary master file
Systems Manual
Transaction file
User's Manual
Vertical integration

Discussion questions

1. Suppose you were responsible for developing a new accounts receivable application for a medium-size organization of medium complexity having a variety of accounts. Describe the development team you would like to have appointed.

2. What are the responsibilities of management, system analysts, and programmers in the design process?

3. Describe some of the tools of systems design.

4. What are the main components of a good computerized report for management?

5. Explain how flowcharts are used in designing an information system? Why are decision tables not always used?

6. What are the advantages of assigning to a steering committee responsibility for the design of a large and complex system?

7. What is the role of an accountant and auditor in the design phase? Why cannot accounting and auditing considerations be left until implementation and operations?

8. What are procedures? What role do they play in an information system? When should procedures be designed? Who should be responsible?

9. What is the significance of forms in an information system? Describe different types of forms. Who should design forms?

10. What are the objectives of a systems flowchart?

11. Suppose an application were designed to incorporate a Sales Order File for batch processing. What changes will be necessary for real-time processing?

12. What types of files (master, transaction, and so forth) would be required for the following types of processing:

a. Payroll?

b. Accounts receivable?

c. Student admission?

d. Student grades?

For each of the four cases, what storage media would you use?

13. List the components of a document package? Why should they be in distinct modules for user, programmer, operator, and so forth?

14. Describe the importance of documentation.

15. When should documentation begin and end within the development cycle?

16. Who should be responsible for documentation?

17. Why is documentation so unpopular? Can it be subcontracted?

18. What are the components of a Procedures Manual?

19 What are the differences between system feasibility documentation, program documentation, and system documentation?

Exercises

1. Design detailed outputs for the file in Exercise 1, Chapter 10 for managerial use.

2. Draw a systems flowchart for Exercise 1, Chapter 10.

3. Draw a programming flowchart for the system in Exercise 1, Chapter 10.

4. Is the file in Exercise 1, Chapter 10 a master file or a transaction file? Is any other file required for this application?

5. Design a form for collecting the data for Exercise 1, Chapter 6.

6. Consider an environment using tapes for accounts payable processing. Tape A is the master with information on all the vendors and amounts owed; Tape B is a transaction file with the day's transactions of amounts paid to vendors during the day. At night, in batch, the master tape is updated by the transaction tape giving the remaining amounts due to vendors. What tapes result in output? What happens to tapes A and B? What is used for the next day's processing? What happens if the new master tape is lost or destroyed in error?

7. What is the difference between a systems flowchart and a programming flowchart? Draw an example of each. Assume any one application for both flowcharts.

Selected annotated bibliography

Cougar, J. Daniel; Mel A. Colter; and Robert W. Knapp. *Advanced Systems Development/Feasibility Techniques.* New York: John Wiley & Sons, 1982, 506 pp.

If you could read only one book on design techniques, this would be the one. It includes a number of articles on design written by authorities in the field. Start with the survey by Colbert on the evolution of the structured methodology, pages 73–96. Boehm, Gane and Sarson, Stevens, Myers and Constantine, and Orr are also authors recommended. Since the authors are proponents of a specific design approach and critic of others, the book helps the reader compare techniques and gain a perspective to design methodologies.

Herchauer, James C. "What's Wrong with System Design Methods? It's Our Assumptions." *Journal of Systems Management* 29, no. 4 (April 1978), pp. 25–29.

The author criticizes the common assumptions: dominance of information technology; humans are inferior to machines; noncomputer technology is not optimal; and humans lack understanding of using computer technology. The author recommends a sociotechnical system of information and communication within the complexity of an existing organizational structure. The author's design methodology is highly output- and user-oriented.

Meyers, Gibbs. "Forms Management." *Journal of Systems Management* 27, nos. 9–11 (September–November 1976).

This is a series in three parts on forms management. Part One discusses the use of forms for greater organizational efficiency and smoothness of operations; Part Two is on the design of business forms; and Part Three is on cost-saving techniques for designing 10 different types of forms, including form construction and production.

Mixon, S. R. *Handbook of Data Processing Administration, Operations and Procedures*. New York: AMACOM, Division of American Management Association, 1976, pp. 127–258.

This text includes eight chapters on systems design: input forms design, output/report design, DED, systems control, data base design, program functions, modular programming, and program specifications design.

Rubin, Martin L. *Introduction to the System Life Cycle* Vol. 1. New York: Brandon/Systems Press, 1970, pp. 61–100.

This is a multivolume handbook with a chapter in Volume 1 on systems design, including sections on detailed analysis, design decisions, design objectives, and systems specifications. The next two volumes are on documenation forms and standards.

Stevens, Wayne P. *Using Structured Design*. New York: John Wiley & Sons, 1981, 209 pp.

This book is on the theory of structured design, not implementation. The author discusses structured charts, design modules, and evaluation criteria of good design, such as cohesion and coupling. Stevens argues that structured design results in reduced development and maintenance costs, and increases the usability of modules.

Teichroew, Daniel, and Z. Gackowski. "Structured System Design," *Ideas for Management*. Cleveland: Association for Systems Management, 1977, pp. 45–58.

Teichroew has long been associated with a project at the University of

Michigan for automating the design and implementation of an information system. In this article, a computer-aided technique for structured documentation and analyses of an information system are described; numerous charts are used. Highly recommended for one view of the future of automated design. Tiechrow's work can also be found in *Systems Analysis Techniques* edited by J. D. Couger and R. W. Knapp published in 1974 by John Wiley and Sons. This book also includes chapters on HOSKYNS, ISDOS, TAG, SOP, ADS, and SYSTEMATICS.

Weinberg, Gerals M. *Rethinking Systems Analysis and Design*. Boston: Little, Brown, 1982, 193 pp.

This is not a conventional textbook. The style is light, breezy, and anecdotal yet the text is filled with advice on the pitfalls and problems that arise during the analysis/design process. The book is meant to be a supplement to more structured material on the subject.

Yourdon, Edward. "The Second Structured Revolution." *Software World* 12, no. 3 (1981), pp. 10–15.

A good review of structured analysis and design and their integration with structured walkthrough. Good advice on how to sell the structure to management and technicians is also included, as is implementation advice.

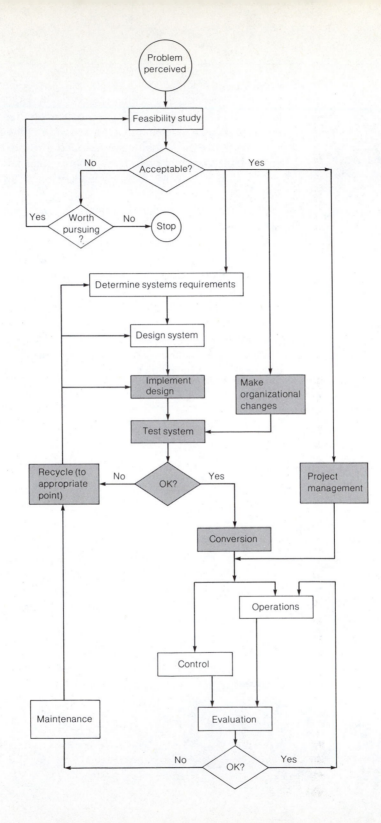

Implementation, testing, conversion, and evaluation of systems development

14

Computer programs are 90 percent debugged 50 percent of the time.

Computer Graffiti

Following design of the new system, implementation takes place, although it is not always possible to pinpoint exactly where design ends and implementation begins. Programming the solution, for example, is usually a major activity of implementation but some development teams provide so much detail in the design phase that programmers need only translate each design specification into a computer instruction. Other teams, however, merely specify logic in general terms when designing the system, leaving implementation of this logic to programmers.

Hardware installation and testing are other activities of implementation. Organizational changes are also initiated in this phase of development and files prepared. Then the system is tested and the development process evaluated. Finally, conversion takes place. Figure 14.1 is a network design showing implementation activities in relation to testing, conversion, and evaluation.

This chapter is the last in Part 3 describing the development process of an information system. Some aspects of design and implementation are mentioned only briefly in this part, to be examined in detail in Part 4 about management of an information system. Problems of operations, evaluation, maintenance, and redevelopment, for example, are discussed in Chapter 15; quality control and security are the subjects of Chapter 16; behavioral and organizational questions, the crux of successful implementation, are in Chapter 17; and distributed data processing is the subject of Chapter 18.

Implementation

Programming activities

All computerized information systems require programming effort. The main program(s) must be written so that the system produces the information expected. At the same time, programs for storing data, checking data, and maintenance must also be prepared. Once the needs of management have been spelled out,

Figure 14.1
Partial network diagram of programming, testing, and conversion

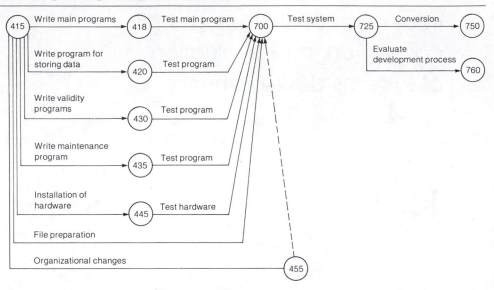

programming is left to programmers. A detailed discussion of this technical activity is beyond the scope of this text. However, it should be noted that not all programs needed for the new system have to be written by the firm's programmers. Software programs, designed to perform a specific or general-purpose function, can be purchased. Many are available for functional information systems, such as marketing, advertising, and financial accounting, and for solving operations research problems. The value of such packages must be weighed against their cost and the expense of adapting them to local equipment configurations.

Hardware selection and installation

Responsibility for the selection and implementation of hardware for large and medium-size computerized systems is generally delegated to hardware and systems personnel. However, operational managers are increasingly assuming the responsibility for selection of minis, micros, and input-output equipment. The principles of analysis described in the feasibility study should be used in evaluating costs versus benefits when making equipment decisions.

Site preparation, installation, and testing of the new equipment are also part of this phase of implementation. These activities may be complex and technical for larger systems. An IBM manual[1] lists 222 activities in a critical path diagram for installation of a computer system, for example.

In the field, sequencing of hardware activities varies. Figure 14.2 is a sample

---

[1] IBM, *Management Planning Guide of Data Processing Standards,* No. C20–1670–1 (White Plains, N.Y.: International Business Machines Corporation, n.d.), p. 13.

Figure 14.2
Equipment-related activities

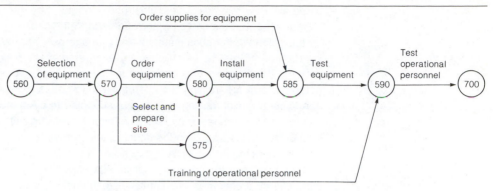

network diagram, representing the common practice. In any given situation, sequencing will be a function of equipment complexity, the time available for project completion, and the level of knowledge and experience of existing personnel.

File preparation

File specification was discussed in Chapter 13 and file design in Chapter 6. The implementation of a file according to file specifications is done in one of two ways: **file creation** or **file restructuring.** Files are created from new, or predominantly new, raw data. Collection of this data may require special forms and procedures. Large volumes of data may be collected on special mark-sense sheets or on documents that are optically scanned. If coded or collected from documents, the data must be converted to machine-readable form. Whatever the approach to data collection and conversion, the data must be stored on storage media chosen for the new file. File creation is done by a special program, sometimes called a **start-up program.** Either before or after storage, the file must also be validated and checked for completeness.

In file restructuring, an old file is converted into a new one. Restructuring may be triggered by the addition of data elements and consequent expansion of a file, the need for additional width of one or more data elements, the rearrangement of data elements to facilitate processing, the need to change format to conform to a new standard form, or the need to revise an old file to make it complete and accurate.

To restructure a file, selected parts of the old file have to be retrieved and added to newly created raw data or new derived data calculated from other files. A start-up program can also be written for this purpose. It should contain special checks like subtotals, totals, and cross-totals to ensure that no data is lost in the restructuring process. Also, special procedures must be adopted so data generated during the time the old file is being converted to the new one is not lost. This problem is critical when transactional data is being continuously generated in real-time systems. Again, as with newly created files, restructured files must be checked for data validity and completeness.

Organizational considerations

Many new information systems require organizational changes. Positions may be eliminated, others created, and the job descriptions of employees altered to incorporate new responsibilities. Restructuring jobs may affect departmental span of control so that the firm's organization chart may change.

After planning for such changes and management approval of the plans, training programs must be established to teach employees how to operate the new system. This involves preparation of teaching materials and selection of personnel to perform the training. An alternative to in-house training is to send employees to commercial training institutes or schools run by manufacturers.

Figure 14.3 is one example of sequencing **training** activities. Note that each type of training is based on the specifications drawn up in the design phase. Activity sequencing, however, will vary from project to project. A small organization, for example, may train a single individual for updating, equipment operation, and input/output procedures, so consecutive training sessions rather than parallel sessions would be required. The project manager will determine sequencing based on the nature of the project and the resources (time and personnel) available for training.

If the firm lacks system analysts, they may have to be hired from outside the firm, but often it is more difficult to train a person in the intricacies of the com-

Figure 14.3
Activities related to training and operation

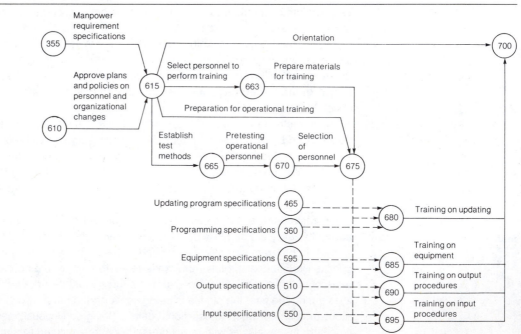

pany's power structure, its practices, terminology, and procedures than it is to train as an analyst a person already within the organization. Furthermore, loyalty to the firm of an outsider is hard to assess, whereas the loyalty of an individual already in the firm's employ is known. For these reasons, many managers prefer to train analysts from existing personnel, selecting individuals who show interest and aptitude for this work.

But what makes a good analyst? The main desirable characteristics are: an inquisitive mind, a flair for detail, ability to work with people at all levels, an open mind, logical ability, thoroughness, resourcefulness, imagination, and ability to communicate (orally and in written documentation). Technically, system analysts should be knowledgeable about such computer subdisciplines as hardware, software, data structures, and data management. Also, the analysts must have good business backgrounds so that they can communicate readily with management and the applications staff. However, since these fields are growing, becoming increasingly complex and specialized, no system analyst can be expected to have expertise in all these areas. If the EDP department is weak in one of these subdisciplines, consultants may have to be hired when selecting equipment, developing specialized software, making feasibility decisions, or even when orienting and training operating personnel.

Orientation, the introduction of users to the new system, should also take place during implementation. Organizing orientation would be similar to the organization for training. Traditionally, orientation has been directed exclusively toward managers and supervisors. However, to ensure systems effectiveness, workers and clerks in affected areas should also participate, though the material covered should be modified according to the level of personnel being oriented. Orientation should establish favorable attitudes toward the new system once employees know how the system operates and how each operation contributes to final results.

The content of the orientation sessions should include:

1. Objectives of system
    Short term
    Long term
    Relationship to:
      Organizational goals
      Overall systems goals
2. Limitations of system
3. Systems environment
    Applications
    Equipment
4. Process of development
    Nature
    Stages
5. Resources required
    Time

Critical path
Monetary
Personnel
6. Role of
User
Systems personnel

Testing the solution

The testing process involves comparison of desired performance (as stated in the users requirement specifications) with actual performance, identifying deviations and eliminating them outside the allowed tolerances.

First, the actual system test must be planned. This means preparing the test data and selecting knowledgeable persons who represent the users to perform the test.

Reliability testing standards state the allowable occurrence of error in processing. For example, one error in a thousand may be the reliability specification of a warehouse inventory system. If the system, when tested, exceeds this error allowance, the system will have to be redeveloped or testing conditions reestablished. This is an example of the iterative recycling nature of the development process: design, test, redesign, retest, and recycle until the test is satisfactory; or, state systems specifications, design, test, restate specifications, redesign, and retest. (Some steps in the development process have been excluded to emphasize the relationship between design and testing.) **Performance testing standards** include specifications of response time, throughput, and staff and equipment efficiency. **Load specifications** state the factor of safety needed for peak periods, emergencies, and future expansion.

Next, test data must be collected. The team must decide how **test data** will be generated, what data to use, and the amount of data required. In many cases historical data is available for testing. For example, in converting from a manual to a computer system, the new system can be tested against the results of the old, using data collected in the past. However, in projects performing functions never done before, test data must be created. This should be done by the manager who can anticipate the conceptual problems and exceptions that may arise and need testing, in cooperation with the systems designer, whose experience makes it possible to anticipate operational problems.

What data to use and how much to use is a problem of sampling. A well-designed sample produces results as significant as those from the data collected from the population as a whole, and processing of the sample is cheaper and faster as well. Unfortunately, few people working with systems have training or applied experience in empirical experimental techniques. It may be necessary for the development team to add consultants knowledgeable in experimental design when test data is being prepared. Also, the consultants could help with the entire scope of testing, which should extend from the collection of input to the usage of output.

Levels of testing

Testing a new system is done at four levels: components, functions, subsystems, and systems.

Component testing is checking the parts of the system, such as a piece of equipment, the performance of an individual operator, or the effectiveness of a form, procedure, or program (for example, when desk-checking a computer program, the methodical manual check of each output, watching for omissions and possible misinterpretations, is one type of system component test).

Sometimes a component cannot be isolated. For example, one person's work may be so integrated with that of other employees that testing the individual's output would not be meaningful. In this case, the component to be tested would be the aggregate work of a group of employees.

The testing phase should begin with component testing because it is easier to identify errors and problems at this level than it is to isolate problems when testing interrelated components. Also, the earlier a problem is detected, the less effort is required to correct it.

Function testing is at a higher level of aggregation, measuring the performance of related components in a functional subsystem. This level of testing should be done after components of the function have been tested individually and found satisfactory.

Subsystems testing evaluates how related functions operate. For example, in testing an input subsystem, input procedures, input preparation, validity checking, and procedures for correcting errors would be assessed. Testing at this level checks the interrelationships of functions tested individually earlier.

Systems testing, checking overall results (that is, the performance of all subsystems in aggregate), is the final test phase. This can be done by **pilot tests, parallel runs, or simulation.** These three alternatives were described in Chapter 13.

The four testing levels are illustrated in Figure 14.4. The terms will perhaps be more meaningful when a practical example is given. A financial system can be subdivided into financial subsystems of accounting, manufacturing, engineering, marketing, and inventory subsystems. Each of these subsystems has many func-

**Figure 14.4
Levels of testing**

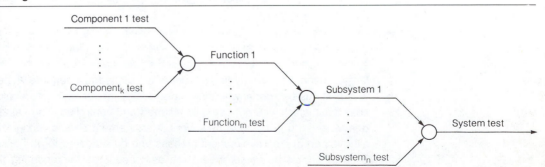

Figure 14.5
Share of effort in the development of an information system

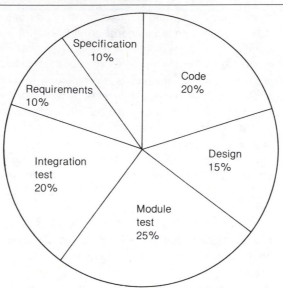

SOURCE   M. V. Zelkowitz, "Perspectives on Software Engineering," *ACM Computing Surveys* (New York: Association for Computing Machinery) 10, No. 2 (June 1978), p. 198.

tions. The accounting subsystem includes accounts payable, accounts receivable, general ledger, costing, assets, liabilities, income, expenses, and tax functions. Each function is further subdivided into components. The payroll function includes wages, social security, W2 form, editing, balancing, journal, register, check writing, and payroll statement components. Testing begins at the component level of this hierarchy, continues at higher levels of aggregation, and ends up with the total systems check.

Testing is a labor-intensive activity and takes a great share of the total effort required for the development of a computerized information system. This is reflected in Figure 14.5, which shows that testing takes about 45 percent of the total development effort.

The testing process ends when test results at the system level are satisfactory. Unsatisfactory testing requires recycling, as in Figure 14.6, where possible cycles are depicted. In complex systems, the value of *n* may be 3 or 4. If *n* is larger, responsibility may lie with users who failed to adequately specify needs, with systems personnel who did a poor design job, or with the development process itself which was not carefully planned and controlled. The value of *n* is seldom 1, even with capable personnel. Management should recognize that recycling is part of the development process and be prepared for it. Formal recycling controls should be established, such as procedures for recording the need for

Figure 14.6
Recycling of testing process

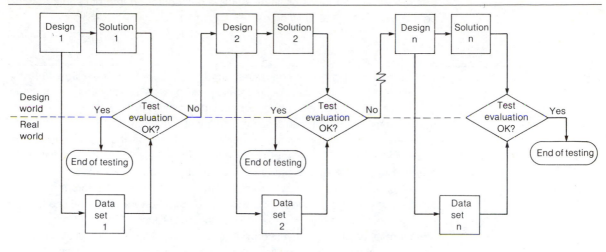

change and documenting modifications accomplished. Information about these changes must then be channeled to affected groups.

At the conclusion of favorable testing, the test results should be presented to management for approval. This is management's final check to see that the system satisfies goals and objectives for the system. By formalizing user acceptance, the development team minimizes the possibility that users will complain at a later date that the system fails to satisfy requirements.

Testing responsibility

Responsibility for testing lies with both users and systems personnel. Users can best formulate the conditions for **outside testing,** for example, examining systems response to varying conditions of input, including instability and overload. **Inside tests,** examining the structure of the system for completeness, consistency, reliability, and linkages, fall to systems personnel, particularly programmers.

Sometimes the individual performing a job does the testing. For example, programmers generally **debug** programs[2] they have written, though programs can also be tested by system designers who know the system and can anticipate some of the problems. To ensure objectivity, it is advisable to leave testing to analysts assigned to other responsibilities in the firm who have not participated in the development of the new system. A side benefit is that the expertise the tester acquires during testing serves as job enlargement for the analyst, while

---

[2] This term originates from the early days of computers when vacuum tubes were used. One such computer gave false results. The programmers spent many days trying to trace the error but with no success. Then, by accident, an operator found a bug on a contact that was causing the machine to malfunction. The bug was removed and the program, once debugged, worked perfectly.

giving to the firm backup personnel knowledgeable in the system. In cases of programs involving funds or an accounting procedure, an internal auditor should be involved in the test function.

Conversion

The development process concludes with the cut-over or **conversion** from the old system to the new. Old documentation and outdated forms and files must be withdrawn and equipment no longer required removed. Any delay in removing unnecessary equipment can result in additional rental costs.

There are many approaches to conversion. Three of the most common are shown in Figure 14.7. The **sequential approach** means the complete switchover from old to new system is made on a given date. Sometimes old and new systems are run in **parallel** for a period of time. Large and complex information systems are generally phased in one **module** or **subsystem** at a time, bottom-up, even though the design may be top-down. This reduces the work load on personnel responsible for conversion and at the same time helps isolate problems of the new system while minimizing the consequences of potential system failure.

Phasing in the new system must be carefully planned. Orientation and training sessions should have been completed. Manuals should have been distributed to affected personnel, and employees of departments involved in the changeover should be briefed on the scheduled cut-over date.

There is a tendency among users to delay phasing out old systems. Continuation of a parallel run beyond the planned schedule, for example, gives users

Figure 14.7
Approaches to conversion

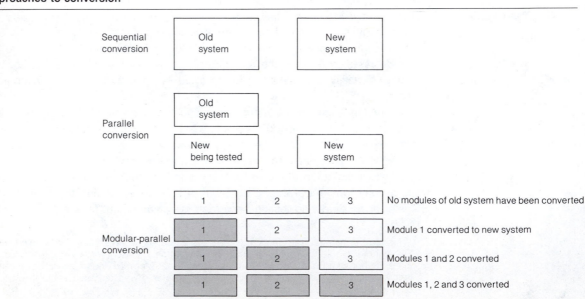

an added sense of security. This costly practice should be discouraged. Once the new system has achieved desired performance levels, the old system should be discontinued. Confidence in the new system will develop only when it stands on its own.

Evaluating the systems development process

Before the development team is dispersed, **evaluation** of the systems development process should take place. Mistakes should be identified and analyzed as to why they were made and how they could have been avoided. The purpose of such an analysis is not to exchange accusations and recriminations, but to learn from the past so that similar mistakes won't be repeated when future information systems are developed. The efficiency and effectiveness of the new system should be scrutinized and the benefits versus costs assessed. A critical review of the need for recycling during the development process, of liaison and communication problems that arose and of schedule slippage, should lead to improved procedures and approaches for other projects.

Summary

Design and implementation of an information system are closely allied. The exact point where design ends and implementation begins is difficult to pinpoint. Generally, however, implementation is left to technicians following design guidelines made during the design phase. Programs are written, files prepared (either created or restructured), equipment purchased and installed, and orientation and training sessions take place. Testing, a comparison of expected operational performance with desired performance as stated in the systems specification stage, follows. This testing stage provides an opportunity for further training of employees who will eventually be responsible for operation of the new system.

The actual tests are done on several levels—component tests, functional tests, subsystem tests, and tests of the entire system. All functions must be tested, including those of hardware, input data, input instruments, formats, codes, feedback, programs, training, and procedures for both normal and exceptional conditions. Performance must be evaluated not only for content quality but for timing and sequence as well, using the safety factors specified in the specification stage. During testing, management must make sure that the new system performs as desired and needed.

Training is an important part of implementation. It has a long period of gestation and must be started early. Conversion should take place as soon as the new system achieves desired performance levels. All interested personnel should be carefully and regularly informed of the status of conversion and project completion. Silence and absence of information can start rumors resulting in low morale.

Testing and conversion cause a period of organizational strain and disruption. Unforeseen difficulties arise, and recycling is generally required. Recycling is usually done under great pressure of time, requiring higher work loads than usual. Normal service is unavoidably affected. The stress of conversion can be minimized if such problems are understood and anticipated and if the phase-out of the old system takes place swiftly on schedule. Organizational breakdowns are most likely to occur during long parallel runs.

A final duty of the development team is to present an evaluation of the development process to management. This report should include mistakes and insights of both users and system personnel to aid future teams in formulating new information systems for the firm.

Key words

Component testing	Parallel conversion
Conversion	Parallel runs
Debug	Performance testing standards
Evaluation	Pilot tests
File creation	Reliability testing standards
File restructuring	Sequential approach
Function testing	Simulation
Inside tests	Start-up program
Load specifications	Subsystem testing
Module	Systems testing
Orientation	Test data
Outside tests	

Discussion questions

1. Distinguish between:
   a. Creating and restructuring a file.
   b. Training analysts and orientation of management.
2. Describe four programming activities.
3. Describe different approaches to conversion.
4. Describe five sources of file changes that would require updating of the files.
5. What redesigning of an information system is necessary for an expected change of equipment?
6. For whom should orientation sessions be planned?
7. Why should management be trained in systems use?
8. Why should systems orientation permeate the organization?
9. What type of training should be provided to managers and supervisors?
10. What are the activities of implementation of an EDP project?
11. How can the systems implementation be humanized?
12. Why is testing necessary? Should testing be done after each component of the system is implemented or should the testing be done for each subsystem or the total system? What are the advantages and limitations of each approach?

13. Distinguish between:
    a. Pilot and parallel testing.
    b. Component and subsystems testing.
    c. Subsystems and systems test.
    d. Historical data and test data.

14. How should the training differ in content, depth, detail, and terminology for managers, supervisors, operators, and data clerks?

15. Suppose that the completion of programs for a project were scheduled for December 1, but on October 1, two programs in COBOL were each three months behind. What action would you recommend? What if the December 1 deadline could not be changed?

16. What training options do companies have?

Exercises

1. Write a program to produce the report requested in Exercise 1, Chapter 10. Specify procedures needed in operations.

2. Read Dan Appleton, "A Manufacturing System Cookbook, Part 3," *Datamation* 29, no. 9 (August 1979), p. 130 ff. Do you agree with the author's list of characteristics for successful and unsuccessful implementation? How would you rank these characteristics? Substantiate your ordering.

3. Fill in the network diagram provided on page 320, naming the activities in the proper sequence.

   a. Write main program.
   b. Dummy.
   c. Dummy
   d. Conversion.
   e. Write other program.
   f. Install equipment.
   g. Dummy.
   h. Dummy.
   i. Test main program.
   j. Select equipment.
   k. Orientation of management.
   l. Test other program.
   m. Test equipment.
   n. Dummy.
   o. Dummy.
   p. Test system.
   q. Test all programs.
   r. Test operational personnel.
   s. Specify manufacturer requirement.
   t. Dummy.

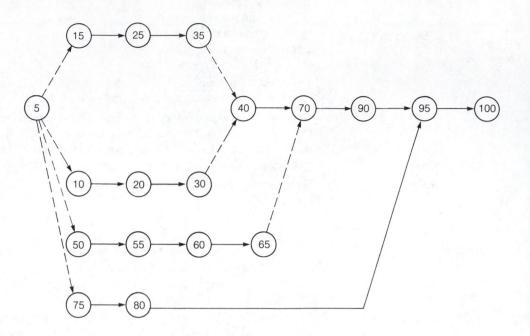

Selected annotated bibliography

De Marco, Tom. *Controlling Software Projects*. New York: Yourdon Press, 1982, 284 pp.

This book discusses ideas for managing and controlling a systems project. It is helpful for both users and analysts.

Essiek, Vicky. "Systems Testing: An Effective Management Tool." *National Report: Computers and Health* 4 (May 20, 1983), pp. 5–7.

The environment is health care but the principles of testing, tuning, and quality assurance are applicable to all businesses.

Lehman, John H. "How Software Projects Are Really Managed." *Datamation* 25, no. 1, January 1979, pp. 119–29.

This is a mine of statistics collected from a stratified sample of 37 computer users. The article includes numerous statistical tables covering the management not just of software but of the entire development cycle of an information system. It discusses methods of estimating costs and schedules, documents required, project team composition, personnel turnover, testing tools, aids and methodology used, and approaches to project planning and control.

Mixon, S. R. *Handbook of Data Processing Administration, Operations, and Procedures*. New York: AMACOM, 1976.

This text has an excellent chapter on system testing (pp. 259–70). It discusses the organization of testing, system test plan, test data development, and acceptance testing. There are many checklists provided. The book also has good sections that relate to implementation: project implementation (pp. 45–125) and documentation standards (pp. 271–354).

Scharen, Laura L. "Improving System Testing Techniques." *Datamation.* 23, no. 9 September 1977, pp. 115–17 ff.

The author strongly argues that systems testing should follow a standard set of procedures. Extensive checklists for preparation, test operations, unit-test evaluation, system test evaluation, and acceptability test are provided.

Squire, Enid. *Systems Design.* Reading, Mass.: Addison-Wesley, 1980, 346 pp.

Pages 258–61 are on testing: test time, test data, test exceptions, full test, and acceptance tests.

Weinberg, Gerald. *The Psychology of Computer Programming.* New York: Van Nostrand Reinhold, 1971, 288 pp.

This book, a classic in the field, initiated the concepts of structured walk-through and egoless programming.

Yourdon, E. *Structured Walkthroughs.* New York: Yourdon Press, 1978, 137 pp.

This book describes peer testing during development, citing many examples of proper (and improper) testing. The author claims that peer testing reduces debugging and maintenance. Yourdon has popularized this technique through his writings and by holding seminars on the subject at his consulting company.

MANAGEMENT OF AN INFORMATION SYSTEM

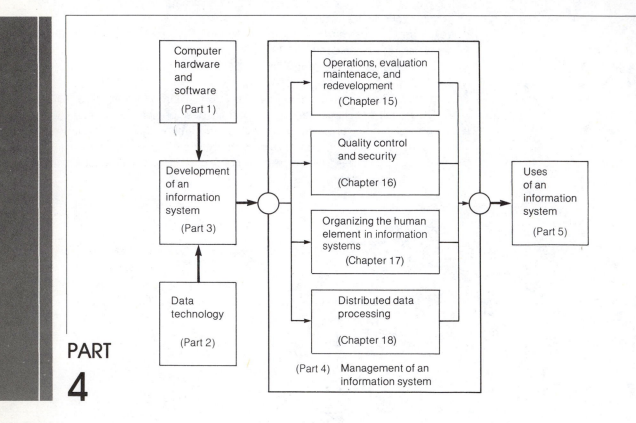

Computer hardware and software (Part 1)

Development of an information system (Part 3)

Data technology (Part 2)

Operations, evaluation maintenace, and redevelopment (Chapter 15)

Quality control and security (Chapter 16)

Organizing the human element in information systems (Chapter 17)

Distributed data processing (Chapter 18)

(Part 4)   Management of an information system

Uses of an information system (Part 5)

PART

4

Part 4 is closely related to Part 3. In fact, it is difficult to separate the two since many aspects of management of an information system (such as evaluation, redevelopment, control, and organization) need to be planned when the system is being designed. Yet integration of all the material in Chapters 15 through 18 into a discussion on development would have been cumbersome indeed. The operational considerations which are raised in Part 4 must be well understood by the development team and this knowledge must be used in determining design specifications. However, the organizational problems raised in Part 4 also affect daily operation of the system, which explains why the material is introduced following sections on development. An overview of the chapters in this part is shown in diagram form on the facing page.

Chapter 15 examines operations, evaluation, maintenance, and redevelopment. Normal operations include periodic evaluations for efficiency and effectiveness, but evaluation may also be triggered by user complaints or changes in EDP management. Should systems performance prove unsatisfactory, either maintenance (minor modifications) or redevelopment (major redesign), following the steps of develop-

ment described in Part 3, will also be required. Chapter 15 also discusses evaluation criteria and modification methodology.

Control measures are designed to prevent inadvertent errors in processing and breaches in system security. Procedures, corporate policies, software, and specialized hardware all can contribute to control. In Chapter 16, aspects of information systems vulnerable to security violations and susceptible to error are identified and control recommendations are outlined.

The human element of a computerized information system must also be managed. Schemata for organizing EDP departments are described in Chapter 17. How the mobilization of EDP personnel has changed as computer technology has evolved is also explained. In addition, this chapter discusses the problem of human resistance to computers and recommends ways to overcome this resistance.

Chapter 18, on distributed data processing (DDP), is an extension of Chapter 17, describing in detail an alternative organizational structure for processing. A separate chapter has been devoted to this topic because of the newness and importance of DDP and the effect DDP has on equipment, software, and personnel in the management of information systems.

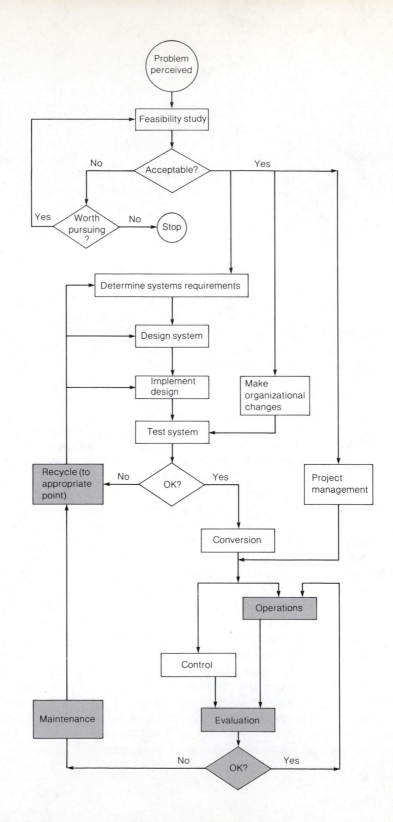

Operations, evaluation, maintenance, and redevelopment

15

I firmly believe that the maintainability of a system is a direct function of how well it was developed initially; the success of any maintenance effort is directly related to the management attitudes surrounding it.

Louis A. Rose

Once a system is developed and converted, operations begin. In many business organizations, operations are performed by an EDP department. Operations should be evaluated periodically, where evaluation is the comparison of actual performance with objectives. When a predetermined level of error tolerance is exceeded, system modification is necessary. The corrections themselves are technical matters. What concerns management is evaluation leading to a decision to modify the system, and control of modification procedures.

Modifications may be minor, called **maintenance,** or major, requiring **redevelopment** of the system following the cycle of development that was discussed in Chapters 11–14. In this chapter, the interrelationship of operations with evaluation, maintenance, and redevelopment is discussed. Evaluation criteria are listed and the methodology of maintenance and redevelopment is described.

Operations

Operations in small systems (for example, operations using a minicomputer) are administered by line management. In large systems and systems with a common data base, however, a specialized department handles operations. Organizations differ in how this department is named. It may be called a Computer Center or Data Processing Department. In this text, the term EDP (Electronic Data Processing) department will be used.

A prime responsibility of EDP departments is **efficiency** of operations, efficiency being the ratio of output to input. Efficiency of operations is dependent on good documentation of procedures including:

1. Run sheets for computer operators.
2. Instructions for error correction during operations.

3. User procedure manuals.
4. Library procedures.
5. Project control procedures.

Optimization of operations means either maximizing output within a given departmental budget, or minimizing input for the production of a required output. How hardware (CPU and peripherals), software (system and application programs), the data base, and EDP personnel are deployed will determine results. The department may change equipment or reorganize existing equipment in a new configuration to improve efficiency, organization logic may be revised, software rewritten, the data base restructured, and/or data on storage devices reorganized. All of these technical decisions will affect both efficiency and critical factors of performance, such as timeliness, accuracy, and quality of information,[1] factors by which users measure the **effectiveness** of the information system. Whenever **evaluation** of the system shows that either efficiency or effectiveness have dropped below acceptable levels, corrective action must be taken.

Evaluation of operations

Evaluation of operations may be initiated periodically or may occur when changes in EDP management take place. (Mobility is high in EDP management due to competition among businesses for qualified, experienced EDP personnel.) Users may also request a review of operations when dissatisfied with service.

Factors considered in the evaluation of operations include:

1. Timeliness of operations and reports generated.
2. Validity and completeness of reports.
3. Achievement of predetermined acceptable levels of operations.
4. Frequency of errors or discrepancies.
5. Response time required to meet users' requests.
6. Effectiveness of measures to control data and protect both security and privacy of information.
7. Software performance.
8. Reliability of system.
9. Achievement of long-range goals.
10. Frequency of unscheduled downtime and its percentage of total scheduled time.
11. Availability and usefulness of documentation.
12. Degree of incorporation of latest technology.
13. Quality and turnover of EDP personnel.
14. Availability and effectiveness of training programs.
15. User perception of EDP quality and service.
16. Openness of communication lines between users and EDP personnel.

---

[1] For formal measures of these factors, see David P. Norton, and Kenneth G. Rau, *A Guide to EDP Performance Management* (Wellesley, Mass.: Q.E.D. Information Sciences, 1978), p. 310.

Many of the above factors can only be measured subjectively. But much data can be collected on operations to assist management in the evaluation process. For example, **hardware monitors** can collect data on the utilization of the CPU, peripherals, and data that can be analyzed to identify bottlenecks, downtime, and saturation conditions of channels, storage devices, and other peripherals. **Software monitors,** such as account or auditing programs, can provide management with information on how the systems resources have been used, by whom, and for what application. **Monitor programs** embedded in software may keep track of application programs demanded, languages favored, as well as software features and routines used. Such data is useful for analysis but has a price tag since the cost of processing this data must be considered. Monitors can also interfere with optimal operating efficiency.

Monitors aid in the evaluation of EDP operations in the aggregate, but have limited value in reviewing the efficiency and effectiveness of individual applications. Generally users are less concerned with overall operation of a system than with application specifics. Methods of evaluating each application (or subsystem) are described in the next section of this text.

Evaluation of applications

The evaluation of input, process, and output for applications is conceptually similar to the evaluation of general operations. What differs is that user management is responsible for the evaluation process. Users, not EDP personnel, determine the efficiency and effectiveness of the application. An unsatisfactory assessment of performance will lead to maintenance or redevelopment.

Efficiency

In the development of an application, analysts try to maximize output for a fixed input, or minimize input for a fixed output. They are often able to identity areas in which output can be substantially increased at very little marginal cost. Once the system is operational, however, users can often spot inefficient design features. Data preparation, for example, is still a very labor-intensive activity, constituting a high recurring cost. Users are frequently able to recommend changes in procedures, redesign of forms, or program modifications that will help reduce this cost (recommendations that should have been made, but were not, during design). The run time of application programs is also a cost that users are highly motivated to reduce. Rewriting programs, perhaps using a clever algorithm, restructuring data, and better utilization of hardware to reduce processing time are technical improvements that users, analysts, and programmers often initiate to improve efficiency.

Effectiveness

The objectives stated in the feasibility study and in the detailed specification of systems requirements are compared to actual performance to determine the effectiveness of an application. One problem with this measure of effectiveness is that the objectives themselves may be outdated, invalid because of internal or external environmental changes, or because the decision maker has reordered priorities. In such cases, user objectives must be restated in detailed operational terms. To do so, users must follow the procedures for determining objectives that were originally followed during the developmental cycle of the application.

Monitors can assist in the collection of quantitative data used to evaluate effectiveness, but qualitative evaluation requires a survey of user attitudes. Questionnaires are one method of gathering user opinion. Sometimes users are asked to rank their responses on a scale of 1 (very satisfied) to 5 (very dissatisfied). The answers of all users can then be weighted. Interviews are another technique for gathering user opinion on application effectiveness. Observation and study of documentation, such as logs recording complaints or error frequency, can also be used.

In addition to measuring performance against stated objectives, users should be asked to evaluate the application in general terms. The answers to the following questions would be a good indication of the effectiveness of the system.[2]

1. Have original system objectives been undesirably compromised in an attempt to satisfy other objectives the system was designed to encompass?
2. Is all system output used?
3. Are meaningful data reduction and exception reporting techniques employed to produce digestible, usable decision-oriented information?
4. Do adequate procedures exist governing preparation and control of input data?
5. Does the system employ sufficient data edits and audits?
6. Are precision standards and the accuracy of system results understood by users?
7. Are processing turn-around times satisfactory?
8. Are processing delays frequent in occurrence?
9. What is the general level of confidence placed in system output by the users?
10. Is obsolete or unused data retained in system files unnecessarily processed?
11. Is processing logic straightforward, easily understood, and properly documented? Are routines unnecessarily complicated?
12. Do adequate processing operation procedures exist?

The process of evaluation and monitoring is summarized in Figure 15.1. Changes in operations to improve effectiveness and efficiency are sometimes called **fine-tuning.** A 25-percent improvement in efficiency is not uncommon; 100-percent improvement is not unknown. With constant technological development in hardware and software, the importance of regular evaluation cannot be overstressed. Internal and/or external evaluation teams may be used, depending on the size and complexity of the operation. One study reports that outside evaluators are used by three out of five large companies, and two out of five small and

---

[2] Adapted from J. G. Kirzer, "A Model for System Design," *Journal of Systems Management* 23, no. 10 (October 1972), p. 30.

medium-sized companies. Regular evaluation should identify problems before **crash maintenance** is required. Balancing cycles of evaluation and maintenance is part of **maintenance management,** the subject of the last section of this chapter.

Maintenance and redevelopment

Maintenance and redevelopment are illustrated in Figure 15.2. The process begins when an application (system or subsystem) is ready for implementation (Box 1) at the conclusion of the development cycle. After operations begin (Box 2), the system is evaluated (Box 3). If satisfactory, procedures are established for periodic reevaluation, or reevaluation is initiated by users or analysts (Box 6). If modification is needed (Exit NO, Symbol 4) then a decision must be made whether the modification required is major or minor (Symbol 7). Minor design changes are made (Box 8), and these changes, once implemented (Box 9), are tested (Box 10). Satisfactory results lead to documentation (Box 12), and operations (Boxes 1 and 2). Major modifications, however, require redesign of the system following the stages outlined in Chapters 11–14 (Box 13).

The questions unanswered by the flowchart are: Why does the need for modification arise, and when should modifications be undertaken? What criteria de-

Figure 15.1
Efficiency and effectiveness of computer application

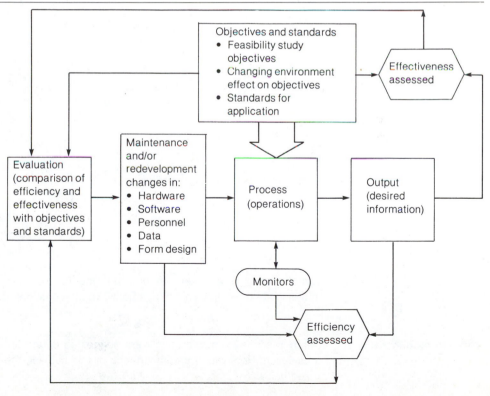

Figure 15.2
Process of maintenance and redevelopment

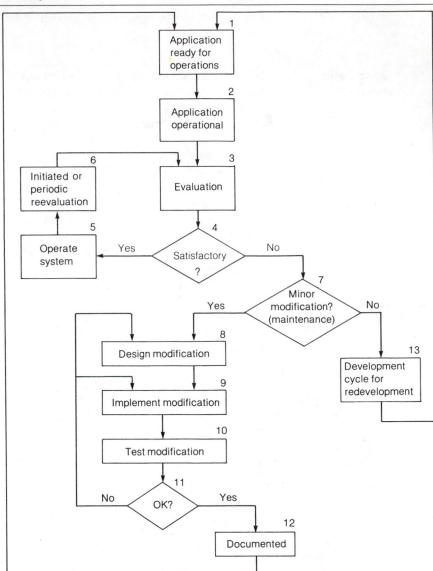

termine whether maintenance or redevelopment are required? What are the problems of maintenance management? These questions will now be addressed.

System modification

Many reasons for modification were suggested during the earlier discussion on evaluation. Because of the importance of this subject, the reasons are summarized below.

Modifications imposed by external environment

New laws or changed government regulations are two reasons systems must commonly be modified. Competitors may also so alter market conditions that system redesign must be initiated. Flexible programs can be written that make modification part of routine maintenance when regular changes in the external environment are anticipated, such as revision of tax rates, but sometimes unexpected modification is required.

Modifications initiated by user management

System modification is sometimes triggered by a change in the management and user environment. A different style of decision making may lead to the need for a different threshold of information (level of information detail). Or management may simply learn to use information systems more effectively. An increase in awareness of a system's potentialities often causes management to place increased demands on the system. Policies of an organization may change requiring new algorithms for calculations, such as new depreciation methods. Or, frequent errors and inconsistencies resulting from poor systems specification, bad design, or hasty and incomplete testing may become apparent to users when the system is put into operation. A user may also have a wish list of features to be added to the system when finances permit.

Modifications initiated by EDP personnel

A system generally requires modification when new equipment is acquired. For example, more storage would mean a larger data base and increased processing would be feasible. Technological advance in the computer industry is swift-paced. Organizations adopting new technology or merely expanding their systems with more sophisticated computers will find that their information systems need modification.

Analysts also may detect errors in a system resulting from poor design and implementation or invalid assumptions once the system is operational. EDP personnel, like management, may also have a wish list not included in the original development because the design was frozen or because development resources were lacking at the time. The list might include reorganization of data, new output form design, or even new programming solutions. Generally these ideas were conceived and documented during development. Once the system is made operational, the suggestions are renewed and reevaluated, and often the changes proposed are added during regular maintenance or redevelopment cycles.

Maintenance and redevelopment management

Every firm needs a policy to differentiate between maintenance and redevelopment, to answer the question posed in Symbol 7 of Figure 15.2. In general, minor modification is defined as a change that affects few users, one that does not require much effort or many resources (not more than one month of a senior programmer's time or two days of the time of a senior analyst). Maintenance jobs can also be defined as routine or expected tasks, or preventive action to minimize errors. Some firms add adjustment to new equipment to the category of maintenance, including the training of user personnel in the new technology. In contrast, redevelopment requires a major allocation of resources and personnel. Many firms have a committee to help draw the line between minor and major modifications, an important distinction because procedurally the two may differ since minor modification may skip some of the stages of development.

Once the maintenance tasks are defined, responsibility must be assigned and resources allocated. (An estimated 30–70 percent of all systems effort goes to maintenance). Usually authority to review and evaluate operations, and responsibility for approving minor modifications, are given to a senior EDP analyst or an internal auditor. A committee composed of the DBA, an auditor, and users' representatives generally assigns priorities to maintenance requests and reconciles conflicts between user departments, settling jurisdictional problems of maintenance when they arise. The committee also sets guidelines for identifying emergency maintenance and establishes rules for maintenance control. This latter activity, **maintenance control,** is exceedingly important since statistics show that security violations often occur during maintenance procedures. There is also a tendency to cut corners in maintenance work to get to more exciting projects. Control of maintenance procedures should ensure that one job is fully completed before the next is begun.

Even routine maintenance should not skip the steps outlined in the development cycle of an information system. Too often there is a tendency to hastily patch programs, to omit the need specification and testing stages due to time pressures. This can lead to monumental blunders, such as the error that resulted when a university programmer patched a grade report, and in the process, changed the statement numbers of the program. Figure 15.3 is a flowchart showing both the original statement numbers (to the left of each box) and modified numbers (to the right). The "Go To" statement, however, remained unaltered. The program was run without testing. As a result, 14,000 grade reports were mailed by the university to the first student on the list, L. C. Able, instead of grade reports being sent to each of the university's 14,000 students. In this case, the original fault lay with the maintenance programmer who skipped an important step in the development process—testing. But maintenance procedures were also inadequate since a supervisor should have caught the error. And it is incredible that no one running the program, printing results, bursting and decollating the reports, and stuffing envelopes caught the mistake. Similar errors can occur in business environments. Mistakes of this nature can be expensive, disruptive, and ruin an organization's credibility.

All modifications, both major and minor, must be economically justified. The cost of development is a sunk cost, so the justification is based on a marginal analysis: that is, the additional marginal cost compared to the marginal benefits of modifications. The techniques of economic analysis described in the feasibility study apply.

When a system has been repeatedly modified, often by different programmers, it becomes cumbersome and inefficient to operate. You might compare the

Figure 15.3
Partial flow chart of a program carelessly maintained

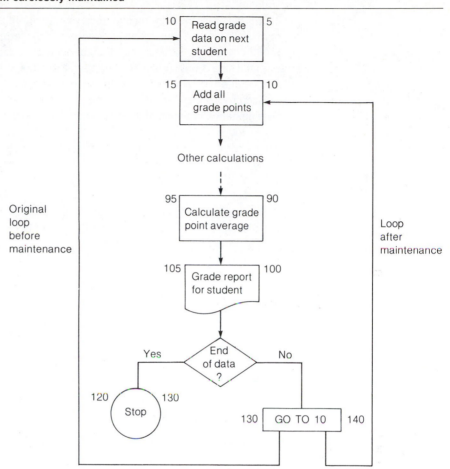

NOTE   the numbers on the left are those before maintenance, those on the right after maintenance.

system to an old car which becomes increasingly unreliable and costly to maintain with age. Some systems are junked as are old cars but others can be redeveloped. A redevelopment decision should be economically justified, but in practice the decision is often judgmental. The resulting redevelopment, however, can sometimes be supported since integrating new technology should make the new system cost-effective.

There is a strong correlation between high standards in the original development process and low maintenance. Planning ahead for equipment and software compatibility, for example, will obviously reduce maintenance. Errors and inconsistencies should be identified and corrected during testing of the system, before it is made operational and the errors become a problem of maintenance. Rigid statements of documentation should also reduce time and effort required to make changes.

One major problem in maintenance management is finding and retaining personnel with the skill and patience needed to trace errors and weaknesses of programs. Correcting, testing, and documenting changes are often less interesting than attacking a new project from an analyst's point of view. The need for maintenance often results from inadequate documentation, patchwork design, and unrealistic procedures. Senior programmers and analysts who should be engaged in maintenance because of their experience and skill generally shun maintenance duties. Job enlargement, giving analysts maintenance responsibilities in addition to other duties, is one solution to this problem. Rotation has other advantages as well since a pool of analysts for maintenance provides systems backup in addition to a variety of approaches and fresh solutions to maintenance problems.

Maintenance is costly and takes a large share of effort when compared to the effort spent in the initial development of an information system, as shown in Figure 15.4. Note that the shaded part of the figure is the effort required for the initial development, corresponding to Figure 14.5.

Summary

After an information system has been implemented and is operational, periodic changes will be required to keep it running efficiently and effectively. The altered state of variables both within the organization and in the external environment may mean operations no longer meet the objectives of the system. Minor changes are called maintenance. Major modifications are called redevelopment.

The need for maintenance or redevelopment is identified during evaluation of

Figure 15.4
Effort distribution

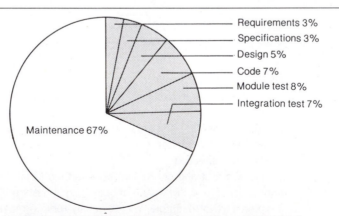

Requirements 3%
Specifications 3%
Design 5%
Code 7%
Module test 8%
Integration test 7%
Maintenance 67%

SOURCE   M. V. Zelkowitz, "Perspectives on Software Engineering,"
ACM Computing Surveys (New York: Association for Computing Machinery) 10, no. 2 (June 1978), p. 202.

**Figure 15.5
Development cycle**

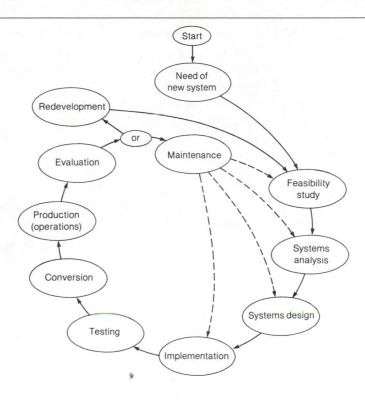

a system's performance. Evaluation is the comparison of actual with expected performance. When the need for major modification is indicated, a decision for redevelopment should be made by a committee that includes user representatives and EDP personnel responsible for maintenance.

Maintenance and redevelopment are extensions of the development process described in Chapters 11–14 (see Figure 15.5). The development cycle is never ending, triggered whenever evaluations indicate that performance is unsatisfactory. Evaluation should be regularly scheduled. It may also be initiated by dissatisfied users and EDP personnel.

Key words

Crash maintenance	Maintenance
Effectiveness	Maintenance control
Efficiency	Maintenance management
Evaluation	Monitor programs
Fine-tuning	Redevelopment
Hardware monitors	Software monitors

Discussion questions

1. What is system maintenance?

2. What is system redevelopment?

3. How are system maintenance and system redevelopment related?

4. How long can the life of an information system be extended by modification and redevelopment? How can it be determined whether such maintenance is cost-effective?

5. Describe how an information system is evaluated. When should evaluation take place? Who should be responsible?

6. What is a monitor? What are the functions of monitors?

7. How can components of an information system, such as hardware, software, and procedures, be evaluated separately? Is such evaluation desirable?

8. What is the role and the importance of maintenance programmers? Why is maintenance often an unpopular assignment?

9. What is the difference between efficiency and effectiveness of an information system? How can they be evaluated?

10. What personal qualities are needed in a maintenance programmer?

Selected annotated bibliography

Adler, Cyrus. "How to Keep Automated Equipment Up and Running." *Office Administration and Automation* 44, no. 5 (May 1983), pp. 29–31.
Ways to increase uptime through routine maintenance and careful use of automated office equipment are described.

"Bibliography of 1982 Performance Literature," *EDP Performance Review* 11, no. 3 (March 1983), pp. 1–31.
This is the ninth in annual bibliographies published by *EDP Performance Review* indexing performance-related literature during the preceding year.

Biggs, Charles L; Evan G. Birks; and William Atkins. *Managing the Systems Development Process.* Englewood Cliffs, N.J.: Touche Ross, 1980, 408 pp.
This book includes sections on system refinement and tuning, postimplementation review, and ongoing maintenance, pp. 229–52.

Harnett, John. "Who's Taking Care of the System?" *Computerworld* 17 (August 24, 1983), pp. 43–46.
Different types of service options are described, including third-party, mail-in, walk-in, remote diagnostics, and self-service.

Herzog, John P. "Systems Evaluation Technique for Users," *Journal of Systems Management* 26, no. 5 (May 1975), pp. 30–35.
This article is specifically addressed to the line manager and describes a scoring system by which a system can be evaluated in terms of problems solved, objectives satisfied, and reliability of input, output, and processing.

King, William R., and Jaime I. Rodriques. "Evaluating Management Information System." *MIS Quarterly* 2, no. 3 (September 1978), pp. 43–52.

This article describes an evaluation model that measures attitudes, value perceptions, information usage, and decision performance. The model is applied to a strategic planning information system.

Lesson, Margorie. *Computer Operations Procedures and Management.* Chicago: Science Research Associates, 1982, 608 pp.

This book describes operations of a computing center with detailed discussions on hardware, peripherals, operating systems, microsystems, and time sharing. It is designed as a text, with each chapter ending with a summary followed by discussion questions, team and group projects, a glossary, and a study guide.

Luit, Peter. "Why You Shouldn't Neglect Systems Maintenance." *Canadian Data Systems* 8, no. 2 (February 1976), pp. 37–38.

An excellent brief discussion on the importance of maintenance. Conditions that impair the effectiveness and efficiency of a system are listed and ways in which companies can organize for maintenance are suggested.

"Maintenance: The Third Party Approach." *Which Computer 7, no. 5 (February 1983), pp. 64–68.*

The variety of services provided by third-party maintenance organizations is outlined.

McGraw, John F. et al. "How Productive Is Your System?" *Small Systems World* 10, no. 8 (September 1982), pp. 18–20.

The reasons why companies are not effectively using their hardware are identified, and tip-offs which indicate degraded computer performance are described. The use of hardware and software to monitor productivity is recommended.

Shaeffer, Howard. *Data Center Operations.* Englewood Cliffs, N.J.: Prentice-Hall, 1981, pp. 190–264.

This book has two chapters relevant to computer operations: "Data Center Workflow and Job Scheduling," and "Resource Allocation." Many samples of forms used in computer centers are included. The text is detailed, perhaps more approriate for a professional computer center manager than for a corporate manager.

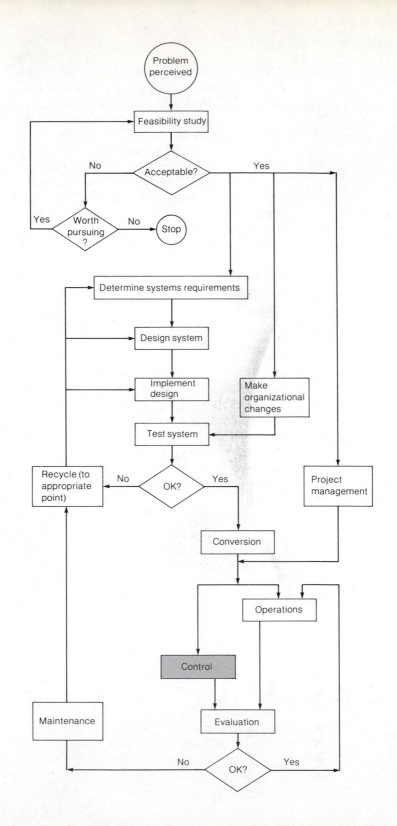

Quality control and security

16

A society with a high level of automation must eventually frame its laws and safeguards in such a way that computers can police the actions of other computers.

James Martin

Information systems should be controlled for accuracy, timeliness, and completeness of data. Procedures must be adopted and checkpoints established to guard against unintentional human errors, such as the use of an outdated code, the wrong input tape, or incorrect output distribution. Some errors are built into the system by poor design; many result from careless programming.

Preventing such errors is one aspect of control. Security, protecting information from unauthorized access and illicit use, is another. The need for control and security of business data predates the use of computers. For example, marketing strategies and product development have always been closely guarded business secrets. However, the volume of confidential data processed by information systems today means the rewards for theft or industrial espionage are of a higher magnitude than in the past. Consider, for example, the large sums of money being transferred daily by EFT (electronic fund transfer). Furthermore, modern data communications technology makes remote theft a distinct possibility. Computerized systems can be breached from a location thousands of miles from a data base. In addition, many persons today have a knowledge of computing systems, a knowledge that can be used for nefarious purposes.

Another reason control is so important is that never before in history has it been possible to make so many mistakes in so short a time. Undetected errors compound at an alarming rate due to the rapidity of computer calculations and the repetitious nature of computer operations. No wonder the issues of control and security occupy so much management attention.

The determination of technical control measures is generally the responsibility of EDP personnel. However, management should specify control standards, identify the data that needs protection, and specify the degree of control and security needed after weighing costs versus benefits and considerations of risk.

Protection of data

Data must be protected from accidents and natural disasters as well as from intentional theft. A breakdown in an air-conditioning system may result in loss of computing capabilities. Fires, floods, hurricanes, even a heavy snowfall causing a roof to collapse can cause destruction of data and valuable equipment. Poor machine maintenance may be at fault. Human errors, such as inadequate input preparation, poorly drawn user specifications, programming oversights, or careless machine operation, may also cause failure of the system to provide needed information.

Establishing control measures for the above is far less taxing than protecting information systems from intentional damage or theft. Disgruntled employees have sabotaged computer operations in the past; so have members of the public. Computers have been shot, short-circuited with metal objects, also doused with gasoline and set afire. Damages for acts of vandalism alone run into the millions.

Industrial espionage and fraud are other security threats that are hard to control. When all computer equipment and data were centralized, physical access to the system could be controlled, but with widespread use of teleprocessing networks, data is in far greater jeopardy. Communication lines can be infiltrated through **wiretapping** (electromagnetic pickup of messages off communication lines); **masquerading** (pretending to be a legitimate user to access the system); **piggybacking** (interception and switching of messages), and **reading between the lines** (engaging the system illicitly when a user is connected to the computer but is "thinking," and the computer is idle). Infiltration may involve manipulation of data, the alteration of computer programs, pillage of data, or unauthorized use of the computer itself. A few years ago, a 15-year-old boy was charged with felony, grand theft, and vandalism for using 200 hours of unauthorized time, worth about $10,000, at the University of California at Berkeley, accessed from a second-hand terminal costing $60. In another case of remote entry fraud, 277 freight cars of Penn Central, worth over $1 million, were diverted to a spur track and sold.

Most cases of fraud are kept hush-hush since firms are reluctant to announce their losses to the public. But observors agree that computer crime is on the rise. Common crimes include adding, altering, and deleting transactions; file changes; program changes; and improper operation. In cases reported, detection has often been accidental, not the result of established EDP control measures or auditing. Professionals predict that computerized systems will be assaulted with increasing frequency in the future. The saying, "Temptation makes a thief," appears to be applicable to computer theft. The increasing use of telecommunications, the large amount of data being processed, and huge sums of money involved in electronic transfer make computer theft highly lucrative. Unfortunately, cheap microcomputers and teleprocessing capabilities favor the embezzler rather than the controller.

Countermeasures to threats

Security of an information system should be tight, the detection of fraud not dependent on luck. Validation of data and coding are measures to counter threats to computer systems. These have been discussed in earlier chapters of this text. Access control and auditing are additional countermeasures that will be examined in greater detail at this point.

Access control

For centralized CPUs in batch mode, access control is easily achieved. The computer center can be physically closed to unauthorized personnel—a closed shop, denying unauthorized personnel the capability of submitting jobs to the computer. Badge systems, locked doors, a guard at the entry: all procedures common to restricted areas in security-sensitive factories or research divisions can be adopted. In addition, the computer can reference an access directory, described in Chapter 8, when use of the data base is requested.

With telecommunications, access control has three dimensions: (1) **identification:** verifying the identity of the user requesting service; (2) **authentication:** verifying the user's right to access a requested file or portion of the data base; and (3) **authorization:** verifying the type of access permitted—that is, read, write, update, or no access. A security matrix stored in the computer can control dimensions 2 and 3. (See Table 8.4 for a sample.) The user's identity may be verified by a machine-readable badge, a voice print, fingerprints, or handprints, though such equipment is expensive at the present time. More common is the use of **passwords.** The secrecy of passwords can be guarded by frequently changing the password, by using a system to generate passwords for each user or by techniques for generating passwords for each session, called **session passwords.** The user can also be identified by a project or account number, and be constrained by time locks (system operational only during specified times), hardware locks (physical locks on machines), and the amount of computer time allocated per job. In addition, the security matrix may control the access to the data base of each individual terminal. For example, the terminal in the data base administrator's office may be the only one permitted to access all files and programs, and the only terminal that has access to the security matrix itself.

Auditing

There are two approaches to auditing: auditing around and through the computer. Auditing is used to detect accidental errors as well as fraud.

Auditing around the computer

In this approach, output is checked for a given input. It is assumed that if input is correct and reflected in output, then the processing itself is also correct. The audit does not check computer processing directly, hence the term **auditing around the computer.** This type of audit does not require computer expertise. Instead, traditional auditing methods and techniques are used: that is, tracing who did what, when, in what sequence.

The problem with this approach is that processing errors may exist even though no errors are apparent in input and output. Furthermore, computer calculations provide few intermediate results for auditors to check by traditional trailing methods.

Auditing through the computer

To check both input *and* process, **auditing through the computer** can be made. This auditing approach may use test data, auditor-prepared programs, auditor-software packages, or audit programming languages.

Use of test data   In this technique, a selected set of data is checked for reasonableness, validity, and consistency. Auditors search for extreme conditions, out-of-sequence data, out-of-balance batches, and so forth, the type of errors frequently found when testing application programs. The accuracy of the computer program itself in performing calculations is examined, and operation procedures used by the firm are scrutinized and checked for consistency with corporate policies.

Auditor-prepared programs   In this approach, specially written programs prepared by the auditors are used to check specific conditions and to identify situations that need further study and analysis. The programs also spot check for unauthorized manipulations by programmers and operators, and provide listings of before and after changes which facilitate auditing.

Auditor-software packages   Standard auditing programs can be purchased. These are not as specialized as programs written by auditors for a specific information system but they are less expensive and relatively easy to use.

Audit programming languages   Special programming languages can be used to generate output needed by auditors. System 2170, for example, developed by the accounting firm, Peat, Marwick and Mitchell, is a language that can be learned in about one week, and has 21 audit commands.

All "through the computer" auditing approaches create problems when used on real-time systems since sample data can get mixed with the live stream of data unless extreme care is taken and expensive precautions are adopted. One solution to this problem is to create a representative set of data that represents the company and use it for auditing independent of the live data system. This approach is referred to as the **mini-company approach** since the test data base is a miniature representation of the company.

Auditing approaches should be decided during the early stages of development of an information system. For example, the generation of reports to trace calculations on intermediate results and generation of listings of exceptional and suspicious situations can be programmed with little effort during the design phase. Grafting these auditing and control features after the system is operational is both expensive and disruptive. At the time design specifications are under consideration, auditors must indicate output needs; specify decision rules of computations (e.g., rounding rules); establish editing; backup and recovery procedures; and set document and testing standards. Auditors should also participate in testing the system and have a voice in the decision of system acceptance. Once the system

Figure 16.1
Rings of control and security defenses

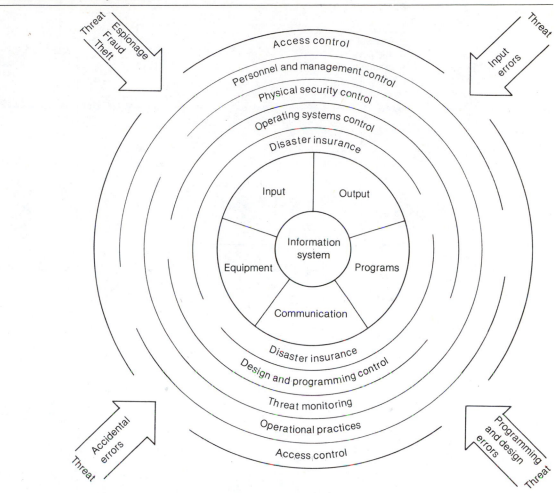

SOURCE Adapted by permission of the *Harvard Business Review*. Exhibit from "Plugging the Leaks in Computer Security" by Joseph J. Wasserman, (September–October 1969), p. 124. Copyright, © 1969 by the President and Fellows of Harvard College.

is operational, auditors play a role in control and evaluation throughout the life cycle of the system.

An auditor of a computerized information system should be not only a competent accountant and auditor, but also knowledgeable about computer systems, especially the implementation of data bases, documentation, data security, and recovery. In addition, programming skills are needed since computer programs are used in the audits themselves, COBOL being the language most commonly employed. For example, programs control calculations, comparisons, and verifi-

Figure 16.2
Stages of processing and quality control points

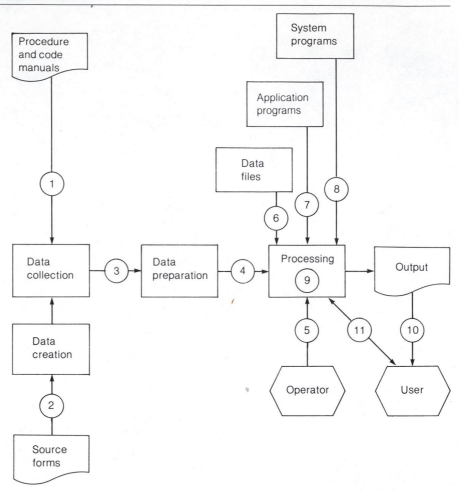

cations. They perform intermediary operations (such as sampling and extractions) and also perform the functions of monitors to collect data on operations.

There are many texts on the subject of computers and auditing.[1] What needs to be stressed here is that computers are used by auditors in auditing computerized systems. But current computer audit techniques are not as advanced as the technology being audited and the computer profession shows no sign of waiting until auditors catch up.

[1] See Delroy L. Cornick, *Auditing in the Electronic Environment* (Mt. Airy, Md.: Lomond Books, 1981, 316 pp); Donna Hussain and K. M. Hussain, *Information Resource Management* (Homewood, Ill.: Richard D. Irwin, 1984, pp. 299–316); and Joseph Sardinas et al. *EDP Auditing: A Primer* (New York: John Wiley and Sons, 1981), 209 pp.

How much control and security?

In deciding how much control is needed to protect a computerized information system from inadvertent errors and security violations, the monetary cost to implement control measures must be considered as well as the psychic cost of delays and inconvenience from controls. Companies can go too far, causing production to fall off because computers are so difficult to access by bona fide users and because procedures to monitor errors impede performance. A well-conceived system of control can be visualized as rings of protection (see Figure 16.1), designed uniquely for each system, with complex controls when the cost of data loss by accident or criminal intent is high.

Every information system should include in its design control points for monitoring the system. Figure 16.2 shows where controls are needed, where information systems are most vulnerable to security violations and most susceptible to error. The remaining sections of this chapter will be a commentary on each of these control points. Potential threats to data quality and security at each point will be discussed, countermeasures to these threats will be suggested, and the personnel responsible for control will be identified.

Control points

Control of procedure and code manuals (Circle 1, Figure 16.2)

Table 16.1 summarizes the common sources of errors when using procedure and code manuals. Usually errors in the use of manuals are the result of poor documentation or carelessness in their use. Since manuals are valuable, they should be kept in a safe location and their use should be carefully monitored. Many businesses assign someone on the staff of the data base administrator as the keeper of code manuals. This individual coordinates assignment of codes according to the needs of users to eliminate redundant coding schemes and is responsible for establishing all codes needed by the system. Publication, maintenance, and distribution of a uniform code manual are also responsibilities of this individual.

One usually associates the theft of manuals with national security violations. For example, in 1981, the sale of a manual containing cryptographic codes was revealed. This sale was made by a U.S. soldier to the Soviet Union for $131,000. In today's computerized world industrial espionage is also a problem of major dimensions and manuals are a major target. In 1983, the Japanese firms, Hitachi and Mitsubishi, were charged with paying $648,000 for stolen manuals on IBM products. The two companies agreed to a payment of $300 million to IBM in settlement, and have given IBM the right to scrutinize their related new products for a period of five years. Two U.S. firms have also been implicated in the case. IBM has sued NAS and National Semiconductor Corporation for $2–$5 billion in damages for allegedly aiding Hitachi in stealing the manuals. The publicity given this case has served a useful purpose: many firms have tightened the security of their manuals.

Form control (Circle 2)

A common method of collecting data for an information processing system is through the medium of forms. Though error-free data collection may be impos-

Table 16.1
Control of manuals

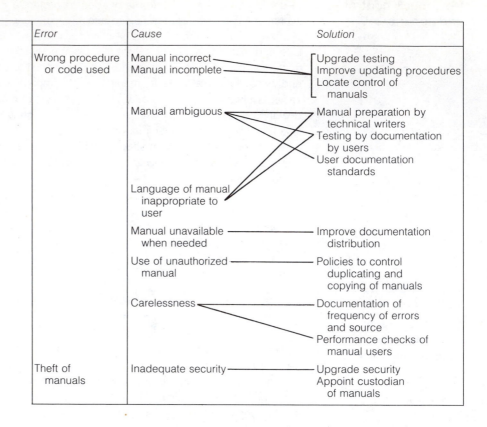

Error	Cause	Solution
Wrong procedure or code used	Manual incorrect Manual incomplete	Upgrade testing Improve updating procedures Locate control of manuals
	Manual ambiguous	Manual preparation by technical writers Testing by documentation by users User documentation standards
	Language of manual inappropriate to user	
	Manual unavailable when needed	Improve documentation distribution
	Use of unauthorized manual	Policies to control duplicating and copying of manuals
	Carelessness	Documentation of frequency of errors and source Performance checks of manual users
Theft of manuals	Inadequate security	Upgrade security Appoint custodian of manuals

sible, errors can be minimized by having well-designed forms with easy-to-follow directions. Analysts who design forms and program input validity checks are primarily responsible for controlling errors at this checkpoint. **Turnaround documents** are being increasingly used by businesses to reduce errors. For example, banks provide customers with deposit slips already printed with their names, addresses, and account numbers. Only spaces for date and amount need to be filled. By reducing the amount of information the customer must provide, the opportunity for error is minimized. Other examples of turnaround documents are the tear-off sections of utility and credit card bills that must accompany bill payment, and preprinted complaint forms that come with mail order merchandise. Table 16.2 summarizes frequent causes of errors in filling out forms and possible control solutions.

Data collection (Circle 3)   One of the more important points in data control is data collection. Data collection is not only the source of many careless errors, but is also the focus of much criminal activity.

**Table 16.2
Form control**

Error	Cause	Solution
Forms filled incorrectly	Directions ambiguous	Forms prepared by analysts experienced in form design
	Format poor	Upgrade testing, including testing by user groups
	Substitute or unauthorized person filling out forms	Distribution and collection controls
		Require identification of user
	Poor motivation	Instructions should emphasize positive benefits of correct data and negative effect of wrong information
	Carelessness	Use of turnaround documents
		Validity check of data during processing (a solution at Circle 9)

**Table 16.3
Data collection control**

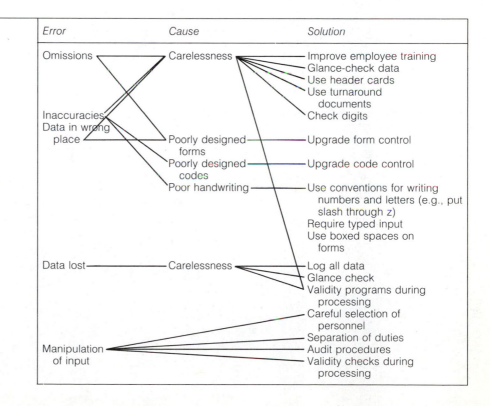

Error	Cause	Solution
Omissions	Carelessness	Improve employee training
		Glance-check data
		Use header cards
		Use turnaround documents
Inaccuracies		Check digits
Data in wrong place	Poorly designed forms	Upgrade form control
	Poorly designed codes	Upgrade code control
	Poor handwriting	Use conventions for writing numbers and letters (e.g., put slash through z)
		Require typed input
		Use boxed spaces on forms
Data lost	Carelessness	Log all data
		Glance check
		Validity programs during processing
Manipulation of input		Careful selection of personnel
		Separation of duties
		Audit procedures
		Validity checks during processing

For example, a Blue Cross-Blue Shield claims examiner mailed forms to relatives who filled them in with real names and policy numbers to defraud the system of $128,000. In another recorded case of fraud, 11 employees of the County Department of Social Services in Los Angeles issued checks to themselves using terminated welfare accounts. Other cases of manipulation of input data include: an IRS clerk who awarded a relative unclaimed tax credits; the theft of $100,000 from a bank account using the MICR number found on a discarded deposit slip; and a conspiracy between an accounting clerk and grocer resulting in a theft of more than $120,000 over the years by issuing false invoices for undelivered food. Inadvertent errors can be equally harmful to an organization. The code of equipment costing $20,000 was erroneously used to code the price of 50 manuals of that equipment. This mistake resulted in an inflated inventory value of one million dollars. Table 16.3 summarizes common errors in data collection and suggests possible control solutions.

Data preparation (Circle 4)

Errors in data preparation occur when data is incorrectly converted into machine-readable form. Control is exercised by the department responsible for the data preparation. Recommended control measures are summarized in Table 16.4.

Ways to detect error and procedures to correct mistakes are not all that is needed. The source of the errors should be traced and procedures amended so that the same errors do not recur. By reorganizing the location of data preparation, for example, one firm reduced input errors from 15 percent to 2 percent. Originally, clerks had coded information on forms from user transactional records, the forms later being used to key input at the EDP center. By moving EDP input

**Table 16.4
Summary of data preparation errors and solutions**

Error	Cause	Solution
Incorrect data	Poorly written keypunch instructions	Upgrade procedures manual, include visual aids
	Hardware error	Proper maintenance
	Carelessness	Verification of keypunching by a second operator
		Use of check digits
Card handling errors (cards misplaced, put out of order, damaged, or duplicated inadvertently)	Carelessness	Glance check
		Validity programs
		Upgrade employee selection and training
	Poor procedure	Upgrade procedure testing
		Log data

clerks to user departments, coding forms were eliminated and input keyed directly from source documents. This procedural change, with responsibility for data preparation no longer shared (each department blaming the other for errors), helped reduce input errors significantly.

Operations (Circle 5)

Though employees can be trained in emergency procedures should flood, earthquake, fire, or an explosion interrupt operations, a safeguard for an information system against such disasters is backup data files stored in a secure vault at another location. Also, complete backup processing facilities at another computer center tested for restart and recovery may be provided. Backup is good insurance against sabotage. Incidents of willful damage to computer equipment and data files have augmented in recent years, particularly in industries engaged in politically sensitive research, for example, nuclear energy or chemical warfare.

In handling sensitive information, the following basic operating precautions are also recommended. There should always be two operators present. This is a good security measure, and a good safety practice as well. Work schedules should be changed frequently so that no single operator handles the same programs for a long period of time. No employees should be assigned processing tasks when a conflict of interest might arise (for example, bank employees should not handle programming that will affect their accounts). Finally, proof of authorization and sign-in/sign-out controls for handling sensitive files should be initiated and neither programmers nor analysts should be assigned routine operating tasks.

Though many controls are needed to prevent malicious intrusion during operations, information systems being exceedingly vulnerable during this activity, most breakdowns and errors can be traced to lax procedures and careless operators. And these incidents can be costly, indeed. For eample, the running of an accounts payable program using an out-dated price list cost one firm $100,000. Another expensive mistake: A bank shredder fed a printout of sensitive data on depositors with the line of print parallel to the blades instead of at right angles. As a result, strips of readable confidential data were thrown in the trash where they were spotted, retrieved, and peddled at a local bar by a drifter. The cost to the bank: reward money for return of the strips and an incalculable loss of customer confidence.

More stringent control procedures could also have prevented the following incident. A Chicago hotel mixed address tapes, sending letters to vendors instead of to past guests explaining recent hotel renovations and urging the guests to return. Instead of goodwill, the hotel received irate calls from vendors whose spouses were citing the letters as evidence of their infidelity.

Failure to test control procedures produced the following fiasco. When a fire broke out in a computer center, employees discovered that narrow doors barred passage of fire extinguishing equipment.

But who was to blame when a corrosive leak in an air-conditioning system destroyed a computer several floors below? It simply isn't practical to devise con-

**Table 16.5
Control of operations**

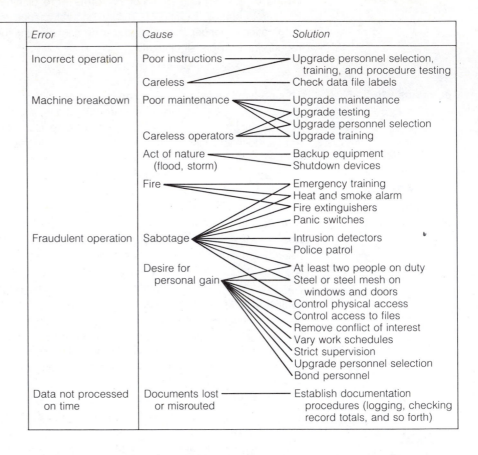

Error	Cause	Solution
Incorrect operation	Poor instructions	Upgrade personnel selection, training, and procedure testing
	Careless	Check data file labels
Machine breakdown	Poor maintenance	Upgrade maintenance
		Upgrade testing
		Upgrade personnel selection
	Careless operators	Upgrade training
	Act of nature (flood, storm)	Backup equipment
		Shutdown devices
	Fire	Emergency training
		Heat and smoke alarm
		Fire extinguishers
		Panic switches
Fraudulent operation	Sabotage	Intrusion detectors
		Police patrol
	Desire for personal gain	At least two people on duty
		Steel or steel mesh on windows and doors
		Control physical access
		Control access to files
		Remove conflict of interest
		Vary work schedules
		Strict supervision
		Upgrade personnel selection
		Bond personnel
Data not processed on time	Documents lost or misrouted	Establish documentation procedures (logging, checking record totals, and so forth)

trol methods for *all* possible threats to an information system. Controls are costly, and too many controls can impede operation. The controls summarized in Table 16.5 are those most frequently adopted for operations.

Data files (Circle 6)

If data files are centrally stored, a librarian generally is assigned responsibility for control. Otherwise the owner of the data is responsible. Table 16.6 summarizes the types of control needed to protect data files.

There are numerous cases of errors and fraud relating to data files cited in computer literature. Stolen programs have been held for ransom. Disgruntled employees have maliciously scratched or destroyed tapes. At the Arizona State Finance Center, a backup card file was used for making Christmas decorations. An employee moving files to storage in another organization wedged the vault open but forgot to remove the wedge after the move was complete. Though the vault was fireproof, a fire swept through the open door and destroyed hundreds of tapes.

Table 16.6
Control of data files

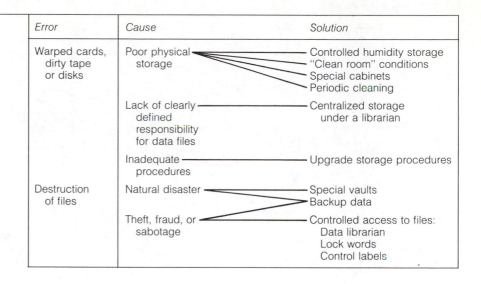

Error	Cause	Solution
Warped cards, dirty tape or disks	Poor physical storage	Controlled humidity storage "Clean room" conditions Special cabinets Periodic cleaning
	Lack of clearly defined responsibility for data files	Centralized storage under a librarian
	Inadequate procedures	Upgrade storage procedures
Destruction of files	Natural disaster	Special vaults Backup data
	Theft, fraud, or sabotage	Controlled access to files: Data librarian Lock words Control labels

In most cases, destruction of data files can be attributed to lax security. Since files are particularly vulnerable to industrial espionage, the need for data safeguards at this control point is vital.

Programming controls (Circles 7,8)

Many mistakes in computerized systems can be attributed to faulty programming. One bank, for example, lost $300,000 by paying customers interest on 31-day months. In another case, an omitted hyphen in programming caused a rocket being tested to head for Rio de Janeiro. It had to be destroyed mid-flight, at a loss of $18,500,000. Unintentional errors may result from an incorrect algorithm, erroneous programming logic, or a cause as minor as one out-of-sequence programming statement. Training care, strict adherence to standard programming procedures, and proper documentation should minimize such problems.

The controls summarized in Table 16.7 should trace inadvertent errors and also help prevent fraud. Control measures should be initiated and enforced by EDP personnel responsible for systems analysis and programming. Unfortunately, programming fraud is exceedingly difficult to detect and the crimes themselves are often quite ingenious. The first federal prosecution of computer crime in 1966 was against a bank programmer who programmed the system to omit his name from a list generated daily of overdrawn accounts. He withdrew large sums of money before being caught. Control measures, however, did not bring about his downfall. The overdrafts were detected only when the computer broke down and the bank had to revert to manual processing.

Another programmer assessed a 10-cent service charge to each customer and put the amounts in a dummy account under the name of *Zwicke*. By chance, a

Table 16.7
Programming controls

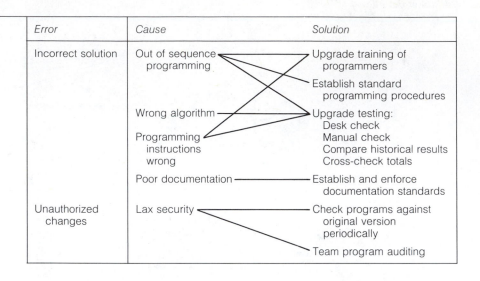

Error	Cause	Solution
Incorrect solution	Out of sequence programming	Upgrade training of programmers
		Establish standard programming procedures
	Wrong algorithm	Upgrade testing: Desk check Manual check Compare historical results Cross-check totals
	Programming instructions wrong	
	Poor documentation	Establish and enforce documentation standards
Unauthorized changes	Lax security	Check programs against original version periodically
		Team program auditing

PR man decided to award a bonus to the first and last name on the firm's alphabetical list of customers. The bogus Zwicke was accordingly discovered.

Nibble theft, stealing small amounts of money over a period of time, is more difficult to detect than bite-size fraud, the embezzlement of large sums. The latter can be uncovered by auditing and checking for unreasonable values or control totals. But no matter how well designed the controls, someone will think up a new technique for cheating the system. Constant vigilance is required, especially when technology changes and new hardware and software are used.

Processing (Circle 9)

At the time of processing, data which passed control points 2, 3, and 4 can be reevaluated by computer programs. Validation programs, described in Chapter 7, can check for completeness, accuracy, format, range, reasonableness, consistency, sequence, and number of transactions. Input errors can also be detected during processing when self-checking codes are used.

Processing control, the responsibility of EDP personnel, is closely related to operations control. Measures that specifically guard against careless processing are listed in Table 16.8.

Output (Circle 10)

Output is the product of all input and processing. If proper control is exercised in each of the steps discussed earlier, the output should be free of error. But most firms add output controls in an information system's design to cross check for errors that may have slipped past earlier controls. Responsibility for these controls is divided between EDP personnel producing output and managment using the output. These controls are summarized in Table 16.9.

**Table 16.8
Processing controls**

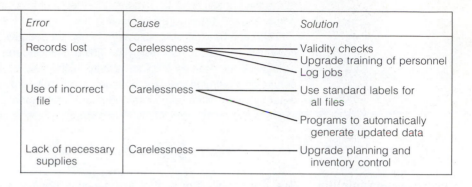

Error	Cause	Solution
Records lost	Carelessness	Validity checks
		Upgrade training of personnel
		Log jobs
Use of incorrect file	Carelessness	Use standard labels for all files
		Programs to automatically generate updated data
Lack of necessary supplies	Carelessness	Upgrade planning and inventory control

Many output mistakes can be caught by cursory sight checks. For example, a payroll run of checks issued without decimal points could be easily spotted by an alert operator since the amounts would be unreasonable. In addition, many of the validation programs used for input can be run to control output.

**Teleprocessing
(Circle 11)**

Access controls discussed earlier in this chapter are one method of protecting data during teleprocessing. The use of cryptography, transformation of data, protocols, packet switching, parity checks, and self-checking codes, described in Chapters 5 and 7, are additional control techniques.

The vulnerability of computer systems to intrusion though telecommunications lines was illustrated in 1983 when data bases at Los Alamos National Laboratory in New Mexico, at Security Pacific Bank in California, and the Sloan Kettering Cancer Center in New York were all accessed by a group of "hackers" in Milwaukee. These young people, aged 15–22, belonged to the 414 Gang (named

**Table 16.9
Output control**

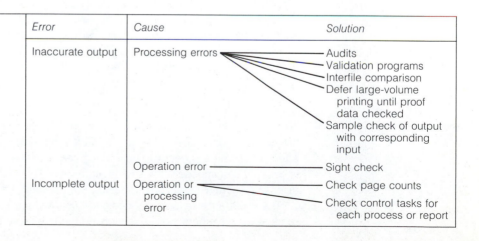

Error	Cause	Solution
Inaccurate output	Processing errors	Audits
		Validation programs
		Interfile comparison
		Defer large-volume printing until proof data checked
		Sample check of output with corresponding input
	Operation error	Sight check
Incomplete output	Operation or processing error	Check page counts
		Check control tasks for each process or report

after the area code of Milwaukee). They penetrated telecommunications security at the three institutions to demonstrate their technical wizardry, not for money or personal gain. They were just "having fun."

This case has helped publicize the need for security agents trained to uncover computer crimes. It has also highlighted the inadequacy of our present legal framework for defining criminal activity in the field of computing. Finally, it has served as a warning that telecommunications may prove an Achilles heel to computer systems. More resources and more professional attention must be devoted to system security, particularly to telecommunications security, in the future.

Control responsibility of management

The responsibility for control and security of information is ultimately management's. A firm's survival is at stake when decisions are based on inaccurate data or when losses must be absorbed due to sabotage or theft. Goodwill and a firm's reputation for quality service are also threatened when controls prove inadequate. Though EDP personnel participate in technical control decisions, it is up to management to identify needed points of control, to establish and document procedures, and to assign personnel to enforce these procedures. In designing an overall security plan, information needing protection must be identified, resources for this protection must be allocated, and corrective actions must be outlined for procedure revision should the security prove inadequate. Regulations should be flexible, selective, effective, and enforceable.

Control of an information system is facilitated by dividing the system into five basic functions: programming and systems development; handling input media; operation of data processing equipment; documentation and file library; and distribution of output. The duties of employees should not cross these functional lines. When no single individual performs all the steps in a transaction, the opportunity for fraud is diminished. If controls at one level are bypassed, errors can be detected at the next control point. This separation of duties may not be practical in small institutions, but the principle should be followed whenever possible.

All controls should be periodically reviewed and problems that have arisen analyzed. What types of errors occurred? At what cost? Why? Could the errors have been prevented? How? Depending on the answers to these questions, controls should be tightened (or relaxed).

Summary

This chapter examines controls for documentation, forms, data collection, data preparation, operations, data files, programming, processing, and output. A management dilemma is deciding how much control is necessary. Too much control is costly: it can impede work and affect morale. Too little control permits inaccuracies and security infractions, reducing the usefulness of the system.

The importance of carefully designed controls cannot be overstressed. Most readers will have personally experienced the frustration of trying to correct a billing error resulting from inadequate control procedures. Indeed, a major source of public distrust of computers can be traced to such experiences, the feeling consumers have that they are being victimized by computerized systems. In a survey reported by Sterling,[2] four or more contacts were required by one third of the individuals negotiating clarification or solution of computer errors. Billing mistakes were by far the most common category of error (81 percent), the types of errors falling into the following categories:

Payment not credited	7.9%
Incorrect amount of payment credited (overcharged)	12.8
Incorrect amount of payment credited (undercharged)	4.3
Billed for already settled account	7.3
Charged for nonexistent expenditure	29.9
Not given credit on returned item	5.5
Charged interest without cause	14.0
Billing error caused by misdirected bill	7.3
Other	10.9
All billing errors	100.0%

Distribution of error by type of transaction was as follows:

Credit service and special credit card	16.7%
Oil company (heating, gasoline)	9.9
Utility company (gas, phone, electric)	16.7
Department store	22.2
Mail order business	16.0
Insurance	1.9
Bank or savings institution (not including checking)	4.3
Checking account	4.9
Government (municipal)	0.6
Government (federal)	2.5
Other	4.3
All errors	100.0%

Since a firm's reputation depends on the quality of its customer service, inadequate controls over computerized information can lead to decrease of clients, a decline of profits, and a loss of goodwill.

Control measures should be planned, implemented, tested, and evaluated during the development of an information system. It is both expensive and disruptive to add controls at a later date. However, whenever computer fraud is reported, security experts must devise counter procedures to prevent future incidents of the same nature. Unfortunately, firms are reluctant to publicize security breaches lest their credibility suffer. This means that analysts designing security measures are not always aware of the tricks and techniques used by perpetrators of fraud to breach information systems

The widespread use of home computers makes information systems today even more vulnerable to security infractions than in the past since every terminal has the potential for infiltrating information networks. As the number of computers in-

---

[2]T. D. Sterling, "Consumer Difficulties with Computerized Transactions: An Empirical Investigation," *ACM Communications* 22, no. 5 (May 1979), pp. 285–87.

Table 16.10
Countermeasures for threats to security

Access control
Authorization/authentication,
  (e.g., passwords,
  cards)
Hardware locks
Logging access
Time locks
Librarian control of:
  Data
  Programs
  Documentation

Processing controls
Transformation of data
Ciphering/deciphering
Validity checking
Control totals
Form control
Procedure control
Backup
  Equipment
  Personnel

Physical controls
Vaults
Fire extinguishing equipment
Physical restrictions to:
  Peripherals
  Libraries
  CPU

Organizational controls
Separation of duties
Rotation of duties
Bond personnel
Identify disgruntled personnel
Train personnel
Remove conflicts of interest
Disaster insurance
Background check
Appoint security officer

Monitoring controls
Auditing
  Internal
  External
Standards
Testing

creases, applications expand, and data bases grow, preventing and detecting computer crime will become an even greater problem. Laws need to be written defining computer crime such as:

1. The introduction of false data into a computer.
2. The use of computer facilities for unauthorized or illegal purposes.
3. The alteration or destruction of a computer, its information, or files.
4. Electronic burglary of money, financial instruments, property, services, or valuable data.

Though some state and federal laws do cover these areas in part, comprehensive federal legislation is lacking. Such legislation would be an important deterrent to felons and a valuable mechanism for the prosecution of computer-related crimes.[3]

Common countermeasures to security threats are summarized in Table 16.10.

Key words

Auditing around the computer
Auditing through the computer
Authentication
Authorization

Identification
Masquerading
Mini-company approach
Passwords

[3]Linda M. Marquis and Virginia M. Moore, "Proposed Federal Computer Systems Production Act," *DPA Journal* 50, no. 12 (December 1980), pp. 29–32.

Piggy-backing   Session passwords
Processing control   Turnaround documents
Reading between the lines   Wiretapping

Discussion questions

1. Identify methods of access control to:
   a. The data base.
   b. Programs.
   c. The CPU.
   How effective is each control?

2. What is an audit trail? How is it different in a computerized business firm compared to a noncomputerized firm?

3. How does auditing through a computer compare to auditing around a computer?

4. Distinguish between:
   a. External and internal control.
   b. Organizational and administrative control.
   c. Process and operational control.
   d. Physical and access control.

5. Comment on the statement: A computer system adds to the probability of errors, fraud, and destruction of data and information.

6. Describe types of crimes perpetrated against computerized systems.

7. Describe five situations in which personal identification might be required before access to a computer is granted. In each case, which of the following methods would you recommend:
   a. I.D. card?
   b. Password?
   c. Signature identification?
   d. Hand form indentification?
   e. Voice identification?
   f. Handprint identification?

8. Comment on the statement: Computers never make mistakes. People do.

9. What are some of the common causes of errors in computer systems? Classify them in terms of:
   a. Source.
   b. Motivation.
   c. Importance.
   d. Difficulty to trace.
   e. Difficulty to correct.

10. Why is privacy of data important to business clients and customers? What other segments in business are affected and why? How can each problem be successfully approached?

11. How can the conflict between need for data privacy and need for data access be resolved? What tradeoffs can be made?

12. What is a password? Are passwords cost-effective? When should passwords be used?

13. Give two examples of unexpected results that might be produced because of:
    a. Malfunction.
    b. Mistakes.
    c. Fraud.
    d. Theft.
    e. Sabotage.

    How might security be improved to prevent incorrect results caused by a? By b, c, d, and e?

14. What are some common abuses of computerized information systems? How can these abuses be prevented?

15. What is the difference between the design and implementation of controls? Where does each start and end? How do they overlap?

16. Has your privacy been invaded by business computers? How can invasion of privacy be prevented?

17. Can a computer system ever be completely secure? What are the tradeoffs in costs? What are the social and nonmonetary costs?

18. Can error-free data be guaranteed? Can error-free results be guaranteed? Explain your answers.

19. Identify control points where measures should be taken to ensure security of data. Explain what measures you would require and why?

20. How can careless errors be reduced?

21. What should be management's role in planning system security?

Exercises

1. Assume that a firm has a privacy policy that states that salary data should be known only to the immediate supervisor of employees and higher level managers. Design controls to implement that policy.

2. Read about a case on computer fraud.
    a. How was the fraud discovered?
    b. What levels of management were involved?
    c. Why was the crime not uncovered by auditors?
    d. Why did it take so long to discover?
    e. How could the crime have been avoided?
    f. How can a system be designed and operated to prevent such a crime from recurring?

Selected annotated bibliography

ACM Computing Surveys 11, no. 4 (December 1979), pp. 281–413.

This is a special issue on crypotology and data encryption addressed to the nontechnical reader. The articles recommended include one on the history and state of the art on application of encryption to secure data bases, communications, and networks, and one examining cryptographical weaknesses.

Allen, Brandt. "The Biggest Computer Frauds: Lessons for the CPAs." *The Journal of Accountancy* 143, no. 5 (May 1977), pp. 52–62.

This is an analysis of cases of computer abuse described in a study by Stanford Research Institute. The author explains how such examples of fraud can be prevented and how the accounting profession can aid in preventing criminal activity.

Argyris, Chris. "Organizational Learning and Management Information Systems." *Data Base* 13, nos. 2 & 3 (Winter-Spring 1982), pp. 3–11.

Argyris describes organizational learning systems that inhibit error detection and corrections. He examines implementation of MIS and argues that implementation does not deal ". . . with the fact that there are inner contradictions embedded in organizations that cannot be eliminated because they are inherent in the use of information. . . ."

Comer, Michael J. *Corporate Fraud.* London: McGraw-Hill, 1977, 393 pp.

A comprehensive book on the classification, concealment, detection, and defense against corporate fraud. Thirty cases of computer crime (pp. 153–88) are described and many cases analyzed.

Computer 16, no. 7 (July 1983), pp. 10–95.

This is a special issue devoted to computer security. S. R. Ames, Jr. and P. G. Neuman present an excellent introduction to new technologies. C. E. Landwehr discusses the best technologies available and projects for trusted systems under development. Other articles are on the following topics: securing a distributed system, statistical data bases, multilevel systems, and multiprocessor microcomputers.

Diraff, T. E. "The Protection of Computer Facilities and Equipment: Physical Security." *Data Base* 10, no. 1 (Summer, 1978), pp. 15–24.

A good discussion of considerations of location, access control, personnel control, and systems recovery as they relate to physical security of an information system.

Howe, Charles L. "Coping with Computer Criminals." *Datamation* 28, no. 1 (January 1982), pp. 118–28.

According to the author, "Too often MIS managers concentrate on hardware and software rather than on personnel as a means of checking computer abuse." Howe outlines a plan for security against fraud, including means to thwart theft of computer time.

La Bjork, L. A., Jr. "Generalized Audit Trail Requirements and Concepts for Data Base Applications." *IBM Systems Journal* 14, no. 3 (1975), pp. 229–45.

This article hypothesizes what information must be retained in the audit and presents a scheme for organizing the contents of the audit trail so as to provide the required functions at minimum overhead. Types of audits, audit assumptions, time domain addressing, time sequences required to support versions of data, and audit trails and their implementation are discussed.

Parker, Donn, and Susan Mycum. "Computer Crime." *ACM Communications* 22, no. 4 (May 1984), pp. 312–15.

Two professionals in the field discuss the nature and future of computer crime.

Perry, William E. "Designing for Auditability." *Datamation* 23, no. 8 (August 1977), pp. 46–50.

Perry argues that internal audit functions of the system must be considered throughout the development cycle, starting with project definition and extending to conversion. The author also identifies conditions necessary before internal auditing of a computerized system is effective.

Pritchard, J. A. T. *Risk Management in Action.* Manchester, England: National Computing Center Ltd., 1978, 160 pp.

An excellent discussion of the tradeoffs in security management of a computing center. Discusses the identification and measurement of threats, countermeasures, auditing, contingency planning, and a risk control program.

Sardinas, Joseph; John G. Burch; and Richard Asebrook. *EDP Auditing: A Primer.* New York: John Wiley & Sons, 1981, 209 pp.

This is an introduction to EDP auditing. Discussed are tagging, tracing, computer-assisted audit techniques, audit software, Integrated Test Facility (ITF), and Parallel Test Facility (PTF). There are also good sections on controls for operations, administration, documentation, and security.

Ware, Willis H. "Information Systems Security and Privacy." *ACM Communications* 22, no. 4 (May 1984), pp. 325–31.

This article discusses the nature of privacy, the "people threat," the question of leadership, and the need for a national commission to study problems related to privacy and security.

Weber, Ron. *EDP Auditing: Conceptual Foundation and Practice.* New York: McGraw-Hill, 1982, 643 pp.

The author focuses on control framework, the techniques of evidence collection, and how evidence itself should be evaluated. It is the author's premise that a good auditor must be better at business than clients. Many detailed and technical aspects of EDP control are discussed, such as concurrency, cryptography, kernel programs, data dictionary, and rollbooks. This is an impressive text.

Organizing the human element in information systems

17

More than machinery, we need humanity.

Charles Chaplin
in the film, *Modern Times*

Though computerized societies are often pictured as machine-dominated, with humans insignificant in the production of information and in decision making, in fact, computers exist to serve people, to aid humans in reaching decisions. Furthermore, a computer requires a large number of professionals and support personnel for the execution of a given task (see Figure 17.1). Input, be it data, operating instructions, or application programs, is initiated by humans. It takes skilled analysts to assess the needs of users and to convert these needs into bits, the only medium understood by machine. Collection and updating of data are iterative human activities. Skilled programmers are needed for the preparation and evaluation of operating instructions, and many technicians are required for operating and servicing the computer itself. Output must be interpreted and evaluated by management, and then both must be distributed and stored. Without analysts, application and system programmers, systems engineers, operators, and librarians to provide ancillary services, a computer simply cannot produce the information that users request.

This chapter opens with a discussion of the organization and mobilization of EDP personnel, including departmental organization, and vertical and horizontal relationships of EDP departments with other divisions of a firm. The nature of human resistance to computers is then analyzed and steps to minimize this resistance proposed. The chapter concludes with a brief introduction to human engineering.

| Location of EDP | Firms vary in their placement of EDP on their organization charts. Figure 17.2 shows six alternative plans of organization. |

When data processing was in its infancy and applications were limited, Case

**Figure 17.1
Computer-human interaction**

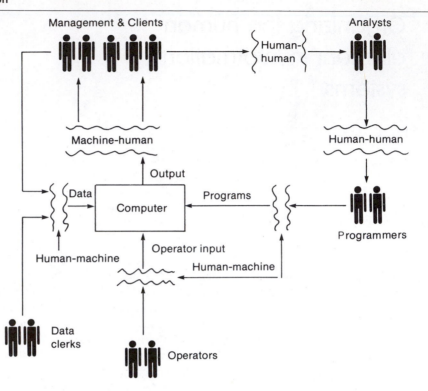

1, EDP as a subdepartmental unit, was common. However, as more resources were devoted to computers and applications became diversified, EDP rose in the organizational hierarchy of most firms, with personnel reporting directly to department heads (Case 2) or division chiefs (Case 3). Since payroll and accounting applications predominated in the 1950s, EDP often fell under the jurisdiction of a firm's comptroller.

As the need for expensive data processing resources grew, sharing of data and equipment across divisional lines was initiated to cut costs in many firms. This gave impetus to the centralization of data processing, the establishment of EDP departments reporting directly to top management (Case 4). Still another organizational schema is the use of service bureaus to supplement a company's internal computing facilities or to handle all of its data processing (Case 5).

Though centralization is still a common schema, a flip-flop back to decentralization has become an increasingly attractive alternative as a result of the dramatic drop in the cost of computers in recent years and the development of **distributed processing** (Case 6). Distributed data processing (DDP) is the subject of the next chapter in this book, chapter 18.

Many variables, such as equipment needs, personnel considerations, and data base use influence management's choice of EDP location. Economies of scale

Figure 17.2
Alternative locations of EDP within a firm's organization structure

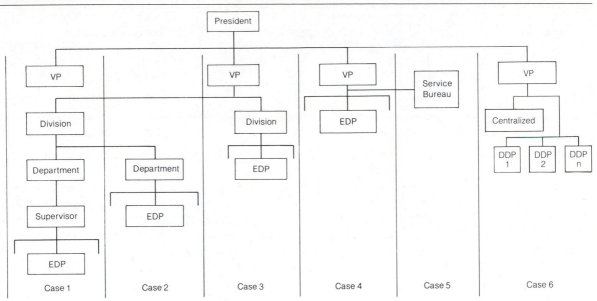

and Grosch's law[1], that computer effectiveness is proportional to the square of cost, were factors that promoted **centralization** in the past, but technological developments of microelectronics and the dramatic drop in the cost of computers have given impetus to **decentralization** in recent years.

On the other hand, decentralized personnel may be more vulnerable to high turnover. In addition, many firms claim that they are better able to attract and retain competent personnel when equipment is easily accessed at a central location. But this latter argument has lost some of its validity with the common use of terminals, telecommunications, and remote job entry. Furthermore, firms supporting decentralization counter that distributed centers are more sensitive to users and are better able to implement and maintain applications. Though common data bases are often centralized, modern technology permits segmented, replicated, and/or distributed bases under local control.

All of the arguments for and against centralization are discussed in greater depth in Chapter 18. The point to be made here is that there is simply no conclusive advantage to either centralization or decentralization of all EDP departments. What often tips the scale are personalities and/or the existing organizational structure of a firm. A strong manager may insist on retaining control of all resources necessary for profit making, including EDP. Reorganization may be re-

---

[1]For a discussion of Grosch's Law, see William F. Sharpe, *The Economics of Computers* (New York: Columbia University Press, 1969), pp. 314–22 and Daniel P. Siewiorek et al., *Computer Structures: Principles and Examples* (New York: McGraw-Hill, 1982), pp. 60–61 and pp. 889–91.

Table 17.1
Some alternative centralization-decentralization combinations

Alternative	Development personnel	Equipment and operation	Development activities	Data base	Planning
1	C	C	C	C	C
2	D	C	C	C	C
3	D	D	C	C	C
4	D	D	D	C	C

C = Centralized.
D = Decentralized.

sisted even when decentralization is indicated because of new equipment or expanded operations.

A combination of centralized and decentralized EDP functions is quite common (see Table 17.1). Planning is generally centralized even under distributed data processing to ensure equipment compatibility and to minimize duplication of effort. Alternative 4, compromising between user demand for decentralized operations, development activities and personnel, and the value of centralized control of the data base and planning has become increasingly popular in recent years.

EDP relationship with user departments

To facilitate coordination between functional departments that are heavy users of computers and EDP personnel, many companies place these departments under the jurisdiction of a single vice-president in their organizational charts (see Figure 17.3). The vice-president's title varies from firm to firm, though VP for Information Services is frequently used. This plan of organization helps coordinate teleprocessing by EDP personnel with telecommunications under the Director of Communications, for example. It minimizes bureaucratic red tape for record managers who handle large volumes of computer output and rely on EDP equipment for retrieval and storage. A link with EDP ensures access to analysts and programmers for planners, reference service personnel, and word processor users. In deciding placement of EDP within a firm's organizational structure, the horizontal relationship of EDP with user departments is as important as EDP's vertical integration in the organization's hierarchy.

EDP departmental organization

The development of increasingly sophisticated computer equipment and the expansion of computer applications in business have led to changes in the need for EDP personnel and altered job descriptions over time. In early EDP shops, a single employee often functioned as analyst, programmer, and operator. As the demand for computing services grew, operations became a full-time job and a programmer-analyst was added to the staff. By the early 1960s, computers were performing tasks that required system programmers, application programmers, and system analysts.

Figure 17.3
Organization chart for a VP for information services

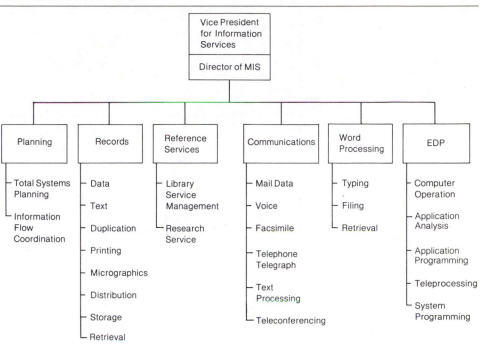

By the late 1960s, specialization was needed in all EDP positions. The generalist could no longer keep abreast with technological advances. Qualifications for all EDP positions were upgraded. Operators, for example, needed experience with online real-time, multiprocessing and multiprogramming environments, and some knowledge of data management and programming as well. Programmers specialized in either scientific or business applications while business programmers in large organizations were specialized in functions, such as accounting and production. Likewise, EDP staff expanded to include system programmers, maintenance programmers, data base programmers, and functional analysts. Though computers have eliminated many manual jobs for workers, a multiplicity of new positions to provide ancillary computer services has been created. Coordinating the activities of these numerous positions and providing job backup have become major managerial problems.

Figure 17.4 shows diagrammatically how EDP personnel configurations have changed since computers were introduced in the 1950s. The temporal evolution corresponds to the growth of EDP departments in size. That is, firms with limited EDP may consolidate operation, programming, and analysis in one position even today: the job array at the base of the figure corresponds to that found in large EDP departments. Note that some jobs listed for the 1970–1980s are not offshoots of earlier positions but are completely new. These include the data base administrator; specialists for applications, such as numerical and process control;

Figure 17.4
EDP personnel configurations

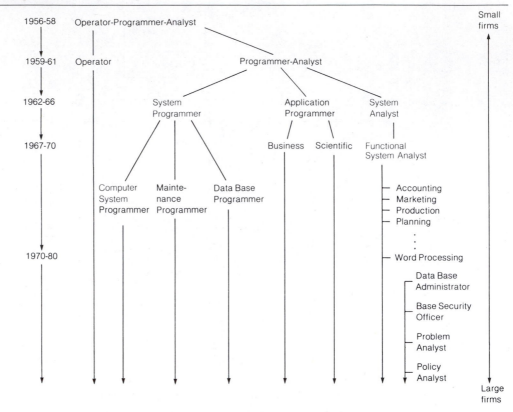

problem analysts, who might be compared to earlier time-and-motion-study experts; and policy analysts, who evaluate EDP input and output for policy implications.

The organizational structure of EDP departments, which has changed over the years as a result of altered staff configurations, has also been affected by a redefinition of the role and responsibilities of EDP personnel and users. For example, when computers were first introduced, users participated in the development of new information systems but EDP departments had the major responsibility for the development effort. In the 1980s, however, widespread use of decentralized and distributed processing will shift some systems development to users. The EDP role will become largely advisory. Hardware selection, acquisitions, installation, operations, and maintenance will also be transferred to users. One reason this transference of responsibility is possible is that less technical knowledge is needed for the operation of today's minis, micros, and packaged systems than was required for early models of computers.

A switch in roles has also occurred with reference to data base control. Originally local data was kept by users. With the centralization of EDP and the advent of common data bases, data processing departments assumed jurisdiction over data. However, today's minis enable local sites to manage local data, and distributed data processing technology permits users to control replicated and/or segmented parts of the common data base as well. So users have again assumed data base responsibility.

All of these shifts, summarized in Figure 17.5, have required constant readjustment in the structure of EDP departments. For example, systems development was the responsibility of EDP departments until the mid-1970s, when it shifted to users. Responsibility for the data base, however, rested with users in 1950–60, moved to EDP departments 1960–75, then back to users after 1975. In the 1980s, EDP at the corporate level commonly includes systems planning, and coordination and maintenance of the common data base. This necessitates compatibility of hardware and systems development at all levels. Users are responsible for hardware, software, and development of their information systems. They have also inherited problems of human engineering, meshing human with machine. Formerly, this was the responsibility of EDP management.

Figure 17.5
Changing responsibilities of user and EDP departments

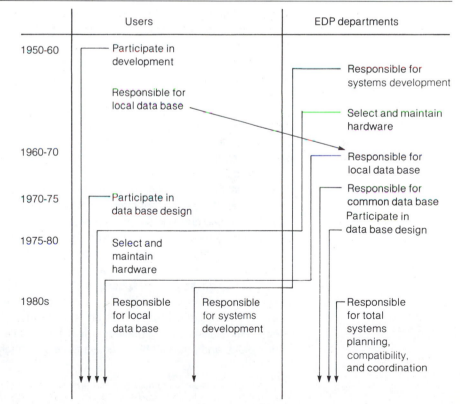

Nature of human resistance

In the preceding section of this chapter, changes in the location, structure, and duties of EDP departments were discussed. These changes, reflecting the expanded role of computers in business, have disrupted the traditional power structure in many firms. Some employees have lost jobs; others have been transferred to learn new skills in different working environments. Every change—even changes for the better (that is, higher pay, better working conditions, job enlargement)—evokes **human resistance.** Empirical evidence shows opposition to computerized information systems is the rule, not the exception. This should come as no surprise to managers, for the phenomenon of resistance to change has been well documented in business. For example, the Hawthorne Study at Western Electric in the 1920s noted that factory conditions alone did not explain worker attitudes. Actions perceived as a threat to job security triggered a strong emotional response. Another example is the negative reaction by managers when techniques to apply mathematical and statistical methods to decision making were first introduced by management scientists.

The resistance to computers is found at all levels of an organization. Though an assembly line worker may have different reasons for fearing computers than management does, the reaction is no less intense. Both groups are disturbed by disruption of the status quo. Procedures change, jobs gain or lose status, and totally new relationships must be forged as departments are restructured in accordance with the expanded role of machines. Resistance can often be traced to job insecurity, fear of displacement, or loss of income. But personal ego and feelings of self-esteem are also involved. It is a blow for workers to learn that their former duties have been reassigned to machines in the interests of efficiency, to find computerized systems installed without warning.

Managers themselves realize that fundamental changes are required in their personal styles of management, their thought patterns, and their job behavior when computerized information systems are installed. Many feel increasingly hemmed in, believing that their choices are restricted, since informations systems seem to centralize all important decisions. Local managers resent having daily goals defined, the action to achieve these goals specified, and performance evaluated by a system in which personal relationships play no role. Furthermore, the information produced by the system may reveal staff incompetence, or provide data that managers would prefer to suppress. For example, a report by one company comparing monthly sales showed a correlation between low performance and the deer season. Managers lax in controlling unexcused absences of hunters were easily identified.

A final explanation for managerial resistance is that computers alter the decision-making process. Decisions are no longer based on intuition but on data provided by the system. This type of decision making requires a different type of conceptual thinking. Many managers find their former style of decision making under attack and are not able to adjust to new technology in time.[2]

---

[2]Some authors predict automation of management. See John E. Steeley, Jr., "When Management Is Automated," *Datamation* 24, no. 4 (April 1978), pp. 172, 174, 176.

Some individuals express their opposition to computers by quitting their jobs. These are usually people the firm can least afford to lose since only those with good qualifications have job mobility. Those who remain may express resistance by griping, sloppiness, failure to meet deadlines, and possibly even sabotage of data. Sometimes resistance is mobilized by unions. Most often it is simply a reluctance, a hesitation, a lack of confidence in the new system that slows achievement of projected benefits. How to overcome this resistance is the subject of the next section.

Overcoming resistance

A sensible approach is to anticipate and identify pockets of resistance. For example, studies show that the intensity of resistance is proportional to the age of an employee and the number of years an individual has performed the task to be consigned to machine. The degree of planning, education given to employees affected by the change, and the rate of the introduction of change also affect resistance intensity. Policies should be adopted in the early stages of planning a new system to defuse this hostility. The policies selected will depend on the nature of the resistance. For example, if it's economic, a combination of policies to relocate, reclassify, and retrain personnel, as well as liberal policies on compensation or early retirement, should help. If resistance is a function of the rate of change, pacing implementation of the new information system to allow time for readjustment should be a solution.

Often, seemingly irrational resistance to computers is based on a lack of understanding of machine capabilities. Orientation sessions and in-house training are two techniques that help change employee attitudes. Change in attitude also occurs when employees participate in systems development, helping identify problems, and the need for additional information. When possible solutions are proposed by the development team, employees begin to see computers are valuable business aids, and the mystique, the fear of the unknown, fades.

In many cases, resistance is based on employee resentment of computer specialists. Technicians often appear insensitive to users, talking in computer jargon, using acronyms that have no meaning to laymen, showing contempt when proposed solutions are not readily accepted. Instead of using tools of persuasion, they dictate change, ignoring psychological factors altogether. Indeed, many computer technicians lack the most elementary aspects of common sense and tact in dealing with people.

The personality of programmers has been described by Dick Brandon, a well-known author and EDP consultant as follows: "The average programmer is excessively independent—sometimes to a point of mild paranoia. He is often eccentric, slightly neurotic, and he borders upon a limited schizophrenia."[3]

Perhaps Brandon's description is too severe, but an antagonism between users

[3] Quoted in Jac Fitz-enz, "Who Is the DP Professional?" *Datamation* 24, no. 9 (September 1978), p. 125.

and computer specialists is indeed very common.[4] The problem is further aggravated by the fact that programmers and analysts have high mobility, their turnover rate deterring the development of company loyalty and deep interpersonal relationships.[5]

In some instances, resistance may prove beneficial. If management and the development team examine the objections of employees and improve the proposed system by listening to constructive criticism, resistance can serve a useful purpose. Perhaps technicians have not paid enough attention to human needs in designing the work environment, perhaps the stress has been on technology, ignoring the human-machine interface on which success of the new system depends. A careful assessment of employee objections may help avert a costly flop. Those who assume that all resistance is the grumbling of malcontents do their firm a disservice.

Once management has decided that the proposed information system is, indeed, in the best interests of the firm, steps should be taken to change the attitude and behavior of employees resisting implementation. Change may be **participative change,** from within the individual, or be initiated by management, called a **directive change.**

A participative change starts with new knowledge (formal education, self-instruction, or observation), knowledge that kindles new attitudes which, in turn, affect behavior—first individual, then group behavior. Such change can be nurtured by the environment. For example, it may be corporate policy to reward employees financially if they join educational programs. A directive change is imposed by management. Policies are formulated that require alteration of group behavior (e.g., all employees are *required* to attend orientation sessions), which in turn should alter the attitude of individuals and their knowledge.

Which of these two approaches works best in an EDP environment? Generally a participative change is most desirable. Self-motivated employees tend to infect others with their enthusiasm, and their willingness to try new ideas often serves as a catalyst to a change in attitude of co-workers. But when no employees voluntarily engage in activities that lead to an alteration of behavior, management must implement strategies to encourage an attitude change. Figure 17.6 shows that the impetus for change comes from opposite points in participative and directive change, but that the end results are the same.[6]

| **Human factors** | What makes human resistance to computers different from the resistance of human to machine during the industrial revolution and later automation is that EDP |

---

[4] Ibid., pp. 124–28. In a profile of computer personnel, Fitz-enz examines the DP professional in terms of Herzog's five motivators: achievement, recognition, work, responsibility, and advancement. See also D. Couger, J. Daniel, and R. A. Zwacki, "What Motivates DP Professionals?" *Datamation* 24, no. 9 (September 1978), pp. 116–23.

[5] R. A. McLaughlin, "That Old Bugaboo, Turnover," *Datamation* 25, no. 11 (October 1978), pp. 97 and 99.

[6] This conceptual framework originates with Mayo and is well discussed in Paul Hersey and Kenneth H. Blanchard, *Management—A Behavioural Approach* (Englewood Cliffs, N.J. Prentice-Hall, 1977), pp. 2–3, 280–84.

Figure 17.6
Participative and directive changes

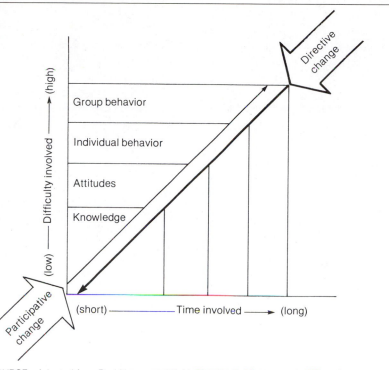

SOURCE   Adapted from Paul Hersey and K. H. Blanchard, *Management of Organizational Behaviour: Utilizing Human Resources* (Englewood Cliffs, N.J.: Prentice-Hall, 1977), pp. 281–82.

adds two more dimensions to the human machine relationship: specialized computer hardware and software. As illustrated in Figure 17.7, EDP requires machine-software interface (A), human-software interface (B), human-machine interface (C), and human-machine-software interface (D).[7]

Human factors, sometimes called **man-machine studies (ergonomics** in Europe) is a field currently researching human-computer relationships.[8] Some of the problems and recommended solutions are quite mundane. Are work stations comfortable and pleasing? The arrangement of furniture and work space around a terminal can affect user morale: an inconvenient layout may contribute to employee errors. The size of the keys, the angle of the screen, the flickers on the screen, the size of the characters on the screen, and color of displays are all important to the user.

---

[7]For a similar diagram and an excellent discussion, see Gloria Grace in her preface to a special issue on human considerations in information processing, *Human Factors* 12, no. 2 (March–April, 1970), pp. 161–64.

[8]See K. D. Eason, L. Damodaran, and T. M. Stewart, "Interface Problems in Man-Computer Interaction," in *Human Choice and Computers,* eds. E. Mumford and H. Sackman (Amsterdam, Netherlands: North-Holland Publishing, 1975), pp. 91–105.

Figure 17.7
Relationship between human, machine, and software

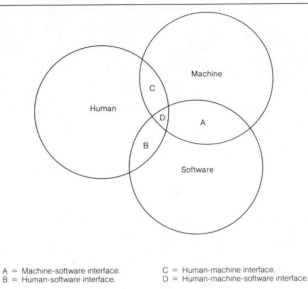

A = Machine-software interface.   C = Human-machine interface.
B = Human-software interface.   D = Human-machine-software interface.

Many human engineering problems arise from the diverse and wide range of knowledge and computer experience of information system users. Managers use computers primarily for output, but the same machine must serve clerks (who use terminals primarily as input devices), professionals (analysts, programmers), and product designers using CAD (computer-aided design). Technicians designing computerized systems see information problems that need resolution, and manipulate hardware, software, and technology toward this end. They often fail to recognize the communication barriers of nonprofessionals with computers, the need for interactive and conversational modes, and the need for techniques, training methods, and documentation aids to assist users in taking full advantage of the potential of computers for problem solving. Computer experts tend to be highly rational and mechanistic in their thinking. They often deny the existence of individuals who see broad patterns and total pictures rather than well-bounded problems that can be solved by computer. As a result, systems design is not always appropriate for all classes of users.

The literature on human engineering is quite extensive (over 1,000 references as early as 1971), a clear indication of the importance of this subject. Management should keep abreast of current research in this field since no computerized information system can achieve its full potential as a tool in management decision making when aspects of human engineering are ignored.

Summary

Figure 17.2 shows alternative organizational plans for EDP departments within a firm's hierarchy. Their location has been influenced over time by the expanding nature of EDP responsibilities and the introduction of new technology, such as DDP (distributed data processing) which permits decentralization of data processing. Even within EDP departments, organization has not remained static. As the demand for information has increased, a multiplicity of new jobs to provide ancillary computer services has been created. Job descriptions have also been continually altered in response to technological developments. At the present time, for example, DDP and the widespread use of minis have shifted many former responsibilities of technicians to users.

The growth of EDP has not proceeded smoothly in all cases, however. Employee resistance to change, fear of job displacement, and unwillingness to learn new procedures and skills have hindered the development of information systems. How to eliminate human resistance and design computers with human-machine interface is the subject of much research at the present time.

Key words

Centralization
Decentralization
Directive change
Distributed processing
Ergonomics

Human factors
Human resistance
Man-machine studies
Participative change

Discussion questions

1. Why are some people against automation?

2. Why is there resistance to computerized information systems by:
   a. Managers?
   b. Data clerks?
   c. Clients/customers?

   How does each group react? What can be done to reduce the resistance from each group?

3. Describe the skills required for computer processing and comment on:
   a. Their relative importance.
   b. The changing demand.
   c. The supply of persons with these skills.

4. What is the difference between human factors in computer processing and human engineering of information systems?

5. What are the problems of human-machine interface in computer processing? Give examples in business and propose solutions.

6. What steps should be taken to improve the probability that an information system will be accepted by users?

7. How can resistance to computerized information systems be overcome?

8. How and why is the involvement of users in development useful in reducing resistance to computerization?

9. Does computerization support the centralization or decentralization of management in a business firm?

10. How are the personnel problems in EDP departments unique?

11. Where in the organization structure of a business firm should EDP be located? Justify your answer.

12. How would you organize EDP in terms of organization structure, span of control, and supervision?

13. What are the major functions to be performed at an EDP installation? What personnel is required to perform these functions?

14. What are the advantages of having a single analyst-programmer rather than an analyst and a programmer?

15. What personal and professional qualities are required by each of the following employees:
    a. Computer programmer?
    b. System analyst?
    c. Data clerk?
    d. Computer operator?

    What schooling is necessary for each job? What on-the-job training is required?

16. Why is there a high turnover among computer personnel? How can this turnover be minimized?

17. Why is displacement important when a computerized information system is initiated? What are the variables that affect the importance of displacement?

Exercises

1. What personnel would be required for generating the report in Exercise 1, Chapter 10 and implementing the policy in Exercise 1, Chapter 16? Would a firm have to hire personnel specially for these tasks?

2. Suppose you are consulting for a firm about to initiate an EDP center with 50 persons, including 20 programmers to operate a batch as well as an OLRT computer system for marketing. What EDP organization structure would you propose? What employees will be needed?

3. Read R. Boguslaw, *The New Utopians* (Englewood Cliffs, N.J.: Prentice-Hall, 1965). The author calls computer people the new utopians, the social engineers of our times. What dangers does Boguslaw identify? Do you agree with Boguslaw's hypothesis?

4. Identify the principal jobs in business data processing and compare them in terms of:
   a. Education required.
   b. Experience required.
   c. Relationship to user management.

d. Position in the organizational structure.

e. Salary range.

Selected annotated bibliography

Chadwin, Mark Lincoln, and Edward M. Cross. "Personnel Management for a Special Breed: The Data Processing Professional." *Personnel Administrator* 28, no. 8 (August 1983), pp. 53–59.

The authors suggest that data processing employees require special handling. Techniques used in the management of other office personnel are often inappropriate for DP personnel.

Chapanis, Alphonse. "Computers and the Common Man." In *Information Technology and Psychology: Prospects for the Future,* Richard A. Kasschau et al., eds. Houston Symposium 3., New York: Praeger Publishers, 1982, 260 pp.

The author discusses the problem of improving computer software. He uses statistics derived from several user polls in support of his ideas. Error messages, help utilities, and obtuse porgramming languages come under his attack. This is a useful article for persons interested in basic human factor issues.

De Boever, L. "The Myth of User-Friendly Computing." *Computer-World* 16, no. 34 (August 23, 1982), pp. 1–8.

The author argues that user-friendly systems seldom meet the claims of vendors and often fail to satisfy the needs of the end user, especially users at the managerial level. Many users lack typing skills for entering input and want to be able to browse through online data, though they may lack complete knowledge regarding how to operate the system. There are numerous software packages that claim to meet the needs of such users. De Boever believes such packages are incomplete and inadequate.

Kotter, John P., and Leonard A. Schlesinger. "Choosing Strategies for Change." *Harvard Business Review* 57, no. 2 (March/April 1979), pp. 106–14.

An excellent article on the causes of resistance and strategies for overcoming it.

Licker, Paul S. "The Japanese Approach: A Better Way to Manage Programmers." *Communications of the ACM* 26, no. 9 (September 1983), pp. 631–36.

Licker discusses Theory Z, Japanese style. That is, stressing lifetime employment, nonspecialized career paths, collective decision making, and other holistic matters.

Moynihan, John A. "What Users Want." *Datamation* 28, no. 4 (April 1982), pp. 116–17.

Moynihan believes that "humans and machines can make beautiful music together," but only if the system is designed with the user in mind. This article summarizes results of an empirical study on human-machine interface, listing 11 desirable characteristics of an interactive system.

Tomeski, Edward A., and Harold Lazarus. *People-Oriented Computer Systems*. New York: Van Nostrand Reinhold, 1975, 299 pp.

The authors argue that computers have failed to serve people and organizations. The book is a plea to vendors and users to adopt policies and practices that will make computerized information systems sensitive and responsive to human and social needs.

Zaltman, Gerald, and Robert Duncan. *Strategies for Planned Change*. New York: John Wiley & Sons, 1976, 404 pp.

This book is based on extensive interviews with over 75 professional change agents. Changes in computer systems as well as organizational change and innovation diffusion are discussed. Among the issues presented are planning change, resistance to change, social problems, and ethical dilemmas.

Distributed data processing

The present state of things is the consequence of the past.
Samuel Johnson

Distributed data processing (DDP) is one way of organizing equipment and personnel to implement a management information system. Generally, a decision to utilize this processing structure is made during the development stages of a new information system, but sometimes an ongoing system is converted to DDP. In either case, operations shift from a centralized EDP center to dispersed locations. This chapter describes in detail how daily operations and management are affected by this change. The material could have been included in Chapter 17, but has been allocated a separate chapter due to the newness of this processing organization and the importance of this approach for the 1980s and beyond.

DDP combines features of both centralized and decentralized processing. Managers view this innovation with some apprehension, however, since widespread use of DDP will change organizational structure and patterns of corporate decision making. This chapter provides background information on the evolution, architecture, and features of DDP and identifies implementation considerations.

Evolution of DDP

When EDP was first introduced, firms commonly established small data processing centers in divisions needing information. These centers were physically dispersed and had no centralized authority coordinating their activities. Data processed in this manner was often slow to reach middle and top management, and frequently failed to provide the information needed for decision making. In addition, this type of organization structure did not take advantage of Grosch's law, a law applicable to early computers which states that the increase in the computational power of a computer is the square of the increase in costs, that is, doubling computer cost quadruples computational power. Processing by small dispersed computers was, therefore, unnecessarily expensive. Furthermore, due to the scarcity of qualified computer specialists, the centers were often poorly run.

The need for centralized computing facilities was soon recognized. Firms hoped that costs would drop, that information processing would be responsive to management needs, that the delivery speed of information would increase, that redundancy in processing and files would be eliminated, and that security and control of information would be tightened. However, not all of these expectations were realized when centralization took place. Lack of communication between users and analysts continued to exist. Users felt isolated from the computing facilities, complaining that analysts were unresponsive to their needs and resenting the hours required to justify and document requests for service. The bureaucracy created often proved inept at mediating conflicting interests. Analysts chaffed at criticism, believing that the length of time required for systems development was simply not understood by users.

This dissatisfaction led to reconsideration of dispersed processing. Technological developments in the meantime made DDP economically feasible. Minicomputers with capabilities exceeding many former large computers were now on the market at low cost. Chip technology had increased CPU and memory capacity while reducing computer size. Strides in telecommunications meant that no processing center would be isolated. In addition, experience with data processing had given users confidence that they could manage and operate their own processing systems. By the late 1970s, DDP was a commercial reality.

What is DDP?

Distributed data processing is the linking of two or more processing centers **(nodes)** within a single organization, each center having facilities for program execution and data storage. However, this definition—which excludes computer networks like ARPA (Advanced Research Projects Agency) and EFT (Electronic Fund Transfer) because they serve many clients in business, industry and government—is still evolving.

The link provided by DDP permits centralized control over policies and processing while the system retains the flexibility of decentralization. The facilities at sites are tailored to local needs and controlled by local management, avoiding the rigidity of centralized hardware and personnel, while integration of the sites minimizes duplication of effort.

Distributed systems vary in architecture, software, protocols, controls, and data transmission capabilities according to the needs of the organization served. A number of equipment configurations will now be discussed.

Equipment configurations

The difference between DDP and earlier dispersed processing is the link between processing centers. Formerly, stand-alone computers processed information: DDP involves a network of processors. Figure 18.1 shows sample DDP configurations. In the **star network,** failure of the central computer impairs the entire system. The **ring** structure overcomes this problem, for rerouting is possible should one processing center or its link fail. The ring allows interaction and **offloading**

Figure 18.1
DDP configurations

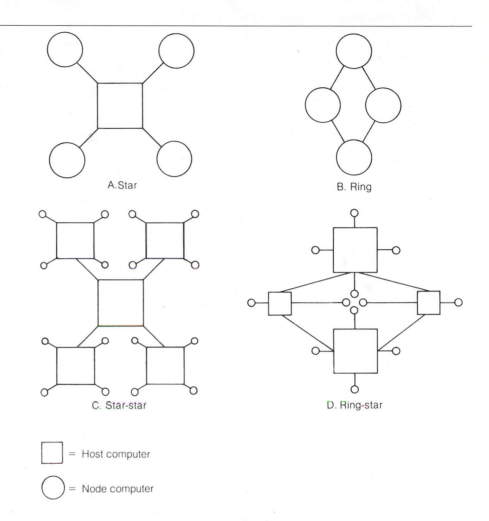

A.Star

B. Ring

C. Star-star

D. Ring-star

☐ = Host computer

◯ = Node computer

(the transference of processing from one site to another) without dependence on a central host. Both star and ring configurations are essentially **horizontal systems,** that is, each processor is an equal. The hardware may be unique at each center, which means that equipment may be purchased from any number of vendors, an advantage when the market responds to technological developments and new models are made available. But this flexibility has a negative aspect: it increases problems of linkage and compatibility between nodes. There are combinations of rings and stars, like star-star and ring-star as shown in Figure 18.1, C and D, respectively, but the basic weaknesses remain.

Hierarchial distribution is the configuration that many firms prefer since it requires the least reorganization, corresponding to the hierarchial structure that is already in existence within the corporation. This system, illustrated in Figure 18.2,

Figure 18.2
Hierarchical distributed data processing

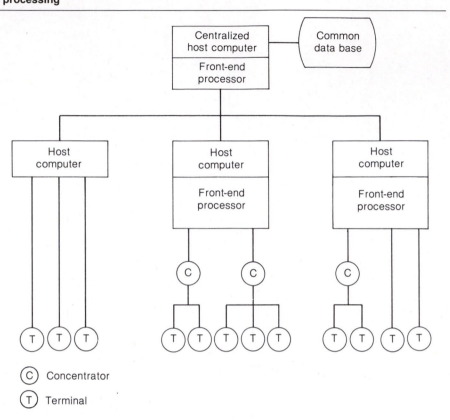

C   Concentrator

T   Terminal

has a central host computer and common data base with minis and micros at dispersed sites. Generally, all equipment and software are supplied by the same vendor, minimizing problems of compatibility between nodes. Because many computers have either a fail-safe capability (ability to continue operations in spite of breakdown due to the existence of backup) or a **fail-soft capability** (the ability to continue with a degraded level of operations), a breakdown in the hierarchy does not incapacitate the entire system. All computers have independent processing capabilities to some extent. Of course, the exact configuration of any hierarchial system of DDP would vary according to the needs of the organization being served.

Systems architecture   DDP, regardless of configuration, requires a system for data control, for resource sharing, and for coordination of dispersed processing. Procedures, software, hardware, and personnel are all needed to support DDP. How these resources are combined is part of the **systems architecture.** Systems architecture is not merely a design. It includes protocols for running DDP as well.

Many computer vendors market architectural systems. Vendors design software for specific equipment to encourage purchase of that hardware. Lack of industry standards and rapid changes in technology create problems of equipment interface with network systems. Users often find that only one network architecture can be adapted to their equipment configurations.

The most widely used architecture is **SNA (Systems Network Architecture).** IBM first introduced SNA in 1974 for hierarchial distributed processing.[1] In 1978, the IBM 8100 was placed on the market, a computer specifically designed for DDP using SNA. Because of IBM's dominance in the computer industry, its investment in SNA and the 8100 has legitimized DDP as a concept and made it a commercial reality. An important feature of the 8100 is that it is a stand-alone computer designed for online processing and need not be linked to a host computer. Furthermore, installation does not require technical expertise. As an IBM press release notes, ". . . portions of the new system can be installed by users—with a set of easy to follow directions—in much the same way as a basic household stereo system might be set up."[2]

DDP data bases

There are many ways to organize DDP data bases.[3] All data can be centralized, or processing centers can keep segments of the data base. Sometimes dispersed centers keep data needed for local processing that replicates data stored in the central repository. A **hybrid approach** to data organization is also possible in which dispersed processors keep both segmented and replicated data. These approaches to data base organization will be explained next.

Centralized data base

When dispersed processors draw all data from a centralized data base, transmission costs are high. This system is appropriate when infrequent access to the centralized data is needed and when updating needs to be strictly controlled.

Segmented distributed data base

Under this system, parts of the data base are stored at dispersed sites. The segments might be data from a function or data pertaining to a geographic area. The data is segmented according to local processing needs so that each site is basically independent though other sites may draw on the distributed data base as a shared resource.

---

[1] For detailed study of SNA, read R. J. Cypsen, *Communications Architecture for Distributed Systems* (Reading, Mass.: Addison Wesley, 1978), 711 pp.
[2] Quoted by Larry Woods, "IBM's 8100: First Impressions," *Datamation* 25, no. 3 (March 1979), p. 142.
[3] For a further discussion of this subject, see a set of articles on distributed data bases in Burt H. Leibowitz and John H. Carson, *Distributed Processing* (Long Beach, Calif.: IEEE Computer Society, 1978), pp. 381–444.

Replicated distributed data base

When more than one dispersed processor needs the same data, a common approach to data base organization is to store the data base at a central repository with duplicate segments needed for local processing stored at decentralized computers. This is called a **replicated distributed data base.** The local bases used for processing, including online real-time operations, are then periodically used to update the centralized data, which in turn updates all distributed data bases.

Some large regional banks adopt this system. Central processing takes place after banking hours and distributed data bases are then created for branch offices. These latter bases are essentially working files used for local transactions, such as deposits and withdrawals. At the end of each working day, the central data base is again updated and the cycle begins once again with the creation of (updated) distributed data bases for the branch offices.

In general, the centralized data base has all control and summary data bases, whereas transactional data and local data are in the distributed data bases. Branch offices might still have to access the centralized data during the course of the day. This would occur when a customer of the bank wished to cash a check at a branch that did not have a record of his or her account, for example. In this case, the transaction would have to be routed through the central data base.

One advantage of replicated data bases is that they provide backup, so the system is less vulnerable should failure at the central location occur. An additional advantage is that systems are more responsibe to local needs when data is managed locally. (An advantage that applies to segmented data bases as well.) In particular, maintenance and updating of large and complex data bases are more effective when sections of the bases are under local control. Certain types of processing are also more efficient. For example, retrieval by indexes requires careful cross-indexing. Personnel on location with a need for the retrieved data will be more highly motivated and more knowledgeable about the task than programmers at a centralized data base.

A major problem with replicated distributed data bases is minimizing redundancy. For efficient processing, no more data than absolutely necessary should be stored at remote sites, but the exact need of distributed centers for data is not easily determined. Another problem arises when more than one dispersed processor attempts to access the same data at the same time from the central data base. Such concurrent communication problems also occur with segmented distributed data bases when two processors attempt to access the same data at the same time. Much research is currently being conducted in this area.

Hybrid approach

Some firms combine a segmented and replicated approach to organization of their data bases—the hybrid approach. For example, a national business may segment the base geographically, and then provide branches within each region with replicated data from geographical headquarters. Warehouse inventories are often controlled in this manner.

In a DBMS environment, both distributed DBMSs and a central DBMS are

Table 18.1
Illustration of grid analysis

Informational Sites / *Needs*		A	B	C	D
Process	1	X	X	X	X
	2	X			
	3		X	X	
Files	1	X			
	2	X	X	X	X
	3			X	X

possible. Though the distributed systems would satisfy local needs, the central DBMS would have the overall schema of the entire logical data base, and be concerned with problems of security, integrity, and recovery for all data, including data at distributed centers.[4]

When to implement DDP

Distributed data processing is not applicable to all organizations. How does a firm decide whether DDP is appropriate? Unfortunately, there is no formula or precise rule to guide management in reaching a decision about DDP implementation. However, firms with geographically dispersed outlets, firms with a matrix structure rather than functional organization, multinationals, project-based companies (such as construction firms), and conglomerates have organizational structures that lead naturally to decentralization and the distributed mode.

In less obvious cases, a grid analysis may help determine the appropriateness of DDP. A sample is shown in Table 18.1. Here a hypothetical firm with sites A, B, C, and D (X axis) has informational needs satisfied by Processes 1–3 and Files 1–3 (Y axis). The informational requirements of each site are marked on the grid. Since Process 1 and File 2 are required by all sites, centralization of their processing is indicated. Since Process 2 and File 1 are needed by only a single site, they are clear candidates for the distributed mode while Process 3 and File 3 are possible candidates.[5]

However, management must assess the impact of DDP on the firm before DDP is implemented. How will DDP affect corporate decision making? Is DDP economically feasible? Usually, consideration of DDP as an alternative to centralized processing in use may be triggered by dissatisfaction with current operations. Management must decide whether dissatisfaction will be remedied, in fact,

---

[4]See Bruce G. Lindsey, "Single and Multi-site Recovery Facilities." in *Distributed Data Bases*, I. W. Draffan and F. Poole, eds. (New York: Cambridge University Press, 1980), pp. 247–84 and Eduardo B. Fernandez et al., *Database Security and Integrity* (Reading, Mass.: Addison-Wesley Publishing, 1981), pp. 267–288.
[5]See P. J. Down and F. E. Taylor, *Why Distributed Computing?* (Oxford, England: The National Computing Center, 1976), p. 41.

by DDP and whether the benefits of DDP will be worth the cost and disruption which reorganization entails. Implementation considerations which go into a DDP decision are discussed below.

Costs

One component of cost is CPU hardware. Today's micros and minis are dropping in price while increasing in computing power due to recent technological advances. This means DDP is economically feasible for many businesses that formerly could not afford dispersed processors.

Terminal hardware is also dropping in cost, but as users demand more sophisticated units, such as intelligent terminals with local processing capabilities, actual terminal expenditures may rise. Figure 18.3 shows a cost curve for various types of terminals.

At the present time, transmission costs are not dropping as dramatically as the cost of hardware, so it is tempting to install additional processors in the distributed mode rather than transmit data to a centralized computer. High transmission costs in the past were due, in part, to the monopolistic character of the transmission industry. However, federal regulation of the communications industry is changing. Firms implementing DDP should periodically make a financial reassessment of their equipment configurations. In all likelihood, communication costs will drop in the future.

Cost elements other than hardware and data communication facilities are software, processing staff requirements, end user staffing, and training. If should be recognized that .5 to 1.0 percent of a firm's budget is allocated to data processing as a norm in largely centralized organizations. When a firm chooses DDP, processing costs may increase to as much as 5.0 percent.[6]

In general, DDP proves economically feasible when:

1. A high remote transaction rate exists.
2. Remote sites have a total mass data storage capability of at least 40 megabytes.
3. A distributed local data base will handle most local needs. (No more than 20–30 percent of data base access requirements from other locations.)
4. Data transmitted is much smaller than local data use.
5. Sharing would improve overall organizational efficiency.

At present, small, high-powered, dedicated computers are proving cost-efficient when the central computer is overloaded, but, of course, every situation must be examined on an individual basis.

EDP reorganization

Distributed data processing requires that EDP personnel be shifted to dispersed centers for operations. Responsibility for systems development, security, and ac-

---

[6] George A. Champine et al., *Distributed Computer Systems: Impact on Management, Design and Analysis* (Amsterdam: North-Holland Publishing, 1980), p. 307.

Figure 18.3
Cost of terminals for varying degrees of distribution

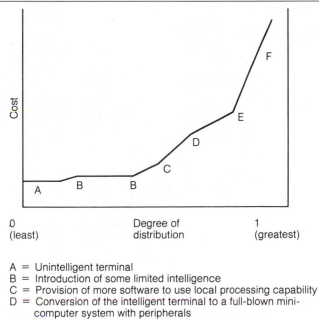

A = Unintelligent terminal
B = Introduction of some limited intelligence
C = Provision of more software to use local processing capability
D = Conversion of the intelligent terminal to a full-blown mini-
      computer system with peripherals
E = More software to process more applications locally
F = Tending towards complete independence from the central site

SOURCE   P. J. Down and T. E. Taylor, *Why Distributed Computing?* (Oxford, England: The National Computing Center, 1976), p. 78.

quisitions may also be transferred to local managers. The EDP staff at the corporate center will be dismantled, managers will loose empires, and new sets of interpersonal relationships will have to be forged. One sample organization chart for a firm with DDP is shown in Figure 18.4.

How far to go with decentralization often depends on human factors rather than economic and technological considerations. Will managers accept a redefinition of their responsibilities or will jealousies undermine DDP service? Is competent staff available to manage and operate local computing sites? Will employees agree to transfer to distributed centers? Will distributed processing promote greater efficiency and happier staff relationships once the trauma of reorganization is passed?

Conversion to DDP is much easier in a receptive environment, but the key to DDP success in all firms is careful planning and competent management of DDP networks. The next sections of this chapter will discuss these topics.

Planning for DDP

This section focuses on planning issues that are unique to DDP—how to decide the jurisdiction of local nodes, and how to coordinate operations and management in a firm with semiautonomous processing centers.

Figure 18.4
Organization chart with DDP

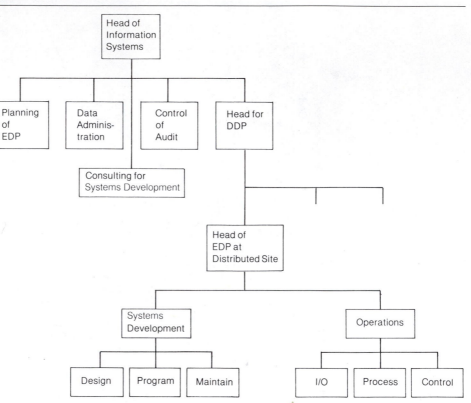

A cardinal rule in establishing a DDP center is to include users in the **planning task force.** This task force should develop a series of master plans which describe the flow of information within the organization under DDP and how responsibility for this flow is to be divided. These should include:

1. A master plan that outlines goals, functions, schedules, performance levels, and expenditures for each node and the center.
2. A master system design which details the structural relationship of nodes to the center, the communications subsystems to be used, standards for hardware and software, and protocols for synchronization and security.
3. A master management plan which describes the degree of autonomy granted node managers, training plans, career development paths, possible job rotations, and control procedures.[7]

Planning for DDP structure is largely dependent on the technology available and forecasts on equipment to be expected in both the short- and long-term fu-

---

[7]For more on this subject, see Champine et al., *Distributed Computer Systems,* pp. 318–19.

Table 18.2
Sample DDP structure: distribution of activities between center and nodes

Center	Distributed node
Overall planning of:	Local planning for processing
Corporate systems	
Policy determination	
Resource needs	
Compatibility	
Planning and control of:	Planning and control of:
Major software	Local software
Global security	Local security
Global standards	Local standards
Common data base	Local data base
Management and control of:	Management and control of:
Central resources	Local resources
Network management of:	
Design	
Operations and control	
Maintenance	
Budgeting of central and network expenditures	Budgeting of local spending
Systems quality control	Local quality control
Systems audit	Local audit
Hiring/coordinating systems personnel	Local personnel management

ture. The nature of the business, top management's organizational philosophy, stage of growth of the firm, existing organizational structure, and management style also have a bearing.

There are three organizational variables in distributed processing which must be planned: degree of centralized control, hardware configurations, and data base distribution. At one extreme, a firm might choose to distribute only limited functions; at the other, total distribution and decentralization of processing with complete profit and loss responsibility assigned to local managers. In most cases, a firm will choose a position somewhere in between.[8]

The hypothetical firm described in Table 18.2 is one example of DDP. Here, the central staff has global responsibilities. That is, central management sets standards for planning and controls, is responsible for system maintenance and network design, prepares budgets, and assigns staff. This results in uniform standards throughout the organization, flexibility in personnel placement and utilization (small processing centers do not need nor can they afford the full-time services of on-site hiring and maintenance personnel), systems backup, and centralization of major financial decisions. Managers on site have control over local planning, local resources, and local processing.

Another approach is to assign specific functions to individual nodes. For example, the New York office of a firm might be responsible for policy and resource planning, the Chicago office responsible for the common data base and quality

---

[8]For a good discussion of alternatives, see Grayce M. Booth, *The Distributed System Environment: Some Practical Approaches* (New York: McGraw-Hill, 1981).

Table 18.3
Sample DDP structure (distributed functions)

Function \ Site	New York	Chicago	San Francisco	London
Planning				
Need assessment	X			
Policy determination	X			
Resource				
Compatibility	X			
Acquisitions	X			
Major spending	X			
Common data base		X		
Standards			X	
Major software development				X
Network management			X	
Quality control		X		
Auditing	X			

control, San Francisco for standards and network management and so on. Table 18.3 shows this concept. Under this structure, duties assigned to the center in Table 18.2 are distributed among the nodes.

These two examples are oversimplifications, for in practice, many firms have mixed processing modes, combining features of centralized, decentralized,[9] and distributed processing. For example, Hewlett-Packard manufactured 4,000 products in 38 plants in 1978, and had 172 sales offices around the world. The company's 1,400 computers served 4,500 employees, mixing all processing modes. For example, materials, services, legal reporting, and employee benefits were centralized; customer service, inventories, payroll, and personnel decentralized; with production information, orders, and accounts receivable handled by the distributed mode.[10]

Management of DDP

The management of distributed processing can be divided into the areas of static and dynamic control. Because firms may differ in network configurations, the location of managers responsible for these controls may vary from one firm to another, but both types of control are necessary in DDP systems. **Static control**

---

[9] Decentralized processing refers to physically separated, stand-alone processing entities.
[10] See Cort Van Renssalear, "Centralize? Decentralize? Distribute?" *Datamation* 25, no. 9 (April 1979), p. 90.

deals with equipment, data base structure, and applications whereas **dynamic control** concerns monitoring, testing, interfacing, and security.

With regard to static control, compatibility is the key issue. Equipment guidelines and language standards are essential. For example, management might decide that all equipment should support an ANSI standard version of COBOL, or that all hardware used for scientific processing provide a standard FORTRAN compiler. Data bases for applications must be designed for integration and interface protocols must be established for information exchange. Above all, management must check to see that duplication of effort is avoided.

Dynamic control involves monitoring the network so that problems or failures at each node can be detected and corrected. Each component of a DDP system should have self-test facilities to assist in isolating the source of problems. A veritable arsenal of security measures is needed in managing the transmission of data over long distances because the possibility of wiretapping and electrical interference must be added to conventional security issues, such as access, integrity of data, privacy, threat monitoring, and auditing. In addition, statistics should be collected on the system and use patterns analyzed to help identify potential network weakness.

Because of the complexity of distributed data processing, many firms today assign one person from top management with the specific responsibility of **network administration.** Obviously, a person in this position would need managerial and technical skills of the highest order since issues such as compatibility of hardware, language choice, division of the data base, and personnel and system security (issues that affect the entire operation of the firm) would be within the manager's jurisdiction. The duties assigned to this position also include error detection and correction, equipment monitoring, and traffic monitoring.

Risks and rewards of DDP

The initiation of DDP involves a multiplicity of risks. Among the more common are poor systems design resulting from inexperience, redundancy among nodes, problems with interface, costs that are hidden or that escalate, and employee resistance to change. Companies may have technical, personnel, and organizational problems coordinating multiple vendors and models of equipment. They may lack sufficient personnel to staff the different nodes, and have problems attracting professionals and training employees in DDP. Privacy, security, and standardization become major managerial headaches.

The rewards, however, are many. Harry Katzan cites increased system responsiveness, planned growth, resource sharing, a data base customized to organizational patterns, and improved reliability.[11] Information sharing, the ability to incorporate new services and technologies with ease, longer system life expectancy based on increased adaptability, and possible integration of multiple sys-

---

[11] Harry Katzan, *An Introduction to Distributed Data Processing* (New York: Petrocelli Books, 1978), 242 pp.

tems into networks are other advantages. Certainly, increased motivation among distributed staff should be included in this list of benefits. Travel expenses should be reduced and the importance of geographical location of facilities diminished. In addition, distributing responsibility among departments will reduce pressures on top management.

Future of DDP

The future of DDP is clouded due to uncertainty in two major areas: federal regulations and standards. Though recent court decisions enable both AT&T and IBM to enter the field of data communications, of benefit to DDP users since competition between these corporate giants should lower communication costs, the FCC's stance on DDP is unclear. Lack of agreement over network standards is also an impediment to DDP research and development. The Europeans utilize X.25 standards: the Americans, SNA and SDLC (Synchronous Data Link Control).[12] DDP will not be widely implemented until universal standards are adopted and DDP equipment and software of competing manufacturers can be integrated into a single DDP system.

Once DDP is cost-effective and hardware, systems architecture, and communications are integrated into reliable and robust systems, DDP will become more viable. Advances are being made in distributed data base technology and software so that data can be accessed with ease no matter where it is stored in the distributed network. Solutions to problems of deadlock and optimal routing of queries are presently being researched. Future systems must be less vulnerable to failure and more easily restructured in response to growth or changed informational needs. DDP applications will undoubtedly broaden from current use for data entry and validation to full office automation and shop floor control.

DDP should give computing power to large segments of the population heretofore lacking efficient and speedy access to information processing. Indeed, DDP's greatest impact may be democratization of the computer. Already personal computers are in the price range of many households and their widespread use means that computers are no longer the prerogative of corporate boardrooms and the business elite. When the computing power of personal computers is extended through low-cost networks, the mysticism of computers should disappear entirely.

Summary and conclusions

DDP takes computing power from one large centralized computer and disperses this power to sites where processing demand is generated. The equipment used is a mix of terminals, minis, and small business computers integrated by appropriate system architecture. Some computers are being especially designed for DDP applications. The computers themselves can be linked in a variety of configurations, such as star, ring, or hybrid configurations, though the hierarchical structure with fail-soft capability is more common.

---

[12] See F. P. Corr and D. H. Neal, "SNA and Emerging International Standards," *IBM Systems Journal* 18, no. 2 (1979), pp. 244–62.

Distributed processing offers firms an increasingly wide range of organizational alternatives as opposed to the former black-and-white choice of centralization or decentralization. The willingness and ability of EDP personnel to manage local computer centers, and advances in chip technology and telecommunications have made DDP feasible.

Deciding when to distribute depends on how much processed data is needed by the corporate center and how much is utilized at branches. One rule of thumb states that distributed processing is indicated when 20 percent of the processed information is needed by the center and 80 percent at local sites. Other factors indicating the need for DDP are decentralization of responsibility, distributed functions, and limited information flow to headquarters.

A major advantage of DDP is that systems can begin simply and grow modularly. DDP can also be adapted to various organizational structures and modified when necessary to adapt to changing patterns in the flow of information. These and other advantages are listed in Table 18.4. Limitations appear in Table 18.5. Most of the technological limitations will be overcome in time. The computer industry is already researching systems architecture, equipment, software, and data base management systems in response to users' needs and technological needs. Resistance to change will slow the spread of DDP, but once a firm restructures its data porcessing, and new relationships and power structures are forged, DDP will prove its value to users as well as to technical personnel.

One final word. DDP requires the total commitment of top management. Special staffing and new positions, such as data base administrator and network administrator, should ease systems implementation and operations, but the involvement of management in planning for DDP and setting standards and controls is essential to ensure that the system meets the firm's needs. Though many of the planning decisions are technical, they should not be delegated exclusively to technicians. Coordination, integration, and control are keystones to DDP success and these are the responsibility of management.

Table 18.4
Advantages of distributed data processing

1. Offers decentralized processing and satisfies desire for local autonomy and local application development. Facilitates user accessibility to computer centers.
2. Local control over needed segments of the data base is retained at the distributed centers.
3. Quality of input and processing is improved because of greater sensitivity to local conditions.
4. Users feel analysts at dispersed sites are more responsive to their needs.
5. Enables modular growth with little disruption at central site.
6. Enables use of different equipment at sites, provided interface problems are resolved.
7. Provides stand-alone operations with fail-soft capability for hierarchical structures and alternative routes for ring structures.
8. Provides middle management at distributed level with unique, relevant, and timely information, and consequently a measure of independence from top management.
9. Enables use of heterogeneous equipment and resource sharing, including dynamic load balancing (by moving around and distributing load) to maximize throughput.

**Table 18.5
Limitations of DDP**

1. Can be more expensive than centralized processing in spite of low-cost minis, largely because of the cost of transmission, software necessary for DDP, and the overlapping of equipment (especially disks in cases of replicated data bases).
2. The interface of expensive equipment from different vendors at dispersed nodes is a problem, for equipment may differ in instruction sets and operating systems.
3. Most existing software packages are designed for stand-alone computers and need to be adapted for DDP.
4. Communication systems of DDP are vulnerable to security violations.
5. National and international standards for network communication do not exist, causing problems of interfacing and implementing DDP.
6. With autonomous distributed sites, corporate standards of development, integration, and data bases are more difficult to enforce.

Key words

Centralized data base
Distributed data processing (DDP)
Dynamic control
Fail-soft capability
Horizontal systems
Hybrid approach
Network administration
Nodes
Offloading

Planning task force
Replicated distributed data base
Ring network
Segmented distributed data base
Systems Network Architecture (SNA)
Star network
Static control
Systems architecture

Discussion questions

1. Describe the essential elements of a distributed processing system.
2. What are the characteristics of DDP?
3. When would you select a star computer configuration as opposed to a ring or hierarchical configuration? Why? Give examples of each in business and industry.
4. What configuration of computer equipment in a DDP environment would you select for the following situations:
    a. A bank with many branches?
    b. A wholesaler with many warehouses?
5. What problems arising out of personnel conflicts and power struggle should be expected in the transition from centralized EDP to DDP? What can be done to minimize the harmful effects?
6. What are the problems of control, security, and privacy to be expected in a DDP environment? How can one overcome such problems?
7. What are the role and importance of telecommunications and teleprocessing in a DDP environment?

8. Comment on the following statement: DDP democratizes computing by making it more accessible.

9. What is distributed in DDP?

10. Can DDP be implemented in modules? Explain.

11. What effect will DDP have on organization structure, management style, and the decision-making process in business?

12. What is involved in the conversion from centralized EDP to DDP? What additional equipment, software, or personnel will be required under the new structure?

13. What type of business or industrial environment lends itself to DDP?

14. In planning for DDP, what types of master plans should be formulated?

15. Describe the difference between dynamic and static control in DDP. Does the type and degree of control vary among businesses and among different firms within an industry?

16. What is the role of a network administrator?

Exercise

1. Would you want the systems in Exercise 1, Chapter 10 and Exercise 1, Chapter 16 to be processed at a central facility or a distributed facility, assuming both options were feasible? Explain your choice.

Selected annotated bibliography

Booth, Grayce M. *The Distributed System Environment: Some Practical Approaches*. New York: McGraw-Hill, 1981, 286 pp.
This book, written by a practitioner from Honeywell, has neither an IBM bias nor the theoretical bias of an academician. Good sections on distributed network architectures, distributed systems structures, and design considerations are included.

Champine, Goege A. *Distributed Computer Systems: Impact on Management, Design, and Analysis*. Amsterdam: North-Holland Publishing, 1980, 380 pp.
Comprehensive coverage of distributed processing, including excellent chapters on human interface in distributed systems (Chapter 6) and the management of distributed systems (Chapter 15).

Chorafas, Dimitris N. *Databases for Networks and Minicomputers*. New York: Petrocelli Books, 1982, 281 pp.
Chapter 19, "Supporting a Distributed Environment," is especially recommended (pp. 267–78). The needs for standards, documentation, and coordination in distributed data networks are emphasized.

Draffan, I. W., and F. Poole, eds. *Distributed Data Bases*. New York: Cambridge University Press, 1980, 374 pp.

This text reviews data base theory, discusses problems associated with the setup and administration of distributed data base systems, and attempts to suggest solutions. The book is based on lecture notes for an advanced course on distributed data bases organized by the editors and held at Sheffield City Polytechnic in England in 1979.

Durniak, Anthony. "Special Report: New Networks Tie Down Distributed Processing Concepts." *Electronics* 51, no. 3 (December 1978), pp. 107–20.

An excellent article on network architecture, including both American and foreign approaches. Somewhat technical but not difficult reading.

Fernandez, E. B.; R. C. Summers; and C. Wood. *Database Security and Integrity.* Reading, Mass.: Addison-Wesley Publishing, 1981, 320 pp.

This book is for readers with some technical background in the computing field who have an interest in data base security. Privacy requirements, data base concepts, policies and models of data base security, auditing and controls in a data base environment, and enforcement design are among the topics covered. These topics are relevant to a DDP environment.

Hessinger, Paul R. "Distributed Systems and Data Management." *Datamation* 27, no. 11 (November 1981), pp. 178–82.

The author discusses how distributed processing is affected by the technology of mainframes, minicomputers, distributed processors, operating software, DBMS, and data communications networks.

Liebowitz, Burt H., and John H. Carson. *Distributed Processing Tutorial,* 2d ed. Long Beach, Calif: IEEE Computer Society, 1978.

This book is neither a tutorial nor is the text limited to a discussion of DDP. It is a set of over 50 articles on topics such as communications, networks, intelligent terminals, multiprocessors, and distributed data bases. As with most sets of readings, it is a mix of excellent and mediocre articles. But overall, it is a good collection, including both survey-type and technical articles.

Lorin, H. "Distributed Processing; An Assessement." *IBM Systems Journal* 18, no. 4 (1979), pp. 582–603.

This article discusses the potential benefits and pitfalls of DDP: centralized management, historical relationship of DDP with online systems, the reliability and growth of fail-soft systems, and adjusting DDP to the organization structure of the firm. Lorin concludes, "We do not know, in general, whether complexity will increase or decrease distributed processing systems, or how operational costs will evolve. We are just discovering an art."

Patrick, Robert L. "A Checklist for System Design." *Datamation* 26, no. 2 (January 1980) pp. 147–53.

This article is an excerpted version of the author's *Design Handbook for Distributed Systems,* discussing 15 ideas on systems design (out of 186 ideas in the book). He describes how each idea has been successfully implemented in practice. The article is especially good on the human factors of designing and implementing a distributed system.

Thierauf, Robert J. *Distributed Data Processing.* Englewood Cliffs, N.J.: Prentice-Hall, 1978, 305 pp.

The fact that a textbook is published on this new and controversial topic is an indication of the importance of this subject and its approaching maturity. This book includes some material from the author's previous work, *Systems Analysis and Design of Real-time Management Information Systems*. Both books are packed with lists, tables, and diagrams and text is tightly written.

Warren, James D., Jr. "Think Ahead to Avoid Distributed Confusion." *Small Systems World* 7, no. 6 (June 1982), pp. 28–29.

Warren discusses five approaches to installing a DDP system. He concludes that successful DDP requires hybrid management—a mix of local management with centralized top management.

USES OF AN INFORMATION SYSTEM

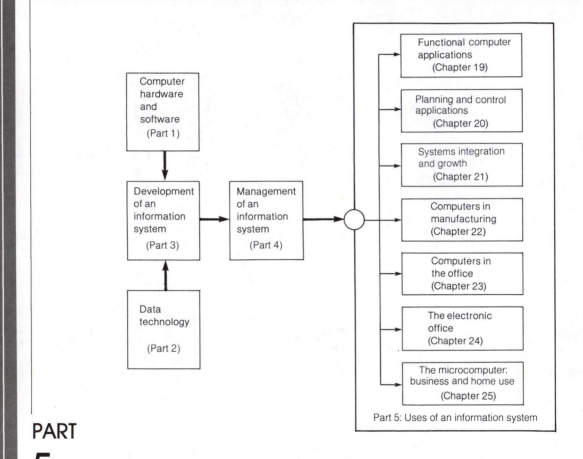

PART 5

Computer hardware and software (Part 1)

Development of an information system (Part 3)

Data technology (Part 2)

Management of an information system (Part 4)

Functional computer applications (Chapter 19)

Planning and control applications (Chapter 20)

Systems integration and growth (Chapter 21)

Computers in manufacturing (Chapter 22)

Computers in the office (Chapter 23)

The electronic office (Chapter 24)

The microcomputer: business and home use (Chapter 25)

Part 5: Uses of an information system

The overview of Part 5 appears in diagram form. Most information systems are at the operational level of a business. In Chapter 19, four case studies are presented to show functional computer applications: airlines reservations, a travel agency, a hotel, and a car dealership. The chapter also describes expert systems and public online data bases.

Computerized decision making by middle and top management for planning and control, the subject of Chapter 20, often requires decision support systems with data management, analytical, and interactive capabilities. Other special features that need to be considered in planning and control information systems are the scope of data, time horizon, degree of quantification, degree of detail, mode of operation, and display media. A brief discussion on artificial intelligence attempting to answer the question, "Will machines replace management?" concludes the chapter.

Although functional applications discussed in Chapter 19, and control and planning applications discussed in Chapter 20 can be developed and maintained independently, integration of subsystems to encompass all levels of management is more effective. Chapter 21 introduces horizontal, vertical, longitudinal, and total systems integration, discussing their implementation and analyzing the advantages of each type of integration. The chapter concludes with a section on growth, describing how a firm's capacity to absorb computer technology can influence speed and direction of growth.

Chapter 22 analyzes specialized and somewhat advanced computer applications in manufacturing. One section is devoted to "smart" products. Another to the automation of manufacturing processes, including numerical control, use of robots, and process control. The chapter also reviews the use of computers in product design.

Chapter 23 describes advanced office applications of the computer, including electronic mail, teleconferencing, the war room, electronic fund transfer, and word processing. Chapter 24 focuses on the integration of computerized office functions and presents a scenario of the electronic office of the future.

Use of business and home microcomputers is the subject of Chapter 25. Capabilities of microcomputers, selection criteria, and management problems are considered. Ways a microcomputer can assist a manager, supplementing corporate mainframes, are outlined. Uses of a microcomputer by families for home banking, shopping, and as a reference tool are also described.

Chapter 26 tells of the impact of computers on management: how the task mix of managers has been changed by computers; how corporations have been restructured, eroding power bases and altering the span of control of many managers; and how computers have altered decision making. The chapter also looks at issues of growing concern to managers as a result of computerization.

Finally, Chapter 27 looks at the future of computing. Technological innovations we can expect in the 1990s are described. The book closes with a brief description of the ways an information society may change our lives.

Functional computer applications

19

. . . the greater the power at our disposal the greater the number of insoluble problems we can solve.

Jacques Stern

The use of a computer in a function (such as accounting, marketing, finance, manufacturing, or production) is known as a **functional computer application.** Payroll, invoicing, asset depreciation, inventory forecasting, scheduling, labor distribution, and job costing are examples of such applications. Some applications are strictly at the operational level. Others assist management by making decisions formerly made by executives, such as production scheduling, or provide information needed for decision making, such as sales information, job costing, or forecasting used in planning.

After listing sample functional applications using computers in business, this chapter introduces two recent applications: expert systems and online public data bases. A case study approach is used to discuss other functional applications.[1] Airline reservations, travel agencies, a sample hotel, and a car dealership are the cases examined.

Airline reservations has been selected since most readers are familiar with this application and because there are many spin-off applications, such as reservations for hotels and credit authorizations, EFT, loan payment processing, message switching in telecommunications, police car dispatching, and teller postings in a bank. One system chosen for study is SABRE of American Airlines since this was the first large-scale commercial real-time system developed. But all airlines today have systems similar to SABRE. For equipment configurations necessary for reservations, the United Airlines system will be examined. Also, the use by small travel agencies of inexpensive minis requiring little training will be explored.

---

[1] For books with details on functional systems, see A. L. Eliason and K. D. Kitts, *Business Computer Systems and Applications* (Chicago: Science Research Associates, 1979), chapters 4–18; and Raymond McLeod, Jr., *Management Information Systems,* 2nd ed. (Chicago: Science Research Associates, 1983), pp. 381–508.

Hotels, in many ways, resemble airlines for similar reservation systems are required, and both use computers for subsystems, such as accounting, general ledger, and payroll. However, hotels have many unique computer applications, such as monitoring energy consumption. A case study will be presented to demonstrate computer use in a medium-size business in a hotel chain.

Finally, the chapter discusses computer use by an automobile dealer. This example has been selected because of the diversity of input and output required by small businesses.

General business functional systems

A sample list of functional computer applications for business appears in Table 19.1 Some of these applications will be discussed in detail in later chapters. For example, computer use in manufacturing is the subject of Chapter 22 and office applications appear in Chapter 23. Many applications in Table 19.1 involve automation of business record keeping that was formerly done manually by clerks. Other systems have changed the ways business is conducted, providing information and services that only computers can provide. To keep abreast of functional software applicable to a given business, managers generally rely on system analysts, software vendors, and trade periodicals.

Expert systems

Most computer applications consist of programs and data. **Expert systems** add another component: a knowledge base. This knowledge base is data and information on a given topic which makes the system an expert on that topic. When combined with software that enables the computer to recognize problem patterns, to analyze data, and to apply decision rules, the expert system can solve problems within a limited domain. It can also explain the reasoning leading to problem solutions.

In all cases, the system acts as a consultant to the user. Data on the environment is solicited from the user through an interactive dialog. The system then draws on its knowledge base to determine what operators (arithmetic or Boolean) should be used to produce results and recommendations. The knowledge base consists of relevant facts, a historical base of actions of human experts within the problem domain taken under specific sets of circumstances, and **heuristics** (rules of thumb for evaluating facts and inferring meaning). The latter are gathered from cooperating professionals working in the field and written into programs as IF-THEN-ELSE rules.

Many expert systems have been developed in scientific fields. For example, DENDRAL is used for the spectrographic analysis of gases. MYCIN diagnoses blood and meningitis infections, then suggests antibiotic therapies for treating the infections. Expert systems are also being developed for businesspersons. DIP-

Table 19.1
Sample of computer operational applications in business

Accounting and finance
Accounts payable
Accounts receivable
Asset accounting
Auditing
Billing
Budget analysis
Budgeting
Capital budgeting
Cash disbursements
Cash receipts
Check writing and
  reconciliation
Cost accounting
Equipment inventory
Funding
General ledger
Invoicing
Payroll
Purchasing
Warranty administration

Administration
Facilities control
Information retrieval
Operations research
  models
Personnel records
Record keeping
Recruiting
Regulatory reporting
Skills inventory
Training management
Wage and salary
  administration
Word processing

Agribusiness
Farm and crop rotation
Financial and accounting
Optimal feed blending
Optimal fertilizing program

Banking
Automatic cash dispensing
Bill-paying service
Checking account
Credit card subsystem
Electronic fund transfer
Investment analysis
Loan management
MICR routine
Mortgage control
Proof and reconciliation
Savings accounts

Construction
Design analysis
Project control (CPM, PERT,
  GERT)
Scheduling of labor and
  materials
Stress and strain calculations

Financial
Cost accounting
Financial reporting
Ledger accounting
Payroll
Tax accounting

Hotel and restaurant
Accounting
Auditing
Billing
Checkout subsystem
Energy control
Inventory control
Personnel management
Registration
Reservation
Room service

Insurance
Actuarial computation
Claims
Customer policy records
Dividend management
Estate planning
Revenue management
Risk analysis
Underwriting

Manufacturing
Bill of materials processing
Equipment inventory
Inventory control
Job costing
Labor accounting
Materials control
Numerical control
Plant and tooling
Process control
Production scheduling
Purchasing
Quality control
Robots
Routing and standards
Shop floor control
Simulation models
Smart products
Stores control
Tool control
Vendor file

Table 19.1 (concluded)

Marketing
Advertising and promotion
Client file
Credit control
Dealer analysis
Forecasting—short- and
   long-range
Market research
New product scheduling
Order entry
Physical distribution
Sales analysis
Sales control
Warehouse control

Purchasing and order entry
Billing
Inspection
Invoice matching and payments
Materials procurement
Ordering
Pricing
Receiving

Real estate
Financial computation
Investment portfolio analysis
Listing services
Mortgage loan accounting
Property management
Tax analysis

Research and development
Computer-aided design
Engineering control
Engineering scheduling
Experimentation control
Product testing
Product control
Scientific computing
Simulation

Reservations
Airlines
Car rentals
Camping
Hotel
Theaters

Retailing
Accounting
Auditing
Billing
Credit checking
Inventory control
Marketing analysis
Point-of-sale subsystem
Sales forecasting

Word processing

Utilities
Accounts receivable
Customer billing
Facilities
Maintenance accounting
Maintenance scheduling
Rating

METER ADVISER assists in oil exploration. XCON can be used to diagnose computer malfunctions, and MECAO is used for problem solving in the machine industry. TAXADVISOR provides estate-planning tax advice. It has 275 production rules for advising clients on planning alternatives, such as whether to purchase gas and oil shelters. TAXMAN evaluates the tax consequences of certain types of corporate reorganizations. A sampling of other expert systems in current use or under development is listed in Table 19.2.

Much attention is currently being focused on expert systems, a relatively new field of endeavor in computer science. In business, the emphasis is on expert systems to assist operational decision making. Because of the many behavioral variables and relationships that cannot easily be quantified in planning and control situations, the development of useful expert systems in these areas is more difficult than in a limited domain, such as disease diagnosis.

The ultimate goal of computer professionals is to move beyond expert sys-

Table 19.2
Sample expert systems in current use or under development

System	Knowledge domain	Function performed
AUDITOR	Business	Assists auditors in assessing a company's allowance for bad debts
CADUCEUS	Medicine	Diagnosis, internal diseases
CRIB	Computing fault diagnosis	Advises faults in computer hardware and software
EDP AUDITOR	Business	To assist auditing advanced EDP systems
EL	Electrical industry	Analyzes electrical circuits
HASP/SIAP	Defense	Passive sonar surveillance system
HASP (SU/X)	Machine acoustics	Problem solving
MONITOR	Business	24-hour currency information service providing international exchange rates to traders
PECOS	Programming	Problem solving
PROSPECTOR	Mining	Mineral exploration—evaluates sites for potential deposits
RI	Computing	Configuring the VAX-II/780 computer system
SACON	Engineering	Advises structural engineers in using structural analysis program MARC
SECHS	Chemistry	Search
TICOM	Programming	Computer-assisted method of modeling and evaluating internal control systems

tems to **knowledge information processing systems (KIPS).** KIPS will combine the problem solving ability of computers, the algorithmic power of decision models, the know-how of experts, and artificial intelligence (machine learning and self-modification of programs).[2]

Public online data bases

In January 1984, there were over 1,700 **online public data bases** accessible for a prescribed fee to computer users. This number is continually growing—over 133 new data bases were added to the list in the last six months of 1983 alone.

These data bases cover a wide range of subjects. Data bases of interest to

---

[2] Artificial intelligence is discussed in greater detail in the following chapter.

businesspersons include bases that provide banking and financial information, stock market quotations, abstracts of articles in trade journals, patent information, and data on individual corporations or specific industries. (See Table 19.3 for sample bases relevant to business management.) For a complete listing of data base services available, one would have to consult a directory. One such directory is an online public data base itself.

One cannot generalize about data base services since each producing company attempts to offer unique specialized features to attract customers. For example, SOURCE offers time sharing in addition to some of the services listed in

Table 19.3
Sample online public data bases relevant to business management

Product	Producing company	Information provided	Update frequency
ABI/Inform	Data Courier, Inc.	Abstracts and citations on business and management	Weekly or Monthly
BI/Data	Business International Corporation	Annual time series data on international economics and finance	Daily
DISCLOSURE II	Disclosure, Inc.	Financial information on publicly held corporations	Weekly
Dow Jones News & Retrieval	Dow Jones, Inc.	Full text of *Wall Street Journal, Barrows,* SEC reports, and general financial information	Continuously
DUNSPRINT	Dun & Bradstreet, Inc.	D & B financial reports on U.S. businesses	Daily
Historical Dow Jones Averages	Dow Jones, Inc.	Daily quotes by date are accessible on transportation, utilities, and 65 stock companies	Periodically
INNERLINE	Bank Administration Institute	Banking and financial information	Varies with data base
MANAGEMENT CONTENTS	Management Contents, Inc.	Abstracts and citations on business and management	Monthly
MEDIA GENERAL FINANCIAL SERVICE	Media General Financial Service, Inc.	Financial information on over 3,000 companies and 170 industries	
NEWSNET	Newsnet, Inc.	Full text of over 120 business-oriented newsletters and specialized subjects	Varies with newsletters
PATSEARCH	Permagon International Information Corp.	U.S. patent abstracts and citations	Weekly
SOURCE	Source Telecomputing, Inc.	Variety of business and consumer-oriented data bases and computer services. Input from United Press International (UPI), *New York Times,* Prentice-Hall, and others	Varies with data base and service

Table 19.3. DIALOG, with over 80 million items of stored information, is perhaps the largest data base service. One special feature offered by DIALOG is SDI (Selective Dissemination of Information) which matches key words drawn from each user's profile with key words in a directory of references. As a result, references customized to the special interests of each client can be recommended. PROMT, with bibliographical citations from business literature on international trade, production, new products, and regulations, is one data base accessible through DIALOG. TRADEMARKSCAN, covering over 600,000 registered and pending U.S. trademarks, is another.

Case studies

Airline reservations

The need for a computerized information system for reservations was recognized by American Airlines in 1954 because the company was finding it increasingly difficult to maintain accurate and timely manual records of passengers. The conventional system of assigning agents quotas for seats was also unsatisfactory. When local agents sold out their seat allotments, passengers were often lost to the airlines due to delays in locating a vacancy held by an agent in another part of the country. Lost revenues resulted.

It took 10 years of development and more than $30 million to make the desired computerized **central reservation system** operational.

When placed in operation, the system, called SABRE, worked as follows. A client inquired about a flight. The agent keyed the coded flight number and proposed date of travel on a terminal. An average of 2.3 seconds was required before the agent received information regarding seat availability and answers to client questions, such as total plane capacity, number of seats in first class, meals served, and plane connections. Once the client reached a decision on flight and date, this information was keyed along with the client's name, phone number, number of seats requested, and passengers' names. Special service needs, such as a salt-free diet, a wheel chair, or assistance in boarding, car rental, and escorts for children changing planes, were added to the client's record. After a code to identify the agent was entered, a key was pressed which signaled the terminal to print out the input message for visual recheck by the agent. If no mistakes were identified, the reservation was confirmed and the reservation transaction completed.

In addition to making reservations and keeping passenger records, SABRE had control functions. For example, the system would not accept incorrect data, such as a code for a nonexistent flight or a family booking where the number of names did not match the number of seats requested. Incomplete input was also refused. Should a flight be canceled, each agency having made bookings was informed and told which clients to notify. The system automatically released seats when a cancellation was made. If a passenger desired a connecting flight, the system made the reservation, even on another airline. This latter service was provided for more than one third of all passengers.

Reservation information was also used internally by the airlines. For example, the information provided caterers with estimates of the number of meals to be

Table 19.4
Functions performed by an airline information system

Provides information to potential customers on flight times, fares, and availability, as well as information on routes, schedules, hotels and car rentals, meals in flight, movies, and so forth.

Makes cargo reservations.

Maintains passenger inventory and availability lists.

Maintains passenger waiting lists, confirmation, cancellations, and no-show lists.

Keeps track of special requirements for wheelchairs, pets, and so forth.

Checks in passengers.

Generates tickets, including self-service issuance of tickets using credit cards.

Prepares boarding manifests.

Provides a meal count prior to departure.

Makes cargo load calculations prior to departure.

Makes passenger load and trim calculations prior to departure.

Calculates an optimal passenger route (for minimum time or minimum fare).

Provides information for:

Crew scheduling.

Maintenance scheduling.

Integrates automated ticketing, boarding control, and baggage delivery at all airports.

Keeps profile of passengers, including information on seat preferences (aisle, window, nearness to exits, smoking or nonsmoking), choice of drink, special dietary requests, wheelchair needs, and so forth.

Navigates the route for the pilot to optimize fuel consumption, given the number of passengers, cargo weight, wind velocity, wind direction, and air and cloud currents.

Integrates the microprocessors in an aircraft.

Integrates maintenance and monitoring of crucial parts of the airplane under stress or strain.

Schedules pilots and flight attendants, giving consideration to their preferences and seniority within the constraints of time flown and projected earnings.

Provides automatic rerouting when bad weather exists or in the event of flight cancellations.

prepared, arrival and departure desks received passenger lists, and flight control were given weight and loading information which also guided management in assigning crew and maintenance personnel. Furthermore, the system kept accounts of funds receivable for each day, month, flight, and route. Such statistical data was exceedingly useful to management for planning. SABRE processed all flight information received from dispatch centers, adjusting scheduled flights and stops as well.

Reservation systems similar to SABRE are now standard in the airlines industry. The original SABRE has been completely redesigned, incorporating new technology and additional information services, but before it was replaced, other airlines had improved upon SABRE, developing more sophisticated systems, leapfrogging over American Airlines to become leaders in automation. Both Eastern and United, for example, used CRT terminals, which provide faster and quieter output than typewriters, before American made the switch.

In 1980, United Airlines' hardware supported a fleet of 370 aircraft, operating over 20,000 flight miles, and involving 49,000 employees. The computer system processed information on all phases of operation, including the generation of management and control reports on passengers, cargo, crews and personnel, scheduling, and equipment utilization. Systems characteristics included:

The capacity to process 36,000 reservations per hour.
A real-time response of less than two seconds 50 percent of the time; four seconds 90 percent of the time.
Average dialogue: two and a half to three minutes.
Average input message: 15 characters.
Average response: 130 characters.

Sequential transaction files were retained as backup and the entire real-time data base was copied once a week as additional backup. The purpose of these performance statistics and Table 19.4, summarizing functional subsystems of airline information systems, are to demonstrate the speed and capabilities of an OLRT system. Pressures of competition are continually upgrading services offered. For example, calculation of fares and ticket printout by computer are presently being implemented. Some airlines already provide self-servicing ticket machines at airports. The magnetic strip on the back of accepted credit cards provides information that is used to verify credit, create a billing record, and issue a ticket in the card holder's name. The variety of fares and discounts available impedes total implementation of self-service ticketing at this time.

What slows new applications is the problem of systems integration, the subject of Chapter 21. Because of the size of the airline industry, development and integration of new subsystems take years of planning and the allocation of substantial resources.

Reservations by travel agents

Airline reservations today are made primarily by travel agencies. No longer do most passengers buy their tickets directly from the airlines. In 1984, approximately 80 percent of the 20,500 travel agents in the United States utilized minicomputers or terminals with access to airline reservation data bases. Some agencies are connected to the data base of a single airline used frequently. Others are connected to a single data base that is connected to other airline data bases in turn. Another common agency reservation system is a computer connection to airline clearinghouses. The fastest reservation option and one with fewest errors and least noise is direct access to the data bases of a set of airlines. As might be expected, this is also the most costly service.

More than 80 percent of automated reservations for U.S. flights are made by agents using SABRE, the reservation system of American Airlines, APOLLO of

United, or PARS of TWA. Since these reservation systems have only limited flight information about competitors, small carriers are at a disadvantage. In 1983, 16 airlines complained to the Public Works and Transportation Committee that reservation systems marketed by the major airlines to travel agents represented unfair bias.

Reservations for international flights are serviced by SITA (the French acronym for Airlines' Worldwide Telecommunications and Information Services). This reservation system serves 248 airlines (both large and small carriers) flying to 950 cities in 154 countries. In addition to online reservations, SITA provides Bagtrac (a baggage tracing service), Bahamas (a baggage handling and management service), meteorological information, and personnel training.

How do these reservation systems work? The SABRE system designed by American Airlines for travel agencies today is essentially the same system described earlier. It requires about a week of training for personnel to learn procedures for calculating the numerous options for fares and for mastering the large number of codes utilized. This system is utilized by Schmal Travel, a travel agency in the town of 50,000.

A sample of the coding as it appears on the passenger hard copy given by Schmal to clients and as it appears on the input terminal (with slight modifications in format) is shown below:

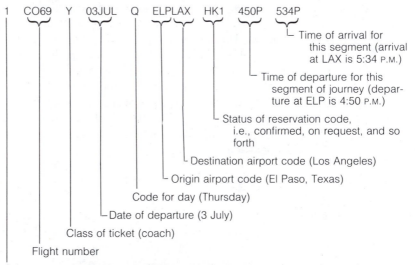

The system also prints a schedule for passengers (see sample, Table 19.5), though many clients find this output hard to read, preferring a simple typed schedule with only essential noncoded information including travel date, flight numbers, and arrival and departure times.

The cost of American's reservation system (two CRT terminals and one printer) to Schmal Travel is $690/month with line charges paid by the airline. The salary of one clerk performing the same services would be approximately $700/month

Table 19.5
Sample output for airline reservation

```
*A
 1.1HUSSAIN/K M DR ──────────────────────── Name of passenger
 1 CO  69Y 03JUL Q ELPLAX HK1   450P  534P  ⎫
 2 CI   7Y 03JUL Q LAXHND HK1  1020P  700A  ⎬ Information on
 3 PA   2C 10JUL Q NRTLAX HK1   730P 1205P  ⎬ 4 segments of
 4 CO  74Y 10JUL Q LAXELP HK1   200P  533P  ⎭ the journey
T-TAW10DEC/ ─────────────────────────────── Date of reservation
P-ELP915-882-3836-A ─────────────────────── Phone number of agent
ELP505-646-1206-0 ───────────────────────── Phone number of passenger
N-07                                        ⎫
CALL DR FOR RECFN                           ⎬ Other codes required
R-P                                         ⎬ for tracing the record
C3V*MS 1719/290CT RCS6KX H                  ⎭ and reconfirmation
```

Note the highly formulated and coded form. The codes are sometimes obvious, such as 03JUL = 3d July. Codes such as HND = Haneda Airport in Tokyo, and NRT = Narita Airport, also in Tokyo, are less obvious. All data is coded in a prescribed sequence and format, requiring a trained person to operate the system.

plus fringe benefits, so on strictly economic grounds, the system is cost-effective. Intangible benefits include faster and more accurate information, less monotonous work for clerks, and greater customer satisfaction. An increased load by the agency could improve the cost-benefit ratio because one printer can service two additional terminals. The principal disadvantage to travelers is that the system is biased toward American Airline reservations, providing less information on competing flights.

Hotel computer applications

It was stated in the chapter introduction that an airline reservation system had spin-off applications for hotel reservations. Hotels also use computers for applications such as accounting, inventory, and payroll. These applications will now be discussed in the context of an actual case study. The hotel chosen for the study, Hotel West (a fictitious name) is a private business, though part of a chain, in a town of 50,000. It has 200 rooms, 175 employees, and a variety of facilities, including an indoor pool, conference rooms, banquet halls, shops, bars, and a restaurant servicing primarily upper-middle class families and traveling businesspeople.

Hotel reservations

The input required for hotel reservations is name, address, phone, date and time of arrival, length of stay, number in party, room preference (size, price, location; e.g., poolside, quiet wing), and special services requested (crib, wheelchair). Because desk clerks and receptionists are generally unskilled and not permanent staff, reservation equipment is designed to be simple to operate. In Hotel West, a terminal with a standard typewriter keyboard is used for entering name, address, and phone number of the client, and a special-purpose terminal with 76 keys and 16 lights is used to input other reservation data. These two terminals appear in Figure 19.1. Though this latter terminal appears confusing at first glance, it is actually easier and faster to operate than airline reservation systems. For example, when an October booking is requested, the clerk need not remember a month code (such as 10) but merely presses the key marked Oct. in a group of 12 keys for months set in a row. Additional keys represent other crucial data, such as code keys for hotel identification, date, number and type of rooms required, or action requested (cancel, reserve), and all related keys are grouped together. The lights identify the status of the equipment (ready, in use), availability of different types of rooms (single, double), and room availability in nearby hotels. Equipment so specialized is expensive and can only be justified if the number of reservations and hotel size are sufficiently large to permit it to be cost-effective.

Reservations for a room at Hotel West can be made by another hotel in the chain or reservations can be made by the client calling a reservation center. When Hotel West initiates a room request on behalf of a customer for a room at another hotel in the chain, a computer tie-in with central reservations checks availability. Confirmation of the reservation and a copy of notification to the hotel in question are messages that the operator in Hotel West receives as printout, and which the client can use as a reservation confirmation. Table 19.6 shows how such a request is coded. The terminal used for telephoning reservations is shown in Figure 19.2.

Figure 19.1
Two terminals for hotel reservations

Courtesy International Business Machines Corporation

Table 19.6
Sample hotel reservation dialogue

Mr. John Doe, staying at Hotel West, asks the desk clerk to make reservations at another hotel in the chain, Hotel Polka, code 352 for June 5th for one person for two nights for a single room with guaranteed payment. Doe's address is 4943 Karen Drive, Las Cruces, NM 88001. Telephone 505-523-1427.

INPUT
TYPED BY
CLERK:

Doe, John   (name of guest, last name first)
4943 Karen Dr.   (street address)
Las Cruces, NM 88001 (City, State, Zip code)
5055231427   (Area code plus phone number)
SK   (operator's initials for Kathy Stacy)

Clerk also keys in data on the special terminal, 352 for the hotel code, June 5 for the date of arrival, the 1 key for the number of rooms required, 1BD 1PR key for 1 bed for one person, and the 2 key for the two nights desired, the action key AVAIL to inquire about availability of the room, and finally, the ENTER key to enter the data for processing.

COMPUTER
MESSAGE
CONFIRMING
RESERVATION
AT HOTEL
WEST:

CONF 1RM 1BD 1PR 2NT MON JUN 05
GUARANTEED PAYMENT DUE IF NOT CANCELLED
BEFORE 6PM

MESSAGE
TO HOTEL
POLKA:

SOLD 1RM 1BD 1PR 2NT MON JUN 05
GUARANTEED PAYMENT
4943 Karen Dr.
Las Cruces, NM 88001
SK

Figure 19.2
Keyboard of terminal for hotel reservations

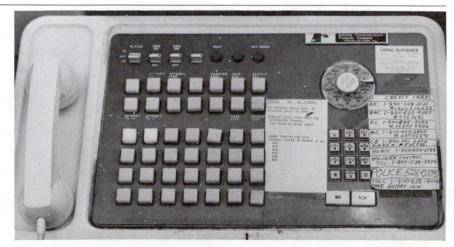

If the requested hotel has no bookings available, central reservations will supply data on room options at the nearest hotel in the chain. Table 19.7 is a sample output message conveying information on alternative hotel booking possibilities.

The tie-in to central reservations costs Hotel West $8,000 per year with $1 charged for each reservation made by the system. Line charges vary from one chain to another, some underwriting the expense as part of their service to member hotels. One can measure the gain from a centralized reservation system since many of the figures are available for a cost-benefit analysis: cost of reservation service, number of rooms reserved through the system, income from reservations, income otherwise lost from unoccupied rooms. However, intangible benefits, such as convenience to customers, should also be recognized.

The central reservations network can also be programmed to provide other information services as well. In 1979, when gas shortages discouraged travelers, one hotel chain relayed information on filling-station hours, and dollar and volume limits per vehicle of stations within a five-mile radius of each hotel in the 1,500-member chain. Travelers or hotels could phone to obtain the information. The purpose was to prevent cancellations or empty rooms by providing information on gas availability to clientele.

Other business applications

Hotel West also has a minicomputer for other business applications that is independent of the reservation system. This minicomputer has five CRTs: a main office terminal, three at points of sale (restaurant and bars), and one at the housekeeper's station. These terminals are used for room assignments, registration, and billing (front desk activities), and for processing payroll, accounts receivable, general ledger, cash posting, printing of statements, and management reporting,

Table 19.7
Sample of information on alternative hotel accommodations

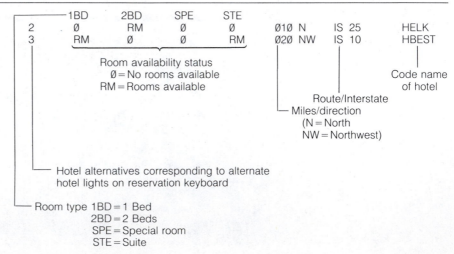

as well as energy and inventory control (backroom accounting). Larger hotels often have two computer systems for these functions, separating front desk and backroom accounting, and also providing backup in the backroom computer should the frontroom system fail at the check-in counter.

Hotel West's minicomputer is located in an alcove of the front office. Maintenance and training are provided by the small out-of-state firm that installed the equipment and developed the software, Communications Diversified, Inc. This firm, with only 45 professionals, can compete with large conglomerates like IT&T because it specializes, providing software packages that apply to only a few industries. The hotel management software, for example, required little modification to fit Hotel West's needs, whereas the purchase of a general business application package would have required Hotel West to hire a programmer or system analyst to adapt the package to local conditions. This specialization of software entrepreneurs, coupled with the drop in the price of minis, is what has made computer applications cost-effective for small businesses.

In the following sections, several of Hotel West's specialized business applications will be described.

Room status

In order for a desk clerk to assign rooms to clients, the status of hotel rooms (occupied or empty) must be known. At Hotel West, room status is one report provided by the minicomputer. To obtain room status information, the clerk first requests the display of a menu of reports or programs on the CRT of the front desk terminal by pressing a key code to this effect. From this list, the code for room status report is determined. This code is keyed and the RETURN key pressed to indicate end of choice of report. The terminal will then display the number of rooms available on any given date (up to 20 years in the future) and rooms currently ready for occupancy by room number and type (single, double). Occupancy status is updated in real-time mode from the housekeeper's terminal as maids complete cleaning. This information not only serves the front desk for registrations, but pinpoints the location and progress of each maid, and identifies rooms ready for inspection.

Registration and check-out

Registration is done on the CRT by the front desk clerk. The input required, listed in Table 19.8, is keyed line by line from top to bottom, the terminal validating each entry by character and range validity checks. When a required field is not provided, the system locks (does not proceed) until all required information is entered. In processing registrations, the computer updates the room inventory, informs the housekeeper (on a terminal) of the room assignment, and generates a guest folio of all registration information keyed by room number. Included is such data as time and date of check-in which the computer automatically records. A guest account is also created (room rent and tax) to be updated in real time for charges, for example, telephone calls or restaurant bills.

At check-out, the computer will print an itemized customer bill upon a simple

Table 19.8
Terminal input for hotel registration

Number of days stay

Guest's name (Last, First)

Guest address _____

                       Street   City   State   Zip

Number in party

Rate

Representing

Method of payment code

(1. Cash, 2. Prepayment, 3. Credit Card, 4. City Acct.)

Credit Card   _____

                   Number   Date expires (MM/YY)

keyed command by the desk clerk. When payment is received, the clerk enters the method of payment (cash, check, credit card) and amount into the system for auditing purposes. The computer automatically updates the room inventory and signals the housekeeper that the vacated room is ready for cleaning.

Check-out using the computer system is fast and accurate, saving the client time since the system instantly generates the bill. But registration by computer takes longer than traditional manual registrations primarily because more information is requested, information that the desk clerk manually keys into the system.

Control applications

Stock inventory, especially food and beverages, is one important control function performed by computer at Hotel West. Another is auditing: shift audits (done three times a day) and the night audit (an audit summary of all three shifts). The audits list all transactions, amounts, mode of payment, transaction clerk, and shift supervisor. These computer audits eliminate the need for daily bookkeeping by an accountant. In addition, the audits serve as financial reports to management. Table 19.9 lists still other types of reports generated by computer at Hotel West.

In addition, the computer regulates energy consumption at Hotel West. Upon registration of a client, room heat (or air conditioning) is automatically turned on: at check-out, the system turns heat off. Air circulation in unoccupied rooms is also maintained by automatically switching on heat or cooling periodically. At Hotel West, the computer is programmed to control energy demand during peak periods. To reduce energy surcharges, heat is switched off for short time spans when energy demand reaches a predetermined level. The computer also regulates power-consuming devices, such as pumps, lights, and signs. This automation and control reduces energy consumption at Hotel West, saving an estimated 15–30 percent on the hotel's energy bill.

Table 19.9
Hotel's referance and control reports

For front desk
  Directory of guest folios for any date
  Directory of quests' names for any date
  Inventory of rooms available for any date
  Folio details for any guest
  Advance deposits received
  No shows
  Stayovers
  Arrivals
  Advance deposit transferred
  Entire content of current room folios or city accounts
  Check-out listings

Guest accounting
  Folio copies for each check-out
  Shift audits
  Credit card account totals
  Shift audits for each POS terminal
  Account code summaries for each POS terminal
  Room summary balance due and method of payment

Inventory control report

Energy consumption report

Wake-up service
Wake-up is automated, the computer telephoning clients at the time requested.

Videotex service

Hotel West also subscribes to videotex service, providing guests with terminals that interact with public data bases. Weather, restaurant and entertainment guides, help wanted ads, and local sales are examples of information that can be obtained through this service. Guests can also make airline reservations from the terminals and access the *Dow Jones News and Retrieval* data base for stock market quotations. In addition, electronic mail can be sent to guests at other hotels in the chain since all of the hotels belong to the same network. (The chain has over 500,000 videotex terminals at hotels around the country.)

Guests pay for this service: a fixed charge plus a fee based on length of time at the terminal. Programming skills are not required. After turning on the system and typing in credit card information, guests follow menus on the screen to access the information they desire. The keyboard has 12 special function keys that are easily mastered, including ENTER, YES, NO, and HELP.

The effectiveness of hotel applications

Are the functional applications and information generated by the computer at Hotel West cost-effective? Though costs can be determined, many benefits are hard to quantify (see Table 19.10). One simply cannot subject the benefits to a rigor-

Table 19.10
Hotel's cost-benefit analysis

Cost
  $1,000/room for hardware and software (one-time costs)
  $700/month for maintenance
  $8,000/year for tie-in to national reservation system,
      including communications

Benefits
  Energy expenditure reduction of 15–30 percent
  Increased employee productivity
  Real-time accounting including restaurants and telephone
  Personalized, fast service to client
  Accurate information regarding room availability
  Control and reference reports

ous monetary analysis. One can merely say that management, knowing costs, deems the computer systems worthwhile.

Hotels that cannot afford their own computers may choose a less expensive option: participation in a multiuser hotel computer system. Such systems provide reservation and guest accounting services. They may also keep track of guest telephone calls and point-of-sale terminals in the hotel's bars and restaurants. Such a system cannot be customized to the individual environment or problems of client hotels, but for standard applications, it generally proves satisfactory.

Because the costs of computer hardware and software are continually dropping, we may see expanded hotel applications in the future. Hotels in convention cities may adopt systems dedicated to complex reservation services. For example, citywide hotel networks may be established with access terminals in major U.S. cities so that bookings for all conference attendees can be made by conference organizers with ease. Hotels may also adopt systems to provide personalized service to guests. For example, they may collect data on guest preferences so that returnees will find their rooms stocked with their favorite soap and shampoo, the radio tuned to music they like, and their home-town newspaper on the table.

An automotive dealer

Not all businesses can afford a mini or require real-time capabilities. Many turn to a computer utility for processing business information. The car dealer in the following study is a case in point. Though this businessman has net assets over $2 million and employs 65 persons, he utilizes a computer located 1,700 miles from his car lot for accounting reports, entering all data online from the terminal (shown in Figure 19.3) and receiving output, including periodic management reports, on that same terminal overnight. This terminal has all of the features of a typewriter terminal plus many lights and special keys. In addition, it utilizes two cassettes simultaneously for input or output, and storage.

The input mode is conversational, the system asking for relevant data. Incorrect data, such as alpha characters in a numeric field, will cause the system to

Figure 19.3
Terminal for auto dealer accounting application

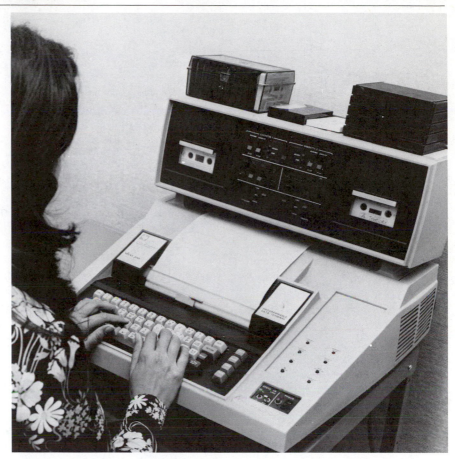

lock up until corrections are made. If data is suspicious but not necessarily incorrect (e.g., sales price less than cost), a light and beep alert the operator though the coded data will be accepted.

Let us trace an input transaction. Invoice No. 26772, for a part costing $4.46 is manually assigned a control number (CTL 170) by the accounts payable clerk, and the department to which it is charged is coded (1250). The invoice data is then keyed onto the termnal in the format shown in Table 19.11. The system's responses are explained above the code line: the operator's below.

All input is transmitted online to the computer utility (and a copy for the dealer is stored on cassette) where it is processed overnight. The output is transmitted to the dealer before 8:00 A.M. the next morning, where it is recorded on tape. Daily output is generally coded, used for reference, checking, or operational control by employees familiar with the codes. The output may also be processed by

Table 19.11
Sample input dialogue

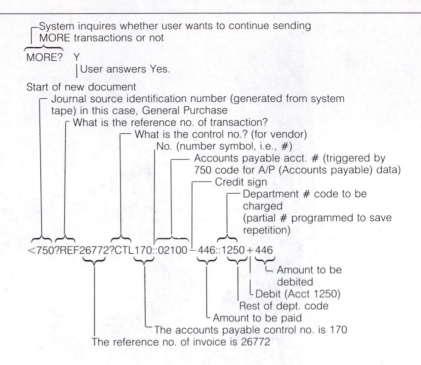

computer, according to a prescribed format programmed on a second cassette. This auto dealer has seven programs on tape for performing editing, summary, and utility functions.

The computer service also periodically generates and mails reports, such as a listing of deviations between forecasted and month-to-date sales, inventory control reports, and accounting reports, such as a balance sheet and profit and loss statement. One such report is shown in Table 19.12. This is a financial statement, completed and printed by computer monthly and annually. The balance sheet and profit and loss statement are necessary for businesses in all industrial sectors if they are public corporations, for they are required to file this information with the Securities and Exchange Commission. In this case, the auto dealer is not a public corporation but the information is useful for internal control, auditing, and tax purposes.

Another sample report, Analysis of Accounts Payable, is shown in Table 19.13. This report show transactions from Lohman Auto Parts, including invoice 26772 used in Table 19.11. In addition to listing date, source number, and invoice number of each transaction with vendors, the report shows total payments, the closing balance, and year-to-date purchases.

Note that this report is not coded. Since it is mailed, not sent by telecommunications, length is not an overriding cost consideration. Readability is more im-

Table 19.12

Blank financial statement report for auto dealer to be completed by computer

Table 19.13
Sample accounting report for auto dealer

```
                                        ANALYSIS  OF  ACCOUNTS  PAYABLE                                              10/31/79
                                               REPORT # 15                    ACCOUNT #   02100                      PAGE  12

  CTL                      TELEPHONE                  REF    OPENING           CURRENT               CLOSING     YEAR-TO-DATE
  #    VENDOR  NAME        NUMBER     DATE  SRC        #      BALANCE      PURCHASES   PAYMENTS        BALANCE     PURCHASES

  169  L C RADIATOR SHOP   524-4152  09-28                   261.00-
                                     10-04  750    38547                  17.50-
                                     10-04  750    39872                  20.00-
                                     10-04  750    39860                  24.75-
                                     10-19  600     1867                               261.00
                                     10-29  750    38980                  31.16-
                                     10-31  750    38991                  12.50-
                                     10-31  750    39756                  40.00-

                           * TOTAL *                                                              145.91-     2,358.97-

  170  LOHMAN AUTO PARTS   523-7559  09-28                    88.88-
                                     10-09  600     1721                                88.88
                                     10-17  750    26715                   6.28-
                                     10-22  750    26772                   4.46-
                                     10-22  750    26393                   4.47-
                                     10-22  750    26739                   4.52-
                                     10-23  750    26850                   2.19-
                                     10-24  750    26887                  40.50-
                                     10-24  750    26786                  44.40-
                                     10-24  750    26829                  46.65-
                                     10-25  750    26919                                14.49

                           * TOTAL *                                                              138.98-     2,968.73-

  171  LORDS LOCKSMITHING  524-3651  09-28                    43.00-
                                     10-09  600     1722                                43.00
                                     10-15  750     4241                   7.50-
                                     10-16  750     4079                  14.04-
                                     10-31  750     4096                  32.00-

                           * TOTAL *                                                               53.54-       871.15-

  173  MAC TOOLS OF LAS CRUCES 524-4535 09-28                   .00
                                     10-09  750   517435                  33.80-

                           * TOTAL *                                                               33.80-        73.11-

  174  MANNIES             524-3646  09-28                     .00
                                     10-24  750    12110                   2.34-

                           * TOTAL *                                                                2.34-        22.40-

  176  MESILLA VALLEY LINC MERC 526-2481 09-28              235.47-
                                     10-11  750     2306                   4.73-
                                     10-11  750    27320                  11.66-
                                     10-11  750    27337                  23.48-
                                     10-11  750    27310                  71.40-
                                     10-19  600     1878                               235.47
                                     10-23  750    27333                   1.91-
```

portant than condensation. But for daily input and output, coding is essential. Though data per transaction is small, total volume to be processed is large. Coding reduces input time, the need for storage space, the duration of computer processing, and the expense of data trasmission. In addition, coding classifications facilitate processing and reporting, and minimize the danger of ambiguity.

The way these reports reach the dealer (coded output transmitted by telecommunications, and noncoded reports sent by mail) is depicted in Figure 19.4.

Cost-benefit analysis for accounting applications

The costs and benefits of computer accounting services in this case study are summarized in Table 19.14. Though costs are $7,970 higher than tangible benefits, this dealer estimates intangible benefits at $52,000, making the system cost-effective. The manager claims that the major benefit of information provided by the computer is timely reporting, a benefit which can only be given a subjective value. Other benefits, however, are tangible. For example, 90 percent of claims against car warranties are paid within 14 days when processed by computer. The remaining 10 percent must be documented by mail with an average of 35 days elapsing before payment is received. The early payment of claims increases cash flow and working capital, producing a saving for this dealer of $4,200 annually.

Intangible benefits include increased inventory control. Information on inventory is of value to all businesses, but a car dealer's inventory represents many

Figure 19.4
Flow of data and information to the auto dealer

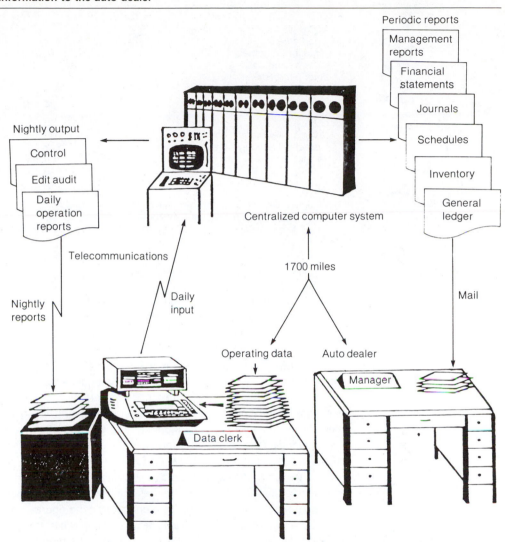

Periodic reports

Management reports

Financial statements

Journals

Schedules

Inventory

General ledger

Nightly output

Control

Edit audit

Daily operation reports

Centralized computer system

Telecommunications

1700 miles

Nightly reports

Daily input

Mail

Operating data

Auto dealer

Manager

Data clerk

thousand dollars per car type. Close monitoring of inventories, peak sales months, and customer preferences is essential in this high turnover and high cash-flow business.

Other compuer applications

In addition to utilization of a computer service for accounting reports, the car dealer has a minicomputer for making computations regarding auto financing. This mini serves the financial manager (sometimes called contract officer) of the firm in determining monthly payments for a client once auto and accessories are selected.

Table 19.14
Cost-benefit analysis for accounting applications (annual)

Cost

Payroll, including fringe benefits of part-time data clerk	$ 7,680
Rental of equipment	16,200
Transmission cost	420
Other (supplies, and so forth)	110
Total costs	$24,410

Benefits

Savings over manual costs of doing essential accounting and inventory reports	$12,240
Benefits from faster accounts receivable	4,200
	$16,440
Intangible benefits estimated by management of the additional reports and sales resulting from faster ordering	$52,000
Total benefits	$68,440

Monthly payments depend on a number of variables: rate of interest, trade-in value, credit-life or disability insurance costs, starting date of payments, cash down payment, number of payments, and so forth. Tax and license fees must also be reckoned. The computer speeds answers to such questions as, "What will be my monthly payment if I put $1,500 down instead of $500? If I play over 20 months instead of 24?" By hand, the answers to such questions take an average of 16–18 minutes to calculate, and errors occur on an average of once every 15 computations. The minicomputer takes about one minute to arrive at and print answers with an average of one input entry error per 1,000 entries. The use of the minicomputer thus saves considerable time for both client and financial manager and proves more accurate as well.

The minicomputer also assists in contract preparation. Once the amounts to be specified in a contract are decided between client and agent, a lapse time of 1–2 hours is required for contract preparation if the figures are typed into a contract by a secretary. This includes a wait period while the secretary completes priority assignments and 8–12 minutes of actual typing. The minicomputer can prepare the same contract document much faster. The financial manager selects the contract form desired by a one-digit code and keys in the variables in a given sequence. The content format is stored in computer memory. The entire document is printed with the variables inserted, ready for the customer's signature in approximately 3 minutes.

With each contract, numerous forms and letters are generated by the agency (see Table 19.15). Again the minicomputer is utilized. It inserts names and address of customer, odometer reading, stock number of auto sold, and so forth, in appropriate spaces in standard letter and document formats. For example, a let-

Table 19.15
Forms and letters prepared for auto dealer

Title application

Power of attorney

Odometer statement

Agreement on insurance

Credit-life and disability

Tax affidavit

Bank draft for mortgage and loan payoff

Thank-you letter to customer

ter of thanks to the customer is prepared, the content of which varies, depending on whether a new car or second-hand model was purchased. Once an operator keys the type of purchase, the computer collates prewritten paragraphs with customer name and address and prints a personalized letter and addressed envelope. (This is a word processing rather than data processing application, a topic to be discussed later in Chapter 23.)

This same mini is also used in inventory control and the preparation of reports on sales per salesperson. Data on sales is stored on a floppy disk, sales agents being represented by the last four digits of their social security numbers. From this stored information, weekly control reports are generated (see Table 19.16). These reports serve as the basis for managerial decisions on quotas, bonuses, vacation schedules, salesperson-of-the-month awards, and so forth.

A cost-benefit analysis of the mini appears in Table 19.17. In view of the fact that the life of the mini is an estimated five to ten years, the mini is clearly cost-effective.

The authors were surprised that payroll is not handled by computer at this dealership. It was explained that payroll was one of the first systems automated at this agency, but by NCR noncomputer data processing equipment. Neither the computer utility nor the mini has taken over the payroll application, a problem of integration to be discussed in Chapter 21.

Table 19.16
Content of one report generated from contract manager's minicomputer

For each salesperson
  Number of cars sold
    Old
    New
  Number of trucks sold
    Old
    New
  Number of deals financed
  Number of credit life policies sold
  Number of extended summer plans
  Ranking

Table 19.17
Cost-benefit analysis of minicomputer application

Cost
Equipment = $38,000; initial investment
Clerk plus fringe
benefits = $13,000/year
Supplies = $500/year

Tangible benefits
Savings of $26,000/year in clerical help

Intangible benefits
Speed of computer in answering "What if"
questions makes great
impression on customer
Reduces errors
Saves the time of contract officers

Summary and conclusions

This chapter introduced functional applications of computers in business. After listing common applications in accounting, administration, banking, insurance, manufacturing, marketing, and other business sectors, two recent specialized applications were introduced: **expert systems** and **public online data bases.**

Expert systems serve as consultants to management. They draw on a knowledge base of facts and heuristics relating to a limited problem domain. After soliciting information on the problem environment from the user (often through an interactive dialogue), expert systems then apply decision rules, many based on heuristics, to the circumstances described in order to recommend a problem solution.

Public data bases (contrasted with data bases maintained for the exclusive use of a single organization) also serve managers. A wide range of information services are currently available online from computer terminals. Fees for data base access may be based on a fixed monthly charge or depend on connect time.

A case study approach has been used to show functional applications in use. Computer applications in airline reservations, a travel agency, a hotel, and a car dealership were examined in this chapter. Table 19.18 summarizes chraracteristics of the applications discussed. In each example, terminals with online capabilities were used. This is by no means the universal mode of operation, though it is becoming increasingly common and proving cost-effective for a wide spectrum of businesses.

The examples cited varied in development effort, dialogue, and the required training of personnel. But all applications had the following advantages:

1. Customer service improved and expanded.
2. The level of efficiency was raised, as sales and office staff saved both time and effort recording information necessary for operations and control.
3. Load potential increased.
4. Information accuracy improved, enhancing the firm's image and reducing losses due to errors.
5. The query and interactive capabilities provided the right information at the right time to the right person.

Table 19.18
Summary of characteristics of functional applications
discussed in Chapter 19

Characteristic	Airline reservations		Hotel (non-reservation) applications	Auto dealer	
	Airline	Travel agent		Accounting	Contract management
Mode	OLRT	OLRT	OLRT	Online input and batch output	Online and batch
Use of teleprocessing	Yes	Yes	No	Yes	No
Nature of input	Coded	Coded	Menu	Coded but prompted	Formatted but not much coded
Nature of output	Coded	Coded	Listings, tables, and reports	Listings, tables, and reports	Letters, contracts, and reports
Levels of application	Operational	Operational	Operational and control management	Operational and control management	Operational and control management
Location of computer system	Owned Centralized	Accessed	On site and rented	Utility	Owned on site
Size of computer "on site"	Large	None	Mini	None	Mini
Data base	Own data base accessed	Central base accessed	Local data base	Data sent by teleprocessing	Local data base
Capital costs	High	None	Small	Almost none	Small

Key words

Accounting applications
Airline reservation application
Auto dealer application
Backroom accounting
Central reservation system
Contract manager applications
Cost-benefit analysis
Functional computer application

Expert systems
Heuristics
Hotel computer applications
Knowledge information processing
  systems (KIPS)
Online public data bases
SABRE system
Travel agency applications

Discussion questions

1. Give three examples of computer applications in different functional areas in business. In each case, identify:
   a. Output.
   b. Input.
   c. Equipment required.
   d. Mode of processing used (batch, OLRT, etc.).
   e. Functions performed.
   f. Benefits achieved.

2. Give examples of information systems that are used for:
   a. Calculations.
   b. Storage and retrieval.
   c. Report generation.
   d. Combination of above.

3. Describe briefly the operational information generated by all information systems for:
   a. Production.
   b. Marketing.
   c. Research development.
   d. Personnel.
   e. Accounting.
   f. Finance.

4. What are some of the problems of operational management in business that can best be resolved by a computerized system?

5. What are common business functions? Can data files be organized to correspond to these functions?

6. What effect will the point-of-sale (POS) terminal have on marketing?

7. Discuss functional applications of computers in the following industries:
   a. Airline.
   b. Banking.
   c. Construction.
   d. Insurance.
   e. Real estate.
   f. Retail.
   g. Agriculture.
   h. Government.

8. Identify functional applications relating to personnel records in a business firm.

9. List three computer applications. Identify their common characteristics.

10. List five functions in a business that are currently done manually and should be done by computer. In each case, specify the reasons you think the functions should be computerized.

11. Is it possible for a manual system, such as the airline reservation system in the United States, to be cost-effective? (Manual reservations exist in many countries, including the Soviet Union.) Specify the reasons for your answer.

12. Suppose that you were in charge of an MIS in a large car rental firm without any computer system. Suppose further, your firm has just been bought by a conglomerate owning an airline with a sophisticated airline reservation system. How could you adapt the airline reservation system to car rental operations? What functions could it perform?

13. Suppose that you were given a large interest in Hotel West described in this chapter. What other ways could the computer be used if any? Explain.

14. Why is it difficult to measure all the benefits of a functional system? Are there different approaches you would follow in different environments? Explain.

15. List five new computer applications in business in the last two years.

16. For what level of management and for what functions are expert systems most appropriate? Give examples in manufacturing and other businesses.

17. In your opinion, what is impeding the widespread use of expert systems? How can use constraints be removed?

18. Widespread use of expert systems is not feasible or desirable. Comment on that statement.

19. Give examples of how public online data bases can serve management.

20. If a feasibility study in your firm showed that access to a public online data base would cost $60,000 in initial cost, and $10–15,000 per year thereafter, would you recommend the service?

Exercise

1. How would you classify Exercise 1, Chapter 10? Is it functional? Is the application at the operational level?

Selected annotated bibliography

Eliason, Alan L., and Kent D. Kitts. *Business Computer Systems and Applications*. 2d ed. Chicago: Science Research Associates, 1979, 348 pp.
This text examines operational applications in business. In each case, the application is described, output and input displayed, data elements in the file listed, systems flowcharts presented, and the implications to management discussed. These are not case studies but actual data is used. This book is a detailed walk-through of the design stage of the development process.

Flanagan, Patrick. "Need Information? You Name It, Data Bases Supply It." *Office Administration and Automation* 64, no. 3 (April 1983), pp. 42–48.
An excellent survey of the many data bases that can be accessed by a terminal or a telephone line. This article discusses General Electric Information, the Dow Jones News/Retrieval, and the *Wall Street Journal* Transcript Service.

Gessford, John Evans. *Modern Information Systems Designed for Decision Support.* Reading, Mass.: Addison-Wesley Publishing, co., 1980, 511 pp.

This text has six chapters on computer applications in business, including systems for administration, payment, financial control, operations data, planning, and strategic information. The applications are described with varying detail, but many are explained by flowcharts and lists of file contents.

Haden, Douglas H. *Total Business Systems: Computers in Business.* St. Paul, Minn.: West Publishing, 1978, 463 pp.

This textbook has chapters on computer applications, retail systems, one-statement booking, motels, hotels, Standard Oil of Ohio, Norwich Pharmaceutical, Cuyahoga County Welfare Department, Blue Shield, Provident Insurance, and United Airlines. These applications cover businesses of all sizes using different modes of processing (online, OLRT, and batch). The cases are well researched and described.

"Hotel Systems." *Which Computer?* 6, no. 7 (October 1982), pp. 50–55.

This is a British journal and its context is the United Kingdom, but the principles discussed are appliable to the United States. The article discusses processing needs, processing equipment, and staff training for three categories of hotels: less than 50 beds, 50–300 beds, and over 300 beds. Billing, POS terminals in restaurants, and automatic telephone accounting are applications examined. Numerous case studies are cited.

Michaelson, Robert, and Donald Michie. "Expert Systems in Business." *Datamation* 29, no. 11 (November 1983), pp. 240–46.

The basics of expert systems and many myths that surround them are discussed. TAXADVISOR and TAXMAN are two of the systems described.

McLeod, Raymond, Jr. *Management Information Systems,* 2nd ed. Chicago: Science Research Associates, 1983, 669 pp.

Part Four of this book describes functional information systems used by managers of marketing, manufacturing and finance companies. Both input and output subsystems of each functional system are examined.

Stefik, Mark et al. "The Organization of Expert Systems." *Artificial Intelligence* 18, no. 2 (March 1982), pp. 135–73.

An excellent overview of expert systems and expert system applications.

Thierauf, Robert J. *Effective Management Information Systems.* Columbus, Ohio: Charles E. Merrill Publishing, 1984, 558 pp.

This book combines a theoretical and practical look at effective management information systems. Chapters 12–15 discuss marketing, manufacturing, accounting and finance, and personnel subsystems.

Planning and control applications

20

The biggest single need in computer technology is not for improved circuitry, or enlarged capacity, or prolonged memory, or miniaturized containers, but for better questions and better use of answers.

Author unknown

This chapter contrasts computer assistance in decision making for control and planning with computer applications at the operational level as described in Chapter 19. First, the chapter classifies control decisions, describing the types of problems computers can solve. Then data needs at different levels of management are analyzed. Finally, special design features required by decision support systems for middle and top management are examined, features not required for functional applications. **Spreadsheets,** a sample planning application of computers, are introduced. The information system used by American Airlines for planning and control is also presented as a case study. The chapter concludes with a brief discussion on **artificial intelligence** in answer to the question, "Will computers replace management in making planning and control decisions in the future?"

Management decisions classified

A decision is a choice among alternatives. Some business decisions are judgmental, based on intuition. But many others can be stated in terms of decision rules, the problems being well structured and conceptually simple. Software used to make programmed decisions is possible for this latter type of problem, the assistance of computers being particularly valuable when structured problems must be solved routinely and repeatedly. A **nonprogrammed decision** is generally required for nonstructured, complex problems with variables that cannot easily be quantified.

To answer the question "What control and planning decisions can be and should be made by information systems?" one must first classify decisions and then check the applicability of computerized solutions to each classification. Robert Anthony divides business decision making for control and planning into operational control, management control, and strategic planning:

1. **Operational control** is the process of assuring that specific tasks are carried out effectively and efficiently.
2. **Management control** is the process by which managers assure that resources are obtained and used effectively and efficiently in the accomplishment of the organization's objectives.
3. **Strategic planning** is the process of deciding on objectives of the organization, on changes in these objectives, on the resources used to attain these objectives, and on the policies that are to govern the acquisition, use, and disposition of these resources.[1]

When analyzing decisions at each of these levels, one finds that problems arise requiring both programmed and nonprogrammed solutions. For example, prediction models can be programmed for management control. However, hiring, layoff, and the assignment of personnel are nonprogrammed management control decisions for, at the present time, no decision theory exists that permits the statement of personnel decision rules. This may change. In 1969, Herbert Simon predicted that by 1985, "we shall have acquired an extensive and empirically tested theory of human cognitive processes and their interaction with human emotions, attitudes and values."[2] And Norbert Wiener predicts that whatever humans can do, the computer of the future will also do, though he does not specify a point in time when information systems will automate all decision making.[3]

Not all experts accept these views, however. Many believe that there are areas of business decision making that can never be automated. Psychologists such as W. R. Reitman call such problems "ill-defined."[4] The term "ill-formed" is used by computer scientist L. Uhr.[5] In the context of architectural design, Ritter refers to the "wicked problem."[6] "Many management commentators prefer the classification "ill-structured."

Though time may prove Simon and Wiener correct, at present, individuals, not computers, make decisions that require the ability to recognize and infer patterns for nonquantifiable data variables, especially human variables. Table 20.1 rep-

[1] Robert N. Anthony, *Planning and Control Systems: A Framework for Analysis* (Cambridge, Mass.: Harvard University, Division of Research, Graduate School of Business Administration, 1965), pp. 16–18.

[2] J. M. Bergey and R. C. Slover, "Administration in the 1980s," *S.A.M. Advanced Management Journal* 34, no. 2 (April 1969), p. 31.

[3] Ibid., p. 26.

[4] W. R. Reitman, *Cognition and Thought* (New York: John Wiley & Sons, 1965), pp. 148–64.

[5] L. Uhr, *Pattern Recognition, Learning and Thought* (Englewood Cliffs, N.J.: Prentice-Hall, 1973), pp. 268–84.

[6] For an excellent discussion of Ritter's characteristics of the problem, see Lawrence F. Peters and Leonard L. Tipp, "Is Software Design Wicked?" *Datamation* 22, no. 8 (May 1978), p. 127. See also Derek Partridge, "A Philosophy of 'Wicked' Problem Implementation," *Proceedings of the AISB/GI Conference on Artificial Intelligence* (Hamburg, West Germany: 1978), p. 245.

Table 20.1
Classification of decisions

Function / Type of decision	Operational control	Management control	Strategic planning
Programmed	1	3	5
Nonprogrammed	2	4	6

NOTE   Though all problems in Cells 1, 3, and 5 are theoretically programmable, the shaded area approximates current computerized problem-solving effort.

resents the structure of decision making today showing the amount of decision making theoretically programmable that is actually computerized. The actual percentage of programmed versus nonprogrammed decision making varies from one industry to another, but approximately 80 percent of all decisions are programmable, given the current state of the art, especially in such areas as accounting, finance, and manufacturing.

Peter Keene and Michael Morton, who equate structure with programmed decisions and nonstructure with nonprogrammed decisions, would add an intermediate layer to Table 20.1: semistructured problems. "These are decisions where managerial judgment . . . will not be adequate, perhaps because of the size of the problem or the computational complexity and precision needed to solve it. On the other hand, the model or data alone are also inadequate because the solution involves judgment and subjective analysis. Under these conditions the manager *plus* the system can provide a more effective solution then either alone."[7]

Keene and Morton also point out that there are no rigid divisions between cells as shown in Table 20.1 since factors, such as time available for decision making, may require a nonprogrammed solution when the writing of a programmed solution would also be possible. In addition, the use of operations research techniques and the development of new technology continually blur arbitrary divisions: yesterday's ill-structured problem may be solved by computer today.

Table 20.2, listing sample control and planning business problems that fall into structured, semistructured, and nonstructured categories, should be studied with Keene and Morton's criticism of arbitrary divisions in mind. The chart is included to provide examples of applications with programmed solutions, and to show types of problems for which software is of no assistance to managers in decision making at the present time.

Decision-making stages

How can problems solvable by computer be identified? How can management determine whether programmed solutions are feasible? Problem solving, accord-

[7] Peter G. W. Keene and Michael S. Scott Morton, *Decision Support Systems: An Organizational Perspective* (Reading, Mass.: Addison-Wesley Publishing Co., 1978), p. 86.

Table 20.2
Sample decisions classified by level of decision making

Type of decision	Operational control	Management control	Strategic planning
Structured	Inventory control Accounts payable Accounts receivable Queuing Sequencing Plant scheduling Transportation models Assignment models	PERT/GERT for project control Linear and mathematical programming for resource allocation Prediction models Inventory control Break-even, marginal or instrumental analyses	Resource allocation using mathematical programming
Semistructured	Cash management Bond trading	Short-term forecasting Budgeting Marketing models Long-term forecasting	Capital acquisition Portfolio analyses New product planning Mergers and acquisitions
Unstructured	Designing products	Hiring and firing Predicting consumer preference	R & D planning

ing to John Dewey, requires answers to three questions. What is the problem? What are the alternatives? Which alternative is best? This corresponds to Herbert Simon's division of the decision-making process into three stages: intelligence, design, and choice (see Figure 20.1). Only after gathering intelligence and analyzing options will the structure of the problem be revealed and the applicability of information system decision models become apparent. Each of these stages is described in greater detail below.

Intelligence[8]

Intelligence in this context is defined as in the military: the gathering of information. Data must be collected on objectives, organizational constraints, resources available, and on the external environment (for example, competition and legal framework). Study of this data, recognizing patterns and trends, leads to the next phase, design.

Design

When examining alternative courses of action, mathematical and statistical models for decision making should be considered. See Table 20.3 for a list of models commonly used in solving business problems. The models fall into three categories: those that utilize the data base but can be manually processed; those that utilize the computational capability of computers but utilize external data; and those that process computer data kept in the data base.

The first group includes simple prediction models, trend analysis, and break-even analysis where simple plotting of data stored in the data base is sufficient.

---

[8] For an excellent discussion of this phase of decision making, see Gordon B. Davis, *Management Information Systems* (New York: McGraw Hill, 1974), pp. 322–30.

**Figure 20.1
Stages of decision making**

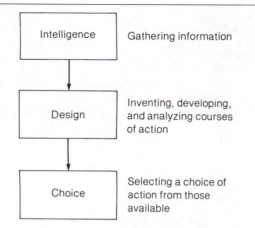

Intelligence	Gathering information
Design	Inventing, developing, and analyzing courses of action
Choice	Selecting a choice of action from those available

Models requiring the computing capability of computers but utilizing external data form a far larger group. PERT and GERT for project management fall into this category. Even though only simple mathematical operators are needed (add, subtract, multiply, divide, compare), numerous computations are required, and computations for each set of data are run repeatedly during the life of the project to produce a variety of reports (sorted by earliest target date, by highest slack, by management responsibility, and so forth). In addition, speed is a factor of considerable importance. For models with similar characteristics, a computer is indispensable.[9]

Mathematical programming for resource allocation is another model in the second group. Computers are valuable in solving this type of problem, for not only must a large number of calculations be performed, but the calculations themselves are cumbersome, requiring coefficients correct to stated decimal places. The mathematics involving matrix manipulation is also complicated. Here again the data utilized is primarily external.

Repetitive calculations are also needed for simulation models and sensitivity analysis, problems that again are best solved by computer.

The final group of models includes those that utilize both the data base and processing capabilities of computers. An example is inventory models where data on demand, lead time, and supplies are provided by the data base and numerous complex calculations are made.

After analyzing the problem, it may become apparent that information systems cannot provide a solution. Instead, data is manipulated, risks evaluated, and alternative solutions postulated based on management's past experience, knowl-

---

[9]Computer programs for OR (operations research) models are often provided by the vendor of large computers or sold by software houses. In the case of CPM/PERT, there are some 87 programs available. See Perry Peterson, "Project Control Systems," *Datamation* 25, no. 6 (June 1979), pp. 147–53.

Table 20.3
Taxonomy of decision-making models

1. Using data base:
   Simple prediction models
   Break-even analysis
   Marginal analysis
   Incremental analysis

2. Using computing capability of computer:

PERT/GERT	Sequencing
Mathematical	Plant scheduling
programming	Plant location
Queuing	Exponential smoothing
Inventory	Transportation models
Simulation	Assignment models
Sensitivity analysis	

3. Using computer and data base:
   Budget simulation
   Inventory
   Markovian chain
   Multiple regression for prediction

edge, perception, creativity, and intuition. Several solutions should be developed, including solutions with probability associations indicating the chance of success for each decision.

Choice

The final decision will be generated by computer when information systems are applicable. In semistructured situations, a model may be of assistance by classifying and displaying relevant information that will aid management in making a nonprogrammed decision. For example, a sensitivity analysis may indicate the consequences of changes in selected variables and parameters. Nonstructured problems will require judgmental decisions.

Note that in all types of decisions, choice is essentially a human activity. Even programmed decisions are based on rules and criteria originally established by the decision maker.

Decision support system

When information systems are used to assist management in problem solving, the term **decision support system (DDS)** is used to describe the human-machine interplay in reaching decisions. In spite of the predictions of early commentators (Leavitt and Whistler in 1958;[10] Simon in 1965),[11] computers have not replaced management, not even middle management, though it is argued that growth at this middle level has not kept pace with management growth at other levels of

---

[10] H. J. Leavitt and T. L. Whistler, "Management in the 1980s," *Harvard Business Review* 36, no. 6 (November–December 1958), pp. 41–48.
[11] Herbert Simon, *The Shape of Automation for Man and Management* (New York: Harper & Row, 1965).

corporate organization. Instead, computers complement management, aiding, not eliminating, the decision maker. Today managers rely on computers ranging from small microcomputers to sophisticated OLRT systems with a DBMS accessible by conversational high languages.

Differing informational needs

How do planning and control decisions vary from one organizational level of decision making to another? Entire textbooks have been written on this subject. But briefly, planning by top management determines *what* must be done, direction by middle management specifies *how* it is to be done, and operations *do* it. The feedback of *what* is done in operations is then evaluated and controlled. These activities and the levels of management responsible are graphically illustrated in Figure 20.2, with arrows indicating the continual recycling of information throughout the corporate structure. This is a theoretical framework. In practice, the responsibilities of management vary from one industry to another and depend on management style.

Each level of decision making for planning and control requires different data. For example, Table 20.4 shows informational needs according to functions at the levels of operational control, managerial control, and strategic planning. Before information systems can be designed, the nature of information required at each level of decision making must be explicitly stated in operational and quantitative terms. Variables include: type of questions asked, time horizon of data, the information environment, degree of quantification, degree of detail, mode of operation, and display media.

**Figure 20.2
Functions of planning and control by different levels of management**

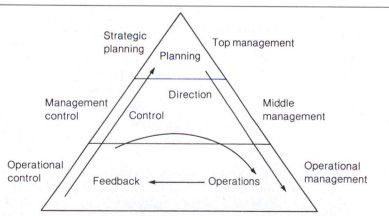

At left: Anthony's framework of business decision making.
At right: Corresponding levels of management.

Table 20.4
Information needed for operational control, management control, and strategic planning

Type of information	Operational control	Management control	Strategic planning
Accounting	Accounts payable Accounts receivable Costing	Budgeting reports with discrepancies and exceptions	Budget projections
Finance	Cash on hand	Investment alternatives	Long-term financial needs
Manufacturing	Engineering specs Work-in-progress Work to be started	Equipment loading and utilization Optimization of resources Performance measurement	Product enlargement Resource allocation
Marketing	Sales orders (A/R) Sales distribution	Projection of sales	Projection of markets and products
Purchasing	Inventory on hand Physical distribution Orders (A/P)	Inventory control Vendor evaluation	Planning new sources for purchasing
Personnel	Personnel records	Union negotiation	Manpower projection
R&D	R&D work-in-progress and its schedule	R&D progress reports for monitoring	Evaluation of long-range pure and applied research

Type of question asked

A computerized information system must answer different types of questions according to the levels of management being served. Operational management wants descriptive responses to questions that ask What is? Planners want answers to What if? (for example, What will happen if parameter X is increased by 2 percent?).

The distinction is important to systems development because different resources are required for solutions to different types of questions. A descriptive report can best be written in COBOL, RPG, or such languages as BASIC, PL/1, APL, or FORTRAN. "What if?" questions usually require simulation models using languages like GPSS and SIMSCRIPT. Query and conversational languages, such as those described in Chapter 3, are also appropriate for planning and control. In addition, familiarity with such special techniques as the Critical Success Factors (CSF) and Business System Planning (BSP) developed by IBM, is required of analysts developing systems for planning and control. Unfortunately, analysts and programmers specialize. Those who are knowledgeable and skillful in designing descriptive information systems generally have little experience with languages and techniques appropriate for planning models.

Time horizon of needed data

Operational management is concerned with current information. Today or this week. The timeliness of data can be crucial. Strategic planning looks ahead 1–10 years, depending on the volatility of the business. Management control falls in between. Current data must be compared with horizontal and longitudinal data to identify undesirable discrepancies in order for corrective action to be triggered. The time horizon is generally 1–5 years, though some middle managers evaluate monthly or yearly data only.

Informational environment

The source of information for decision making varies at the three levels of management. Generally, internal information relating to performance is generated from the data base for operational control, though some external information, such as the price of raw materials and lead time for delivery, may be required.

As one moves upward in management hierarchy, the need for internal information decreases and more external information must be evaluated in reaching decisions. Strategic planning requires data from demographic and industry studies, as well as information on sources and suppliers of materials, data regarding government regulations (federal and state), data on competitors' policies, and data on customer preferences. Formerly such external data was not included in the data base. It was too voluminous. The cost of converting it into machine-readable form was excessive, and retrieval systems were inadequate. Recent advances in computer technology have altered this situation. There has been a drop in hardware costs, and data, such as industry reports or macro data on the economy, is now available on tape or readable by OCR readers.

Retrieval of relevant information, however, remains a problem. It can be done to some extent by a manager on a terminal using conversational and dialogue languages such as those discussed in Chapter 3. Computer input on microfilm also aids in the retrieval of management information in much the same manner as online inquiry systems. In addition, special computer programs can be written to retrieve information. But then there is the problem of analyzing and interpreting the information for its policy and planning implications. This is part of intelligence in decision making referred to earlier and also part of nonprogrammed decision making.

Degree of quantification

Whereas operational and managerial control requires numeric data, strategic planning places a heavy reliance on subjective data, such as qualitative evaluations of products and services.

Degree of detail

Operational management needs detailed information such as sales per sales representative, quantity of each product sold, or cost figures for each unit in production. At the level of management control, figures on branch or division performance are required. For strategic planning, information must be further aggregated, providing decision makers with figures for the organization as a whole. Once the lowest level of aggregation is identified and common definitions of data elements accepted by management throughout the organization, software can process data at any level of aggregation specified. Often operational information must be accurate to two decimal places. But future projections cannot be calculated with the same degree of accuracy. Tolerance ranges for information accuracy are another difference in the degree of detail required by the three levels of management.

Another aspect of detail is **exception reporting.** This is information on deviations, both good and bad, from expected or targeted values. Such deviations may alert managerial control to problems in need of solution, or may result in rewards, such as bonuses when sales exceed quotas. Sometimes exceptional reporting triggers a decision by top management to revise policies and procedures.

An information system that provides exception reporting saves middle management from having to monitor *all* phases of operation. The use of information systems for making decisions based on exceptional data is known as **management by exception.**

Mode of operations

By definition, real-time systems are those that generate information so fast that the results of computations are useful in guiding a physical process. OLRT has its primary use at the operational level for businesses with continuous processes where changes in the environment will have important consequences.

Strategic planners in the past generally relied on overnight batch processing. Today's planners, however, are more dependent on instantaneous results, utilizing the inquiry capability of OLRT. This capability can be provided by a war room or a communications center, though the reduced cost of terminals and minis means many managers today are installing OLRT in their corporate offices.

Display media

All levels of management use printouts for long reports, and will, in all likelihood, have access to a CRT and/or a typewriter terminal for short reports. Operational and control management utilize interactive display terminals sometimes with plotting and graphing capabilities. In addition, microfilm or microfiche units to display historical or archival data are frequently employed. Strategic planners have a greater need for graphic displays. Since their requirements need not be online information, the graphics can be generated.

Management style and threshold

There are still other factors which contribute to the type of information needed by management: style and the threshold of information desired by an individual manager. Driver and Rowe[12] classify managers into four groups: the **flexible manager** who relies heavily on intuition and personal affability; the **decisive manager** who makes quick decisions after examining alternatives and summary data, satisfied with a "good enough" decision; the **hierarchical manager** who makes up his mind after evaluating lots of data, seeking the "best solution"; and the **integrative manager** who uses logic to sift through data and alternatives.

[12] Michael Driver and Alan Rowe, "Decision Making Styles: A New Approach to Management Decision Making," in *Behavioral Problems in Organization,* ed. Cary Copper (Englewood Cliffs, N.J.: Prentice-Hall, 1979), chapter 6.

Figure 20.3
Different information thresholds

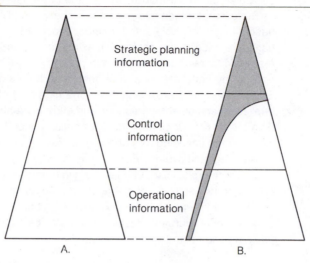

These differences in style pose a dilemma for designers of information systems because tailoring a system to one style of management may mean redevelopment when managers change.

The **threshold of information** desired also varies from one manager to another. In Figure 20.3 the shaded area A represents a manager who relies on exceptional information, staff reports, and summary presentations prepared specifically for top management. In contrast, B is a manager at the top level who also utilizes selected detailed information on control and operations in reaching decisions. Of course, many other variations exist, the shape of the shaded area depending on an individual manager's personality, style, span of control, and professional background, as well as on factors such as the complexity of the organization and the confidence of the manager in the abilities of subordinates. A good information system is one that can be easily modified when changes in management style or threshold occur.

Independent or integrated systems?

From the preceding discussion, it is clear that managers at the three levels of decision making require different information. Operational control needs are largely descriptive, internal, current, quantitative, and detailed, demanding a high degree of accuracy. Strategic planning information is primarily prescriptive, external, qualitative, aggregated, directed toward the future, with a wide range of accuracy permissible. Management control lies in between. These different needs suggest that three separate information systems might be advisable. Indeed, managers have often insisted on tailored information systems for they have not wanted to share information nor been willing to conform to the rules, definitions, and procedures of common information systems. Computer analysts have encouraged this posture in the past because of limited processing and memory capability of computers and their inability to manage large data bases.

But computer technology has now changed. DBMSs have been developed to handle large data bases and memory capacity has expanded. At the same time, hardware prices have dropped, making use of the new technology economically feasible. Meanwhile, problems with parallel independent systems have been recognized by both managers and analysts. The inability to relate data at different levels is a serious drawback. So is the high cost of parallel systems in terms of duplicated equipment, personnel, and effort in creating, verifying, and maintaining data bases. Most important, the information generated by parallel systems is often inconsistent: impeding, not abetting, decision making.

An integrated system, on the other hand, collects and validates raw data only once before processing. The resulting information is refined and reformatted, percolating to higher levels of management, the same basic information being shared by all bona fide users. The next chapter, Chapter 21, discusses integrated systems in detail. But first, design features to be included for the special needs of planning and control will be discussed.

Design features for planning and control

Design features specifically required for a decision support system at the level of planning and control include access to the data base through data management, and both analytical and interactive capabilities.

Data management

In complex business environments, a DBMS capability is required if planning and control decision makers are to effectively use the data base. But planners also need languages that are analytical and have conversational capabilities, such as those discussed in Chapter 3, and also languages with query capabilities for a DBMS, such as the software discussed in Chapter 9. There are software and languages that have been designed for business decision making approaching such capabilities. TROLL and TSP, for example, have excellent econometric capabilities though they do not have very good capabilities for accessing and using large data bases.

Analytical and modeling capability

Available data that cannot be analyzed has little value. Analysis may be done by statistical packages (including packages utilizing standard operations research techniques), or specially written software. Programming should correspond to the human thought process and aid decision makers by suggesting solutions. The system should also encourage "factoral" thinking. That is, large problems should be factored (subdivided) into smaller subsets of decisions. Also, the computer should assist managers in interpretation, what Newell and Simon describe as "bringing the problem-solving methods into effective correspondence with each problem-solving situation."[13]

Many systems are being developed to help planning and control managers analyze problems. For example, STRATANAL is useful in planning corporate strategies and GIDS (Generalized Intelligent Decision System) has the "ability to comprehend English-like queries and subsequently formulate models, interface appropriate data with these models, and execute the models to produce some facts or expectations about the problem under consideration."[14] AIDS (An Interactive Decision System), written in common BASIC, rationalizes the judgmental process on a broad range of topics,[15] and GMIS (General Management Information System) uses an interactive relational data base management system and a high level language SEQUEL (discussed in Chapter 3) to give it enhanced analytical and statistical capabilities.[16]

Interactive capability

A decision support system that utilizes human-computer interaction (a dialogue with the computer) is particularly helpful for problems with the following characteristics, problems commonly found in planning and control.

1. The problems are not known in advance.
2. Solutions are open-ended (that is, there is no single correct answer).
3. Problems can be factored and tackled incrementally.
4. Limited human patience is a major consideration.
5. The data is rapidly changing.
6. The policymaker's perception is also changing over time.
7. The problem is complex and needs raw data analysis, transformations, projections, and so forth.
8. The environment is dynamic.
9. Decisions must be made rapidly.

Though problems at the operational level often meet the above criteria, a decision support system is primarily used for decisions that are more abstract—complex problems as found in management control. A DSS is also used for prob-

---

[13] Allen Newell and H. A. Simon, *Human Problem Solving* (Englewood Cliffs, N.J.: Prentice-Hall, 1972), p. 91.

[14] Robert H. Bonczek, Clyde W. Holsapple, and Andrew B. Whinston, "Computer-Based Support of Organizational Decision Making," *Decision Sciences* 10, no. 2 (April 1979), pp. 268–91.

[15] Peter R. Newsted and Bayard E. Wynne, "Augmenting Man's Judgment with Interactive Computer Systems," *International Journal of Man-Machine Studies* 8, no. 1 (January 1976), pp. 29–59.

[16] See Thomas D. Truitt and Stuart B. Mindlin, *An Introduction to Nonprocedural Languages: Using NPL,* (New York: McGraw Hill, 1983), 493 pp. This book also has appendixes on FOCUS, RAMS, NOMADZ, and INQUIRE. For another excellent reference on query languages, including SQL, see British Computer Society, *Query Languages: A Unified Approach,* (London: Heyden and Sons, 1981), 105 pp.

lems in strategic planning that need to be graphically portrayed for easy assimilation and comprehension.

Designing interface equipment that provides interactive capabilities requires a knowledge of human engineering. One strategy, for example, is to lock out the user at selected points in the human-machine dialogue. This forces the user to concentrate on the problem for a given time period before proceeding with the solution. Presumably the delay ensures better decisions. Some critics, however, believe delays, intentional or otherwise, add a factor of distress which negatively affects the quality of decisions. Unfortunately, studies of human behavior have a long gestation period. By the time issues are resolved, computer technology has changed and the answer is often irrelevant.

Sample planning application: Spreadsheet use

A good example of a computer program to assist management in planning and control is the use of electronic spreadsheets. Because they are used extensively in planning, spreadsheets are sometimes called planning language. A computer program that does spreadsheet calculations replaces the drudgery of manual ledger-sheet calculations and reduces errors. Furthermore, the computer allows a manager to ask "What if?" questions, and will then calculate a whole new set of values in answer. For example, a manager might want to know how a change in the rate of inflation or change in interest rates might affect the firm's financial ratios. Answers will be swiftly calculated following any changes to the parameters of the spreadsheet matrix on the terminal screen.

Table 20.5
Selected list of applications of electronic spreadsheets

Administration
  Employee benefit strategies
  Feasibility studies
  Personnel needs
  Salary structures
  Union negotiations

Finance
  Budgeting
  Cash flow
  Choice of financing strategy
    purchase, lease, rent or
    combination)
  Income statements
  Investment analysis
  Portfolio analysis
  Profit planning

Marketing
  Advertising policies
  Planning of market strategies
  Pricing policies
  Product mix
  Sales forecasts

Manufacturing
  Capacity planning
  Cost analysis
  Facilities planning
  Labor mix
  Plant configurations
  Production mix
  Scheduling

Planning
  Acquisition strategies
  Goal setting
  New venture strategies
  Organizational configuration
  Strategic planning

Figure 20.4
Evolution of spreadsheets

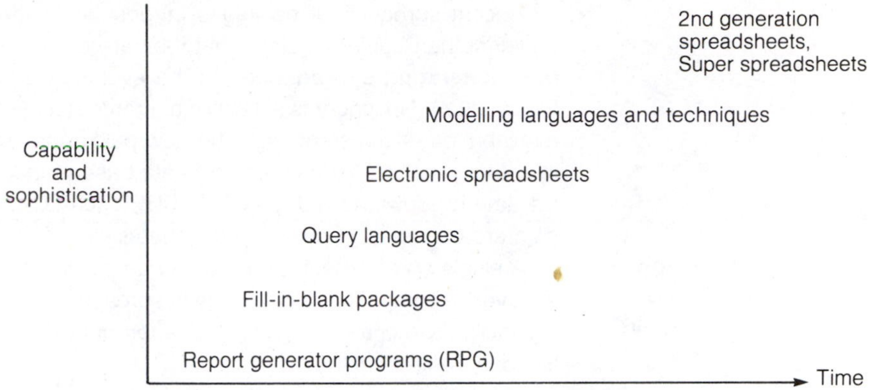

A common use of spreadsheets is forecasting—each row in the matrix will represent a variable, each column a period of time. Spreadsheets can also be used for budget preparation, cash flow status, currency conversions, expense reports, job-cost analysis, income statements, profit plans, salary costs, and sales forecasts. Other applications are listed in Table 20.5. Note that spreadsheets have functional applications as well as planning and control applications. They are useful whenever tabular (grid or matrix) calculations are called for.

Most commonly, spreadsheet programs are purchased as packages. VISI-CAL, the earliest package on the market, derived from earlier fill-in-the-blank programs and languages (such as RPG) designed to assist managers. Query languages were a further evolution. When VISICAL was introduced, the benefits of electronic spreadsheets were quickly recognized. By 1983 VISICAL had sold over ½ million copies and many competitors had entered the market, including CUFFS,

Table 20.6
Criteria for selecting a spreadsheet package

Cost
Support
Documentation
Screen characteristics
Systems characteristics
Edit functions
File handling
Menu characteristics
Search method
Calculations performed
Output characteristics
Graphic capabilities
Color choice
Corporate data base integration
Teleprocessing integration
Word-processing integration
Hardware requirements

EMPIRE, EXPRESS, IFPS, MULTIPLAN, MODEL, and SIMUPLAN. In fact, over 50 spreadsheet packages could be purchased in 1983.

Recent spreadsheet packages introduced to the market are so much more powerful than earlier versions that they are called **super spreadsheets,** or **second generation spreadsheets.** (The evolution of spreadsheets is illustrated in Figure 20.4). No longer is a 128K mainframe necessary—spreadsheets today are available on microcomputers. The new packages are also user friendly and flexible. Many include text processing, data base management systems, color graphics, and windows. LOTUS, 1–2–3, SUPERCALC, and VISICALC-advanced version are examples of super spreadsheets.

A single spreadsheet package can be purchased by a firm and shared by executives. Another option is to access spreadsheet packages through a time-sharing facility. Criteria for selecting an appropriate spreadsheet for a given firm are listed in Table 20.6.

Case study: Airline use of systems for planning and control

Chapter 19 described a functional application of an airline information system: reservations. This section will briefly describe AAIMS used by American Airlines for planning and control. This system, which was called AEMS (Airline Econometric Modelling System) when it was first introduced, was operational as early as 1970. By 1972, the system adopted a new name, AAIMS (An Analytical Information Management System), while its jurisdiction extended to include operations research modeling, and reports on traffic analysis, freight administration, flight departures, maintenance engineering, and economic regulation needed for management control and strategic planning. Studies and forecasts performed by the system appear in Table 20.7. The system also performed many statistical routines, some of these being listed in Table 20.8.

AAIMS is user-operated and user-controlled, requiring no knowledge of programming. The system prompts managers in an interactive conversational mode using industry terminology, not computer jargon. It is a computational system with a repertoire of 60 verbs, including DISPLAY, PLOT, MINUS, and TIMES—the computations being tested for validity and consistency. The AAIMS system is also a retrieval system, using coded commands. For example, P5; AA; SYS; 5136; 6401 will generate an operating expense quarterly report (code P5) for American

Table 20.7
Studies and forecasts in AAIMS

Aircraft utilization	Productivity measurement
Financial ratios	Revenue/yield
Load factors	Seating configuration
Market shares	Traffic and capacity growth
Operating statistics	Unit costs

Table 20.8
Statistical routines used in AAIMS

Graphic analysis	*Time series analysis*
Time-series plots	Exponential smoothing
Scatter diagrams	Moving averages
Statistical analysis	Period-to-period ratios
Correlation	Year-end totals
Descriptive statistics	Year-over-year ratios
Regression	

Airline (AA) systems (SYS) personnel expenses (code 5136) related to the DC–9–30 (code 6401).

This description of AAIMS is already outdated. Like all computerized information systems, AAIMS has continually evolved and improved. Will such planning systems ever replace middle or top management? What are the limits of a computerized information system? This chapter concludes with a discussion on artificial intelligence, the capacity of machines to perform functions normally associated with human intelligence.

Artificial intelligence

A major problem in a discussion of whether computers will ever match human intelligence is defining the term *intelligence*. Computers are intelligent if intelligence is reasoning, adaptability, or the ability to solve structured problems, to work mathematical equations, or prove theorems in geometry. The computer's intelligence even outstrips that of humans (according to this definition), insofar as a computer possesses the ability to process numerical data at superhuman speed without error or fatigue, and the ability to store and retrieve far larger amounts of data than can be handled by the human mind.

Sometimes a capacity to learn is defined as a key characteristic of intelligence. Can computers learn? Arthur Samuel answered this question affirmatively with his checkers program in the 1950s. This program included rules of thumb to identify and incorporate successful game strategies so that the computer improved its game in time. At first, Samuel, a mediocre player, beat the machine, but the computer "learned" and soon was able to defeat checker champions.

When defining intelligence as the ability to think and be creative, again the question of semantics arises. Does a problem such as, "What is the minimum number of colors needed for countries on a world map so that no two adjacent areas have the same color?" require thinking? If so, machines can think since the answer, 4, was generated by computer in 1977. Computers have constructed original proofs in Euclidean geometry and can design electric motors, activities many professionals define as "creative."

Alan Turing's solution to this controversy has been to establish a test for thinking. He suggested an individual match wits with a computer and with another person communicating through a terminal. If computer performance cannot be distinguished from human performance, the machine thinks. There have been many applications of Turing's test premise. In 1978, for example, David Levy played chess against a computer version, Chess 4.7, at an international chess match. He was unable to determine whether he was competing against a human or machine, a proof according to Turing, that a computer can think.

One criticism of Turing's test lies in the nature of communication used. But perhaps the premise of the test is also at fault. Why should a machine have to be equal to humans before it can be called creative and intelligent? After all, a plane cannot fly as well as a bird, but nevertheless flies. Without doubt, computers today contribute greatly to management decision making and problem solving. Machine intelligence, called **artificial intelligence,** still has a limited problem-solving range. But perhaps computers will be used to make design improvements in hardware and software, so that future computers may eventually equal or even surpass human problem-solving capabilities. We may produce what Jack Good calls the **ultra-intelligent machine (UIM),** which might in turn make design improvements, creating a second generation of UIMs, and so on, and so on.

Joseph Weizenbaum, an eminent computer scientist, argues in his book, *Computer Power and Human Reason* for a halt in research on artificial intelligence.[17] He believes our society cannot handle the social, psychological, ethical, and human implications of artificial intelligence, foreseeing culture shock many magnitudes greater than that described by Alvin Toffler in *Future Shock.* But can we stop development in artificial intelligence? And should we? Management at present benefits greatly from decision support systems, and most professionals support further research to extend the problem-solving range of machines. Weizenbaum, however, reminds us that trust, courage, and sympathy cannot be programmed. Do we want all human emotion excluded from decision making?

Exactly how artificial intelligence will alter society and businesses remains unknown. What is known is that computers assist and supplement human intelligence in problem solving, and that computers will play an expanded role in business decision making in the future, even at the higher levels of management.

Summary

Not all problems can be solved by computer. Programmed solutions are feasible for structured problems, computer assistance in decision making being most effective when speed is essential and a large number of routine, repetitive computations must be performed.

Information systems for control and planning must provide a different type of

---

[17] For another strong criticism of artificial intelligence, see Hubert L. Dreyfus, *What Computers Can't Do* (New York: Harper & Row, 1972), p. 259, and a reply by Senon W. Pjlyshyn, "Minds, Machines, and Phenomenology: Some Reflections on Dreyfus' 'What Computers Can't Do,' " *Cognition* 3, no. 1 (1975), pp. 57–77. Two sides of the argument (Weizenbaum's, "Once More, the Computer Revolution," and Daniel Bell's, "A Reply to Weizenbaum") are also presented in Tom Forester, *The Microelectronic Revolution,* (Oxford, England: Basil Blackwell, 1980) pp. 550–72. Pages 575–76 of this book provide a guide to further reading on the controversy.

Table 20.9
Differences in information content required by three levels of management

Nature of information	Operational control	Management control	Strategic planning
Question asked	What is? (descriptive)	What was, is, and will be? (descriptive and prescriptive simulation)	What will be? What if? (prescriptive) simulation)
Time horizon	Current (What is happening today and this week?)	Past and current	Future (What will happen in 1–5 years?)
Information environment	Mostly internal current information: Resources Utilization	Some internal and some external: Past and current performance Predictive future information	Highly dependent on external information
Degree of quantification	Quantitative	Quantitative	Not quantitative

data than information systems at the operational level. Variables include types of questions asked, time horizon of data, informational environment, degree of quantification, and degree of detail (see Table 20.9). In addition, information systems must respond to differences in the mode of operation in reaching decisions at the three levels of management, and to preferences regarding display media. Management style and threshold are also factors to be considered in a system's design. Special features required for planning and control decision support systems are data management, an analytical and modeling capacity, and interactive capability.

At present, computers complement, support, and extend a decision maker's range but management is in no immediate jeopardy of being replaced by machine. Too many "wicked problems" exist, defying programmed solutions. However, research in artificial intelligence, data management, linguistics, and psychology will undoubtedly expand the role of machines in decision making in the future.

Key words

Analytical and modeling capability	Degree of quantification
Artificial intelligence	Design
Data management	Display media
Decision-making stages	Exception reporting
Decision support system (DSS)	Flexible manager
Decisive manager	Hierarchical manager
Degree of detail	Informational environment

Integrative manager
Intelligence
Interactive capability
Management by exception
Management control
Mode of operations
Nonprogrammed decision
Operational control
Programmed decisions

Second generation spreadsheet
Semistructured problems
Spreadsheet
Strategic planning
Super spreadsheet
Threshold of information
Time horizon of data
Type of questions asked
Ultra-intelligent machine (UIM)

Discussion questions

1. Describe five examples of computerized systems used by middle management. In each case, identify:
   a. Information provided.
   b. Models used (if any).
   c. Nature of information (quantitative or qualitative).
   d. How the information can be used.
   e. Benefits (of the information).

2. What is exception reporting? Cite an example. Specify the trigger rules for initiating such a report.

3. Can a computer be a catalyst in management decision making? If so, how?

4. What can middle and top management do to ensure and maximize the beneficial use of computers?

5. Can techniques of operations research and management science be used in an information system? Cite examples. In each case, identify the model used and the function performed.

6. Can decisions be programmed? What decisions cannot be programmed? Give examples of programmed and nonprogrammed decisions in a business firm where the primary activity is:
   a. Marketing.
   b. Production.
   c. Service.
   d. Financial.
   e. Consulting.

7. Can a computer think? What kind of an impact will computers have on middle and top management? Will they help or hinder the decision-making process?

8. What is a model? What is simulation? What is a simulation model? How can such a model be used in business? Cite four examples of simulation models identifying the functions performed by computer.

9. Can computers make managerial decisions? How can the unintentional decisions be avoided?

10. What is the difference between algorithmic and heuristic decision making? In what business situations are each type of decision made? Which type of decisions do computers make?

11. Give six examples of models used by computers in business problem solving. Is the main reason for using the model to:
    a. Compute quickly and accurately?
    b. Process large masses of data?
    c. Correlate the data in the common data base?
    d. Compute complex mathematical relationships?
    e. Combination of the above?

12. Describe the different informational needs of middle and top management in terms of:
    a. Source.
    b. Aggregation.
    c. Period covered.
    d. Accuracy.
    e. Other considerations (specify).

13. Suppose Hotel West were part of a large chain under your management. What information would you require from each hotel in the chain for purposes of planning and control?

14. What types of decisions can computers make that humans cannot? Explain.

15. What are the comparative advantages of computers over humans in making business decisions and vice versa? How will these relative advantages change once computers become faster and cheaper with greater information storage and retrieval capabilities?

16. Will advances in artificial intelligence result in replacement of middle and top management? Describe the nature of advances that would promote such a situation.

17. How will traditional structure of management hierarchy change because of computers? What adverse effects will reorganization have and how can these be minimized or eliminated?

18. How can spreadsheets be used in your field? What features and capabilities would you want?

19. What is the difference between a planning language and a spreadsheet? How can both be used in planning? What other uses do they have? Which managers should use them?

Exercises

1. Suppose the manager in Exercise 1, Chapter 10, wanted to:
   a. Compare the sales of each salesperson with that of the average last month.
   b. Compare sales by each salesperson by age group to establish a predictive relationship.

What additional input, if any, would be required? Are applications (*a*) and (*b*) at the operational, planning, or control level? Would these applications be cost-effective? State assumptions you need to make.

2. Read Joseph Weizman, *Computer Power and Human Reason* (San Francisco, Calif.: W. H. Freeman, 1976), or one of Weizman's articles on artificial intelligence, such as "On the Impact of the Computer in Society," *Science* 1,176, no. 4,035 (May 12, 1972), pp. 609–14. List arguments against future research on artificial intelligence.

3. Sketch a spreadsheet that you think will be useful in your field. Specify the parameters in column 1, variables for other columns, and the relationships for calculating variable values.

Selected annotated bibliography

Alter, Steven L. *Decision Support Systems: Current Practice and Continuing Challenges,* Reading, Mass.: Addison-Wesley Publishing, 1980, 316 pp.
This Ph.D thesis is a supplement to *Decision Support Systems: An Organizational Perspective* by Peter G. Keene and Michael S. Morton. It includes many cases of DSS implementation, such as AAIMS of American Airlines. A good discussion of difficulties in systems usage, implementation patterns, strategies, and implementation risk factors is presented.

Denise, M. Richard. "Technology for the Executive Thinker." *Datamation* 29, no. 6 (June 1983), pp. 206–16.
This article touches on a broad range of topics including software functions to satisfy management needs, software solutions, modeling languages, packages for DDS, the integration of decision support, and the implementation and audit of decision support systems.

Dickson, Gary W. "Management Information Systems: Evolution and Status." In *Advances in Computers,* Marshall C. Yovits, ed. New York: Academic Press 1981, pp. 1–39.
The article is an excellent overview of MIS. Of particular interest is the discussion of the relationship between MIS and DDS. An extensive 9 page bibliography is included.

Evans, Christopher. *The Mighty Micro.* London: Victor Gollancz, Ltd., 1979.
This book looks at short-term computer technology (up to 1990) and also makes long-term predictions for 1991–2000. Included are three chapters on intelligent machines. These chapters discuss the pros and cons of artificial intelligence. The author represents the minority of computer scientists in his opposition to artificial intelligence. His views are worth reading.

Hirsch, Alan. "New Spread-sheet Packages Do More Than Model." *Mini-Micro Systems* 16, no. 7 (June 1983), pp. 205–16.
Hirsch argues that the first generation spreadsheet packages are giving way to integrated second-generation packages. Four of these (MBN; 1–2–3; Microsoft/Microplan; and Advanced Version of Visicalc) are compared. A list of 41 vendors and an excellent glossary is included.

Huber, George. "Cognitive Style as a Basis for MIS and DSS Design: Much Ado About Nothing." *Management Science* 29, no. 5 (May 1980), pp. 567–79.

The author reviews studies of the cognitive style and concludes that the cognitive approach is not especially fruitful.

Keene, Peter G., and Michael S. Morton. *Decision Support Systems: An Organizational Perspective*. Reading, Mass.: Addison-Wesley Publishing, 1978.

An excellent book in a series on decision support. It traces the underlying theory, discusses models for DSS, and then their implementation (including design, evaluation, and strategies for DSS development).

Kingston, Paul L. "Generic Decision Support Systems." *Managerial Planning* 29, no. 5 (March–April 1981), p. 11.

This article presents a good overview of DSS and describes how a computer system can meet the needs of volatile environments, such as those subject to government regulation and economic uncertainty.

Lasdan, Martin. "Make Room for Executive Workstations." *Computer Decisions* 14, no. 12 (December 1982), pp. 116–25.

The author analyses and refutes arguments about why top managers should not use computers. Ways in which to persuade reluctant executives to use computers are suggested.

Naylor, Thomas H. *Corporate Planning Models*. Menlo Park, Calif.: Addison-Wesley Publishing, 1979, 390 pp.

A good book on models for planning and control, integrating a discussion of decision-making models with a look at the informational needs of management and information systems.

Rector, Robert L. "Decision Support Systems: Strategic Planning Tool." *Managerial Planning* 31, no. 6 (May–June 1983), pp. 36–40.

The focus of this article is on application areas, documentation, and how DSS should be introduced and taught.

Rhyne, Lawrence C. "Strategic Information: The Key to Effective Planning." *Managerial Planning* 32, no. 4 (January–February 1984), pp. 4–11.

This article is highly recommended. It discusses different types of information needed for various types of planning (e.g., budgeting, long-range and strategic planning). Good tables are included.

Rockart, J. F., and M. E. Treacy. "The CEO Goes On-Line." *Harvard Business Review* 60, no. 1 (January–February 1982), pp. 82–88.

Examples of CEO going online are given. The authors think this is a trend that will continue and offer reasons why.

Weizenbaum, Joseph. *Human Power and Human Reason*. San Francisco, Calif.: W. H. Freeman, 1976, 300 pp.

This is a powerful assault on artificial intelligence from a prominent researcher. It is a provocative book to read even if one disagrees with the author's views.

Williams, Andrew T. "The Graphsheet Contenders." *PC World* 1, no. 1 (January 1983), pp. 124–33.

This article, addressed to corporate decision makers, helps them select spreadsheet packages. Packages discussed in detail are MBA and 1–2–3.

Systems integration
and growth

The purpose of computing is insight, not numbers.

Richard Hamming

21

Computer applications at the operational level were discussed in Chapter 19; control and planning applications in Chapter 20. Many of these applications can be developed and maintained independently though integration of subsystems is far more efficient and effective.

Integration of an information system is the unification of subsystems through linkage. Integrated systems may consist of integrated hardware, the integration of CPU and peripherals, or the integration of hardware and software. Integration may occur at a centralized location only, or include distributed processing sites. Integration may be of data and words. This chapter does not discuss technical aspects of resource integration. Rather it first focuses on the logical organization of integrated functional subsystems. It then describes how subsystems logically integrated serve business by giving management access to data bases designed for different classes of users. As shown in Figure 21.1, linkage of subsystems can give management access to decision support data bases, functional data bases, and expert system data bases.

Integration leads to growth of information systems. How users and analysts evaluate growth perspectives will also be discussed in this chapter along with the effect of technology on growth.

Types of logical integration

This section describes four types of logical integration: **horizontal, vertical, longitudinal,** and **total systems integration.**

Figure 21.1
Data base linkage and integration for different classes of users

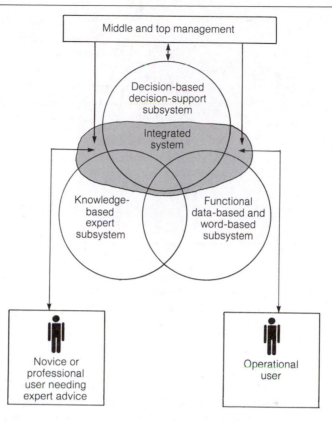

Horizontal integration

A firm with three levels of decision making (operations, control, and planning) has horizontal integration when functional information subsystems, such as production, marketing, accounting and finance, are integrated at one level, as illustrated in Figure 21.2, sharing a common data base. There does not have to be direct linkage between all files to achieve integration as long as **chaining** exists. That is, key data elements can be used to link Files 1 and 3 indirectly as long as Files 1–2 and 2–3 have direct links.

Integration has two advantages: data stored in several files can be correlated and used to generate new information otherwise not available; and collection, preparation, storage, and processing of duplicate data are eliminated. An example of horizontal integration is the use of sales information in a marketing file to send invoices for payment collection, an accounting function. Another example would be the use of the sales file to determine production quantities and schedules.

In the past, it was necessary for a manager to spend a great deal of time combining information contained in operational reports prepared in different functional

Figure 21.2
Horizontal integration at different levels of management

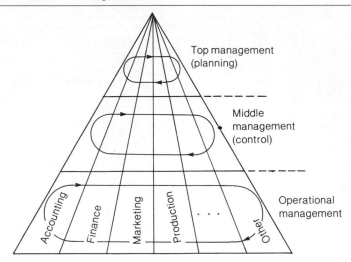

areas. Often these reports were produced in a manner which made it necessary to re-sort the information so that meaningful correlation could be produced from different functional areas. Now all this can be done automatically in an integrated system.

Vertical integration

In vertical integration, an information system for a single function (e.g., production) serves all levels of management but is not integrated with other functional systems (see Figure 21.3). For this type of data flow, common definitions or definition equivalencies are essential. For example, if the code for married were 1 in the operational personnel file, and M in the planning personnel file, this must be known at the time of data access. Such information is stored in tables for automatic reference by the computer, a process known as **table look-up.**

One advantage of vertical integration is efficiency, for data needs to be collected only once for use at all levels of management. Consistency, accuracy, and timeliness of information are added benefits since the information conveyed to control and planning is working operational data aggregated by software for management's needs. Information and feedback also flow in two directions, a feature lacking in horizontal integration

Longitudinal integration

Another dimension of integration is time. Managers are interested not only in operations today, but in past trends (such as trends in demand, supply, and performance). Such data is needed for evaluating performance (comparing past with present records) and is useful when making predictions for future values of sales, market share, production, and so forth. Longitudinal integration need not be for

Figure 21.3
Vertical integration

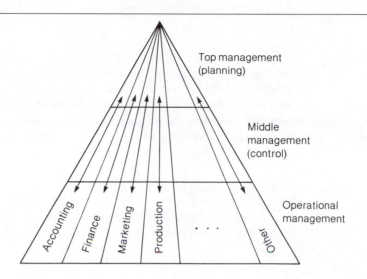

the entire system, as illustrated in Figure 21.4, but may be for only selected functions of the system. The time period for longitudinal integration is shown in Figure 21.4 as five years, but this will vary from one firm to another depending on the nature of the product and industry.

Unfortunately, past data is not always available when needed. It may not have been collected, may be lost, or simply may be aggregated in units not comparable with present data. Integration over time requires both completeness and continuity of data, called **data integrity. Equivalence tables** can be used if the incompatability is a trivial coding difference and software can generate compatibility when new classifications of data are composites of two or more former classifications. But disaggregation, such as the division of account x into x_1 and x_2 means that the new x_1 has no historical counterpart. Such disaggregation of codes should

Figure 21.4
Longitudinal integration

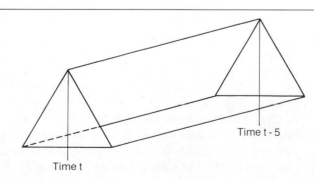

therefore take place only when absolutely necessary, with managers aware of the fact that this disaggregation will disrupt continuity of data.

Total system

Most firms want horizontal *and* vertical integration so that data is shared by all functions and information flows between all levels of management. When longitudinal integration is also incorporated, the system is referred to as a **total system,** or an **integrated management information system.** Sometimes the acronym MIS (meaning management information system) is also used, though this latter acronym has many other interpretations and connotations.

Examples of integrated and nonintegrated systems

In Chapters 19 and 20, computer applications were described for an airline, travel agency, hotel, and automobile dealership. Each of these applications will now be reexamined for horizontal, vertical, and longitudinal integration.

Airline integration

The airline reservation application discussed in Chapter 19 was integrated horizontally with such related functions as aircraft loading, meal catering, crew scheduling, aircraft maintenance, and so forth. Baggage control, however, was omitted. Why? Primarily because of the large capital investment needed to develop scanners for data collection on luggage which varies in size, shape, material, and position. At the present time, most airports lack the special facilities required for computerized baggage control.

Another application that can be integrated horizontally with airline reservations is hotel reservations. For example, the data base of Best Western Hotels is being integrated with United Airlines so that reservation services can be offered. It takes planning and capital investment for such integration, but the advantages are recognized by both airlines and passengers. Undoubtedly other hotel chains, car rentals, and tour companies will be integrated with airline reservations in the future.

Chapter 20 described the DSS for American Airlines called AAIMS. This system has been extended to all U.S. carriers, providing horizontal integration of airlines, so that the Civil Aeronautics Board can receive compatible reports from all carriers under its jurisdiction. AAIMS consists of an extensive standard data base, with files for traffic capacity, head count, and financial data, the latter including income, expense, and balance sheet data with the data itself broken down into six dimensions: airline, marketing, function, account, aircraft, and time. See Figure 21.5 for the hierarchical structure of this data base. One path in the data hierarchy, expense, is traced through all six dimensions.

This system enables the calculation of expenses for every airline for each marketing entity for every function and account, for each aircraft type, and for different time periods, such as daily, or quarterly. Reports specified by the CAB are used by the entire airline industry, including the airlines themselves, the Air

Figure 21.5
Data base structure for AAIMS

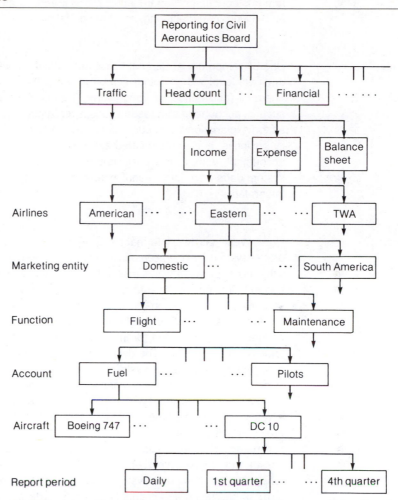

SOURCE   Adapted from Richard L. Klaas, "A DSS for Airline Management," *Data Base* 8, no. 3 (Winter 1977), p. 3.

Transport Association, and even engine and airframe manufacturers. Quarterly reports vary from 50–75 pages per airline, depending on company size, aircraft type, and route structure.

AAIMS is also longitudinally integrated, containing over 20,000 monthly and quarterly time series data values, each set covering four to ten years. The AAIMS system has the capability of manipulating the time series data for forecasting and prediction, partly because of the language used—APL (A Programming Language), an interactive language with a powerful vector manipulation capability. But this time series orientation, while it is a strength, is also a weakness because it limits modeling capabilities, such as simulation. Still, the AAIMS reporting system has conceptually many applications in industries other than the airline, such as banking, manufacturing, and transportation.

Travel agent

Use of computers at Schmal Travel is a strictly functional application at the operational level with no other computerized subsystems at higher levels of management (and hence no integration). The agency has no horizontal integration, such as accounting with reservations, even though such software is available, the stated explanation being cost. An unstated reason is that Schmal Travel is a family business, and an automated accounting application would have replaced the accountant, who, in this case, is the son-in-law of the owner. The reservations system does have longitudinal integration because the accessed data base is so integrated.

Hotel West

Hotel West has two information systems: reservations, and a horizontally integrated system for operations, including registration, accounts, payroll, and so forth. Why this separation when reservations should logically be integrated with registration? The answer is that software for the two systems came from different sources (the reservation system developed by the chain, and the applications programs developed by a software company, Communications Diversified, Inc.), neither system designed for integration with the other. As a result, the two systems are incompatible. The desk clerk at Hotel West manually enters reservation data into the registration system since there is no linkage between the two systems. In hotels where reservations and registration are linked, guests merely verify registration data that has been processed by computer from the original reservation request, sign the registration form, and pick up the key without having to provide duplicate information at check-in.

Energy regulation could be an independent application handled by a microprocessor, but at Hotel West, energy is integrated horizontally with other operational functions. The computer system also generates management reports for control (e.g., on utilization and distribution) but its vertical integration does not extend to planning, for no planning models are needed for this type or this size of business. Expansion and planning decisions are based on the judgment of the manager, not on a computer model of business data.

Longitudinal integration exists at Hotel West but integration includes future reservation data (up to 20 years in advance), not past data needed for forecasting, as most firms require.

Auto dealer

The auto dealer described in Chapter 19 has three independent information systems: a NCR data processing system for payroll, a minicomputer for sales contracts, and a terminal connected to a computer utility for accounting and inventory applications. The processing modes of these three systems differ and the hardware is incompatible. Why? Because the systems evolved independently and the software purchased has no integration capability. The manager recognizes the need for horizontal integration, but says separate systems have been beneficial, giving the company operating experience with modules and subsystems, preparing them for a larger integrated system which they hope to acquire in the future. The manager is currently studying alternative integrated systems, talking with other dealers to learn their experiences and recommendations, and waiting for hardware and software costs to drop. Asked if vertical integration and a decision support system for planning is contemplated, the manager answered no. The control reports presently generated are adequate, and future sales can be predicted by studying economic indicators, the money market, and interest rates without the need for a planning model. The value of DSS was recognized, however, the manager being particularly impressed with DSS retrieval capabilities and the advantage of being able to ask "What if?" questions, such as, "How will demand for pickups change, given shifts in population? Industry?" But the acquisition of DSS is a distant goal.

Planning for an integrated system

A total system is not always required. For example, the auto dealer cited above has no need for vertical integration. This is true of many small firms. The sample case studies also reflect another truism. Many firms fail to integrate systems even when the need is apparent. The primary reason for this is lack of compatible hardware, particularly when subsystems are implemented by minicomputers. In addition, subsystems with their own data base require software and linking data elements, perhaps even a DBMS, to implement and maintain an integrated data base. Such integration requires planning, as described in Part 3 of this text, and coordination of personnel. The more people involved, the more complex the planning becomes, for a linear increase in personnel means a geometric increase in cross currents and interaction. There is one path for two persons, three paths for two, six paths for four, ten for five, and so forth. Note that the fifth person increases personnel by 25 percent, whereas the paths increase 66.6 percent. This phenomenon, called the **geometric organization syndrome,** adds to the time and resources that must be allocated to integration. Furthermore, in the past, firms have been unable to find systems personnel with knowledge of structured programming and skill in analysis and design combined with a business background to implement integration. This is changing. There are now over 60 schools and colleges of business in the United States with formal MIS undergraduate programs giving students a good foundation in business principles while providing training in programming and systems analysis.

Another impediment to total integration is that few businesses have the monetary and human resources to implement large integrated systems all at once. Instead, modular systems are added and integrated gradually within an overall plan for an integrated system. Large, complex, mature firms with subsystems already in operation find that vested interests and entrenched personalities impede systems integration. The difficulties of implementation, however, should not fore-stall integration efforts. With planning, time, and patience, a total system can be achieved.

Case study of subsystems integration

When total integration is not financially feasible, limited integration is often pos-sible. Integration of subsystems related to the flow of materials needed for pro-duction can be implemented by the **Materials Requirements Planning System (MRP),** for example. In this system, products that need to be produced, quan-tities, and times of production are specified in a Master Production File. This in-formation, combined with data from a Production Requirements File and Mate-rials Availability File is used to calculate materials needed for each product, and to ensure that materials are ordered and available at the time of production, no

Figure 21.6
The MRP system showing link between subsystems and files

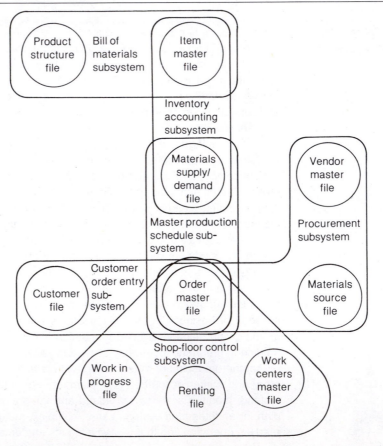

later and no earlier. This reduces the investment in inventory and maintains the flow of materials without which production would be slowed or even stopped.

The integrated MRP System is shown in Figure 21.6. Subsystems include inventory accounting, production scheduling, shop floor control, procurement, customer order entry, and bill of materials. Several models used by middle management are part of the system, including an economic order quantity model for production, least unit cost model, least total cost model, and a part-period balancing model.

MRP integrates not only horizontally but vertically between operational and control management levels. The system orders materials (expediting some orders, canceling others), allowing for discounts. It does both production shop scheduling and vendor scheduling, and enables management to react promptly to changes in the master schedule or market availability of materials. These prompt reactions are facilitated not only by performance reporting and accounting reporting but by status reports on demand and supply schedules of materials.

An advanced version MRP, called MRPII, has two additional features: capacity planning and execution of work orders. It can be implemented companywide, standardizes interdepartmental transactions, enforces a master-production schedule, and reduces waiting time for finished jobs. It can simulate daily operations to identify potential bottlenecks and can prepare reports on production hours and production units. These features add to the cost of hardware, software, and training. In 1984, training for MRP II was an estimated $150,000 for the first year. Total implementation cost varied from $250,000 to over $4 million.

Advantages of MRP are summarized in Table 21.1 MRP requires discipline and careful handling of bills and supply orders. In fact, "The extreme operating discipline placed on inventory managers and material planners by MRP may cause cultural shock to the point of passive or active resistance by these groups—the very same people MRP is supposed to help."[1] Most firms implementing MRP, however, find that the system is extremely helpful to management, well worth the cost.

Table 21.1
Advantages of MRP

Purchasing problems rare, such as failure to order needed supplies on time
Shortages uncommon
Emphasis shifted from expediting orders to de-expediting orders
Three month projections common (Without MRP, monthly projections necessary)
Inventory cost reduced $\frac{1}{4}$ to $\frac{1}{3}$
Consistent on-time delivery of products
Overtime cut by up to 50 percent
Calculation of materials requirement reduced to 2 days (Without MRP, calculation of
    materials requirement can take up to 13 weeks)
Engineering changes easy to accommodate

---

[1] William S. Donelson, "MRP—Who Needs It," *Datamation* 25, no. 5 (May 1, 1979), p. 187.

Advanced information systems

Advanced information systems are integrated systems designed to incorporate change without disrupting information flow and generation of reports. Equipment configurations may vary, and so will decision-support models, languages, hardware, and data base organization. One firm may limit advanced information systems applications to planning, inventory control, and scheduling: another to production and accounting. However, basic components of advanced information systems will be common as listed in Table 21.2.

An example of an advanced information system is the use of the simulation model for planning shown in Figure 21.7. This model can determine consequences when different subsets of internal and planning variables are manipulated in a given environment. First, the manager analyzes and evaluates the firm's performance (Box 3) in the context of its societal environment (Box 2), which is determined by external variables, such as manpower and labor unions. (Box 1). The evaluation may lead to a reassessment of goals and objectives (Box 4), which in turn affects company priorities and policies (Box 5). A trial set of planning variables selected by management (Box 6) is then entered as input, the planning model simulating results (Box 7) based on data in the common data base (Box

**Figure 21.7
Simulation model for planning in an advanced information system**

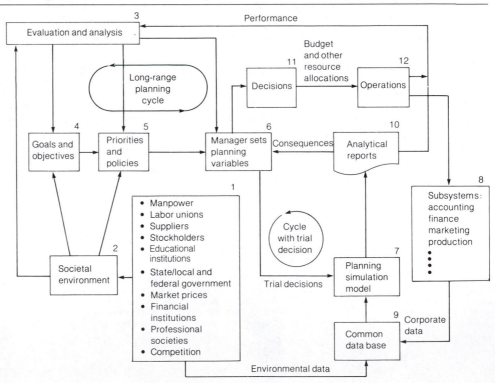

Table 21.2
Components of an advanced information system

Data entry
Data entry is commonly online real time. Traditional input devices are used as well as graphic terminals, voice entry devices, and optical scanners. Entry devices are "intelligent." They allow for different formats of data, modes of processing, and check for validity, consistency, and integrity of data.

Conversational computing
A conversational mode allows users to carry on a dialogue with the computer using a very high level language. (4GLs can be expected in the future.) End users can retrieve data, update data, process data, and solve problems using menus or a high level command structure.

Output
Output may appear on the screen or be printed in hard copy as text, a table of numbers, or graphics using up to 128 colors.

Data bases
Local data bases at distributed nodes or centralized common data bases may be used. Files are integrated so data on all functions are easily accessible for use in planning, control, and operations. Data may cross national borders. A DBMS controls data access, security, integrity, backup, and recovery. As a result, end users need not be concerned about the physical organization of data, media compatibility, choice of storage devices, or optimal access paths. Modes of processing (e.g., batch, online, and real time) are also controlled by a DBMS.

Integration
Corporate data required by multiple users is integrated into a single information system allowing efficient and effective use of data by employees at all levels of the corporate hierarchy. Integration includes hardware integration (CPU and input/output devices), data and words, and software (e.g., graphics, spreadsheets, and expert systems).

Decision Support Systems (DSS)
DSSs use mathematical and statistical models of operations research and management science to solve managerial problems in planning and control. The systems are capable of making inferences. They facilitate exceptional management by identifying deviations that need management attention and intervention. They integrate the decision maker's value system and judgments into an interactive real-time decision-making process.

9), which is composed of both environmental data (Box 1) and corporate data from subsystems (Box 8). The results of the calculations are then displayed as analytical reports (Symbol 10).

After reviewing the consequences of the trial decision, the manager may wish to change the values of the planning variables and recalculate consequences. The cycle of Boxes 6–10 continues until the decision maker is satisfied with results. Decisions are then translated into budgets and resource allocations (Box 11) and the plan put into operation (Box 12). The analytical reports from the planning model are evaluated (Box 3), with the planning cycle repeated periodically.

Integration across national borders

System integration (both limited and total system integration) in firms with foreign operations may result in **transborder data flow.** This flow has been the subject of much political controversy, leading to national restrictions on data flow. As expressed by Louis Jorvet, Magistrate of Justice in France, "Information is power, and economic information is economic power. Information has an economic value and the ability to store and process certain types of data may well give one country political and technological advantage over other countries. This, in turn, may lead to a loss of national sovereignty through supranational data flows."[2]

Some Third World countries are concerned that cultural and institutional bias accompanies data flow, fearing that imported information may not be in their national interest. Other countries fear loss of employment when multinationals integrate systems. It is estimated that Canada will have lost 23,000 jobs worth $1.5 billion by 1984 due to system integration of U.S. firms with Canadian outlets.[3]

To control transborder flow of data, many countries have passed restrictive legislation. In France, for example, a fine of $400,000 and five years of prison are the penalties for transborder data flow of what is defined as "sensitive." In England, the post office has the right to read all transmitted messages, a right that implies that firms must share their cryptographic codes. In Italy, a proposal has been made that transmission cost be proportional to the volume of messages, which could increase transmission costs tenfold. Some countries require that all transborder data flow be handled by public carriers. This results in loss of control by the user and often means degraded service. A data act in Sweden in 1973 empowers a Data Inspection Board to approve all transmissions of personal data crossing its borders. There are over 20 countries with data privacy acts, many using legislation as a way to monitor data for their own economic and political objectives.

Fortunately, standards are now emerging for transborder flow. The OECD (Organization of Economic Cooperation and Development), of which the United States and Canada are members, has adopted guidelines on transborder data flow covering collection and use of data, data quality, security, openness, individual participation, and accountability.[4]

| Growth paths | As subsystems are added and integrated, information systems grow. The direction of growth is a management decision influenced by users' requests for additional applications, analysts' recommendations for expansion, available technology, and the size and complexity of the existing system. The **growth path** favored by users may prove inadvisable from a technological standpoint, however, or such factors as lack of operational expertise within the firm may preclude new applications favored by analysts. The considerations to be weighed by management in choosing a growth path are described in detail below. |

---

[2] Quoted by John Eger in "Transborder Flow," *Datamation* 24, no. 12 (November 15, 1978), p. 50.
[3] Rein Turn, "Transborder Data Flow," *Computer World* 14, no. 9 (March 3, 1980), p. 62.
[4] International Information Flow Guidelines," *Information Retrieval and Library Automation* 18, no. 8 (August 1982), pp. 1–2.

Criteria determining priorities of growth

In recommending priorities for growth, users usually rank potential applications on the basis of the following criteria:

Projected tangible payoff.
Projected intangible payoff.
Time and cost of implementation.
Opportunity costs.
Human factors
Development risks.
Potential impact on competitiveness.
What other companies have done.
Placement of application in project sequencing.
Requirements of local, state, or federal legislation.

When analysts list priorities for growth, they choose applications on the basis of:

Ease of implementation.
Contribution to learning.
Minimal operational problems.
High visibility and a large number of users.
Contribution to an integrated system.
Experience and capabilities of EDP personnel.
Support of top management.
Minimal resistance of personnel.

Not included on these two lists is a factor that is often decisive in choosing which applications are implemented: personal and financial power. The saying, "Whoever has the gold gets first priority," is relevant, for generally the priorities of financial officers, who control funding and often have organizational responsibility for computer operations, are adopted. The fact that financial applications are usually the first implemented may be justified since many such applications are structured, repetitive, serve multiple users, have a high cost-benefit ratio, and involve a large volume of transactions. However, many other applications have the same characteristics. When implementation decisions are made in committee, power, including vocal power, wins.

Often the growth of information systems is impeded by lack of available resources or technological limitations. Projects high on a list of priorities may have to be delayed, whereas minor applications low in priority may prove feasible. Furthermore, **Nolan's growth curve,** described next, is a significant factor in determining a firm's ability to assimilate computer technology.

Nolan's growth curves

According to Richard Nolan, information systems (reflected in EDP costs), follow a S curve through four stages of learning and growth: initiation of EDP, expansion, control formalization, and integration. This curve is the same shape curve

Figure 21.8
Growth curves postulated by Nolan

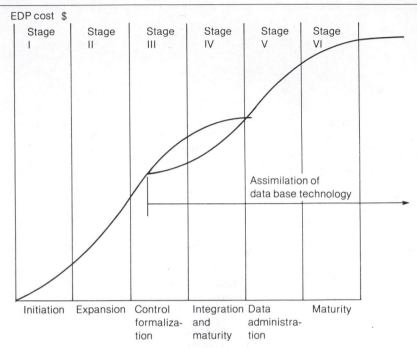

SOURCE   Richard L. Nolan, "Thoughts about the Fifth Stage," *Data Base* 7, no. 2 (Fall 1975), p. 9.

used by Arnold Toynbee to explain the histories of societies, and by others to explain success patterns of peoples and organizations, product development, market development, and the absorption ot technology. That is, slow early acquisition of knowledge and skill is followed by a period of rapid learning and growth, then a slowdown in learning rate, and a final plateau. For EDP, however, Nolan adds a second S to the curve and two more growth stages (data administration and maturity) to include the assimilation of data base technology (see Figure 21.8).

Tables 21.3 to 21.5 describe characteristics of management and organization during Nolan's six growth stages.[5] These include equipment variations, and differences in types of applications and modes of processing. These are listed to show readers that implementation decisions on new applications have a relationship to the phase of growth an organization has reached. Some applications desired by users and analysts may be inappropriate due to the firm's lack of maturity and experience, or lack of appropriate technical personnel.

It is often asked whether a firm can leapfrog over stages of growth. This is

---

[5] For details, see Richard L. Nolan, "Managing the Crises in Data Processing," *Harvard Business Review* 57, no. 2 (March–April 1979), pp. 115–26.

Table 21.3
Applications in the six growth stages

I	II	III	IV	V	VI
Initiation of decentralized jobs	Proliferation of applications	Consolidation of application. Some networks	Selected data base application. Individual networks	Integrated data resource management. Integrated switched networks. Satellite transmission. Integrated voice data, facsimile, text editing	
Initiation of: Payroll, Accounts payable, Accounts receivable	Initiation of: Budgeting, Cash Management, Inventory, Materials control, Marketing, Order processing, Purchasing, Stores control	Initiation of: Cost analysis, Scheduling, Financial and capital investment planning. Personnel	Initiation of: DSS, OLRT, CAD, Process control, Numerical control	Initiation of: Electronic office, DSS for strategic planning, Advanced robots and CAM, Word processing, Personal computing	Refinement of: Text management, CAI, Heuristic modeling
Selected reduction of cost and labor-intensive jobs	Initiation of: Data base and telecommunications, Minis and micros			Integration of data base, telecommunications with minis and micros	

Table 21.4
Processing mode in the six stages of growth (percentage)

Modes of processing	Stages					
	I	II	III	IV	V	VI
Batch	100	80	70	50	20	10
RJE		20				
Data communications processing				40	60	60
Data base processing			15			
Inquiries processing			10			
Time sharing			5			
Personal computing				5	5	5
Mini and micro computing				5	15	25
Total	100	100	100	100	100	100

SOURCE   Reprinted by permission of the *Harvard Business Review*. Exhibit from "Managing the Crises in Data Processing" by Richard L. Nolan (March–April 1979). Copyright © 1979 by the President and Fellows of Harvard College; all rights reserved.

Table 21.5
Organizational mode for the six stages of growth

Function	I	II	III	IV	V	VI
DP organization	Decentralized	Centralized computer	Centralized computer	DDP, utilities	Data resource management	
DP control	Lax, to encourage utilization	Lax, but controlled to facilitate growth	Formalized to contain supply of services	Formalized control to match demand with supply of resources Steering committee	Formalized control to contain demand	Formalized control to balance supply with demand
					Data administration	
User attitude and responsibility	Hands off	Superficially enthusiastic	User directly involved and accountable for quality and value added		User and EDP jointly accountable for quality and effectiveness of system	

possible in small firms when software is purchased for a minicomputer. Such firms are often pressured by competition to adopt real-time systems as was Hotel West, described in Chapter 19, which started with a centralized online real-time system and integrated accounting applications without experiencing earlier stages of EDP development. The auto dealer, however, was more cautious and followed Nolan's growth curve (using a minicomputer in decentralized functional applications).

Larger firms may also skip growth stages if management and analysts have learned their lessons elsewhere. But leapfrogging is inadvisable in most cases. Generally, large complex businesses opt to follow an orderly growth curve, as did American Airlines with SABRE and AAIMS.

Nolan's growth curves are theoretical. In actual practice, the slopes of the *S*'s vary from one organization to another, depending on the firm's ability to absorb computer technology. The term **absorptive capacity** originally applied to economic development: the recognition that underdeveloped countries need an infrastructure, knowledge, and discipline to absorb massive aid. EDP also requires learning and experience before a firm can operate and manage a sophisticated integrated system. The lessons learned in extending applications progressively, adding new equipment and software with each phase of growth, enable firms to absorb and effectively utilize EDP technology. This absorptive capacity will affect the slope of each firm's growth curve.

Furthermore, no single growth curve can describe a firm's level of development in all applications at any given point of time. Instead, a series of parallel growth curves may be required. For example, a firm may be in Nolan's second stage in implementing word processing, the third stage in telecommunications, and fourth in its applications portfolio. Each organization's mix will be unique. Nevertheless, growth should be orderly, with a long-range systems plan for EDP expansion.

Summary and conclusions

Integration of subsystems requires the linking of files and compatibility of data. This integration can be horizontal, vertical, or longitudinal. When these three types of integration are combined, the system is a total system or an integrated MIS. The three dimensions of a total system are shown in Figure 21.9.

Integration can be initiated top-down as discussed in Chapter 12. The top-down structured approach has the advantage of ensuring that the organizational goals and objectives filter throughout the design of the system.

Integration reduces the redundancy of data; eliminates duplication in preparation, validation, storage, updating, and filing; and permits calculations and report generation from multiple files for the production of information not previously available.

An example of limited integration described in this chapter is MRP, Materials Requirements Planning System. This system integrates procurement, customer order entry, bill of materials, production scheduling, shop floor control, and inventory accounting to minimize the cost of materials inventory and to ensure that materials required for production are available when needed. The components of advanced information systems are also described.

Systems integration of firms with foreign subsidiaries results in transborder data flow. Many countries consider this flow a threat to their sovereignty and have reacted by passing restrictive legislation on data transmissions.

Growth of EDP systems is stimulated by integration. The growth path favored by users may not be that recommended by analysts, for the two groups evaluate potential applications on the basis of different sets of criteria.

The ability of a firm to assimilate computer technology will also influence speed and direction of growth. The growth curves postulated by Nolan, representing six stages of development, apply to most firms. However, because of recent ad-

Figure 21.9
Three dimensions of total integration

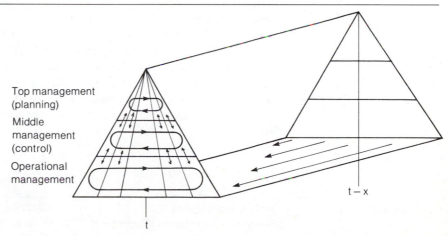

Top management
(planning)

Middle
management
(control)

Operational
management

$t - x$

t

Figure 21.10
Current and possible future growth curves

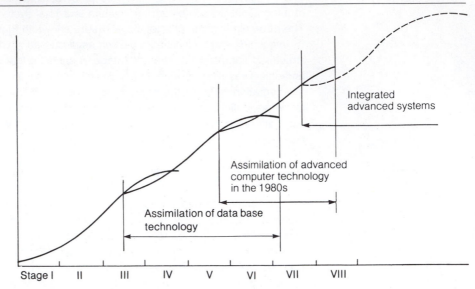

Integrated
advanced systems

Assimilation of advanced
computer technology
in the 1980s

Assimilation of data base
technology

Stage I   II   III   IV   V   VI   VII   VIII

vances in computer technology, new growth curves need to be added to those postulated by Nolan, as shown in Figure 21.10. Note that in this figure, the curve representing assimilation of data base technology is overlapped by a curve representing the assimilation of advanced technology. As in the earlier stages of growth, the same pattern of learning is followed (though the time lapse may vary): slow early acquisition of knowledge and skill, followed by a period of rapid learning and growth, then a slowdown in learning rate, and a final plateau or a falling off. The advanced computer technology to be assimilated includes numerical control, process control, computer-aided design, computer-aided manufacturing, word processing, robotics, lasers, voice synthesis, glass fibers, and terminals with conversational, graphic, and intelligent capabilities.

Yet another curve (shown in dotted lines in Figure 21.10) is in the making. This curve represents the merger of telecommunications with information processing and the advent of integrated advanced computer systems incorporating artificial intelligence. We are talking about wired homes, offices, and cities and computers that learn, that are able to do not only what we tell them, but what we want them to do.

Key words	Absorptive capacity	Chaining
	Advanced information systems	Data integrity
	Airline integration	Equivalence tables

Geometric organization syndrome
Growth path
Horizontal integration
Integrated management information
  system
Longitudinal integration
Materials Requirements Planning
  System (MRP)

MRP II
Nolan's growth curves
Table lookup
Total system
Transborder data flow
Vertical integration

Discussion questions

1. What is an integrated system?

2. "A total MIS is a myth." Comment. Justify your position.

3. What is the difference between an MIS and an information system used by management in business?

4. What are the essential prerequisites of an MIS?

5. Why is a total MIS difficult to achieve in a large and complex organization?

6. Can an MIS be achieved modularly? Or must it be implemented all at once?

7. How are the basic functions in a business firm related to one another? How can they be integrated in an information sytem?

8. What are the stages in the growth and use of computer systems? Is it necessary to follow all the stages in sequence?

9. Why must a firm go through stages of growth for an information system?

10. What is the shape of the growth path for EDP operations? Is the same growth path followed for all types of applications or does each application have a unique path?

11. Distinguish between:
    a. Horizontal and vertical integration.
    b. Vertical and longitudinal integration.
    c. System and subsystem.
    d. Total information system and MIS.

12. What determines the boundaries of a system and subsystem?

13. What are the advantages and disadvantages to systems integration?

14. Can systems integration be achieved during operations after experience is gained with the system or should it be planned in the stage of system design?

15. Is it desirable and practical to plan and strive for a total system? Why?

16. Is the SABRE system a total system? If not, why not?

17. Why are many business systems not integrated even under desirable conditions? What is needed to achieve an integrated system?

18. Do you believe that there will be a third S curve above the two curves suggested by Nolan? Where will it start and end? For what industries? What will trigger and sustain a third curve?

Exercises

1. Can the applications in Exercise 1, Chapter 20 be independent of Exercise 1, Chapter 10, or should the applications be integrated? How can this integration be accomplished?

2. Suppose that your firm is planning a computerized information system for marketing and production records. Should this system be integrated with the finance file or should the system and the file be separate? Is integration beneficial to the manager? Explain.

Selected annotated bibliography

Clark, Mike. "MRPII and the Small Manufacturing Company." *Manufacturing Engineering* 92, no. 1 (January 1984), pp. 62–64.

The author states that the size of a company appropriate for MRPII depends on how tightly the company is able to structure its production process.

Computer Technology Review.

This journal, started in 1980, has a subtitle: *The Systems Integration Sourcebook*. The magazine publishes articles on the integration of subsystems, including architecture, human interface, software, communications, control, and devices.

Dickson, Gary W. "Management Information Systems: Evolution and Status." In *Advances in Computers*. C. Marshall Yovits, ed. New York: Academic Press, 1981, pp. 1–37.

Dickson, a professor at the University of Minnesota, brings a scholarly viewpoint to the subject. He discusses the concept of MIS, support mechanisms, and research. Included is an extensive bibliography of 235 items including classics in the field going back as far as 1967.

Haden, Douglas H. *Total Business Systems: Computers in Business*. St. Paul, Minn.: West Publishing, 1978. 463 pp.

This text describes many applications of integrated and total systems.

King, William R. "Integrating Computerized Planning Systems in the Organization." *Managerial Planning* 32, no. 1 (July-August 1983), pp. 10–13.

This article discusses mission, objectives, constraints and strategies for each type of system. When planning, each of these factors must be considered.

Newman, P. S. "Towards an Integrated Development Environment." *IBM Systems Journal* 21, no. 1 (1982), pp. 81–107.

The author proposes an approach to systems integration and recommends consistent development and execution as solutions to problems of cost-control and effectiveness of applications. The article includes a discussion of systems description languages, high-level languages, application generators, and new data models. There is also an excellent bibliography of 60 items.

Nolan, Richard L., ed. *Managing the Data Resource Function,* 2nd ed. St. Paul: West Publishing, 1982, pp. 1–20.

Nolan, the originator of the theory of growth curves in computer processing, discusses his more recent views on the subject. Steps of growth and strategies for managing growth are examined.

Parsons, Gregory L. "Information Technology: A New Competitive Weapon." *Sloan Management Review* 25, no. 1 (Fall 1983), pp. 3–13.

Parsons discusses the competitive impact of information technology and presents guidelines to integrate information technology with a firm's strategy.

Strassmann, Paul A. "Stages of Growth." *Datamation* 22, no. 10 (October 1976), pp. 46–50.

An excellent discussion of growth theories (including Nolan's and Withington's), their limitations and refinements, as well as growth trends.

Computers in manufacturing

22

Computing machines perhaps can do the work of a dozen ordinary men, but there is no machine that can do the work of one extraordinary man.

E. B. White

Computers are used to generate reports for operations, control, and planning in all functional areas of a business, including manufacturing. In addition, computers can be added as components to manufactured products, giving the products intelligence. This will occur with increasing frequency in the future and the capabilities of intelligent products will become more sophisticated as research in artificial intelligence is applied to product development.

Computers can also be used to automate manufacturing processes: for example, numerical control, the use of robots, and process control to monitor a continuous operation. They are also used in product design. The development of intelligent terminals with color graphic capabilities has made the latter use increasingly common. CAD, computer-aided design, can be implemented without other computer applications in manufacturing, but when integrated, CAD provides input for the other applications in manufacturing.

All of these diverse uses of computers in manufacturing, either as integral parts of a manufactured product or as a tool in the actual manufacturing process itself, will be discussed in this chapter. The nature and need for each computer application will be identified, the advantages and limitations will be presented, costs and hardware/software needs will be evaluated, and future use of each application will be considered. The importance of these subtopics differs with each application so that the emphasis and sequence of subtopics in each section will vary.

This chapter closes with a look at automated factories and makes predictions for future use of computers in manufacturing.

Report generation

In manufacturing, as in all functional areas of a business, information must be gathered on operations for purposes of evaluation and control. Managers also require data for planning future production. Computerized information systems for job costing, production scheduling, shop floor control, equipment inventory, and so forth are common in manufacturing concerns. Table 19.16 (in Chapter 19) lists other operational computer applications that can be applied to manufacturing; Chapter 20 describes the use of computers to assist managers in planning and control.

Smart products

Computers can also be used as a component in a manufactured product. A **smart product** has a microprocessor embedded in its design which gives the product arithmetical capabilities, the ability to make choices (logic), and memory. Such products entered the market as a result of chip technology which has made microprocessors inexpensive. Microprocessors of the type used in many smart products range in price from $2 to $5, depending on their capabilities and the lot size of production. Furthermore, microprocessors are tiny and reliable. Because they still need protection from oil, dust, and vibrations, manufacturers are constantly seeking to improve their design so that in the near future they will be robust, and be able to withstand rough environments. Examples of smart products include the following:

Smart taximeters

A microprocessor can keep track of charges for up to five persons sharing a cab, each passenger with bags traveling to a different destination (luggage handling per piece is added to each bill).

Smart scale

A microprocessor has the capability of calculating the exact postage of weighed, packages once the destination (either zip code or country code) is keyed in. The scale's postal rate charts are stored in the microprocessor's memory. The use of a smart scale saves labor costs, replacing employees that were formerly needed to calculate postal rates. An estimated 8 percent of all outgoing commercial mail is stamped with excess postage, so the accuracy of a smart scale is also a money-saver.

A smart-scale variation is one that will calculate the amount of calories in food being weighed. The user keys in a code identifying the food placed on the scale. (Code tables are supplied by the manufacturer.) Then a microprocessor embedded in the scale uses information in its memory on calorie values to calculate the number of calories in the food on the scale. Such a scale is of value to people with health problems who want to control their calorie intake, such as persons who are overweight or diabetic.

Smart phone

A smart phone can store both emergency numbers (fire, police) and frequently used numbers, and will dial them when users press a specific key. The phone microprocessor will also keep dialed numbers in memory until a call is connected. Upon receipt of a busy signal, the line will be monitored until free and the call then automatically redialed. In addition, the phone can serve as an answering service, recording incoming messages for later reply, and can also be used as a home intercom system.

Smart microwave oven

Many ovens have time-bake capabilities but the timers cannot be set with great accuracy for the setting options are generally 5-minute blocks. Smart ovens can be set to the second, and can furthermore be programmed to perform a sequence of activities. For example, the user may preset a microwave oven to first defrost 4 pounds of rump roast for two minutes, followed by a 25-minute time delay for temperature equalization, and a cooking period of 56 minutes at temperature level five, and finally, an indefinite keep-warm at "hold" until the meat is served, and the oven turned off. It took Amana four years to develop its smart microwave oven, but being the first among oven manufacturers to apply microprocessors to cooking, it was breaking new ground. Additional Amana smart products should take less development time. Each industry must acquire knowledge and experience in electronic-oriented production if it plans to produce smart products.

Smart clock

A smart clock can also be programmed to perform a sequence of activities. For example, the clock might be set to buzz gently at 6:38 A.M.; to turn on both the radio and coffee pot at 6:40 A.M.; to automatically retune the radio dial to music with a fast rhythm at 6:51 A.M.; and to ring the alarm loudly at 6:55 A.M.

Smart pilot

Microprocessors can be a cockpit aid to pilots by taking readings on temperature, wind velocity, direction, and engine performance, then calculating optimum altitude for minimum fuel consumption, given the number of passengers. Flight testing has shown a fuel saving of 2–5 percent when such calculations are made.

Smart TV

TV game programs can be stored on cassettes and displayed on TV screens by microchip processors. Favorite TV programs can be recorded and stored for later replay. A smart TV connected to a phone is able to access information on theater bookings, weather, sales, and even information in the *Encyclopaedia Britannica*. Some of these services are offered by VIEWDATA in Great Britain. Viewtron is a similar service under development in this country. With keyboard and interface, the smart TV can become a rudimentary home computer.

Future of smart products

Smart products will have even greater potential when chip technology merges with voice recognition technology. Imagine the convenience of departing for work after having left verbal instructions with a home computer to vacuum the house at 4:30 P.M. in preparation for dinner guests. The computer would turn on the vacuum at the prescribed hour and direct its path according to the house floor plan stored in its memory. Unexpected objects would be detected by a TV camera and appropriate deviations made. After cleaning all rooms, the vacuum would return to the closet and the computer would record a message to the effect that the task has been completed.

It is not the lack of technology that limits applications of smart products. Rather high program development costs limit the number of smart products on the market. Sales must either be voluminous so that the fixed initial cost is shared by many users, or multiple uses of programs in other products must be found. Sometimes additional applications of the microprocessor in a product will add to its appeal at little extra cost. For example, the smart clock might be used for thermostat control, or locking house doors at night. Smart products will sell only if the price is right and price is directly related to quantity produced and sold. Manufacturers must, therefore, be shrewd in assessing customer preferences and needs. There is great scope for creative designers and salespeople in the smart-product marketplace.

Robots

Another use of computers in manufacturing is the addition of microprocessors to machines in order to automate control of machine processes. A machine composed of sensing devices, links and joints that performs specific manual tasks governed by a microprocessor(s) is a **robot.** Robots are usually manipulators designed to move materials, tools, or devices through programmed motions. In general, a single robot is capable of being programmed to perform a variety of tasks.

Robots are of particular value for tasks that are structured and highly repetitive. For example, industrial robots are used for spot welding, material handling (e.g., stacking parts), machining, and assembly. Robots can be found spraying paint, assisting in die-casting operations, and packing cartons. They can bore holes accurate to 0.002 inch and do so up to 10 times faster than their human counterparts with a reliability factor of 97 percent. One robot, PUMA (Programmable Universal Machine for Assembly) can load and unload the parts from furnaces, presses and conveyors; weld, spray, grind, and drill; then test its own work. Also, robots can shelf merchandise after reading and matching the code on the products with shelf codes.

On farms, robots sow seeds. In lumber camps, they saw branches. Prototypes are being developed for home use: to walk the dog, collect the mail, pour drinks, and protect against intruders. One restaurant even advertises a robot receptionist. It can sense the number of guests waiting to be seated, scan empty tables for one to fit the party size, seat the guests, take orders, and serve food.

Robots are of particular value in environments that are dangerous or hostile to man. Following the 1979 nuclear accident at Three Mile Island, robots were used to take samples to determine whether the degree of radioactivity was high and possibly dangerous to humans. Robots have also been used extensively in space exploration.

To date, most of the workers who have been replaced by robots have been retrained and placed in other operations. Attrition has kept firms from having the problem of surplus labor. However, as applications expand, the problem of worker displacement will become more acute. Today assembly workers constitute 17 percent of the U.S. work force and inspection workers another 12 percent. These are two areas where robots can function effectively. Some experts predict that robots will eventually replace 65 percent to 75 percent of the current factory work force.[1]

Many reasons are given for installing robots. They have proved remarkably adept at increasing productivity (raising productivity by a factor between 3–5), reducing waste, and maintaining quality. They do not report late for work, get sick, or tire. Service is uninterrupted by shift changes or coffee breaks. Robots neither demand pay hikes nor rally against management. In the automobile industry, American robots cost approximately $5.50 an hour contrasted with union labor of roughly $18.50 in wages and benefits. By 1990, nearly half of the final assembly of cars is expected to be done by robots. Similar figures demonstrating the cost-effectiveness of robots in production lines can be cited in many manufacturing areas.

The robotics industry is relatively new—some compare it to the minicomputer industry of the early 1960s. The 1985 market should be $214 million, up from $68 million in 1980. By 1990, the American market should be worth $2 billion. Many U.S. corporations that plan to be big robot users in the future, for example, IBM, General Motors, and Bendix, are starting production of their own robots. GM plans to spend over $1 billion for 14,000 robots by 1990. Japan is currently a leader in the population of robots, and in the ratio of robots per employee in manufacturing (two-fifths of the robots in the developed world are in Japan), but Japan, at present, lacks the technical support and service needed to export their robots.[2]

The explosive growth of the field of robotics can be traced to a number of factors:

1. The dramatic reduction in the price of microchips.
2. Rising wage scales of workers, making the use of robots economically viable.
3. Improved technology that has made robots more intelligent and flexible, able to perform a wide variety of activities.
4. The manufacture of robots by growing numbers of established and new corporations. This has meant robot availability and competitive prices.

---

[1] Leopold Froehlich, "Robots to the Rescue," *Datamation* 27, no. 1 (January 1981), p. 96.
[2] "Quicker than R2D2," *The Economist* 290 no. 7325 (January 21, 1984), p. 63.

The sections that follow provide a closer look at the capabilities, limitations, and potential of robots.

How do robots work?

A photograph of an early industrial robot appears in Figure 22.1. The main components of a robot are schematically represented in Figure 22.2. Data is collected on the environment through a sensor, a device such as a photo cell with an am-

Figure 22.1
Shakey, the robot developed at Stanford Research Institute

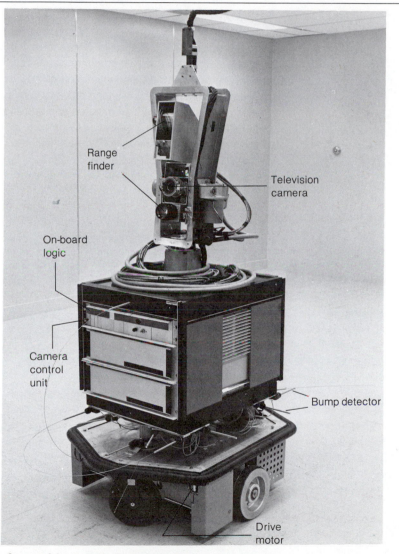

Range finder

Television camera

On-board logic

Camera control unit

Bump detector

Drive motor

Courtesy Systems Research International

Figure 22.2
Components of a robot

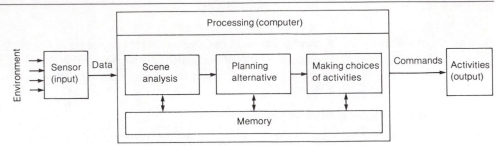

plifier having on-off light sensitivity. The sensor locates objects and a range finder determines their distance. Three-dimensional data is collected so that spatial images of the objects and their motion can be determined.

The data from the sensor is then processed by computer. First, scene analysis is performed. Light and shade patterns and densities are studied by the computer and spatial relationships of objects determined. TV cameras are sometimes used as sensors but their current effectiveness is limited since technology for processing data from pictures is not highly developed. Next, alternatives for performing necessary actions are evaluated, given the environmental context by a procedure called **context-dependent processing.** That is, information stored in the memory of the computer regarding operational steps must be coordinated with environmental data collected by the sensors, so that the optimal strategy for the operation can be determined. Techniques incorporating artificial intelligence are used to analyze the data and choose the best operation alternative. The actual choice is then translated into commands to direct an actuator that performs the desired activity.

This activity may require robot arm movement. Figure 22.3 shows a sample robot arm. Maneuverability of such an arm will depend on arm sensors and size.[2] A warehouse, for example, might need arms for handling fragile items and arms with different capabilities for large, heavy crates.

Limitations

Robots are activated by toggle switches, push buttons, joysticks, handlebar controls, or instructions from a keyboard. Though some voice recognition software has been developed, robots that can receive verbal instructions have limited capabilities at the present time. Instructions accepted are of the following nature: go higher, stop, repeat last step, go two inches backward, and so forth. At present, robots have limited dexterity of movement. Robot sensors (tactile, sight, and sound) are also limited in their ability to recognize patterns and identify objects to be manipulated.

Robots are still not cost effective for many types of activities. Trained employees are still needed to identify defective, soiled, worn, deformed, or cracked parts found in an assembly line. Robots also are unable to assist in assembly lines

Figure 22.3
View of the arm of a robot

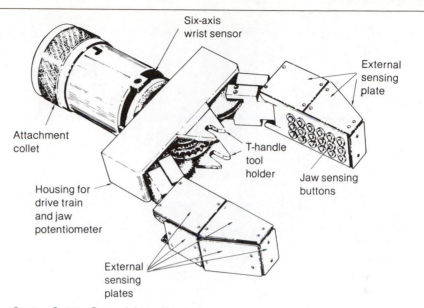

Courtesy Systems Research International

where turn-around parts are handled and they do not always recognize parts assembled in the wrong position. In addition, robots are still unable to coordinate activities with other machines in an autonomous multirobot environment.

More robotics research is needed in the areas of tactile sensing, vision, pattern recognition, and search strategies. Customers want robots that can handle a knife with the skill of a neurosurgeon yet hold slippery objects and be able to cradle such fragile objects as eggs. Another area that needs research is how to balance high technology with human values, how to utilize robots without creating social turmoil because of labor displacement. What will be the social consequences of widespread use of robots? Many observers believe that technologists must tread cautiously as we move from a labor-based industrial society to an automated postindustrial one. It is time for our society to evaluate carefully the social implications of a robot world.

Future of robots

We can anticipate more complex robots in the future—robots with many arms working in concert. We can also expect future robots to respond to high-level languages and have sophisticated sensory capabilities. It is expected that the use of robots and microprocessors will help make U.S. industry more competitive on the world market, both in the price and quality of goods. The actual contribution of robots to productivity will depend on the nature of industry. Figure 22.4 shows industries where robots can be the most effective.

**Figure 22.4
Where robots could help**

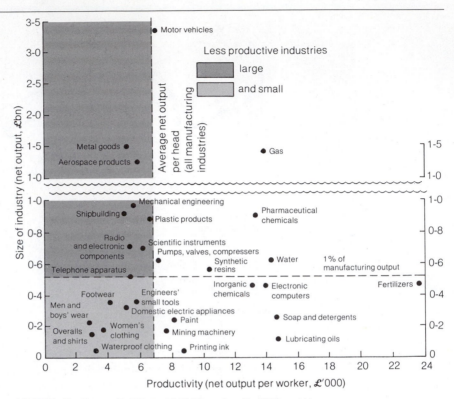

SOURCE   *The Economist* 273, no. 7106 (November 10, 1979), p. 111.

Though expanded robot applications will indeed affect workers and consumers alike, robot self-regeneration will have the biggest impact on our future. Self-regeneration means that robots will be used to construct robots, that intelligent computers will be used to design and improve robots *and* improve the design of machines to produce robots. However, major engineering advances are needed before we have such capabilities.

Numerical control (NC)

Computers played an important role in the manufacturing process itself. Formerly, operators had a far larger role on the factory floor than they do today. In the 1940s, for example, all drilling machines were manually controlled. Metal was placed in the machine by an operator who set the tool for the exact operation to be performed and turned on the power. Later the metal was removed, or perhaps turned, so new operations at different angles could take place and tools were adjusted for wear and tear.

In the 1950s, the operator's role was eliminated by hard-wired circuitry. In the

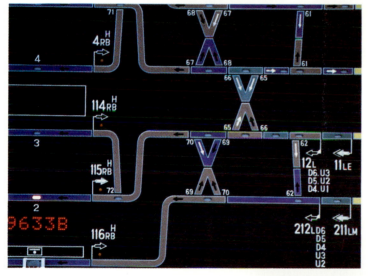

Train dispatchers are using a computer to control the movement of Japan's high-speed bullet train. A panel displays all of the information needed about train operating conditions on the entire line. *Courtesy of Japanese National Railways.*

The location of train number 9633B is shown in this closeup section of a panel used to control movement of Japan's bullet trains. *Courtesy of Japanese National Railways.*

Computer graphic displays are used at a center responsible for controlling the distribution of electricity. *Courtesy of Ramtek.*

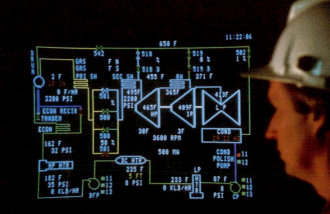

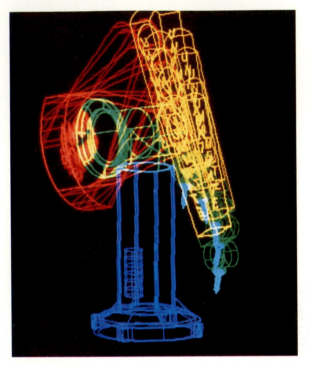

Six-axis robot programs can be generated offline and simulated graphically to verify arm extents and articulations, and identify potential collisions. *Courtesy of Computervision.*

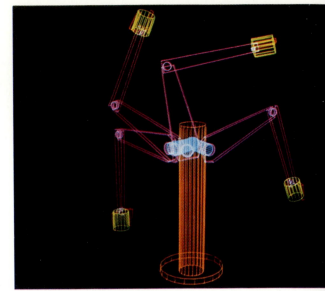

A multi-frame display of a pick-and-place robot arm, photographed directly from a computer screen. *Courtesy of Evans & Sutherland Mechanical Dynamics, Inc.*

Graphics are used to simulate lane changes of a Ford Bronco II. Components such as steering, suspension, bushings, and tires are represented in detail. *Courtesy of Evans & Sutherland and Mechanical Dynamics, Inc.*

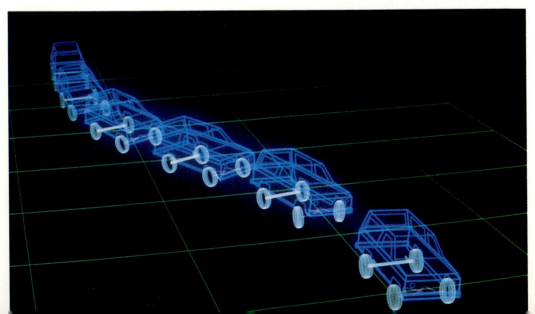

COMPUTER APPLICATIONS

Brokers on the Stockholm Stock Exchange sit before terminals. This is one of the world's most modern, and most quiet, stock exchanges. *Courtesy of Ericsson.*

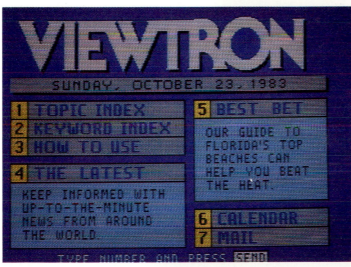

In Florida, Viewtron offers customers a wide-range of home computer services. *Courtesy of Viewtron*

COMPUTER APPLICATIONS

Architects, designers, and engineers can develop and refine mathematical building models at interactive graphic terminals in their work areas. Software is available that blends three-dimensional computer graphic capabilities with architectural design and drafting techniques. *Courtesy of McDonnell Douglas Automation Company.*

A customer online order processing system automates and integrates basic distribution functions: order entry, customer information, pricing, order processing, inventory control, purchasing, receiving, warehousing, shipping control, invoicing, accounts receivable, sales analysis, and information inquiry. Online video terminals and printers are located conveniently at the client site for time-saving order processing. *Courtesy of McDonnell Douglas Automation Company.*

1960s, computers began controlling tools for machining as shown schematically in Figure 22.5. A computer generates instructions for operations on paper tape or other input modes such as magnetic tape cartridges, cassettes, and floppy disks. The instructions may be coded sets of holes in cards or magnetic spots on tape representing numerical data which tell the machine what operations to perform. From this, the name **numerical control** was derived. In many cases, instruction preparation takes place on offline equipment, far away from the factory floor. The instructions are subsequently fed into a **controller** attached to a given machine which is a smart product or a full-fledged computer. The controller interprets the instructions on the tape and generates appropriate impulses that govern the positioning and operation of the tools. It even selects the necessary tools. For example, in boring a large hole, a series of small holes must be drilled. The numerical control machine will select the optimal number and tool sizes needed to perform the task as well as the optimal sequence, and then position the tool by three coordinates and dictate the speed of the drilling. The computer can also be programmed to make allowances for wear of the tool as experienced human operators do.

The precision of numerical control machines makes them invaluable. For example, in making a turbine blade which tapers in thickness to a fine edge, the blade can be tooled within a fraction of a millimeter of design specifications. If the same machine were needed for another similar operation, a new tape could be fed into the controller to direct the new operation.

Automation of factory machines has reached a high level of sophistication. It

Figure 22.5
Offline numerical control machines

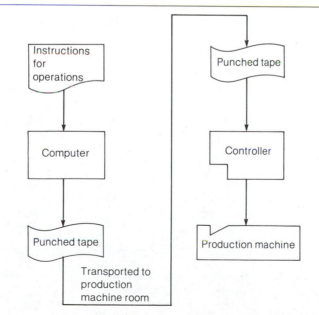

is currently possible to draw on a graphic terminal the shape of a two-dimensional machine cut desired. A printer will list the coordinates of the drawing, which are then converted on a keyboard device into punched paper tape, which is then fed into a controller which activates the cut on a numerical control machine and monitors it for accuracy. In the online version, the image drawn on a terminal can be converted directly to instructions for the NC machine.

More complex operations in three dimensions can be programmed in special languages, such as APT (Automatically Programmed Tool). Many factory operations have been programmed by software vendors and are available as software packages that can be adapted to a variety of production tasks. Large firms often have a library of programs for different operations, different combinations of which may be used to automate complex sets of operations.

Configurations for numerical control machines

One configuration of numerical control machines, represented schematically in Figure 22.6, is for **direct numerical control (DNC)** by a single large computer over different tools and production equipment. This centralized system was favored in the late 1960s and early 1970s when computers were expensive, but conflicts in priorities and delays often occurred since a single computer was often overburdened and subject to breakdown.

Microtechnology of the late 1970s made distributed and decentralized computers economically feasible. A computer used for NC costing $350,000 in 1965

**Figure 22.6
Direct numerical control machines**

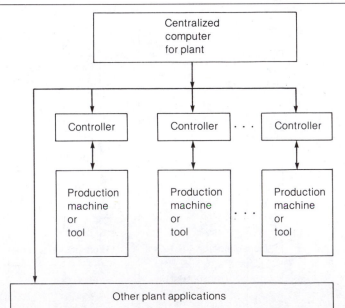

Figure 22.7
Network of dedicated numerical control machines

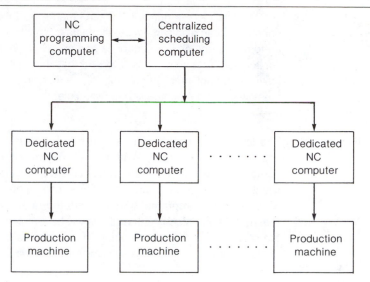

dropped to $35,000 in 1970. By 1975, the cost was $3,500. Cost has reached a plateau, not dropping much below this figure, but the cost/performance ratio has continued to improve. That is, "bells and whistles" have been added that have kept the price relatively stable. Computers used for NC today are also of improved quality, increased reliability and flexibility, better integrated, and easier to use and maintain. More microprocessors are now embedded in NC machines so that more tasks can be automated. These additional features have been added in response to customer demands. The price/performance ratio has continued to improve because of technological advances and the pressures of competition among manufacturers.

Soon, one computer per production machine or tool may be a reality. Distributed computers dedicated to a special task are optimized in design, which contributes to cost reductions. The use of distributed computers also permits relatively autonomous modular growth of numerical control assembly lines. New equipment can be added without disruption to the line, a departure from the "throwaway" philosophy that prevailed in earlier days when entire systems were uprooted when new numerical control machines were installed.

A schema for a **dedicated numerical control** system is shown in Figure 22.7. In this schema, a centralized computer schedules operations and monitors a number of numerical control computers attached to dedicated different production machines, thereby maximizing throughput and minimizing waiting time between jobs. The main purpose of the central computer is to coordinate and optimize the work of all numerical control machines, thereby improving overall plant efficiency. The **scheduling computer** receives its numerical control instructions from a NC programming computer on which NC programs are written online. Once debugged, these programs are forwarded by the scheduler to the appropriate NC machine for production.

The computers in numerical control machines, in addition to directing machine operations, can also run diagnostic tests to ensure that the operational steps are performed in the proper sequence and on schedule. For example, they can monitor temperatures and torques to see that they fall within allowable limits. Such testing need not interrupt the work of the machine but can be fitted into time segments when the machine is otherwise idle.

Future of numerical control

The low cost of minicomputers and microprocessors will definitely increase the use of numerical control. What is presently needed is the development of new numerical control architecture with software and diagnostic packages for new applications. The greater use of distributed computers in tools and machines, each with stored NC programs, will eliminate the need for most human operators on the factory floor. Machine operations will be directed by commands keyed in from the console of a central computer. In this automated environment, manual operations would be limited to restocking raw materials and removing finished products.

Process control (PC)

Another application of computers to production is **process control (PC).** Unlike numerical control which deals with the manufacture of a discrete product or process (such as cutting a sheet of metal or milling a part), process control monitors a continuous activity, and checks key variables to detect variations from prescribed allowable tolerances; for example, monitoring the production of chemicals, the manufacture of paper, or the generation of electricity. When deviations of prescribed norms occur, corrective action is quickly taken (in real time) and/or human operators are alerted to prevent production from falling below standard, the ramifications of which could be serious, varying in magnitude according to the nature of the process being monitored.

The concept of process control is not new. What *is* new is the low price of computers, making computerized process control economically feasible for many plants that once could not afford it. The first process control computer cost $300,000 in 1958. In 1976, the price was $3,000, a decrease in cost by a factor of 100. As in numerical control, the price of process control is stabilizing, but the price/performance ratio has continued to improve as a result of increased reliability, better quality and the addition of bells and whistles.

Process control is another example of how microtechnology has reshaped jobs performed by factory workers.

Nature of process control

The basic structure and components of a process control system are shown in Figure 22.8. In this figure, manipulated variables and disturbances represent input, while intermediate and control variables are output.

Figure 22.8
Basic inputs and outputs of a process control system

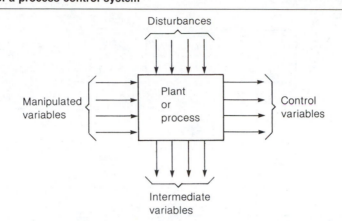

Manipulated variables are predominantly the flow of raw materials, but temperature and process would also be examples of variables that fall in this category. Disturbances may be environmental, such as air temperature and humidity, or relate to the quality of raw materials. Since adjustments must be made to assure uniformity of the product when variables occur in the environment or materials, these input variables are labeled **disturbances.**

It is the computer's role to evaluate performance of the system, to ensure that the process keeps within prescribed limits of factors such as production rate, product quality, and dimensions of product. These output variables, which must be constantly monitored, are called **set points.** Since set points for the limits must be controlled, the term control variables is used. The computer also checks intermediate variables, (the output at given points during production), again comparing the results with predetermined standards. The purpose of process control is to adjust manipulated variables to keep the system operating within the set points of control variables.[3]

To control a process, three components are necessary: **sensors,** a processor, and an **actuator.** Figure 22.9 shows how these components are interrelated. Sensors gather information on intermediate and control variables. The computer compares this information with set points stored in its memory to determine whether corrective action is necessary. If so, the actuator is instructed to make necessary adjustments to the manipulated variables. These adjustments have also been predetermined, based on given conditions, and instructions for corrections are also stored in computer memory. The corrections are then monitored by the sensors and the process reevaluated by the computer in a new control cycle.

How often factory processes should be monitored is an important manage-

---

[3]The terms *manipulated variables* and *control variables* are often confused. Though manipulated variables are under the control of a factory anager, control variables are preset by higher management and are not within the floor manager's jurisdiction.

Figure 22.9
Components of process control

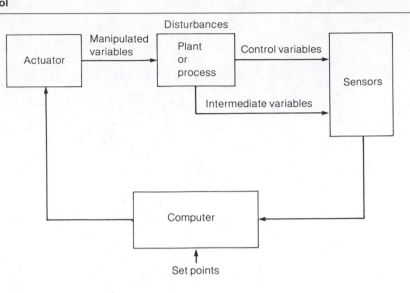

ment decision. Frequent process control ensures high quality of output, but also entails high computing costs. There is also the possibility that conflicting demands for computing service may arise if several factories and/or several processes are being monitored by a single computer at frequent intervals. Timing for sampling must be balanced against the cost of sampling and how critical the control loop is to the manufacturing process. One rule of thumb that is widely applied is: sample every second for flow loops, every 5 seconds for pressure loops, and every 20 seconds for temperature loops. But each industry is unique and production methods vary, so optimal sampling frequency will obviously vary.

Equipment required for process control

Process control requires an online real-time computer, one that has the capability to activate sampling at timed intervals and take immediate corrective action. Because continuous processes have a long start-up time, breakdown can be exceedingly disruptive and expensive. Computer backup and recovery capabilities are therefore essential. The process control system must include a digital computer with an analog-digital converter so data on flow and changes in pressure and temperature, for example, can be analyzed.

Though many processes can be controlled by one computer, microtechnology has reduced computer costs so much that it is now economically feasible in many cases to dedicate a computer to a single control process. If the dedicated digital computer is directly connected to sensors and actuators, it is called a **DDC (direct digital computer).** In a fully automated system, a number of DDCs would be controlled by **supervisory computers** which would be governed by a scheduling computer, which in turn, would be regulated by a centralized computer. A schematic representation of such a hierarchy appears in Figure 22.10.

The purpose of supervisory, scheduling, and central computers is to coordinate process control so that production will be optimized in accordance with management objectives while making periodic production adjustments when necessary in response to external constraints and changes. To take all these factors into consideration requires complex software indeed. Programs should be written in efficient assembler language, but more and more programmers favor higher level language, such as FORTRAN, at the DDC level, trading machine efficiency for ease of use.

Process control in the future

Process control is becoming increasingly attractive as strategy for production and manufacturing, primarily because of the reduced cost of computer processing as a result of microtechnology. With greater development of software packages written in high-level languages, usable on a variety of equipment and applicable to a wide range of problems, process control will certainly expand. Program packages

Figure 22.10
Hierarchy of computers for process control

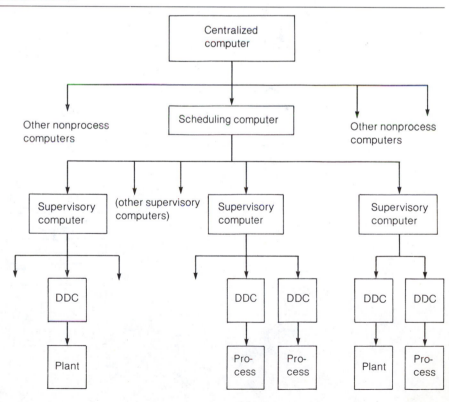

under current development will perform diagnostic and maintenance monitoring in the future, help optimize processing, and provide management with needed data and comparative information for control purposes.

Computer-aided design

Another production application for computers is **computer-aided design (CAD)**. A design on a visual device, such as a graphic terminal, can be scaled, moved around on the screen, and rotated in desired perspectives. The computer can perform calculations on the critical variables of a design and can also determine the effect of design alterations and modifications. Specifications can be stored in computer memory and then integrated with numerical control for actual manufacture of the designed product. Of course, there are many degrees of CAD sophistication. In this section, the discussion of CAD will open with a look at CAD hardware and software, followed by examples of industrial use, and an analysis of cost. Finally, CAD problems and future prospects will be examined.

Figure 22.11
Evolution of CAD hardware

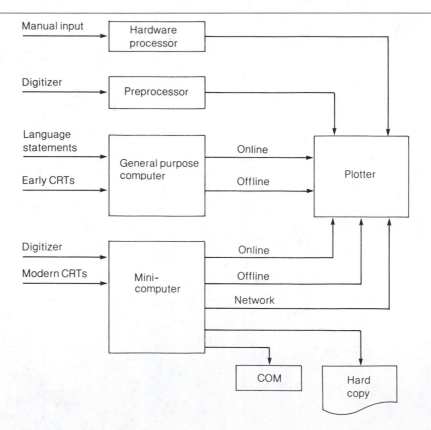

Evolution of CAD hardware

A view of the evolution of CAD hardware is shown in Figure 22.11. Early keyed manual inputs were replaced by **digitizers** that used a hand-held pen-like device to trace diagrams and convert them into signals. These signals were processed by preprocessors (and later by computers) and converted into alphameric data.

Later versions of CAD introduced high-level programming language statements and the use of a CRT with either offline or online plotting for product design. Hardware developments in recent years have given designers improved plotting and CRT equipment, minicomputer networks, and time-sharing facilities.

The graphic capabilities of CRTs were first recognized in the early 1960s in a doctoral dissertation, "Sketchpad," by Ivan Sutherland. Since then research has refined CRT graphics. Circles and geometric shapes can be drawn or preprogrammed on CRTs and called to the screen by keying a command, then figures can be moved, scaled, or rotated by designers. A light pen sketch of these figures can be geometrically corrected (e.g., a circle can be drawn accurately for a given radius, or a hand-drawn line straightened). In addition, some modes of hardware offer designers 128 color choices. Texture can be added by a method called **collage.** A mix of texture and color, called **image mixing,** can give a screen design the illusion of a three-dimensional figure. A more recent development in CAD is that image manipulation, collaging, and mixing can now be done by a minicomputer, either as a stand-alone mini or in a mini network. Specifications can then be sent to a printer, plotter, photo machine, or stored on microfilm for reference and further processing.

CAD software

The intelligence of CAD systems resides in software. Though approximately 1,600 CAD programs developed under NASA funding are in the public domain, many manufacturers prepare their own programs. In addition, graphic packages are available from software houses.

CAD software aids in new product design by providing timely and complete information about proposed designs (that is, materials, weight, costs, performance criteria, and so forth). Such information is needed quickly, at the time new ideas are conceived, not hours or days later when the designer has turned to other projects. This quick access of information and feedback increases productivity by keeping designer involvement and interest at a peak, focusing designer attention on a single project. As a result, design lapse time is considerably shortened and any necesessary changes to correct design errors can be quickly accomplished.

Increased designer productivity resulting from CAD was shown in a comparative study made of two firms that had contracted to design a complex traveling wave tube. The firm with CAD assembled 15 tubes and 10 qualifying prototypes in six months at a cost of $30,000 for software. The other firm, which used the conventional trial-and-error design process, built over 100 tubes at a cost of of $300,000 and at the end of a year, did not have a single prototype that met specifications.[4] Of course, in this case both designers and design environments differed, so perhaps factors other than CAD influenced results, but there is considerable empirical evidence that CAD increases productivity by a factor of 6 to 15.

Firms using CAD systems can store their designs in a data base for archival purposes. These stored designs can be used as working drafts for future modifications, or for reference by other authorized designers working on similar design problems. Software may also be developed to integrate design specifications with production, coordinating and automating the steps leading from design to manufacture of the new product.

Applications of CAD

Despite the high cost of CAD equipment and software, many firms believe that the reduction of time spent in designing products makes CAD cost-effective. As might be expected, the computer industry is in the forefront of CAD use. LSI (large-scale integration), for example, was primarily designed by CAD.[5] In other industrial applications, CAD has been used to:

> Design and proportion bottle shapes, perform modeling and volume calculations for bottle molds; generate tooling of fixtures, jigs, and pumps, and prepare engineering drawings for a bottle molding and manufacturing facility.
>
> Generate technical illustrations, both 2D and 3D, for instrument housings, assemblies, schematic and wiring diagrams, layouts, and so forth, for use in technical manuals of an electronics company.
>
> Perform the mechanical design and layout of gear boxes, axles, springs, drive shaft, and so forth, for the undercarriage of truck models.
>
> Design specifications for production machines of a company specializing in the manufacture of electrical wire fittings and plumbing fittings for the construction industry, since these machines cannot be purchased commercially.
>
> Generate high-quality, accurate engineering drawings to be used to perform manufacturing and assembly operations in an automotive firm. The drawings include designs of sheet-metal parts, electrical schematics, wiring diagrams, control panels, and so forth.
>
> Produce layout drawings for architectural design, including plumbing, electrical, and heating for office buildings and factories.

In all the above applications, CAD is used to advantage both in the original product design and in later changes made in response to new contract specifications or altered marketplace preferences. All firms claim that the reduced drafting turn-around time provided by CAD gives them a critical competitive edge.

Note that the above applications in manufacturing are independent of numer-

---

[4] Max J. Schindler, "Computer-Aided Design by Trial and Error—Just Find the Software," *Electronic Design* 12, no. 6 (June 7, 1977), p. 44.

[5] For details, see William Rosenbluth, "Design Automation: Architecture and Applications," *Computer* vol. 9, no. 2 (February 1976), pp. 12–17.

Figure 22.12
Relationship of CADD and numerical control

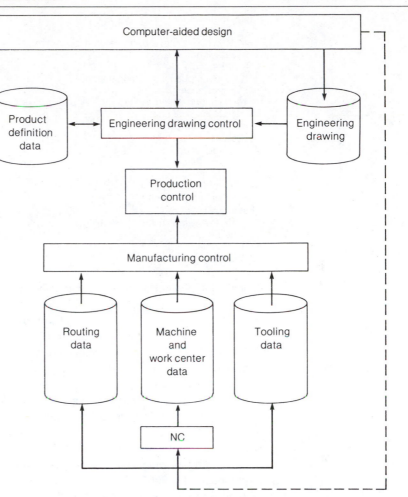

ical control. However, numerical control and CAD can be integrated. Figure 22.12 depicts such an integrated production process. Engineering drawing control receives data on product definition that is used to produce engineering drawings. (If computerized equipment is used in the drafting, the process is called **CADD—computer-aided design** and **drafting.**) This is shown in the top half of the figure.

The lower half is concerned with manufacturing. Data on product design is sent to the numerical control program where data on routing (the sequence of operations), machine and work center data (the data on the machine to be used in each work center for producing each product), and tooling data (what tools are needed for each production stage) are specified. This data is needed for manufacturing control and production control. The direct link between CAD and nu-

Table 22.1
Automated factory components

```
Automated Factory
    Engineering Automation
        CADD (Computer-aided design and drafting)
            • design
            • drafting
        CAE (Computer-aided engineering)
            • simulation
    Manufacturing Automation
        NC (Numerical control)
        PC (Process control)
        Robots
            • production
            • distribution
            • raw materials
            • semifinished products
            • finished products
    Factory MIS
        MRP (Materials resource planning)
        Costing
        Personnel
        Planning
```

merical control is not essential to manufacturing (hence the broken line connection), but it is the ultimate objective of an integrated system.

The integration of numerical control with other operations in manufacturing is called **computer-aided manufacturing (CAM).** Integration with CAD is referred to as **CAD/CAM.** The extended meaning for this terminology is not yet accepted by everyone but in such a rapidly changing field, names must constantly be adjusted to cover new developments or expanded operations. Unfortunately, name changes seldom keep pace with dynamic technology like computer technology.

Firms differ in the amount of computing resources they allocate to CAM and CAD. CAD/CAM systems range from simple systems on microcomputers to more elaborate ones on mainframes with as many as 20 workstations. The 1984 cost of a mini with four workstations was approximately $500,000. A mainframe could be purchased for $600,000 with an additional $12,000 to $20,000 required for each associated workstation. Some firms use time sharing for their CAD/CAM. Others develop customized software which can cost as much as a half million dollars for a basic system, and double that amount for more advanced systems.

Justification for such costs is that CAD/CAM improves productivity—often by a factor of 3 to 20. Errors are reduced and quality is enhanced. Of course, the break-even point will vary among industries and functions. But calculation of this break-even point is difficult, at best. Prices of hardware and software can be calculated, but how can a dollar value be given to better product design? In the application examples of CAD listed earlier, the firms cited found improved product design and design turn-around time more than offset hardware and software costs. CAD results in savings because of improved drafting and drawing capabilities as well. A cost study by Daniel Mullen shows a CAD saving/cost ratio of 2 : 1 (for a project of $154,000/year).

Advances in CAD will upgrade cost-effectiveness and future technological developments will further reduce turn-around time from design to production. But a burden has been placed on designers who now find that industrial design requires knowledge about computers. A designer must learn about software capabilities and limitations, and must be able to communicate with a computer, to structure problems that the data base and the software can solve. The field of design now includes human-machine interface. As with all new technology, it will take time before the full benefits of CAD can be exploited.

The automated factory

Attempts to automate factories can be traced back to the invention of the Jacquard loom in 1808. But it has been in the last three decades that most of the technology for factory automation has been developed. Numerical control machines reached the marketplace in the early 1950s, industrial robots in the early 1960s, and interactive CADs in the 1970s. Microtechnology has added to computer capabilities, while advances in telecommunications have abetted innovative equipment configurations by interconnecting computers and peripherals in scattered locations. Furthermore, online real time has given us the control technology required for full factory automation.

An automated factory means automated engineering, automated manufacturing, and automated factory information systems. Activities that fall into each category are listed in Table 22.1 although, of course, variations may occur from fac-

Figure 22.13
A factory LAN system seen connected to other nets and devices

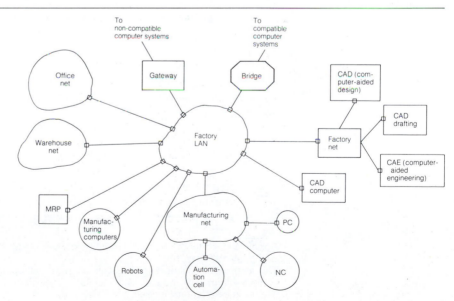

tory to factory. Computerized machines will replace many workers in the design of products and the manufacturing process, will monitor operations, will provide online real-time control of processes, and will integrate information on all aspects of manufacturing to facilitate management decision making.

Such automation requires a **local area network (LAN)** to join design and drafting devisions, the factory floor, warehouse operations, and office. A schematic representation of a factory LAN is shown in Figure 22.13.

Information subsystems are needed throughout the factory. Computers can be used for material requirements planning, inventory control, warehouse costing, sales management, and control of personnel, quality, facilities (e.g., scheduling, maintenance, utilization). Computers can smooth job movement, optimize resource allocations, and make adjustments for retooling and unexpected shifts in orders. **Computer-integrated manufacturing (CIM)** is the term used to describe factorywide MIS.

CIM is one weapon U.S. manufacturers can use to improve their competitive position in the world. Japan, South Korea, Taiwan, Brazil, and Malaysia all employ sophisticated technology to capture markets. Many of these countries have a lower wage scale than the United States which enables them to produce goods at less cost than American equivalents. Aging equipment in many U.S. industries further undermines the ability to compete. If we are to survive, we must implement innovative computer technology. CIM may be the key to continued American leadership in manufacturing.

Predictions for future in manufacturing

The president of General Motors was quoted in 1978 as saying, "I think it is fairly safe to say that within ten years computers will control about 90 percent of all machines in GM's manufacturing and assembly plants. This doesn't mean computers will be replacing men nearly as much as it means that they will be helping our employees to do a better job.[6]

Certainly there is every indication that the use of computers in production will grow dramatically in the future. A Delphi study[7] conducted jointly by the University of Michigan and the Society of Manufacturing Engineers makes the following predictions:

By 1987
    15 percent of assembly systems will use robot technology.
    20 percent of all companies will use computer-aided design.
    66 percent of all manufacturing companies will find computerized management information systems suitable for their use.
    About 38 percent of all manufacturing systems will be equipped with di-

---

[6] Robert W. Decker, "Computer-Aided Design and Manufacturing at GM," *Datamation* 24, no. 5 (May 1978), p. 160.
[7] This technique requires respondents to express their opinions on a numerical scale. They are then informed of the statistical results of answers in relation to their responses. This process is iterated until there is a stability of opinion.

agnostic sensors and associated software for implementing indicated changes or actions.

Software information for locating every individual part in a manufacturing facility will be in wide use.

The expanding use of computerized controls will permit prime contractors to transmit cookpiece configurations via leased wire to subcontract shops, and thereby reduce or eliminate the use of blueprints by 10 percent.

By 1988

50 percent of all direct labor for small component assembly will be replaced by programmable automation.

80 percent of all in-process and finished products will be controlled by computer.

30 percent of all manufacturing plans will be automatically generated by computers.

50 percent of all work force on the floor will be skilled persons operating automated plants.[8]

Summary and conclusions

There are many applications of computers in manufacturing. Some are data processing applications as discussed in Chapter 19—the generation of management and operational reports on such production subsystems as ordering, materials handling, and product control. Numerous other applications that increase production efficiency include the use of microprocessors for such activities as the regulation of current amperage and speed to machine motors, or making energy-saving adjustments according to the load on the motor. In this chapter, specialized production applications were discussed; the use of computers in smart products, robots, process control, numerical control, computer-aided design, and automated factories.

Smart products have embedded microprocessors that give them intelligence for decisions or choices based on calculations the computers perform. Robots are smart products used in industry. Initially they were introduced to replace employees in dangerous, unpleasant, monotonous, or inhospitable environments. But they now are used in all types of production activities since robot prices have dropped while labor costs are on the rise. Even skilled jobs like welding and assembly line work can now be done by robots.

In numerical control, computers direct machines for such operations as boring, planing, or milling. Each machine may have an individual microprocessor under the control of a supervisory scheduling computer. Computers also process analog data provided by sensors in continuous processes found in such factories as steel and paper mills. Microprocessors check sample data against standard performance criteria and initiate corrective action if necessary. As in numerical con-

[8]See *Delphi Forecast of Manufacturing Technology* (Dearborn, Mich.: SME Technical Division, 1977), 94 pp.

trol, process control computers can be linked in a network so as to optimize overall plant production and throughput.

Computers are also used in product design. Critical variables in design can be simulated, and design alternatives studied from varying perspectives. CADD can also provide drawings and specifications for production that can be integrated with numerical control for the automation of all steps from design to manufacture of a product.

A **factorywide management information system (FMIS)** coordinates computer subsystems throughout the company. FMIS facilitates proper planning, timely monitoring, and adequate control. Once all steps in manufacturing (design through distribution of finished products) are automated, and this automation is integrated with a factorywide MIS, **computer-integrated manufacturing (CIM)** is achieved. That is:

$$CIM = CADD + CAM + FMIS$$

Automated factories will disrupt the labor force. Workers will be displaced and will have to find new jobs. This will occur particularly among blue-collar employees, but managers will also be affected. The primary argument in favor of increased automation is that it increases productivity. At a time when the U.S. industrial edge is being seriously challenged by other nations, American manufacturers must automate to remain competitive. However, in addition to the social problems which arise from automation, there are many economic and technical issues to be resolved. For example, automated factories require high capital investment.

The incompatibility of many microcomputers also limits the ability to exploit micros to full advantage in the factory. The large number of micro manufacturers, 4,000 in the United States alone, is one reason for this incompatibility.

Though the United States is an acknowledged leader in computerized automation, both quantitatively and qualitatively, we presently lag behind many nations in the industrial use of robots. ASEA, a robot designed in Sweden and produced in Japan, is more sophisticated than any robot produced in the United States. Volvo in Sweden and Peugot in France use highly complex robots in their factories, perhaps the most sophisticated robots in the world.

One reason Japan is being increasingly successful in computer technology and applications is that the Japanese government has supported private business in computer use and manufacturing. At the end of the 1970s, a three-year annual subsidy of $360 million was given Japanese business for the coordination of computer development. The Japanese government has also launched a $50-million project to foster the use of robots in industry. In the United States, advances in computer technology rely almost exclusively on private enterprise.

A great surge in smart products will occur when voice output units are economically feasible for mass production at low cost. These units added to microprocessors will result in a proliferation of new products. Imagine a stove which gives oral recipe directions or a thermometer that recommends clothing on the basis of weather conditions. How about a freezer that announces food needing restocking? The production of such items will not only create new jobs but will add enjoyment and comfort to our lives.

Key words

Actuator
CAD/CAM
Collage
Computer-aided design (CAD)
Computer-aided manufacturing (CAM)
Computer-aided design and drafting (CADD)
Computer integrated manufacturing (CIM)
Context-dependent processing
Controller
Control variables
Dedicated NC computer
Digitizer
Direct digital computer (DDC)

Direct numerical control (DNC)
Disturbances
Factorywide management information system (FMIS)
Image mixing
Local area network (LAN)
Manipulated variables
Numerical control (NC)
Process control (PC)
Processor
Robot
Scheduling computer
Sensor
Set points
Smart product
Supervisory computers

Discussion questions

1. What is a smart product? What is a smart terminal?
2. Discuss functional applications of computers in manufacturing in:
   a. Design of product.
   b. Manufacture of product.
   c. Testing of product.
   d. Control of manufacturing process.
   e. Performance of product.
3. What are the implications of CAD for the manufacturing process?
4. How can robots be used in:
   a. A house?
   b. An office?
   c. Manufacturing of a part?
   d. An assembly plant?
   e. A continuous industrial process?
5. There are more industrial robots in Japan than in the United States, yet some of those are manufactured from U.S. patents. Why is this the case? What limits robot use in the United States?
6. What are the economic and social implications of industrial robots?
7. What is the difference between numerical control and process control? Give examples (other than from text) of each.

8. How can numerical and process control be used in fully automating production? What industries and tasks are most appropriate for each type of control? Give examples from industry.

9. What is the potential of CAD in industry in the United States? How will CAD use vary between industries? Why this variance?

10. What is needed to integrate NC, PC, and CAD? What would be the effect of this integration?

11. What is the effect of CAM on:
    a. Productivity?
    b. Competitiveness?
    c. Unemployment?
    d. Society?

12. Comment on the statement: A computer is nothing but a fast arithmetic machine. It is an obedient intellectual machine that can do only what it is told to do.

13. Describe briefly smart products not mentioned in the book now available on the market.

14. Do you believe that the government should support research in robotics and the development of automated factories, or is this the province of private enterprise? How will advances in these two areas affect the U.S. position in world markets.

Exercise

1. Draw a diagram showing the use of robots:
   a. In an assembly plant.
   b. In an office.
   c. In production.
   d. In connection with numerical control.
   e. In connection with process control.

Selected annotated bibliography

Albus, James S. "Robots in the Workplace: The Key to a Prosperous Future." *Futurist* 17, no. 1 (February 1983), pp. 22–27.

According to Albus, robots will become cheaper and more sophisticated. They will increase productivity and quite possibly make all of us rich. When? Over the next two centuries, though many changes will take place by the 1990s.

Another article in this same issue, "The Potential Impact of Robots," discusses the displacement of humans and the changes such displacement will bring to our social structure.

Argote, Linda; Paul S. Goodman; and David Schkade. "The Human Side and Robotics: How Workers React to a Robot." *Sloan Management Review* 24, no. 3 (Spring 1983), pp. 31–41.

This case study of one factory focuses on workers' psychological reactions to robots and the emotional stress employees experience when robots are used.

Ayers, Robert and Steve Miller. "Industrial Robots on the Line." *Technology Review* 85, no. 3 (May/June 1982), pp. 34–47.

The author predicts that more sophisticated robots will replace almost all operators in manufacturing by 2025 (about 8 percent of today's work force) and will perform a great number of routine manufacturing jobs.

Beavers, Alex N., Jr. "Factory Automation." *Mini-Micro Systems* 15, no. 12 (December 1982), pp. 222–29.

According to Beavers, the need to boost productivity has forced companies to automate and integrate design engineering with machine control, process control, and management information. Excellent diagrams support this short, but meaningful, discussion.

Foulkes, Fred K., and Jeffrey L. Hirsch. "People Make Robots Work." *Harvard Business Review* 62, no. 1 (January–February 1984), pp. 94–102.

Introducing robots successfully to the workplace depends largely on management decisions: how soon, where, and how many.

Gerwin, Donald. "The Dos and Dont's of Computerized Manufacturing." *Harvard Business Review* 60, no. 6 (March–April 1982), pp. 107–116.

A good, general, nontechnical description of computer-aided manufacturing. This paper also discusses why a company should install CAM equipment in stages and as modules.

Groover, Mikell P. *Automation, Production Systems, and Computer-aided Manufacturing.* Englewood Cliffs, N.J.: Prentice-Hall 1980, 601.

This book surveys various topics on the subject of production automation and related systems. These topics include numerical control, industrial robots, computer-aided manufacturing, process monitoring and control, group technology, and flexible manufacturing systems. The author also discusses the concept of combining automated flow lines with numerical control machines under computer control.

Hegland, Donald E. "Building Blocks—Technology for the Automated Factory." *Production Engineering* 29, no. 6 (June 1982), pp. 66–85.

This article defines and describes the components of computer-controlled manufacturing applications. See also "Building Blocks—Putting the Automated Factory Together," pp. 56–64, in which the concept of the automated factory is examined. The author argues that if manufacturing companies are to survive, they must think of the manufacturing process as a series of data processing operations.

Hudson, C. A. "Computers in Manufacturing." *Science* 215, no. 4534 (12 February 1982), pp. 818–25.

This article discusses computer evolution, manufacturing automation, robotics, fostering innovation, human factors engineering, and the sociological impact of automation.

Inglesby, Tom. "New CAD/CAM Entries Have Designs on the Future." *Infosystems* 29, no. 11 (November 1982), pp. 56–62.

The author reviews the entry of mainframe manufacturers into the exploding market of CAD/CAM systems, though manufacturers of speciality systems are still competitive. The beneficiaries of this competition are the designers of industrial and commercial products.

Johnson, J. "Pushing the State of the Art." *Datamation* 28, no. 2 (February 1982)), pp. 112–17.

CAM-1, an organization of hardware manufacturers, persons from software houses, and CAD/CAM practitioners, is discussed. CAM-1's goal is the push-button factory—a factory in which products are designed and simulated by computer, and manufactured by computer.

Lerner, Eric K. "Computer-Aided Manufacturing." *IEE Spectrum* 18, no. 11 (November 1981), pp. 34–39.

Lerner discusses the use of CAM in a flexible machining system (FMS). He evaluates CAM limitations in this context including lack of versatility, heavy burden of maintenance, difficulty in automating assembly, need for large investments, and market uncertainty. According to Lerner, FMS workers in Japan are having to work faster to keep up with new computerized machines.

Sullivan, Mortimer J. "The Right Jobs for Robots." *Manufacturing Engineering,* 89, no. 5 (November 1982), pp. 51–56.

The article includes blueprints that look technical but are easy to understand. The article describes how robots handle a variety of jobs including complex assembly tasks. Tips on selecting the best robot for highest productivity (return on investment) are included.

Teicholz, Eric and Peggy Kilburn. "Low-cost CADD at Work." *Datamation,* 29, no. 1 (January 1983), pp. 103–10.

This article has fine introductory material on computer-aided design and drafting systems. CADD improves drawing management, maintenance, and error reduction, according to the authors. Experiences with CADD systems costing less than $100,000 are discusses as are vendor and maintenance problems

Thompson, Harry B. "CAD/CAM and the Factory of the Future." *Management Review* 72, no. 5 (May 1983), pp. 27–28.

How CAD/CAM in a computer-integrated manufacturing environment will change the way businesses are planned, organized, and managed is discussed. Written from management's perspective.

Computers in the office

Office automation is long overdue. In the past decade, productivity has increased significantly in manufacturing, but not in office work. Although 40 percent to 50 percent of an organization's operating costs are generally for office work, automation is often brought to this work arena last. Office costs may be as high as 70–85 percent of operating expenses in some service organizations. Without office automation, these percentages are certain to rise. One reason is that salaries for white-collar workers are increasing faster than they are for blue-collar workers. Another is that the demand for office work is increasing so that the number of employees in offices is on the rise. Approximately 55 million of the 1985 workforce of 104 million will be office workers. Each year the number of reports and forms that businesses must submit to governmental regulatory agencies and tax authorities grows. Processing such information is extremely costly. In 1983, the 48 largest U.S. corporations spent an average of $54 million on office work.[1]

Since companies depend on information processed by office workers, most managers are seeking ways to improve the availability, timeliness, and accuracy of such processing. At the same time, they are seeking ways to reduce costs. Office automation is the solution.

The value of office automation is supported by a study by Booz-Allen & Hamilton published in 1980. In this study, the day-to-day activities of 300 managers and professionals in 15 major organizations were recorded and analyzed. They concluded that sound cost-benefit justification can be made for office automation, savings equal to as much as 15 percent of pretax operating income. In addition, time savings of more than 9 percent per year can be achieved within 2 years. Sixty-five percent of the savings in the study were attributed to (1) character-en-

---

[1] Randy J. Goldfield, "Achieving Greater White Collar Productivity in the New Office," *Byte* 8, no. 5, May 1983, p. 164.

coded mail; (2) internal/personal information retrieval; and (3) the use of word processing to originate and edit documents.

This chapter will discuss how the use of computers for electronic mail, teleconferencing, the war room, electronic fund transfers, and word processing increases productivity. These applications can be implemented independently or integrated in an electronic office. In this chapter, each application will be treated independently; the integrated approach in an electronic office is the subject of Chapter 24.

Electronic mail

Using computer technology, especially teleprocessing, to transfer messages is called **electronic mail. Instant mail** is another term used, emphasizing the speed with which messages are conveyed. Though speed is lacking in conventional mail delivery, the U.S. Postal Service provides home delivery of mail at low cost. Electronic mail can be delivered only to other computer terminals at a cost exceeding postal rates at the present time, but electronic mail may overcome cost limitations in the near future. This section will discuss electronic approaches to message transfer, the efforts being made to increase public convenience, and the prospects of electronic mail in the future.

Use of electronic mail

Businesspersons in all fields have a vested interest in the development of inexpensive electronic mail since many firms conduct a large share of their business by mail. One division of a $500 million company reports that it generates an average of 800 printouts daily, many of which are duplicated for distribution, requiring 1.3 tons of paper monthly, and a mail room staffed by five full-time clerks. This commitment of resources to mail is not uncommon.

The telephone is another communications device on which many firms rely. Busy signals, no answer, or equipment failures can be very costly to businesspersons. Electronic mail equals telephone communications in speed yet permits the storage of the message should the intended party be unavailable.

There are many **modes** of electronic message transfer that can be categorized as electronic mail. A message sent from one computer terminal to another is only one of these modes. Mailgram, a joint venture of Western Union and the U.S. Postal Service for overnight delivery of business messages, is another. So is TELEX by Western Union, and FAX. The latter electronically transmits text or graphic materials to a service such as Datapost, which then sorts and packages the messages by zip codes in 25 cities and gives them to the post office for next-day delivery. FAX currently has problems of machine compatibility and is slow in transmission, taking between ½ to 6 minutes to transmit a document copy comparable in quality to a Xerox copier. The process is also costly. A document page in facsimile form requires 200,000 bits. That is 1,000 times the number of bits required for a typical telegram, and 60 times that of a typical office memo.

Electronic mail requires that the addressee have access to a computer for receipt of messages. Currently, electronic mail is used predominantly for telegrams, memos, and short office messages, Citibank of New York City has an operational service, and several national networks for electronic mail exist, such as the **ARPA (Advanced Research Projects Agency),** though ARPA was originally designed to facilitate the sharing of hardware, software, and data resources. In 1969, when it was initially put into operation, the network consisted of only four terminals for the U.S. Department of Defense. By the 1980s, thousands of users had access to the expanded network as a substitute for telephone calls, letters, memos, and even conferences, the latter being multiperson dialogues transmitted to and from several network stations.

When host computers on the ARPA network are not of the same manufacture or model, an interface is required. **Interface message processors (IMP)** then handle and route messages in packages to connected host computers, the speed of transmission varying between one and two seconds. Connected terminals which have terminal IMPs are called **TIP.**

The exact capabilities of electronic mail systems vary, depending on their hardware and software configurations, but the following scenario is technologically feasible at the present time and may become commonplace.

Scenario of use of electronic mail

The secretary's office has a CRT-typewriter terminal with a programmable 10-key pad sitting on a desk cleared of paper stacks. When the secretary keys a message into the computer, it is validated by a spelling-checking routine, centered, and spaced with both right and left margin justification by software. Input messages are addressed to an individual, or keyed by subject to be sent to all persons on a distribution list for that key. A hard copy of the message is automatically printed for the files, and the message itself conveyed to the CRT of the addressee(s) on which an identification number of the intended recipient flashes to announce the arrival of a message. The message itself appears on the screen, once a code or password is keyed into the computer identifying the recipient, the code or password which matches that specified by the sender. After reading the message, the receiver can have it stored or deleted. When more than one message has arrived, a request for a list of senders to be displayed on the CRT can be keyed. The recipient can then decide in which order the messages should appear on the screen, or simply command last-in-first-out (LIFO), or the reverse, first-in-first-out (FIFO).

A traveling sales representative or manager may carry a portable terminal for communications with the home office, or use equipment at branch offices to query the home electronic mail box. Messages received may be rerouted from the home terminal to the traveler, who can then relay instructions electronically to a secretary regarding what responses to make. A draft message can be modified or corrected, then transmitted to the terminal of the addressee directly, with a hard copy of the message produced for home office files or stored in computer memory. If the intended recipient of the message does not have access to a terminal, the message can be directed to a computer service in the vicinity of the addressee, which prints a hard copy in batch processing and mails the message to the addressee for next-day delivery.

Sometimes a manager wishes to reference previous correspondence when drafting a message response. The computer can retrieve past correspondence or memos by subject, key word, name of addressee, date, or a combination of identifiers when programmed to do so. Other information from the data base can be referenced, extracted, and chained to standard letter formats to constitute a message.

Advantages and disadvantages of electronic mail

Electronic mail increases secretarial performance by a factor of between two and three. Retrieval and file management capabilities are particular strengths. In addition, the system is quieter than conventional typewriters and reduces the need for office storage since cabinets with filed correspondence can be replaced by computer memory. Firms with computerized information systems already possess most of the hardware needed. It is only when terminals or minicomputers are used exclusively for electronic mail that hardware becomes a significant cost consideration.

In spite of obvious advantages, managers tend to be ambivalent in their attitudes towards electronic mail. They like the speed, retrieval, and cross-indexing capabilities—being shielded from constant interruptions by jangling phones—and receiving and responding to messages when convenient. But management styles must change. Margin notes can't be jotted when messages appear on a screen, mail can't be taken home for late night work sessions. Nor can management pass copies of messages to associates in conferences unless hard copies are printed, in which case one *raison d'être* of electronic mail is defeated. Furthermore, electronic mail eliminates the need for voice or personal contact in many business situations. Gregarious businesspeople miss the human interplay lost when visual messages replace a phone call or a visit with an associate.

Future of electronic mail

The extent to which telecommunications will be allowed to compete in mail and message transfer with the U.S. Postal Service will determine the future of electronic mail. Cost will become competitive with traditional delivery once competition is allowed, since large-volume message handling will reduce transmission costs and be incentive for innovative technological developments. Once firms are allowed freedom to use electronic resources for communications, systems will be designed for transmission not only of data and text, but voice, video, and facsimile as well. Communication centers will be structured with integrated equipment, procedures, and data processing resources. Business will find it necessary to revise its whole approach to office communications, for electronic mail will become merely one feature of an electronic office (discussed in Chapter 24).

The future of electronic mail will also depend on how television is combined with computer technology. A VIEWDATA system already exists in England in which TV screens serve as terminals for display of requested information. Were this system expanded and widespread, messages sent by electronic mail might be received by TV owners, but in the United States such a system would further erode the prerogatives of the Postal Service. Television receipt of electronic mail would also require considerable refinement of existing TV equipment, since at the present time, TV does not have the resolution to reproduce fine print, or even a letter in small fonts.

Teleconferencing

Whereas electronic mail is primarily for two-party communication, **teleconferencing** serves multiperson communication, linking conference rooms within a large company, or conference rooms between firms. Terminals provide access to the firm's data base and serve as electronic flip charts, displaying specially prepared materials stored in the base for participants at distant locations (information that might be presented on a flip chart at a conventional conference). Subgroups with access to terminals can communicate during the teleconference, and even "whisper" bilaterally. Travel time and travel expense can be eliminated. A study by Ferrera and Niles, comparing the cost of visual teleconferencing with travel in the New York-Chicago-Washington triangle, found a 1.2 advantage in teleconferences for a group of two; and advantage of 32 for a group of six.[2] Computers can also provide a recording of proceedings in teleconferences and give participants flexibility in scheduling meetings.

However, many executives prefer live meetings, relying on interpersonal relationships for conducting business. Teleconferences require the development of new communication skills on the part of individuals.

War room (multimedia center)

War rooms originally served the military, being large halls with maps and multiple display screens where battles were planned and, more recently, strategies simulated, as in the SAGE system. NASA used the war room concept when establishing a communications and information center for space flight at Houston. Large businesses today have **multimedia centers,** an equivalent to military war rooms, where OLRT systems retrieve and process information needed for decision making and models simulate answers to "What if?" questions. Information is displayed on CRT screens, many of which have graphic and color capabilites. Top management, for example, might use the center to display statistics for the firm's predicted share of the market for five years, and then simulate "What if?" questions to weigh alternative marketing strategies. Or the center might be used to simulate results were a PERT chart for a major project altered. Sometimes such centers add teleconferencing capabilities, closed circuit TV, videotapes, and other types of equipment to aid management decision making. The war room concept was used by the consortium Alyeska during construction of the Alaskan

---

[2] Joseph Ferrera and Jack M. Niles, "Five-Year Planning for Data Communications," *Datamation* 22, no. 10 (October 1976), p. 53.

pipeline. It also serves small companies, such as Gould Corporation of Rolling Meadows, Illinois.

Electronic fund transfer (EFT)

In 1965, Thomas J. Watson, then chairman of IBM made the following prediction:[3]

> In our lifetime we may see electronic transactions virtually eliminate the need for cash. Giant computers in banks, with massive memories, will contain individual customer accounts. To draw down or add to his balance, the customer in a store, office, or filling station will do two things: insert an identification into the terminal located there; punch out the transaction figures on the terminal's keyboard. Instantaneously, the amount he punches out will move out of his account and enter another.
>
> Consider this same process repeated thousands, hundred of thousands, millions of times each day; billions upon billions of dollars changing hands without the use of one pen, one piece of paper, one check, or one green dollar bill. Finally, consider the extension of such a network of terminals and memories—an extension across city and state lines spanning our whole country.

This prediction is today much closer to reality. Technology for such electronic transactions exists, but resistance by individuals, banks, corporate firms, and regulatory agencies has slowed implementation. Known as **electronic fund transfer (EFT)**—an unfortunate name since the term implies physical transfer of funds—transactions are completed by computer and telecommunications. Information on checks (payee, amount, account number, check writer, depositor, institution) converted into electronic impulses is sent from one bank to another, a process known as **check transaction.** The check itself, that is, the paper on which the information is written, is not physically moved from one location to another. EFT can eliminate the need for checks altogether if transactions are done on terminals such as **point-of-sale systems (POS)** in restaurants or department stores.

Terminals can be used not only for fund transfers but to check bank balances to see whether customers do, in fact, have adequate funds to pay for purchases, or to check customer credit, reducing the risk of bounced checks. Systems can also check for reported stolen credit cards and monitor for possible stolen cards by analyzing frequency of use. While providing EFT service, terminals in retail stores can also collect information of interest to market planners and help monitor inventories. Other terminals can be used for automatic payment of bills, payment of insurance premiums, and cash dispensing.

EFT uses

Potential EFT users fall into three categories, These are organizations transferring funds through a bank, banks themselves making interbank transactions, and

---

[3] Reprinted by permission of IBM.

individuals in need of banking services. (In this context, banking includes all depository institutions, including savings and loan associations and credit unions). How these three groups might use EFT is described below.

Organizational use of EFT

Organizations which regularly write large numbers of checks (for payroll or accounts payable, for example) can use EFT profitably, eliminating check writing for these applications entirely. Accounts payable information can be keyed on tape, listing names of payees, accounts, and banks to which deposits should be sent. This information can be sent electronically to the nearest **automated clearing house (ACH),** a computerized version of the traditional check clearing house. The ACH then transfers funds into banks where vendors hold accounts, sending the information on through the ACH network for nonlocal banking institutions if necessary. The transactions to the depository institutions are completed by the close of the banking day.

EFT between banks

In terms of monetary value transferred, banks use EFT more than any other group. Early experiments with EFT included Fed Wire, CHIPS (Clearing House Inter-Payments System), and Bank Wire, a system developed by the Monetary and Payments System Committee of the American Banking Association. Bank Wire II replaced Bank Wire in 1978, after a $10- million, three-year study. The revised system is 30 times faster, sending 18,000 messages per day between 185 member banks and the Federal Reserve with a daily value of transferred funds exceeding $20 billion.[4] The system sends administrative messages and miscellaneous reimbursement messages in addition to fund transfers. The system is being constantly reviewed for greater capacity, faster speed, lower costs, and better security. It has a 100 percent redundancy, with its backup system capable of switching into operation within seconds.

SWIFT (Society for Worldwide Interbank Financial Telecommunications) has provided international EFT service between banks since 1973. The system is a ring network connecting major cities with backup circuits to provide alternative EFT routings should the primary circuits fail. Figure 23.1 illustrates this concept. The dark lines in this figure represent primary circuits, the broken lines backup. Should New York–Brussels be inoperative, electronic funds destined to Brussels could be transferred from New York through Montreal and Amsterdam.

EFT use by individuals

Individual EFT transactions can also take place on terminals. These terminals, frequently located in retail stores (POS terminals) instantly debit a customer's account and simultaneously credit the keyed amount to a merchant's account. Terminals can also perform many of the functions of a bank teller. Called **automatic**

---

[4]Edith Meyers, ''EFT: Momentum Gathers,'' *Datamation* 24, no. 10 (October 1978), pp. 53–55.

Figure 23.1
Segment of SWIFT ring network

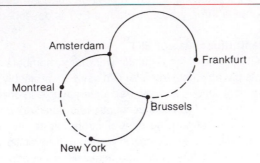

teller machines (ATM), these terminals can accept deposits or payments on loans and bills, can authorize transfer of funds from one account to another, and dispense cash. They can also retrieve financial data from the data base for reference. When placed in a shopping mall, 24-hour service for routine banking operations is available to the public. (Tax counseling, loans, and investment services still require a visit to a bank.) In the past, ATMs have had problems keeping supplied with money for cash dispensing. One solution to this problem has been to place ATMs near supermarkets that wish to keep cash supplies minimal for security reasons. Regular deposits by the markets at the ATMs keep the terminals solvent.

Resistance to EFT

Terminals for the electronic transfer of funds have raised legal and regulatory issues. Court battles are being fought over laws regarding interest payments and branch banking, for example. The uncertainty of the law has caused many banks to be cautious, if not to resist, the use of EFT. Resistance also stems from the high cost of EFT, loss of float, problems regarding privacy and security of data, and fear of monopolistic control. Each of these considerations will now be discussed.

Legal issues

Whether terminals performing banking functions are, in fact, branch banks subject to branch banking regulations was contested in 1974. A decision by the Comptroller of Currency, who regulates banking activity, stated that terminals did not constitute a branch, but a court challenge later partially overruled the comptroller, based on an interpretation of the McFadden Act passed in 1927. All parties recognize that laws as outdated as the McFadden Act need revision to fairly regulate computers in banking.

In 1974 Congress created the National Commission on Electronic Fund Transfers. The commission was directed to recommend legislation providing for the development of public and private EFT systems. The commission held hearings for two years, providing a forum for industry, professional, and consumer groups to voice their views on EFT.

In 1978 the **Electronic Fund Transfer Act** became law. This legislation regulates the issuance of access devices, initial disclosure of terms and conditions for EFT accounts, liability of consumers for unauthorized transfers, documentation of transfers, preauthorized debit and credits, and procedures for error resolution.

Not all legal issues have been resolved by the 1978 EFT Act. For example, additional legislation will be required before interstate EFT or nationwide EFT networks can be established.

The fact that EFT strains the resources of small institutions due to the high cost of terminal equipment also has legal implications. Small businesses find themselves unable to offer EFT services which large institutions can afford. Many states have passed mandatory sharing laws for EFT terminal equipment, but the Department of Justice has recently declared these laws in violation of antitrust legislation. Here, again, legislators must grapple with the implications of EFT in a free enterprise system.

Given the inadequacy of present laws and uncertainty over future legislation, it is not surprising that resistance to the spread of EFT exists.

Cost

The capital cost of EFT is high. Citibank, for example, has spent $150 million on its EFT network. An IBM study estimating 1985 EFT equipment needs forecasts 32,000 ATMs and 50 ACHs to handle 15 percent of all check-type payments through direct deposits, and 400,000 POS terminals to replace another 6 percent of the check volume. The total cost: $2.7 billion.[5]

Float loss

There is generally a four-to-seven-day interval between the time a check is written and the time a check is cashed. The value of checks or drafts in transit and not yet collected is known as **float.** In effect, float constitutes an interest-free loan to check writers during this period. Many corporate firms invest float amounts in short-term loans, in many cases using sophisticated mathematical models to optimize the employment of float funds. Both advantages, interest-free loans and short-term investments, are lost with EFT since the speed of electronic processing reduces float to one day. Of course, if all payments were made by EFT, the loss of float funds would be regained by accounts receivable. There is even the possibility that EFT would be profitable should accounts receivable exceed accounts payable. But firms have no control over how clients pay their bills. A company using EFT for bill payment but receiving income by traditional checks stands to lose money. No wonder cash managers oppose EFT.

---

[5]Frederick W. Miller, "Checkless Society Gets Closer," *Infosystems* 26, no. 3 (March 1979), p. 52; See also Earl Boatright, "Electronic Funds Transfer: Why the Benefits Outweigh the Costs," *ICP Interface: Banking Industry* 8, no. 2 (Summer 1983), pp. 14–16.

On the other hand, fast processing of transfers and exact information on the status of funds enable firms to reduce demand deposits and mobilize idle money. Funds can be transferred on a daily basis. This movement will have an important effect on our economy because of the magnitude of funds involved ($20 trillion in checks per year translates into $54.8 billion for a one-day float). A detailed discussion of macro effects of EFT is beyond the scope of this book, but briefly, increased demand for demand deposits and the conversion of liquid holdings into "near-money assets," such as Treasury bills and commercial paper, would cause a rise in profits and a corresponding rise in the GNP. The normal increase in income velocity of money (the ratio of GNP to demand deposits and currency) is 3–3.5 percent a year. Should EFT cause a spurt in this velocity by encouraging the flight of demand deposits, the Federal Reserve would initiate policy to curb the exodus and help bankers hold on to their demand balances. It might recommend payment of competitive interest rates on demand deposits, for example, but this would require a change in the legal framework of current banking practices and would profoundly affect all financial intermediaries.

Privacy and security considerations

The ease with which financial records can be accessed by EFT raises concerns about individual privacy and the security of financial data. EFT systems have all the security problems generic to data processing systems as discussed in Chapter 16 and two additional weak spots: input identification and telecommunications.

Many terminal systems for EFT are accessed by a plastic card identifying the user's account, but the danger of theft or loss of a card makes this control inadequate. Keys can be stolen for locked terminals and a determined thief will breach a password code. Voice, hand form, or fingerprint recognition are the best security. However, such systems are not economically feasible at the present time.

The use of codes and both encryption and decryption equipment help protect data in transmission. Fewer incidents of attempted theft are reported with EFT than with conventional methods of fund transfer, but the potential loss per incident is much greater. The vulnerability of telecommunications and the limit of liability to the customer prescribed by law makes many financial institutions cautious about embracing EFT.

In an effort to protect privacy of financial data, Congress passed the 1978 Right to Financial Privacy Act, incorporating recommendations of the Privacy Protection Study Commission for safeguarding records of individuals and small partnership customers of financial institutions from unauthorized governmental access. In addition, the Electronic Fund Transfer Act, requires financial institutions to periodically document to customers all transfers. Maximum liabilities and steps for the correction of error are also prescribed. There is still concern that individuals are not adequately protected by legislation in the electronic age, that EFT is an additional threat to individual privacy. This is another reason that resistance to the EFT exists.

Concern over monopolies

Small banks and thrifts are afraid EFT will lead to concentration of deposits in fewer and fewer banks. There is some evidence to support this concern. For example, Chase Manhattan estimated in 1977 that over $50 million of the $250 million received by EFT would have gone to smaller banks were it not for the bank's EFT service. Alarmists see Citibank spreading westward and Bank of America eastward, swallowing smaller financial institutions in their paths. Though antitrust laws, and legislation regarding branch banking, should prevent bank monopolies, resistance to EFT is partially based on this fear.

For many employees, receipt of a paycheck is the best part of the work week. A check in hand or cash in pocket gives a sense of well-being and accomplishment that is lost in electronic fund transfer. For such individuals, cash and checks will remain the primary media for monetary transactions, though such persons will probably use cash dispensing terminals and other services of EFT, such as credit verification. A greater effort to humanize EFT, for example, designing pleasing terminal environments and providing personnel to assist users, should help reduce consumer resistance to EFT.

Pros and cons of EFT

Table 23.1 summarizes the advantages of EFT and the reasons EFT is resisted. The fast processing of EFT is cheaper than handling cash, credit cards, and checks. Credit card processing exceeds 50 cents per transaction, with every indication that this cost will rise. The equivalent transaction by EFT costs only seven cents and this cost should drop with improved technology.

**Table 23.1
EFT pro and con summary**

Party	Advantages	Reasons for resistance to EFT
Corporate firms	Better cash management	Loss of float
Supermarkets and retailers	Quick check- and credit-card approval, which contribute to higher sales and market share	Capital costs
Financial institutions	Low cost of processing electronic transactions Automated teller machine services	Fear of monopolies Insecurity of data
Consumer	Provides convenience of: Automatic cash dispensing Direct deposits Direct payments of bills Home terminal transfer	Loss of float Potential loss of privacy Lack of "in-hand" cash

A benefit not listed in Table 23.1 is that street muggings and hold-ups should occur less frequently when most transactions are by EFT rather than the actual physical exchange of money. Individuals will simply not carry cash to be stolen.

Word processing (WP)

Word processing is another major application of computers for office management. The data processed is not numbers but text. With office costs rising yearly, businesses have begun to recognize the value of WP, a computerized system of hardware and software for transforming ideas into printed text. Computers can compose and format correspondence, and can edit, revise, update, duplicate, and file data for memoranda, contracts, reports, manuals, and reference materials. Word processors can also automate conversion of documents into machine-readable form, provide copy storage, and facilitate the flow of information in an office through reference and retrieval capabilities. In short, WP aids document creation and record keeping. Statistics comparing the cost of documents without and with word processing appear in Table 23.2. When WP equipment is linked to communication equipment, a further benefit, electronic mail, is possible.

Nature of word processing

An overview of word processing is shown in Figure 23.2. Input may be in the form of printed material, such as documents, or mail converted into machine readable text by means of **OCR (optical character recognition)** or facsimile equipment; it may be gathered by voice recognition equipment; or may be entered by key-stroking on a hard copy terminal or CRT system, a process similar to typing. Word processors may also draw upon data (text) stored in computer memory for input. For example, a computer memory can store an encyclopedia of statistics, quotations, standard responses to common queries, and text previously processed. Information from trade journals may also be extracted and placed in storage for reference, or articles may be entered in their entirety after being indexed for retrieval. There are currently 100,000 magazines on the market. Computer retrieval of information in these magazines helps businesspersons keep abreast of the latest developments in their fields for future document generation.

**Table 23.2
Relative cost of document**

	Without WP	With WP
Large documents	71	38
Small documents	68	42
Graphical documents	59	27
Document with equations	330	103
Forms	189	47

SOURCE   John Herrmann, ''Boeing's Work Stations Have the Right Stuff,'' *Management Technology* 1, no. 8 (December 1983), p. 48.

Figure 23.2
Overview of word processing

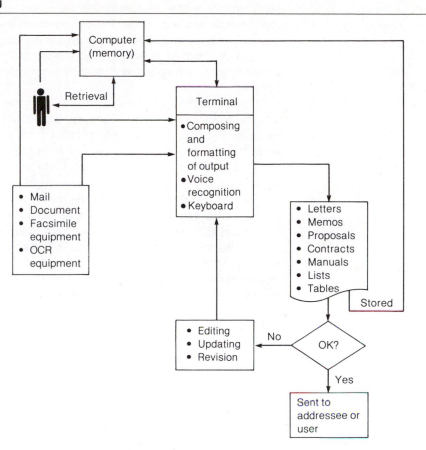

The text chosen for output is formatted under software control. This includes centering, left and right justification, and horizontal and vertical spacing on a page. In conventional text preparation, 38 percent of all copy goes into the wastebasket because of typewriting errors. The nervousness a typist feels, particularly near the end of a page when an error will require retyping the entire page, is eliminated in word processing since corrections can be made one letter, one word, one line, or one paragraph at a time after the page is typed, the word processor making all the necessary format adjustments for corrections automatically. Insertions and deletions can also be performed easily by one command. A dictionary stored in the memory unit can be referenced quickly to check on spelling and syllable divisions.

Text stored in memory, once edited, can be reproduced without mistakes, a tremendous saving over conventional typing where each retyped copy is subject to error. However, text in memory may have to be updated or revised. A final check must, therefore, take place after the output text is composed to be sure all editing has, in fact, been done. The document can then be printed. When the text has been prepared on a CRT, a code releases the text from the screen into memory and starts the printing. A second page of text can be composed while the first is being printed, or can be stored in auxiliary memory for later printing in batch mode if desired.

When the output is correspondence, the computer can be programmed to personalize letters, with names, addresses, and salutations added to the text. This capability was available in the mid-1960s with the magnetic tape Selectric Typewriter. What makes WP different is that sentences or entire paragraphs can be extracted from the data base and collated with other information provided through dictation, or reading by an OCR device in preparing the text. A change in wording, such as substituting the words "recreation vehicle" for "trailer" whenever it appears in the text can be done by a simple command under program control. Names and address lists can be drawn from computer memory, and letters for a selected list printed, such as letters to vice-presidents in a particular industry in zip code 88001. The system may also be directed to print letters and envelopes with a font chosen from a large variety of styles and sizes. In addition, the system can keep track of time spent on each job to facilitate charging customer accounts for service. This feature is particularly valuable for law and consulting firms.

If the word processor has telecommunications equipment and addressees have terminals, electronic mail with instant delivery can be transmitted instead of preparing copies of text. Text storage can be in the computer memory, on microfilm, microfiche, floppy disk, or a computer peripheral instead of hard copy.

General Mills is an example of a company using WP for correspondence. Some 10,000 letters composed from a set of 550 paragraphs stored in memory are mailed each month in response to letters regarding Betty Crocker products. The letters appear customized. So do documents, such as contracts and manuals, prepared by word processors. The wide variety of office applications for word processors, and their speed, accuracy, and convenience are reasons business people are turning to this office use of computers.

When word processing?

Word processors will never replace secretaries entirely. Personal correspondence and documents directed to a particular situation or recipient require conventional methods of preparation. WP is of value primarily for documents with a large receivership, for messages that are repetitive, and for documents that must be regenerated periodically with only minor revisions and updating of text. For such documents, word processing reduces lead time up to 50 percent, and proofreading by 10–95 percent. In addition, reproductions are highly accurate and have cosmetic formatting and lettering.

The need for word processing should be established by a cost-benefit analysis before firms invest in the equipment. Fortunately, WP can be acquired in modules so that receptive departments can initiate word processing and demonstrate its value to other departments in the firm.

Computer resource requirements of word processing

Current hardware for WP falls into one of four categories:

1. Stand-alone hardcopy WP
    This system, with limited editing and processing capabilities, can produce repetitive letters and merge prerecorded text on cassettes to produce hard copy. This system is "blind," permitting no visualization of the text before the output is produced.
2. Stand-alone display WP
    Composition and editing are done on a CRT screen with a minicomputer editing and processing the text. The system is intelligent, with many of the capabilities described earlier in this section.
3. Terminals
    Terminals attached to a large computer system with word processing software provide users with shared-logic WP. Users who share a centralized system pay less for hardware and software, but problems of equipment conformity, CPU availability, and priorities inherent in all sharing systems arise.
4. Time-shared services
    WP services may be provided to customer firms by computer utilities. Time-shared services are appropriate when word processing volume is small, when sophisticated equipment for pictorial or graphic processing is required, or when access to large data banks is needed, such as access to libraries of manufacturing, engineering, or architectural specifications. Large firms might combine internal time-sharing systems with contracted external time-sharing.

Regardless of CPU, WP requires extensive memory hardware. Text requires more space than numerical data since the size of field and record length are variable, not fixed as in many data processing applications. This means that text cannot be stored sequentially in predetermined fields, but must be kept in random storage linked by pointers. The software required for this type of access is not new nor limited to WP. What is new is the software to retrieve and then edit textual data. The newspaper industry has made large investments in software for composition and text editing, so firms can acquire WP packages for as little as $40 per month lease or $200 purchase. Sophisticated packages, however, cost up to 40 times as much.

What is still lacking is adequate software to integrate WP with data processing telecommunications and applications, such as electronic mail and teleconferencing. Also needed are packages for quick retrieval of correspondence and memorandum from a context index (or by subject, names, or dates).

Future of word processing

At present, word processing technology exists and the equipment itself is easy to operate. Secretaries already trained in the use of magnetic tape Selectric Typewriters show little resistance converting to WP, and productivity of WP is high.[6]

However, there are problems that limit widespread use of word processing systems. The capital cost is high; equipment ranges from $5,000–200,000. Units cannot be justified economically unless systems do more than simply replace typists. Applications, such as filing and retrieval, electronic mail, account and record keeping, appointment scheduling, selective dissemination of information, trade magazine browsing, and so forth, must be added. As more and more applications are developed and as secretaries become competent in their use, the market demand for WP will increase. With greater demand, economies of scale will send prices tumbling down.

WP also raises organizational questions. What units should be responsible for WP? Should WP and EDP be integrated? Secretaries may resist being assigned to a clerical pool for sharing WP equipment and managers may prefer private secretaries to the impersonality of WP. With WP, verbal exchanges in the office are replaced by instructions on a CRT typewriter terminal, and users must rely on the magnetic image of data on a screen instead of paper copies of text that can be handled. Users must also learn to index and code data for storage and procedures for retrieval. Though changes in long-established habits and work patterns will take time, increased office reliance on word processors is definitely the trend of the future.

Summary

Electronic mail, teleconferencing, war rooms, electronic fund transfer, and word processing are five computer applications that are restructuring office work in business. Electronic mail is still in its infancy. Since a large percentage of mail delivered is generated by computers and destined to business and government with computer access, office-to-office message transfer will be the first widespread implementation of electronic mail. Service networks, which receive messages electronically destined for individuals in their area, mailing these messages for overnight delivery, may be next. But the extent to which federal regulatory agencies permit the electronic industry to compete in communications will determine the future of electronic mail.

The impact of computers in the office is felt in other ways as well. Teleconferencing and war rooms are changing managerial methods of gathering information for decision making. Electronic fund transfers revise accounting procedures for accounts payable and receivable, minimizing the handling of checks and cash. The alteration of traditional relationships between savings and loan institutions and banks, the potential rise of banking monopolies, and the accelerated income velocity of money under EFT are some of the side effects that have legal ramifi-

---

[6]Eleanor W. Jordan, "Impact of Computers on Company Productivity," *Journal of Systems Management* 33, no. 7 (July 1982), pp. 25–27, and Mark W. McElroy, "The Productivity Myth," *Infosystems* 29, no. 6 (June 1982), pp. 140–41.

cations. Corporate managers must also contend with losses of float funds due to the speed of electronic monetary transactions, and the possibility that security and privacy of financial data may be breached due to the vulnerability of telecommunications networks. The adoption of EFT requires new office procedures, revised job descriptions, retraining of personnel, and a change in the physical environment of business offices.

Word processing has an equally disruptive effect on traditional patterns of office management. WP can be used not only for text preparation of correspondence, contracts, manuals, memos, and so forth, but can be used for retrieval of data needed for decision making, whether it be internal data from the data base (such as transactional accounting or corporate financial data) or external data from a linked data base (such as stock market and economic reports or data from *The Wall Street Journal* and other daily newspapers). An office with integrated computer applications is called an electronic office. This is the subject of the next chapter.

Key words

Advanced Research Projects Agency (ARPA)
Automated clearing house (ACH)
Automatic teller machines (ATM)
Check transaction
EFT between banks
Electronic fund transfer (EFT)
Electronic Fund Transfer Act
Electronic mail
Float
Instant mail

Interface message processors (IMP)
Mode
Multimedia center
Office automation
Optical character recognition (OCR)
Point-of-sale systems (POS)
Teleconferencing
TIP
War room
Word processing (WP)

Discussion questions

1. Why has the U.S. Postal Service recently abandoned its electronic mail program?

2. Will electronic mail and EFT require a greater degree of centralization than is now allowed by antitrust laws?

3. Should government-sanctioned monopolies (e.g., the telephone company) be used to provide standardized EFT/electronic mail services?

4. Will advances in electronic office technology eventually make the use of paper obsolete for office purposes (e.g., money, letters, and office documents)?

5. What new communication skills are required by teleconferencing?

6. To what degree is the "human element" necessary in teleconferencing systems? How can a cybernetic environment be humanized?

7. What are the weak points of a computerized credit and moneyless society? How can these weak points be controlled?

8. What are the effects of EFT as seen from the following viewpoints:
   a. Micro?
   b. Macro?
   c. Economic?
   d. Social?

9. Can EFT systems be made as secure as present-day fund transfer systems (e.g., checks and drafts)?

10. Should the government implement a nationwide EFT network?

11. What is the difference between data processing and word processing?

12. Comment on the statement: Word processing will do for society what data processing did earlier.

13. State the ways in which computers will affect your chosen major field of interest. Explain.

Exercises

1. Read K. L. Kraemer and K. W. Colton, "Policy, Values and EFT Research: Anatomy of a Research Agenda," *ACM Communications* 22, no. 12 (December 1979). List topics on EFT research relevant to businesses.

2. Collect articles from newspapers or magazines describing computer applications or implications of computer use. Analyze the effect of these news items on business and society.

3. Keep a log for a week of all your activities that involve a computer. Analyze the impact of computers on your personal life.

Selected annotated bibliography

Boatright, Earl. "Electronic Fund Transfer: Why the Benefits Outweigh the Costs." *ICP Interface: Banking Industry* 8, no. 2 (Summer 1983), pp. 14–16.
Boatright argues that banks must provide secure and convenient EFT services to stay competitive with other financial institutions.

Getz, C. W. "MIS and the War Room." *Datamation* 23, no. 12 (December 1977), pp. 66–70.
This article has a detailed discussion of the use of a control room for operations and management. The author argues that EDP resources can be used by management for appreciating, knowing, and analyzing data through a management control system using the war room as a nerve and communication center.

Guynes, Steve. "EFTs' Impact on Computer Security." *Computers and Security* 1, no. 1 (January 1983), pp. 73–77.
Security issues discussed in this article include the need for an integrated approach to assessing risks of EFT, designing cost-effective protection, and implementing the plan without undue financial risk to the company or loss of services to the customer. The context is banking, but the principles and approaches apply to firms using EFT as well.

Heinmiller, Robert. "Use Electronic Mail: Save Time and Money, Get More Work Done." *Industrial Research and Development* 25, no. 6 (June 1983), pp. 83–85.

The author, the president of a company specializing in electronic mail, discusses the subject of electronic mail.

Husbands, Bernard. "Electronic Mail—Applications for Management." *Journal of Systems Management* 33, no. 8 (August 1982), pp. 6–8.

The author suggests how the conference table can be turned into an electronic forum, or, if not careful, "a battlefield of personalities, a wasteland of productivity and a cemetery of unvoiced ideas."

International Data Corporation Special Report. "Productivity and Information Systems for Tomorrow's Office." *Fortune* 104, no. 5 (September 1980), pp. 40–53.

An interesting article with good statistics.

Jordan, E. W. "Impact of Computers on Computer Productivity." *Journal of Systems Management* 33, no. 6 (July 1982), pp. 25–27.

This article is the users' viewpoint on the impact of computers on office productivity. Most articles present the viewpoint of the professional computer analyst. This article helps give the other side of the picture.

McCartney, Laton. "Teleconferencing Comes Down to Earth." *Datamation* 29, no. 1 (January 1983), pp. 76–81.

According to the author, "The new technology is not just for top companies with enormous budgets. There is now a variety of modest-priced options and approaches open to the user." These options are discussed. The article includes a graphic layout for a sample system.

Strassman, P. A. "The Office of the Future: Information Management for the New Age." *Technology Review* 82, no. 3 (January 1980). pp. 54–65.

The author states that most of the uses for office automation to help clerical staff have already been discovered. This article emphasizes how office information can aid managers and technical/professional workers.

Zaki, Ahmed S. "Regulation of Electronic Fund Transfer: Impact and Legal Issues." *ACM Communications* 26, no. 2 (February 1983), pp. 112–17.

Relevant statutes are introduced and analyzed. Problems areas are also discussed at both the state and federal level.

The electronic office

24

Once we are able to have messages delivered instantaneously, the way we utilize them changes completely.

James Martin

The **electronic office** has many names. It is sometimes called an automated office, an office system, or the office of the future. These names signify a change in the nature of office work. A modern office is no longer a place but a system—an electronic system. This system claims higher office productivity, more detailed and easily accessed data and information, and faster communications both within and between organizations at low cost.

Today, American businesses are faced with climbing administrative costs (up 10–15 percent a year).[1] By 1990, annual expenditures for white-collared personnel will reach an estimated $2 trillion.[2] Figure 24.1 shows that the number of persons in the work force who can benefit from equipment to increase office productivity is on the rise. Fortunately, the price of important components in an electronic office is dropping. Communication equipment is down 11 percent annually, computer hardware logic down 25 percent, and computer memory down 40 percent.

This chapter describes the tasks performed by an electronic office, and the equipment components needed to perform these tasks. In addition, the problems a manager faces when implementing an electronic office are examined.

Office tasks

Before the value of office automation can be assessed, activities performed in an office need to be studied and electronic equipment identified that is used to perform these activities. In Table 24.1, office work is analyzed for a firm of 1,700 employees that produces both consumer and industrial products. The percentage

---

[1] For details, see International Data Corporation Special Report, "Productivity and Information Systems for Tomorrow's Office," *Fortune* 104, no. 5 (September 1980), pp. 40–53.
[2] See James Martin, "Successful Office Automation," *Computer Decisions* 13, no. 6 (June 1981), pp. 56–70.

of time spent in each office activity is listed for three levels of employees. Secretarial and clerical activities are further detailed in Table 24.2.

Electronic office components

Activities in these lists that are most affected by electronic technology are **data creation, data capture, processing, output creation, output distribution,** and **scheduling.** For example, the creation of input in machine-readable form by offline data processing equipment or an online terminal with a dialogue or interactive mode can replace conventional office procedures for recording and storing data. Data capture refers to machine-reading of hard copy data from correspondence, documents, forms, reports, or memos. Electronic processing replaces filing clerks and storage cabinets, and speeds computations and retrieval of data. It minimizes clerical tasks and time spent in report generation when terminals have word processing capabilities.

In an electronic office, output may appear on a terminal screen or be printed according to programmed instructions, often replacing the need for typing pools. Software can prepare charts and tables, check spelling by validation programs,

**Figure 24.1
Changes in the work force**

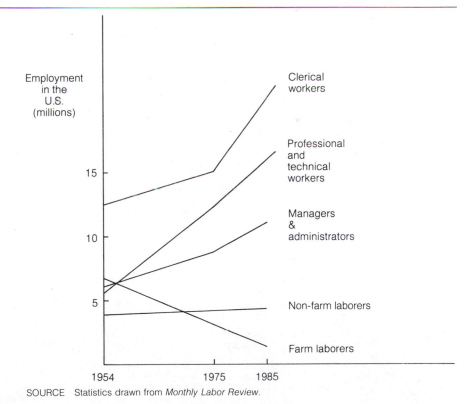

SOURCE   Statistics drawn from *Monthly Labor Review*.

and regulate spacing, headings, footnotes, and so forth in reports. Electronic mail, as described in the preceding chapter, will alter traditional office communications patterns. Even scheduling of meetings and conferences can be done electronically. For example, if updated calendars of employees and their fields of specialization and areas of responsibility are in the data base, the participants who should attend meetings on a given subject can be identified by a program and the meetings scheduled so that no one has a conflict. The computer can also coordinate travel arrangements with meetings (recommend departure time from office, flights, and so forth), prepare an agenda, retrieve relevant documents, and even send reminder notices to participants automatically.

The electronic components that can perform office functions are listed in Table 24.3. It is from this list that equipment and software will be selected for office **workstations,** a workstation being a configuration of electronic equipment and software designed for employees according to their work assignments. For example, an administrative secretary may require file management capabilities; a correspondence secretary, a keyboard terminal for handling electronic mail, an output device for printing quality hard copies and word processing. A manager, however, might need a light pen and a push button terminal with interactive

Table 24.1
Office activities performed by different employees: Percent of time (average)

	Level			
Activity	1	2	3	All
Dictation to secretary	4.9%	1.7%	0.4%	1.9%
Dictation to machine	1.0	0.9	0.0	0.6
Writing	9.8	17.2	17.8	15.6
Proofreading	1.8	2.5	2.4	2.3
Mail handling	6.1	5.0	2.7	4.4
Telephone	13.8	12.3	11.3	12.3
Scheduled meetings	13.1	6.7	3.8	7.0
Unscheduled meetings	8.5	5.7	3.4	5.4
Planning or scheduling	4.7	5.5	2.9	4.3
Traveling outside headquarters	13.1	6.6	2.2	6.4
Copying	0.1	0.6	1.4	0.9
Reading	8.7	7.4	6.3	7.3
Calculating	2.3	5.8	9.6	6.6
Conferring with secretary	2.9	2.1	1.0	1.8
Filing	1.1	2.0	2.5	2.0
Retrieving filed information	1.8	3.7	4.3	3.6
Using equipment	0.1	1.3	9.9	4.4
Other	3.1	6.7	11.4	7.7
Total number in sample	76	123	130	329

Level 1 = Upper management.
    2 = Other managers and manager equivalent personnel.
    3 = Nonmanagerial personnel.

SOURCE Adapted from: G. H. Engel et al., "An Office Communication System," *IBM Systems Journal* 18, no. 3 (1979), p. 403, © 1979 by International Business Machines Corporation.

Table 24.2
Secretarial and clerical activities: Percent of time spent (average)

	Secretary	Clerk
Writing	3.5%	7.3%
Taking shorthand	5.5	
Typing	37.0	7.8
Proofreading	3.9	
Mail handling	8.1	
Bulk envelope stuffing	1.4	
Pick up or delivery	2.2	0.8
Copying or duplication	6.2	3.9
Filling out forms		8.3
Telephone	10.5	9.2
Scheduling and dispatching		1.2
Meetings or conferring with principals	4.3	1.9
Checking documents		10.4
Looking for information		10.2
Keeping calendars	2.6	
Reading	1.7	2.9
Calculating		10.3
Filing	4.6	5.9
Pulling files	2.8	
Collating/sorting	2.6	5.2
Using equipment	1.3	6.3
Other	2.0	8.4

SOURCE   Adapted from: G. H. Engel et al., "An Office Communication System," *IBM Systems Journal* 18, no. 3 (1979), pp. 404–6, © 1979 by International Business Machines Corporation.

graphics, a planning language, and spreadsheet capabilities. Professionals may need hardware with color, graphics, or voice input/output.

Hardware and software configurations will also differ according to the employee's knowledge about computing and the reasons why computers are chosen over traditional office procedures. Table 24.4 summarizes why many secretaries, executives, and professionals use computers and lists factors that affect equipment/software configurations for each group. It is up to management to install appropriate workstations for maximum effectiveness at minimum cost.

Most of the components of an electronic office have been described in general terms in other parts of this text. In the next few sections, the special application of electronic equipment and software to office tasks are examined. Because compatibility of equipment and software purchased from a number of vendors is a major problem for office managers, many companies are turning to consulting firms for the feasibility, selection, and installation of automated office equipment and procedures.

Software

An important requirement of software for office applications is ease of use. Knowledge of computers and experience in programming should not be necessary. This means complex sets of commands must be avoided, English-like languages should be employed, and the system should be tolerant of errors, able to prompt when input is omitted, and both edit and validate data. Furthermore, a

Table 24.3
Components of an electronic office

Data creation and capture
  Computer console
  Keyboard terminal
  CRT terminal
  POS terminal
  Light pen
  Voice recognition unit
  Graphic unit
  Data tablet
  Telephone
  Pattern recognition unit
  Micrographic reading equipment
    (for microfilm and microfiche)
  OCR
  Card reader
  Tape reader

Processing
  Routine software
  Scheduling capability
  Indexing systems
  Retrieval systems
  Personal calendar system
  Information packaged services
    (for example, on industry status,
    stock market, newspapers, journals)
  English-like query languages

Processing (continued)
  Interactive languages
  Interactive graphics
  Bibliographical search capability
  Word processing
  CAI (Computer-assisted instruction)
  Decision support systems

Output
  Printer
  Plotter
  CRT display units
  COM
  Audio

Copying and distribution
  Electronic mail
  Intelligent copiers
  Smart facsimile devices
  Automatic typesetting
  Teleconferencing
  Integrated communication of data,
    word, voice, graphics, and images
  Networks access
    internal
    external

large choice of programs should be available for performing routine office tasks. For example, software might include existing programs such as SCRIPT for formatting letters; PROOFER to check spelling, LABELPRT to print labels; CIPHER to invoke DES for encryption, CALENDAR to announce events taking place in the building; GETNEWS for retrieval, using keywords; PREP2 for help in preparing files; HELP to query online manuals; MAIL to provide standard headings for correspondence; and REMEMBER to store messages for future reminders. TTF might also be available for composing multicolumn pages, and YMFP for formatting technical text. YMFP, for example, uses the Bell Lab language EQN to print formulas such as

$$y = \sum_{x=1}^{5} \frac{1}{x^4}$$

for which the following command would be needed:

eq *y = sum of x =* 1 *to* 5 *over x* sup 4

In addition to the above software,[3] the electronic office of the future will need **query languages,** languages with a dialogue capability as discussed in Chapter 3.

---

[3] For details, see A. M. Gruhn and A. C. Hohl, "A Research Perspective on Comptuer-Assisted Office Work," *IBM Systems Journal* 18, no. 3 (1979), pp. 432–56.

Table 24.4
Computer use by white-collared personnel

		Secretaries	Executives	Professsionals
	User	Secretaries, clerks, administrative assistants	Middle and top management	Scientists, engineers, and technical personnel
	Main use	Word processing	Query of information	Computations with data
	Secondary use	Electronic filing	Some interactive computing (e.g., asking WHAT-IF?)	Interactive graphics
		Data base access	Data base browsing & analysis	
		Letter quality output	Soft screen output	
		Create documents	Read documents	
		Calender/schedule (input initiation)	Calender/schedule (access & modify)	
		Electronic mail	Electronic mail access	
			Access to public data base	
		Teleprinting	Teleconferencing	Image processing
	Voice output	Not desired	Sometimes desired	Not needed
	Intensity of use (importance of ergonomics)	Very high	Low to moderate	Moderate to high
	Background in computers			
	• Knowledge	Little	Little/moderate	Knowledgeable
	• Familiarity	Low to high	Low to moderate	High
	Use of color	Not necessary	Sometimes desirable	Often desirable
	Software needed	Word processing packages	• High level/AGL • Query languages • Packages spreadsheets planning inputs	• Scientific languages, (e.g., BASIC, Pascal, FORTRAN) • Specialized languages, (e.g., APT, PROLOGUE) • Simulation languages, (e.g., GPSS, SIMSCRIPT)
	Motivating factor	Productivity increase Effectiveness	Competitive forces Fashionable	• Ability to do more interactively and more quickly

Figure 24.2
Daily paper on desk of an average clerical employee in the United States

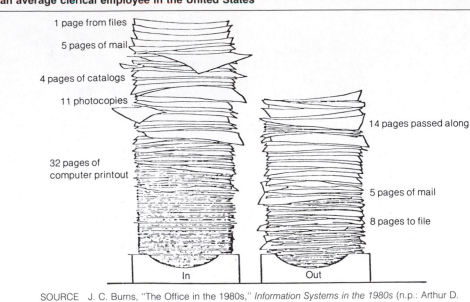

1 page from files

5 pages of mail

4 pages of catalogs

11 photocopies

32 pages of
computer printout

14 pages passed along

5 pages of mail

8 pages to file

In   Out

SOURCE   J. C. Burns, "The Office in the 1980s," *Information Systems in the 1980s* (n.p.: Arthur D. Little, 1978), p. 22.

These will help clerical staff determine what information is needed and assist in online retrieval.

Security should be part of office software as well. Passwords, for example, might be programmed to ensure that only bona fide users have access to the system. Pattern recognition stations will undoubtedly be used in the future, granting access to the data base by speech, fingerprints, or hand forms, but currently such equipment is too expensive for common use and not sufficiently developed to be foolproof.

Processing, storage, and retrieval

The amount of paperwork necessary for traditional processing, storage, and retrieval of office information is staggering (see Figure 24.2). In addition to the clutter of correspondence, memos, reports, and computer printouts, indexes of state and federal regulations must be on hand, and most managers keep trade journals and reference material on their shelves. Microfilm and microfiche can greatly reduce volume and storage cost, but information on film is not always easy to access and read, and space is required for specialized reading equipment. Direct computer storage can reduce storage space for office documents and information. For example, the computer can process and store electronic mail for reference and later retrieval, passing along pages or copies of documents to specified individuals through telecommunications for screen reading, eliminating hard copies altogether. Reports can be stored in memory, their existence indicated by a menu of reports that can be flashed on request onto a CRT screen. Terminals may be connected to services such as The Source for transmission of stock market prices, industry surveys, market surveys, or even newspapers and magazines.[4] By the late 1980s, it is predicted that many electronic journals will be available which eliminate the delay of publication and distribution, transmitting articles to subscribers as soon as they are written.

Information stored by computer must be indexed for retrieval, and potential users need to understand retrieval procedures. Some indexing may be automatically generated by software, such as the indexing of correspondence by name of addressee, date, and reference number. In many cases, however, a clerk may have to assign key words from content. In addition, the storage media, length of storage, and security/privacy levels for access have to be identified. **Coding** speeds this process but codes need first be designed by analysts, then learned by users. It should be apparent, therefore, that though the computer eliminates much paper shuffling, it creates new operational and management problems. But the demand for retrieval programs will undoubtedly spur software firms in the development of such programs as independent packages or as part of a generalized office management package.

The components used by managers for office applications can be multipurpose, serving other managerial needs as well, such as project control, forecasting, and planning. For example, a manager's office workstation may include decision support models on graphic terminals such as PERT and GERT. The terminal used for scheduling may also serve computer-assisted instruction.

Copying and distribution components

Copying information for distribution is an important office function. Stencil and spirit duplications were common in the past; more recently, copy machines have become widely used. In an electronic office, the need for hard copies will not be totally eliminated. Contracts, for example, will still be required for customer signature and not all clients will have workstations for receipt of electronic copy. But electronic office technology includes a fast online intelligent copier that responds to electronic signals from a CPU or from a terminal. A nonimpact printer can also be used which burns text on a photoconductive drum, converting the text to paper by a toner. Magnetic cards control spacing, justified margins, and pagination. Electronic mail, of course, will revolutionize correspondence and interoffice communications, as will teleconferencing.

Technological improvements in copier equipment and message delivery systems can be expected in the future because large businesses such as Xerox, 3M, and Kodak in graphics and copiers, and IBM and AT&T in computers and communications are all competing to increase or at least protect their markets. For example, IBM has developed the 6670 Information Distributor, basically a copier/printer machine, but one capable of performing a number of office functions. At its simplest level, the 6670 is an ordinary copier capable of producing 36 pages

---

[4] See Marvin Karnbluh, "The Electronic Office: How It Will Change the Way You Work," *The Futurist* 12, no. 3 (June 1982), pp. 37–42.

Figure 24.3
Configuration of an IBM 6670 word processing system

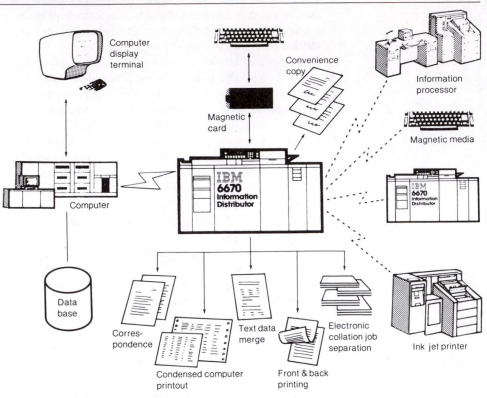

Courtesy International Business Machines Corporation

per minute. But it can also receive input from mag cards or from a remote but communicating computer or word processor which can be combined with other material to create original documents, output being in a variety of fonts and formats. The capabilities of the system are shown in Figure 24.3.

Other corporate giants will undoubtedly develop competing subsystems, providing the consumer with a wide choice of equipment components. One can expect that the electronic office of the future will encompass a wide variety of copy and distribution equipment. However, offices will not necessarily have the same equipment configurations. Small businesses may choose typesetting copy equipment as peripherals to their computers, whereas large firms may connect copiers in intrafirm and/or interfirm electronic networks. Intrafirm networks can be financially justified in large companies since an estimated 90 percent of the paper that crosses office desks is internally generated.

Office integration

Data, text, and images in a common data base should be organized and integrated for easy access and retrieval by authorized users, be they secretaries, executives, or professionals. This organization and integration can be done by software: for example, a DBMS or special software, such as OBE (Office-By-Example), an IBM product that unifies data processing, word processing, graphics, and report preparation with electronic mail.[5]

Another aspect of integration is linking CPUs and peripherals located in scattered locations. Here the solution is compatible hardware, along with appropriate software and protocols. Local area networks (LANs) described earlier in this text provide the linkage. Such networks are essential for applications such as electronic mail, teleconferencing, and EFT. Figure 24.4 is a sample equipment configuration for an electronic office including LAN linkage.

Systems to integrate office functions are already on the market. In 1984, DEC advertised a system integrating data and word processing with intelligent copiers/printers, typesetters, and electronic mail. Wang was selling a network to integrate DP, WP, image, and audio processing. Such systems are designed to provide users with choice of input and output media for a variety of applications using whatever hardware configurations fit user needs.

Implementation of the electronic office

The implementation of electronic technology requires capital investment in hardware, the allocation of resources for software development, environmental planning, organizational changes, the development of standards and managerial skill in smoothing the transition to electronic processing, all topics discussed in other chapters of this text.[6] Table 24.5 summarizes activities specially related to the implementation of an electronic office.

It is often more difficult to implement computer technology in an office than in functional applications. On the factory floor or in a warehouse, employees are fairly homogeneous. In an office, however, there is a wide range in the status of personnel—from clerks who receive minimum wages to highly-paid corporate executives. There is a wide range in the motivation among office workers, in their knowledge base, social class, salary level, and need for computers on the job.

In planning for an electronic office, close attention must be paid to human factors. The system must be customized to meet the needs of a diverse group. Workstations are usually designed for specific categories of office employees— the configuration of hardware/software for secretaries is quite different from the configuration for executives or professionals.

Training in the use of the electronic office is also part of implementation. Again, the diverse nature of office staff presents a problem, since each group of user needs a different type of training.[7] Training should help overcome resistance to

---

[5] For details, see N. M. Zloof, "Office-by-Example: A Business Language that Unifies Data and Word Processing and Electronic Mail," *IBM Systems Journal* 21, no. 3 (March 1982), pp. 272–304.

[6] For details on mission, organization, and staffing, see L. W. Hammond, "Management Consideration for an Information Center," *IBM Systems Journal* 21, no. 2 (1982), pp. 131–61.

[7] See C. V. Bullen et al., "A Case Study of Office Workstation Use," *IBM System Journal* 21, no. 3 (1983), pp. 351–69.

Figure 24.4
Equipment configuration in an electronic office

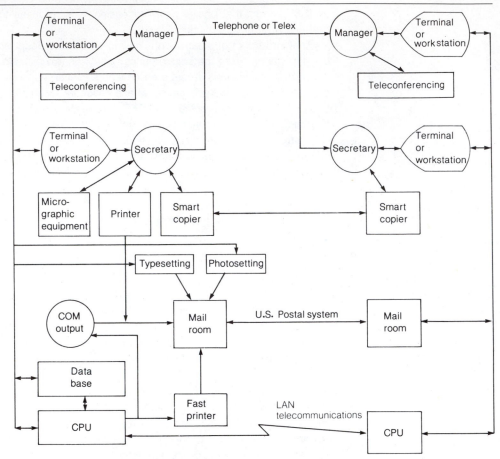

NOTE   Not shown are detailed telecommunication interfaces.

computer technology. Many companies encounter strong opposition to altering the traditional secretary-manager bond. When McGraw-Hill Publishing first attempted to introduce an electronic office, resistance was so intense that the company was forced to withdraw its implementation plans.

Some companies supplement formal training with an information center.[8] This is a walk-in facility where users can seek the advice and help of computer experts. (Such centers usually serve all users in the business, not just office personnel.) The center should be staffed with friendly people so that the employees do not feel hesitant or inhibited in asking for help. An information center which employees find threatening, demeaning, or insulting obviously defeats its purpose.

[8]See William Clarke, "How Manpower With Litle DP Know-How Learn to Go Online With the Company Data Base," *Management Review* 72, no. 6 (June 83), pp. 8–11.

Table 24.5
Implementing an electronic office

Developmental considerations
  Indexing
  Directory maintenance
  Filing and retrieval subsystems
  Text and file transmission protocols
  Security and privacy of data
    protocols
  Equipment use procedures
  Integration of EDP, WP, and
    telecommunications
  Short-term plans within long-range
    system plan
  Capital investment

Environmental considerations
  Space
  Reorganization

Environmental considerations (cont.)
  Aesthetics
  Noise reduction
  Security

Organizational considerations
  Changes in job content
  Changes in supervisory relationships
  Displacement of personnel
  Unemployment
  Training
  Human factors
    Fear of work invisibility
    Resistance to change
    Fear of machines
    Social isolation

A workday in an electronic office

Here is a scenario from a day of work in an electronic office. Upon arrival at work, the manager (Adams) requests a CRT display of the day's calendar. A request for a list of correspondence is keyed on the terminal at Adams's workstation, letters chosen in order of importance from a display menu, their contents read on the screen. A dictaphone is used for replies to be sent by hard copy. Other responses are typed online and delivered by telecommunications to the addressee. One response requires a meeting with Williams. Adams types a message on the terminal to the office secretary asking that a meeting be arranged later in the day.

Adams then keys a request for a list of jobs to be done. Included in the list is a message from the office of project control stating, "Project B85 Activity 10–15 completion due yesterday. Off schedule." Adams displays the PERT chart on the screen, locates activity 10–15 on the critical path, and retrieves the name of the employee responsible (James) from a menu for the PERT program. A message is typed to James, delivered directly to his workstation, requesting an explanation for the delay.

Manager Adams is alerted to the receipt of an urgent communication by a two-star flash on the screen. Secretarial messages such as "Meeting with Williams OK for 15:30 today," or "Dictated correspondence ready for signature," receive a one-star flash. A buzzer and screen announcement interrupt work at 9:55, reminding Adams of a teleconference scheduled for 10:00. Reports and documents needed for the meeting have been automatically retrieved and transmitted to the teleconference room, hard copies preprinted when so specified.

After lunch, correspondence prepared by the secretary is called to the screen, changes are made where necessary. The workstation is linked to an information network, so by a touch of a button, Adams is able to obtain accounting and financial information, current news reports, directories, and other pertinent information. A CAI (computer-aided instruction) course on electronics is sandwiched between scheduled meetings. A list of outstanding tasks keeps Adams informed of jobs that require attention, but priorities are decided by Adams, not by the computer. One activity, listening to conference proceedings on tape, is prepared for the homeward car journey. The tape is fed into a speech compressor that accelerates the proceedings to reduce listening time.

In conventional offices, 35 percent of an executive's time is spent on the telephone, responding to correspondence, and traveling. An increase in productivity in any one of these areas would be a significant saving. In Adams's electronic office, no jangling telephones or drop-in visitors interrupt the pace of work. Adams is alerted to important communications but can delay receipt until convenient. Little time is lost waiting for files to be located or reports typed. (The use of word processing increases typing productivity itself by an estimated factor of 10). And telecommunications, including teleconferencing, eliminate the need for much business travel.

The electronic office, however, is less personal than conventional offices since social contacts are minimized. Adams has few opportunities for chats with co-workers, few excuses for walks down the hall. This all-work environment requires self-discipline and both a willingness to interact with machines and knowledge of their capabilities. Successful implementation of electronic technology in offices will require a major adjustment in the skills, work habits, and attitudes of all office personnel.

Case study results

Electronic offices do exist, although implementation has been limited to date. At IBM, experience with electronic offices in two divisions over a four-year period has led to the following observations:[9]

1. An electronic office improves the quality of office services.
2. Operations are efficient, a savings of 5.25 percent in the time of the principal (manager or professional user); a 15–35 percent savings in secretarial time.
3. Five to ten hours of personal instruction to new employees reduce frustration with electronic components and provide the background needed for new personnel to follow regularly scheduled training courses.
4. Managers tend to initiate their own reference sequences. This apparently reduces the impersonality of the system, giving individuals a sense of having a system of their own, responsive to unique needs.
5. Users are able to cope with the new tools of an electronic office and able to incorporate these tools into established work patterns.
6. Enthusiasm grows as computerized aids augment in numbers and sophistication.

Another study done by Booz-Allen & Hamilton shows that enhanced decision making is the prime benefit of office automation, as ranked by those exec-

---

[9]G. H. Engel et al., "An Office Communications System," and A. M. Gruhn et al., "A Research Perspective on Computer-Assisted Office Work," *IBM Systems Journal* 18, no. 3 (1979), pp. 402–31 and 432–56, respectively © 1979 by International Business Machines Corporation.

utives polled who had implemented electronic office technology. The executives also listed higher managerial and clerical productivity, an improved competitive position, and the ability to pinpoint managerial accountability as additional benefits of importance.[10]

Future of the electronic office

World sales of electronic office components are on the rise (see Figure 24.5). New equipment for office applications is also under development. For example, **intelligent workstations** are projected with private switchboards that will store messages and forward calls. So are multifunction units that are either stand-alone

Figure 24.5
Growth in sales of electronic office components

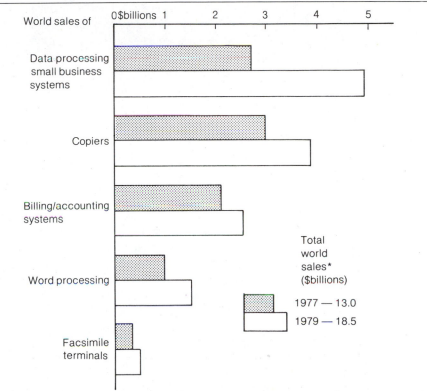

* Total for all electronic office products.

SOURCE *The Economist,* 273, no. 7113 (December 29, 1979–January 4, 1980), p. 56.
Data from *The Economist's* research unit.

[10] See Harvey L. Pappel, "The Automated Office Moves On," *Datamation* 25, no. 13 (November 1979), p. 75.

intelligent machines that can "talk" to one another, or machines integrated with larger office systems.

Laws, especially in the field of telecommunications, and the development of international equipment standards, will largely shape the electronic office of the future. For example, an international standard to regulate fax and facsimile machines was drafted in the late 1970s. At that time, Japan had 250,000 fax machines (word processing is less useful to Japan than fax machines due to the large character set in the Japanese language); the United States, 150,000; and Europe, 65,000; based on different standards. The draft standard regulating compression of data and rates of transmission should spur equipment development in the fax industry and promote tie-ins between industries across national frontiers.

Another international standard allows the scanning of more than one line at a time with a two-dimensional code and transmitting only differences between the two consecutive lines. This improves speed and gives better resolution of data. Further improvements would enable these machines to be intelligent, able to "talk" to one another, and to a central computer with a common data base. The central or shared computer designed not just for data processing but also for word processing, large data bases data base machines, and information retrieval, will then make the electronic office not only more efficient but more effective and with easier and faster access.

Summary

Office costs in the 1970s rose without a corresponding increase in productivity. The steady drop in the price of minicomputers, terminals, and storage devices coupled with the development of word processing and micrographic technology have provided the business community with a feasible alternative to the conventional labor-intensive office: the electronic office.

Today, terminals and micros are replacing typewriters, intelligent copiers are linked by telecommunications, and OCRs and microfilm readers scan documents and correspondence. Messages are sent by electronic mail, and magnetic storage and retrieval systems are reducing the need for filing cabinets. The response time in decision making is decreasing as stacks of paper are eliminated. Use of teleconferencing is minimizing travel by management. We can expect widespread implementation of these features in the years ahead.

Although computer technology speeds office information processing, the transition to new equipment and procedures is costly. Capital investment is high, and psychic costs must be taken into consideration. Resistance to machines and fear of change can affect employee morale and productivity. Managers may find that the solution of technical problems during the transition period will require less managerial skill than solving human problems caused by the disruption of traditional work patterns and relationships.

In this chapter, the components of an electronic office have been described. These components, when integrated with office information systems and data processing systems, can be part of a total information system for a firm.

A logical extension of electronic office technology is placing workstations in employees' homes. Providing personal computers may be less expensive than brick, mortar, and overhead of an office. Such a change would affect not only office structure, but family life, transportation, and urban development as well.

Key words

Coding	Output creation
Data capture	Output distribution
Data creation	Processing, storage, and retrieval
Electronic office	Query languages
Electronic office components	Scheduling
Intelligent workstations	Workstations
Office integration	

Discussion questions

1. List several dangers of the future computerized office.
2. List functions of the office that computers cannot perform well.
3. Comment on the following statement: An electronic office is more effective and more efficient than a conventional office.
4. In what areas can bottlenecks in office procedures be eliminated by computers?
5. What are some of the unique problems of an electronic office? What special human engineering problems arise?
6. List the advantages of a desk terminal or minicomputer in an office compared with the traditional office system. Examine these advantages from the viewpoint of a:
    a. Secretary.
    b. Clerk.
    c. Manager
7. How can a computer assist in the following areas:
    a. Correspondence?
    b. Information storage, filing, and retrieval?
    c. Text production, such as preparation of manuals?
    d. Conferences?
8. Why is it difficult for computers to retrieve information about correspondence?
9. Why is there resistance to an electronic office? What groups of people resist and why? How is this resistance manifested?
10. Some persons claim that computers, especially home computers used for office work, will create new office jobs. Others claim that computers will cause unemployment among office workers. Which claim do you think is true? Explain your choice.

11. Do you agree with the following statement? The computer will remove tedium and monotony from offices and make office work more creative, stimulating, pleasant, and easy. Justify your answer.

12. If workstations were being designed for you as manager and for your secretary, what features (hardware and software) would you want included?

13. If a teleconferencing network were established between offices in your building and 20 branch headquarters throughout the country, what features would you like the network to have?

Selected annotated bibliography

Byte 8, no. 7 (July 1983), pp. 40–129.
This is a special issue on Videotex. An introductory survey and tutorial are followed by articles on PRESTEL, NAPLS, standard graphics on a microcomputer, graphics as artistry online, problems of security, and use of Videotex on personal computers.

Cohen, A., and E. Cohen. "Computers: Ergonomics and the Electronic Office." *Architectural Record* 107, no. 11 (September 1982), pp. 45 ff.
The publication of this article in this magazine is an indication that office automation is affecting almost all disciplines.

Connell, John J. "Is there an Office of the Future?" *Management Technology* 1, no. 5 (May 1983), pp. 22–31
A major educational effort is needed at all levels of management to explain office tools that improve productivity. These tools will change over time. The term "office automation" is inappropriate, according to the author, since many office workers see their work as creative, not something to be automated.

Giuliano, Vincent E. "The Mechanization of Office Work." *Scientific American* 247, no. 3 (September 1982), pp. 148–64.
The author believes that substitution of electronic processing to replace paper is inevitable. A major factor is that the cost of computer processing is dropping substantially. Giuliano argues that productivity, job satisfaction, and service to the customer will be improved by office mechanization.

Grove, G. "Telecommunications in the Electronic Office." *Telecommunications* 15, no. 7 (July 1981), pp. 30–31.
This article discusses the differences between centralized, distributed, and local networks in the integrated electronic office.

Lasden, Martin. "Make Room for Executive Workstations." *Computer Decisions* 14, no. 12 (December 1982), pp. 116–26.
This article puts to rest many of the arguments given against the use of computers by executives. It also gives suggestions for encouraging top-level management to use computers.

MacFarlane, David. "What You Get When You Buy Office Automation." *Datamation* 29, no. 2 (February 1983), pp. 102–18.
Criteria to be used in evaluating integrated office systems are identified. There is also a comparison of systems from 19 major vendors. This article will soon

be outdated, but it is the type of article of great value to businesspersons. Periodicals can keep one updated regarding computer equipment if one keeps on the outlook for articles such as this one.

Mankin, Don; Tora K. Bikson; and Barbara Gutek. "The Office of the Future: Prison or Paradise?" *Futurist* 16, no. 3 (June 1983), pp. 33–36.

The authors believe that management, not technology, determines working atmosphere.

This issue has three other recommended articles: on office work in the future, telecommuting, and shopping for the office computer.

Martin, J. "Successful Office Automation." *Computer Decisions* 13, no. 6 (June 1981), pp. 56–70.

This article stresses human considerations when automating an office, and emphasizes that there needs to be careful education of users at all levels.

McElroy, M. W. "Productivity Myth." *Infosystems* 29, no. 6 (June 1982), pp. 140–41.

A sobering view that many factors other than increased productivity should be considered before computers are used in an office.

Mokhoff, N. "Local Data Nets: Untying the Office Knot." *IEEE Spectrum* 18, no. 4 (April 1981), pp. 57–59.

Contains good charts of some of the available local area networks and their relationship to office automation.

Olson, Margrethe and Henry C. Lucas, Jr. "The Impact of Office Automation on the Organization: Some Implications for Research and Practice," *ACM Communications* 25, no. 1 (November 1982), pp. 838–47.

Eighteen research propositions on the nature of the changes in work are discussed. The effect of such changes on individuals, groups, and organizational structures are examined. This thought-provoking article is for the serious reader.

Walsh, W. A. "Clustered Systems Integrate Information." *Word Processing and Information Systems* 18, no. 10 (October 1981), pp. 21–34.

One message of this article is that you do not have to be discouraged if your system is not totally integrated. Partially integrated systems also have great utility.

The microcomputer: Business and home use

25

The computer revolution is the most advertised revolution in world history. Yet one of the funny things about it is that we probably still underestimate its impact.

Hersh Weiner

In the early days of computing, computers dedicated to different functional applications were common. When powerful general-purpose mainframes were developed, computing became centralized to take advantage of economies of scale. The advent of minis in the 1970s led to distributed processing. Today, microcomputers are reshaping the way in which information is processed. Sales of mainframes and minis have reached a plateau and may even be in decline. The 1980s are the decade of microcomputers.[1]

A **microcomputer** (or **micro**) is a low-cost, small but complete computer system built around microprocessors. Today, 32-bit micros are as powerful as earlier minis and mainframes but cost far less. Since micros are easy to use, this computational power is available to users without having to channel requests for information through analysts and programmers. No longer must users rely on computer professionals who are often overloaded with work and unresponsive to users. With the microcomputer, decision makers have computational autonomy. Micros are proving to be valuable tools of management, extending a manager's scope and vision, while facilitating decision making. They are also useful as personal computers in the home.

This chapter discusses the capabilities of microcomputers, the criteria for selection, and micro management concerns. Sections are also devoted to the use of micros in business and in the home.

Capabilities

There are three levels of functional architecture for microcomputer systems: **individual (stand-alone)**, **work group**, and **cross-functional integrated micros.**

[1] For two other viewpoints on this subject, see Martin Healey, "Junking the Mainframe," *Datamation,* 29, no. 8 (August 1983), pp. 120–36 and Malcolm L. Stiefel, "Minis Are Still King of the Hill," *Mini-Micro Systems* 15, no. 4 (April 1982), pp. 127–40.

Micros at the first level are stand-alone computers with independent data bases. Such micros have no online backup and no way to access additional computing power for peak load periods.

A stand-alone microcomputer dedicated to a single user is satisfactory for home use and for small businesses. However, micros serving multiusers as a shared resource, with a common data base and possibly communications to remote peripherals through a LAN, are becoming increasingly common as tools of business. Many businesspersons select 16-bit machines built around a high-performance microprocessor or several linked microprocessors. Powerful operating systems are favored, such as CP/M, and multimode high-speed printers are generally required.

Owning a micro appropriate for a small business is like owning a compact car. Though the compact is adequate, the owner may want access to a luxury car on occasion and have need for a truck at times. A second car as backup is helpful when the compact breaks down. Although an individual or work group micro might meet processing needs of a given business most of the time, access to additional hardware/software is sometimes desirable and users might benefit from data sharing. The answer is to link micro workstations to a computer network which provides backup and permits sharing of computing resources—the integrated micro of level three.

Level-three micro systems can be quite complex. A communications network links micros and peripherals and permits users to share data. Some systems access public data bases, such as Dow Jones News and Retrieval Service. Some are used for electronic mail. With an additional layer of software, micro systems can interface with minis and mainframes. This gives the micro user access to the computing power of larger computers.

Systems architecture for all of the above capabilities did not exist when microcomputers were introduced in the 1970s. Packages for common functional applications were sold (e.g., payroll, inventory), but micros had limited value as all-purpose tools in a specialized business environment.

Today, however, sophisticated microcomputer operating systems are on the market, for example, UNIX by Bell Labs.[2] Micros can handle many diverse programs and run multiple programs simultaneously. Telecommunications, data base management, financial modeling, and planning packages are all available on microcomputers. Such specialized software packages as programs for law offices, dentists, and wholesale houses, are also available, supplementing accounting and inventory packages of the past. Table 25.1 is an example of the type of information a pharmacist can access on a micro. A similar wide range of software can be purchased for micros in most business fields.

Table 25.2 lists advantages and limitations of micros. Most of the limitations will be overcome by advances in technology in the future. Already a 64-bit processor for microcomputers is under development. We can also expect powerful

_____
[2] See David Fiedler, "The UNIX Tutorial, Part 1: An Introduction to Features and Facilities," _Byte_ 8, no. 8 (August 1983), pp. 186–212.

DBMSs for micros in coming years. By the end of the 1980s, micros may have the computing power and speed of many present-day mainframes. Some observers predict that parallel and interconnected micros may eventually replace mainframes altogether.[3]

Selecting a micro

In selecting a micro, user **needs** and **constraints** should be first ascertained, then **systems requirements** specified. Many articles and books have been written on the subject of hardware acquisition.[4] Procedures for purchasing a micro may be less formal than for the purchase of a mainframe, and selection may be left to the user instead of to a computer professional. However, many of the same type of questions should be asked. How will the micro be used? What special features are desirable (e.g., color, special keyboard, network access capability)? How much money can be spent? A list of factors a potential micro buyer should consider appears in Table 25.3.

The next step should be a study of the micro market. The features in Table 25.3 should be evaluated and compared on models by different manufacturers. When models with appropriate hardware have been identified, cost, software, and vendor services/reliability should be considered. Though time-consuming, this approach to selection will ensure that the micro purchase meets user needs.

In practice, customers seldom canvass the market thoroughly before selecting a micro. One reason is the size of the market—over 150 manufacturers were selling

Table 25.1
Use of a micro in a pharmacy

Daily prescription labelling
Daily prescription audit
DEA-controlled substance reports
Doctor activity list
Drug reorder notification
Drug content reference lists
Generic drug and formulary lists
Interaction audit
Insurance profile
List of prescription by:
    Selected doctor
    Selected drug
    Selected customer
Patient data base
Periodic update
    Report
    Analysis
Year-to-day revenue and expenditure accounting

---

[3] See Irene Shaw Nesbitt, "Move It To A Micro," *Datamation* 29 no. 10 (October 1983), pp. 188–94.

[4] See Hillel Segal and Jesse Berst, *How to Manage Your Small Computer* (Englewood Cliffs, N.J.: Prentice-Hall, 1983), and Donna Hussain and K. Hussain, *Information Resource Management* (Homewood, Ill.: Richard D. Irwin), 1984, Chapters 6 and 7.

Table 25.2
Advantages and limitations of microcomputers

Advantages	Disadvantages
Easy to access and use	Stand-alone micro has no backup or
Processing power rapidly growing	access to other computers in
Full control of operations and	periods of overload
applications	Limits on:
Few environmental constraints	Size of program used
Low cost:	Language of program
Start up	Software packages available for
Run time	certain models
Independence from central computing	Speed of processor
system	Processing power of 16 bit (and
Computing power available when	smaller) machines
needed and not shared with others	Less established vendors than vendors
No need to contribute to overhead for	of minis and mainframes
shared computing resources	Some programs less portable than
Variety of packages increasing	programs for larger computers
	To enhance micros, need
	communications link to access:
	External CPUs and peripherals
	External software systems
	External common data bases

micros in the mid–1980s. Even with the expected consolidation of the market (it is predicted only 50 micro manufacturers will survive into the 1990s), few customers have the time (or take the time) to make a comprehensive market analysis. Another reason is that many customers have no computing background. They don't know the meaning of bits or understand the importance of memory size, DBMS, ROM, or other technical features. They are intimidated by computer jargon and computer salesmen. Instead of canvassing the market themselves, they rely on the advice of friends or business associates, or may just make a purchase to "keep up with the Joneses."

Customer loyalty also influences many sales. Businesspersons place a high value on the past reliability and services of vendors. They may be cautious about buying a new product from an untried manufacturer even when the product may represent the current state of the art. LISA, a powerful, innovative, user-friendly micro designed for business, was not widely sold—perhaps for this very reason. The manufacturer, Apple, could not gain the confidence of prospective buyers.

To capitalize on customer loyalty, many manufacturers design new products for existing clients rather than enter new markets. Hewlett-Packard and National Cash Register, for example, compete only in the business professional market. The demonstrated staying power of familiar vendors influences sales as well. No buyer wants to purchase hardware from a firm with a tenuous future. How can users expect service, customer support, or future systems integration if competition threatens the survival of their micro manufacturer? Still another ramification of customer loyalty is that many manufacturers have introduced IBM-PC-work-alike computers, hoping to lure customers from IBM. Other vendors concentrate on IBM-PC-compatible products.

Table 25.3
Microcomputer selection criteria

Hardware
    Bit size
    Internal memory
    ROM or PROM capacity
    Speed
    Keyboard (shape, size, characters)
    Screen size
    Color capability
    Graphic capability
    Pointer (cursor, mouse)
    Printer capability
    Network access capability and interfaces
    External device interfaces
    User friendliness
    Computer size and portability
    External storage
      Media
      Type of disk drive
      Capacity

Software
    Choice and cost of packaged software available
    Level of language access
    Capabilities:
      DBMS
      Word processing
      Spreadsheets
      Windowing
    Operating system

Vendor
    Reliability
    Reputation
    Services offered

Other
    Cost
    Documentation
    Type of equipment (general purpose, professional or
      personal computer)
    Portability
    Servicability (easy access to service, spare
      parts available)
    Human factor considerations (ease of use, comfort)

In the acquisition of micros, price does not appear to be as crucial a selection factor as it is for many other products. In fact, the micro market may well be inelastic, insensitive to price reduction. (Drastic price slashing could not save Texas Instruments in the home computer market.) Furthermore, IBM's PC Jr., introduced in late 1983, was priced much higher than competitive products but still quickly captured a large share of the personal computer market.

Sometimes a specialized feature sells a micro. A particular spreadsheet program or preference for a mouse may influence a customer's choice. Sometimes it is the operating system that is important to a buyer. CP/M has dominated the

8-bit market but UNIX is favored by many 16-bit micro buyers and may become the de facto standard for the 32-bit machine. UNIX is appropriate for time sharing and supports simultaneous program development in BASIC, FORTRAN, Pascal, and other languages. Sometimes compatibility with other computing resources that already belong to the customer is the decisive factor in selecting a given micro.

In summary, features, compatibility, cost, innovation, reliability, and vendor reputation are factors to consider when selecting a micro. Customers assign different weights to each of these factors based on their knowledge of computers, the time they have available to devote to the selection process, and past experience with vendors. Unfortunately, there are no good rules-of-thumb to guide micro buyers. The large size of the micro market adds to the buyer's dilemma.

Managing microcomputers

The selection, operation, and maintenance of mainframes and minicomputers are generally the responsibility of computer professionals. The selection, operation, and maintenance of autonomous or semi-autonomous micro systems are generally the responsibility of users. This applies to corporate micros as well as to micros for small businesses and the home. Micros are designed to be "friendly" to attract clients without a computing background. No full-time technical support staff is required.

Nevertheless, many micro users find the need for technical assistance on occasion. They may require help in defining needs and selecting appropriate hardware. Guidance in planning for the collection of data, in selecting software, in designing systems security and backup may also be necessary. Periodic systems maintenance can only be done by trained technicians. When micros are part of a network, communications problems require the services of a specialist.

Generally, hardware vendors have **service centers** to provide their micro customers with technical assistance of this nature. Service representatives will help plan an appropriate system, technicians will install the equipment, training sessions and manuals will be provided, a hot-line for answering customer queries will be available, and maintenance contracts will be a customer option.

In a corporate setting, an **information center** for micro users is useful. Staff for the center may be regular members of the computer department responsible for corporate mainframes and minis, or hired especially for this service role. The purpose of the center is to provide users with technical assistance and training.

A wide variety of problems are brought to information centers. Users may need advice on how to format input for a spreadsheet program, how to debug a program, or how to run equipment. Sometimes the problem is in the nature of a crisis; sometimes help in long-range planning is needed.

Micro users who approach the center may be at different stages of Nolan's growth curve. An important responsibility of the center staff should be to help users understand the total picture—how each micro system fits into the information needs of the company as a whole. While aiming for self-sufficiency of the micro user, center staff should promote integration of information systems within the firm.

Table 25.4
Microcomputer applications

Accounts receivable/billing	40.0%
Text editing	28.4
Mailing lists	22.9
Financial planning	18.3
Stock/investment analysis	9.2
Sales tracking	8.3
Payroll/personnel	7.3
Inventory	7.3
Database	5.5
Graphics	4.6
Program development	3.7
Invoicing	3.7
General ledger	2.8
Scheduling/communications	1.8
Business records	1.8

SOURCE   Greggory Blundell, "Microcomputer Market Soars On All Fronts," *Data Communications* 12, no. 3 (December 1982), p. 90.

Use of micros in business

In 1985, a micro with 64K bytes of random access memory, 400K bytes of online storage, a keyboard, a CRT, and application programs for word processing and accounting could be bought for about $5,000. Such micro systems are satisfactory for most small business needs. The cost of supplementary business software bought off-the-shelf ranges from $100–$1,500. Programs in great demand for small businesses include turnkey software for spreadsheets, word processing, data base applications, and simple business graphics. Common applications for micros are listed in Table 25.4.

Micros, with off-the-shelf software systems, can be useful tools of management in large businesses as well. Many programs run on corporate minis during the 1980s could be processed by a micro at a tenth to a twentieth of the cost and effort needed to install and program a mini. Furthermore, managers could run micro programs without the assistance of a computer professional.

Why would a business manager use a desk-top micro? For making complex calculations required when needed to reach decisions in financing, tax planning, mergers and acquisitions, or investments. For sorting and cross-referencing notes in product development, marketing, and sales. Project managers find micros useful in scheduling work assignments and keeping track of development costs. With a micro, systems managers can often obtain quick solutions to user problems.

Teletex and videotex, which disseminate verbal and pictorial information electronically for visual display on a video screen, can also be of value to decision makers. **Teletex** broadcasts text and graphics as part of a television signal, providing a one-way information service. **Videotex** systems have two-way capabilities, allowing users to send as well as receive signals. These services may be public, such as Prestel and Viewtron described later in this chapter, or private. IBM, DEC, and Buick are sample companies with in-house videotex systems which can be accessed from desk-top micros. (See Table 25.5 for a description of these

Table 25.5
Sample private in-house videotex systems

	Videotex
	(Private in-house system)
IBM	DEC
More than 3,000 frames of information	2 networks
Voice capability	(1 for color interactive graphics)
	200 locations

Both have the following services:
Electronic bulletin board
Electronic mail
Employee training
Order processing
Teleconferencing
Electronic encyclopedia
Electronic calendar and schedule
Access to:
Public data bases (e.g., Dow Jones News and Retrieval Service)
Travel agencies and airline schedules
Security dealers
Specialized merchandise catalogs

systems.) In the mid–1980s, DEC used its service primarily for access to catalogs of printed material, including hardware manuals, sales promotion literature, and business forms. A user of DEC's system could punch in an order of selected catalog items which the central computer would print as a shipping order.

Videotex is particularly suitable for information leading to a transaction such as a phone call, letter, or purchase. It includes lists of names, addresses, stock quotes, items for sale, classified ads, and so forth. Videotex might also be used to provide a manager with facts, numbers, survey and financial information, and market projections either as background material or information leading directly to decision. Videotex can also add to a manager's awareness of factors that might contribute to a business decision by providing information of general interest, such as newspaper articles and reports.[5] One way to assess the value of micros to business is to study sales figures. In 1982, micro sales reached $3.06 billion. Of this amount, $1.99 billion represented the business market. The pie chart in Figure 25.1 shows the type of businesses using micros.

The limited processing capability of micros is a drawback to heavy-duty business use. However, technology is being developed to link micros with mainframes, called **mainframe terminal emulation.** The micro user can then log on to the mainframe as if using a dumb terminal and access the computing power of the mainframe.

At the present time, there are three main applications for such linkage. The most common is to provide users with access to financial planning package, such as IPS, and end-user-oriented file management systems, such as NOMAD, FO-

---

[5]Bert Latamore and Paul B. Finney, "Videotex: A Tool for Decision Makers," *Management Technology* 1, no. 8 (December 1983), pp. 22–29.

**Figure 25.1
Business use of micros**

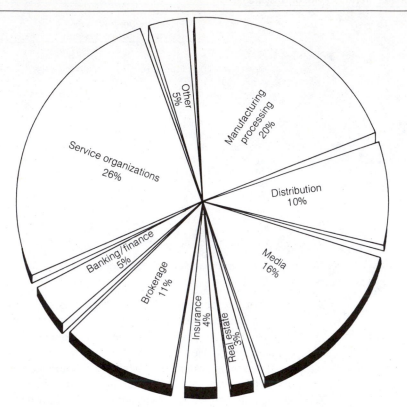

SOURCE   Greggory Blundell, "Microcomputer Market Soars On All Fronts," *Data Communications,* 12, no. 3 (December 1982), p. 90.

CUS, and RAMIS. Stand-alone micros lack the capacity to process such programs. A second usage is to access external data bases, such as Dow Jones, Dialog, or The Source. Finally, a micro user within a corporate setting can access turnkey systems developed in-house for employees in other departments when linked to the company mainframe.

In the near future, it is expected that micros will become active front-end and back-end processors for large-scale corporate mainframe applications. For example, a micro may replace a data entry terminal at a branch office, becoming a front-end processor. When not needed as a data entry station, it can be used for word processing or spreadsheet functions. As a back-end processor, the micro might be used to edit reports and distribute them electronically.

Micros may also become major users of in-house data communications networks in coming years. With a micro-mainframe link, employees can access data stored in a central corporate data base to process an application developed for, and run on, a micro.

In the mid–1980s, many technical problems with terminal emulation were still unresolved, the micro-mainframe marriage not yet successful. User expectations exceeded the state of the art. Since the connection of micros to corporate mainframes is a priority of most data processing managers, both hardware and software personnel are focusing on problem solutions. One can expect the micro-mainframe connection to live up to its billing in the near future.[6]

Business microcomputers in the home

Many microcomputers are used at home for business purposes. Authors, for example, often write books on word processors they maintain at home. Commercial artists with home studios may use the graphic capabilities of micros. Many programmers write and debug programs from an office at home, while salespersons frequently keep samples in a spare room where a micro is placed for completing reports and updating financial records.[7]

With telecommunications to connect remote micros to corporate data bases, micros at home will grow in importance as professional computers. The electronic office described in Chapter 24 could consist of a network of micros located in employees' homes (a mode of work called **telecommuting**). This would minimize the need for downtown office space, a savings to the firm, and reduce work-related expenses for employees (transportation to work, parking, dress clothes, restaurant meals, and so forth). Work schedules would also be more flexible. For example, persons who function best at night might choose 9:00 P.M. to 4:00 A.M. to be on duty. The schedules of workers need not overlap since all communications would be sent and stored by the terminal for retrieval at each employee's convenience. Urgent messages could be brought to the attention of even off-duty employees by being flashed on the screen, a flash reinforced by an audio buzzer. A weekly work contract, specifying hours on duty, might be keyed in Monday morning to assist a scheduling program in coordinating teleconferences.

The need for meetings and conferences would still exist, however. In all likelihood, employees would have to spend several days a month at the central office. The annual Christmas office party is another get-together that electronics can't replace—at least, not yet. It should also be recognized that electronic home offices are not feasible for all firms. Service industries, for example, rely on personal contact. Controllers of large and expensive manufacturing equipment will have to remain on site.

Electronic home offices will expand the nation's available work force. Flexible scheduling will enable parents to work who have childrearing responsibilities that keep them home. Many handicapped persons will be added to the labor pool. The employment of more part-time workers may prove cost-effective if the capital investment of a home workstation plus the wage is less than the value of the

---

[6]See David Ferris, "The Micro-Mainframe Connection," *Datamation* 29, no. 11 (November 1983), pp. 126–139.
[7]See Patrick Kenaly, "Product Profiles: Desk-Top Personal Computers," *Mini-Micro Systems* 16, no. 9 (August 1983), pp. 153–56.

worker's contribution. This enlarged work force will result in more competition for jobs. It is possible that unions, to protect members from unemployment, may resist.

The nature of supervision will change with home electronic offices. Less personal contact between boss and employee may reduce motivation and lower productivity. It will be easy to lodge a complaint, but also easy to ignore it. Employees may be more readily fired when management does not know individual or family circumstances first-hand. But this is merely speculation. The actual effect of home electronic offices on employer-employee relationships will take a long time to access.

The automobile industry, highway builders, and office construction firms will all be adversely affected by widespread implementation of electronic home offices. Telecommunications industries, however, will benefit. There will also be a positive benefit to the nation in terms of energy conservation. Just think how much gasoline will be saved when employees no longer drive to work. With the elimination of rush-hour traffic, pollution will also diminish.

The home personal computer

The sale of desk-top micros designed primarily for personal use (commonly called **personal computers**) began in the late 1970s. At the present time, most of the units are stand-alone computers. They are easy to install, operate, and maintain. In addition, the cost is within budget range of families. A variety of applications programs is available for personal computers. The software is conversational or menu-driven with both editing and retrieval designed for "casual users." The potential market for personal computers is an estimated 75 million U.S. households.

Table 25.6 is a partial list of functional software currently available for stand-alone home computers. Most people with personal computers purchase software packages but some owners write programs themselves. On occasion, quality programs of this latter type are bought by vendors, then resold under the vendor's trademark to the general public. Writing such programs is difficult since the instruction set of micros is limited and the memory smaller than in larger computers.

When telecommunications connect personal computers with a network of other computers and data bases, home micros have unlimited potential applications. (See Table 25.7 for sample applications.) One innovative application is being im-

Table 25.6
Applications for a stand-alone personal computer

- Address records
- Calendar, diary, appointments, and reminders
- CAI (computer-assisted instruction)
- Check-book balancing
- Christmas card list
- Computations
- Correspondence
- Dictionary and thesaurus
- Games and home entertainment
- Homework
- Invitations and menus
- Inventory record and control
- Tax record keeping

Table 25.7
**Applications of a home computer using
a telecommunications network**

Static informational services

Addresses	Investment information
Airline information	Library search information
CAI	Matching (dates, tennis
Car rental	partners, and so forth)
City information	Medical diagnosis
Dictionary, thesaurus,	Real estate information
encyclopedia	Restaurant information
Electronic newspaper	Shopping information
Employment information	Sporting conditions
Entertainment information	Stock market information
Games	Telephone numbers
Housing, education, and	Travel information
welfare information	Vocational counseling
Income tax preparation	Weather information
Insurance information	Yellow pages

Interactive services

Access to local officials	Medical counseling
Advertising and ordering	Psychiatric counseling
merchandise	Public opinion polls
Bidding at an auction	Quiz shows
Computer-assisted instruction	Reservations (airline, hotel,
Consumer guidance	theater, and so forth)
Debates on political issues	Shopping
Entertainment guide	Television ratings
Gambling	Travel counseling
Job counseling	Voting

plemented in Europe by France. It has nationalized post, telephone, and telegraphic services. Government officials have calculated that the cost of printing and distributing phone books, coupled with the salary of 4,500 operators to provide directory assistance, is greater than the cost of providing each phone household with directory assistance by computer. In 1982, the 10-year program to equip all French telephone subscribers with a micro terminal to retrieve directory information was initiated.

The following sections discuss home banking, home shopping, and home access to data base services from micros. The technology for these applications already exists and is being implemented in test cities in the United States. Widespread implementation will have profound social implications.

Home banking

Were EFT extended to the home, the personal computer would act essentially as a POS terminal. Payments of bills for utilities, loans, charge accounts, even tax payments could be transacted from a personal computer. The payers would first have to be identified by a password or unique account number, either keyed or read by machine from a card, but once identification was acknowledged by the machine "shaking hands," the transaction would instantly take place, a record being kept of all transactions at the bank which would make the actual fund transfers.

Home shopping

Another potential use of home micros is shopping. If information on a store's inventory could be accessed by a personal computer, a customer could obtain information on goods, prices, quality, size options, and special features—information such as one would commonly find printed in a store catalog. If pictures of goods were in the store's data base and the home user's terminal had graphic capabilities, products could be displayed, rotated, and scaled. After comparing offerings at several stores, an order could be placed through the home micro by menu-directed or parameter-driven systems, home delivery specified, and payment authorized through EFT. Such home shopping is not yet available in most communities, but this is not because technology is lacking. It is primarily because not enough computers are in homes to make such systems cost-effective.

Home shopping, once it becomes widely implemented, will change our current advertising and marketing practices. For example, stores themselves may reorganize, eliminating salespersons and goods on display, becoming warehouses instead. In addition to reduced overhead costs, shoplifting would no longer be a problem. How will home shopping alter the shape of cities? Streets, highways, parking, and city centers would all be affected.

In the future, entrepreneurs may market access to data bases that match "wanted" requests with available goods and services. Do you wish to rent a cottage on the French Riviera during the month of July? Do you have cocker spaniel puppies for sale? Are you searching for a babysitter for New Year's Eve? This kind of shopping also has potential for home computers.

Data base services

Terminal access to information of public interest, such as weather reports, latest stock market quotations, or movies being shown at local theaters, is another potential use of personal computers. Such information, collected and stored by entrepreneurs, can be accessed for a small fee by home computers connected to **data base services.** Widespread implementation will require telecommunications networks, but already such services are operational on a limited basis, such as The Source and Micronet.

Prestel is an example of an information service that has been available to subscribers in Great Britain since 1979. This system provides over 180,000 pages of information on shopping, entertainment, exhibitions, gardening, travel, and news. The pages themselves are displayed on the family TV screen, transmitted to customers for a fee based on the number of pages accessed and telephone line charges. Users request information by keying appropriate codes on a device with buttons for numerical input, a device that resembles a TV remote control unit and calculator combined. (See Figure 25.2 for a schematic representation of Prestel). Prestel does not have the capability of general-purpose computing, such as financial analysis or word processing.

Figure 25.2
Representation of the Prestel system

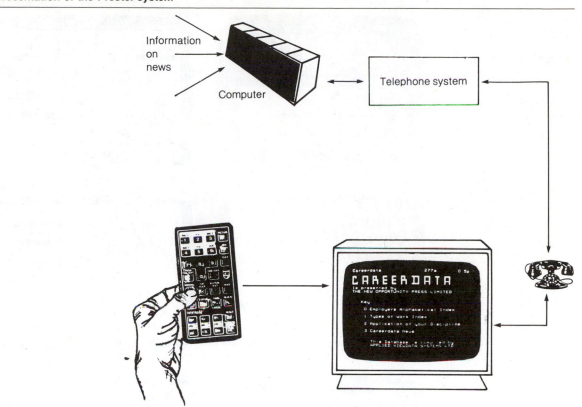

In 1983, Viewdata Corporation of America, a subsidiary of Knight-Ridder Newspapers, introduced south Florida to **Viewtron,** a subscription graphics-based service similar to Prestel. Among the services offered are local and national news, home banking, electronic mail, a link to brokerage firms, home shopping, games, school lessons, sports coverage, reference to sections of the World Book Encyclopedia, weather forecasts, gardening tips, travel information, recipe ideas, entertainment guides, and stock market quotes. Figure 25.3 shows sample Viewtron menus and output.

The terminal used by Viewtron consists of two parts: a small control unit attached to a TV set that plugs into a phone jack and a wireless keypad. The family TV screen is used to receive Viewtron information. The 1984 terminal price was $900: the monthly subscription rate, $12 per month. In addition, telephone line charges of approximately $1 per hour of access time were billed customers by Southern Bell. Viewtron plans to extend services to 35 metropolitan areas once it is established in Florida.

In 1984, IBM, CBS, and Sears announced a joint venture in the videotex business. They intend to send data to home computers instead of using "dumb" ter-

Figure 25.3
Sample Viewtron output

minals (TV screens) with no computing capability as in Viewtron. Such a venture should promote IBM PCs and provide a market for Sears to merchandise its catalog and financial-services products electronically. CBS will contribute its experience with advertisers, news, textbook publishing, and educational software operations. The potential market for such a service is uncertain. Obstacles to be overcome are high costs and need to change consumer shopping habits.

When data services themselves are part of a computing system, a matching response to a user request for information will be feasible. An individual's reading profile might be matched with a list of recent library acquisitions, or golf partners identified with a given handicap. The accuracy of any match is subject to programming decision rules, the data stored in the data base, and the correctness and completeness of data input in the query. With so many variables, the quality of information provided will differ from one data service to another. The home computer owner will have to be as careful "shopping" for information as shopping for quality merchandise.

A major advantage of computer information services over directories, indexes, or other traditional references is **selective processing.** For example, were the San Francisco telephone book in a computer's data base, all persons living on Sunset Drive could be listed, or a list could be generated of all restaurants that serve seafood. In addition, the computer can assist individuals in their search for information by ensuring through menu selection that all necessary input is entered in the system in the correct sequence.

Summary

This is the decade of the micro. The continual drop in the price of micros and their increased computing capability has had a major impact on information processing in business and in homes. Micros give individuals with no technical background or prior computing experience computing power. Micros are low cost, user-friendly, and easy to operate. Software packages exist to meet information processing needs of small businesses, and often serve managers in large corporations as well. As personal computers, micros are found in many homes.

Before selecting a micro, users needs and constraints should be ascertained, then systems requirements specified. Next, the micro market should be surveyed. Cost, features, compatibility, innovation, reliability, and vendor reputation should all be evaluated. Support services offered by vendors are also important since micro users do need technical assistance on occasion. Many large corporations have information centers to help micro users within the firm resolve problems that arise and to provide training.

When stand-alone micros are connected by telecommunications with other computers or large external data bases, the range of potential micro applications expands dramatically. In a business, such linkage gives the micro user access to the processing capability of larger computers, access to external data bases, and access to in-house turnkey systems developed for other employees. The electronic home office is also feasible. Such offices will affect the size of the labor force, urban development, transportation, the relationship of employer to employee, and personal work patterns.

Much software has also been developed for home use of personal micros. Address records, calendars, games, homework, and tax records are sample applications. When the home micro is connected by a telecommunications network to external computers and data bases, teleshopping, home banking, and access to data services are possible.

Although some technological problems still remain to be resolved before these applications become commonplace, problems and obstacles are predominantly political (regulatory), social (resistance to change and fear of computers), and financial (cost of developing the telecommunications infrastructure required.)

Key words

Business micro use	Prestel
Cross-functional integrated micros	Selective processing
Data base services	Service center
Home shopping	Stand-alone micro
Home micro use	Systems requirements
Individual micro	Telecommuting
Information center	Teletex
Mainframe terminal emulation	Videotex
Microcomputer (micro)	Viewtron
Needs and constraints	Work group micro
Personal computer	

Discussion questions

1. Distinguish between:
   a. Personal computers for home use.
   b. Micros for business use.
   c. Minicomputers.

2. What specifications are needed for a micro for a family, a small business and for a corporation? Discuss differences in:
   a. Make.
   b. Storage capacity.
   c. Processing speed.
   d. Peripherals.
   e. Software.
   f. Other capabilities

3. What factors do you think are important in the selection of a micro? Can you rank them? Would your criteria vary for:
   a. Micro for office use in a large organization?
   b. Micro for a small business?
   c. Micro as a home computer?
   d. Micro used as a business computer at home?

4. Describe how microcomputers can be used in:
   a. Small businesses.
   b. Large corporations.
   c. At home.

5. The microcomputer will have a sociological, psychological, and economic impact on individuals and on society. Comment on this statement.

6. Discuss problems of hardware, software, and maintenance when micros are used in a small business.

7. What are the potential effects of micros on business? How can adverse effects be minimized?

8. What will be the effect on society of electronic home offices? Discuss the following implications:
   a. Economic.
   b. Technical.
   c. Effect on employment.

9. Why is it desirable to increase public acceptance of micros?

10. Explain the national infrastructure required if linkage between micros, peripherals, and data services for business and home use are to become commonplace.

11. How can videotex be used by business managers?

12. How can microcomputers be used in business training? How is this use dependent on the type and size of business or industry? Is such training cost-effective?

13. How will EFT affect and be affected by microcomputers? What are obstacles to EFT extension to small and large businesses? How can these obstacles be removed?

14. What will be the economic implications of the microcomputer on:
    a. GNP?
    b. Work week?
    c. Employment?
    d. Displacement?

15. Describe the interrelationship between public data bases and microcomputers? How can this interrelationship be of benefit to individuals, business, and society?

16. What is slowing the integration of micros? To what extent is that desirable? How can obstacles to integration be overcome?

17. How will widespread use of micros change society? State any assumptions that you can make.

Selected annotated bibliography

Blundell, Greggory, S. "Bringing in Personal Business Computers." *Small Business World* 10, no. 9 (September 1982), pp. 24–31.

The author argues that managers should learn how to use micros now while they are still predominantly stand-alone computers. This will prepare them for the networking to come which has great potential for business.

———. "Microcomputer Market Soars On All Fronts." *Data Communications* 12, no. 3 (December 1982), pp. 88–94.

Blundell discusses the distribution of microcomputers by application, user, manufacturer, and year of shipment. The statistics cited in the article are interesting. For example, Blundell states that the cost per connection of ETHERNET dropped from $2,000 in 1982 to close to $400 in 1985 with a cost of $350 projected for 1987. This is a special issue of *Data Communications* devoted to micros. Other articles discuss micros in networks, the IBM PC, and user expectations for micros.

Cooper, Michael S. "Micro-based Business Graphics." *Datamation* 30, no. 6 (May 1, 1984), pp. 99–105.

Cooper compares eight PC graphic software packages and argues that they are not as simple as their advertisements imply. Rather, they are sophisticated, powerful, and user-friendly business tools. Use of the software can reduce the cost of slide preparation 90 percent over traditional methods.

Datamation staff report. "Adventures in Microland." *Datamation* 29, no. 11 (November 1983), pp. 153–56.

Advertising gives users expectations beyond what micros can deliver. What users want is access to mainframe computing power. This article describes the headaches and frustrations of data processing personnel when trying to resolve the technical problems of linking micros to mainframes.

Ferris, David. "The Micro-Mainframe Connection." *Datamation* 29, no. 11 (November 1983), pp. 126–39.

Ferris describes the voracious appetite of users for micro-mainframe connections, applications for such connections, and makes predictions for future developments in terminal emulation.

Forester, Tom, ed. *The Microelectronics Revolution.* London: Basil Blackwell Publishers, 1980, 589 pp.

This book includes articles on use of micros in smart machines (pp. 103–24); microprocessor applications (pp. 125–29); micros in consumer products (pp. 130–37); use of micros in industry (pp. 138–51); and micros in the classroom (pp. 152–58).

Hedberg, Augustin. "Choosing the Best Computer For You." *Money* 2, no. 11, (November 1982), pp. 68–112.

This article will assist the nontechnical person in choosing a micro. Applications, peripherals, interfaces, and software are discussed. Specifications for 38 different products are given.

Jacobsen, Herb, and John Cordullo. "Information Centers: Boon or Bane?" *Management Technology* 1, no. 5, (September 1983), pp. 45–48.

The implementation and use of information centers are subjects of this article. The need of a plan, resources, and the importance of cooperation between user communities and data processing personnel are other topics covered.

Lodahl, Thomas M. "Micro-Power for Managers." *Management Technology* 1, no. 8 (August 1983), pp. 28–35.

This article discusses the architecture, network potential, portability, and price of small computers.

Martin, James. *Viewdata and the Information Society*. Englewood Cliffs, N.J.: Prentice-Hall, 1982, 293 pp.

The author has written over 20 books on computing, including several on teleprocessing. This provocative book describes Viewdata today, and looks at potential future applications.

Petruzzelli, Vito G. "The Infor Center—A Powerful Tool for Modern Times." *Data Management* 22, no. 2 (February 1984), pp. 20–21.

The author argues that the infor center concept is user-driven but that leadership and direction from top management are essential. This is the lead article to five other short articles on the information center in this issue.

Small Business Computers.

This is a journal that should be read by persons with an interest in automation in small businesses. Readers will find that many articles included relate to business use of micros. Technical topics, such as modems, communications, and software testing, are addressed for nontechnical readers.

Impact of computers on management

We shape our tools, then they shape us.

Author unknown

Computers are changing the nature of work everywhere. The storage of information on disk and tape has altered the ways that records are kept. Word processing has transformed office communications, while robots, numerical control, and process control have revolutionized the factory. Articles in the popular press describe the competition between cities for high-tech industries and describe the plight of the unemployed, displaced by computers. The media focuses less attention on the impact of computers on business management. Yet this impact is profound. Computers have changed the role of managers as decision makers. Not only has the type of decisions a manager makes been altered by computerization but also the manner in which decisions are made.

This chapter opens with a discussion of the changed role of modern managers. Altered managerial span of control and the erosion of traditional power structures as a result of computerization are also discussed. Another impact of computers examined in the chapter is the changed knowledge base required by managers today: computer know-how as well as conventional business management skills are needed. The chapter closes with a discussion of issues that take more managerial time today than formerly: security, privacy, and legal concerns. This chapter reviews, integrates, and expands some of the concepts introduced in earlier chapters.

Computer impact on managerial task mix

The **mix of tasks** a manager performs has been modified by computers. For example, word processing is replacing conventional office procedures for the creation of correspondence, documents, reports, and memos. Electronic processing is speeding computations and retrieval of data. Traditional office communication patterns are being transformed by electronic mail while teleconferences have re-

Table 26.1
Computer-induced changes in office work

Without a computer	With a computer
Typing	Word processing
Human memory	Auxiliary memory of computer
Manual filing	Computerized record-keeping
Manual search and human recall	Information retrieval
Keeping calendar manually	Automated calendar with prompts
Postal service	Teleprocessing
Estimation from experience	Estimation through quantitative models
Manual supervision and control	Exceptional reporting
Specialization of tasks	Functional and integrated systems
Judgment, intuition, and experience	Testing alternatives, simulation, and planning models
Manual drawing	Graphic display
	Interactive displays
Use of old or current data	Use of real-time data
Conference attendance (in person)	Teleconferences

duced the necessity for a lot of business travel. Additional computer-induced changes in office work are listed in Table 26.1 All of these changes influence the jobs of office managers, and of all managers who use office services.

Another example of the changed task mix is the fact that computers have added new responsibilities to a manager's workload. In every department or organization where computers are used, managers must:

1. Establish a climate receptive to computers. This includes planning programs and policies to dissipate resistance to change.
2. Make acquisition decisions regarding the rental, lease, or purchase of computer hardware.
3. Select packaged software or participate in development of in-house programs.
4. Hire and evaluate a staff trained to use computer equipment.
5. Establish orientation and training programs for nontechnical staff.
6. Organize departmental use of data, peripherals, micros, and telecommunications equipment.
7. Establish goals for both short- and long-range plans for computer use.
8. Budget for computer processing.
9. Set standards and procedures for computer use.
10. Monitor, control, and evaluate computer operations for effectiveness and efficiency.
11. Develop security measures for protection of information resources.
12. Provide for integration of departmental computing resources with the resources of other organizational units.

These duties require up-to-date knowledge about computers. This means that managers will have to gain a degree of computer expertise in order to remain in

Table 26.2
Distribution of work before and after MRP

Tasks performed	Percentage of work	
	Before MRP	After MRP
Expediting	50%	13%
Unexpediting (forestalling early deliveries)	3	13
Negotiations	5	18
Search for cost reductions	10	19
Interviews	12	17
Ordering	20	20

their jobs. By changing the nature of managerial work, computers have changed the education required to become a manager.

Still another result of computerization is elimination of many time-consuming structured activities that once occupied a large amount of a manager's time. Such jobs as scheduling are now done by computer, and done more efficiently than in the past. This means that managers have more time for creative work.

For example, Table 26.2 shows how computers have changed the job of purchasing. Before the advent of a software for materials resource planning (MRP), purchasing managers spent approximately 50 percent of their time expediting orders. After MRP, this figure dropped dramatically to about 13 percent. The time saved is used in negotiations and in looking for ways to effect cost reductions and to revise delivery dates.

MRP linked to other information-generating systems can change the nature of managerial work throughout a corporation. Inventory management, scheduling, and manufacturing are all related to the purchase of materials. Managers responsible for these activities find MRP frees them from time-consuming paper work, so that they, too, can restructure their jobs.

Similar examples of the changed task mix of managers as a result of computerization can be cited for all managerial levels in most functional areas throughout business and industry.

Effect on decision making of top management

It should be noted that top management has been less affected by computer technology than operational and middle management. One reason is that many of the problems of top managers are neither structured nor capable of being programmed for computers. Top management generally deals with complex problems—problems with variables that cannot easily be quantified. Personnel decisions (hiring and firing) fall into this category. So do decisions regarding overall goals and policies. Promoting innovation, motivating the work force, and resolving disputes are part of the executive domain. These duties require the type of decision making that cannot be automated. Table 26.3 lists activities of top, middle, and operational management and shows how the impact of computers differs at the three levels of decision making.

Table 26.3
Impact of computers on functions of management

	Top management	Middle management	Operational management
Identify areas of improvement	Scant	Scant	Some
Analyze these areas	None	Scant	Some
Develop alternate solutions	Scant	Moderate	Moderate
Evaluate alternate solutions	Scant	Moderate	Moderate
Implement decision	Some	Moderate	Heavy
Job content	Some	Moderate	Major
Job numbers	None	Scant	Moderate

SOURCE   Concept adapted from Jerome Kanter, *Management-Oriented Management Information System,* (Englewood Cliffs, N.J.: Prentice-Hall, 1982), p. 180, 182.

As shown in the table, top management continues to make many decisions without computer assistance. However, managers at the upper levels of an organization do receive reports based on operational and control information generated by computer, and their use of planning and control models is becoming more common. Computer **decision support systems (DSS)** are of particular value to top management in finding solutions to problems where managerial judgment alone is not:

> . . . adequate, because of the size of the problem or the computation complexity and precision needed to solve it. On the other hand, the model or data alone are also inadequate because the solution involves judgment and subjective analysis. Under these conditions the manager plus the system can provide a more effective solution than either alone.[1]

Top management should guard against total reliance on heavily processed data, data that filters out emotion, feeling, sentiment, mood, and all of the irrational nuances of human situations. According to John Gardner, effective management and decision making often depend on judgments based on the very elements that have been filtered out. The manager who makes intuitive decisions that are just below the level of consciousness often has a clearer vision of reality than managers who base decisions solely on data that has been sampled, screened, compiled, coded, and expressed in statistical form, since that process omits or seriously distorts all "information that cannot readily be expressed in words or numbers or cannot be rationally condensed into lists, categories, formulas, or compact generalizations."[2] The corporate executive glued to the computer console who ignores the subtleties of human interaction is indeed an Orwellian parody of what effective management should be.

---

[1] Peter G. W. Keene and Michael S. Scott Morton, *Decision Support Systems: An Organizational Perspective* (Reading, Mass.: Addison-Wesley, 1978), p. 86.
[2] John Gardner, *Self Renewal; The Individual and the Innovative Scoiety* (New York: Harper & Row, 1965), pp. 78–79.

Table 26.4
Calculation of the computerization coefficient for different levels of management

	Percent susceptible to computerization	Top management		Middle management		Operational management	
		Percent of job devoted to	Weighted value	Percent of job devoted to	Weighted value	Percent of job devoted to	Weighted value
Plan	30%	70%	21%	20%	6%	5%	1.5%
Organize	15	10	1.5	10	1.5	5	1.0
Staff	25	10	2.5	10	2.5	5	1.5
Direct	5	5	—	20	1.0	20	1.0
Control	80	5	4	40	32.0	70	56.0
Computerization quotient			29%		43%		61%

SOURCE   Jerome Kanter, *Management-Oriented Management Information System* (Englewood Cliffs, N.J.: Prentice-Hall, 1982), p. 290.

Computer impact on management task mix quantified

The preceding section discussed the impact of computers on management in general terms. Can this impact be quantified? Jerome Kanter has attempted to do so. He divides management into **five functions, planning, organizing, staffing, direction,** and **control,** and has given each a number indicating susceptibility to computerization. He has also assessed the percentage of time spent in each function by operations, middle, and top management. A weighted value for each function is then determined and a computerized coefficient derived for each level of management. (See Table 26.4.) According to Kanter's calculations, 29 percent of top management's functions, 43 percent of middle management's functions, and 61 percent of operational management's functions can be computerized.

This analysis is simplistic insofar as it does not allow for industry differences or variations over time. Kanter's conclusions are also based on highly subjective weight assignments and they were reached based on data from the 1970s. Nevertheless, many commentators would argue that Kanter's percentages are reasonable approximations of the actual contribution made by computers to decision making at the three levels of management. The analysis is also useful because it stresses that not all managerial functions can be computerized and that the mix of functions at a given level is what determines the limits of computer assistance.

In coming years, as more operations research models are put into use and as progress is made in artificial intelligence, many functions not currently susceptible to computerization may become so, and Kanter's percentages will have to be changed. But we are not yet close to Herbert Simon's prediction that, ". . . we shall . . . (acquire) an extensive and empirically tested theory of human cognitive processes and their interaction with human emotions, attitudes and values."

Nor is Norbert Weiner's prediction—that whatever man can do, a computer will also do—likely in the near future. Managers are still needed to recognize and infer patterns from nonquantifiable variables, especially human variables, to in-

Figure 26.1
Traditional and computerized approaches to operating a drilling machine

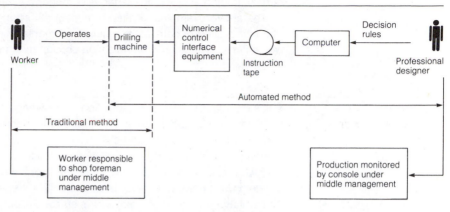

terpret information, to evaluate divergences between planned and actual performance, and to determine corrective actions. Even programmed decision making requires managers to initially think through problems and establish decision rules for problem solutions. As Peter Drucker states:

> We are beginning to realize that the computer makes no decisions; it only carries out orders. It's a total moron, and herein has its strength. It forces us to think, to set the criteria. The stupider the tool, the brighter the master has to be—and this is the dumbest tool we have. . . . It shows us—in fact, it compels us—to think through what we are doing.[3]

Altered managerial span of control

Another area where the impact of computers on managers is felt is in the number and level of employees a manager supervises. In automated factories, for example, drilling machines were formerly operated by workers following blueprints: the shop floor was managed by a supervisor. In many firms today, instruction tape (the blueprint) is fed into numerically controlled machines, machines which do the drilling without worker intervention. The semiskilled or skilled workers who once operated the drilling machines have been replaced by professional designers who prepare the instruction tape. The supervisor has been replaced by a worker who monitors production on a machine console. Figure 26.1 illustrates how such changes have affected the span of control of the production manager.

When computer-aided manufacturing is integrated with computer-aided design, the production process is automated one step farther, making additional changes to managerial responsibility. Should CAD/CAM result in displacement of workers, such as machine operators, while keeping constant the number of man-

---

[3]Peter Drucker, *Technology, Management and Society* (London: Heineman, 1970), pp. 147–48.

agers, managerial control will narrow. Should the company choose to eliminate some managerial jobs and redistribute responsibility among the managers who remain, the job scope of the latter will broaden.

The above examples of altered managerial **span of control** are not unique. The introduction of computers requires reorganization of entire departments and whole firms. Whenever reorganization occurs, managerial jobs are restructured.

Realignment of corporate power structure

Shifts of **power** within an organization occur when computers are introduced. As traditional power bases erode, managers must deal with bruised egos, jealousy, and resentment. Management skill in reducing tension and restoring harmonious interpersonal/interdepartmental relations is taxed to the limit.

P. J. Hickson and others have identified **four vairables** associated with corporate power: **links to others, irreplaceability, dependency,** and **uncertainty.**[4] All four have a bearing on computer operations. Computer departments are linked to many functional departments through such applications as payroll or accounting. These functions are irreplaceable. Other departments depend on computing as well, particularly when integrated systems have been implemented. Computer planning models and programs for control and decision making also reduce uncertainty among users. As a result of these factors, power gravitates to persons with computer expertise, leaving many persons in traditional positions of power but with diminished status.

Another source of resentment stems from the fact that computer departments often win in the brisk competition for scarce corporate resources. Computers require major capital investments and large operating budgets. These needs cut into the funding available for noncomputer activities, yet most departments believe that their programs deserve equal corporate support. Once again, management time and diplomacy are required to mediate conflicts of interest and temper rivalries.

Sometimes hostility to computer departments and personnel can be traced to unrealistic expectations of users, to poorly drawn system specifications, or projects behind schedule. Unfortunately, computer professionals often work in a crisis atmosphere and find that they have no time to develop positive relationships with users. Labor unions sometimes exacerbate existing tensions. Managers who cannot cope with the heightened social and psychological tensions accompanying computerization may find the very survival of their firms at stake.

Need to develop computer know-how

Managers today must develop **computer know-how** to be effective. Chapters of this text have described how computers can assist top and middle managers. The

---

[4]P. J. Hickson, C. R. Henings, C. A. Lees, R. E. Schneck, and J. M. Pennings, "Strategic Contingency Theory of Interorganizational Power," *Administrative Science Quarterly* 16, no. 2 (June 1971), pp. 216–729.

benefits described, however, are often not realized because managers resist using computers. Yet even a positive attitude toward computers is not enough. Full exploitation of computer potential requires knowledge of computer capabilities and limitations. Too often business managers do not utilize computing resources at their disposal to full advantage. Managers who received their business training before the computer revolution or attended institutions that did not offer computer science courses must today compensate for their lack of computing background by enrolling in computer courses, attending seminars, talking with consultants and vendors, and reading computer literature. Many are also turning to information specialists for on-the-job help.

Information specialists are either computer scientists knowledgeable about business and management, or individuals drawn from operations research who have acquired an expertise in computers and data bases. The information specialist is hired to control the flow (and sometimes the content) of computerized information to management.

Information specialists wield far more power than is apparent from a firm's organizational chart. They decide how information is presented (flashed on a terminal screen or buried in a printed report), how data should be correlated, what processing mode to use, the form of output, and which models are appropriate. Such decisions may subsequently limit the range of choices open to management. Although officially serving as technical advisers, information specialists can become decision makers of considerable importance.

Hiring a computer specialist does not exempt managers from the need to learn about computers. If managers take no role in planning, developing, and implementing computer systems, delegating such responsibilities instead to specialists, they may lose decision-making prerogatives by default. This is not to suggest that management should dispense with the services of information specialists. On the contrary, they are a valuable resource. But managers themselves need to develop computer know-how. They should authorize delegated decision making and should carefully define, monitor, and control the work of information specialists.

Issues of growing concern to managers

Computers have added to the complexity of issues that have always been a responsibility of managers. This section will discuss the impact of computers on security, privacy, and the law, and describe how the role of managers has changed as a consequence.

Security

Most commercial, industrial, and financial organizations process and transmit proprietary and sensitive information in the course of their daily activities. The **security** of such information has traditionally been a concern of management. However, with the creation of vast data banks, instantaneous retrieval capabilities, and worldwide teleprocessing, data is today more vulnerable than ever. As a result, managers must devote far more attention to the issue of data security (and to the security of all computer resources) than formerly. They must spend time and effort designing and implementing measures to prevent inadvertent computer error, criminal access, machine malfunction, and safeguard resources from natural disasters. (Chapter 16 discusses such measures.) A greater share of an organization's budget and more people must also be allocated to security. Computer technology has not only changed the nature of the problem of security, but has changed the amount of time and effort that managers must spend on the problem.

Privacy

Computers are able to collect, store, and retrieve large amounts of data, including data of a personal nature. The American public considers no right more sacrosanct than the right to **privacy.** No wonder the public is alarmed at the ease with which personal dossiers are assembled and stored by computer. No wonder the public is demanding control over dossier input, access, and use. In the United States, over 445 million individual records exist in credit agencies, commercial banks, mailing list data banks, and in the Social Security Administration. The federal government itself has more than 3.8 billion records. According to a 1978 survey by Louis Harris & Associates:

> The privacy issue is not solved or fading away. It is going to become more intense in the next decade, as privacy serves as the handle with which a still considerably alienated public seeks to define and install greater measures of individual or social control over an organizational systems whose powers have been vastly increased by computer uses in the last 20 years. . . . Most Americans now see privacy as one of the central "quality-of-life" issues of our times.[5]

The 1971 Fair Credit Reporting Act does provide some federal safeguards against privacy abuse, as does the the Privacy Act of 1974 which sets guidelines for the collection, maintenance, use, and dissemination of information by federal agencies. Although private business is not bound by the 1974 act, most business managers today are cognizant of privacy issues and sensitive to client anxiety regarding the confidentiality of records used in the course of a firm's daily operations. Many companies have adopted and publicized privacy policies to assure their customers that privacy is a managerial concern. (See Table 26.5 for IBM's four principles of privacy.) As with security, managers today are spending much more time on the issue of privacy than in the past and delegating a larger share of corporate resources for privacy protection.

The following are activities that occupy managers responsible for privacy in a computerized environment. Managers must:

---

[5] Alan F. Westin, "The Impact of Computers on Privacy," *Datamation* 25, no. 24 (December 1979) pp. 190 and 193.

1. Develop privacy standards.
2. Identify "sensitive" data. Data descriptions must be added to sensitive data elements so that they can be easily extracted from the data stream for control inspections and correction. Use of this data for new applications must receive managerial approval.
3. Verify the accuracy, relevance, and timeliness of data.
4. Implement data security measures.
5. Establish correction routines and procedures to handle challenges to data accuracy.
6. Redevelop old subsystems to include privacy protection and monitor development projects to ensure that privacy standards are met. This includes the design of new information systems to report on sensitive data, and both log and monitor use of such data.

Table 26.5
IBM's policy on privacy

**Four principles
of privacy**

For some time now, there has been a growing effort in this country to preserve the individual's right to privacy in the face of expanding requirements for information by business, government, and other organizations.

In searching for appropriate guidelines, private and governmental groups have explored many avenues and considered many aspects of the privacy question.

As a company with a vital interest in information and information handling, IBM endorses in their basic purpose four principles of privacy that have emerged from various studies, and which appear to be the cornerstones of sound public policy on this sensitive issue.

1. Individuals should have access to information about themselves in record-keeping systems. And there should be some procedure for individuals to find out how this information is being used.
2. There should be some way for an individual to correct or amend an inaccurate record.
3. An individual should be able to prevent information from being improperly disclosed or used for other than authorized purposes without his or her consent, unless required by law.
4. The custodian of data files containing sensitive information should take reasonable precautions to be sure that the data are reliable and not misused.

Translating such broad principles into specific and uniform guidelines will, of course, not be easy. They must be thoughtfully interpreted in terms of the widely varying purposes of information systems genrally.

In particular, the proper balance must be found between limiting access to information for the protection of privacy on one hand, and allowing freedom of information to fulfill the needs of society on the other.

But solutions must be found. And they will call for the patient understanding and best efforts of everyone concerned. In this search, IBM pledges its full and wholehearted coooperation.

IBM

Courtesy of International Business Machines Corp.

Many firms appoint a special officer to plan for data privacy, to coordinate privacy polices with legal requirements, and to oversee privacy policy implementation. Since security measures that protect data from inadvertent error or fraudulent use serve goals of privacy as well, a single individual may be assigned responsibility for both the privacy and security of computer resources. But managers at all levels must work closely with this individual in planning and implementing privacy/security measures.

Legal issues

Computer science is dynamic, yet state and federal legislatures, responsible for providing legal guidelines for use of computer technology, move slowly. As a result, the computer industry and computerized firms lack an adequate up-to-date legal framework for operations. Most laws regulating the sale and use of computers were originally written for other purposes and are therefore subject to interpretation. (Antitrust statutes, copyright laws, and laws regulating contracts, patents, trade secrets, tort, privacy, theft, freedom of information, and communications.) Often organizations are not sure what legal protections exist with regard to computer activity and they are not clear what actions constitute violations of the law. This presents management with a real dilemma: how to aggressively compete in the computer arena without overstepping ill-defined legal boundaries.

IBM, in particular, has been a defendant in court battles since the early days of computing. The company's size and leadership in pricing have made it a target for much antitrust litigation. But IBM is not the only company that has had to defend itself in court. Managers in many companies must spend large amounts of their time consulting with lawyers to assess the legal ramifications of corporate decisions and both time and organizational resources are often spent fighting legal challenges. Though it is widely agreed that the passage of comprehensive legislation on computer use and abuse would serve business, there is controversy whenever a specific piece of legislation is proposed. It is hard to reach consensus regarding the amount of regulation needed and the type of regulations to codify into law.

Nevertheless, some federal legislation on computer abuse is in sight. In 1984 the U.S. House of Representatives passed H.R. 5616, the Counterfeit Access Device and Computer Fraud and Abuse Act. The House vote of 393:0 shows that the bill had ample bipartisan support. Supporters of the bill believe that it fills a gap in federal criminal statutes, which do not specifically prohibit computer crimes.

The bill establishes that unauthorized access of computers used by the federal government or in interstate or foreign commerce is a federal felony if the offender gains more than $5,000 a year or obtains classified national security information. The penalty is up to 10 years in prison and a fine of $10,000 (or up to two times the amount of the illegal financial gain). The bill also creates three misdemeanor categories:

1. Unauthorized access to computer financial data bases protected by law.
2. Unauthorized use or tampering with computer data that affects interstate or foreign commerce.

3. Unauthorized use, modification, or disclosure of data in a computer that is owned or operated by the federal government.

Sponsors of the bill warn that this crime bill is only the first step in protecting sensitive information in the computer age. They recognize that, even if the bill becomes law, more comprehensive legislation will be needed in the future.

Summary and conclusions

Computers are changing the nature of a manager's work and altering methods of decision making. Managers are also being displaced by computers, though the threat of unemployment is less acute at top levels of managment than at operational levels, and far fewer managerial jobs are jeopardized by computers than are workers' jobs. (See Figure 26.2.) There are still too many "wicked" problems for management to resolve, problems that defy programmed solutions because their variables cannot easily be quantified. However, research in artificial intelligence, data management, linguistics, and psychology will undoubtedly expand the role of computers in decision making and lead to further managerial displacement.

The immediate concern of corporate management is to learn how to utilize computers to best advantage. This may be as simple as phrasing questions differently or as complex as adopting a whole new mind set, a whole new approach to problem solving. More and more managers are turning to information specialists for assistance in maximizing the use of computing resources. At the same time, the widespread use of minis and micros allows managers to access information and even do simple programming without the intercession of program-

Figure 26.2
Displacement caused by computerization

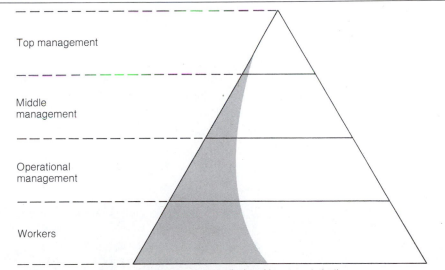

Top management

Middle management

Operational management

Workers

NOTE   The shaded area represents employees displaced by computerization.

mers and analysts, giving management a measure of independence from computer professionals.

Computers have changed the task mix of modern managers. Many monotonous, repetitive jobs formerly done by managers have been computerized (inventory control, for example) freeing managers for more creative activities. Less paper shuffling means more time for conferences, interviews, and personal contacts with employees; more time for planning; and more time for evaluating programs and service.

Since computers have also changed the jobs of professionals and blue-collar employees, organizations have been restructured. As a result, some managers find their span of control is broader than formerly, while others have more limited responsibilities.

Computer departments and computer personnel are today becoming power centers indispensable to normal operations. This has upset the traditional power structure in most firms and has led to conflicts, rivalries, and corporate dissension. While computers have contributed to the problem-solving ability of management, it should be recognized that they have created management headaches as well.

Key words	Computer know-how	Privacy
	Information specialist	Power variables:
	Legal issues	Links to others
	Management functions:	Irreplaceability
	Planning	Dependency
	Organizing	Uncertainty
	Staffing	Security
	Direction	Span of control
	Control	Task mix

Discussion questions

1. What negative impact have computers had on management?

2. How can the adverse effects of computers on decision making be minimized? How can the benefits be enhanced?

3. How have computers altered decision making at the following management levels:
   a. Top?
   b. Middle?
   c. Operations?

4. Will the impact of computers on management vary with:
   a. Size of firm?
   b. Style of management?
   c. Content of management?
   d. Qualifications of managers?

5. Do computers turn managers into conformists? Do managers lose their:
   a. Individuality?
   b. Creativity?
   c. Self-confidence and self-assurance?
   d. Independence of thinking?

6. How are managers affected by the addition of a:
   a. DBMS?
   b. Online real-time system?
   c. Query language and interactive processing?
   d. Simulation language?
   e. Word-processing workstation for secretary?
   f. Teleprocessing?
   g. Artificial intelligence?

7. How has computer technology affected the quality of decision making? The quality of management?

8. How can manager's knowledge of computing contribute to:
   a. Decision making?
   b. Control of the negative impact of computers?
   c. Improved efficiency and effectiveness of computer usage?

9. Why do managers feel threatened by computer technology? What can be done to alleviate management fears?

10. Why are junior managers more favorably oriented to computer systems than their seniors?

11. Which levels of management have been the most and least affected by computer technology? Why? Do you expect this to change in the near future? Why?

12. Can laws prevent or reduce computer crime? If so, how?

13. Why is privacy of data important to business clients and customers?

14. How can the conflict between need for data privacy and need for data access be resolved? What trade-offs can be made?

15. Has your privacy been invaded by business computers? How can such invasion of privacy be prevented?

16. Are laws in the United States adequate for discouraging and punishing:
    a. Computer crime?
    b. Privacy violations?

Selected annotated bibliography

"A New Era for Management." *Business Week,* no. 2787 (April 25, 1983), pp. 50–86.

This is a special report including articles on the shrinking of middle management (pp. 54–61); how computers remake the manager's job (pp. 68–70); and who will retain the obsolete manager (pp. 76–80).

Bushkin, Arthur L., and Samuel I. Schaen. *The Privacy Act of 1974: A Reference Manual for Companies.* McLean, Va.: Systems Development Corporation, 1978, 183 pp.

The subtitle is an apt description of the book. It discusses the coverage of the act, basic compliance requirements, technical considerations for implementation, and the establishment of appropriate safeguards.

Drucker, Peter. *Technology, Management and Society.* London: Heineman, 1969, 209 pp.

This well-known author refers to the impact of computers on business in many of his books. Chapter 10, "The Manager and the Moron," in the above text, is a sample reference. In *Age of Discontinuity,* approximately 100 pages are devoted to computers and the knowledge industry. Drucker frequently writes for journals on computers as well. See *Fortune* (November 1980), *Harvard Business Review* (May 1971), and *Foreign Affairs* (August 1978).

Hoffman, Lance J., ed. *Computers and Privacy in the Next Decade.* New York: Academic Press, 1980, 250 pp.

This book is a set of readings and commentary written by well-known experts in the field (e.g., W. H. Ware, Paul Armer, Rein Turn, Abbe Mowshowitz.) The topics are balanced and provocative. Included are articles on privacy, the personal computer, EFT, transborder flow, and nonuniform privacy laws. Problems and issues arising from the preservation of individual autonomy and the protection of public order in future decades are also addressed.

Hoffman, Lance J. *Modern Methods for Computer Security and Privacy.* Englewood Cliffs, N.J.: Prentice-Hall, 1977, 255 pp.

This a continuation of a series of books and articles on this subject by Hoffman. It is a cram course in security threats and countermeasures. The legal aspects of privacy are discussed as well as the transformation of data to maintain privacy by traditional hardware and software methods. The book makes an excellent reference. It is technical but written in nontechnical language. Questions and sample answers are included for each chapter.

Hutzler, Laurie H. "The Legal Ramifications of Information Privacy." *Administrative Management* 43, no. 8 (September 1982), pp. 36–38.

Managers should consider the legal risks involved when the personnel records of organizations are computerized. The problem of designing systems to ensure the confidentiality of personal information is discussed.

Lucas, Henry C., Jr. *The Analysis, Design, and Implementation of Information Systems.* New York: McGraw-Hill, 1981, 419 pp.

Chapter 4 is recommended. It discusses the impact of computers on organizations and individuals, and also discusses changes in the distribution of power that arise as a result of computerization.

Simon, Herbert. *The Shape of Automation for Men and Management.* New York: Harper & Row, 1965, 11 pp.

Simon is an organization theorist who has contributed greatly to heuristic programming. He has written numerous books on computers such as the above title. *New Science of Management Decision* is another useful reference. Look for his work in magazines as well.

Smith, Robert Ellis. "Privacy: Still Threatened." *Datamation* 28, no. 10 (September 1982), pp. 297–306.

Ellis argues that privacy protection is complicated, yet an issue that must be addressed now, if we are to save future generations from coping with "Big Brother."

Ward, Tom. *Computer Organization, Personnel and Control.* London: Longman, 1973, 134 pp.

This book gives the British view of the effects of computerization. Chapter 6, "The Impact of Computers on the Company," is recommended.

Computers in our future

27

Traveler, there is no path, paths are made by walking.
Antonio Machado

Any description of the state of the art in computing is soon obsolete. Each day, announcements are made of new hardware and software. The computing industry itself has a volatile record of entries and exits. The attempts by newcomers to break into the market with innovative products coincide with the departure of familiar firms and product lines. New ideas are publicized, then fail to reach their promise. In 1983, for example, IBM abandoned on-going research in Josephson junctions, long heralded as the hardware technology of the future, while Osborne, a leading microcomputer manufacturer, close to production of the first voice input-output micro, filed for bankruptcy. Both events were totally unexpected by computer watchers.

Nevertheless, it is not as difficult to look ahead in computing as one might think. It generally takes a long gestation period from the invention of new computer technology to commercial application of that technology. Although sometimes in error, computer specialists can usually identify promising lines of research and predict the spin-off applications.

Making such predictions is not an idle pastime—it serves a useful purpose. We need to plan and prepare for technology of the future. Our social institutions move slowly and humans are resistant to change. If we are to assimilate computer technology without organizational turmoil or social disruption, we must start now to make adjustments in our patterns of thinking and approaches to management.

This chapter describes the advances in technology and trends in computing that can be expected in the future. Fifth generation computers are discussed as are intelligent management information systems. The chapter concludes with a look at some of the broad social implications of information technology.

Technology trends

The raw power of computers needs to be harnessed. Processing speeds already far surpass our ability to process input data or deliver output. To print pages of numeric output at the processing speed of the CRAY computer would require a paper feed running at 250,000 mph—a velocity that would cause the paper to burn. Graphics are one solution to output-bound machines since a curve can represent thousands of numbers. Shading and shadows that add perspective to graphics require even more data, speeding the display of output.

Input/output technology is the focus of much research at the present time. We can expect to utilize the findings of researchers in artificial intelligence to construct smart terminals, optical/laser readers, and speech recognition devices in the future. Plasma screens may replace cathode ray tubes as output devices since they facilitate the display of graphic and pictorial material.

Future hardware advances may also include the replacement of silicon chips by chips made of a gallium-arsenide compound. This switch will increase computing speeds two to five times. Another advantage is that circuits on gallium arsenide require only $1/100$ the power needed for a given circuit on silicon. Intensification of integrated circuits can also be expected. Computers will be smaller, cheaper, more reliable and robust, and far more powerful. Maintenance may become a matter of replacing rather than repairing defective parts. Standardization will evolve and vendors will pay more attention to equipment compatibility. Optic

Table 27.1
Areas of research for fifth generation computers

Hardware Architecture
   Gallium arsenide chips
   VVLSI (very very large scale integration)
   High speed numerical computation
   Data base machines
   Distributed function architecture
   Wafer-scale chip

Software Systems
   Intelligent programs
   Intelligent problem solving and inference system
   Intelligent inferface software
   Natural language communication systems
   Question-answer systems

Systems Technology
   Knowledge data base management system
   Intelligent input/output system
   Image recognition
   Speech understanding
   Expert systems
   Online testing
   Fault logging
   Self-diagnosis

Systems Organization
   Priority of human factors
   Mechanism for influencing perceptions
   Improved user interface and communication facilities
   Maximize effectiveness, but not necessarily efficiency

fibers will be used in telecommunications, replacing telephone lines and coaxial cable. Satellite and packet switching will improve data communications while progress will be made on a network infrastructure to link computers and data banks throughout the country.

Computers will proliferate in the future and demand for software will soar. The growing popularity of personal computers for small businesses and homes has created entirely new markets for software. In addition, users, who lack the resources to write programs, are demanding a wide range of off-the-shelf packages. Hardware manufacturers recognize that they must supply more than basic operating systems and data base management software to keep equipment sales growing. They have entered the software market in competition with established software companies, studying customer needs and writing application programs to meet those needs. In the past, competition in the computer industry centered on hardware; in the future, software may well be the battleground.

Workstations in the 1990s will be built around 32-bit micros, each system custom-designed and user-friendly, connected to other workstations through LANS and satellite networks. Large numbers of micros may be integrated to work in parallel, matching supercomputers in processing capability. As systems gain in complexity, top management will spend more time coordinating and integrating systems, while distributed data processing will shift implementation and supervision of operations to users. Management styles will be altered by information technology and so will the design, production, and marketing of products.

Fifth generation computers

Table 27.1 is a selected list of current research topics in computing. Results from these areas will be incorporated into computers of the future, making these computers fundamentally different from computers of the past. A fifth generation computer system has already been targeted for the 1990s by the Japanese. If the project is successful, it will threaten U.S. preeminence in information processing.

How will the **fifth generation computer** announced by the Japanese differ from predecessors? Figure 27.1 illustrates the basic concept of the system, the major features of which are described below.

A primary difference is that the Japanese plan to incorporate a **knowledge base** in their new computer. A knowledge base consists of stored facts plus IF-THEN rules that allow information to be created from the basic facts. Whereas current data bases store information explicitly, knowledge bases represent data in a dynamic fashion. A good example of this difference is the problem of representing family relationships in a data base. In the structured data base common today, all of the relationships must be entered. In a knowledge data base, inference rules allow relationships to be derived (e.g., IF (PARENT X Y) and (BROTHER X Z), THEN (UNCLE Z Y). The bulk of information stored in the knowledge base is inferred in this manner. When facts are added to the base during use, the structure and interrelationships among facts will change—changes that the user does not have to initiate. Indeed, the end user may be unaware that the changes have taken place.

Figure 27.1
Overview of the fifth generation computer system

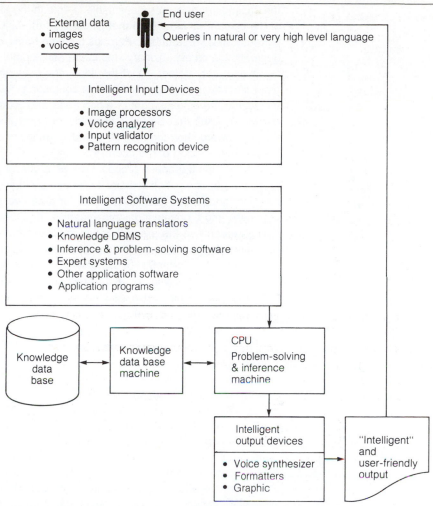

Another goal of Japanese computerization is use of **natural languages** for queries (e.g., Japanese or English) in addition to a 4th generation language based on PROLOGUE. (Not formal computer languages, such as FORTRAN or COBOL.)

A third aim of the Japanese is to incorporate both **artificial intelligence and expert systems** in their fifth generation system. (An expert system consists of a problem-solving component that uses inference rules to draw conclusions from a knowledge data base—inference rules and a knowledge base that a specialist in a given field of expertise has formulated.[1])

---

[1] See Larry R. Harris, "Fifth Generation Foundations," *Datamation* 29, no. 7 (July 1983), pp. 148–56.

There has been much discussion among computer scientists about whether the Japanese project is feasible within the announced time frame. Some say that the Japanese goals are unattainable, a "pie in the sky." Others argue that many of the goals may indeed be met since all of the objectives and technologies are currently being researched. Perhaps the time frame is overly optimistic, but a fifth generation is an evolutionary step in the development of computers. Another factor favoring the project is that the Japanese government provides subsidies and other incentives to private industry in computing. As a result, a long-range commitment to the development of a fifth generation computer is possible. American computing firms that do not receive direct government support are much more oriented toward short-term profits. However, many of our computer scientists share the Japanese vision of the future.

Whether the Japanese proposal will be a challenge, a catalyst, or a blueprint in the field of computing remains to be seen. Although American computer firms have not announced production plans for a fifth generation system to match the Japanese effort, private industry, academia, and the U.S. government are undertaking research in the areas that the Japanese have already singled out. Some observers suggest that one impact of the fifth generation announcement was to push forward the formation of Microelectronic and Computing Technology, a U.S. consortium of 14 computer and semiconductor computers. This consortium is collectively developing advanced hardware/software technology for its partners to use in product development.

Intelligent MIS systems

Fifth generation computers will give managers **intelligent management information systems (IMIS).** By IMIS, one means decision support systems coupled with intelligent information provided by a knowledge data base and expert systems. There will be interaction between the decision maker and the computer through a micro or a terminal. This includes interaction in order to recognize and state the problem to be solved, interaction when specifying goals and constraints, when formatting input, and when selecting a model to reach a problem solution. Simulation models will give managers the opportunity of projecting results from alternative action plans. Whatever model is chosen, an output formatter will be able to provide managers with a numerical solution, a graphic solution, or a solution in text as a result of word processing. Figure 27.2 is an illustration of IMIS components.

A major benefit of IMIS will be to help managers limit information. Managers today risk being overwhelmed by information glut. They can lose their focus and waste time sifting through masses of irrelevant, nonessential data, or data available at the wrong time. An IMIS will help a manager recognize what problems need to be solved and access (or generate) appropriate information for solutions when needed. For example, if sales slump, a manager will be able to utilize an IMIS to help determine the factors that might contribute to lower sales. This will

Figure 27.2
Overview of an intelligent MIS

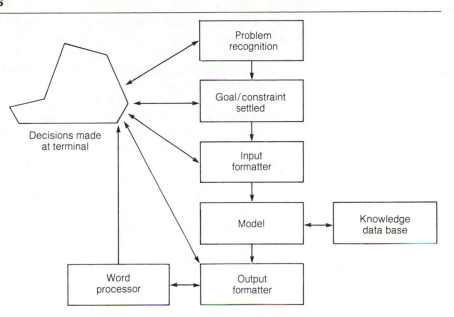

narrow the parameters of the problem. When calling on the data base for sales information, the system will again assist the manager, this time helping frame the request so precisely that only needed data is, in fact, involved. Through prompts, what might be general requests such as, "Give me Oakland sales data," might be reformatted to, "Give me a product listing where slippage has been greater than 5 percent during the period April 15–June 15, 1984 in Oakland, California." In addition, the system will be capable of drawing inferences to assist the manager in evaluating information (e.g., call attention to the sales of competitors) and will utilize expert systems in reaching cause-effect conclusions. In other words, more effective use of information will be encouraged rather than more information. It is possible that the future IMISs will also store profiles of managers that describe their background and experience. The computer will respond to requests for information according to who initiates the request. That is, the information supplied will be at an appropriate level of sophistication for comfortable, efficient and effective assimilation by the manager, based on the computer's assessment of the manager's ability derived from the manager's profile.

Other trends

In addition to the advances mentioned in the preceding sections, other changes in computing are on the horizon. We will see greater use of embedded microprocessors in consumer and industrial products in the future. Microcomputers for business and personal use will become as commonplace as telephones. The emphasis will be on friendly computer systems designed for users with little background or experience in programming.

Integration of systems is another trend. A distinction between word and data processing will no longer be made. Telecommunications will link homes and offices while systems that serve home banking, home shopping, and other family needs will also be appropriate office tools. Information resources will be available to everyone, not limited to a computer elite.

We can also expect some resolution to the controversy over artificial intelligence (AI). As we learn more about the nature of learning and technical progress is made in such fields as natural language understanding, expert systems, speech recognition, and vision recognition, debate will be focused on how best to utilize AI—not whether AI research should be abandoned to prevent future shock. We will redefine intelligence to include person-tool relationships. Information systems will be designed to maximize the contribution of both humans and machines. For example, the human contribution will include flexibility, creativity, and decision making when solving problems with incomplete information, or when dealing with evaluation of systems.

Finally, more time will be spent listening to users, more effort designing systems to meet user needs. In the past, computer systems have required professional staffs for programming, inputting data, operating equipment, and maintaining hardware. Data processing personnel once stood between users and the information needed to achieve corporate goals. Unfortunately, analysts and programmers were often insensitive to user concerns and intimidating to persons lacking computer expertise. Today, a shift in systems design orientation is taking place. Hardware and software are being designed for ease of use although, as a result, machine efficiency must often be sacrificed. Corporate managers have learned that successful systems are those that give users, not technicians, priority.

Information systems of the future will focus on:

1. User service.
   Information specialists will spend more time and effort becoming acquainted with user concerns, their problems, and user environment. Mechanisms to influence and measure perceptions will also be established (e.g., user performance index, independent audit, user sign-off, complaint box).
2. User relations/communications.
   Although computer professionals will be leaders in introducing users to information technology appropriate to corporate objectives, users and managers will participate in setting application priorities. Procedures to facilitate interaction between users and technical personnel will be initiated.
3. People, not machinery.
   Priority will be given to effectiveness of information systems versus efficiency. Responsibility for information systems will shift to users where practical. Organizational structure will be fluid enough to allow change as infor-

mation technology evolves. Furthermore, computer professionals will be recognized as valuable computing resources. Programs to minimize their turnover, such as training and career development, will be initiated.[2]

Social change

When a telecommunications infrastructure exists to link computers, peripherals, and data base services throughout the country at an acceptable price, individuals will have access to information whenever they want it on almost any subject they request. Where access restrictions occur, they will be based on privacy and security considerations, not retrieval or communications limitations. Ease of access will be accompanied by a dependence on computers to organize and control masses of data, giving structure to what would otherwise be information pollution. How will such an information society change our lives?

According to John Naisbitt, author of *Megatrends,* America is being restructured by information technology. Computers are reducing our dependence on hierarchical power structures in favor of informal interaction between people. This link allows individuals to help one another, to exchange ideas and knowledge without channeling communications through a restrictive bureaucracy. An informal network-style management is evolving to replace former centralized authority. Individuals are beginning to rely more on themselves than on institutions. One might characterize these changes as evolution from a managerial society to an entrepreneurial society.

Naisbitt also believes that information technology is leading us to participatory, rather than representative, democracy. Computers assist voters in accessing information. Information contributes to a better informed electorate. We can expect a groundswell of initiatives and referenda as the public becomes more informed on issues and demands that its leaders become more responsive to voter opinion. Political power once concentrated in the old industrial cities of the North will diminish. Computers are fostering economic growth in the South and West, encouraging population shifts away from former industrial strongholds.

Another trend identified by Naisbitt that can be attributed to information technology is that society is becoming one with a multi-option orientation. Computers expand the number of choices available. There are more than 752 models of trucks and cars sold in the United States and one New York City store stocks 2,500 types of light bulbs. Naisbitt believes that the idea of multiple-options has spilled over to other areas of our lives, for example, religion, the arts, and food. Individuality is being promoted, and society is becoming more receptive to cultural and racial diversity.

Altogether, Naisbitt identifies 10 restructuring trends and suggests ways in which

---

[2]The importance of the human element of information systems is supported by the research of John Rockart, who has studied critical success factors that determine whether companies meet corporate goals. See John Rockart, "Chief Executives Define Their Own Data Needs," *Harvard Business Review* 57, no. 1 (January–February 1979), pp. 81–93.

systems managers can assume the lead in moving their companies into the information era.[3] Many persons disagree with Naisbitt, but one cannot dispute that his ideas are thought-provoking and lead to lively debate.

Clearly, an information-rich society holds promise as well as dangers. Though computers help reduce drudgery and add to our leisure, they threaten the jobs of America's work force. While greater access to information may liberate human creativity, cherished values may be lost in a computerized society. We may gain a better perception of reality, or discover that the need to select and manage information is responsible for creating "virtual realities" that do not reflect the actual state of the world.

As suggested by Ashley Montagu and Samuel Snyder:

We are now faced with a new ultimate weapon. This is the computer whose potential impact may surpass that of all of man's earlier devices. Many deplore the computer and some even fear it as more monster than machine. Whatever we think of it, however, we must adjust to it. This does not imply resignation, but rather that we must understand the true nature of this latest of man's inventions and learn how its powers can be combined with our own abilities to be used to the best advantage of humanity.[4]

Summary

By studying current research and development, one can determine future directions of automation. We may have fifth generation computers by the end of this century—computers with rapid processing speeds that can be queried in natural languages. Intelligent systems (e.g., self-diagnosis), intelligent input/output devices (e.g., output formatters), knowledge data bases, and expert systems will also be incorporated into fifth-generation computers. In addition, computing and communications will become even more closely allied. This will promote the development of computer networks for linking dispersed terminals, peripherals, and data banks.

Figure 27.3 shows how computing has evolved since the 1960s, each stage of development leading to new advances. As technology has increased the speed of information processing, lowered costs, and facilitated information access, American business has undergone change. Jobs have been created, restructured, and eliminated. Employer-employee relationships have been altered and executives have had to change their management styles. Smooth conversion to computer systems often depends more on astute management of the human element than on solving technical problems. Indeed, the ability of companies to successfully utilize information technology to meet their goals in the future may well depend on giving user concerns priority over machine efficiency.

;[3]For a summary of Naisbitt's 10 megatrends by Daniel Cougar, see *Computerworld* 18, no. 5 (February 6, 1984), pp. 33–40.
[4]Ashley Montagu and Samuel Snyder, *Man and the Computer,* Philadelphia: Auerbach Publishers, 1972, pp. 1–2.

Figure 27.3
Evolution of computing

	1960s	1970s	1980s	1990s
	• Mainframe ————————→		• Supercomputer	• 5th Generation Computers
		• Minicomputer ———		————————————→
			• Microcomputer	————————————→
				• Intelligent Systems
				• Expert Systems
	• Time Sharing	• O L R T	• Distributed Processing	————————————→
		• Transaction and Integrated Processing	• Clustered Workstations	• Parallel Processing
	• Low Level Languages	• High Level Languages	• 4 GL (4th Generation Languages)	• Very High Level Languages
	• Functional Data base	• DBMS	• Relational Data Base	• Knowledge Data Bases
	• Simple Functional Systems	• Integrated ————————→ Functional Systems		• Integration of Micros DP, WP, and Telecommunication

Key words

Artificial intelligence (AI)

Expert system

Fifth generation computer

Intelligent management information system (IMIS)

Knowledge base

Natural language

Discussion questions

1. Which trends in computing do you think should be encouraged and reinforced? How?

2. Which trends in computing are undesirable? Why?

3. How can business organizations and business managers prepare for the social changes that information technology will foster in the future?

4. How will advances in artificial intelligence affect:
   a. Products in the future?
   b. How companies are organized and managed?

5. What will be the impact of fifth generation computers on management?

6. What role should the U.S. government play in developing a fifth generation computer? Provide subsidies to private industry? Fund research by the Department of Defense? Other?

7. Should the U.S. computer industry be exempt from antitrust legislation in order to strengthen its competitive posture? What steps should be taken to help U.S. firms meet the challenge of the Japanese computer industry?

8. What is a user-friendly computer system? What features should be included in such a system?

9. Do you agree that past computer systems have been oriented toward technology while future systems will be people-oriented? Is such a shift in orientation desirable? Should it be encouraged? How?

10. What are the characteristics of an intelligent MIS? Is IMIS desirable?

11. Comment on the statement: The gap between computer technology and management is wide and growing.

12. Is computer literacy important for business managers? Why? To what extent? How can computer literacy be achieved?

13. Are you optimistic or fearful regarding the future role of computers in business and society? Explain your views.

Selected annotated bibliography

Deken, Joseph. *The Electronic Cottage*. New York: Bantam Books, 1981, 386 pp.
A description of how the computer revolution will change the character of American homes.

Dertouzos, Michael L. and Joel Moses, eds. *The Computer Age: A Twenty-Year View*. Cambridge, Mass.: MIT Press, 1979, 491 pp.
This is a collection of articles on future trends and socioeconomic effects brought about by computer technology. Selection for inclusion in the book was based on articles to complement or reply (even counter-reply) to one another.

Evans, Christopher. *The Mighty Micro*. London: Victor Gollanacz, 1979.
Part Six of this book looks ahead to the years 1991–2000. It describes the impact computers will have on our lives socially, politically, and psychologically.

Hamrin, Robert D. "The Information Economy." *Futurist* 16, no. 4 (August 1981), pp. 25–25.
This article, written by a policy analyst, surveys the future impact of computers on industry and trade.

Johnson, Jan. "Can They Do It?" *Datamation* 29, no. 7 (July 1983), pp. 161–70.
Four experts (from MIT, CRAY, Applied Data Research, and Arthur D. Little) assess Japan's fifth generation computer project.

Kasschau, Richard A.; Roy Lachman; and Kenneth Laughery, eds. *Information Technology and Psychology: Prospects for the Future*. New York: Praeger Publishers, 1982, 260 pp.
Contributors to this book are drawn from government, industry, and academia.

Lecht, Charles P. *The Waves of Change*. New York: McGraw-Hill, 1979, 194 pp.
This book is written by a computer scientist, a practitioner with a journalistic flair.

Lias, Edward, J. *Future Mind.* Boston: Little, Brown, 1982, 299 pp.

The subtitle of this book is *The Microcomputer—New Medium, New Mental Environment.* Of particular interest is the chapter entitled, "Future Mind: Toward the Year 2040."

Martin, James. *Telematic Society: A Challenge for Tomorrow.* Englewood Cliffs, N.J.: Prentice-Hall, 1981, 244 pp.

Martin, a specialist in telecommunications, discusses how computer networks will affect factories, homes, and cities in the future. He forecasts changes in medicine, delivery of news, shopping, and other fields.

McCorduck, Pamela. "Introduction to the Fifth Generation." *Communications of the ACM* 26, no. 6 (September 1983), pp. 629–30.

The author discusses the Japanese fifth generation computer project and Japanese competition with the U.S. computer industry. This issue has three other recommended articles on fifth generation computers.

———. *Machines Who Think.* San Francisco: W. H. Freeman, 1979, 375 pp.

No, the title is not in error. The author, a journalist, has written about the history of artificial intelligence and the controversy surrounding it. She has interviewed the main contributors to AI and describes their research and views, often using their own words. The questions raised by this book are as provocative as its title.

Teich, Albert H., ed. *Technology and Man's Future* 3rd ed. New York: St. Martin's Press, 1981, 420 pp.

Articles in this text are on technology—forecast assessments, control of technology, and ways to reshape technology.

Toffler, Alvin. *The Third Wave.* New York: William Morrow, 1980, 544 pp.

The author of *Future Shock* has again written a book to shock readers. Chapters discuss the intelligent environment, the electronic cottage, the rise of the prosumer, the personality of the future, and 21st-century democracy.

Weil, Ulric. *Information Systems in the 80s.* Englewood Cliffs, N.J.: Prentice-Hall, 1982, 383 pp.

Weil discusses products, markets, and vendors (including Japanese vendors) in the 1980s.

Zvegintzov, Nicholas. "Nanotrends," *Datamation* 29, no. 8 (August 1983), pp. 106–16.

Future direction of systems is identified and discussed. Topics covered are functionality, add-on, compatibility, and tools.

Appendix: Glossary in prose

This glossary will introduce information systems terminology in a meaningful context. The definitions are informal, designed to give the reader an intuitive appreciation and understanding of computers and information systems. An index at the end of this glossary will enable quick reference to the line on which each term is used or defined. A conventional glossary in alphabetical sequence follows.

Equipment

One of the earliest examples of mass processing of data was the use of   1
a **punched card** by Herman Hollerith in 1890 to process census data.   2
Since then the card has been produced in very large quantities by IBM.   3
It is referred to as an **IBM card** or a **Hollerith card.** The card has 80   4
columns. Holes are punched in each column according to a code to   5
represent a character of data. The cards are then fed into special equip-   6
ment, passing one at a time between **photo cells** carrying electric cur-   7
rent. Wherever the punched holes appear, the current passes through   8
the card. The characters represented by the holes are then read by ma-   9
chine in the form of electrical impulses and interpreted as the characters   10
the holes represent, be they data or instructions on how to process data.   11
Hollerith is credited with inventing the first machine for **data pro-**   12
cessing (DP). By data processing, one means the manipulation of data   13
following a sequence of instructions to achieve a desired result. Early   14
DP involved simple processing, such as adding, subtracting, and clas-   15
sifying data. Handling cards required much special equipment. A **key-**   16
punch, used like a typewriter, punched holes in a **data card** to repre-   17
sent data or processing instructions; a **verifier** identified errors in   18

keypunching; a **reproducer** generated duplicate cards and had the added 19
capability of moving columns of data to another position on a card; a 20
sorter classified cards according to coded data classifications; and a 21
collator merged data cards, combining two similarly sequenced sets of 22
cards into one set. These devices are sometimes still used in process- 23
ing, but today their use is primarily for preparing data for a computer. 24
They are referred to as **input** and **peripheral equipment.** The latter also 25
include devices that handle processing results, called **output equip-** 26
ment. These include a **printer** that prints results in single or multiple 27
copies; a **decollator** that separates the carbon sheets from the multiple 28
sheets of output paper, called a multiple **ply** paper; and a **burster** that 29
breaks the perforations in the sheets, creating pages from the long con- 30
tinuous sheets of paper. 31

The equipment mentioned above was originally used for accounting 32
purposes. Those machines using electric impulses became known as 33
electric accounting machines (EAM) or **unit record equipment** be- 34
cause each input card used by the machines usually represented one 35
record of data. Since EAM equipment was used for automating office 36
processing, use of the equipment was called **automatic data process-** 37
ing (ADP). 38

Much of this equipment is no longer used to perform the functions of 39
data processing, having been replaced by a **computer,** an electronic 40
machine that is capable of complex operations with data at fanatstic 41
speeds. The computer is **electronic** because the processing is done by 42
the movement of electronic pulses rather than electrical or mechanical 43
means as in ADP or EAM. Computer processing is therefore referred to 44
as **electronic data processing (EDP).** 45

The early computers in the 1950s performed arithmetic operations that 46
were measured in **milliseconds** (thousandths of a second). As comput- 47
ers developed, the time for operations was reduced to **microseconds** 48
(millionth of a second). It is currently measured in **nanoseconds** (bil- 49
lionths of a second), and will soon be measured in **picoseconds** (a 50
thousandth of a nanosecond). Processing is done by the **central pro-** 51
cessing unit (CPU) of the computer. The CPU has three parts, the 52
arithmetic and logical unit that performs arithmetic calculations (such 53
as add and subtract) and makes choices (Yes and No); the **internal** 54
memory unit that stores information temporarily; and the **control unit** 55
that selects the order of operations and coordinates the other units. 56

One type of electronic computer is a **mainframe,** a large general- 57
purpose computer, the type of computer used by corporations and gov- 58
ernment agencies. It is capable of processing most of the information 59
processing needs of the organization it serves. **Minicomputers** are not 60
as powerful, or large. **Microcomputers** are low-cost computers small 61
enough to be placed on desks. They can be used for business applica- 62
tions and are also used in many homes as **personal computers** to keep 63

track of household inventories, bank accounts, games, or other items. 64
Although microcomputers can be tailored for several different applica- 65
tions by programming, the tasks can only be performed one at a time in 66
contrast to minicomputers that can simultaneously perform multiple tasks. 67
Microcomputers are also slower and have less memory than minicom- 68
puters. 69

A **microprocessor** is not a **general-purpose computer** like the min- 70
icomputer. It is hand-wired by electrical connections to perform a special 71
task such as controlling a car carburetor or controlling a factory opera- 72
tion. A microprocessor is extremely small, the size of a fingertip, and 73
requires very little energy to operate. It may consist of one or more **chips** 74
of a **semiconductor** such as **silicon** with circuitry etched into it that en- 75
ables it to perform computations like a computer. These chips, when as- 76
sembled and related together, form an **integrated circuit (IC).** Large- 77
scale integration of circuits may consist of 10–20,000 **transistors** on one 78
or several chips, each transistor performing the function of the earlier 79
electronic tube, which was a small electronic device capable of pro- 80
cessing data coded in **binary values** (values of 0 or 1). 81

When peripheral devices are in direct communication with the CPU, 82
they are referred to as **online equipment.** Examples are **printers** that 83
produce output and **terminals** that both receive input and produce out- 84
put directly from the CPU. Terminals may be **typewriter terminals** or 85
cathode ray tubes (CRT). A **CRT terminal** looks much like a television 86
set sitting on top of a typewriter. The terminal may be physically part of 87
the computer (in which case it is called a **console**) or it can be located 88
apart, connected to the computer by direct cable or by telephone (in which 89
case, the terminal is said to have **remote access**). With telephone 90
transmission, terminal data must be converted into telephone signals 91
which are then reconverted into data acceptable to the computer. This 92
is done by a **data phone** with a **data transmission set.** The data phone 93
in this case performs the function of an **interface** between the terminal 94
and the telephone lines. 95

Other examples of computer-related equipment, also called **periph-** 96
eral devices, are a **plotter** that plots input graphically; a card reader 97
that reads punched cards; a **magnetic ink character recognition** reader 98
(MICR) used in bank accounting, that reads coded symbols such as those 99
that appear on bank checks; and an **optical scanner** or **optical reader** 100
that recognizes marks and special characters on such documents as in- 101
voices. The characters read can be of different styles and sizes, referred 102
to as **fonts.** Some of this equipment is not directly connected to a com- 103
puter. Such equipment is called **offline equipment.** 104

The equipment discussed in this section may be grouped in many 105
combinations or **configurations.** All computer-related equipment is re- 106
ferred to as **hardware.** 107

Software

In contrast to hardware, physical objects that can be touched, there is 108
software, written as **programs,** that are stored on an input medium such 109
as cards. A program instructs the computer on the **algorithm** to be used; 110
that is, the specific computing procedure to be followed in order to achieve 111
the desired results and the sequence in which the operations are to be 112
performed. Computational operations such as adding, subtracting, find- 113
ing logs and square roots, and rearrangements of data are done quickly 114
and accurately by computers without further manual intervention. 115

Programmers are individuals who write programs instructing the 116
computer what to do. The computer only recognizes electronic pulses 117
which can be generated by a language using numbers for its instruc- 118
tions. Such a language is called **machine language.** Machine language 119
is a **low level language,** in contrast to **natural languages** such as En- 120
glish, which are **high level languages.** There is a spectrum of program- 121
ming languages in between. The closer the programming language is to 122
a natural language, the higher it is in the computer language hierarchy 123
and the easier it is for programmers to write. Low level languages are 124
more difficult to write but are more efficiently run by the computer. A very 125
low level language is called a **micro-code.** This term should not be con- 126
fused with codes and programs for microprocessors, which are referred 127
to as **micro software.** 128

High level programming languages have to be interpreted and trans- 129
lated into machine language to be understood by a computer. This is 130
done by special machine language programs that convert a program 131
written in a high level language into machine language. These sets of 132
conversion programs are called **compilers, assemblers, translators,** 133
and **interpreters.** Other computer programs govern the scheduling of 134
programming **jobs** and automate the relationship of the computer to its 135
peripheral devices. These programs are called **monitors** or **supervi-** 136
sors. Still other computer programs perform "household" duties (fre- 137
quently performed operations of a computer such as label checking and 138
listing an information file). These are called **utility programs.** 139

The compilers, assemblers, translators, interpreters, monitors, super- 140
visors, and utility programs are collectively referred to as **system pro-** 141
grams and are frequently provided together with computer equipment 142
by the manufacturers. These programs are distinct from **application** 143
programs that are typically provided by the user. Both system and ap- 144
plication programs constitute what is known as **software.** Sometimes 145
software is used to redefine a computer's hardware. These programs 146
and the affected hardware are known as **firmware.** 147

System programs are called **operating systems.** The operating sys- 148
tem along with the hardware configuration is unique for each computer 149
model. This is why programs run on one computer system cannot al- 150
ways be run on another. If two computer systems can run the same set 151
of computer programs, they are considered **compatible** with one an- 152

other. One system can then serve as a **backup** for the other in the event 153
of a breakdown. Another type of backup is duplicated data files and pro- 154
grams in case the originals are accidentally or maliciously altered, de- 155
stroyed, or stolen. 156

Many firms custom-develop **application software.** That is, they write 157
in-house programs to solve problems. However, software **packages** can 158
also be purchased for standard applications, such as payroll processing. 159
These are offered for sale by **software houses.** A common business 160
package is a **spreadsheet program** that facilitates business planning. 161

Most computer programs are written by the user or programmers and 162
are written in one of the higher-level programming languages. Whereas 163
each computer model has its specific machine language, standard pro- 164
gramming languages can be used for writing programs for many types 165
of computers. There are tens of high level programming languages. 166
COBOL and **RPG** are most commonly used for information systems and 167
business data processing. Many languages are used in scientific pro- 168
gramming though **FORTRAN** is most common in the United States and 169
ALGOL is popular in Europe. Some languages serve dual purposes, being 170
used for both scientific and business data processing. Examples are **PL/1** 171
and **BASIC.** Languages like **APL** and **BASIC** are also **conversational** 172
or **interactive languages,** enabling fast responses on a terminal. Of in- 173
terest to business management are **simulation languages** like **GPSS** 174
and **SIMSCRIPT,** that are designed specially for business problems in 175
planning and control. Some languages are appropriate for nonnumerical 176
processing such as text processing. **SNOBOL** and **LISP** are examples. 177

Data

As mentioned earlier, programs are sets of instructions for processing 178
data. This data must be organized and managed so that it can be effi- 179
ciently and effectively processed. This is known as **data management** 180
or **file management.** Organized data is a **data base,** also called a **data** 181
bank, consisting of a set of **integrated files.** A file is a set of records; a 182
record is a set of **data elements** where a data element is a fact or an 183
observation with a value that the user needs to record. Each data ele- 184
ment is represented in a **data field,** which was historically a set of **data** 185
columns on a data card. There are 80 such data columns per card, each 186
representing a **character** of data. A set of characters can be **alphabetic** 187
(A to Z), **numeric** (0–9), **alphanumeric** (or **alphameric**) such as the 188
license plate AEJ472, special symbols such as $ * +, or a combination 189
of all these types. For the character to be understood by the computer, 190
it must be machine-readable. That is, the character must be represented 191
by a set of **bits,** which are **binary digits** of 0 or 1. A set of electric cur- 192
rents can be made to represent these digits by being off (0) or on (1). 193
By changing these states we can represent bits, which are combined to 194

represent unique characters. For example, the number 9 can be repre- 195
sented in binary digits as 1001 (on-off-off-on). Similarly, letters and sym- 196
bols can be represented by a unique permutation of 0 and 1 bits. In this 197
way, bits can be made to represent the entire **hierarchy of data** from 198
data elements, records, and files to the entire data base itself. 199

A data element is usually the lowest level of data a manager uses. 200
Each of these data elements is defined in a **data element dictionary** 201
(DED) prepared specially in each business according to its data element 202
needs. In large information systems, these data elements have to be 203
classified, indexed, and organized so as to facilitate their access and 204
use. This function is performed by a **data directory.** The data directory 205
and the DED are then used by a set of computer programs to structure, 206
access, and manage the data base. This is known as a **data base man-** 207
agement system (DBMS). There are many such systems sold by com- 208
puter manufacturers and **software companies.** These include **TDMS,** 209
MARK IV, TOTAL, ADABAS, IMS, and **SYSTEM 2000.** 210

There are basically two types of DBMS. One uses a high level En- 211
glish-like programming language that enables a manager to **query** the 212
data base, retrieve data, and structure output to facilitate decision mak- 213
ing. The second type handles application programs. Both are indepen- 214
dent of data storage techniques. Administering the DBMS and acting as 215
a liaison between users and the data base are persons called **data base** 216
administrators. 217

Data and programs to be processed are stored on a **storage** or 218
memory device. There are many types of such devices. One is called 219
core. It is part of the CPU equipment and is referred to as **internal stor-** 220
age (internal to CPU) or as **primary storage.** It is supplemented by ad- 221
ditional storage on an **external memory device.** An example is a **mag-** 222
netic tape similar to that used in tape recorders. Tape is especially 223
suitable for recording data that must be processed and retrieved **se-** 224
quentially, such as payroll. Some processing and retrieval is done in 225
random order, allowing any word in the memory to be accessed. The 226
memory device appropriate for such **random processing** is a **disk** which 227
is similar to a phonograph record. On small computers, a smaller and 228
less rigid disk, called a **floppy disk** or **floppy,** is used. The tape **(mag-** 229
netic or **paper tape)** and the disk are referred to as **auxiliary, secon-** 230
dary, or **external storage.** 231

Data is stored on tapes or disks as **bits** when representing one char- 232
acter, or stored as **bytes,** sets of bits. The size of a byte is eight bits. 233
Data is also stored as a **word** which varies with computer manufactur- 234
ers but is between 8–64 bits. Large data bases are measured in **tons** 235
of data where a ton is 40 billion bits of data. Many businesses have tens 236
of tons of data. The capability of storing large amounts of data not only 237
enables the use of large data bases but also enables the use of large 238
and complex programs, some being many million bits in size. 239

Some data is kept in a **common data base.** This data is collected 240
and validated only once, then stored to be shared by all bona fide users 241
in the organization for many purposes. Such a system is **integrated.** There 242
are many types of integration. **Vertical integration** is sharing of data by 243
all levels of management even though this may be confined to one func- 244
tion only, such as marketing or production. Other systems are integrated 245
at one level of management but integrated for all functions at that level. 246
Such integration is called **horizontal integration.** There is also integra- 247
tion over time, called **longitudinal integration,** which is used, for ex- 248
ample, in making sales projections based on the past five years of data. 249
When an information system has all three types of integration it is then 250
called a **total system** or a **management information system (MIS).** 251

Information systems

Thus far, computer technology, hardware, software, and data bases have 252
been discussed. If these components are organized as a whole to pro- 253
duce desired information, an **information system** is created. An **MIS** 254
system produces information needed by managers for planning as well 255
as for control and operational functions. However, information systems 256
are not a panacea for all of a manager's informational needs. They do, 257
however, provide information that can contribute to better and more ef- 258
ficient decisions. 259

The careful reader will note that the term "MIS" has been defined in 260
two ways in this glossary. There are still other definitions, Many terms 261
used in this book have more than one definition, especially such terms 262
as *implementation* and *development.* This is because computer science 263
is a relatively new field. It will take many years to develop a universal 264
standardization of terms. The **American National Standards Institute** 265
(ANSI) is one organization presently working on this problem. 266

Information systems are developed in **stages,** each consisting of a 267
set of jobs called **activities.** The first group of activities (first stage) of 268
the developmental process is a **feasibility study,** which examines al- 269
ternative approaches to producing information for practicality within con- 270
straints of the organization. A **constraint** is a factor that places a limit 271
on what is possible. 272

Once an alternative is chosen by management, the next stage in the 273
developmental process is for the manager to define information needs 274
specifically in order for the system to be designed to meet these needs. 275
The **design** starts with the specification of the user's need of **output;** 276
that is, determining what information the system should generate. From 277
the output needs, the **input,** the resources put into the system, can be 278
deduced. This includes a determination of equipment, data, and proce- 279
dures needed to produce the output. The **procedures** are sets of in- 280
structions and rules governing the human-machine (user-computer) re- 281
lationship. 282

The designed system is then **implemented.** This includes writing | 283
programs to manipulate data in order to generate the desired output. The | 284
system is then **tested,** comparing actual performance with desired per- | 285
formance. Further **debugging,** locating and correcting errors, may be | 286
necessary. Once the system performs as expected, it is **documented,** | 287
a process of stating all relevant facts about the system. This documen- | 288
tation includes **decision tables** which specify the logic of the **decision** | 289
rules and **flowcharts** which show the logic and the flow of data. The | 290
documentation and programs are then deposited in a **program library** | 291
and are handled and controlled by a **librarian.** | 292

The system, when satisfactorily tested and documented, is then **con-** | 293
verted, the old system being **phased out** and the new system made | 294
operational. | 295

Management of an information system

Computer operations have many **modes** of operation. One is **batch** | 296
processing, which involves collecting jobs into a **batch** before they are | 297
processed. Another is **time sharing,** where users take turns being ser- | 298
viced. However, due to the fast processing speeds of modern comput- | 299
ers, users are serviced almost instantly, giving each individual the illu- | 300
sion of having the machine to oneself, **dedicated** to one's use. Time- | 301
sharing systems are used largely by programmers and users for scien- | 302
tific computations. Some businesses require a **real-time system,** which | 303
searches its data base and gives results in time to affect the operating | 304
environment. | 305

Developing, operating, and maintaining an information system re- | 306
quire professional personnel, the most important being the **system an-** | 307
alyst, also referred to as **system designer** and **systems engineer.** Within | 308
a development team, expertise in synthesizing systems is necessary as | 309
well as a knowledge of **operations research** or **management science,** | 310
the use of mathematical and statistical techniques for finding the **opti-** | 311
mal (best) solution in application programming, and experience in data | 312
management. The team of system analysts must also have some | 313
knowledge of **mathematical** and **numerical analysis** as well as knowl- | 314
edge of computer hardware and operating systems, though it may call | 315
on **hardware and system programming specialists** for help when | 316
needed. | 317

A system analyst may do computer programming but often this re- | 318
sponsibility is assigned to a **programmer,** a professional at writing pro- | 319
grams. If the logic and flow of the program have been specified in detail, | 320
the actual writing of the program can be done by a lower-level program- | 321
mer called a **program coder.** Another type of **coder** is a clerk who rep- | 322
resents lengthy data by shorthand **codes,** for example, representing colors | 323
by numbers (for example 1 for red, 2 for orange, 3 for yellow, and so | 324
forth). | 325

Keypunched data is prepared by a **keypuncher.** The cards are then 326
sometimes processed on EAM equipment by a **tab operator.** Other 327
professional and technical personnel involved in systems work are **sys-** 328
tem programmers, and **control clerks,** who check and control the quality 329
of input and output. The checking of output should be done after each 330
run, processing of data by computer in the expectation of getting de- 331
sired output. If the output meets prescribed standards, it is distributed to 332
authorized personnel. 333

The **run time** of modern computers is a small fraction of time com- 334
pared to the **response time,** the time elapsed from the moment the in- 335
put starts being read to the moment the output is produced. Response 336
time includes the wait before the CPU is available and the time required 337
for reading and printing. When input-output operations are slow com- 338
pared to the time spent on computations, the full capability of the com- 339
puter is not utilized. Such computer systems are **input-output bound.** 340
Machines that are limited in computing capabilities are **compute bound.** 341

In addition to the response time, preparation of input takes time, as 342
does control of output and its distribution. These are, relatively speak- 343
ing, more time-consuming and error-prone operations than computer runs, 344
since they are **people-intensive,** jobs done manually by people. 345

One other concept concerns **lapse time.** This is the time required from 346
the start of a job to the finish, which is not the same as the time actually 347
spent on the job. For example, a manager may spend ten minutes mak- 348
ing a decision but it may take three weeks of preparation before the 349
necessary data is assembled on which the decision is based. The lapse 350
time in this case is three weeks, ten minutes. Lapse time in preparing a 351
computer program is often much longer than the actual time spent writ- 352
ing the program, for included are the hours spent in debugging. Ex- 353
tended lapse time for preparation is one reason why the development of 354
information systems takes so long and why they must be planned with 355
adequate **lead time** for development. 356

During operations, the system is **controlled** for quality of information. 357
This includes checking of input data for validity, completeness, accu- 358
racy, and errors. Controls are also designed to protect against such in- 359
tentional tampering of data as fraud and theft, but **security** against 360
tampering is not always completely successful. Part of the problem is 361
that design procedures and training for control do not keep up with ad- 362
vances in technology, especially hardware developments. 363

During operations, the system is regularly evaluated. This **evaluation** 364
is based on both efficiency and effectiveness. **Efficiency** refers to the 365
relationship between input and output while **effectiveness** refers to the 366
successful achievement of critical factors of performance set by the user. 367
Examples of critical factors are **accuracy,** a specified percentage of 368
freedom from error; **timeliness,** the availability of information when 369
needed; and **completeness,** the availability of all relevant data. 370

Computer applications

Computers process data and perform calculations to generate informa- 371
tion. Often during the operation of a system, the data changes. The re- 372
cording of this change is a **transaction.** A file containing transactions is 373
called a **transaction file** or **detail file.** It is used to change the data on 374
the **master file.** This is done in a sequential order. The reflection of the 375
new transactions on the master file is called **updating** and periodic up- 376
dating of a master file is referred to ás **file processing.** The deletion of 377
irrelevant data is **purging** of data. Such processing takes place at the 378
operational level of a business; for example, payroll accounts receiva- 379
ble or payable, or deposits and withdrawals from a bank. Other com- 380
puter applications are needed at the **control** and **planning levels** in- 381
volving middle and top managers. At these levels, statistical and 382
mathematical computer models of decision making and special pro- 383
gramming languages such as **GPSS** and **SIMSCRIPT** are needed. 384

In addition to producing information and performing calculations, 385
computers have other applications in business and industry. They are 386
used to control operations. **Numerical control** is **discrete** where dis- 387
tinct operations are controlled, such as the movement of a lathe or drill. 388
Another type of control is **process control** for continuous operations such 389
as those found in a refinery or a steel rolling mill. For such control, **minis** 390
(minicomputers) and **micros** (microcomputers) are used. These may be 391
independent computers that have **stand-alone capabilities.** Other 392
computer systems are designed for limited operations, such as game 393
computers or for use in **smart products.** Some stores have **terminals,** 394
each capable of recording sale and calculating the remaining cash to be 395
paid, and are connected to a central computer. These terminals, called 396
point-of-sale terminals (POS terminals), are sometimes **interactive,** 397
asking and answering questions in a **conversational mode.** 398

There are many other applications of terminals served by a central 399
computer. One example is **computer-assisted instruction (CAI),** where 400
terminals are used for teaching and drilling. Another is **computer-aided** 401
design (CAD), where products are designed on terminals. Such termi- 402
nals are CRTs having **graphic** capabilities on which the user can draw 403
and combine lines, symbols, and curves. Objects thus drawn can be 404
scaled, that is enlarged or contracted, or rotated, and objects can be 405
moved to any part of the screen. Once the desired shape or design is 406
drawn, a mathematical description of the design is stored on paper tape, 407
which can then be used on numerical control equipment to automatically 408
direct the production of the actual product designed on the CRT screen. 409

Some terminals have memory and are programmable. These are called 410
intelligent terminals. These may be miniature stand-alone computers 411
that are used, for example, in accounting applications, data entry, data 412
checking, and even for **cash dispensing.** The latter will dispense cash 413
on request after verifying that one's bank balance will cover the amount. 414
Others dispense cash on a credit card and can communicate in several 415

languages, selecting the preferred language of the user by reading a code   416
symbol on the credit card. Intelligent terminals can also be used for **credit**   417
checking when accepting checks as in a grocery store. Some are con-   418
nected to a bank and will instantly debit your account for the amount of   419
the check. Funds are then transferred electronically from the buyer's to   420
the seller's account, a process called **electronic fund transfer (EFT).**   421
Similarly, funds may be transferred between banks electronically. With   422
more common use of EFT and intelligent terminals, the United States   423
may become a **cashless** and **checkless society.** This will require a   424
greater use of **teleprocessing,** the processing of data at a remote point.   425
For this, the use of **telecommunications** via telephone lines or even   426
satellites for the transference of data between remote points is neces-   427
sary. Connections between a central computer with intelligent terminals   428
and other computers enable computing power to be distributed to de-   429
centralized points and locations. This is called **distributed data pro-**   430
cessing.   431

Sometimes computers are interconnected and share peak loads much   432
like the grid connecting electric power stations. Another similarity with   433
electric power stations is when a **computer utility** sells computing power   434
to customers much as a power utility sells electricity. Both systems have   435
high equipment costs and require many customers to reduce the unit   436
cost. Some businesses, however, are hesitant to use a computer utility   437
because they fear the loss of control over the **security** of their data. Se-   438
curity in this context is protection against unauthorized access.   439

Security in an information system is sometimes breached by accident   440
or error on the part of a programmer or operator, though often the breach   441
is by sabotage or theft. There are two types of computer theft. One is   442
bite theft, a one-time theft where a large dollar amount is stolen by un-   443
authorized access to computerized accounts with the thief disappearing   444
or attempting to escape. The other is **nibble theft,** where the thief takes   445
small amounts over a period of time, hoping never to be discovered. A   446
classic example is the salami technique in which a programmer **trun-**   447
cated small amounts in paychecks and transferred the amount to his   448
personal account.   449

Information systems thus far discussed have been data processing   450
systems. Some systems, however, process words or text. These are called   451
word processing systems. A common use of this computer application   452
is typing correspondence and the preparation of manuals. Text is stored   453
in the computer, displayed on a CRT, and then corrected by **text edit-**   454
ing capability. The text, once corrected, does not have to be retyped,   455
thereby reducing labor and errors that may occur in the retyping.   456

Most of the input for word and data processing is currently typed on   457
a terminal keyboard, or read by optical scanning devices. However, in-   458
put equipment is under development for **voice recognition, picture**   459
processing, handwriting recognition, and even **signature recogni-**   460

tion. In each of these areas, there is an infinite set of possibilities. The | 461
problem is one of identifying the uniqueness of patterns, a subject known | 462
as **pattern recognition.** Pattern recognition does not depend on for- | 463
mulas or algorithms but uses rules of thumb, called **heuristic problem** | 464
solving. Heuristics are also used when writing computer programs for | 465
composing music, solving integration problems in mathematics, and for | 466
playing games of chess. Some computer programs **learn** from experi- | 467
ence, improving their performance, as in Arthur Samuel's checkers-playing | 468
program. Much research is being done to make computers approach the | 469
natural intelligence of human beings. This field of research is called **ar-** | 470
tificial intelligence. | 471

The Japanese have announced that they plan to introduce a **fifth** | 472
generation computer in the 1990s that incorporates artificial intelli- | 473
gence. This will be a **super-supercomputer** thousands of times faster | 474
than computers today, and will be supported by **intelligent input** and | 475
output devices, and **knowledge systems,** the latter being computer | 476
programs that use inference procedures to solve difficult problems. If the | 477
computer incorporates **expert systems,** providing the user with knowl- | 478
edge and advice that human experts might offer, and the user has ac- | 479
cess to decision models, managers in the 1990s will have access to **in-** | 480
telligent MIS or **IMIS.** | 481

The next decade will see expanded use of **public data bases.** These | 482
data bases are compiled, indexed, and updated for customers willing to | 483
pay a fee for access to them. They may provide weather information, | 484
entertainment listings, news, and shopping tips of general interest, or fo- | 485
cus on business data, such as patent information. A **telecommunica-** | 486
tions network is required for customers to access public data bases. | 487
For short distances, **local area networks (LAN)** suffice, an example of | 488
which is **Ethernet.** LANs linked by telephone or satellite are needed for | 489
long distances. | 490

Implications

Computers, with or without artificial intelligence, affect our ways of prob- | 491
lem solving and decision making. Managers need to learn how to effec- | 492
tively use this extension of information. In the future, computers may re- | 493
place some managers at the operational and middle levels of | 494
management. There will also be displacement of high-level manage- | 495
ment, though this will occur less frequently because these managers are | 496
usually concerned with problems that cannot be easily solved by com- | 497
puters. Computers will also replace factory workers and clerks at the op- | 498
erational level, resulting in **unemployment.** In some cases, persons may | 499
lose a job because of computers, but gain a job in computing itself. This | 500
displacement often requires retraining. The fear of losing jobs as well | 501
as ignorance of computing often lead to **resistance,** a behavior that is | 502
common in the computer revolution. | 503

Decision making will change in the future. Since the price of computing has dropped, distributed data processing is becoming economically feasible. This shifts much decision making to distributed nodes. However, data used by more than one user or group may still be processed by headquarters. A **common data bank** reduces the cost per unit of processing and also increases the effectiveness of processing by correlating data from different files.

Theoretically, a national data bank is possible. It could **integrate** files on individuals and businesses, combining such records as taxes, FBI information, credit bureau ratings, medical records, and so forth. However, many Americans believe that such large data banks violate individual **privacy. Security** of data is also an issue. While security is a technological problem, privacy involves ethical and moral values. Privacy concerns have led Congress to reject the idea of the national data bank and instead to enact the 1974 Privacy Act. This act gives individuals the right to know what personal data is collected and how it is to be used by the government. Furthermore, there are controls for the validity and completeness of data. The act applies only to federal agencies, but it has been used as a framework for state laws on data privacy, and for federal laws covering the private sector, including education, health care, and business.

There are other legal problems unique to computers that are currently being defined in court: the liability for computer errors and computer fraud; patenting of software; the use of computer media as evidence; and perhaps most important, interpreting antitrust laws in relation to computer manufacturers. Old laws need to be redefined and new ones enacted.

Along with the legal implications, there are social implications of the still emerging computer industry. The combination of EFT credit terminals with personal and home computers will affect the way we do our shopping, influence urban development, and the growth of shopping centers. The use of **numerical control, robots, electronic mail, electronic offices, teleconferencing,** and **process control** will affect our nation's productivity. These and other computer applications currently being developed will have a significant impact on how we do business and even on how we live in the future.

Index to glossary in prose

Glossary

This glossary includes operational definitions of basic computing terms. Since precise technical definitions too often obscure meanings, the definitions in this list have been written in simple terms. Readers wishing a complete technical glossary of computer terms should consult such dictionaries as the *American Standard Vocabulary of Information Processing* published by the American National Standards Institute. Dictionaries of computer terms can be found in many libraries.

abacus: beads or balls which slide back and forth along wires on a frame, used as counters or memory aids for doing arithmetic.

acceptance test: a test for evaluating the capabilities and performance of a system in terms of specifications predefined by the user in the systems specification stage.

access: (1) the manner in which files or data sets are referred to by the computer. See **direct access, random access, remote access,** and **serial access;** (2) the process of obtaining data from storage.

access time: the period of time between a request for information and the availability of that data.

accumulator: a hardware register that holds the results of arithmetic, logical and I/O operations.

accuracy: correctness, freedom from error.

Ada: programming language originally developed by the Department of Defense for use in embedded system applications in the military services. Used today for many other applications as well.

address: name given to a specific memory location, either within the computer (memory address) or on the storage media (disk address), where information is stored.

ALGOL (ALGOrithmic Language): a modular structured programming language used by persons involved in scientific and mathematical projects.

algorithm: a step-by-step process for the solution of a problem in a finite number of steps. Usually developed in an outline or by a tool of analysis before coding begins.

alphanumeric: alphabetic, numeric, and punctuation characters (but not special symbols like $).

American National Standards Institute (ANSI): an organization sponsored by the Business Equipment Manufacturers Association (BEMA) for the purpose of establishing voluntary industry standards.

analog: using measured physical variables, such as distance, rotation, or voltage, to represent and correspond with numerical variables that occur in a computation.

analog computer: (1) a computer in which analog representation of data is mainly used; (2) a computer that operates on **analog data** by performing physical processes on these data. Contrast with **digital computer.**

analog data: data represented in a continuous form, as contrasted with *digital data,* represented in a discrete (discontinuous) form. Analog data are usually represented by means of physical variables, such as voltage, resistance, and rotation.

analog signal: a continuous electrical signal representing a condition (such as temperature or the position of game control paddles). Unlike a **digital signal,** which is discrete, an analog signal can be any frequency or strength.

analyst: see **system analyst.**

APL (A Programming Language): powerful interactive language for scientific and mathematical computations.

application program: a program written for or by a user that applies to the user's own work.

application software: software programs that perform a specific user-oriented task, such as balancing production or payroll processing. Application software can be either purchased as a package or custom designed by a programmer.

APT (Automatically Programmed Tool): a language for programming numerical control machines.

architecture: (1) the structure of a system. Computer architecture often refers specifically to the CPU; (2) a specific choice of representation, inference, and control strategies.

arithmetic and logic unit (ALU): the element in a computer that can perform the basic data manipulations (arithmetic, logic, and control functions) in the central processor.

arithmetic operations: binary operations of addition, subtraction, multiplication, and division. Also operations with negative and absolute values.

array: an arrangement of elements in one or more dimensions.

artificial intelligence (AI):   (1) the ability of a computer to imitate certain human actions or skills, such as problem solving, decision making, perception, and learning; (2) a subfield of computer science that is concerned with symbolic problem solving; (3) an attempt to program computers so that they behave intelligently.

assemble: to prepare a machine language program from a symbolic language program by substituting absolute operation codes for symbolic operation codes, and absolute or relocatable addresses for symbolic addresses.

assembler: a computer program that converts (or translates) assembly language programs into a form (machine language) that the computer can understand. The assembler translates mnemonic instruction codes into binary numbers, replaces names with their binary equivalents, and assigns memory locations to data and instructions.

assembler language: a programming language in which the programmer can use mnemonic instruction codes, labels, and names to refer directly to their binary equivalents. The assembler is a low level language since each assembler language instruction translates directly into a specific machine language instruction.

attribute: a characteristic. For example, attributes of data include record length, record format, data set name, associated device type and volume identification, and use.

audit trail: the procedure of tracing the steps in processing data to ensure that results are within either expected or standardized limits.

auditing around the computer: checking output for a given input.

auditing through the computer: checking both input and computer processing. May use test data, auditor-prepared programs, auditor-software packages, or audit programming languages.

auditor: person authorized to make a formal periodic examination and check of accounts or financial records to verify their correctness. A computer auditor may also be assigned to verify the correctness of computer information processing to ensure that processing conforms to the firm's goals, policies, and procedures (policies with regard to security and privacy.).

authentication: verifying the user's right to access a requested file or portion of the data base.

authorization: verifying the type of access permitted, for example, read, write, update, or no access.

automatic data processing (ADP):   (1) data processing largely performed by automatic means; (2) by extension, the discipline that deals with methods and techniques related to data processing performed by automatic means; (3) pertaining to data processing equipment, such as electrical accounting machines and electronic data processing equipment.

automation: use of self-operating equipment, electronic devices, and so forth to replace human beings in production, inspection of parts, control of work processes, or performance of routine or repetitious work.

auxiliary operation: an offline operation performed by equipment not under control of the central processing unit.

auxiliary storage: (1) data storage other than main storage. For example, storage on magnetic tape or direct access devices. Synonymous with **external storage** and **secondary storage;** (2) a storage that supplements another storage. Contrast with **main storage.**

backup: (1) copying of one or more files onto a storage medium for safekeeping should the original be damaged or lost; (2) redundant equipment or procedures used in the event of failure of a component or storage medium.

bandwidth: the difference between the lower and upper limits of the wave frequencies that can be transmitted over a communications channel. A high bandwidth means more data can be transferred in a given time interval.

bar code recognition: a form of machine-readable encodation formed by vertical bars and spaces. A scanner measures the presence or absence of a reflection over time to determine bit patterns of characters. See **optical character recognition.**

BASIC (**B**eginner's **A**ll-purpose **S**ymbolic **I**nstruction **C**ode): a relatively easy-to-use programming language that is available in many small computer systems.

batch processing: a traditional method of data processing in which transactions are collected and prepared for processing as a single unit.

baud: a measurement of communication speeds between devices. Generally means bits transferred per second. Divide the number by 10 to translate to characters per second.

binary: the basis for calculations in all computers. This two-digit numbering system consists of digits 0 and 1 which are represented in the computer as the presence or absence of pulses.

bit: the contraction of "binary digit," the smallest unit of information that the computer recognizes. A bit is equivalent to the presence or absence of an electrical pulse (0 or 1). Bits are usually grouped in **nibbles** (4), **bytes** (8), or larger units.

block: a set of things, such as words, characters, or digits, handled as a unit.

blocking: combining two or more records into one block.

Boolean: (1) pertaining to the processes used in the algebra formulated by George Boole; (2) pertaining to the operations of formal logic.

bridge: a simple connection between LANs that share homogeneous equipment and protocols. See **LAN.**

broadband: a communication channel having a bandwidth greater than a voice grade. Allows higher speed data transmission.

buffer: a storage area in memory or in a peripheral that is used for temporary storage of data awaiting further processing.

buffer storage: equipment linked to an input device in which information is assembled from external storage and stored ready for transfer to internal storage.

bug: a mistake in a program or in an electrical circuit. Eliminating the mistakes is known as **debugging.**

bus: (1) a circuit used for transmitting data or power. Often one which acts as a common connection among a number of locations; (2) a path over which information is tranferred from any of several sources to any of several destinations.

business data processing: data processing for business purposes, for example, recording and summarizing the financial transactions of a business.

business information system: an information system within an organization that supports one of the traditional functions of business. The system can be either an operations or management information system.

byte: a group of bits (usually 8). A byte can be used to represent one character (number or letter) of information, all or part of binary numbers, and machine language instructions.

CAD/CAM: an integrated system of computer-aided design and computer-aided manufacturing.

calculator: generally and historically, a device for carrying out logic and arithmetic digital operations of any kind.

canned program: a software package developed and made available (sold by software houses or provided free by vendors) to multiple users who have similar needs and problems.

card code: combinations of holes on a punched card to represent characters or combinations of small magnetic fields on magnetic cards.

card column: the vertical set of punching positions on an IBM card.

card field: assigned card columns for data.

card punch: a device that will record information on cards by punching holes to represent characters.

card reader: a device that senses and translates into machine code the holes in punched cards.

cassette tape storage: storage of data on a serial device that records magnetically on a removable tape cassette.

cathode ray tube (CRT): an electronic vacuum tube, such as a television picture tube, that can be used to display graphic images, text, or numerical data on visual display terminals.

cell: (1) the storage for one unit of information, usually one character or one word; (2) a location specified by the part or whole of an address and possessed of the faculty of store.

central processing unit (CPU): the part of the computer that controls the execution and interpretation of the machine language processing instructions.

centralization: the concentration of decision making in an organizational structure.

chain: dispersed data records that are linked by means of pointers. The pointers tell where the next record or record segment is located.

channel: (1) a path for electrical data transmission between two or more stations; (2) a hardware device that connects the central processing unit and main storage with the I/O control units; (3) synonymous with circuit, line, link, path, facility. See also **voice-grade channel.**

character: any letter, number, symbol, or punctuation mark.

character reader: equipment that reads printed characters from a document.

check: a process for determining accuracy.

check digit: a digit added to a set of digits used for the purpose of checking the accuracy of input data.

checking program: a specific type of diagnostic (error-discovering) program that examines programs or data for mistakes.

checkpoint: a place in a routine where a check, or a recording of data for restart purposes, is performed.

chip: a thin semiconductor wafer on which electronic components are deposited in the form of integrated circuits.

circuit: a means of communication between two or more points. Normally, the telephone linkage is a two-wire or four-wire circuit.

class: a group of data or information with similar or the same characteristics, and which is often a subdivision of a category.

COBOL (**C**ommon **B**usiness-**O**riented **L**anguage): A high level programming language designed for business data processing on large computers.

code: (1) in data processing, the representation of data or a computer program in symbolic form according to a set of rules; (2) in telecommunications, a system of rules and conventions according to which the signals representing data can be formed, transmitted, received, and processed; (3) to write a routine.

collate: to combine items from two or more ordered sets into one set having a specified order not necessarily the same as any of the original sets. Contrast with **merge.**

command: an order to the computer in the form of words and numbers typed on a keyboard, words spoken into a microphone, positions of a game paddle or joystick, and so forth.

common data base: pooled data integrated for common use as a shared resource.

common carrier: a government-regulated private company that furnishes the general public with telecommunications service facilities. For example, a telephone or telegraph company.

communication: transmission of intelligence between points of origin and reception without alteration of sequence or structure of the information content.

communication line: any medium, such as a wire or telephone circuit, that connects a remote station with a computer.

communication link: the physical means of connecting one location to another for the purpose of transmitting and receiving data.

compatibility: (1) the ability of an instruction, program, or component to be used on more than one computer; (2) the ability of computers to work with other computers that are not necessarily similar in design or capabilities.

compile: to prepare a machine language program from a computer program written in another programming language, by making use of the overall logic structure of the program, or generating more than one machine instruction for each symbolic statement, or both.

compiler: a translation program that converts high-level instructions into a set of binary instructions (object code) for execution. Each high level language requires a compiler or an interpreter. A compiler translates the complete program which is then executed. Every change in the program requires a complete recompilation. Contrast with **interpreter.**

computer: a system designed for the manipulation of information, incorporating a central processing unit (CPU), memory, input/output (I/O) facilities, power supply, and cabinet.

computer-aided design: utilization of a computer for the design or modification of a product.

computer-aided manufacturing: the use of computer technology in operation and control of a manufacturing process.

computer-assisted instruction (CAI): the direct use of a computer for the facilitation and certification of learning—that is, using the computer to make learning easier and more likely to occur (facilitation), as well as using the computer to create a record proving that learning has occurred (certification).

computer-independent language: a programming language that requires translation or compiling to any one of a variety of computer languages.

computer application: the use of a computer to solve a specific problem or to accomplish a particular task. The problem can be a scientific or business problem.

computer code: a machine code for a specific computer.

computer graphics: the use of computer capability to create, transform, and display symbolic and pictorial representations.

computer industry: firms which supply computer hardware, software, or EDP services.

computer instruction: a machine instruction for a specific computer.

computer network: a computer system consisting of two or more interconnected computing units.

computer program: a series of instructions or statements, in a form acceptable to a computer, prepared in order to achieve a certain result.

computer specialist: a person whose occupation is related to providing services in organizations that use computers or in the computer industry. System analysts, programmers, and data base administrators fall into this category.

computing system: a central processing unit, with main storage, input/output channels, control units, direct access storage devices, and input/output devices connected to it.

concentrator: a device that provides communications capability between many low-speed channels. Usually different speeds, codes, and protocols can be accommodated on the low-speed side. The concentrator may have the ability to be polled by a computer, and may, in turn, poll terminals.

configuration: the group of devices that make up a computer or data processing system.

console: that part of a computer used for communications between the operator or maintenance engineer and the computer.

constraint: a restriction.

control: a management function that involves observing and measuring organizational performance and environmental activities and making changes when expectations and standards are not met.

control program: a program that is designed to schedule and supervise the performance of data processing work by a computing system.

control unit: (1) the part of the central processing unit that directs the sequence of operations, interprets coded instructions, and sends the proper signals instructing other computer circuits to carry out the instructions; (2) a device that controls the reading, writing, or display of data at one or more input/output devices.

controller: a device used to manage a peripheral device such as a CRT, printer, or disk drive.

conversational: pertaining to a program or a system that carries on a dialog with a terminal user, alternately accepting input and then responding to the input quickly enough for the user to maintain his or her train of thought. See also **interactive.**

conversion: (1) the process of changing from one method of data processing to another or from one data processing system to another; (2) the process of changing from one form of representation to another; e.g., to change from decimal representation to binary representation.

critical path: the longest time path in a project that has to be done as quickly as possible. Any delay along this path causes the entire project to be delayed.

CRT display device: a display device on which images are produced on a cathode ray tube.

cryptography: the art of writing or deciphering messages in code.

cursor: an electronically generated symbol that appears on the display screen to tell the operator where the next character will appear.

custom software: tailormade computer programs prepared for a specific purpose. Contrast with **packaged software,** in which the programs are written for general purposes.

cycle: (1) an interval of space or time in which one set of events or phenomena is completed; (2) any set of operations that is repeated regularly in the same sequence. The operations may be subject to variations on each repetition.

cylinder: the tracks of a disk storage device that can be accessed without repositioning the access mechanism.

data: facts, numbers, letters, and symbols that become usable information when processed.

data acquisition: the process of identifying, isolating, and gathering source data to be centrally processed in a usable form.

data bank: a comprehensive collection of libraries of data. For example, one part of an invoice may form an **item,** a complete invoice may form a **record,** a complete set of such records may form a **file,** the collection of inventory control files may for a **library,** and the libraries used by an organization are known as its **data bank.**

data base: a collection of interrelated data **files** or **libraries** organized for ease of access, update, and retrieval.

data base administrator (DBA): person delegated authority to coordinate, monitor, and control the data base and related resources, including the **DED** and **DD** systems.

data base management system (DBMS): a generalized set of computer programs that control the creation, maintenance, and utilization of the data bases and data files of an organization.

data capture: a method whereby recorded information is read by an optical reading device and sent to a computer for processing.

data collection: (1) a telecommunications application in which data from several locations is accumulated at one location (in a queue or on a file) before processing; (2) accumulation of data in a form usable by computer.

data definition language (DDL): a computer program used to describe data at a sufficiently high level to make use of a common programming language to access data in a data base management system.

data directory (DD): lists or tables that facilitate quick reference to pertinent information regarding an information system using a DED.

data element: a fact or observation collected and recorded as data.

data element dictionary (DED): defines data elements by use of descripters used to describe characteristics, attributes, and other related information concerning the data element.

data hierarchy: the organization of characters, data elements, records, and files (data sets and subsets) to form a data base.

data layout sheet: used in planning the physical space of data (field width) in data records.

data, machine-readable: concerns data that is acceptable as input to a particular machine.

data management: a major function of operating systems that involves organizing, cataloging, locating, storing, retrieving, and maintaining data.

data manager: software which describes the logical and physical organization of the data base and enables manipulation of the base by programmers.

data manipulation language (DML): a computer program for accessing and modifying the data base.

data medium: the material in or on which a specific physical variable may represent data.

data network: telecommunications network designed specifically for data transmission.

data organization: the arrangement of information in a data set. For example, sequential organization or partitioned organization.

data processing (DP): the manipulation of data by following a sequence of instructions to achieve a desired result.

data processing system: a network of machine components capable of accepting information, processing it according to a plan, and producing the desired results.

data security: protection of computerized information by various means, including cryptography, locks, identification cards and badges, restricted access to the computer, passwords, physical and electronic backup copies of the data, and so forth.

data structure: the manner in which data is represented and stored in computer system or program.

data transmission: the sending of data from one part of a system to another.

debug: to find and eliminate mistakes or problems with software or hardware and eliminate them.

decision support systems (DSS): computerized applications used by management for decision making. These applications often use mathematical and statistical models, such as linear programming, CPM or PERT—models included in operations research and management science.

decision table: a table of all conditions that are to be considered in the description of a problem, together with the actions to be taken. Decision tables are sometimes used in place of flowcharts for problem description and documentation.

decollate: to separate the piles of a multipart form or paper stock.

DED/DD committee: committee that takes responsibility for the content and control of data in an information system.

dedicated: if a computer or piece of hardware is assigned exclusively to one task, it is said to be a dedicated system.

derived data: data obtained by manipulating or processing other data, especially raw data. For example, age may be derived from date of birth and current date.

descripter: a word or phrase used to identify, categorize, or index information or data.

device: in computers, a piece of hardware that performs a specific function. Input devices (e.g., keyboard) are used to get data into the central processing unit. Output devices (e.g., printer or display monitor) are used to take data out of a computer in some usable form. Input/output devices (e.g., terminal or disk drive) are able to perform both input and output of data.

digit: a single character, 0–9, A–Z, or a special symbol such as $, %, ¢, #, or +.

digital: the representation of data using a discrete medium such as sticks, markers, bits, or anything that is counted to determine its value.

digital computer: a computer that operates by using numbers to express all quantities and variables of a problem. In most digital computer systems, the numbers, in turn, are expressed by electrical impulses. Contrast with **analog computer.**

digital to analog converter: device that transforms a computer's digital electrical pulses into a continuous analog signal in order to relay information to or to power some nondigital device outside of the computer.

direct access: (1) retrieval or storage of data by a reference to its location on a volume, rather than relative to the previously retrieved or stored data; (2) pertaining to the process of obtaining data from, or placing data into, storage when the time required for such access is independent of the location of the data most recently obtained or placed in storage; (3) pertaining to a storage device, such as magnetic disk or drum, in which the access time is effectively independent of the location of the data. Synonymous with **random access.** Contrast with **serial access.**

direct access storage device: a device in which the access time is effectively independent of the location of the data.

disk: a circular plate with magnetic material on both sides. This plate rotates for the storage and retrieval of data by one or more "heads" which transfer the information to and from the computer. The computer-readable information may be placed on a floppy or a rigid (hard) disk, and may have information on one or both sides. Also known as diskette or disc.

disk pack: a removable direct access storage volume containing magnetic disks on which data is stored. Disk packs are mounted on a disk storage device.

disk storage: storage on direct access devices that record data magnetically on rotating disks.

display: a visual presentation of data.

display tube: a cathode ray tube on which information appears.

display unit: a terminal device that presents data visually, usually by means of a cathode ray tube.

distributed data base: a data base needed for local processing kept by the processing center at a distributed node.

distributed data processing (DDP): the arrangement of computers within an organization in which the organization's computer complex has many separate computing facilities all working in a cooperative manner, rather than the conventional single computer at a single location. Frequently an organization's central files are stored at the central computing facility, with the geographically dispersed smaller computers calling on the central files whenever they need them.

distributed network: a network in which all node pairs are connected, either directly or through redundant paths through intermediate nodes.

document: a medium and the data recorded on it for human use. By extension, any record that has permanence that can be read by humans or machines.

documentation: (1) the creating, collecting, organizing, storing, citing, and disseminating of documents, or the information recorded in documents; (2) a collection of documents or information on a given phase of development or all development documentation of an information system.

down time: the period during which a computer is not operating.

dumb terminal: a terminal that lacks computing and storage capabilities of its own.

dummy: pertaining to the characteristic of having the appearance of a specified thing but not having the capacity to function as such. For example, a dummy character, dummy plug, or a dummy activity.

dump: to copy or print out certain contents in memory or to transfer information from memory to an external storage device.

duplex: a method of operating a communications channel between two devices. **Full duplex** allows both units to send and receive simultaneously. **Half duplex** allows only one unit to send information at one time.

duplicate: an exact copy or reproduction.

eavesdropping: unauthorized listening in on a telecommunications system.

economic feasibility: a check to see whether expected benefits equal or exceed expected costs.

edit: to modify the form or format of data. For example, to insert or delete characters such as page numbers or decimal points.

effectiveness: system readiness and design adequacy. Effectiveness is expressed as the probability that the system can successfully meet an operational demand within a given time under specified conditions.

efficiency: the ratio of useful work performed to the total energy expended. A system is efficient if it fulfills its purpose without waste of resources.

electromechanical data processing: the use of electromechanical devices, such as typewriters and calculators, to process data into information.

electronic data processing (EDP): processing of data largely performed by electronic devices.

emulation: a technique using software or microprogramming in which one computer is made to behave exactly like another computer.

encrypt: to encipher or encode.

ergonomics: the science of human engineering which combines the study of human body mechanics and physical limitations with industrial psychology.

executive routine: a routine that controls the execution of other routines.

expert system: a knowledge system that performs at or near the level of human experts.

external storage: same as **auxiliary storage.**

fail-safe: ability to continue operations in spite of breakdown because backup processing exists.

fail-soft: ability to continue operations in spite of breakdown but with a degraded level of operations.

fault: a physical condition that causes a device, a component, or element to fail to perform in a required manner.

feasibility study: an analysis to determine whether or not desired objectives of a proposed (information) system can be achieved within specific constraints.

feedback: the return of part of the output of a machine, process, or system to the computer as input for another phase, especially for self-correcting or control purposes.

field: in a record, a specified area used for a particular category of data.

fifth generation computer: term is associated with intelligent supercomputers planned by the Japanese for the 1990s.

file: a logical collection of data, designated by name, and considered as a unit by a user. A file consists of related **records.** For example, a payroll file (one record for each employee, showing rate of pay, deductions, and so forth) or an inventory file (one record for each inventory item, showing the cost, selling price, number in stock, and so forth).

file layout: the arrangement and structure of data in a file, including the sequence and size of its components.

file maintenance: updating the file to reflect changes in information. Data might be added, altered, or deleted. File maintenance also refers to reorganizing files, deleting records that are no longer in use, and so forth.

financial feasibility: a check to see whether funds are available to meet expected costs.

firmware: software that is stored in a fixed (wired-in) way, usually in a read-only memory.

fixed-length record: a record having the same length as all other records with which it is logically or physically associated.

floppy disk: a record of data on a flexible disk.

flowchart: a graphical representation of a procedure or computer program.

font: a family or assortment of characters of a given size and style. For example, large print for preparing transparencies, italicized print for emphasis, and so forth.

format: a specific arrangement of data.

FORTRAN (**FOR**mula **TRAN**slating system): a language primarily used to express arithmetic formulas in computer programs.

fourth generation languages: refers to a class of very high level languages often in an interactive mode. Some come with a DBMS.

front-end processor: processing equipment in a telecommunications environment that can relieve the CPU of certain processing tasks.

full duplex: see **duplex.**

gate: an electronic circuit with two or more inputs and one output, which has the property that a pulse goes out on the output line if, and only if, some specified combination of pulses occurs on the input lines.

gateway: connects LANs with heterogeneous equipment and protocols.

general purpose computer: a computer that is designed to handle a wide variety of problems.

GIGO: common computer acronym for **G**arbage **I**n, **G**arbage **O**ut. Output from a computer is only as good as the data input.

GPSS (**G**eneral **P**urpose **S**ystem **S**imulation): a graphic-oriented language, used for business simulation problems.

graphics: presenting information pictorially rather than alphanumerically.

half duplex: see **duplex.**

handshaking: the electronic process when communicating units query one another to ensure that each is ready for transmission and that information will not be lost.

hard copy: information generated by a computer and normally printed on paper.

hardware: the electronic circuits, memory, and input/output components of a computer system. Components made of steel or metal that one can see and touch. Contrast with **software.**

hash total: a summation for checking purposes of one or more corresponding fields of a file that may be in different units.

header label: a file or data set label that precedes the data records on a unit of recording media.

heuristic: (1) pertaining to exploratory methods of problem solving in which solutions are discovered by evaluation of the progress made toward the final result. Contrast with **algorithm;** (2) plausible, judgmental, "private," not articulated.

hierarchical computer network: a computer network in which processing and control functions are performed at several levels by computers especially suited for the functions performed: e.g., in factory or laboratory automation.

hierarchy of data: a data structure consisting of sets and subsets so that every subset of a set is of lower rank than the data of the set.

high level language: a programming language in which the statements represent procedures rather than single machine instructions. FORTRAN, COBOL, and BASIC are three common high level languages. A high level language requires a compiler or interpreter.

HIPO chart: a design and documentation tool of structured programming.

horizontal integration: the integration of functional information subsystems (e.g.: production, marketing, and finance) at one level of an organization (e.g.: operations, control, or planning).

host computer: a computer and associated software which, although run as a separate entity, can be accessed via a network.

housekeeping: in a program, the taking care of details and repetitive functions.

human factors: physiologial, psychological, and training factors to be considered in the design of hardware and software and the development of procedures to ensure that humans can interface with machines efficiently and effectively.

hybrid computer: a computer for data processing using both analog representation and discrete representation of data.

index: (1) an ordered reference list of the contents of a file or document, together with keys or reference notations for identification or location of those contents; (2) to prepare a list as in (1); (3) a table used to locate the records of an indexed sequential data set.

information: data that is processed and transformed into a meaningful and useful form.

information processing: same as **data processing.**

information retrieval system: a computing system application designed to recover specific information from a mass of data.

information system: a system that utilizes manual, electromechanical, and electronic data processing systems, as well as personnel and operating procedures, to collect and process data and disseminate information in an organization.

in-house: a system for use only within a particular company or organization, where the computing is independent of any external service.

input: (1) the data that is entered into programs; (2) the act of entering data into a computer; (3) data used by programs and subroutines to produce output.

input device: any machine that allows entry of commands or information into the computer. An input device could be a keyboard, tape drive, disk drive, microphone, light pen, digitizer, or electronic sensor.

input/output (I/O): that part or procedure of a computer system that handles communications with external devices.

inquiry: a request for information from storage. For example, a request for the number of available items, or a machine statement to initiate a search of library documents.

installation: process of installing and testing either hardware or software, or both, until they are accepted.

instruction: a set of characters that defines an operation and which causes a computer to act accordingly on the indicated quantities.

instruction set: the set of instructions that a computing system is designed to be capable of performing.

integrated circuit (IC): complete module of components manufactured as single or solid units made by either a film deposition or a diffusion process. Used as logic circuitry or for storage of information. Integrated circuits are contrasted to discrete components such as transistors, diodes, capacitors, and resisters that can be assembled into circuits.

intelligent terminal: a terminal that is programmable and can process its messages. For example, checking validity of input.

interactive: commonly used to describe a software program that provides give-and-take between the operator and the machine. The program may ask a question to elicit a response from the operator or present a series of choices from which the operator can select. Also referred to as **conversational mode.**

interactive program: a computer program that permits data to be entered or the flow of the program to be changed to online real time.

interface: the juncture at which two computer components (hardware and/or software) meet and interact with each other. Also applies to human-machine interaction.

internal store: storage within the computer proper.

interpreter: a translation program used to execute statements expressed in a high level language. An interpreter translates each such statement and executes it immediately. Instructions can be freely added or modified in the user program, and execution may be resumed without delay. Compare with **compiler.**

inter-record gap: an area on a data medium used to indicate the end of a block or record.

iterate: to repeatedly execute a loop or series of steps. For example, a loop in a routine.

job: a specified group of tasks prescribed as a unit of work for a computer. By extension, a job usually includes all necessary computer programs, linkages, files, and instructions to the operating system.

joystick: an input device consisting of a normally vertical stick that can be tilted in any direction to indicate direction of movement.

k: computer shorthand for the quantity 1024 which is 2^{10}. The term is usually used to measure computer storage. It is approximated as 1,000.

key: a field of data in a record which is used for accessing the record.

key data element: data element used to link files.

key word: A significant or informative word in a title, abstract, or text that is used to describe the document.

keyboard: the panel of keys that is connected to a computer and used to enter data. It looks similar to the keys of a typewriter.

keypunch: a keyboard-actuated device that punches holes in a card to represent data.

knowledge system: an intelligent computer program that uses knowledge and inference procedures to solve difficult problems.

language: a set or system of symbols used in a more or less uniform way by a number of people so that they can have communication with and understand one another.

large-scale integration (LSI): the combining of about 1,000 to 10,000 circuits on a single chip. Typical examples of LSI circuits are memory chips, microprocessors, calculator chips and watch chips.

leased line: A line reserved for sole use of a single leasing customer.

level: degree of subordination within a hierarchy, whether the hierarchy be the organizational structure of a business or a set of data.

library: a collection of files and computer programs and routines.

light pen: an input device for a CRT. It records the emission of light at the point of contact with the screen.

linkage: in programming, coding that connects two separately coded routines.

listing: a printout, usually prepared by a language translator, that lists the source language statements and contents of a program. A listing of a file is a printout of the contents of the file.

load: to enter or add to the internal storage of a computer information from auxiliary, intermediate, or external storage.

local area network (LAN): a telecommunications network used to connect computers with other computers, peripherals, and workstations that are in fairly close proximity.

location: a physical place in the computer's memory, reached by an address, where an item of information is stored.

logging: recording of data about events that occurs in time sequence.

logical data element: data element that is independent of the physical data media on which it is recorded. Data elements are grouped by use and meaning.

logical file: a collection of one or more logical records.

logical record: (1) a collection of items independent of their physical environment. Portions of the same logical record may be located in different physical records; (2) a record from the standpoint of its content, function, and use rather than its physical attributes; that is, one that is defined in terms of the information it contains.

loop: the repetitious execution of a series of instructions caused by having the last instruction in the series return the machine to the first instruction in the same series.

low level language: a language that is easily understood by the computer. In a low level language, programs are hard to write (by programmers) but quickly executed by machine. Examples are machine or assembler language.

machine instruction: an instruction in a source language that is equivalent to a specified sequence of machine instructions.

machine language: set of codes representing the instructions which can be directly executed by a computer processor.

machine-independent: pertaining to procedures or programs created without regard for the actual devices that will be used to process them.

magnetic disk: a flat circular plate with a magnetic surface on which data can be stored by selective magnetization of portions of the flat surface.

magnetic ink: an ink that contains particles of a magnetic substance whose presence can be detected by magnetic sensors.

magnetic ink character recognition (MICR): the machine recognition of characters printed with magnetic ink. Contrast with **optical character recognition.**

magnetic tape: a tape with a magnetic surface on which data can be stored by selective polarization of portions of the surface.

main memory: the internal memory of the computer contained in its circuitry, as opposed to peripheral memory (tapes, disks).

main storage: (1) the general purpose storage of a computer. Contrast with **auxiliary storage;** (2) all program-addressable storage from which instructions may be executed and from which data can be loaded directly into registers.

mainframe: a large general-purpose computer with fast processing time appropriate for corporations, research organizations, universities, and governmental agencies.

maintenance: any activity intended to eliminate faults or to keep hardware or programs in satisfactory working condition, including tests, measurements, replacements, adjustments, and repairs.

malfunction: the effect of a fault or unexpected functioning.

management information system (MIS): a computerized information system that processes data to produce information designed to aid in the performance of management functions.

mark-sense: to mark a position with an electrically conductive pencil for later conversion to machine-readable form.

masquerading: pretending to be a legitimate user to access a system.

mass storage (online): the storage of a large amount of data which is also readily accessible to the central processing unit of a computer.

mass storage device: a device having a large storage capacity.

master file: a file that is either relatively permanent, or that is treated as an authority in a particular job.

match: to check for identity between two or more items of data.

matrix: a commonly used method of storing and manipulating data. A matrix format consists of rows and columns of information.

matrix organization: borrows staff from functional divisions—staff that is responsible to the project manager for the life of a project.

medium: the material, or configuration thereof, on which data is recorded. For example, paper tape, cards, magnetic tape.

memory: the section of the computer where instructions and data are stored. Each item in the memory has a unique address that the central processing unit can use to retrieve information.

memory, read-only: a memory that cannot be altered in normal use of the computer.

menu: a list of alternative actions displayed on the terminal for selection by the user.

merge: a computerized process whereby two or more files are brought together by a common attribute.

message switching: a telecommunications application in which a message received by a central system from one terminal is sent to one or more other terminals.

metal-oxide semiconductor: technology for manufacturing semiconductors to produce integrated circuit logic components.

microcomputer: a small but complete microprocessor-based computer system, including CPU, memory, input/output (I/O), interfaces, and power supply.

microfiche: a sheet of microfilm on which it is possible to record a number of pages of microcopy.

microfilm: film on which documents are photographed in a reduced size.

microprocessor: an integrated circuitry implementation of a complete processor (arithmetic logic unit, internal storage, and control unit), on a single chip.

millisecond: one-thousandth of a second.

mini-company approach: use of a representative set of data to represent a company when auditing. Allows audit independent of live data stream.

minicomputer: an electronic, digital, stored-program, general-purpose computer smaller in size than a mainframe.

mnemonic: a short, easy-to-remember name or abbreviation. Many commands in programming languages are mnemonics.

mnemonic symbol: a symbol chosen to assist the human memory. For example, an abbreviation such as mpy for multiply.

mode: a method of operation. For example, the binary mode or the interpretive mode.

model: a computer reproduction or simulation of a real or imaginary person, process, place, or thing. Models can be simple or complex; artistic, educational, or entertaining; serious, part of a game, or a mathematical representation.

modem (MOdulator-DEModulator): a device that transforms a computer's electrical pulses into audible tones for transmission over the phone line to another computer. A modem also receives incoming tones and transforms them into electrical signals that can be processed and stored by the computer.

modify: to alter a part of an instruction or routine.

module: (1) a program unit that is discrete and identifiable with respect to compiling, combining with other units, and loading. For example, the input to, or output from, an assembler, compiler, linkage editor, or executive routine; (2) a packaged functional hardware unit designed for use with other components.

monitor: (1) a microcomputer program that directs operations of the hardware; (2) may also refer to a video display.

mouse: a pointing device used to identify a location on a CRT screen for making additions or changes to data. The pointer is controlled by a person who moves the mouse in two dimensions on a flat surface, such as a table top.

multiplexer: a hardware device that allows handling of multiple signals over a single channel.

multiprocessing: the use of several computers to logically or functionally divide jobs or processes, and to execute various programs or segments asynchronously and simultaneously.

multiprogramming: to permit more than one program to timeshare machine components.

nanosecond: a billionth of a second. Supercomputers have a cycle time measured in nanoseconds. For example, Cray–1 has a cycle time of 12.5 nanoseconds.

natural language: a spoken, human language such as English, Spanish, Arabic, or Chinese. Compare to **programming language.**

network: an interconnection of computer systems, terminals and communications facilities.

node: (1) an end point of any branch of a network, or a junction common to two or more branches of a network; (2) any station, terminal, terminal installation, communications computer, or communications computer installation in a computer network.

numeral: expressing or denoting a number or numbers.

numeric: expressed by a number or numbers. Synonymous with numerical.

numerical control: automatic control of process performed by a device that makes use of all or part of numerical data generally introduced as the operation is in process.

object program (object code): the output from an assembler or compiler; a program in machine language.

offline: used to describe equipment which is neither connected to, nor under the control of, the central processing unit.

offloading: the transference of processing from one system to another.

online: directly connected to the computer and in operational-ready condition.

online processing: processing of input data in random order, without preliminary sorting or batching. Contrast with **batch processing.**

online system: in teleprocessing, a system in which the input data enters the computer directly from the point of origin or in which output data is transmitted directly to where it is used.

operand: (1) that which is operated upon. An operand is usually identified by an address part of an instruction; (2) information entered with a command name to define the data on which a command processor operates and to control the execution of the command processor.

operating system: a collection of programs for operating the computer. Operating systems perform such housekeeping tasks as input/output between the computer and peripherals, and accepting and interpreting information from the keyboard.

operation: (1) the act specified by a single computer instruction; (2) a program step undertaken or executed by a computer. The operation is usually specified by the operator part of an instruction.

operator's manual: directions for running programs and operating equipment.

optical character recognition (OCR): the machine identification of printed characters through use of light-sensitive devices. Contrast with **magnetic ink character recognition.**

optical reader: a device that reads handwritten or machine-printed symbols into a computing system.

optical scanner: (1) a device that scans optically and usually generates an analog or digital signal; (2) a device that optically scans printed or written data and generates their digital representations.

original equipment manufacturer (OEM): a term commonly used to refer to a computer sales organization that has an arrangment to package and sell a manufacturer's product.

output: (1) any processed information coming out of a computer via any medium (print, CRT, and so forth); (2) the act of transferring information to these media.

output device: a machine that transfers programs or information from the computer to some other medium. Examples of output devices include tape, disk, and bubble memory drives; computer printers, typewriters, and plotters; the computer picture screen (video display); robots; and sound synthesis devices that enable the computer to talk and/or play music.

packaged software: a program designed to be marketed for general use that may need to be adapted to a particular installation.

packet switching: the transmission of data by means of addressed packets whereby a transmission channel is occupied for the duration of transmission of the packet only. The channel is then available for use by packets being transferred between different data terminal equipment. Note: the data may be formatted into a packet or divided and then formatted into a number of packets for transmission and multiplexing purposes.

packet switching network: a network designed to carry data in the form of packets. The packet and its format are internal to that network. The external interfaces may handle data in different formats, and conversion is done by an interface computer.

paper tape: continuous strips of paper on which data is stored by way of punched holes.

parallel conversion: operating a new system in a test mode before the old system is fully phased out.

paradigm: an abstract strategy for representing knowledge, drawing inferences, maintaining control.

parallel processing: pertaining to the simultaneous execution of two or more programs.

parity: A 1-bit code that makes the total number of bits in the word, including the parity bit, odd (odd parity) or even (even parity). Used for error detection during data transmission.

parity bit: a check bit appended to an array of binary digits to make the sum of all the binary digits, including the check bit, always odd or always even.

parity check: a check that tests whether the number of ones (or zeros) in an array of binary digits is odd or even.

Pascal: a programming language first developed to teach programming concepts, but its use has extended to business and scientific applications.

password: a secret identification code keyed by the user and checked by the system before permitting access. Each user or group of users has a unique password.

pattern recognition: the identification of shapes, forms, or configurations by automatic means.

peripheral: any unit of equipment distinct from the central processing unit, which may provide the system with outside communications.

peripheral-bound: a system that backlogs because of the slowness of peripheral equipment.

PERT (Program Evaluation and Review Technique): an analysis technique utilized to find the most efficient scheduling of time and resources when developing a complex project.

physical record: a record from the standpoint of the manner or form in which it is stored, retrieved, and moved; one that is defined in terms of physical qualities. A physical record may contain all or part of one or more logical records.

picosecond: one-trillionth of a second.

piggy-backing: interception and switching of messages.

PL1 (Programming Language—version 1): high level language developed by IBM. An all purpose procedure-oriented language for both scientific and business applications.

plot: to draw or diagram. To connect the point-by-point coordinate values.

plotter: a mechanical device for drawing lines under computer control.

plug-compatible: the ability to interface a peripheral or CPU produced by one manufacturer with hardware or software produced by another.

pointer: an address or other indication of location.

point-of-sale terminal (POS): a terminal commonly used in retail stores that serves the function of a cash register while collecting sales data and performing other data processing functions. Such terminals are usually connected online and in real time to a computer.

polling: a technique by which each of the terminals sharing a communications line is periodically interrogated to determine whether it requires servicing.

port: a channel of communication between the central processing unit and a peripheral.

portability: properties of software that permit its use in another computer environment.

preprocessor: a computer program that will prepare for another processing activity.

price differentiation: pricing a product to help favored customers or damage specific competitors: a strategy to enter and/or capture a desired market share.

primary storage: internal storage within a computer.

primitive data: synonymous with **raw data.**

printer: a computer output device that produces computer output on paper.

priority: a rank assigned to a task that determines its precedence in receiving system resources.

private line service: a communications service used exclusively by one particular customer. Also, the whole process of providing private line circuits.

problem-oriented language: a programming language designed for the convenient expression of a given class of problems.

procedure: the course of action taken for the solution of a problem.

procedure-oriented language: a programming language designed for the convenient expression of procedures used in a wide variety of problems.

process chart: a document used to collect information on each step of a process. Used in system development to analyze procedures to be computerized.

processor: in hardware, a data processor.

program: a sequence of instructions directing a computer to perform a particular function; a statement of an algorithm in a programming language.

program (verb): to make a program.

program error: any mistakes or problems in a computer program that keep the computer from performing the proper computations.

program library: a collection of debugged and documented programs.

programmer: person who writes programs.

programmer's manual: descriptions of programs.

programming language: a set of symbols and rules that can be used to specify an algorithm in a computer-executable form.

project management: in information systems development, the planning, coordination, and control of activities during the development from the feasibility study through conversion.

project organization: the creation of a separate organizational unit for the sole purpose of completing a project.

PROLOG (**PRO**gramming in **LOG**ic): language that lends itself to inference making. Used extensively in artificial intelligence.

protocol: the rules governing how two pieces of equipment communicate with one another.

punched card: a card punched with a pattern of holes to represent data.

random access: an access method whereby each record of a file or location in memory can be accessed directly by its address.

raw data: data that has not been processed.

read: to read is to sense the meaning of recorded data on a disk or card for storage and/or processing.

read-only: a type of access to data that allows it to be read but not modified.

reader: a device that converts information from one form into another form.

reading between the lines: engaging a system illicitly when a user is connected to the computer but the computer is idle.

register: the hardware for temporarily storing one machine word.

real time: in synchronization with the actual occurrence of events.

real-time processing: processing data rapidly enough to provide results useful in directly controlling a physical process or guiding a human user.

record: a collection of data items stored on a disk or other medium which may be recalled as a unit. Records may be fixed or variable in length. One or more records usually make up a data **file.**

recovery: to reestablish operations following breakdown of CPU or I/O devices.

redevelopment: recycling the development cycle for major modification of an information system.

refresh: the process of restoring the contents of a dynamic memory before they are lost. Also the process of redrawing (many times per second) the image on a CRT before it can fade from sight.

remote access: pertaining to communication with a data processing facility by one or more stations that are distant from that facility.

remote job entry: submission of job control statements and data from a remote terminal, causing the jobs described to be scheduled and executed as though encountered in the input stream.

replicated distributed data base: a duplicate segment of a data base that is needed for local processing, stored at the local site.

Report Program Generator (RPG): a computer programming language that can be used to generate object programs that produce reports from existing sets of data.

reproduce: to prepare a duplicate of stored data or information.

resistance: in the context of information systems, the act of opposing change which is brought about by the use of computers.

response time: the time required for the system to respond to a user's request or to accept a user's inputs.

robot: a machine composed of sensing devices, links, and joints that performs specific manual tasks governed by a microprocessor or microprocessors.

robotics: study on collection of manipulative devices and sensing devices which cooperate to reliably perform a task.

run: the execution of a program by a computer on a given set of data.

scroll: the movement of a CRT display upward with new lines continually being added to the bottom of the screen.

search: a systematic examination of the available information in a given field of interest.

secondary storage: same as **auxiliary storage.**

security: prevention of access to or use of data, documentation, or programs without authorization.

semiconductor: a substance whose conductivity is poor at low temperatures but is improved by the application of heat, light, or voltage.

sensor: any device that monitors the external environment for a computer. Types of sensors include photoelectric sensors that are sensitive to light; image sensor cameras that can record visual images and transform them into digital signals; pressure sensors that are sensitive to any kind of pressure; sensors that record infrared information; and ultrasonic transducers that produce a high frequency sound wave that bounces off objects and lets the computer calculate the distance between itself and those objects.

separation of responsibility: a management control technique that can be applied to management of information systems. The information system is divided into functions, and employees are assigned duties and responsibilities that do not cross functional lines.

sequence: (1) an arrangement of items according to a specified set of rules; (2) in sorting, a group of records whose control fields are in ascending or descending order, according to the collating sequence.

sequential access: a storage method (such as on a magnetic tape) by which data can only be reached or retrieved by passing through all intermediate locations between the current one and the desired one.

serial: the handling of data, one item after another. In communications, a serial transmission breaks each character into its component bits and sends these bits one at a time to a receiving device where they are a reassembled.

service bureau: provides computing services to customers.

service routine: a routine in general support of the operation of a computer, for example, an input/output, diagnostic, tracing, or monitoring routine.

simplex channel: a channel that is capable of transmitting data in only one direction.

simulation: a computerized reproduction, image, or replica of a situation or set of conditions.

smart terminal: see **intelligent terminal.**

software: a general term for computer programs involved in the operation of the computer.

software maintenance: the adjustment of an existing program to allow acceptance of new tasks or conditions (e.g., a new category of payroll deduction) or correct previously undiscovered errors detected by users.

sort: (1) a procedure to reorder data sequentially, usually in alphabetic or numeric order; (2) the action of sorting.

source program: program that must be translated into machine language before use.

special purpose computer: a computer that is designed to handle a restricted class of problems.

spreadsheet: packaged software used largely, but not exclusively, in planning. Enables quick computation of cells in a matrix given a column of values that changes.

stand-alone system: a computer system that does not require a connection to another computer.

storage: the general term for any device that is capable of holding data which will be retrieved later.

store: to enter or retain data in a storage device.

subsystem: a secondary or subordinate system, usually capable of operating independently.

supervisor: a control routine or routines through which the use of resources is coordinated and the flow of operations through the central processing unit is maintained.

system: usually refers to a group of related hardware and/or software designed to meet a specific need.

system analyst: an individual who performs system analysis, design, and many related functions in the development and maintenance of an information system.

system analysis: the analysis of an activity to determine precisely what must be accomplished and how to accomplish it.

system manual: general information on a system and its objectives (an overview, not details).

table: a collection of data in which each item is uniquely identified by a label, by its position relative to the other items, or by some other means.

tape: inexpensive mass storage medium. Must be accessed sequentially.

tape drive: a device that moves tape past a head.

tape unit: a device containing a tape drive, together with reading and writing heads and associated controls.

task: a program in execution.

telecommunications: (1) pertaining to the transmission of signals over long distances, for example, by telegraph, radio, or television; (2) data transmission between a computing system and remotely located devices via a unit that performs the necessary format conversion and controls the rate of transmission.

teleconferencing: two-way communications between two or more groups (or three or more persons) remote from one another, using electronic means.

teleprocessing: the processing of data that is received from or sent to remote locations by way of telecommunications lines.

terminal: a keyboard plus a CRT and/or printer that can be connected to a computer.

throughput: a measure of the amount of work that can be accomplished by the computer during a given period of time.

time sharing: a method of sharing the resources of the computer among several users, so that several people can appear to be running different computer tasks simultaneously.

top-down development: downward from skeletal outline of program design to the detailed levels, continuously exercising the actual interfaces between program modules. The opposite from developing bottom-level modules first and working up, finally integrating and testing the entire system.

track: the portion of a moving storage medium, such as a drum, tape, or disk, that is accessible to a given reading head position.

transaction file: a data file containing relatively transient data to be processed in combination with a master file.

translator: (1) a device that converts information from one system of representation into equivalent information in another system of representation; (2) a routine for changing information from one representation or language to another.

transmission: (1) the sending of data from one location and the receiving of data in another location, leaving the source data unchanged; (2) the sending of data.

transposition: the interchange of position. May be an exchange of data positions, e.g., 15 instead of 51.

turnaround documents: document produced as output which becomes input when user supplies additional data on the document.

turnaround time: the measure of time between the initiation of a job and its completion by the computer.

turnkey vendor: one who provides a complete system including the computer, software, training, installation, and support.

unit record: a card containing one complete record; a punched card.

update: to modify a master file with current information according to a specified procedure.

user friendly: descriptive of both hardware and software designed to assist the user by being scaled to human dimensions, self-instructing, error-proof, and so forth.

user's manual: procedures for use of an information system written in terms that users understand.

utility program: a program used to assist in the operation of the computer; e.g., a sort routine, a printout program, a file conversion program, and so forth. Generally these programs perform housekeeping functions and have little relationship to the specific processing of the data.

validation: process of checking compliance of data with preset standards and verifying data correctness.

variable: a quantity that can assume any of a given set of values.

vendor: a supplier or company that sells computers, peripherals, or computer services.

very large scale integration (VLSI): in practice, the compression of more than 10,000 transistors on a single chip.

voice-grade channel: a channel suitable for transmission of speech, digital or analog data, or facsimile, generally with a frequency range of about 300 to 3000 cycles per second.

wafer: many silicon chips linked together to increase efficiency and lower cost of production.

wand: a portable scanning device often used in stores and factories to read data for computer processing.

width of field: the amount of space allowed for data in a data record.

window: partial area on a CRT screen for display of program results. Windows allow the simultaneous display of results from more than one program.

wiretapping: electromagnetic pickup of messages off communication lines.

word: a unit of data or the set of characters which occupies one storage location. In most minicomputers, a word is equal to two bytes.

word processor: a text editor system for electronically writing, formatting and storing letters, reports and books prior to printing.

write: (1) to copy information usually from internal storage to external storage; (2) to transfer information to an output medium.

Selected list of abbreviations and acronyms

AA	American Airlines
AAIMS	An Analytical Information Management System
ACH	Automatic Clearing House
ACM	Association of Computing Machinery
ACS	Advanced Communication System
ADABAS	Adaptable DAta BAse System
ADP	Automatic Data Processing
ADS	Accurately Defined System
AEMS	Airline Econometric Modelling System
AI	Artificial Intelligence
ALGOL	ALGOrithmic Language
ALU	Arithmetic and Logic Unit
ANSI	American National Standards Institute
A/P	Accounts Payable
APL	A Programming Language
APT	Automatically Programmed Tool
A/R	Accounts Receivable
ARPA	Advanced Research Projects Agency
ARR	Accounting Rate of Return
ATM	Automatic Teller Machines
AT&T	American Telephone and Telegraph
BASIC	Beginner's All-Purpose Symbolic Instruction Code
BBC	British Broadcasting Corporation
BSP	Business System Planning
C	Centrigrade
CAD	Computer-Aided Design

CAD/CAM	Computer-Aided Design/Computer-Aided Manufacturing
CAI	Computer-Assisted Instruction
CAM	Computer-Aided Manufacturing
CCD	Charged Coupled Devices
CHIPS	Clearing House Inter-Payments System
CIM	Computer-Integrated Manufacturing
COBOL	COmmon Business-Oriented Language
CODASYL	Committee On DAta SYstems Language
COLINGO	Compile On LINe and GO
COM	Computer Output on Microfilm
CPM	Critical Path Method
CPU	Central Processing Unit
CRT	Cathode Ray Tube
CS	Computer Science
CSF	Critical Success Factor
DASD	Direct Access Storage Device
DBA	Data Base Administrator
DBCL	Data Base Command Language
DBMS	Data Base Management System
DBTG	Data Base Task Group
DD	Data Directory
DDC	Direct Digital Computer
DDL	Data Description Language
DDP	Distributed Data Processing
DED	Data Element Dictionary
DED/DD	Data Element Dictionary/Data Directory System
DES	Data Encryption Standard
DML	Data Manipulation Language
DNC	Direct Numerical Control
DP	Data Processing
DSL/ALPHA	Digital Simulation Language/ALPHA
DSS	Decision Support System
EAM	Electrical Accounting Machines
EDP	Electronic Data Processing
EFT	Electronic Fund Transfer
EIS	Electronic Information Services
ENIAC	Electronic Numerical Integrator And Calculator
EVPI	Expected Value of Perfect Information
FAX	Facsimile
FCC	Federal Communications Commission
FDS	Full Development System
FICA	Federal Insurance Contributions Act

FIFO	First-In-First-Out
FMIS	Factory-wide Management Information System
FORTRAN	FORmulae TRANslator
4GL	4th Generation Language
GERT	Graphic Evaluation Review Technique
GIDS	Generalized Intelligent Decision System
GIGO	Garbage In Garbage Out
GIS	Generalized Information System
GM	General Motors
GMIS	General Management Information System
GNP	Gross National Product
HIPO	Hierarchy Plus Input-Process Output
IBA	Independent Broadcasting Authority
IBM	International Business Machines Corporation
IC	Integrated Circuitry
ID	IDentification Number
IMIS	Intelligent Management Information System
IMP	Interface Message Processor
IMS	Information Management System
I/O	Input/Output
IQF	Interactive Query Facility
IRG	Inter Record Gap
IRR	Internal Rate of Return
IRS	Internal Revenue Service
IS	Information System
ISBN	International Standard Book Number
ISDOS	Information System Design and Optimization System
ISO	International Standards Organization
IT&T	International Telephone and Telegraph
JCL	Job Control Language
K	Kilo
KIPS	Knowledge Information Processing System
KWIC	Key Word In Context Index
KWOC	Key Word Out Of Context Index
LAN	Local Area Network
LIFO	Last-In-First-Out
LISP	LISt Processing
LSI	Large-Scale Integration
LSNLIS	Linear Sciences Natural Language Information System

MARS	Multi-Access Airline Reservation System
MIC	Magnetic Ink Characters
MICR	Magnetic Ink Character Recognition
MIS	Management Information System
MOS	Metal-Oxide-Semiconductor
MRP	Materials Requirements Planning System
NASA	National Aeronautics and Space Administration
NC	Numerical Control
NCR	National Cash Register
NPL	Natural Processing Language
NPV	Net Present Value
OCR	Optical Character Recognition
OEM	Original Equipment Manufacturer
OLRT	OnLine Real Time
OR	Operations Research
OS	Operating System
PB	PayBack Period
PBX	Private Automatic Branch EXchange
PC	Process Control
PERT	Program Evaluation Review Technique
PI	Profitability Index
PIN	Personal Identification Number
PL/1	Programming Language 1
POS	Point Of Sale
PR	Public Relations
PSA	Program Statement Analyzer
PV	Present Value
RAM	Random Access Memory
R&D	Research and Development
REQUEST	Restricted English QUESTion-Answering
RJE	Remote Job Entry
ROI	Return On Investment
RPG	Report Program Generator
SBN	Standard Book Number
SBS	Satellite Business System
SCL	Systems Communication Location
SCS	Small Computer System
SDI	Selective Dissemination of Information
SDLC	Synchronous Data Link Control
SEQUEL	Structured English QUEry Language

SIMULA	**SIMULA**tion Language
SMF	**S**ystems **M**anagement **F**acilities
SNA	**S**ystems **N**etwork **A**rchitecture
SNOBOL	Stri**N**g-**O**riented Sym**BO**lic **L**anguage
SODA	**S**ystems **O**ptimization and **D**esign **A**lgorithm
SOP	**S**tudy **O**rganization **P**lan
SQUARE	**S**pecifying **QU**eries **A**s **R**elational **E**xpressions
SSI	**S**mall-**S**cale **I**ntegration
SWIFT	**S**ociety for **W**orldwide **I**nterbank **F**inancial **T**elecommunications
TDMS	**T**ime-shared **D**ata **M**anagement **S**ystem
TELEX	**TEL**etypewriter **EX**change (Western Union)
TIP	**T**erminal **I**nterface Message **P**rocessor
TWX	**T**eletype**W**riter **EX**change Service
UIM	**U**ltra-**I**ntelligent **M**achine
UL1	**U**ser **L**anguage **1**
UP	**U**ser **P**rogram
UPC	**U**niversal **P**roduct **C**ode
VP	**V**ice-**P**resident
WATS	**W**ide **A**rea **T**elephone **S**ervice
WP	**W**ord **P**rocessing

Index

This book has been set Linotron 202N, in 9 point Helvetica and Helvetica Light, leaded 3 points. Part and chapter numbers are 30 point Avant Garde Gothic Medium. Part and chapter titles are 18 point Avant Garde Gothic Medium. The size of the type page is 37 by 48 picas.